War and Society in East Central Europe
Volume XXXVIII

ARMY AND POLITICS IN HUNGARY
1938-1944

Lóránd Dombrády

Edited by Gyula Rázsó
Translated by Eleonóra Arató
Copyedited by Matthew Suff
Typeset by Andrea T. Kulcsár

Social Science Monographs, Boulder, Colorado
Atlantic Research and Publications, Inc.
Highland Lakes, New Jersey

Distributed by Columbia University Press, New York
2005

EAST EUROPEAN MONOGRAPHS, NO. DCLXXIX

The publication of this volume was made possible by grants from

NEMZETI KULTURÁLIS ÖRÖKSÉG
MINISZTÉRIUMA

Nemzeti Kulturális Alapprogram

All rights reserved, which include the right to reproduce this book or portions thereof in any form whatsoever, without the written permission of the publisher.

Copyright © 2005
By Atlantic Research and Publications, Inc.

ISBN 0-88033-577-7
(978-0-88033-577-7)
Library of Congress Control Number: 2006922844

Printed in the United States of America

ATLANTIC STUDIES ON SOCIETY IN CHANGE

NO. 121

Editor-in-Chief, Béla K. Király

Associate Editor-in-Chief, Kenneth Murphy

Editor, László Veszprémy

Table of Contents

Table of Contents..v
Preface to the Series and Acknowledgments................................vii

Part I
The Development of Hungarian Political Ambitions before the Second Vienna Award

Honvéd Chief of the General Staff Henrik Werth
   and the Hungarian Military Policy..3
Differences in Foreign Political and Defense Issues
   between the Government and the General Staff:
   Teleki's and Werth's Discord..24
The German–Polish Conflict and
   the Impact of the War on the Hungarian Military Plans.........55
The Hungarian Military Requests Germany
   to Help Reclaim Transylvania...85
The Impact of the German Western Blitzkrieg:
   Hungary Becomes more Pro-German...................................108
Mobilization and Deployment against Romania:
   The Second Vienna Award..132

Part II
Hungary Enters World War II

Antagonism between the Military Leadership and the Government
   Regarding the Further Development of Military Policy.......209
German Training Units in Transit across Hungary to Romania...232
The Growing German Military and Political Influence...............240

The German Army Prepares for War against the Soviet Union
    and Ignores the Hungarian General Staff............................253
Joining Germany's Attack on Yugoslavia...................................266
The Hungarian Military Command
    Offers Its Services to the Germans..307
Offensive against the Soviet Union..330

Part III
The Failure of the New Hungarian Military Political Experiment

Colonel General Ferenc Szombathelyi at the Head of the General Staff:
    An Attempt to Create a New Hungarian Military Policy......355
German–Hungarian Discussions:
    Putting the 2nd Hungarian Army at Germany's Disposal.....384
The Hungarian–Romanian Discord Intensifies: Aspirations to
    Retain Power in the Case of an Anti-Romanian Action........397
A Radical Turning Point in the Course of the War:
    The Destruction of the 2nd Hungarian Army........................419
Failed Attempts to Break away and the Military Command........439
Hungary's Occupation...507
The Regent's Unsuccessful Attempt to Stabilize His Regime
    and to Break away from the War:
    The Failure of the October 15, 1944, Proclamation..............539

Bibliography..553
The Author...557
Biographies..559
Name Index..581
Place Index...587
Maps by Béla Nagy..591
Volumes Published in "Atlantic Studies on Society in Change"......599

Preface to the Series and Acknowledgments

The present volume is a component of a series that is intended to present a comprehensive survey of the many aspects of East Central European society.

The books in this series deal with peoples whose homelands lie between the Germans to the west, the Russians, Ukrainians and Belorussians to the east, and the Mediterranean and Adriatic seas to the south. They constitute a particular civilization, one that is at once an integral part of Europe, yet substantially different from the West. The area is characterized by a rich diversity of languages, religions and governments. The study of this complex area demands a multidisciplinary approach, and, accordingly, our contributors to the series represent several academic disciplines. They have been drawn from universities and other scholarly institutions in the United States and Western Europe, as well as East Central Europe.

The editor-in-chief is responsible for ensuring the comprehensiveness, cohesion, internal balance, and scholarly quality of the series he has launched. He cheerfully accept this responsibility and intend this work to be neither justification nor condemnation of the policies, attitudes, and activities of any person involved. At the same time, because the contributors represent so many different disciplines, interpretations, and schools of thought, our policy in this, as in the past and future volumes, is to present their contributions without major modifications.

The author of this volume is a distinguished scholar in the field to which the theme of this book belongs to. He is the former director of the Institute of Military History, Budapest and member of the Board of Directors Hungarian Committee of Military Historians.

The appendices were prepared by Andrea T. Kulcsár.

Budapest, March 15, 2005

Béla K. Király
Editor-in-Chief

Part I

THE DEVELOPMENT OF HUNGARIAN POLITICAL AMBITIONS BEFORE THE SECOND VIENNA AWARD

HONVÉD CHIEF OF THE GENERAL STAFF HENRIK WERTH AND THE HUNGARIAN MILITARY POLICY

The period between 1938 and the declaration of war on the Soviet Union in 1941 is registered in Hungarian history as a time when the country's governing system shifted further to the right. Facing a more and more hopeless situation, Hungary's ruling aristocratic circles, oriented towards the West, and Prime Minister Count Pál Teleki himself—who had succeeded Béla Imrédy on February 16, 1939—tried to restrain this accelerating process, fearing an extreme shift to the right and also a growing German influence. The extreme right—supporting the German infiltrating efforts while expecting that they would strengthen their position—turned increasingly openly against Teleki's political goals. Teleki also faced demands from the military leaders and the officer corps, which enjoyed Regent Horthy's support. Boosted by German military successes, the military demanded the tightest possible alliance with Germany and its army, as well as military cooperation. They increasingly resisted Teleki's policy of armed neutrality and the revision of Hungary's borders through Hungary's own strength and without any international obligations. The military was convinced that cooperation with the German Reich was the only way to regain Hungary's lost territory. In order to achieve this, the Reich's support had to be gained: therefore the military demanded a decisive pro-German foreign and military policy and relevant actions from the Hungarian government.

General of the Infantry Henrik Werth stood at the forefront of the army's aspirations.[1] Regent Horthy appointed him *Honvéd* Chief of the General Staff on September 29, 1938, at the suggestion of political circles dissatisfied with Prime Minister Béla Imrédy's increasingly right-wing policy and popularity within the army. However, Werth, who soon became one of the most prominent representatives in the pro-German policy group, was misunderstood by those who trusted him. A decisive point in their backing was that Werth had not had any connection with the exponents of the extreme right's policy either inside or outside the army. He had never supported such views and, what is more, had persecuted them within the army. At the same time his earlier views, expressed orally and in written form, about the relationship between the army and politics did not turn out to be too distant from the views of the people that he was to tame. According to Werth, several factors were crucially necessary for the country: a well-organized mobilization of the regime's powers—based on social unity—to overcome bickering party politics, the maximal development and recognition of the army as the main player in the future of the country, and a political party policy subordinated to these goals, which would take adequate measures to implement them.

In line with his commission Werth considered the urgent development of the army as his top priority. He viewed the opportunity to realize his ideas as the chance of a lifetime. He had little faith in political alternatives and was not willing to depart from his bedrock of views built up during long years of military service and experience, and he tried to enforce them using all means at his disposal. He viewed the politicians'—and therefore, Teleki's—disagreement as the manifestation of a behavior that questioned the primacy of the military leadership in politico-military and professional issues, and thus a danger to the success of the revisionist policy.

Before elaborating on the details of Werth's appointment and his activity as Chief of the General Staff, it seems to be necessary to summarize the stubbornly and systematically held views that underlay his actions and composed the theoretical foundations of his eventually ignominious role.

True to the political ideal that he represented, Werth was not politically interested in the party-political sense of the word. He judged everything according to its military merit, a type of thinking that defined his views. From among different political systems, he supported whichever one relied on the army, since they formed their policies by considering military ideas. In his view it is the primary function of the state to prepare for war and to fight wars successfully, because war has always been a constant factor in the history of mankind. This function of the state can only be realized if all the necessary steps are taken in peacetime in order to make the army efficient and thus, in the case of a war, to make quick or total mobilization of the hinterland and the army possible. Werth considered the Dual Monarchy and, even more so, the German Empire as past guardians of these ideals. He greatly appreciated this heritage and hoped to implement it in the *Honvédség*, a successor to these ideals. After Hitler came to power, Werth's attention turned to the reviving *Wehrmacht*. Although he did not much care for the essence of national socialism, Werth viewed the Hitler regime's cooperation with the German army as exemplary and something to be followed by the Hungarian political system. In contrast, he believed that bourgeois democracies were decadent political formations, incapable of efficient mobilizations, and also incapable of a rapid or successful internalization of war, a failing which would especially badly affect small states.

Investigating the possibilities of territorial revision for Hungary, beginning in the 1920s Werth paid great attention to exploring a future war. He tried to apply the principles of modern military science to the prospects of a future war and to ascertain how it might be fought in the circumstances that Hungary might encounter. Thus, he incorporated the ideas of war without limits and civilian volunteerism into his theoretical and practical activities. As early as the end of the 1920s he professed that Hungary could not avoid the oncoming war, which would be a total war between alliances. Therefore, everything in one's power had to be done so that Hungary, militarily prepared, could stand by the appropriate ally, which would, by all means, help it to recover all the lost territories. Thus Werth considered it the priority of Hungarian foreign policy to develop a strong connection with an appropriate ally or an alliance. Even if he did not spell it out, he anticipated an alliance with the German leadership, which was expected to change the Treaty of Trianon for Hungary. Consequently, while developing his ideas, Werth mostly studied and used German theoreticians, especially von Seeckt. Werth's studies and lectures at the General Staff Academy contributed to the outlook of the Hungarian General Staff and to the deepening of Werth's own German orientation. Thus, his views significantly influenced Hungarian military theory and the principles of military policy to be formed.

The idea that the last war had been lost "politically," and could be explained by a total lack of harmony between the political and military leadership before and during the war, held a significant place among Werth's views, as formulated by his close examination of the war. In order to avoid repeating those mistakes, an accord between the political and military leadership had to be created in a timely fashion. Spearheaded by the military leadership—that is, the General Staff—the necessary internal, external and economic measures were to be undertaken in the area of military preparedness, according to the preset goals.[2]

In order to be successful in his tasks as Chief of the General Staff, Werth planned on relying primarily on the Regent. He was certain that he could win over the Regent—whose certain rights as Supreme Commander were realized through the activities of the Chief of the General Staff, in any case—to his own militarily substantiated views, which, as far as Werth knew, were not far from the Regent's own ideas. As Chief of the General Staff, Werth was subordinated exclusively to the Regent, had reporting duties to him alone, and maintained immediate contacts with him as his official duty. Therefore, he thought, he would have abundant opportunities to check any unappealing decisions that might come even from the government.

Werth openly approached his own General Staff, who more or less knew his views. They were his implementers thus far and, he assumed, respected him. He considered the members of the General Staff to be the élite segment of the military leadership and thus entitled to a privileged place inside and outside the army through the importance of their roles. When taking over his office, he turned to his subordinates with a "command pertaining to the General Staff." He indicated that he would rely primarily on the General Staff, "whose outstanding value, high level of knowledge and exemplary diligence will be of assistance in the extraordinary tasks towering before me." He went on to say that he had the opportunity to educate and to prepare a substantial part of the General Staff "for tasks calling for deeds" and that he had gotten to know others during World War I and during military service with them. Werth asked the members of the General Staff for hard work, for unconditional obedience to their superiors, and for service to those ideas that their oath obliged them to support. He felt it necessary to emphasize the point that he did not tolerate party-based politics.[3]

Werth considered an officer corps of the *Honvédség* that was an efficient and malleable body of soldiers and was united in its conservative views, in being anti-left and anti-Soviet, in its nationalism, in a traditional pro-German attitude, and in demanding the immediate realization of a plan for territorial revisionism, to be of vital importance to the army. It was no secret to him that a number of officers openly endorsed Szálasi's Arrow-Cross Party or other national socialist and racist parties, and that some of them had even sought direct contacts with them. Werth was convinced that these unwanted political tendencies—which he was supposed to restrain—were due to the weaknesses of the former military leadership and to the impatience of the officer corps at the pace of political developments. He assumed that the aspirations that he required of the officer corps—many members of which had sought political opportunities within party programs—would be embraced by his staff, and that the program would vent off accumulated dissatisfactions and would channel energy into the right direction. Werth was led by such considerations in his steps to avoid unwanted political activities. If it was brought to his attention, he confronted officers who had kept ties with political parties, and he tried to prevent any political discussions contrary to army regulations.

Following his taking office, the new head of the General Staff informed his staff about the tasks ahead of them, with the execution of the army's development program within the context of the foreign political situation as the most important one. The *Honvédség* was poorly armed, which made an active military intervention in the German–Czech conflict, as requested by Hitler, impossible, and also continued to preclude being able to use any opportunities arising from the development of the foreign political situation.[4] The speed of the ongoing army development was too slow and lagged so far behind that, under the present circumstances, achieving a combat-ready status had to be pushed into the distant future. Laying the blame on the previous weak military leadership, Werth, in agreement with the new Minister of Defense, General of the Infantry Károly Bartha, who came to office on November 15, 1938, worked out the principles and necessary measures that, in his view, would form the foundation of a dynamic army development once they were adopted and executed.

The demands outlined by Werth can be summarized in the following:
- cooperation between the military leadership and the government should be solidified as soon as possible;
- all the country's administrative and economic measures should be facilitated by legislating and applying suitable military law;
- all civilian interests and needs should be subordinated to the

development of the army and should exclude any feature that contradicts the needs of the army, even to civilian disadvantage;
- the credit framework and the military budget announced in Győr in March 1938 should be substantially increased;
- by adopting government tools, everything should be done to make military-industrial activities more efficient;
- the capacities of the military industries and the undisturbed supply of materials and semi-products should be increased by state loans and grants;
- import opportunities for equipping the army and for the military industries, even at the expense of political and economic concessions made to Germany and Italy, should be created;
- special emphasis should be laid on developing the iron, metal and machine industries, because they are of crucial importance in establishing mechanized forces and the air force;
- it is of crucial importance that the government's foreign policy suit Hungarian interests identical with those of the army;
- the development of the army and its future efficient use towards territorial revisionism can only be envisioned in a close and multifaceted alliance with the Germans;
- for future reference, lessons are to be drawn from the situation concerning the German–Czech conflict, when the *Honvédség* was insufficiently prepared for action;
- finally, the government should not implement measures affecting the army without previously informing and consulting with the Minister of Defense and the Chief of the General Staff.

Following the Munich Accord and the ensuing Hungarian–Czechoslovakian negotiations, Werth spent a tense October waiting and preparing for the military occupation of territories that would probably be re-annexed. He took stock of the forces at his disposal, which were quite weak and could hardly be applied for a serious armed operation.

Although shying away from armed action against Czechoslovakia, the Hungarian government—via irregular troops called the Ragged Guard (*Rongyos Gárda*)—initiated disruptive and destructive armed actions on Czechoslovakian territory. The units were armed during the fall of 1938 and headed by General Staff Colonel Sándor Homlok, Head of the 5th Section of the General Staff. The Ragged Guard contained 900 soldiers organized into 19 battalions, including volunteers from different paramilitary organizations and also drafted reservists commanded by professional officers. Within the 19 battalions, 57 minor action groups were created. The units formed and were equipped in the different barracks of the country, wore civilian clothes, and were concentrated in Vásárosnamény near the border. Following October 6, but before the Hungarian–Czechoslovakian discussions were to start, the first units advanced over the border, beginning at Tarpa. The aim of the action, coordinated with Polish forces, was to demoralize the Czechoslovakian military and to encourage the Hungarian population of those territories to stage uprisings. It was, thus, to prepare the ground for a military attack in case the negotiations did not come to fruition, by raiding bridges, railways and other military targets. The activities went on until January 1939, even following the First Vienna Award, but proved a failure due to the resistance of the Czechoslovakian army and security forces. Thus the units were withdrawn and disarmed.

Following the unsuccessful Hungarian–Czechoslovakian negotiations, the First Vienna Award of November 2, 1938, re-annexed to Hungary 12,400 km² of territory with 1.1 million people of majority Hungarian ethnicity. However, the Award did not satisfy the demands of the Hungarian government or those of public opinion. The extreme right immediately staged an attack against the government and demanded an unambiguous and active pro-German policy to remedy the negligence so far. After his earlier trip to Germany and based on what he had seen there, Prime Minister Béla Imrédy himself decided to accelerate the building of closer connections. His decision was fully accepted by the officer corps, which, referring to disadvantages stemming from their previous military unpreparedness, once again vigorously demanded that all the resources of the country should be involved in serving preparations for the coming war, and that German support should be gained for this end.

It was amidst the intensification of the internal political situation between November 5 and 10, 1938, that the re-annexed territories were occupied by Hungary. During the solemn re-annexation ceremony, the II. Army Corps took possession of the Csallóköz, the I. Army Corps took possession of the Ipolyság area, the VII. Army Corps was involved at Kassa, and the VI. Army Corps took possession of Munkács and Ungvár, all according to former agreed-upon plans.

Prime Minister Imrédy tried to silence the critical voices of the extreme right, dissatisfied with the size of the re-annexed territories, and to consolidate his own situation, by proposing a new territory acquisition mission. After consulting with the military leadership, he considered it possible that the forces occupying the re-annexed territories would be able to change the situation established by the Vienna Award by occupying Sub-Carpathia (Ruthenia). The November 8 session of the Council of Ministers passed a resolution calling for the launching of a military campaign. Seeking German consent, the Hungarian ambassador to Berlin, Döme Sztójay, handed over the Hungarian memorandum to the German Ministry of Foreign Affairs the same day. German Under-secretary of Foreign Affairs Woermann informed him that they had already been informed about the Hungarian intention via the German ambassador to Budapest, Erdmannsdorff. He also informed him that the German government was anxiously watching the intended Hungarian step, because, if the Czechoslovakian army resisted, Germany could not be of assistance to Hungary.[5] The Hungarian government also tried to get information about the Italian reaction. On November 19, the Hungarian military attaché to Rome, Colonel László Szabó, who had been back in Hungary sick, was sent back to Rome to be instrumental in gaining the Italians' consent.[6]

The operative group to direct the planned armed operation included Prime Minister Imrédy, Minister of Foreign Affairs Kálmán Kánya, Minister of Defense Károly Bartha, Chief of the General Staff Werth and Chief of Intelligence (head of the 2nd Section of the General Staff) Colonel Rudolf Andorka, and went into session on November 19 waiting for the Italian agreement. Woermann's statement was not taken into consideration. Werth was very optimistic and hoped for success within two or three days. Andorka was more cautious and calculated that ten days would be needed.[7] Their plan called for the simultaneous intervention of the Hungarian and Polish raiding forces, with the Romanians remaining neutral as secured by the Poles. The attack would be launched by two army corps on November 20. The task of the VIII. Army Corps at Kassa was defense, while the VI. Army Corps, together with the forming mechanized brigades—a regiment of motorized and cyclist troops, a small company of tanks and four motorized batteries—were to swing into action. It was calculated that the two army corps, with their 18 battalions each, would have the upper hand against the heavily demoralized Czechoslovakian force of about 21 battalions, which had already lost the front fortification line. The remaining *Honvédség* forces would secure the area of Csallóköz and Rozsnyó.[8] The day of the attack had to be postponed to November 21—then again to 22—because the VI. Army Corps was late in reaching its launching point.[9]

By the evening of his departure, László Szabó's telephone message had already arrived back in Budapest, stating that

Mussolini—so long as the Germans were not against it—was himself not against the operation. What's more, according to Szabó, Mussolini offered 100 airplanes for the air defense of Budapest.[10]

However, the planned operation had to be cancelled. On November 21 the Hungarian ambassador to Rome, Villani, sent a telegram stating that Italian Minister of Foreign Affairs Galeazzo Ciano, Conte di Cortellazo, had requested that he and Szabó come to his office, where he informed them that the German government had sent them a memorandum expressing the position that the Sub-Carpathian operation ought to be stopped and that the Italians were in solidarity with the German government.

The surprised Minister of Foreign Affairs Kánya immediately turned to Berlin. He expressed his disappointment about the German position, which had come to Rome in an indirect way. He asked for the confirmation of the surprising German position.[11]

The German response was instant. Erdmannsdorff informed Kánya that, according to the German government, if the dubious-sounding military operation were to take place, the Vienna Award would lose its value, because the operation would show disrespect towards the two grantors of the Award. Hungary was expected to observe the judgment of the award.[12]

On November 21 German Minister of Foreign Affairs Joachim von Ribbentrop sent for Sztójay and expressed his disapproval of the Hungarian government's intention. He claimed that so far he had been convinced that the Hungarian government would not act upon this question before further discussions of the issue had taken place. He alluded to the fact that "Czechoslovakia has 14 well-equipped divisions and will launch an attack on Hungary, which would bring about a very critical situation in Hungary, while they [the Germans] will not be able to help." Sztójay argued that the Hungarian government had organized the operation in full knowledge of this fact and that von Ribbentrop considered the Czechoslovakian danger greater than the Hungarian government did. The German Minister of Foreign Affairs ignored Sztójay's interpolation and showered him with all his earlier accusations: the conclusion of the Bled Accord,[13] the Hungarian government's total withdrawal of any military cooperation and operation, the gestures of neutrality towards Great Britain, their intention to rely on two power centers in their international affairs, and, finally, a total lack of trust in the Axis Powers. After all that, Sztójay came to the following conclusion, which he shared with the Hungarian government: "It was a close shave. We should be happy that we survived."[14]

Since Imrédy and the military leadership had built the success of the operation on the fact that the Czechoslovakian army would not be able to regroup its forces and exert a serious resistance once tied down by the German threat, von Ribbentrop's stern tone and veto on the operation forced Imrédy to reevaluate things. He came to the conclusion that the grievances that the Germans had experienced from the Hungarians could only be redressed by some future measures that would please them. Without that, any attempt at a territorial revision could hardly be imagined.

Werth agreed with Imrédy in evaluating the situation, and on November 29 explained to Andorka that "we have to fully surrender to the Germans."[15]

The Chief of the General Staff trusted that the Prime Minister would understand and support his ambitions for the army, since the Prime Minister had himself been the creator of the armament program. Imrédy's political aspirations with regard to concentrating power by taking leadership into his own hands, and introducing government by decree were ideas not too remote from Werth's. However, Werth had just taken office and was occupied with the concentration of forces and military operations relating to the occupation of Sub-Carpathia following the Vienna Award, leaving him little time to clarify his relationship with the Prime

Minister more thoroughly or to evaluate the internal political situation around him. Yet the turn of events soon forced him to make up for his negligence in this area. The intensification of hidden disagreements within the government party following the Sub-Carpathian failure had led to unsettling dissident activities, to the voting down of the government and to its resignation, and then to its recreation, which all shook up the officer corps. Some officers who sympathized with the extreme right hoped for a continuation of Imrédy's "reform policy" and were concerned about the "change of the guard," and thus felt compelled to be more active politically. They paid close attention to the creation of a mass party, the extreme right-wing Hungarian Life Movement (*Magyar Élet Mozgalom*), initiated by Imrédy. The fact that Jenő Rátz, who had retired from the government, was actively involved in running the movement indicated that it could count on the support of the officer corps in addition to the civil servants.

Faithful to his obligations as indicated in his orders to his officers, Werth acted against these more and more direct political activities. He spurned those clap-trapping officers with Arrow-Cross sympathies who endangered military discipline. However, he became unsure when he discovered the Prime Minister's followers and most trusted co-workers among the politically active officers. He was surprised to discover that even in his immediate environment many young General Staff officers had become more and more openly politically engaged. Werth came to realize that he was considered a re-activated and apolitical old fogey who did not understand the spirit of the age and its call. It was not difficult to discover the dismissed Jenő Rátz, the closest confidante of the Prime Minister, behind all this. Moreover, Werth thought that certain officers' confidence in Horthy had been shaken, which he considered an unacceptable development threatening the discipline of the whole army. He made up his mind to call the Regent's attention to it. As Chief of Intelligence Colonel Andorka noted in his diary, "it seems that Werth in his naïve way is going to be tricked by the extremists." When speaking about forcing back the extreme right, Werth mentioned the fact that in his immediate environment he had discovered that the pro-Jewish behavior of the Horthy brothers had given rise to antipathy towards the Regent in certain officers.[16] He also suggested to Andorka that definite measures should be taken, first of all, against the Arrow-Cross officers. Werth also stated that he did not know what to do with Imrédy's followers, who posed an equally great threat towards the army's discipline. They attacked Werth and demanded personnel changes in the military command, and gradually became more powerful in the shadow of the Prime Minister. All these phenomena led Werth to discover the Prime Minister's lack of trust in him.

At the same time, those who hoped that Werth would hinder the extreme right from gaining ground in the military, and who expected him to put a stop to political activity within the army, also lost hope. Werth did not seem to be able to put the army in order, and he appeared indeed to be just an old fogey with no sense for political nuances. Werth was unsuspecting towards everyone and easily influenced politically. This explained, he went on, why there was order in civilian life but complete chaos in the army, as the officer corps' discipline sank to its lowest point. Keresztes-Fischer did not conceal his opinion from Imrédy or Bartha either. Bartha, who at this point in time was trying to serve his Prime Minister without any reservations, defended the officer corps but turned against Werth, and stated that it was little wonder that the Chief of the General Staff could not win over the officer corps, since he considered them a "horde." Andorka noted the following in his diary: "Bartha simply does not want to see clearly and stands on Imrédy's radical line himself. He shuts his eyes and sees everything as beautiful."[17]

Early in January 1939 Werth once again issued a staff instruction in which he tried to prevent the officers from discussing politics:

> ... three months ago, in my instruction as new Chief of the General Staff, I outlined the picture of an ideal General Staff officer and clarified my views about politics. I was very clear in stating that a General Staff officer is not to voice party-political ideas. Our political views are given, because they cannot be different from what is legitimized by the government of the Regent. Each one of the General Staff officers should submit to this policy, should represent it to the outside world, and cannot look left or right in order to save himself in the case of political changes... Discussing politics has still not stopped among the General Staff, while some of you still voice party-political principles and make tendentious political statements contrary to military discipline and to the healthy atmosphere that a serious and important institution such as the General Staff should possess. One more time I emphatically warn every single member of the General Staff to refrain from making political statements... Careless remarks by individuals of this body inherently carry the danger of setting bad examples to troop officers and of inciting them towards similarly careless actions and statements. Therefore, General Staff officers should thoroughly consider what they say and what they do. This applies... especially to senior officers... The act of a senior officer who wants to guide his subordinate or subordinates onto the field of politics, instead of keeping them back, is an unforgivable sin worthy of immediate retribution.

Furthermore, Werth also emphasized the point that those General Staff officers who, contrary to the order, were unable to detach themselves from politics should request their retirement or otherwise, he—Werth—would be forced to send them into retirement. All this did not indicate, he added, that the General Staff should not be allowed or indeed that they would not actually be obliged "to get to know and study the new thoughts of the age."[18]

The instruction did not much change the situation. Werth continued to be at the center of pressure squeezing from several directions. Acting against officers antagonistic towards the government policy sanctified by the Regent would have been simple if it had only been Arrow-Cross people. However, Werth's situation was aggravated by the fact that he had to take measures against some who were influencing the policy of the government in power. Although he was uncertain about navigating in the turbulent waters of the political circle that operated behind the scenes, he soon recognized the growing antagonism between Horthy and Imrédy, and did not hesitate to stand by Horthy.

Toying with the idea of resignation, Werth complained to Horthy about his impossible situation and his worries about the future of the *Honvédség*. The Regent reassured him and, in opposition to Imrédy, confirmed his Chief of the General Staff in his position and reaffirmed his statement that he, Werth, continued to work with the Regent's favor. With the approaching downfall of the Prime Minister, Werth's paralysis towards Imrédy and his followers gradually lessened. Werth's vanity was hurt and so he turned against his assumed greatest enemy, Rátz and his followers in the army. On February 7, in the presence of Minister of the Interior Keresztes-Fischer, Werth outlined to Rátz his destructive role within the army. Werth held him responsible for the army's disintegration.[19]

Werth's actions against Rátz's followers were far from being as complete as could have been expected. Werth was aware that they also enjoyed the support of the Germans and that they were eager to attack him in front of the latter. Besides his own tilt towards the Germans, the latter reason also contributed to his statements that his steps were of domestic interest only and were not against the country's German orientation as urged by the Prime Minister and his followers.

When on February 16, 1939, the Teleki government took office, Werth's situation solidified at the head of the army. Officers of an extreme right-wing bent were now ready to accept the "stiff and apolitical" general whose head they had been after not such a long time ago. All of a sudden Werth found himself surrounded by people loyal to him. The officer corps, which continued to see the realization of their revisionist goals in deepening the relationship with Germany, lined up with him and against the new Prime Minister Count Pál Teleki, who was expected to restrain the country's pro-German foreign policy and commitments as well as any political influence over the military command.

Following the change of government, there were soon signs of differences between Teleki and Werth. Teleki did not look forward happily to the activities of the Chief of the General Staff, but hoped that his loyalty to the Regent, discipline, dedication to the law and regulations, and also his antagonism with Rátz, would be enough to restrain him from extreme pro-German activities.

Werth also soon recognized Teleki as an adversary. He did not hesitate to bring it home to Teleki that he considered political interference by civilians in military affairs beyond a certain point to be obstructive, because it decreased military efficiency. In order to realize his military-political ideas, Werth needed support and a free hand, and if he were not granted them then he would be forced to choose between independent activity and resignation.

The confident conduct of the Chief of the General Staff irritated Teleki, which soon led to tension between them, but it received a favorable response in the military command and, most of all, among the General Staff officers. According to the latter "Werth represented the active military will, as opposed to the government's approach, which tried to find diplomatic ways and kept begging for favors."[20] They agreed with Werth that the Chief of the General Staff had to play a decisive role as the head of the Hungarian military, in order to shape and realize those principles and practices that corresponded to military-political goals. Werth tried to have this approach accepted by those people outside the army who played a role in shaping the policy of the country. He emphasized the point that this was the only way for him to responsibly satisfy his appointment. He saw the government's foreign political and domestic political "uncertainties" as disturbing factors in the attempts to develop stable military-political goals, and considered that these "disturbances" made preparations for maximal effort impossible. This is how such conditions are created as to damage the realization of the main goal—territorial revision. He had been appointed by the Regent and, therefore, he was supposed to give an account of his activities to him. This was the relationship that he tried to play against the politicians, generally with success. And that was how the Chief of the General Staff became a state within the state, as Teleki later complained to the Regent. Werth forgot that the government had a military policy that he was supposed to realize, and not vice versa.

The Teleki–Werth opposition soon took on a personal nature. Werth, a general from Swabian peasant stock, had an instinctive aversion to the aristocrat, famous scientist and statesman, who, as Werth perceived it, considered him a Swabian petty bourgeois, a limited and aspiring sergeant in spite of his rank as a general and his high office. He grasped every opportunity to make up for his inferiority complex towards Teleki. It worked in his favor that for a long time he enjoyed Regent Horthy's confidence, and Horthy overlooked their animosity and tried to diminish it in his own way. It also strengthened Werth's position that he frequently antagonized

Teleki to accelerate the realization of the revisionist goals, which made Werth popular among the officer corps.

With growing concern Teleki watched how Werth's and the military command's sphere of influence increased, and how Werth committed the country to Germany with the knowledge and consent of the Regent, intoxicated by the German successes, and against the government, something which would lead to a tragic end sooner or later.

Notes

1. General of the Infantry Henrik Werth (1881–1952)'s most important positions: Head of Department 6-1 of the Ministry of Defense (1922–1926), Commander of the General Staff Academy (1926–1931), Commander of the 4th Pécs Mixed Brigade (1931–1936), Chief of the General Staff (1938–1941).
2. For more, see *Hadtörténelmi Közlemények* (1977) 1: pp. 5–7.
3. Hadtörténelmi Levéltár (Military History Archive, HL). Eln. Vkf.1. 1938/752.
4. When in August 1938 Hitler elaborated on his plans for Czechoslovakia to Regent Miklós Horthy, Prime Minister Béla Imrédy and Minister of Foreign Affairs Kálmán Kánya, the Hungarian politicians refused to participate in a German military action against Czechoslovakia, citing the unpreparedness of the *Honvédség*. They were afraid of international consequences, found Germany's military strength insufficient to resist a probable Western military intervention, and did not trust Romania's and Yugoslavia's neutrality either. The military command did not think that an attack against the Czechoslovakian line of fortifications with the available forces was possible. According to the evaluation of the Hungarian General Staff, the troops to be mobilized would reach their complete readiness to march only by the end of the year.
5. Országos Levéltár (National Archive, OL). K 64-83-33/a-1400/1938. Rp.
6. Rudolf Andorka, *A madridi követségtől Mauthausenig* (From the Madrid Embassy to Mauthausen) (Budapest, 1978), p. 63.
7. *Ibid.*, p. 64.
8. OL. K 64-83-33/a-1469/1938. Rp.
9. Andorka, *A madridi követségtől...*, p. 65.
10. OL. K 64-83-33/a-1398/1938. Rp.
11. *Ibid.*
12. György Ránki, Ervin Pamlényi, Loránt Tilkovszky and Gyula Juhász, eds., *A Wilhelmstrasse és Magyarország: Német diplomáciai iratok Magyarországról, 1933–1944* (The Wilhelmstrasse and Hungary: German Diplomatic Documents about Hungary, 1933–1944) (Budapest, 1968), p. 328. (164.sz. irat) (writing No. 164)

13. After secret conferences the Hungarian government signed the preliminary agreement with the Little Entente states in Bled, Yugoslavia, on August 22, 1938, which caused Berlin's resentment. In the document the Little Entente states recognized the right of Hungary's rearmament, and in return Hungary gave up hostile intentions against them.
14. OL. K 64-83-33/a-1486/1/1938. Rp.
15. Andorka, *A madridi követségtől...*, p. 70.
16. *Ibid.*, p. 78.
17. *Ibid.*, pp. 79 and 80.
18. HL. Eln. Vkf.1. 1939/711.
19. Andorka, *A madridi követségtől...*, p. 102.
20. Gyula Kádár, *A Ludovikától Sopronkőhidáig* (From the Ludovika [Military Academy] to Sopronkőhida) (Budapest, 1978), p. 343.

DIFFERENCES IN FOREIGN POLITICAL AND DEFENSE ISSUES BETWEEN THE GOVERNMENT AND THE GENERAL STAFF: TELEKI'S AND WERTH'S DISCORD

Even in the middle of the domestic political fights within the government, gaining the goodwill of the German government was of crucial importance for Hungary's élites, in the hope that they would be able to facilitate obtaining Germany's consent to the occupation of Sub-Carpathia. From the German side, signs of accommodation were forthcoming in order to support Imrédy, who had been coming around to the Germans, had organized a fascist-like movement, and had also met with an increasing internal resistance.

The new Minister of Foreign Affairs, Count István Csáky, who followed Kálmán Kánya, was pleased to receive von Ribbentrop's invitation to visit in January 1939. In order to get a more friendly reception before his departure for Berlin, Csáky announced Hungary's plan to join the anti-Comintern pact on January 12 and also held out the prospect that Hungary would withdraw from the League of Nations. Werth and the military command looked forward to the visit with great expectations. They agreed that even if concessions had to be given, German permission for a Sub-Carpathian operation had to be gained. The visit was also considered significant with regard to an increased German support to arm and equip the Hungarian army.

Before Csáky's departure an unexpected border incident at Munkács caused a stir. In the early morning hours of January 6 there was a clash between the Hungarian and the Czechoslovakian border guards, in which even tanks were deployed by the Czechoslovakian side. Although the incident had simmered down by the morning hours and the Czechoslovakian forces withdrew from the Hungarian territories that they had penetrated, in Budapest Imrédy, Csáky and Werth quickly conferred to discuss needed actions. In addition to Csáky, Werth especially showed signs of determination, and he considered the incident to provide a good opportunity to solve the Ruthenian question immediately and radically. He suggested that the I., the II., the V. and the VI. Army Corps be put on alert. Imrédy put a dampener on the mood, saying that Germany would surely not allow an independent operation at that point in time. Such a step would only ruin the chances of the upcoming conferences. Therefore, Werth gave orders to merely reinforce the border guards, as Minister of Defense Bartha informed the Council of Ministers on January 14.[1] Due to a total failure of the ensuing examinations by both sides and due to the impossibility of finding out who the initiators of the clash were, the case of the border incident was set aside. However, Csáky did not fail to reprimand the soldiers for leaving the border open.

The Hungarian Minister of Foreign Affairs incurred reproaches from Hitler upon arriving in Berlin. Hitler also emphasized the fact that although Hungary had been reluctant to move earlier, when Germany had requested it to do so, it had certainly attained its goal with Germany's help: Hungary had been able to validate its territorial claims towards Czechoslovakia. Following that, the ungrateful Hungarian government had wished to initiate an armed operation behind Germany's back. For future reference, Hitler advised avoiding such operations and recommended a more moderated policy towards Yugoslavia and Romania. Without any further ado, he informed Csáky that in the future he expected an unambiguously committed policy towards Germany, a policy also substantiated by actions.

Von Ribbentrop essentially repeated his Führer's accusations and admonitions. At Csáky's inquiry as to what kind of future German plans Hungary could count on, von Ribbentrop gave an evasive reply but felt obliged to emphasize the point that it was in Germany's interest to have a strong Hungary. Alluding to the January 6 border incident, Csáky noted that should it happen again, the Hungarian government might find itself in a situation when it had to shoot back and to push forward. Von Ribbentrop returned this in kind and said that Germany would not stay indifferent if a cannon were fired in Europe; once again, he warned against any unilateral Hungarian step: Germany would not consent to a one-sided solution of the Hungarian–Czechoslovakian border question. He warned Csáky to take measures so that the Hungarian irregular troops active along the border would cease to stir up trouble. Finally, he felt it urgent to mention the usefulness of the Hungarian–Yugoslavian rapprochement and the improvement of relations with Romania.[2]

Whatever was said during Csáky's Berlin visit, it did not hinder Werth in his unquestioning belief in Germany's helpful intentions. In his view, regaining Hitler's benign outlook and regaining deepening connections with Germany were the major results of the meeting. Moreover, improving relations would bring the Germans around to give their consent to the Sub-Carpathian operation. Werth was not alone in this belief. In spite of the Berlin outcome, several military and civilian politicians, and not only extreme right-wing ones, counted on the rapid intensification of German relations and on a radical solution to the Czechoslovakian question. And Hungary would have a role in it as well. Prime Minister Teleki, who in the meantime had succeeded the dismissed Imrédy, also shared in these views. The new government continued to keep the question of the Sub-Carpathian issue on its agenda. During a conversation with Werth, Csáky explained that, in spite of their silence, he did not think that the Germans considered the Czechoslovakian issue settled. And furthermore, they supported the Slovaks' and Ruthenians' striving for independence, in order to facilitate Czechoslovakia's disintegration. In Csáky's view the Germans did not really oppose Ruthenia's annexation to Hungary. As far as Romania was concerned, the Romanian question could be brought to the foreground later.[3]

The semi-official German comments also nurtured the military's and the politicians' conscious evaluation of the Czechoslovakian question. After the official statements, Germany strove to keep Hungary's revisionism, which had failed in November, alive for its own purposes. On February 7 Sztójay quoted an informer close to Hermann Göring—it must have been General Heinrich Bodenschatz, Göring's aide-de-camp—who confidentially informed Csáky, and probably Werth as well, that it was in Germany's interest to annex Czechoslovakia's former Austrian territory in the near future[4] and that the eastern parts could be annexed by Hungary. When Sztójay pointed out that "we should be informed about the date well ahead of time, because in this subject concrete agreements and military discussions are also necessary," his informer answered that the Czechoslovakian liquidation might already happen before April of the same year. Furthermore, he reassured Sztójay that Germany would not get involved in war with the Western countries during the year. To stave off uneasiness about the deployment of the ill-equipped Hungarian army, the informer also noted, as was also reassured by other sources according to Sztójay, that the Czechoslovakian army had been weakened and its heavy artillery had been bought by the Germans and was actually in Germany.

The information coming from Sztójay, which described the nature of the German armaments in detail, and in an exaggerated form, made a major impact on Werth. This information estimated the numbers of the German army as 20 million, with 150–220 divisions. News about the German air force received special emphasis. Sztójay gave information about new airplanes, which could reach the shores of England at any time and which could wage decisive strikes on the bases of the British fleet. According to the German plan, in the case of war "the states of Central and Eastern Europe had to take an immediate and concrete stand with regard to belonging to one of the parties or the other."[5] If one of the states closed its borders, it would be made to support the German Reich by force.

Werth was absolutely in favor of the above conclusion, since he had stated it earlier when speaking about the "war of the future." His first and foremost informer was Ambassador Sztójay, who had been the Hungarian military attaché to Berlin from 1928 to 1935 and then ambassador from 1935 onwards. From the beginning of his service, Sztójay had done everything to facilitate a pro-German Hungarian foreign policy. As military attaché he considered it his duty to deepen the connections between the Hungarian and the German General Staff. Szójay, a former fellow General Staff officer, had had a major effect on Werth in the first half of the 1920s, when Werth was the Chief of the 1st Section of the General Staff and Sztójay was the Chief of the 2nd Section of the General Staff. The two had very close working relations and shared the same views about the future development of the country and the army. During those years Werth increasingly came to respect Sztójay, who carved out a significant political career. Thus Werth came to completely trust and consider Sztójay's military knowledge, which had a wide political horizon as well. Most probably, Werth also considered Sztójay to be a non-official trustee between himself and the political and military circles of the Reich, one who also informed him about confidential issues behind the scenes in Berlin, and who also might have informed the same circles about Werth and the army under him, and about the developing differences of opinions between Werth and the Hungarian government. The intimate exchange of news between Sztójay and Werth took place through personal meetings, through the military attaché to Berlin, and through the members of the Hungarian General Staff who frequently paid visits to Berlin.

Sztójay's ambassadorial reports and analyses never lacked military analyses far beyond what the tasks of an ambassador entailed. He placed the strength and battlefield achievements of the German army at the forefront, in order that they might be considered when Hungarian political decisions were passed, a tactic which was not ineffectual for Teleki either. With all that, Sztójay tried to support Werth's ambitions.

In February 1939 the Berlin information drove the Hungarian political and military leadership to the conclusion that they had to be prepared to take political and military action soon, that they should increase their revisionist propaganda, that, besides preparations for mobilization, the disarmed irregular troops should be placed on a state of alert, and that operations ought to be harmonized with the General Staff of the Polish army. All these things should be done even if they could not count on the operation before April, according to the received information.[6]

Werth, however, did not find the preparations adequate. He had long been preparing for the immediate utilization of an opportunity to act and had been preparing further necessary measures, including the ordering of certain units to alert status. As Andorka wrote in his diary on February 28, it was impossible to explain to him that until the Germans' resistance with regard to Hungarian revisionism was tackled, any kind of military venture, and preparation for it, was hopeless.[7]

Werth's attitude towards urging military preparations did not remain secret in Berlin. On March 5 German *Abwehr* officers Lahousen and Stolz were sent to Budapest to inquire of Andorka about the issues disturbing the development of cooperation between the two armies, such as the Ruthenian issue. During their discussion Andorka called his German visitors' attention to the fact that if Hungary was not free to tackle the Ruthenian question, that issue would be solved by Warsaw and Bucharest.[8]

On March 10 the Chief of the General Staff turned to Prime Minister Teleki and expounded on the Ruthenian question. There were signs that the solution would be of immediate importance. He suggested developing a closer cooperation with the Polish irregular troops. Furthermore, in case a partial mobilization was not possible, he suggested the organization of illegal units of officers and privates within the *Honvédség*, through which Hungary would be ready to perform a surprise occupation of Sub-Carpathia at any time, without having to order a full mobilization and thus attract the attention of foreign countries ahead of time.[9]

With the intensification of the Czechoslovakian question, the Hungarian government also considered it necessary to inquire via Sztójay about the expected German reaction via the German Ministry of Foreign Affairs. On March 4 Sztójay requested of von Ribbentrop that Germany and Italy deliver statements that they recognized Hungary's priority with the Sub-Carpathian territories. The German Minister of Foreign Affairs advised patience and also promised Sztójay that he, von Ribbentrop, would get in touch with the Hungarian government in time before whatever change might occur on the Czechoslovakian issue.

With the attempt to remove the Slovak leader Monsignor Jozef Tiso on March 10, the events leading to the proclamation of an independent Slovakia and the dissolution of the Czechoslovakian state had begun.

Hearing the news, Werth asked for a partial mobilization on March 11. However, the government was cautious and considered it satisfactory to call up two age-groups for a military exercise. They were concerned that the Germans would consider a mobilization as an anti-Tiso measure. Teleki agreed to issue an immediate alarm for the border guard battalions.[10]

The *Honvédség* was caught off-guard by Hitler's message of March 13 that the Hungarian government had a free hand in occupying Sub-Carpathia. The Hungarians were requested to launch the operation in complete secrecy before March 15. Furthermore, they were forbidden to inform the Italians and the Poles as pledged by the Hungarian government. For his help, Horthy was very grateful to Hitler.[11]

Amidst the general euphoria Werth expressed justifiable reservations when he was informed that he had to launch his troops on March 15. He would have liked to ask for a week for the mobilization and for the concentration of the troops, since the preparations for the mobilization of the *Honvédség* alone took 72 hours.[12] The short time at their disposal made the mobilization of reserves impossible, and only the regular military units could be counted on. The operation would have been risky to perform with the new recruits, most of whom had served only since February 1. Undoubtedly, in the case of resistance the 12th Czechoslovakian Infantry Division and the 2nd Mechanized Brigade of the 2nd Czechoslovakian Division could cause serious losses to the occupying Hungarian troops and even might put the whole operation into doubt.[13] Tension about the uncertainty of the situation was not relieved by the news about the Slovakian situation, which included intensified Czech and Slovak conflicts due to demands placed by the independent Slovakian army, clashes between Czech soldiers and the Hlinka Guard, and the rapid deterioration of the fighting morale of units stationed in Slovakia. The Hungarian government and military leadership had not received any information about the German invasion of Czechoslovakia on March 15. Lacking all sorts of information, and with the greatest misgivings, Werth issued the command for the immediate deployment of Hungarian units for the occupying military operation that would start two days later.

The government did not agree with Werth's justified doubts. They feared that if they did not act by the time set by the Germans, they would miss the opportunity. It was also a concern that the head of the Sub-Carpathian autonomous government, Ágost Volosin, on the German payroll, would manage to see that an independent Carpathia-Ukraine would be established. Therefore, on March 14 Csáky handed over an ultimatum to the Czechoslovakian ambassador in Budapest and, in spite of the German interdict, informed Polish Minister of Foreign Affairs Beck that the *Honvédség* would start the following day, in order to use the only possible opportunity.

Since during the short time at their disposal no substantial preparations could be made, on March 15 the units of the mechanized brigades stationed near the border in northeastern Hungary— two hussar regiments, five bicycle battalions and two mechanized battalions (the latter at the very earliest phase of their preparations) joined the operation and crossed the border. The mechanized units were followed by the 24th Ungvár Infantry Regiment and the border guard units. The transports of the 5th, 8th and 17th Infantry Regiments, dispatched from Transdanubia in haste, arrived only on March 16, continuously unloaded in the already occupied area, and joined the advancing forces. What made this possible was the fact that the retreating Czechoslovakian units did not blow up the railway equipment. At the same time the troops of the V. and the VI. Army Corps—stationed in eastern Hungary and mobilized in the meantime—secured the operation in the direction of Romania while the II. and the VII. Army Corps secured it towards the north.[14]

The advancing army did not meet much resistance anywhere. They only had a small clash with the Szics Guard. On March 16 the bicycle units reached the Polish border at Verecke, and on March 17 the mechanized units advancing in the Tisza Valley occupied Kőrösmező while other troops reached Uzsok.

The Hungarian government was very pleased with the success of the operation. Relatively early, March 17, Csáky characterized the events to the Council of Ministers as a done deal, saying that "with Hungary's forceful, determined and quick action, as well as its amazingly dashing performance, our *Honvédség* has gained a lot of prestige both with Germany and Italy and with other countries."[15] In speaking about the foreign political reception, he mostly emphasized the unexpected nature of the situation, which confronted the neighboring countries with a *fait accompli*. In referring to the Western countries, he added that France was more pleased that Sub-Carpathia went to Hungary than it would have been if it had been occupied by Germany. Speaking about Romania, he established that the Romanians did not dare to march in the border area because he, Csáky, had let them know that Hungary would retaliate against any kind of attack.

However, the Hungarian government was not as sure about the Romanian measures as Csáky's words might indicate. They were watching the Romanian movements on the border with great concern, and both they and the soldiers were very pleased that no clash occurred. The Romanians laid claim to villages with a Romanian population north of the Huszt–Berezna–Bisztra line and also laid claim to the Kőrösmező railway. Finally, being isolated and fearing the Germans, the Romanians did not dare to stage an armed incident, yet the presence of the mobilized Romanian troops on the border indicating an interest in attacking put the Hungarian–Romanian relationship on edge.[16]

A general acknowledgement of the situation that had been created by the occupation of Sub-Carpathia only slowly led to the easing of tensions. On March 20 the Hungarian ambassador to Bucharest, László Bárdossy, informed Csáky, quoting Romanian government sources, that Romania had no plans to attack Hungary. His sources indicated that the reason for the mobilization was the great confusion and concern raised by the fear of a possible German or a common German–Hungarian attack.[17] Csáky did not delay the response. He established at the March 23 session of the Parliament's

Foreign Political Committee that the Hungarian government had no plans to launch a military action against Romania. However, the situation would be different should Hungary experience a Romanian attack, but this was at present totally improbable.[18] Following that, it was not until the end of April that both countries withdrew their forces concentrated on the border. However, the Romanian forces withdrawn to peacetime garrisons were kept at an elevated number. Along the whole border, accelerated preparations for fortifications were underway.[19]

Due to information gathered from non-official sources—and confirmed by the General Staff, the Hungarian government was of the view that further opportunities had arisen to re-occupy more areas from the currently forming Slovakian state using the concentrated Hungarian forces. Thus, the Kassa–Eperjes line, the Nyitra and the surrounding area were being considered. The first step was taken on March 23, when Hungarian troops occupied this area in order to secure the Ung Valley from the west. However, no more territory was acquired, because on March 24, at the immediate and vehement protest of the German and Slovakian governments, the Hungarian government cancelled any further advance. Csáky wanted to avoid embittering the relationship with the Germans. Via Sztójay, the government of the German Reich sent a map with the exact line of the new Hungarian–Slovakian border, thereby summarily informing the Hungarian government that they considered the established situation as final.[20]

Troops marching into Sub-Carpathia had hardly arrived at their target locations when Werth's letter was on Teleki's and Csáky's desks. He reported that the occupation of Sub-Carpathia was complete, although the "pacification" of the area would take a long period of time, due to its terrain. As opposed to Csáky's enthusiasm, the Chief of the General Staff qualified the operation as an adventure in military terms. Due to the exigent situation, there was a great imbalance between the task and forces applied to it, and thus the military had been unprepared for the operation. The success was solely due to the performance of the troops and to luck. Werth also called attention to the fact that, following the occupation of northern Hungary, Hungarian troops were in a state of mobilization and that the occupation of Sub-Carpathia had also been planned. It should be noted, however, that the state of alert had been cancelled and that his proposal of March 10 urging that preparations start was not accorded any attention. As Werth continued to complain, two days after making his proposal the political leadership had added requirements on him that could have only been met by undertaking the greatest risk—a coerced deployment of the newly recruited troops. Finally, and after not taking into account the circumstances of how the Germans allowed the occupation of Sub-Carpathia, he called on the relevant politicians by saying "... please inform me about future political goals in time, so that I am able to carry out the military preparations according to plans and in a reliable fashion."[21]

Whatever had happened, it made the Chief of the General Staff cautious; thus, even contrary to the government's desire, he tried to delay the disarmament of the mobilized forces. In the still tense situation, he wanted to preclude the possibility that it might again become incapable of action. However, Minister of Defense Bartha considered the Romanian military measures as defensive and also came to the conclusion, based on events of the recent past, that "an initiative that might propel Hungary into a war in the near future could only be expected from the Axis Powers anyway." After convincing Werth, Bartha proposed to the government on April 15 that the troops on the Romanian border, kept at war strength at great financial sacrifice, be disarmed.[22] Bartha, however, made some concessions to the Chief of the General Staff by being willing to wait with the disarmament "until the Prime Minister returns from his trip to Rome, and to keep the move dependent on the results of political discussions."[23]

However, the demobilization of the troops did take place before the Prime Minister's trip to Rome. In view of Csáky's exposé, the Romanian government ordered the disarmament of older age-groups of its army on April 14. Reciprocally, the disarmament of Hungarian troops also began on April 16.[24]

It was not only the tense Romanian–Hungarian relationship that delayed the earlier demobilization of the troops. In the meantime, the Italian–Albanian conflict had intensified, which also entailed the sudden deterioration of Italian–Yugoslavian relations. On April 5 Csáky informed the narrow circle of the Council of Ministers that the conflict might escalate into war and, consequently, lead to the division of Yugoslavia. In this case a military presence along with Italy might make expansion to the south possible.

On the day before the session of the Council of Ministers, Csáky instructed Villani to inquire of Ciano whether it was possible that Italy would go to war against Yugoslavia. Csáky emphasized the point that the question was raised for the sake of the army, since he was aware that in the case of an Italian action against Yugoslavia it had to be ready. Therefore, a definite Italian stand was needed for any Hungarian action. Concentrating the mobilized Hungarian forces on the country's southern border would take about 48 hours. On the other hand, maintaining the mobilized troops there in vain entailed severe economic costs and would take the money away from the ongoing armament program.[25]

Ciano did not give a definite "yes" to Villani, but did not exclude the possibility of an Italian–Yugoslavian armed clash either, which might make it possible for Hungary to expand to the south.[26]

On April 16, the day after the session of the Council of Ministers, Villani once again contacted Csáky and called his attention to differences within the Italian government and General Staff as regard the Yugoslavian question. Hearing of Csáky's inquiry, Mussolini thanked Villani for the Hungarian offer, but said that, since the Yugoslavs would hardly move against Italy, there would not be any need to utilize the Hungarian troops.[27]

Csáky did not gain the unequivocal support of the Hungarian military leadership for the anti-Yugoslavian plan, because, as he quickly recognized, the Italian ideas clashed with Germany's Balkan policy. On March 21 László Szabó, the Hungarian military attaché to Rome, informed his superiors that the occupation of Czechoslovakia had created an anti-German atmosphere in the Italian public, including fears of the Germans becoming excessively strong. Italian–German interests clashed with regard to Yugoslavia, which put into question the possibility of an Italian armed intervention there. To prevent a German expansion in the Balkans seemed to be vital for the Italians. It was Mussolini's task to get around the worries of the Italian public, as well as certain politicians, and to settle the situation, which had provoked a crisis in the Axis.[28] Werth informed Csáky about the instructions that he had sent to Szabó on March 27, in which he stated that, under the circumstances, the Hungarian military leadership did not find it possible or effective "that we, once again, contribute to or attempt the internal destruction of Yugoslavia with devices used once before."[29]

When they made the offer to the Italians the Hungarian foreign policy planners were motivated by something beyond the hope of gaining territory. In the tense international situation they sought support against the threatening German expansionist ambitions. The deteriorating German–Polish relations, after the annexation of Czechoslovakia and the pressure put on Poland, did not leave any doubt that Germany's next victim was to be Poland. The Hungarian government and the public, rejoicing over the finally materialized Hungarian–Polish border, were placed in an embarrassing situation by the ever-intensifying conflict. The question was whether the situation would deepen into war, how isolated such a war would remain, and what role in it Germany planned for Hungary. The

Hungarian government wanted to stay as far away as possible. In addition to its being difficult to make the pro-Polish public accept any anti-Polish measure, it would also inevitably have led to an open break with the Western powers. The conclusion of the British–Polish mutual assistance pact on April 6, the ratification of the French–Polish accord, and the British–French guarantee pact concluded with Greece and Romania on April 13 did not leave any doubt in Teleki's mind that a German attack on Poland would lead to an armed engagement with the Western powers.

When, between April 18 and 20, Teleki and Csáky brought up the Polish question with Mussolini during their visit to Rome, as well as the issue of likely ensuing German pressure on Hungary, Mussolini reassured them that if that ever happened, it would be the end of the Axis. Hungary could count on Italy's full support. Then unexpectedly Mussolini suggested rapprochement towards Yugoslavia, when, only a few days before, the Hungarian politicians had offered their assistance in a military operation against their southern neighbor. The Duce said that the Italian government would be glad to see an agreement, and requested that the Hungarian government not try to enforce its revisionist demands upon Yugoslavia. He also cautioned the need for tactfulness towards Romania. He was not going to conclude any agreement with Romania behind the back of the Hungarian government, but Hungary should understand that any harassment would drive Romania into Germany's embrace.

Recognizing Mussolini's intention of establishing a balance within the Axis through winning over the small states, Teleki agreed to follow his guidelines: isolating Romania without pushing it towards Germany, and friendship with Yugoslavia, while temporarily putting aside revisionist ambitions towards it.[30]

On April 27, a few days after the visit to Rome, Csáky asked Villani to inform the Italian Minister of Foreign Affairs, before Ciano met von Ribbentrop, about the Hungarian government's position concerning the German–Polish conflict. As he had done before during the Rome discussions, Csáky once again established that Hungary was not in a position to participate directly on the German side against Poland. However, the Hungarian government came up with a new and unique offer that held out the prospect of indirect support of Germany and thus seemed to be applicable to reassure the Germans. At the same time, this offer made it possible to confront Romania and, in a best case scenario, promised at least a partial satisfaction of territorial demands against it. According to plans, in the case of a German–Polish conflict Hungary would institute an immediate mobilization and concentrate at Sub-Carpathia and at other points along the Romanian border, because it was not known what obligations Romania—allied to Poland—would undertake in the case of a German attack. If Romania responded to this Hungarian step with further mobilization of its own, the Hungarian government would come to certain conclusions. Csáky concluded, "In this way we will not directly fight the Poles, because that is a total impossibility due to domestic concerns and, besides, we are also morally opposed to it. But at the same time, the Germans cannot say either that we did not stand beside them. Perhaps in this way the situation can be avoided that over time the German Reich gradually takes everything into its hands, as happened in Czechoslovakia."[31] Considering that our own deployment tied down our railways, we would be compelled to reject the German intention to pass through, he added.

The circumstances of how the above Hungarian offer was formulated are unknown. However, the opinion of the General Staff, which was completely bogged down by the preparations for war against Romania, must have counted as well. Hoping for some support for Hungarian territorial demands in Romania was considered unlikely by the General Staff, so long as Hungary remained completely passive on the Polish question. They had to seek a conciliatory solution that might be accepted by Germany. The more and more shaky Italian position also helped to convince the soldiers. Speaking about the German–Polish conflict on May 1, Mussolini told László Szabó that Italy would be neutral and would deny anyone the right to pass through its territory. But if the conflict could not be localized, Hungary should stand by Germany with its full armed force, just as Italy would do.[32]

Mussolini's position greatly distressed Teleki, who did not believe that the German–Polish war could be confined. He thought it would necessarily escalate into a clash between Germany and the Western powers, which would possibly bring about Germany's defeat. Therefore, "as much as possible Hungary has to stay away from the war and has to beware of being mixed up in an open armed conflict with the Western powers. It has to be prevented that Hungary be subjected to international isolation, as happened after the Great War. And, while relying on the essentially intact armed forces, this is how the regime should be secured through the cataclysm that will, by all means, result in a political and power vacuum in Central Europe."[33] Thus Teleki and his circle considered staying away from the war to be of vital national importance, and wanted to gain the support of the Italians for this objective. He gradually lost faith in the revisionist dreams that might be implemented with the help of the Germans. Also, it was increasingly improbable that Germany, which had become more and more influential in Romanian politics and had gained more and more economic advantages there, could be won over for the revisionist project against Romanian territory.

These hopes decreased further during Teleki's and Csáky's visit in Berlin. Hitler himself received the two Hungarian politicians on April 29. He described to them the goals of his policy at great length, and the slogans placed here and there did not alter the fact that his policy was extremely aggressive. His tone was especially harsh about Poland, and this was underlined by the fact that the German–Polish non-aggression pact had been terminated two days previously. In connection with Hungary he spoke about friendship, and the Hungarian politicians reassured him about its mutuality. Within the framework of this friendship Hitler expressed his wish that Hungary should improve its relationship with Yugoslavia and should consolidate its relations with Romania, even if Hungary "continues not to be able to give up certain rights towards it."[34] Hitler did not mention the Hungarian position in connection with the German–Polish conflict, and Teleki and Csáky thought that they had better not do so either.

In order to ease the two Hungarian politicians' bad mood during the discussion, von Ribbentrop and Göring indicated that Romania was being closely watched, because its behavior was suspicious, and pointed out that Germany had mostly economic interests there. Göring also added that, in his view, Romania belonged to the Hungarian sphere of interest. He did not think that Romania would be able to keep its present composition. Csáky, who had always been receptive to German promises, happily noted that he did not think that the Germans had high hopes with regard to the economic agreement concluded with the Romanians.[35]

After arriving home from Berlin, the Hungarian statesmen worked hard on formulating Hungarian foreign policy by concentrating on favorable German utterances. Even so, it did not change the Hungarian government's intention to carry out the territorial revision with regard to Romania even without German consent. They wanted to continue modernizing the army so that a favorable moment could, hopefully, be attained. The historian Gyula Juhász wrote that "... if conflict between Germany and the Western powers were to evolve into war, the Transylvanian revisionist project should definitely be carried out by using the chaos of war before the war ended. Obviously, the Teleki government built on the conviction that it would be easier to have the winning powers legally recognize the already re-occupied areas—especially if Hungary did not enter the war on Germany's side—than to achieve a Romanian–Hungarian border adjustment at the peace conference."[36]

However, Teleki's ideas met the substantial opposition of growing extreme right-wing forces. Werth did not agree with this way of achieving the revisionist project. He was convinced that it would only happen through Germany, as the military force that would play the decisive role in a future war and in the political reorganization following it. Therefore, he strongly emphasized the need for political and military cooperation with Germany. He was convinced that Hungary should not be left out of the war that was shortly looming large, and that it should participate on the side of a victorious Germany. As it had often proven before, independent military operations provoked the opposition of the German government. And the arming of the *Honvédség* could hardly be done without its support, even at the price of considerable political and economic concessions.

Despite the ban, the Arrow-Cross and pro-Imrédy groups gathered strength within the General Staff, the Ministry of Defense and the troops. The ever-louder pro-German utterances became concentrated in the phrase "we want everything back." Certain General Staff officers already emphasized the necessity of concluding a German–Hungarian accord. Although Werth prohibited it, he was forced often to ignore the extreme expressions of pro-German politics, since he himself believed in their basic elements. Staunchly pro-German officers such as General Dezső László, the head of the 1st Operational Section of the General Staff, and others surrounded Werth and ingratiated themselves with him, although it was not long before they incited people against him. At the same time those such as General István Náday, Rudolf Andorka and others, who tried to moderate Werth's extreme pro-German behavior, were gradually pushed into the background. In June 1939 Andorka resigned, with his post going to Colonel István Ujszászy, who proved to be more permissive towards the growing German influence.

A March 29 discussion of a select few within the General Staff—which was probably closely related to the coded telegram that the Hungarian ambassador to Warsaw sent the same day—well illuminates how the situation had developed. In the telegram the ambassador, András Hóry, informed his superiors about the Polish position on the Danzig question. He wrote that the Poles were not ready to give in to pressure and, if needed, would protect their rights by force of arms. In the case of conflict with Germany they counted on the support of Poland's allies and of the Western powers.[37] Werth found the situation critical from the Hungarian standpoint. He raised the question of Hungary's position in the case of war. Náday and Andorka argued for a consistent stance of neutrality, while Dezső László considered that entering the war alongside Germany and attacking Poland was a possible option to pursue. Werth was uncertain about the situation, which cannot be explained solely by the resistance of the government, nor by the traditional sympathy towards the Poles felt by the public and the army, but must have also included military considerations. Unlike László, Werth was concerned about driving the *Honvédség* into an extended armed conflict when it was at the very beginning of its armament process. On the other hand, he also considered a possible absence from the likely conflict to be even more dangerous. A confrontation with Germany was not to be risked. Therefore, the armament plan should be accelerated, so that the Hungarians could move on.[38]

The reports of Colonel Béla Lengyel, the Hungarian military attaché to Warsaw, also played a part in Werth's assessment of the situation. Lengyel described a picture of an expected Polish–German armed conflict, based on confidential information gained from the Chief of the Polish General Staff and Polish General Staff officers. Should the Germans attack, the Polish army planned to initiate a counterattack with the support of its allies. According to Lengyel's report, the estimated 550,000-strong Polish army was quietly mobilizing and was partially concentrating on the border, ready to advance. In the Polish army the atmosphere was feisty and determined. It was hoped that the operations, when launched, would be joined by France, would tie down significant German forces, and would result in the occupation of eastern Prussia. The Polish Supreme Command considered the time favorable, because, in their view, the armament program of the German army was not yet complete. They considered only the German air force to be dangerous at this point.[39]

The expected outbreak of a Polish–German war and its consequences emerged as troubling factors in the Hungarian army's plans about Romania and plans for an undisturbed process of military armament. A government resolution wanted to accelerate the preparations against Romania. For that Werth asked for new investment loans. He called the Prime Minister's attention to the backwardness of the country's military mobilization and of its war material supply. He also pointed out that the latest Romanian mobilization well demonstrated that the Hungarians were already behind the Romanians, who had increased their advantage by further improvement of the fortification line along the border. Hungarian intelligence reports about turmoil during the Romanian mobilization and about shortages of arms did not much change the unfavorable situation.[40]

The Chief of the General Staff was also very much disturbed by the developing German–Romanian rapprochement and the resulting German support for the armament buildup of the Romanian army, which was in contrast with the repeatedly manifested German reluctance to support the *Honvédség*. While Germany time and time again rejected delivery of heavy armaments and certain war supplies to Hungary, it permitted them to go from Czech arms factories to Romania. On March 25 Sztójay informed the Minister of Foreign Affairs that the German–Romanian economic treaty included a trade of Romanian crude oil to Germany in return for Germany agreeing to ship to Romania the first part of war supplies, which had been ordered earlier from the arms factories in Brno and Skoda.[41] Following that, shipments became constant. This made the Hungarian government increasingly nervous, and forced it to protest to the German government. Some Hungarians viewed the disloyal behavior of the government of the German Reich as justified, and even rationalized it as a response to the Hungarian position over the Polish question. The Hungarian military leadership also embraced and voiced this view when they impatiently demanded that measures be taken in the issue of shipping war supplies.

On June 2 Head of the Political Section of the Ministry of Foreign Affairs Jenő Ghyczy called Sztójay's attention to repeated German gestures towards the Romanians and Slovakians. Romania had an alliance with Poland, which, from the German perspective, "should be of more impact" than the Hungarian–Polish relationship, which was based only on traditional friendship and lacked any kind of formal obligations.[42] In spite of it all Germany supplied significant amounts of war materials to Romania. On June 22 Ghyczy sent Sztójay a detailed list of war supplies shipped so far or expected to be shipped in the near future. Ghyczy asked the ambassador to effectively intervene so that these shipments "would be limited to the minimum possible."[43]

On June 29 Sztójay reported to Ghyczy that, following his instructions, he had repeatedly brought up the issue of the Romanian armament shipments to German Under-secretaries of Foreign Affairs Weizsäcker and Woermann. He had produced the list that Ghyczy had sent and also referred to information gained from trusted sources that at the end of 1941 about 1,000 cannons would be delivered to Romania from the Skoda factory. Sztójay had told them that he was convinced that these guns would mostly be targeted against Hungary. The diplomats had looked greatly surprised and noted that perhaps Romania would not manifest hostile behavior. Sztójay then had referred to the emotional effect on the

Hungarians provoked by continuing shipments, because it meant that support was being given to the enemy of Hungary by the German Reich, which sympathized with Hungary. Sztójay then suggested that Werth, who was getting ready to go to Berlin, bring these issues up with his discussion partners.

Weizsäcker had also made notes of the conference for his superiors, saying that the Hungarians were asking whether shipments of armaments to Romania should not be scaled down.[44]

The evolving situation induced Teleki to take a step that he hoped would call the Germans' bluff and also help Hungary to become involved in the developing German–Italian war economic cooperation. On June 21 Sztójay submitted a memorandum to the German Ministry of Foreign Affairs in which he noted that the Hungarian government was considering the intensified international situation and the importance of reacting quickly in unexpected situations while continuing to work on the development of its national economy. Therefore, Hungary was inquiring whether, in the case of war, in what measure the Axis Powers had considered utilizing Hungarian raw materials. Only if proper information were given about that could preparations to satisfy these needs be made that would not cause disturbances in the Hungarian economy. He added that it was of the highest imperative "that, at least in principle, we commonly establish the framework of the war economy, be prepared for any possibility, possibly know ahead of time what is expected of us in a given situation, and know what we can expect from the two big powers in return. Therefore, it seems to be justified that the relevant military leaders of the German Reich, Italy and Hungary are authorized to conduct conferences on the economic and related military issues of the war economy with each other as soon as possible. Also, they should establish the guidelines to be followed in the following situations:

a) if the Axis Powers together and simultaneously become involved in war;

b) if the Axis Powers individually get involved in war;
c) if Hungary is left out of a conflict for the time being;
d) if Hungary gets involved in war immediately at the same time as the Axis Powers."[45]

Furthermore, the Hungarian government asked the German government to inform it whether it was ready to authorize the Reich's military leadership to engage in an informal discussion on this topic with the Hungarian Chief of the General Staff. General Werth's upcoming visit to Berlin would serve as a good opportunity for this.

Teleki hoped that if Germany accepted the suggestion, it would be willing to actively participate in supporting the Hungarian armament program and thus counterbalance the advantage that the Romanian army had enjoyed by the shipments received thus far. Teleki hoped that this step, which entailed an increased commitment, would soothe the Hungarian military command, which did not cease to harp on the issue that a government-level contract or agreement would much better tie Germany to Hungary and thus disarm German reservations about the Hungarians.

The attempt at rapprochement did not achieve its expected results. On June 30, prior to Werth's visit, the German Ministry of Foreign Affairs had held discussions with Wilhelm Keitel, the Chief of the *Oberkommando der Wehrmacht*, or OKW, about the issue. A decision was made that the Hungarians would not be included in the preliminary war economic talks with the Italians, although they would return to the issue later.

Although no official German response arrived to the offer, Werth still arrived in Berlin with the assignment that during his conferences he should bring up the point that Hungary ought to be involved in the German–Italian war economic cooperation and in any relevant preliminary discussions.

In Berlin, Werth's German hosts tried to convince him about the strength of the German army. What he saw further strengthened his belief in the strength of the German army and further increased his admiration. He met polite and understanding partners in Commander-in-Chief Brauchitsch and others when he raised the issues of the shipments of German war supplies to Romania and of Hungary's desire to join the war economic cooperation. Yet he never received a straightforward response.

Werth took it as a sign of confidence in him that Hitler also received him on July 5. No notes were left of the conversation between them, but it is quite likely that Hitler described to him his grand schemes and Werth listened with appreciation. After expressing his total agreement, Werth could not have asked unpleasant questions about such topics as the suggested war economic cooperation or the nagging Romanian question.

By the time that Werth had returned home, the project assigned to him by Teleki was already unsuccessful. Therefore, already by the second day after his arrival back in Hungary, referring to the discussions during the previous days, Sztójay had to return to the issue of Hungarian cooperation. He asked for a definite reply from Woermann, who avoided a response by saying that these matters pertained not to the military but to the Ministry of Foreign Affairs. Sztójay expressed his hope that there would not stem any "bad atmosphere" from Werth's also raising the issue. Woermann reassured the worrying Hungarian ambassador, but also informed him that it had been brought to the attention of Hungarian Embassy Counselor Lajos Kuhl that "it could not have been discussed according to its merit" during Werth's visit.[46] The Ministry of Foreign Affairs would return to the issue in time.

However, any "discussion of it according to its merit" kept being delayed and slowly disappeared from the agenda. It seems that the German foreign policy was to keep a free hand on the Hungarian–Romanian issue. Supporting the Romanian arms shipments was of importance for Germany, and not just because of Romanian oil. The Romanian army also had a place in its future plans, as opposed to the Hungarian army, which had no part to play, and therefore Germany had no real interest in supporting the Hungarian armament program in any major way. Also, keeping the Romanian shipment issue that so much irritated the Hungarian government undecided became a constant pawn in keeping Hungarian policy initiative at bay and was useful for blackmailing purposes.

As part of military preparations against Romania, on May 8 Werth recommended that Teleki launch the "special operations." He understood that preparations and the execution of planned operations against Romania required that preparatory work begin, and that this might take a long period of time, perhaps even years: "Launching these preparatory steps, which I am listing below, is of crucial importance, is unrelated to the current foreign political situation, and should be done in great secrecy and in with keeping all the necessary precautionary measures, since these cannot be improvised."[47] Within the framework of these operations Werth proposed the development of a cell system in Transylvania, whose responsibility would be to engage in sabotage activities and to destroy transportation, communication lines and industrial sites. He also considered it necessary to establish a self-defense system. Its task would be to hinder the theft of Hungarian possessions and to offer assistance in military administration in areas to be occupied during the military operation. For the time being Werth did not believe that a general uprising of the Transylvanian Hungarians would be viable, since activities relating to it could not be kept in secret and so would lead to foreign political frictions. But he found more plausible preparations for an uprising of the Hungarians along the border and its organization into a cell-based pattern. He also considered it important to launch intensive and conscious propaganda activities. The organizational work should be started by the General Staff.

The conference of a few select people that was convened by Teleki on May 22, 1939, agreed to Werth's proposals. The Prime Minister warned Werth to apply the greatest possible care to his work and asked for continuous information. He required one condition—that the political, religious and economic leaders of the Transylvanian Hungarians not be involved.

In May 1939 Teleki indicated that he desired that the British government recognize the following items: Hungary's territorial demands on Romania, the legality of consequent independent Hungarian political and military measures, and the recognition of his policy in connection with these. He wanted to learn, and be confirmed in his belief, that the British security guarantee extended to the Romanians referred only to Romania's independence and not to the inviolability of its borders. The Prime Minister's instructions to the Hungarian ambassador in London, György Barcza, included paying great attention to feeling out and to possibly influencing British views and intentions with regard to Romanian–Hungarian relations. The Hungarian military attaché to London, Lóránd Utassy, was not idle either. He worked to become informed about the role that Romania played in British strategic ideas, as well as how much Hungarian military political ideas influenced them. On May 4 Utassy reported that on the previous day he had had a discussion with General Staff Colonel Banfield, a Central European expert at the British Ministry of Defense. Utassy complained to Banfield that due to the British security guarantee the Romanians gave the cold shoulder to reasonable Hungarian advances, while their treatment of their Hungarian minority caused more and more problems. Banfield seemed to understand these concerns. He indicated that the British were aware that the Romanian behavior was not up to par and that the British government disapproved of it. The British guarantee gave security in the case of German aggression, and the British would like to further an agreeable solution to the Romanian–Hungarian controversy. He thought that it was of the

Differences in Foreign Political and Defense Issues 51

utmost importance that the Hungarian government call the intransigent behavior of the Romanians to the attention of the British Ministry of Foreign Affairs, since it seemed to hamper the peaceful atmosphere that Great Britain wished to develop. Then Banfield proceeded to confidentially inform Utassy that he had produced a study on Hungary's military political significance in the case of war in the southeastern part of Europe. Its essence was that "Hungary's neutrality is of prime military interest to Great Britain. Feeding Poland with war materials via the Baltic Sea cannot be done and, therefore, only the Dardanelles–Romania route is available. German forces deployed in Hungary could easily cut through the narrow Romanian–Polish common border, and in that way Poland would be completely isolated."[48] Banfield also said that the Foreign Office had also received the study.

The position described by Banfield, which was also reinforced via other sources, did not at all agree with Hungary's plans for an armed operation against Romania. This very much disturbed Teleki and those pro-Western circles who agreed with him. They were very much aware that even if they were willing to make temporary allowances in order to avoid a confrontation with the West, they would not be able to make either their political enemies or the military leadership accept the postponement of territorial revision, or bring these latter to agree to give up the military action that might achieve it. A new idea arose that making clear the consequences in Hungary of the rigid British positions might induce the British to revise their views and to support Hungarian needs more intensively. This might have been what led Barcza, at Banfield's inspiration, to raise the point that it would be useful to elaborate on the Hungarian position with regard to Romania's behavior in the British Foreign Office. Although Britain favored Romania in everything in order to win it over from the Germans, in the given situation it would be in Britain's interest to support a Hungarian–Romanian agreement. The Foreign Office was afraid that, once the

Germans have made up their minds about an attack on Romania, the Hungarian public would be fired up by the hope of receiving back Transylvania and would stand by them, thus putting a great deal of internal pressure on the Hungarian government.[49]

Responding to the June 8 speech of British Minister of Foreign Affairs Halifax, on June 13 Csáky asked Barcza to submit a memorandum to the British saying that the settlement of the Hungarian–Romanian territorial dispute was the prerequisite for a Danube Valley settlement. British Deputy Minister of Foreign Affairs Cadogan, who accepted the memorandum, told Barcza that the British security guarantee did not authorize Romania to demonstrate intransigent behavior towards its neighbors. Cadogan asked for data about the Romanian treatment of the Transylvanian Hungarians and about the deterioration of their situation.[50]

Notes

1. Rudolf Andorka, *A madridi követségtől Mauthausenig* (From the Madrid Embassy to Mauthausen) (Budapest, 1978), p. 84.
2. György Ránki, Ervin Pamlényi, Loránt Tilkovszky and Gyula Juhász, eds., *A Wilhelmstrasse és Magyarország: Német diplomáciai iratok Magyarországról, 1933–1944* (The Wilhelmstrasse and Hungary: German Diplomatic Documents about Hungary, 1933–1944) (Budapest, 1968), p. 347. (177)
3. *Ibid.*
4. Országos Levéltár (National Archive, OL). K 64-81-21-1939. Rp.
5. *Ibid.*
6. Hadtörténelmi Levéltár (Military History Archive, HL). Eln. Vkf.1. 1939/3373.
7. Andorka, *A madridi követségtől...*, p. 108.
8. *Ibid.*, p. 110.
9. OL. K 64-83-33/a-236/1939. Rp.
10. Andorka, *A madridi követségtől...*, p. 114.
11. Ránki–Pamlényi–Tilkovszky–Juhász, *A Wilhelmstrasse és Magyarország...*, p. 368.
12. HL. Eln. Vkf.1. 1939/3402.
13. HL. Eln. Vkf.1. 1939/3373.
14. HL. Eln. Vkf.1. 1939/3529.
15. OL. Minisztertanácsi jegyzőkönyv, 1939. március 17. (Minutes of the Council of Ministers, March 17, 1939).
16. HL. Eln. Vkf.1. 1939/3875.
17. OL. K 64-83-33/a-282/1939. Rp.
18. OL. K 64-83-33/a-306/1939. Rp.
19. HL. Eln. Vkf.1. 1939/3923.
20. OL. K 64-83-33/a-319/1939. Rp.
21. OL. K 64-83-35-354/1939. Rp.
22. OL. K 64-83-35-400/1939. Rp.
23. *Ibid.*
24. Andorka, *A madridi követségtől...*, p. 129.
25. OL. K 64-81-23-378/1939. Rp.
26. *Ibid.*
27. *Ibid.*

28. Gyula Juhász, ed., *Diplomáciai iratok Magyarország külpolitikájához 1936-1945* (Diplomatic Writings on Hungary's Foreign Policy, 1936-1945) (Budapest, 1962-1982), vol. IV: p. 119.
29. *Ibid.*
30. OL. K 64-81-23-426/1939. Rp.
31. Juhász, *Diplomáciai iratok...*, vol. IV: p. 200. (103/a)
32. OL. K 64-81-23-492/1939. Rp.
33. Gyula Juhász, *Magyarország külpolitikája* (Hungary's Foreign Policy) (Budapest, 1969), p. 202.
34. Juhász, *Diplomáciai iratok...*, vol. IV: p. 218. (116)
35. Ránki–Pamlényi–Tilkovszky–Juhász, *A Wilhelmstrasse és Magyarország...*, p. 380.
36. Juhász, *Magyarország külpolitikája*, p. 203.
37. Juhász, *Diplomáciai iratok...*, vol. IV: p. 126. (40)
38. Andorka, *A madridi követségtől...*, p. 123.
39. Juhász, *Diplomáciai iratok...*, vol. IV: pp. 135 and 136. (49 and 50)
40. HL. Eln. Vkf.1. 3875/1939.
41. Juhász, *Diplomáciai iratok...*, vol. IV: p. 111. (27)
42. *Ibid.*, p. 295. (178)
43. *Ibid.*, p. 320.
44. *Ibid.*, p. 341.
45. Ránki–Pamlényi–Tilkovszky–Juhász, *A Wilhelmstrasse és Magyarország...*, p. 403. (221)
46. *Ibid.*, p. 408. (229)
47. OL. K 64-82-27-1017/1939. Rp.
48. OL. K 64-82-27/b-562/1939. Rp.
49. Juhász, *Diplomáciai iratok...*, vol. IV: p. 310. (181)
50. *Ibid.*, pp. 310 (187) and 314 (191).

THE GERMAN–POLISH CONFLICT AND THE IMPACT OF THE WAR ON THE HUNGARIAN MILITARY PLANS

The growing danger of war and the expected behavior of the Western powers induced Prime Minister Teleki to let the country's allies, first of all Germany, know that Hungary was not in a position to enter the war against Poland. He also expressed the conviction that policy among the Axis Powers must be coordinated more closely. In his letters to Hitler and Mussolini in July, Teleki made the Hungarian position very clear.

As could be expected, Teleki's letter enraged Hitler, who dumped a flood of complaints on Hungarian Minister of Foreign Affairs Csáky when the latter met him on August 8, 1939 to try to explain Teleki's letter. Hitler said that in the changed situation he would not be able to support Hungary's territorial revisionist demands, and that he had not counted on Hungary's participation in a war against the Poles anyway. Hence, Teleki's letter was incomprehensible and so was the atmosphere that it created in Hungary. Although he was not authorized, the frightened Csáky asked Hitler to ignore Teleki's letter.

To ease the consequences of rigid isolation, earlier on July 26 Csáky had called the attention of Italian Minister of Foreign Affairs Ciano to the Hungarian position elaborated in April, which, in the case of a Polish–German conflict, envisioned Hungary mobilizing against Romania, something that could no longer be planned.[1]

Amidst the accelerating events, preparing the Hungarian army for the tasks ahead continued at an intense speed. Werth applied all his energies to this goal and tried to take control of all the non-army-related factors that would influence the army's preparations.

He kept an eye on increasing war production in every forum where he could, and on developing a national mobilization plan. He proved to be tireless at building relations with the leaders of the German army—so much so that the number of meetings at different levels between the officers of the two armies multiplied.

Although with less intensity, Werth also tried to keep Italian relations alive. In the first days of August he viewed the military exercise of the Italian army around Turin, and grasped the opportunity to have talks with General Pariani, the Chief of the Italian General Staff. As the military attaché to Rome László Szabó registered in his notes, Werth again brought up the need for cooperation in the fields of war industry and raw materials among the three friendly states, and also touched upon the question of common operational planning. Assuming tight Italian–German military cooperation, Werth hoped that he would learn more from the more talkative Italians about the German plans and intentions—first of all about Romania—not shared with him in Berlin. Werth explained to Pariani that Hungary saw Romania as its only enemy. He went into detail about the weaknesses of the Romanian army, about the Hungarian military preparations, and also about the Hungarian military operational plans. Pariani thought that the plans were good but noted that they should speak about them in detail only if the target of the three countries' operation was Romania. For the time being, he noted, there was no word about such a plan.[2]

Werth followed that by wondering whether a coordinated operational plan against Yugoslavia should be made within Italian–Hungarian cooperative activities. Pariani considered the preparation of an occupational plan realistic for the time being. He also answered with a definite "no" to the inquiry about whether the Italians had any plans—including their ideas about France and Great Britain—that assumed common operations with the Germans.

When the Polish question came up, Werth took a stand against applying Hungarian troops, and Pariani reassured him that the Hungarians would not be involved.

After finishing the discussion Werth suggested that the statements be put down in writing, but Pariani, not wanting to be obliged, rejected the idea. Pariani also suggested that the three of them should meet in October and discuss all the questions further. At that point they would agree on the common operational military targets, which could be France as much as Romania.[3]

Werth returned to Budapest knowing that in the issues that he had raised, and probably in other areas as well, there were no signed Italian–German military agreements. The Italian military leadership was just as uncertain about Germany's intentions as Hungary was. Whatever he saw at the military exercises did not impress him. He had not valued the strength and efficiency of the Italian army much, and now his prejudices against the current Italian ally, going back to World War I, were reinforced. Werth thought that the Hungarian government's policy of winning over the Italians in fact hindered the development of relationships with Germany, which were valued increasingly highly.

However, the Chief of the General Staff's experiences did not influence Csáky, who hurried to Rome on August 18 to raise the idea of an agreement between the Axis Powers and Hungary and to win the Italians over to it. He hoped that it would ease the tense situation. The Hungarian government continued to feel encouraged by the fact that the Italians were uncertain about the Germans' intentions and therefore were unsure of the Hungarians as well. It also felt encouraged by the Italian desire to remain distant from a probable war, due to Italy's military unpreparedness.[4] The desire for conquest via war was not remote from Mussolini's mind, but he did not seem to want to drift into a war for German goals and interests, and was trying to keep his freedom of action, so that he would be able to move forward at a time and under circumstances favorable to him as well. However, the increasingly uncertain Italian leaders, who were afraid of the Germans, did not offer too much solace to the Hungarian Minister of Foreign Affairs. Ciano flatly refused the idea of a joint agreement, fearing its adverse effect on Hitler and expecting bad consequences for Italian–German relations.[5] Csáky also witnessed how uncertain Mussolini was with regard to the development of events and to taking precautionary steps, thus making him unresponsive to Hungarian suggestions. On the one hand, he thought it was possible that the West would not intervene in the war and therefore Germany would be in business, which was something not to miss. On the other hand, he was afraid of Hitler's anger at him if he engaged in something that Hitler disliked.

The tense situation was further complicated for the Hungarian government by the fact that the Soviet government had accepted the German government's offer to conclude a German–Soviet non-aggression pact. The Prime Minister's hope that war would break out between Germany and the Soviet Union vanished. It became evident that there would be no agreement between Hitler and the Western powers at the expense of the Soviet Union. In the new situation Teleki reinforced the point, in a message sent to London, that even though the Hungarian government would not announce the country's neutrality—which would be contrary to its territorial revisionist aspirations and would provoke Hitler's anger—it also would not enter into war against Poland should that country be attacked.

While the Hungarian government tried to secure its neutrality in the looming threat of war by intense diplomatic activity, the military evaluated the situation differently. It interpreted ongoing events as evidence of Germany's becoming stronger. In the wake of the German–Soviet agreement Werth thought that Germany's back was safe against the Western powers. The threat of a two-front war could be eliminated in the case of an attack against Poland. He also thought that in the event of war, Germany would give a free hand to Hungary against the Western-committed Romania. On August 23 he asked Teleki for an emergency meeting of the Council of Ministers so that it could decide about launching the necessary defensive measures against Romania, as justified by the increasing concentration of Romanian units at the Hungarian border.[6] Since August 20 Romanian troop movements could be detected moving towards the Hungarian border. On August 23 an aerial survey reported a movement of troops towards the border.[7] By August 20 the strength of the Romanian army had reached 250,000 in Transylvania and 80,000 in Dobrudja.[8]

The Council of Ministers satisfied the Chief of the General Staff's request of August 23 for a partial mobilization of the *Honvédség* and to keep the troops near the border on alert.[9] Besides the increasing Romanian mobilization, one of the reports issued by the 2nd Section of the General Staff on August 24 also called attention to the concentration of German troops against Poland. This report gave special importance to the concentration of German troops in Slovakia. By August 20 three more divisions had arrived, joining the two German divisions that had been in the Zsolna area since May. These forces were complemented by the 2nd and 3rd Slovakian Divisions.[10]

Csáky immediately instructed Bárdossy to ask the Romanian Minister of Foreign Affairs Grigore Gafencu about the reason for the Romanian troop movements: "Most probably Gafencu will respond that the troop movements are not against us. In this case, try to find out who they are against."[11] During the conversation Bárdossy was supposed to emphasize the defensive nature of the Hungarian counteractions.

Accordingly, on August 24 Bárdossy contacted Gafencu, who really tried to avoid giving a straightforward answer. Gafencu told Bárdossy that Romania was ready to sign a non-aggression treaty with Hungary. When Bárdossy repeatedly asked him, Gafencu denied the reality of any troop movements and claimed that since

May there had not been any changes. He also asked the Hungarian government not to do anything based on false information that would lead to erroneous conclusions. As long as the Hungarians did not attack, they were safe from Romania.[12] Finally, Gafencu acknowledged that certain defensive actions had been in progress, which he justified by the threat of war breaking out between the two power groupings within a few days, and noted that everyone should be prepared for the consequences, including Romania. Romania intended to defend itself from wherever the pressure was coming.

Hearing from Csáky the response of the Romanian Minister of Foreign Affairs, Werth noted that it was totally immaterial whether the Romanian troops were performing a defensive or an offensive troop concentration at the Hungarian border. Hungarian preventive actions were needed in either case.[13]

The Hungarian government's response arrived in Bucharest on August 25. It claimed that it had obvious proof about troop movements towards the Hungarian border and therefore it did not consider the response of the Romanian Minister of Foreign Affairs satisfactory. It was upholding its protest.[14]

At the same time as working with Bárdossy, Csáky also sent Sztójay a telegram asking his Berlin ambassador to relay the Hungarian government's position with regard to the Romanian measures to the German Ministry of Foreign Affairs. It was necessary to call the German government's attention to the fact that the Romanian government had kept its army in a mobilized state since March, even though on March 26 the Hungarian government had informed the Romanians that Hungary would abandon its earlier measures and had not initiated any military actions following that. The Romanian government, once again, had avoided answering the Hungarian government's requests for an explanation. This had hindered the normalization of the relationship between the two countries. And now, "reliable news has come to the attention of the

Hungarian government that mobilized Romanian forces are slowly concentrating along the Hungarian border." Thus, the Hungarian government was forced to implement suitable defensive regulations in the face of these grave and incomprehensible military actions and would hold the Romanian government responsible if "its action launched weeks ago in order to improve the relationship does not bring any results."[15]

The daily reports of the General Staff described more and more Romanian forces arriving along the border. In the meantime, the Hungarian countermeasures were continuing, as the Chief of the General Staff reported to the Prime Minister.

In the evening of August 25 another coded telegram came from Bárdossy, informing the Hungarian government that Germany had asked the Romanian ambassador to Berlin for an explanation about the causes of the Romanian mobilization. The Romanian Ministry of Foreign Affairs connected the Hungarian protests and military preparations with German interest, and saw their military measures justified.[16] In this tense foreign policy situation the Hungarian government was not very happy with the Romanian position, nor with Germany's manner in putting pressure on Romania, Poland's ally. Hungary wanted to avoid at all costs appearing compromised in the eyes of the Western powers. On August 26 Csáky called upon Bárdossy to protest: "We had no idea that the Germans would also take steps. There is no connection between the two steps."[17]

On the eve of the war, the tension between Hungary and Romania served German interests. The German foreign affairs and military command was troubled by some possible joint Romanian–Polish action.

Werth did not see the immediate possibility for Hungarian–German common action against Romania. However, he did think that indirect support of the Germans by means of the mobilization would bring with it a certain kudos that would help cooperation later on and would slightly counterbalance the politicians' rigid behavior on the Polish issue. However, seeing the continued Romanian military concentration—mounted brigades and mechanized units had shown up in Transylvania[18]—Werth also found it plausible that in the case of a German–Polish conflict Romania would give up its cautious behavior towards Germany and take military steps according to its obligations to Poland. If that happened, fearing a Hungarian attack coordinated with the German army, the Romanians could start preventive military operations against Hungary. In this case Hungary could count on Germany's support. Although the shortcomings of the preparations of the *Honvédség* did not make it possible to initiate independent operations, such an action supported by the Germans would create a good opportunity for the military pushing its way into Transylvania. This idea pleased Csáky as well.

At the August 28 session of the Supreme Military Council (*Legfelső Honvédelmi Tanács*), Csáky emphasized Hungary's intention to remain neutral in the Polish–German conflict and justified Hungary's current military actions by the need to counter Romania's previous steps.[19] Yet, these military actions ended on August 29 at 12 p.m.[20] to stress Hungary's neutrality. Due to the ever-increasing scale of the Romanian mobilization, Werth did not agree with the Council's decision.

This decision immediately provoked the Germans, who had been resentful about the dubious Hungarian behavior on the Polish issue. That same day Woermann informed the flabbergasted Sztójay in Berlin that Keitel had cancelled the German war material transports to Hungary as long as the Hungarian attitude remained uncertain.[21] The Germans well knew that this step deeply affected the interests of the *Honvédség*, since it erected a roadblock in the way of equipping the army and would further widen the gap between the Hungarian military leadership and the government. Werth repeatedly noted that the anti-German measures of the government endangered the equipment for the army, the development of its capacities, and the realization of territorial revisionist goals. Once again he was convinced that the influence of the General Staff should be increased against the hesitant government, in order to protect the interests of national defense.

During the end of August, news also arrived from Slovakia about a further acceleration of military preparations there. German and Slovakian troops began to concentrate on the Polish border, beginning on August 28.[22] According to the statements of the Hungarian General Staff, the units of the 5th German Army in Slovakia—with ten to twelve German and two Slovakian divisions—finished their deployment. New air squadrons also arrived at the Slovakian airports.[23]

On September 1 Germany attacked Poland. The Hungarian government immediately ordered the implementation of a state of emergency. The troops of the VI. Hungarian Army Corps began moving to the Romanian border, where they prepared for defense. The Hungarian air force implemented steady aerial surveillance over Romanian territories.[24] Affected by the events, Romania ordered the mobilization of more age groups of the civilian population.[25]

Hardly had the German troops reached the Polish border when von Ribbentrop instructed Ambassador Erdmannsdorff to tell the Hungarian Minister of Foreign Affairs that at that moment Germany was not asking for any armed help. At the same time he assumed that the Hungarian government would not make a declaration of neutrality and, therefore, would leave the field open for any military possibilities that might arise. Von Ribbentrop also asked Erdmannsdorff to try to feel out the Hungarian reaction to events and, in the case of dubious behavior, to exert the appropriate pressure on the Hungarian government.[26]

Csáky gave a sigh of relief at von Ribbentrop's message and hastened to assure him of the Hungarian government's loyalty to the German Reich. Csáky abandoned even the thought of a presumed Hungarian declaration of neutrality and, acceding to German wishes, left the threat of a Hungarian intervention against Romania open.[27]

Werth was especially taken by the idea of "Hungarian possibilities being left open" in von Ribbentrop's message. After evaluating the situation, on September 4 he sent a letter to Teleki and Csáky, telling them that he had information that the Soviet army was concentrating troops on the Polish and Bessarabian borders. If it was the start of Soviet operations against Poland, Romania would most probably send troops to Poland. In this case, Werth wrote, "one has to count on Romania attacking via Sub-Carpathia in order to widen the narrow Romanian–Polish border and thus also to extend its border further west to the River Tisza. This has to be prevented. Therefore, I propose a) that all our border guard units be mobilized except for those on the western border, and b) that all our mobilized forces join up to secure a general troop concentration after a general mobilization." He warned the Prime Minister that it was necessary to take immediate measures, since concentrating all the forces at the border would take five days.[28]

Even if it was originally the intention of the Romanian government to help the Poles, the military events of the first days of the war, the German military's big successes, the retreat of the Polish army and the idleness of the Western allies following the declaration of war all caused the Romanians to reconsider things.

The Hungarian mobilization and the spreading news of the Soviet troop movements at the border of Bessarabia were enough to deter the Romanian government from a careless step.

Werth and the military leaders influenced by him did not recognize that the German military command was intent on playing Hungary and Romania off against each other. Hungary was kept at bay by Romania and it was made sure that no armed conflict would break out that would be contrary to German interests. German foreign policy took especially great care to keep the Hungarian military's intense anti-Romanian feelings directed partly against the hesitant Hungarian government by various conciliatory gestures of its own.

In the meantime the Hungarian government took desperate steps to keep the country distant from the conflict or any compromising actions, the very things that Werth thought would yield advantages. It tried to save the country's neutrality while still maintaining Hungarian territorial demands. On September 3 Teleki sent a letter to Ciano to reinforce Hungary's peaceful intentions towards Romania. In connection with Hungarian territorial demands towards Romania, he asked the Italian government to help in the settling and securing of the issue, preferably through a conference that would serve European stability should any kind of confrontation occur.[29] Contrary to Werth, Teleki saw the settlement of the Transylvanian question according to Hungarian interests to be separate from the present conflict. As Teleki wrote, in spite of everything the Hungarian government was determined to bring the Hungarian-Romanian territorial question to a long-lasting conclusion. "It was willing to undertake any risky action to force the issue if it did not receive a guarantee that its demands towards Romania would be settled at a conference that would also settle Europe's future for the next decade or two."[30] Teleki emphasized the point that the Hungarian government would resort to arms only in the case of emergency if it did not receive a favorable settlement. The government was forced by the fear of future events and public pressure, and this is what justified the military preparations. If Italy were unable to secure a peaceful settlement, "the Hungarian government would still be very grateful if Italy suitably prepared world public opinion for the likely outcome of events, and if it supported Hungary diplomatically.[31]

The Germans did not delay for long in expressing their goals in the new situation to the Hungarian government. As early as September 4 von Ribbentrop asked for and received guarantees via Sztójay that the Hungarian government would not initiate military action against Romania without the agreement of the German government. At the same time, Csáky was invited to discuss the issues in Berlin.[32] The request was surprising, because the government did not want to take immediate steps and Werth wanted to act only together with the Germans. Neither Werth nor Bartha received invitations to the discussion, which might have been a sign to Werth that the Germans had no plans for common action against Romania.

It was unnecessary for von Ribbentrop to dissuade the Hungarian government from careless armed operations, something he very well knew from their often vehemently expressed position. Rather, this step was a gesture towards the Romanians, in whom the German wanted to intensify the inculcation of the idea of a Hungarian threat that could be cleared away only by Germany's shielding arm.

The Romanian government's fear was made apparent by the fact that following September 5 major Romanian emergency drafts took place. The number of mobilized forces reached 650,000 troops. In Transylvania the Romanian forces amounted to three times the strengths of the concentrated Hungarian forces. Hungarian and other ethnic troops of the Transylvanian units were considered to be unreliable and so were replaced by Romanians.[33]

Already on September 4 Csáky asked Bárdossy to protest once again to the Romanian government about the continuous concentration of troops, because they forced the Hungarian government to take up defense positions in spite of its desires. At the same time, Csáky also instructed the Hungarian ambassadors to Rome and Berlin to inform the Italian and German governments about the protest. They were instructed also to call attention to the fact that the direction in which the new troops were looking indicated that the Romanians wanted to occupy the Sub-Carpathian railways, since their own connections with Poland were not satisfactory.

In a September 6 report Sztójay described his September 3 discussion with Under-secretary of Foreign Affairs Woermann, where Woermann made the following surprising statement: "According to news from Bucharest, the Hungarian invasion of Transylvania is imminent." He told Sztójay that the German government would not like to see such an action. Sztójay then told him that the Romanian rumor was unfounded, but also felt obliged to allude to Romania's bad conscience with regard to Transylvania, Bessarabia and Dobrudja.[34]

Bárdossy's confidential message also warned about machinations behind the scenes. "One of my informants had the following confidential information from circles in the German Embassy: Yesterday the Germans asked for guarantees from the Romanian government that it would not support the enemies of the Reich. In return they offered to secure the Hungarian–Romanian border and, moreover, even the occupation of Hungary to prevent an invasion."[35] Bárdossy reported for the second time the same day, indicating that the distrust towards the Hungarian government was growing day by day. "According to my sources, the German military attaché made an attempt to reassure the [Romanian] King that the Hungarians would not attack Romania, or that the Germans would not allow it in any case. Yet there is a general fear that the Hungarians will shortly provoke a conflict."[36] He noted that in Bucharest everyone, including the Germans, thought that it was impossible that the Romanians would have aggressive designs.

Parallel with his visit to Germany, on September 7 Csáky asked the Romanian ambassador to Budapest, Raoul Bossy, not to excite his own government and the Budapest diplomatic corps with news about the Hungarian mobilization. He wrote to Bárdossy in Bucharest that "I was able to prove to him chronologically that they were the initiators of military actions; he did not deny it."[37] Bossy promised Csáky that he would collect information and, in the given situation, was probably honestly reassured with regard to the peaceful intentions of the Hungarian government.

Csáky had secret talks with von Ribbentrop, since, at the request of the German Minister of Foreign Affairs, the meeting was not publicized. Csáky promised von Ribbentrop that Hungary would not do anything against Romania without a preliminary agreement with Germany. Moreover, out of personal eagerness, he also offered a non-aggression pact with Romania, which von Ribbentrop obviously considered unnecessary.[38]

More evidence of the German fear of rapprochement occurred right after Csáky's return to Hungary, when Erdmannsdorff appeared with von Ribbentrop's message, saying that it would not be practical if Hungary accepted a non-aggression treaty offer from the Romanian government. German foreign policy leaders were afraid that if the controversy that they had incited got out of their control, the two relevant governments would venture out to take independent measures.[39]

In the meantime, Sztójay had tried to intervene to restart the deliveries of war supplies that Berlin had stopped. While Csáky was with von Ribbentrop, Sztójay was told that although the political reason for the embargo had disappeared, transportation difficulties continued to occur.[40] It was an unpleasant piece of news for the Hungarian military command, which was ready to conclude that the Germans would not easily forgive the rigid Hungarian position demonstrated on the Polish issue. Werth and Bartha pondered how they could make the relevant German officials reverse their decision and cancel the embargo, even at the expense of having to distance themselves from the Hungarian government's position. Their problems intensified when the Germans thought that it was time to warn the ally that had taken its own road on the Polish issue. In the afternoon of September 9 von Ribbentrop unexpectedly visited Csáky with a request that he had not mentioned two days earlier—that starting on September 10 the Hungarian government allow German troop transportation across a few kilometers of Hungary, between Kassa and Nagyszalánc, on a railway that connected Slovakia and the northeastern Carpathians.[41]

The German request was clearly related to the circumstance that had arisen on the previous day, September 8, when without any notice the airspace over northern Hungary became very active, as German air squadrons flying east serially violated the Hungarian airspace. Sentries and patrols reported 12 incursions during the day, including 90 bombers that flew over the Hungarian territory in various-sized units.[42] Between 5 and 6 p.m. German planes appeared in Kassa's airspace five times, and 48 bombers were registered.[43] On September 9 in the morning hours, 58 planes flew over the Hungarian territory.[44]

On September 10 the Hungarian Council of Ministers rejected the German request as a violation of national honor and also as a grave step that might provoke a declaration of war by the Great Powers. However, no memorandum of protest was ever sent to the German Ministry of Foreign Affairs for violating Hungarian airspace.

Werth anxiously watched these events, fearing that they might lead to a further deterioration of German–Hungarian relations. He understood the nature of the German military steps. He knew that Ribbentropp made his request in order to secure the reinforcement of the German units operating North of the Carpathian Mountains.[45] The reality was that the Kassa railway did not have any impact on the reinforcement of German troops.

The threatening nature of the German air activity over northern Hungary did not escape Werth's attention. He concluded that a very serious situation had developed, which might be difficult to settle. His opinion regarding the Polish question—opposing the government's positions supported by the Regent and public opinion—did not promise to produce any advantage. Without risking his popularity, even within the army, it would have been troublesome to voice anti-Polish views. In the meantime, the development of military events in Poland and the total inactivity of the French and British forces following the declaration of war reassured him in the belief that Germany was the only force that was able "to rule" in the Central and Southeastern European region. The German–Soviet agreement also reinforced him in this view, because it seemed to have sidelined, or at least defused the threat of, the only force that could have stood in the way of Germany's expansion.

The rejection of the German request created a bad atmosphere only within the Hungarian army leadership. Even the government, alarmed by its own step, revised its decision and tried to seek an intermediary position. They were willing to let trains pass along the railway in question, as long as they had locked carriages and were not convoying troops. This, it was hoped, would ease the expected German reprisal.[46]

However, von Ribbentrop did not want to accept the Hungarian offer. He acknowledged the Hungarian rejection with surprising ease and, already on September 10, instructed Erdmannsdorff to inform the Hungarian government that "the rejection of the German request was not iniquitous, and Hungary should remember that Germany had made it possible that the railway in question would belong to Hungary."[47] He also cautioned the Hungarian government that its northern ally could be mobilized at any time against Hungary. It is hard to imagine that on September 10 Tiso's Slovakian government would turn to the Hungarian government, without Germany's urging, to ask for permission to transport Slovakian war materials to eastern Slovakia on railways closed to the Germans. The Hungarian government flatly rejected the Slovakian request. Csáky told Erdmanssdorff that the Hungarian government "might consider the Slovakian proposal as a military attack and would respond accordingly. There are already Hungarian troops dispatched towards the Slovakian border." Csáky also alluded to recent Slovakian official irredentist behavior, which, according to foreign sources, was encouraged by the Germans and seemed to indicate connections between them and the recent Slovakian request.[48]

The foreign policy leaders of the Reich did not wish to further increase the tension. It had achieved its purpose: the Hungarian government once again could be condemnable for the sin of ingratitude by the one "friend" who had helped them achieve their revisionist goals, thereby putting a new trump card into the hands of German diplomacy. Von Ribbentrop made arrangements so that the suddenly intensified Hungarian–Slovakian relationship would now calm down. Under-secretary of Foreign Affairs Weizsäcker denied the news allegedly leaked by German military sources that two Slovakian divisions were concentrating in eastern Slovakia. He also noted that no deployable Slovakian military force seemed to exist.[49] This latter remark obviously did not correspond to reality, since the September 13 situation report of the General Staff spoke about the withdrawal of the 2nd and 3rd Slovakian Divisions from military action.[50]

On September 14, via Erdmannsdorff, von Ribbentrop expressed to Csáky his disapproval of the fact that the Hungarian government might consider military measures in its response to the Slovakian request. "Therefore, I would advise adequate caution to Count Csáky in his actions against Slovakia, which is under our protection. Any kind of unfriendly action towards Slovakia would produce an appropriate reaction in Germany."[51]

In the distrustful atmosphere created by the diplomatic flurries following the rejection of German–Slovakian military transportation across Hungary, and amidst signs of a German–Romanian rapprochement, the Hungarian military leadership and government remained anxious about the continuing Romanian troop movements. In Romania the portion of soldiers drafted reached 75%, and then 80%, of the total mobilization of all potential troops. The strength of the mobilized army surpassed 800,000 and approached 1,000,000.[52] By mid-September an army of fifteen divisions, four mountain brigades and one mounted division were stationed in Transylvania.[53] On September 17 the Soviet Union began marching into eastern Polish territories. Contrary to the Hungarian government's expectations, this step did not produce an immediate regrouping of the Romanian troops to the Bessarabian and Moldovan borders from Transylvania.[54]

The Hungarian government's fears were intensified by Germany's irritation at Hungary's accommodation of Polish refugees and of its general pro-Polish attitude, including that within the army. In an order of September 17, General of the Infantry and Army Commander-in-Chief (*Honvédség Főparancsnoka*) Hugó Sónyi admonished the officer corps, many of whose younger members supported the Poles and made anti-German remarks. News of this behavior reached high-ranking German leaders, provoked protests from them, and threatened to destroy the German–Hungarian friendship.[55] The sympathy of the military was increased by reports from Polish soldiers and civilians streaming into Hungarian territories between September 15 and 22 about the Germans' inhumane treatment of them.[56]

At the end of September the pressure on the Hungarian government increased further. On September 23, speaking about the residue still in Berlin of the Hungarian "sinful" behavior, Sztójay stressed that "our position of not allowing the German troops to cross Hungarian territory, despite the fact that the Chancellor of the Reich indicated that he would be grateful for the help, has taken on the heaviest weight."[57] Following that, Sztójay, who also took part in the anti-Hungarian German campaign with his tendentious reports, reinforced the personal opinions of many in high German circles by quoting a journalist in Göring's circle that after the end of the German–Polish war the Hungarians would turn against Germany. Prime Minister Teleki and his circle did not even try to hide their openly anti-German attitude, he stated.[58]

News from various indefinite sources also raised the idea of a German military action against Hungary, which systematically softened the Hungarians. An example was the news that the Viennese Cartographic Institute had ceased to print Polish maps and had begun printing the map of Hungary at a quick pace.[59]

The spread of rumors evoking the danger of a German invasion was only one tool used by the Germans to put political pressure on Hungary in order to increase its political and economic demands on the nation. Germany saw its most efficient tool in the Hungarian extreme right wing and the Hungarian military command. In the case of a regime change to the right, the Imrédy–Werth–Sónyi–Bartha–Csáky group was to take away power from Teleki, relying on the Regent and the aristocracy. In the analysis of the German security services about Hungarian power relations, should a new regime emerge, the best solution probably would be a "dictatorial government that relies on the military for power" under Csáky as prime minister.[60] The Germans paid close attention to the differences in views with regard to relations with Germany between Teleki, who also held out the prospect of an armed resistance in the case of a German intervention, and the Hungarian military. Therefore they did not really take the Prime Minister's fierce statements seriously, while Teleki himself became increasingly doubtful about the support of the military against the Germans. Both the actions of the Italian ally and the complete passivity of the Western democracies during the German–Polish war also cautioned him about abrupt actions.[61]

The Germans did a lot to show their trust in the Hungarian military and to deepen the connections between the two armies. The Hungarian military delegation, headed by General Lajos Csatay, which paid a visit to the Polish–German front early in October, expressively stressed in its report the close friendship between the Hungarian and German soldiers during the visit: "The Germans received the Hungarian committee with great hospitality and often deferential treatment. [Several other national delegations participated in the tour.] Imparting their experiences, the German officers made several references to the fact that the information given was meant just for the Hungarian committee." They did not stint themselves in extending awards either, which was how Dezső László, head of the 1st Section of the General Staff, received a high award in honor of his "merits."[62]

The extreme right thought that it was now time to increase its influence in the army, and so began to spread illegal pamphlets among the army officers in September. Commander of the VI. Army Corps General József Bajnóczy sent the Chief of the General Staff a fake "evaluation of the situation" pamphlet dated September 15 written by an Arrow-Cross or pro-Imrédy, yet anonymous, military-sounding author who wished to inform the officer corps of the foreign and domestic political situations. The pamphlet was dense with social slogans and demands calling the officers' attention to the "wide horizon" as understood by the author. Attention was called to the increasingly open activities of Hungarian bourgeois politicians who risked the cause of Hungarian territorial revisionism, who fraternized with the Anglo-Saxons and the Jews, and who behaved ambiguously with the German allies and thereby clashed with the military leadership. Furthermore, the author of the pamphlet was obliged to try "to restore the unfortunately shaken but indispensable trust towards the military center." Due to bitterness over missed opportunities and in order to avoid missing future opportunities, the pamphlet concluded with a list of foreign and domestic political, military and economic measures meant to help the country, which mostly coincided with the Werth-defined ideas of the military leadership. These ideas were obviously to be implemented by a right-wing and radical government that would fully serve the views of the military.[63]

It was difficult to reduce the tension between Romania and Hungary. In compliance with his promise to von Ribbentrop, on September 7 Csáky tried to approach the Romanian government, but the ice-cold distrust of the Romanians was a major hurdle. Although it began to concentrate troops on the Romanian–Soviet border in mid-September, the Romanian government did not do it by transferring troops from Transylvania but by yet another wave of mobilization, starting on September 15, which raised the strength of its army to one million troops. Csáky could persuade the Romanians to decrease the strength of their Transylvanian forces and downgrade their alert status only by demobilizing his own troops and by applying German pressure.[64]

Finally, mostly affected by the Romanians' concern about Bessarabia, an agreement was concluded on October 7 to decrease the strength of the Romanian forces stationed in Transylvania.[65] The Romanians began to shift significant forces to Bessarabia. By early November the size of Romanian forces concentrated in Transylvania had fallen to the August 15 level, and those forces remaining in Transylvania were withdrawn to their peacetime garrisons and barracks. This, however, did not mean that the Romanian army had given up on its defensive preparations.[66]

The Hungarian military command's attention turned towards the Soviet–Romanian relationship, and accordingly towards the possibility of cooperation with the Soviet Union. Werth was occupied by thoughts of a possible military operation executed simultaneously with the Soviets, should armed conflict break out due to the intensification of the Bessarabian conflict. He was also interested in using Soviet natural resources for the economy, a possibility that had arisen due to the growing Hungarian–Soviet economic relations. Seeing Germany's rapprochement with the Soviet Union, Werth set aside his resentments and considered utilizing the advantages that the situation presented, and even made necessary. He saw the German–Soviet agreement as a strategic step that marked the spheres of influence between the two powers for a long period of time; in his view, an anti-Romanian step executed in parallel with the Soviet Union could not be contradictory to Germany's interests.

Werth ignored the pro-Romanian statements coming from the German diplomats, and tried to convince Teleki that the possibilities opening up had to be grasped. If the Soviet Union took steps to regain Bessarabia, Hungary also had to enter the scene. In his view, Hungary had to act as long as the majority of Romanian forces were occupied in the east and a possible Romanian–Soviet agreement did not allow the Romanians to concentrate fully at the Hungarian border. Such a Hungarian step would not be opposed by the Germans, as far as Werth saw.[67] In the meantime he also took some measures without the knowledge of the government. At the end of September he allegedly instructed the Hungarian military attaché to Moscow, Gábor Faragho, to begin discussions about cooperation with the General Staff of the Soviet army. However, the instructions never materialized, and the issue soon lost its importance.[68]

Hungarian foreign policy leaders did not consider the situation to be as unambiguous as the Chief of the General Staff did, although they would have liked to give in to the temptation. It was obvious once again that they should turn for advice to the Italians. On September 27 Csáky asked Villani to seek information about the Italian government's views should the Hungarian government not stay idle if the Soviet Union attacked Bessarabia.[69]

By the following day Villani had responded to the Hungarian Minister of Foreign Affairs. Ciano urged moderation on his Hungarian colleague and encouraged him to stay away from conflicts and to establish a friendly connection with neighboring countries. He also noted that Italy was not in a position to offer help to Hungary if the situation did not evolve according to their wishes.[70]

On September 30 Csáky sent a letter to the ambassador to Rome asking him to inform Ciano that there were two possibilities if the Soviet Union should occupy Bessarabia. If the Soviet Union occupied Bessarabia, either peacefully or not, the Hungarians would avoid any kind of interference, since it "would not be useful, because it would mean a common operation with the Soviets!" If, however, an occupation produced signs of chaos, such as the disintegration of the country or anti-Hungarian massacres, then the Hungarians would quickly intervene. In the latter case, "the intervention does not have to be a common operation, and its peaceful character could be documented." Csáky also inquired about the guarantees Italy could give if Hungary accepted the Italian suggestion that "it should refrain from joining any kind of conflict that might have adverse affects on Romania."[71]

The Italians reinforced the Hungarian government's decision to avoid any action in parallel to actions undertaken by the Soviet Union—something strongly pressed by Werth. At the October 5 session of the Council of Ministers the Prime Minister's position opposing common action with the Soviets hardened against the military's position.[72]

Villani's letter of October 7 said that "in connection with Romania Count Ciano was informed in Berlin that as long as Romania retained its complete neutrality—and, by all means, it will do that—it will not be exposed to either a Russian or a German attack, since the two Great Powers did not want to stir up the status quo in the Balkans."[73] Besides the indirect admonition to Hungary, the German message also contained a threat to Romania: "If Romania should violate the neutrality, Russia would occupy Bessarabia, and the Reich would not venture to take action, because it has no common border with Romania. Instead, it would assign

Hungary and Bulgaria to participate in the liquidation of Romania."[74] Ciano continued to offer neutrality.

The decision annoyed Werth, and also Bartha, who agreed with him and who was also voted down at the government session. Their opinion remained unchanged: Hungary should not remain idle. If Russia attacked Romania, Hungary would have to act and occupy Transylvania.[75] Bartha even offered his resignation after suffering this strong setback at the session of the Council of Ministers. Werth's views were fortified by Ujszászy's report indicating that there was great restlessness in Romania due to uncertainty about Soviet intentions. Bucharest felt sure about the operation against Bessarabia. The small-scale Romanian troop transfers that had begun in the last days of September turned into increasingly larger measures east of the Hungarian frontline.[76] Werth took into consideration only those factors that suited his ideas and, contrary to the government, did not take into his calculations the fact that the German and Italian allies had made statements supporting the status quo, and neither did he notice the international incentives and guarantees on which the Romanians counted when they dared to weaken their forces on the Hungarian border. Werth could not hope the Romanians to incite the Germans against themselves by violating the terms of neutrality, so that the Germans would give a free hand to Hungary and Bulgaria to punish them for their disobedience. There were even fewer chances now for the Romanians to act than there had been a month before. After the Hungarian government settled on a decision favorable to them, the Germans did nothing to inform Werth through their own channels, since they grasped every opportunity to maintain and intensify the controversies between the Hungarian government and its military.

In the last days of September the Hungarian military leaders came to believe that it was economically necessary for them to approach the Germans and resolve any outstanding controversies.

It was of vital importance to restart and possibly intensify the supply of raw materials, which was already lagging behind and causing serious shortages and deadline alterations. Therefore, since the Germans had refused to deliver the needed supplies, they had to be appeased, and the sooner the better. Yet one inevitable fact was also recognized: satisfying the ever-growing German economy was the Germans' only measure of vital importance. The German government was well aware that it was easy to blackmail both the Hungarian military and political leaderships sensitive to the question of war supply. The country was willing to make sacrifices and compromises for these supplies. On September 2, right at the introduction of the embargo, Sztójay recommended to the government that "in terms of food deliveries, it would be beneficial to offer a gesture, a spontaneous extra quantity of food beyond what was included in the agreement," to pacify the Germans: "Sooner or later they will ask for it anyway, and we may make a good impression in this way, with beneficial effects."[77] On September 19 Germany submitted a request to the Hungarian government to increase the quantity of food transports and to increase the exchange rate of the Deutschmark. The government tried to connect filling the request with increasing the quantity of imported German war materials. The German side dodged the request. They responded that they did not know their own war supply needs and surpluses yet.[78] Hardly had the Germans begun to fulfill their obligations when another difficulty cropped up. During the Hungarian–German economic discussions of January 1940, the Hungarian party attempted to resist Germany's requests to modify the exchange rate of the Deutschmark, and the Germans once again stopped the war supply deliveries. The military blamed the government for the consequences of denying the Germans' request.

The Hungarian Council of Ministers held a session on economic issues, discussing and debating the causes of the German war supply embargo. The German military attaché to Budapest,

Wrede, informed his superiors about the session. Werth was invited to the session and blamed the government's zigzag policy for what happened. Under such a policy Werth could not be responsible for equipping the *Honvédség* or for the combat readiness of the army. According to Wrede, Werth also offered his resignation.[79]

In a report sent to the Ministry of Foreign Affairs on October 13, Erdmannsdorff also confirmed Wrede's report:

> According to my observations there is tension between the [Hungarian] government and the *Honvédség*. The dissatisfaction of the military is mostly targeted at Prime Minister Count Teleki and Minister of the Interior Keresztes-Fischer, who are blamed for not having a clear attitude towards the foreign political situation. The military also blames them for the war supply embargo introduced by the Germans. Evidently, both the General Staff and the Arrow-Cross have striven to impress German official circles to support their own internal political agenda, eventually, to overthrow the Teleki government... It is obvious that the *Honvédség*'s attitude towards Germany is more positive than that of the Prime Minister and other members of the government. The older age-group of the military, who fought on our side in World War I, and especially the very influential Chief of the General Staff, General of the Infantry Werth, understand the utmost necessity of having to cooperate with Germany. Their attitude is a relief in the sea of unreliability frequently experienced here.[80]

During the January Hungarian–German economic talks, Bartha contacted the head of the German delegation, Clodius, who sent a satisfied telegram to Berlin: "I have discussed the issue of war material transportation with Hungarian military organs... they understand... they are trying to create positive reciprocal services for Germany. They advocated fulfilling various different German demands to the Prime Minister and leading civilian organizations."[81]

The halting German transports and the general difficulties around raw materials purchases induced the General Staff and officials of the Ministry of Defense to raise the issue of taking up economic relations with the Soviet Union, which would solve some of the raw materials supply problems. In the wake of a German–Soviet economic rapprochement, a Hungarian one seemed to be feasible, and commensurate with hoping that it would not meet Germany's opposition.[82] Already on September 26 Bartha raised with Teleki the urgency of entering into negotiations as soon as possible. In November he once again returned to the question of negotiations. He proposed the fulfillment of six months' supply of certain raw materials, amounting to 100 million pengős, in return for certain goods produced by Hungarian industry.[83]

Notes

1. Gyula Juhász, ed., *Diplomáciai iratok Magyarország külpolitikájához 1936–1945* (Diplomatic Writings on Hungary's Foreign Policy, 1936–1945) (Budapest, 1962-1982), vol. IV: p. 378. (240)
2. Hadtörténelmi Levéltár (Military History Archive, HL). Eln. Vkf.1. 1939/4417.
3. Juhász, *Diplomáciai iratok...*, vol. IV: p. 397. (251)
4. Hugh Gibson, ed., *Ciano naplója: 1939–1943: Gróf Galeazzo Ciano olasz külügyminiszter, 1939–1943 teljes, rövidítés nélküli naplói* (Ciano's Diary: 1939–1943: The Full Diary without Shortening of Count Galeazzo Ciano, Italian Foreign Minister, 1939–1943) (Budapest, 1946), p. 130.
5. *Ibid.*, p. 137.
6. Országos Levéltár (National Archive, OL). K 64-82-27/a-751/1939. Rp.
7. HL. Eln. Vkf.1. 1939/4479.
8. HL. Eln. Vkf.1. 1939/4438.
9. HL. Eln. Vkf.1. 1939/4477.
10. HL. Eln. Vkf.1. 1939/4417.
11. OL. K 64-82-27/a-751/1939. Rp.
12. OL. K 64-82-27/a-752/1939. Rp.
13. OL. K 64-82-27/a-ad. 756/1/1939. Rp.
14. OL. K 64-82-27/a-7512/4/5/1939. Rp.
15. OL. K 64-82-27/a-1939. Rp.
16. OL. K 64-82-27/a-754/1939. Rp.
17. *Ibid.*
18. OL. K 64-82-27/a-826/1939. Rp.
19. György Ránki, Ervin Pamlényi, Loránt Tilkovszky and Gyula Juhász, eds., *A Wilhelmstrasse és Magyarország: Német diplomáciai iratok Magyarországról, 1933–1944* (The Wilhelmstrasse and Hungary: German Diplomatic Documents about Hungary, 1933–1944) (Budapest, 1968), p. 430. (249)
20. HL. Eln. Vkf.1 1939/4507.
21. Ránki–Pamlényi–Tilkovszky–Juhász, *A Wilhelmstrasse és Magyarország...*, p. 431. (250)
22. HL. Eln. Vkf.1 1939/4507.

23. HL. Eln. Vkf.1 1939/4735.
24. HL. Eln. Vkf.1 1939/4510.
25. HL. Eln. Vkf.1 1939/4544.
26. Ránki–Pamlényi–Tilkovszky–Juhász, *A Wilhelmstrasse és Magyarország...*, p. 432. (251)
27. *Ibid.*, p. 433. (253)
28. OL. K 64-81-24-848/1939. Rp.
29. OL. K 64-81-27/b-800/1939. Rp.
30. *Ibid.*
31. *Ibid.*
32. Ránki–Pamlényi–Tilkovszky–Juhász, *A Wilhelmstrasse és Magyarország...*, p. 437. (258)
33. HL. Eln. Vkf.1. 1939/4570 and 4582.
34. OL. K 64-82-27/a-815/1939. Rp.
35. OL. K 64-82-27/a-832/1939. Rp.
36. OL. K 64-82-27/a-831/1939. Rp.
37. OL. K 64-82-27/a-825/1939. Rp.
38. Ránki–Pamlényi–Tilkovszky–Juhász, *A Wilhelmstrasse és Magyarország...*, p. 438. (260)
39. OL. K 64-82-27/a-844/1939. Rp.
40. Ránki–Pamlényi–Tilkovszky–Juhász, *A Wilhelmstrasse és Magyarország...*, p. 437. (259)
41. Juhász, *Diplomáciai iratok...*, vol. IV: p. 505. (379)
42. HL. Eln. Vkf.1. 1939/4609.
43. HL. Eln. Vkf.1. 1939/4623.
44. HL. Eln. Vkf.1. 1939/4671.
45. HL. Eln. Vkf.1. 1939/4735/7-10.
46. Ránki–Pamlényi–Tilkovszky–Juhász, *A Wilhelmstrasse és Magyarország...*, p. 440. (263)
47. *Ibid.*, p. 440. (262)
48. *Ibid.*, p. 441. (264)
49. *Ibid.*, p. 443. (267)
50. HL. Eln. Vkf.1 1939/4654.
51. Ránki–Pamlényi–Tilkovszky–Juhász, *A Wilhelmstrasse és Magyarország...*, p. 444. (263)
52. HL. Eln. Vkf.1 1939/4647.
53. HL. Eln. Vkf.1 1939/5121.
54. HL. Eln. Vkf.1.1939/4684.
55. HL. Eln. Vkf.1 1939/4998.

56. HL. Eln. Vkf.1 1939/4732.
57. OL. K 63-472 and 473; Domokos Szent-Iványi, *Emlékirat* (Memoirs), Ráday Levéltár (Ráday Archive), Szent-Iványi hagyaték C/80, p. 231.
58. *Ibid.*, p. 232.
59. *Ibid.*, p. 49.
60. Ránki–Pamlényi–Tilkovszky–Juhász, *A Wilhelmstrasse és Magyarország...*, p. 450. (278)
61. Gibson, ed., *Ciano naplója...*, p. 162.
62. HL. Eln. Vkf.1. 1939/5158.
63. HL. 196/VI.hdt.I.a. 1939.
64. HL. Eln. Vkf.1. 1939/4766.
65. HL. Eln. Vkf.1. 1939/5035.
66. HL. Eln. Vkf.1. 1939/5121.
67. Carlile Aylmer Macartney, *October Fifteenth. A History of Modern Hungary, 1929-1945* (Edinburgh, 1961), vol. I: p. 386.
68. *Ibid.*
69. OL. K 64-82-27/b-881/1939. Rp.
70. OL. K 64-82-27/b-882/1939. Rp.
71. OL. K 64-82-27/b-885/1939. Rp.
72. Macartney, *October Fifteenth*, vol. I: p. 387.
73. OL. K 64-82-27/b-921/1939. Rp.
74. *Ibid.*
75. Macartney, *October Fifteenth*, vol. I: p. 387.
76. OL. K 64-81-23-926/1939. Rp.
77. Juhász, *Diplomáciai iratok...*, vol. IV: p. 471.
78. *Ibid.*, p. 536.
79. Ránki–Pamlényi–Tilkovszky–Juhász, *A Wilhelmstrasse és Magyarország...*, p. 454. (882)
80. *Ibid.*, p. 455. (283)
81. *Ibid.*, p. 471. (299)
82. HL. Eln. Vkf.1. 1939/4817.
83. HL. Eln. Vkf.1. 1939/5131.

THE HUNGARIAN MILITARY
REQUESTS GERMANY
TO HELP RECLAIM TRANSYLVANIA

Teleki and the Hungarian government did not give up on revisionist plans for Transylvania yet. Rather than relying on Germany, they continued to consider the idea of unaided military attempts. While the Soviet Union once again expressed its good intentions towards Hungary, Teleki, supported by Western circles, hoped for the outbreak of armed conflict between the Soviet Union and Germany. Meanwhile Germany's dissatisfaction towards the Hungarian government simply kept increasing.

Werth was convinced that the Hungarian government was missing the opportunity to realize Hungary's territorial demands. He disapproved of the Prime Minister's pro-Western policy, and thought that Great Britain was trying to drive a wedge between the Soviet Union and Germany. Great Britain, in his view, was also trying to cause foreign political difficulties for the Soviet leadership, in order to create internal political and economic tension that might make the Soviet Union unable to fulfill its economic obligations to Germany. In his view, the Soviet Union was seeking a peaceful solution with Romania, but if there were a change in Romania's attitude and it openly joined the Western powers, a Soviet–Romanian conflict would be unavoidable.[1]

It seems peculiar that the Chief of the General Staff, an advocate of unconditional adjustment to Germany, continued to consider armed action against Romania using whatever opportunities were afforded, in spite of definite German warning against it. Among the formative factors of his views was the solid belief that a Hungarian action executed at the right moment would surely gain

Germany's post-facto approval. Moreover, in order to secure the Romanian oilfields, sooner or later Germany would have to pacify the unreliable Romanians. On what did Werth base his views, which were contrary to official German statements and actions? He relied on the information relayed to the General Staff and to him, not officially, but in a tendentious way, by Sztójay, the military attachés and the officers of the German army. The *Wehrmacht*'s authoritative spokesmen suggested that the official German goals with regard to Romania and the expected Hungarian role there were being suppressed for foreign political reasons. They also managed to hint that while they had reservations about the Hungarian politicians, the non-official information was being extended by the highest German circles to the Hungarian military Supreme Command, that they were considered more reliable. To show the truth beyond the stated goals, they often leaked the real parameters about the preparation plans of the German army, which they were to execute depending on how Germany's foreign political goals developed.

The *Wehrmacht*'s plan to invade Romania was complete, and it included a role for Hungarian troops. However, this plan was not announced officially, nor was it reconciled along traditional military lines, since Germany was confident that it would enfold Romania in its camp through political pressure and thus avoid military action. This "non-official" line given to the Hungarians about German foreign policy served two purposes. First, it increased the Hungarian army's confidence in pursuing its own political line, strengthened its pro-German orientation, and further deepened the disagreement between the unreliable Hungarian government and the reliable Hungarian Supreme Command. Therefore, it secured the Hungarian army for Germany as a tool of political pressure. At the same time, by keeping the Hungarian army on alert, it also put pressure on Romania. Werth firmly believed in this German approach, since he was disposed to read the development of international politics according to what conformed to his own ideas. He misjudged the situation and its expected development, and therefore the underlying intentions of Germany and the Soviet Union in connection with their agreement. Werth thought that once Germany gave a free hand to the Soviet Union on the issue of Bessarabia, it would provide the same approach to its Hungarian ally on the question of Romania. He also counted on the division of Romania. He ignored the frequent German threats during the fall of 1939, and thought that they were targeted at the slow and double-dealing Hungarian government.[2] He also totally ignored the reactions of the Western powers, since he did not think that they would have any impact in the region. Their attitude towards the issue of Poland helped to convince him of this. Accordingly, he wished to influence Hungarian policy beyond his nominal role and sphere of authority. Thus, he opposed any measure that would moderate the strained relationship with Romania or might forestall the military's being afforded some future opportunity to act.

Werth's report sent to Csáky on October 15 described his disappointment over missed opportunities and his dissatisfaction with the government's policy and its expected impact. He also described the situation evolving in Transylvania, quoting from military intelligence sources. When the German–Polish controversy broke out, the Transylvanian Hungarians were convinced that Hungary would soon attempt to re-annex Transylvania. Since this did not take place, the atmosphere there had quietened down, but during the weeks of September the belief still held that "we are waiting for a favorable opportunity." However, the ensuing Hungarian troop withdrawals had spoiled the atmosphere among the Hungarians. Many drew far-reaching conclusions and came to "predict a Hungarian–Romanian non-aggression treaty and the abandonment of Hungarian revisionist goals."[3]

Csáky rejected Werth's proposal for radio broadcasts, because around that time the Romanians exposed a Transylvanian plot, resulting in massive arrests and a total liquidation of a support network. A new propaganda campaign on Hungarian Radio would necessarily become connected with the conspiracy, complicating the situation and leading to the jamming of the radios of the Transylvanian Hungarians.[4]

The uncovering of the Transylvanian conspiracy deeply concerned Teleki. In his irritation about disclosure of the groups organized by the 5th Section of the General Staff, he turned to Werth. He was angry because he believed that the directors of the conspiracy were loud-mouthed, saber-rattling soldiers. And his antipathy increased when he realized that Werth had not followed the instructions of May and had failed to keep the Prime Minister informed, did not consult with him on planning, and organized people—among them minority leaders and church officials—against Teleki's specific ban.[5]

On October 22 Werth informed Csáky that only a few of the people arrested actually belonged to the clandestine organization. He also informed him that an investigation was underway about the circumstances of the discovery. Two days later he asked the Minister of Foreign Affairs to instruct Bárdossy to do anything in his power "to defend the arrested, some of whom were connected with my organization."[6]

In order to avoid antagonizing the general situation, the Romanian government made an effort to handle the conspiracy case with the greatest possible self-restraint. The two governments agreed that they would not reveal it to the public. Citing Yugoslavian government sources, the Hungarian ambassador to Belgrade, Bessenyei, reported on November 10 that the Romanian government was doing its utmost to ensure that "the case of the conspiracy discovered in Transylvania not hinder the Hungarian–Romanian rapprochement."[7] As a result of all the effort, most of the participants in the conspiracy (67 people, including all the church leaders in the area) were transferred across the border, so that the

Romanian Military Court brought a verdict against only 15 people in April 1940.

The case of the disclosed conspiracy continued to exert an unpleasant effect on the increasingly cold relationship between the Prime Minister and the Chief of the General Staff. Werth, deeply and unjustly insulted, wrote an indignant note to Csáky with copies to Teleki and Bartha, where he voiced several complaints, about such matters as the fact that Csáky had made a statement in front of one of Werth's "functionaries" that he—Csáky—had had no knowledge of the conspiracy. Werth referred to Csáky's May letter in which he called Werth's attention to the importance of organizing "self-defensive sabotage" units in Transylvania. Werth also alluded to the ensuing conference, where, in their presence and agreement, a resolution was accepted about immediately establishing those units.[8]

Csáky rebutted Werth's insinuation, saying that he had known about and endorsed the plan, but then calling the Chief of the General Staff's attention to details that had apparently not been considered and had now caused unpleasant circumstances in the Hungarian government's foreign policy towards the Romanians and had weakened the organizations of the Transylvanian Hungarians. Csáky also stated that "both the Prime Minister and I asked you that, in the executing organization, no political or economic functionaries of the Transylvanian Hungarians—of their organizations, institutions or churches—be included, nor should the radio be utilized."[9] Csáky also noted that he had asked Werth in vain to inform him about the nature of the Transylvanian propaganda directed by the General Staff and related measures, but this had never happened. It is not known in whose circle the utterance that Werth had found insulting was said—or whether it was said at all. Nor is it known if it was someone who wished to further deepen the existing discord between Werth and Csáky and Teleki. As far as Werth was concerned, it was an attack on him, and the blame for the botched operation was unduly put on him. He felt no urge to investigate things further.

Teleki became increasingly concerned about his deteriorating relationship with Werth, their increasing discord, and the fact that Werth's independent aspirations were being supported by the General Staff and benevolently handled by Horthy. A parallel military policy was surfacing, which deviated from the government's position and which not only endangered the realization of his decisions but also inherently carried the possibility of an open break within the governing élite. He thought that this was very dangerous, given the ever-intensifying foreign political situation. He was concerned that the army would encourage the radical extreme right or perhaps enter into alliance with them. His distrust reached such proportions that he even ignored the information coming from the unreliable General Staff and tried to be informed on military issues through his own channels. He collected information through his ambassadors in different countries about the "phony war" looming in the West, about the strength, equipment, and strategic ideas of the British and French armies, and about the war plans of the Great Powers. And it was through diplomatic sources in the West that he received information about the German army and the assumed intentions of Hitler and the German General Staff.

The Hungarian ambassador to London, György Barcza, gave Teleki information about Great Britain in a series of private letters. He provided a wealth of data about the British army and, most of all, about the strength of the Royal Air Force and the Royal Navy. He described in detail the output of Great Britain's military manufacturing, and also pointed out the orders that the British government had placed in the United States for military goods. Barcza called Teleki's attention to the productive capacity of American industry, which was able to produce 3,000–4,000 airplanes daily. This data and information more and more strengthened Teleki's conviction that Germany could not win a war against the Western powers.[10] He also asked his Italian envoy Villani to perform similar duties. Since Villani was not a military man, he refused to accept responsibility for the professionalism of the reports.[11]

Teleki's distrust went really far. For example, he circumvented the General Staff to obtain information about the Romanian army. He himself wanted to size up the relative military strength of the Hungarian forces and the Romanian army. Bárdossy—via the "confidential" intervention of a General Staff colonel and military attaché, Oszkár Baitz—sent detailed reports about the power of the Romanian air force, its structure, and the quality and characteristics of its airplanes. The Romanian air force of 445 airplanes was far superior to the strength of the Hungarian air force, even if it would be difficult to put their concentrated use against Hungary, since they were scattered at different remote airports.[12]

Teleki's distrust of the attachés was mostly justified. Their reports were not meant to give direct information to the Prime Minister or the Minister of Foreign Affairs. For the sake of their own promotion, the attachés would collect and report only information that the Chief of the General Staff expected and wanted to hear. It was among their assignments, especially in the Western countries, to keep track of the ambassador and his co-workers. This did not remain a secret, and often led to a tense relationship between the ambassador and the military attaché. For example, the atmosphere was pretty bad at the London Embassy—of special importance to Teleki. Ambassador György Barcza and Lieutenant Colonel Lóránd Utassy could not stand each other, and the tension between them further deepened following the outbreak of the war. Utassy did not make a secret of his feelings. He had complained already during the fall of 1939 to his superior, Colonel Ujszászy, who tried to reassure him in a letter that October: "You are not the only one [attaché] who has this problem. There are few exceptions to the rule when there is complete harmony" [between the military attaché and the ambassador]. Ujszászy asked Utassy to adjust to his ambassador in every way publicly, but "you should report, without reservations, your own opinions and news to us in each and every case and then add what the ambassador thinks about it."[13]

The relationship between Utassy and Barcza deteriorated further during the spring of 1940, before Hitler launched his western campaign. On April 16 Utassy wrote the following to his friend Gábor Faragho: "I do not agree with the ambassador's report. He reports whatever he wants; I am following my independent way. All I am saying is that the situation is horrible both within the Embassy and in the local Hungarian (Jewish) community."[14]

In a coded telegram of May 7 Utassy reported to Ujszászy that "in spite of cordial contact, the disagreements between the ambassador and me keep deepening. Affected by his environment and his own mentality, he deliberately describes an incorrect picture in his reports, which he justifies to me by saying that he is counterbalancing Sztójay's pro-German reports." On the same day the surprisingly well-informed Utassy—even well-informed about Barcza's personal affairs—also informed his superior in a letter:

> Since the outbreak of the war there has been a certain disagreement between the ambassador and me. I have not attributed to it any special significance as long as there was any chance that Hungary would retain its neutrality. However, the situation has worsened and at any moment Hungary could be driven into the war... Some of the officials here openly admit that they will not leave England and would rather let themselves be interned here. Just last November the ambassador sent a telegram to his family instructing them to leave Hungary and come to London because, in his view, they would be in a safer personal and material situation... I have every reason to assume that at the crucial moment the ambassador will sabotage or even refuse to comply with the government's decree.[15]

On May 16 Ujszászy responded. He relayed the Chief of the General Staff's appreciation and reassured Utassy that his information about his ambassador was reported only to the Chief of the General Staff and the Minister of Defense and that "we only acknowledge them and do not pass them on." He also instructed Utassy to go to the United States to pursue his intelligence work on Great Britain in case diplomatic relations between Great Britain and Hungary were broken. If the United States broke diplomatic ties with Hungary, then Utassy should return to Budapest.[16]

During the fall months Werth did whatever he could to accelerate equipping the army and increasing the production of war materials. This endeavor coincided with the government's goals, and yet he was not satisfied and wanted a greater effort. He wanted to make the *Honvédség* combat-ready, so as to be able to take advantage of any opportunity that cropped up. Furthermore, his attention was continually occupied by the Soviet–Romanian relationship. In November the Soviet press once again raised the issue of the need to settle the Bessarabian question. Werth immediately voiced the intention of deploying Hungarian troops at the outbreak of a Soviet–Romanian conflict. His hardly secretive opinion induced the Romanian military command to give up on regrouping their forces. They were concerned that in the case of an eastern conflict the Hungarian General Staff would persuade the reluctant Hungarian government to opt for military action. The increasing role of Werth's General Staff and their impact on the Hungarian government was the reason for a growing fear in the region. In his letter of December 14 to Csáky, Bárdossy described information that had originated with the Romanian ambassador to Budapest, Crutescu, but that was also widespread in diplomatic circles. According to this information the Romanian government "counts on a war between us, if not earlier, then in the spring. This is based on the view that whatever the General Staff wants, that happens in Hungary. The General Staff is assuredly preparing for war and, either at the Germans' request or due to other considerations, in spring it will decide that it is time to deploy the army against Romania without asking the government or even against the government's wish."[17]

The well-informed Crutescu, who obviously exaggerated the role attributed to the Hungarian government, also mentioned the fact that the government had forced the General Staff to transfer Colonel Homlok, who had directed the Transylvanian conspiracy, into a different position. In spite of Crutescu's opinion, Colonel Homlok's transfer was not due to the relationship between the government and the General Staff, since it was obviously due to events; he was soon appointed military attaché to Berlin. So Crutescu unknowingly (or deliberately!) poured oil on the fire. Teleki was shocked to hear the news, and expressed his consternation to Werth and blamed his subordinates for the fact that Homlok's transfer was leaked by the General Staff and brought to the Romanians' attention. He spared no words of criticism regarding secrecy within the army. Werth choked with rage at the Prime Minister's criticism and ordered an investigation, which produced no results.

Bárdossy's report of December 12 said that one and a half months earlier the Romanian government had been thinking about decreasing the strength of its mobilized forces, but now they had even put a ban on leave: "According to my sources the Romanian High Command has begun to implement the necessary arrangements for a complete mobilization—as opposed to the 80–90% mobilization until now—so that by January 15 everyone of military age will be under arms and at his post of service."[18] So it seemed that Romania wanted to get ready before spring to avoid being surprised. And, in view of the newly strained Romanian–Hungarian relations, they had arranged that most of their forces would be concentrated on their western border.

The memorandum that Werth gave to the Prime Minister on December 12 could hardly be kept secret from the Romanian government. Werth elaborated on the question of Bessarabia and the expected Soviet actions. Hungary should not stay idle in this situation and would have to attack Romania to occupy all of Transylvania. In the case that the Romanian army was tied down in the east, Werth wrote that the available forces would be sufficient for staging a successful operation against the numerically superior Romanian troops. He expected the Romanians to suffer a serious loss against the Russians, which would make it impossible for them to deploy new and significant forces against the Hungarians, and they might even have to send more troops to the eastern frontline. In this way, the Romanian resistance would weaken and the initiative would fall into the hands of the Hungarians. The total collapse of the Romanian army and the hinterland would further increase the chances of winning for the Hungarian troops. Werth juxtaposed this situation to the patriotic enthusiasm of Hungarian troops, whose armaments had also been improved. He also considered the experiences of the August–September Romanian mobilization, with each wave of mobilization needing 15 days to be completed. The Hungarian mobilization and deployment was substantially shorter, at 4 to 5 days. It was the goal of the Hungarian leadership to retain and increase this advantage and then to use it with a surprise deployment and attack. Neither did it escape his attention that the Romanian troops were not evenly well equipped, with the reserve troops having downright poor-quality arms and equipment. In the case of a two-front war, the Romanians, at the peak of their effort, would only be able to deploy the latter forces in Transylvania.

Teleki, fearing foreign political complications, was skeptical about the calculations of the Chief of the General Staff and was not at all convinced that the *Honvédség* in its current state would be able to re-occupy Transylvania even under the above-mentioned circumstances. The Supreme Military Council discussed Werth's memorandum on December 19 and 22. Mostly Teleki and Minister of the Interior Keresztes-Fischer took issue with it because of the expected foreign political consequences. Werth's proposal was not approved by the Council, but the government did lay down the conditions under which the army's intervention would be necessary: 1) if the Transylvanian Hungarian minority were to come under threat, 2) if a Bolshevik revolution were to break out in Romania, or 3) if Romania were to give up territories without a fight to the Soviet Union or Bulgaria.[19]

Once again it was difficult for Werth to submit to the refusal. Already during the December 22 session of the Supreme Military Council he used the opportunity and retorted in Horthy's presence. He viciously attacked the government, saying that they had hindered mobilization of the country and the development of war production. He stated that although Hungarian industry had been in a state of mobilization since September 1939, it was not yet producing the amount of material required by the army. Production simply had not reached suitable standards in spite of all the efforts. He especially condemned the Ministry of Trade and the Ministry of Industry, which had been reluctant to issue the appropriate instructions. As he stated, individual ministers were in perfect agreement with regard to the affairs of the army, but the high-ranking officials of certain ministries "obviously do not understand the importance of national mobilization, and express not only their indifference but a total disregard. Therefore, they are delaying the quick and smooth execution of issues due to jealousies over bureaucratic turf. They do not keep deadlines ordered by the Supreme Military Council. On the contrary, they consider them insulting. The following statement of a certain official is the most characteristic: 'There is a thaw in the foreign political situation. It is not worth accelerating things. Why are the soldiers so nervous?'"[20]

To change this situation Werth demanded the army's increased participation in the governance of the country and the country's industry. The existing "complicated and obsolete" administration should be reorganized, because it had made it possible for there to be absolutely no acceptance of responsibility, due to a lack of discipline in work, due to the untimeliness of the work done, and due to neglecting deadlines. This could only be achieved if in every relevant ministry "the head of the section for national mobilization is a military person who, through the chief official assigned to direct national mobilization-related affairs, will have both reporting rights and the right to make proposals to the relevant minister. This is the only way that issues related to national mobilization will prevail quickly and safely according to the intentions of the relevant minister. And, furthermore, in this way the unfortunate jealousies regarding spheres of authority will be eliminated... every instance of negligence will be punished."[21] If all these things were not realized, Werth said that he could not take any responsibility for equipping the army or for its combat efficiency. Alluding to the upcoming Hungarian–German economic discussions, Werth also condemned what he called the petty and narrow-minded policy that, by refusing to satisfy the German demands, delayed the transport of German war material. He asked the government for another 300 million pengős as an emergency investment loan in order to expand the armament program.

Werth told the Council clearly which parts of the administration should be reorganized, apart from the planting of interfering soldiers on their necks. On the other hand, he ignored the fact that the multiplying economic difficulties could hardly be solved by political means, by military intervention, or by Draconian measures in the economy. And he refused to acknowledge the obstructive political character of German economic relations, and instead made the Hungarian government responsible for them.

While the military leadership tried to influence the government to move towards a military operation against Romania, Germany continued to disapprove of every step that might lead to a Hungarian–Romanian armed conflict. It was brought to the attention of the Hungarian government that Germany would not idly watch a Hungarian attack against Romania.[22] Several German military activities during the month of December also served to soften the attitudes of both countries, to increase Germany's influence, and to pave the way for the acceptance of Germany's economic demands. Disquieting news about a major concentration of troops came from Slovakia. The local population was informed that the newly arriving, mostly motorized, 700,000 German troops had come "for a rest." At the same time, the Slovakian government was asked to repair the roads leading to Hungary and to reinforce its bridges.[23]

While the official German policy cautioned moderation, the German military command made sure that their Hungarian comrades had a glimpse behind the scenes. The Hungarian military command was confidentially informed that the *Honvédség* might have a role in the occupation of Romania.

On January 17 General Tippelskirch, Head of the Recording Office of the German General Command, arrived in Budapest to meet his colleague Colonel Ujszászy, Chief of the 2nd Section of the General Staff, and to improve cooperative news recording. In order to do that, a German communications officer would be delegated to the 1st Section of the General Staff. Tippelskirch grasped the opportunity to give military political information to Ujszászy. First of all, he reassured him that, although the Germans were forced to use certain western Slovakian facilities for troop deployment, they were not targeting Hungary. The news about troops in eastern Slovakia was not true, but he asked the Hungarians not to release an official denial, because it was desirable to have Romania believe the rumor.

Speaking about the Romanian situation, Tippelskirch said that the German military command believed it unlikely that the Soviet Union would raise the question of Bessarabia in the spring. If indeed it did happen then a Soviet–Romanian conflict would break out, which would upset Romania's internal order. In that case, Germany would do everything in its power to secure the oilfields of Ploieşti, and so quick decisions would have to be made. Military operations would have to be completed within ten days, so that the oilfields could be continuously used. Obviously, Tippelskirch said, if the conflict could be confined locally and Romania did not collapse, it would not be in Germany's interest that Hungary interfere in order to re-annex Transylvania.[24]

Listening to the German general's comments, Ujszászy had the impression that the Germans had already drawn up concrete plans regarding Romania, which, for the time being, they did not want to share with the Hungarian military command. Obviously, the thought also occurred that a preventive German attack against Romania was also possible, even if it were not justified by domestic chaos but by the Romanian government's resistance to the growing German pressure and its reluctance to satisfy German economic demands.

The multilateral, although mostly Hungarian, threat induced the Romanians to turn for help to the Italians, who had become alienated from and jealous of the Germans because of the German–Soviet agreement and because of the growing German influence in the Balkans. On December 23 Romanian Minister of Foreign Affairs Gafencu went to Rome and sought to find out from Ciano what position they would take if the Soviet Union attacked Romania. Seeing Ciano's reluctance to make any sort of binding statement, Gafencu asked him to try to at least impress upon the Hungarians the seriousness of the situation, because the Hungarian threat was forcing the Romanian government to move towards signing an accord with the Soviet Union. Gafencu did not bring up the German threat that lay behind the Hungarian threat. Mussolini also received the Romanian Minister of Foreign Affairs, along with Ciano, and insisted that Ciano intervene with the

Hungarian government according to the Romanian wish. The Duce assured Gafencu about his support and even held out the prospect of some war materials supply to Romania. Ciano agreed to act as intermediary, but also noted that the Hungarian government could hardly be forced to remain idle unless it gained some type of territorial concession from Romania.[25]

As a result, Ciano invited Hungarian Minister of Foreign Affairs Csáky to Rome. Similarly to Gafencu, Csáky came to Rome to secure the Italian ally's support in the strained foreign political situation. Ciano cautioned restraint to his guest and informed him that Italy had decided to support Romania in the case of a Soviet attack. If Hungary offered guarantees to Romania that, in the case of an external attack, it would also not attack, this would meet Italy's approval, and then Hungary could count on the annexation of certain areas along the border zones.

Csáky found the Italian offer acceptable, but only if the annexed territories were proportionately large enough for Hungary to make an impact on the defense of the Carpathians. When asked how the Hungarian government hoped to realize such a request, since the Romanians would offer armed resistance, Csáky's pugnacious response was "we will respond with Hungarian swords to the prospective cannons."[26]

Ciano continued to press the issue of when the Hungarian government would launch a war against Romania, if it saw no alternative, considering the Supreme Military Council's December resolution. Csáky then stated with unscathed determination: "... I don't know, because it depends upon the circumstances. I can only tell you that the Regent and the government have decided that, if Russia attacked Romania and the latter put up an honest and armed resistance to defend Bessarabia or any other border areas, Hungary would not attack Romania from the back."[27] Then he proceeded to list the situations prescribed by the Supreme Military Council that would bring about a Hungarian intervention. Understandably,

Csáky was reluctant to make a statement about an independent Hungarian armed action. However, he pointed out that from a military perspective time was against Hungary. The Germans were transporting increasing amounts of war material to Romania, which could be countered by a parallel increase in Italian shipments to Hungary. The Romanian army's size was increasing and its fortification line was getting stronger. It was in Hungary's interest to settle this issue as soon as possible and, preferably, before the deepening of the European conflict.

During the discussions, Csáky told his hosts that an embittered Italian–Yugoslavian relationship was not in Hungary's interest, since it would damage the chances of improved Hungarian–Yugoslavian relations, a priority with regard to the political and military isolation of Romania.[28] Speaking about the Hungarian–Soviet relationship, he established that Hungary did not feel threatened by the Russians and that no more contested questions remained between the two countries. Yet the Carpathian border would still be strengthened.[29]

The Italian Minister of Foreign Affairs found the outcome of the discussion satisfactory. He was convinced that the Hungarians would not get involved in any military conflicts. Csáky, arriving back in Hungary from Rome, had the chance to assist in Germany's gaining ground in Hungary once again. During the Hungarian–German economic talks, which ended on January 16, the Hungarian government, worrying about the production of war materials and squeezed by the military, was forced into giving concessions. As a result, the Germans made promises to increase the volume of war material supplies to be shipped. The details were registered in a military protocol.

In spite of the German and Italian statements, the Hungarian General Staff continued to believe that a Hungarian armed operation against the Romanians might still be possible in the near future. According to the analysis of the General Staff, for the time being Romania was resisting the expansion of German influence, even though it might induce the armed intervention described by Tippelskirch. Romania was forced into a dangerous politics of balancing and, in spite of what it seemed, was far from changing the direction of its foreign policy or tying its fate to Germany. The Romanian government and the country's public opinion continued to hope for victory by the Western democracies. In the case of an armed conflict, however, since Romania was threatened on three sides and could not count on any Western help, it would therefore not be able to exert any serious resistance. The General Staff believed that this provided an opportunity that Hungary should use. Hungary should offer its services to Germany and should also argue for action against Romania by any political or economic means available. A showdown in the near future would be desirable, in order to avoid the likely situation where Romania—breaking with its current policy—would surrender to the German pressure. This would make the realization of Hungarian territorial revisionist aspirations difficult.[30]

Meanwhile, the intelligence unit of the General Staff continued to collect and summarize reports for the Operational Staff on the relocation, organizational changes and armaments of the Romanian army, as well as the growing fortification line. These reports helped in the preparation of the *Honvédség* for its possible independent campaign against Romania. They indicated that the Romanian army was continuing to receive arms from several sources and that its equipment was also improving. Increasing numbers of Zbroiovka light machine-guns and heavy machine-guns were detected in the possession of infantry units stationed near the Hungarian border, and their firepower was increasing. Armored power was also increasing, with four anti-tank cannons per regiment and the equipping of the mechanized brigades also underway. So far about 70–80 Renault-35 type medium tanks (47 mm cannons) had arrived from France, automobile and airplane material from Great Britain, air force bombs from Holland and Belgium, and raw material from the United States. However, the most disturbing thing was that, in spite of the repeated protests, Germany continued "to deliver every kind of war material under the sun." These were mostly Czechoslovakian materials, but artillery equipment from the Polish booty could also be found among them. On top of all that, news also came that Italy planned to deliver 500 pieces of 47 mm anti-tank guns to Romania. At the same time, the Italian ally was not willing to supply such guns to the Hungarian army, short on anti-tank weapons.[31]

Such a turn of events would have forced the leadership to further accelerate preparations, except that continuously arising difficulties hindered them. The German shipment of equipment for the mechanized brigades—considered to be the major players in a military operation against Romania—was delayed. As the artillery professionals established in January, Hungarian field artillery preparedness was inadequate, unsuitable to destroy Romanian fortifications and only able to paralyze them.[32] Eight 21 cm heavy howitzers from Italy designated for the 101st and 102nd Heavy Artillery Battalions had arrived, but needed serious work so that the guns could be used. This was important because the 101st and 102nd Heavy Artillery Battalions were formed during the fall of 1939 and were to play the role of breaking through the fortification line. The military command also urged the manufacture of 150 mm howitzers.[33]

At the beginning of 1940 the Carol Line of 320 fortifications posed the greatest problem to the Hungarian military and required careful military planning. The Hungarians had to count on disabling 25–30 fortifications in order to open up a planned 7-km wide gate. After an initial assault by the artillery and Ca-135 bomber planes, specially trained commandos were to execute the breakthrough.[34]

Act II of 1939 ordered the abolition of the Supreme Command of the *Honvédség* by March 3, 1940. General of the Infantry Hugó Sónyi retired. Werth convinced the Regent to abolish it in order to simplify the system and to make the command structure more efficient. His aim with this professionally justifiable measure was to eliminate what had been a co-commander from beside him and with whom, thus far, he had had to share the command of the *Honvédség* and who had tied his hands. Teleki recognized his goal and was concerned about a further increase in the Chief of the General Staff's power. He did not agree that the measure was just "an internal affair" of the military, even if sanctioned by the Regent. Both then and later on Teleki several times failed to convince people about the benefits of restoring the original system. On March 10 General of the Infantry Vilmos Nagybaczoni Nagy was appointed the Commander of the 1st Hungarian Army, the strongest field army of the *Honvédség*. It was supposed to play a decisive role in the expected military operations.

Teleki was also concerned about news of the German military movements in Austria and Slovakia as obvious proof of increasing pressure on Hungary and Romania. Rumors were spread among the German and Slovakian armies and the Slovak population that the German military in Slovakia and the Slovakian army would shortly occupy Slovakian territories previously annexed by Hungary, and that the Slovakian army had already taken steps to begin mobilization.[35]

The Hungarian government tried to elicit a straightforward response from the Germans about their intentions towards Romania and about Hungary's role in that action. The Hungarians were especially interested in the possibility that the Soviet Union might get involved because of Bessarabia, and in the probable effect of any possible ensuing German military measures to secure the Romanian oil. German diplomats tried to dodge these questions. On February 23 Sztójay inquired about these issues with

Weizsäcker, who did not seem to be as communicative or informed as the earlier representative of the German General Staff in Budapest had been. Weizsäcker said that the Soviet Union's southeastward initiative was very unlikely. He immediately returned the question, asking whether the Hungarian government had any relevant information, which he would be eager to hear himself.[36]

Similar feelers were sent out to Rome as well. At the end of February Villani paid a visit to Ciano. The Italian Minister of Foreign Affairs stated that he did not think that there would be a German–Romanian war. Germany would not have to get the oil, under agreement in any case, in this way. Ciano said that if Germany did want to occupy Romania and wanted to do it by marching across Hungary, in his view then, as Villani saw it, "we would commit suicide if we resisted. Therefore, we have to endure such a deployment." Villani was also warned by Ciano that "we should not do anything together with the Reich, because it would have very serious consequences. Let us not enter [Romania] together with the German troops, but let us wait until they finish the operation, and only then let us occupy Transylvania, saying that we have to take care of the defense of the Transylvanian Hungarian population. In this way we would not join the war and yet would still prevent Transylvania shifting from Romanian rule to German rule." Villani knew that the position that Ciano recommended would hardly meet with the agreement of the Germans, an opinion that he voiced in his memorandum about the conversation: "I am sure that it will not be easy to get the Germans' agreement for the separate action, but I did not share this qualm with Ciano."[37]

Notes

1. Hadtörténelmi Levéltár (Military History Archive, HL). Eln. Vkf.1. 1939/3038.
2. *Ibid.*
3. Országos Levéltár (National Archive, OL). K 64-82-27-937/1939. Rp, and HL. Eln. Vkf.1. 1939/5121.
4. OL. K 64-82-27-937/1939. Rp.
5. OL. K 64-87-27/b-950/1939. Rp
6. OL. K 64-87-37/b-954/1939. Rp.
7. OL. K 64-82-27/a-1000/1939. Rp.
8. OL. K 64-82-27-1017/1939. Rp.
9. *Ibid.*
10. OL. K 64-83-35-977/1939.
11. *Ibid.*
12. OL. K 64-82-35-20/1940. Rp.
13. HL. Documents of the Military Attaché to London.
14. *Ibid.*
15. *Ibid.*
16. *Ibid.*
17. OL. K 64-86-27-2/1940. Rp.
18. OL. K 64-83-35-877/1939. Rp.
19. Carlile Aylmer Macartney, *October Fifteenth. A History of Modern Hungary, 1929-1945* (Edinburgh, 1961), vol. I: p. 389.
20. HL. Eln. Vkf.1. 1939/21/OM.B.
21. *Ibid.*
22. Dezső Saly, *Szigorúan bizalmas* (Strictly Confidential) (Budapest, 1945), pp. 112 and 130.
23. Gyula Juhász, ed., *Diplomáciai iratok Magyarország külpolitikájához 1936-1945* (Diplomatic Writings on Hungary's Foreign Policy, 1936–1945) (Budapest, 1962-1982), vol. IV: p. 679. (516)
24. *Ibid.*, p. 675. (514)
25. Hugh Gibson, ed., *Ciano naplója: 1939–1943: Gróf Galeazzo Ciano olasz külügyminiszter, 1939–1943 teljes, rövidítés nélküli naplói* (Ciano's Diary: 1939–1943: The Full Diary without Shortening of Count Galeazzo Ciano, Italian Foreign Minister, 1939–1943) (Budapest, 1946), pp. 187–188.

26. OL. K 64-85-23-39/1940. Rp.
27. *Ibid.*
28. *Ibid.*
29. György Ránki, Ervin Pamlényi, Loránt Tilkovszky and Gyula Juhász, eds., *A Wilhelmstrasse és Magyarország: Német diplomáciai iratok Magyarországról, 1933–1944* (The Wilhelmstrasse and Hungary: German Diplomatic Documents about Hungary, 1933–1944) (Budapest, 1968), p. 470. (279)
30. HL. Eln. Vkf.1. 1940/3414.
31. *Ibid.*
32. HL. Eln. Vkf.1. 1940/3152.
33. *Hadtörténelmi Közlemények* (1972) 4: pp. 750–751.
34. HL. Eln. Vkf.1. 1940/3169.
35. OL. K 149-1940-1-5007/A XXII. 513/1940/19.
36. OL. K 64-88-35-179/1940. Rp.
37. OL. K 64-85-23-1840/1940. Rp.

THE IMPACT OF THE GERMAN WESTERN BLITZKRIEG: HUNGARY BECOMES MORE PRO-GERMAN

During the first days of March, 1940, Sztójay showed up with important news that raised great interest both in government and military circles, although for different reasons. Germany was preparing with full force to launch its western operation. Germany was preparing to mobilize nearly one million soldiers and already had 200 divisions. Although the disposition of German forces along the western front was not known, there were already between 60 and 70 divisions deployed on the Belgian–Dutch border, according to one Belgian source.[1]

The Hungarian military assumed that, parallel with the western campaign, the German army might occupy Romania, in order to secure its vital oil resources. Then Hungary could also intervene, as outlined earlier by Tippelskirch. In the military's view, the Romanian regime would probably collapse. In reaction, this would induce the Soviet Union to raise its demands in connection with Bessarabia and Bukovina.

It is not known how informed Teleki was of the details about the ideas formed jointly by the Hungarian and German General Staffs earlier. But at that point in time the Chief of the General Staff gave him a detailed report about the German military's goals and the expected role of Hungarian troops in it, thereby eliciting his immediate disagreement. Teleki still supported the Supreme Military Council's December resolution that the criteria for common German–Hungarian action were that the German steps be called forth by the Soviet Union's intervention against Romania, and that the common actions be preventive actions. In this way Teleki hoped to give the issue an anti-Soviet edge, which might place the Hungarian cooperation in an acceptable light to the Western powers. He did not even want to hear about the situation, in which Germany, irrespective of a Soviet intervention, would occupy Romania in order to secure its oil even in the case of British military disembarkation there. In such an action Germany might ask for permission to deploy forces across Hungary and for the active participation of Hungarian troops.

As Csáky summarized in his notes about the April 6 meeting, during the discussion no final solution was reached between Teleki and the military. Teleki did ask Werth to take up relations with the General Staff of the German army, to make careful inquiry about their goals, to make them aware of the Hungarian position, and to conduct negotiations according to that position. Werth was supposed to establish right at the beginning of discussions that any kind of agreement between the two armies would be realized only in the case of a Russian advance, where the Hungarian "participation in this case would obviously assume an anti-Comintern basis."[2] Once again Teleki tried to bring the issue to a plenum that included the Italians, saying that, considering the military issues, a Hungarian–German–Italian discussion would be needed to deal with all the issues and to reach an agreement.

Teleki also thought it important to find out whether the German military High Command had any information about Russian plans against Romania. He also wondered whether the German measure was targeted to precede the Soviet Union's actions and whether it was meant to secure the oil. He assumed that the Hungarians would be judged differently by the Western powers if Hungary participated in the German occupation of Romania under the pretext of a preventive action against the Soviet Union. Teleki did not pay attention to the other possibility—for him unfavorable although decisive for the German military High Command—that the Romanian oil should be secured especially in case the British disembarked a military force in the Balkans.

According to the first military plan, the one most favorable to the Hungarians, which was supposed to have been initiated by Werth, German troops would advance to Moldova via eastern Galicia and Bukovina by utilizing the Hungarian railway across Sub-Carpathia, while Hungarian troops would secure the German flank by occupying Transylvania. Teleki recommended that it be clarified who would secure the Hungarian right wing in the case of a Yugoslavian reaction. Since Italy could be expected to do that, discussions with them were crucial.

Teleki, who was sensitive to the possibly necessity of transporting German troops across Hungarian territory, would have liked to make a gesture, no matter how unfeasible, to the Western powers. Thus, he wanted the German General Staff to agree that "... the transit of German troops be under Hungarian command when on Hungarian territory, because we cannot march into Transylvania with the impression that the Germans have acquired it for us. This would cause difficulties for the Hungarian government in the future."[3] Teleki deluded himself with the false hope that such a step would avoid or at least diminish the appearance of cooperation with the Germans. He also wanted to clarify along which lines the German troops would cross Hungary, how long they would take advantage of Hungarian transport, and how the German troops were to be supplied and reinforced. It was important for him to clarify these questions because, contrary to the military, he counted on the Romanian campaign dragging out. Nor had he discarded the idea of a British–American declaration of war.

Teleki had doubts about whether Werth would negotiate with the German General Staff according to his—Teleki's—instructions, since the Germans seemed to have made a bigger impact on him than Teleki had. Therefore, he did not exclude the possibility that, behind his back, Werth had already made commitments to the Germans, which might force the Hungarian government into a situation that would lead to a final break in relations with the West.

Csáky, who was also inclined to make allowances to the Germans, did not very much believe in the success of Teleki's ideas. Otherwise he would not have made the suggestion that Teleki not make Hungarian cooperation dependent upon Russia's actions, and nor would he have asked Teleki to consider "that in the case of cooperation, it would be desirable to ask the Germans to sign a non-aggression and eternal friendship accord with us."⁴

Teleki wanted to call attention to the expected German demand and to state the Hungarian government's position in connection with it. Once again he sought understanding and protection from the Italians. Two days after the talks with the military leaders, he sent his trusted man, Lipót Baranyai, to Rome to inform Mussolini about the events, about the Hungarian government's views, and to try to find out the Duce's views. Ciano noted in his diary on April 18 that Baranyai had told him about the big turmoil in Budapest because "the German General Staff is trying to win the confidence of the Hungarian General Staff. Using the pretext that Russia will soon occupy Bessarabia, Germany intends to occupy the Romanian oilfields and asks for free transit across Hungary. The price of this permission would be Transylvania. The tricky question for the Hungarians is whether they will allow them through or offer resistance. In either case, Hungary's freedom is over. To fulfill the request would spare them from destruction and devastation, but if they fought, it would prepare them for rebirth in the future."⁵ Ciano cautioned Baranyai and Villani, who had argued for refusing the German transit request, to fulfill that, and accompanied them to the Duce, who proved to be very reserved. He said that he stood with Germany without any reservations, and was prepared for the fight against the British and the French, and once again proposed that they accept the German offer. Ciano immediately sent a telegram to Berlin asking whether indeed what the Hungarians described was true.

After receiving a negative response from Berlin and also having received the news about the German attack on Denmark and Norway, the Italian dictator received Baranyai and his company for the second time. Quoting the German denial, he argued that "the Hungarians should keep their calm and moderation and should accede to the German request." Neither expecting nor hoping for this response, according to Ciano the Hungarians "went so far as to ask whether, in the case of military resistance, they could count on an Italian help. Mussolini smiled and said, 'How can you imagine that, when I am Hitler's ally and intend to stay one?'"[6]

In parallel with the Budapest and Rome discussions, the German General Staff was considering the occupation of Romania. Lieutenant Colonel Winter, from the Operational Section of the German General Staff, received the assignment from General Halder, Chief of the *Wehrmacht*'s land forces, to devise a study plan, in case a British military disembarkation took place at Thessaloniki, and so that the Germans could take steps to secure the Romanian oil.[7] Winter submitted the results of his work to Halder on April 8. According to this plan, starting from Thessaloniki, the British would reach the Danube within six days by mechanized forces or between three weeks and 28 days by infantry, unless—as was most probable—the Bulgarians resisted the British crossing their territory. A British division disembarking at Constanţa could reach Galaţi and Brăila within 48 hours, which would make it possible to close down the Romanian oil ports—so important from the German point of view. In addition, advancing British warships could prevent German control of the Iron Gate (at the Danube). The voyage between Constanţa and the Bosphorus would take only 24 hours.[8]

Winter considered that five days were needed for the Germans to make counter-arrangements to deploy German troops to the Romanian border. Following that, and depending on the Romanians' behavior, Winter considered 8 to 17 days necessary to occupy the country. If the planned western campaign had not begun by then and mechanized units could be withdrawn from the west, the regrouping and deployment of forces would take ten days, but the occupation itself could be executed within a shorter period of time. The deployment of parachutists could also modify the execution of the occupational plan. Vienna would serve both as a launching point and as a base for replacement of men and material. The Hungarian position would influence things, since the deployment would happen across Hungarian territory and even Hungarian units might be used. It is not clear what Winter thought the participation of Hungarian units would be dependent upon.[9]

On April 7 Major Kinzel, the Chief of Section of the Eastern Armies of the German General Staff, arrived in Budapest to unofficially inform the Hungarian General Staff about German military plans concerning Romania and to learn about the Hungarian position. The day after the Teleki–Werth discussion, official connection between the Hungarian and German General Staffs was established. Accordingly, on April 9 Kinzel informed Halder about the developments—the Hungarian General Staff did not raise any objections against the German transit, but requested participation in the occupation in return. In particular, the Hungarians wanted to participate in northern Transylvania as liberators. Following that, Halder asked for a precise professional opinion from his colleagues about the preparedness of the Hungarian military and about the usefulness of the Hungarian troops.[10]

On April 15 Werth, enthused by the German successes in northern Europe and by the possibility of participating in the expected occupation of Romania, sent a letter to Horthy urging a more decisive pro-German stand and substantial actions. Alluding to Teleki's pro-Western policy and to his own reservations about it, Werth explained to Horthy, who was himself carried away by the successes of the Germans in northern Europe, that "the German–Italian friendship seems to be a lasting one and the Axis is strong. Final victory is evident and, although the wheel of fortune is ever-turning, one could make predictions about the final outcome of the war. In this war Germany is more prepared than the Allies. After conquering the Scandinavian countries, Germany will not have raw material problems. Material resources at Germany's disposal make the German victory probable and its defeat out of the question. But even if Germany did not win the war, its military force cannot be destroyed by the Allies. Therefore, Hungary has to stand by Germany in this fight right now. It is time for us to give up neutrality, to intervene in the war on Germany's side, and to realize the re-annexation of the annexed territories. If, after our open joining with Germany, it were to lose the war, we could still retain the re-annexed territories, because the Allies could conquer them only at a very great expense and would not be able to send large forces to the Danube Basin to dismember Hungary after the war."[11]

Based on the Chief of the General Staff's ongoing pro-German attitude, it was not surprising that after the end of the Scandinavian campaign and before the beginning of the western one Werth believed in the success of Germans' further conquests without reserve. Why, however, he thought that the Scandinavian successes would solve Germany's raw material problems is less clear. In his letter Werth clearly spelled out his self-justifying opinion, which he continued to voice in military circles until the final collapse, that if Germany lost the war, it would still not lead to its total collapse. By the end of the war the victors would also have reached the end of their strength and Hungary would not have to pay a heavy price for the advantages gained through the Germans.

Teleki considered Werth's letter to the Regent and his circumventing him—Teleki—as an open attack on his own foreign policy efforts. He pointed out the dangers stemming from such occurrences, and tried to impress Horthy to restrain Werth. "Make sure that the soldiers do not engage in politics... I am not sure that Germany will win, and therefore it is not convenient for us to side with them. If we have had a narrow escape so far, let us not ruin it at the last moment. I think that our political action was good; it is dangerous to divert from the current direction."[12]

The Prime Minister's satisfying "political action" had not been at all as successful as he had dreamed. Furthermore, he could hardly count the army among his supporters. He did not know whether Werth had taken up a position contrary to his instructions before meeting Kinzel, but his intuition did not promise anything good. Unfortunately, it is not known to what extent Werth informed Teleki about his discussions with Kinzel.

Teleki's enemies were heartened by the British reception of his initiatives. The Hungarian government brought the probable plans of the Germans to cross Hungary to the attention of the British, indicating that the Germans could also execute them by force, should the Hungarians deny them permission. The denial could also serve as a pretext for the Germans to place a Hungarian government in power that served them in every way instead of the present one. If a good compromise could be reached, however, the Hungarian government could control the German transit and the amount of time that they spent in Hungary. All this, however, could only occur if Romania was attacked by the Soviet Union, which was very unlikely. The Hungarian General Staff was having technical discussions with the German General Staff so that drastic steps by Germany against Hungary could be avoided. Therefore, the Hungarian government found it necessary to ask whether Great Britain was willing to promise to show disinterest towards the re-annexation of Transylvania by Hungarian troops in the case of proper Hungarian behavior after the war or at any other convenient time.[13]

To Teleki's great disappointment, the British government reacted very strongly. Having been convinced that the German occupation would happen in any case, and not only in reaction to Soviet steps, at the instruction of his government the British ambassador to Budapest demanded that Teleki promise that Hungary would resist the German transit attempt by force of arms. Should it do so, he the ambassador held out the possibility of help from the Western powers. Teleki refused to accede to this rigid—one could say cynical—position, saying that small states had already been destroyed in the past when they had trusted in British help. Teleki's disappointment was further increased when the British made a condition for maintaining the transportation of certain overseas materials to Hungary.[14]

The contact with London regarding the issue of German transit did not remain a secret from the Germans. They were aware that the Hungarian government was not going to accept the British conditions, but it was a good opportunity for them to create an unsavory atmosphere—through the Hungarian army and the Hungarian extreme right—and to attack the government, which had been unsuccessful in reaching a pact with the British. They mostly targeted the British offer to lift the raw materials blockade against Hungary. Due to the approaching end of the first phase of the armament program and due to the sea blockade, Germany's influence over the increasingly troubled Hungarian industry and economy had grown. The economic advantages of overseas imports supported by Great Britain would have countered this political and economic squeeze, which could have been increased by the Germans at any time.

On April 30 Clodius, who had been attending conferences in Budapest, told Teleki that, for political and economic reasons, Germany expected that Hungary would offer its raw material surpluses from any origin to Germany, since the Hungarian armament program was dependent on its goodwill. Teleki acknowledged this without any opposition and assured Clodius of his cooperation. He most certainly did it with less enthusiasm than Werth, who, according to Clodius, "has always been Germany's trusted friend and expressed his honest admiration at Germany's achievement in Norway. In connection with the British economic war, he declared that every Hungarian soldier knew that Hungarian armaments were only possible with Germany's help and could only be completed with Germany's help. That is why the Minister of Defense and he, Werth, had always been in support of the intensification of German–Hungarian economic relations, and will also be ready in the future to oppose any contrary actions."[15] In summary, Clodius stated with great satisfaction that Hungary was engaged in a politics of solidarity with Germany and Italy and would draw the necessary economic consequences stemming from this relationship.

As is known, Hungarian military leaders did whatever they could to try to support the Hungarian armament program by making sure that the German economic demands were accepted. Werth and Bartha went so far as to make irresponsible economic promises behind the back of the government to underline their requests in connection with the needed armaments. Werth also brought up the issue of war material supply during Kinzel's visit and tried to underline this by mentioning the preparation of the *Honvédség* for probable cooperation with the German army. In general, Werth attributed the fact that the German war supply deliveries kept faltering, and that the Germans turned a deaf ear to requests for tanks, airplanes, and so on, to the Hungarian government's turncoat policy. He told Teleki and other politicians that if Hungary charted a political course that made its loyalty as an ally evident, then Germany would cease to support the Romanian army with weapons.[16] Repeated references by German official circles to the importance of the Romanian oilfields and army did not convince Werth, a true believer in allied relations, that Romania could be a more valuable ally than Hungary for Germany. Yet the increasing quantity of oil flowing through Hungary to Germany did not leave any doubt about it. As the 2nd Section of the General Staff reported, just between April 20 and June 25, 1945, 4,418 wagons of oil and oil derivatives were delivered via Hungarian railways to their destinations in Germany. Furthermore, this quantity was complemented by the shipments on the Danube.[17]

Since no official step from the German government took place in connection with the transit transportation issue, Teleki found it necessary to clarify it with the Germans. On April 17 he wrote a letter to Hitler and asked whether, with regard to the events in the Balkans, the government of the German Reich found it necessary to convene a conference including Italy "so that all the three states will be prepared for every possibility, so that no surprise would occur, and they would not have to face completed facts."[18] Hitler's reaction is known from a note in Halder's diary from April 24, the day that he reported to Hitler about the military preparations for Romania. Hitler thanked him for the careful plan and, while looking through the Hungarian references, revealed his opinion about Hungary's role. He felt that the tripartite discussions should not take place, because they might give rise to different rumors. He had already informed the Duce, who was also against the discussions. He found it worrisome that Hungary wanted to use force against Romania, which would be contrary to Germany's interest. And since the Hungarians were not able to execute an independent military action, they would be defeated. In its present state the Hungarian army could fight for three days at the most. And following the unavoidable defeat, the Hungarian government's first reaction would be to turn to Germany for help. It was in Great Britain's interest to set the Ploieşti oil sources on fire in order to bar Germany from its oil source. Whoever set them on fire—it might be the Hungarians—was all the same to him. So they should be secured by all means, including political or military, so that the oil shipments would be undisturbed at least until the following spring. Hitler had already called Mussolini's attention to the ungrateful Hungarians, who had not sacrificed anything thus far, who were also unable to fight by themselves because of Yugoslavia, and who could cause trouble with their quibbling in the Balkans, which would not be in Italy's interest either. The Hungarians' action might lead to the Soviet Union's appearance in the Balkans as well.

Hitler's distrust towards the Hungarians also included the Hungarian troops' participation in the occupation of Romania. For the time being, he did not think that it was practical to hold extensive General Staff discussions with the Hungarians, and only recommended conferences about the railway transportation across their territory.[19]

Following Kinzel's visit Werth waited impatiently for the continuation of discussions between the two General Staffs on a higher level. He was afraid that the German leadership, more and more distrustful of Teleki, would oppose Hungary's participating militarily in the occupation of Romania. He put out feelers to find out the Germans' intentions. On April 26 Colonel Ujszászy had discussions with Halder. Although the details are not known, according to Hitler's instructions Halder must have been close-mouthed and avoided taking a definite position on issues of greatest interest for Werth.[20] Fearing that he would suddenly be placed in a position difficult to handle, Werth continued his efforts.

On May 7 Colonel Sándor Homlok, the military attaché to Berlin, showed up at Halder's door and asked for information about the expected cooperation against Romania. At that point in time—on the eve of launching the western campaign—Halder proved to be more informative. The impending military operations made the issue of securing the Romanian oil topical. The uncertainty about Romania's behavior and the British appearance in the Balkans forced the German General Staff to make urgent preparations for the occupation of parts of the Balkans, and so a clarification of the Hungarian role also became important, because the German troops would be tied down in the west. First of all, Halder stated that the tripartite conferences raised by Teleki would not take place. It was in Germany's and Italy's common interest that there be peace in the Balkans. However, certain preparations might be necessary to ensure peace, but they were of a theoretical character for the moment. Yet the following related issues would come up, in which

Hungary should secure the deployment of German troops, should secure the use of railways, roads, airports and communication devices if they became important for the German army, should provide troops ready to advance to the Romanian territories from the north while the Germans advanced from the south, with the zone border being the Bihar Mountain region, should use its own equipment, as would Germany, and therefore should not count on the support of German artillery or air force. Halder also said that Bulgaria might participate in the operation. He did not want to share further details because, if action became imminent, there would be need for thorough discussions between the two General Staffs. The cooperation was to be handled discreetly and no written agreement would be drawn up.[21] Halder also asked Homlok to share the details with Werth only.[22]

The General Staff of the *Wehrmacht* apparently did not pay attention to Hitler's suggestion of caution, and counted on the Hungarian troops' participation. It was assumed that the western campaign would tie down the majority of German forces and the remaining forces would not be sufficient for a quick and smooth execution of the occupation plan, especially in the case of Romanian resistance.

Finally, Werth received a message (Homlok's) that measured up to his expectations. He was looking forward to receiving concrete instructions and was ready to comply with Halder's wishes and to carry out the necessary instructions even if it required not informing the government or not requesting its consent. The German General Staff soon contacted him. In the middle of May, at their request, the organizer of Hungarian military transportation, General Staff Major Kálmán Kéri, traveled to the German Headquarters following the start of the western campaign. There Kéri had discussions with General Thomas about the German military needs and contingency plans for the transit of German troops across Hungary. After Kéri's return to Hungary, preparations were immediately begun. According to the German occupation plans, about three army corps had to be transported to the area of Békéscsaba and Gyula. Since the railway stations of the area could not receive the troops and were unsuitable for quick unloading, Hungary began the construction of unloading ramps on open railways suitable for armored and mechanized units. The transport of German troops across Hungary had to be organized so that it would not disturb the transportation of mobilized Hungarian troops deployed to northern Hungary.[23]

The connection between Werth and the German General Staff did not remain a secret from Teleki. This more open opposition from Werth further deepened the differences with the Prime Minister, who hoped that transporting the Germans could be avoided, or at least that its foreign political impact could be reduced. Although he took more and more open steps that carried the danger of an open breakup with the Prime Minister, Werth nonetheless considered himself to be supported by the army, a major part of the nation's political and public life, and even by the consent of the Regent. He was also aware that his adversary could not openly act against him, since that would lead to an open confrontation with the Germans. Werth visualized the not-so-distant future, when he, at the head of his troops, would enter Transylvania as liberator, which would be his ultimate justification against Teleki and his followers.

In the meantime he did whatever he could to convince Teleki about the necessity of cooperation with Germany. Another rejection might have serious consequences, would endanger the re-annexation of lost territories, and might end up in a confrontation with the Germans.

Solymossy assured Ujszászy that he was inclined to be pro-German and, therefore, he was not biased when he described the German leadership's and public's attitude towards Hungary as distrustful. Whoever assumed altruism in the policy of Hitler's Reich—preoccupied exclusively with its own aspirations for power—would be an idealist. The Third Reich frowned upon Hungary because it did not take a radical stand against the Jews or liberal tendencies, did not utilize its economic resources rationally and purposefully with regard to a higher national economy, allowed personal interests to dominate issues, allowed Anglophile tendencies to prevail in the divided Hungarian public view and in administrative and economic issues, which made Hungary unreliable from a German point of view, and did not have the type of industrial development that would not endanger German imports, along with the needed quantities of the agricultural exports. Therefore, non-official and party circles and the majority of the German army "cannot be considered to be pro-Hungarian. Moreover, a certain contempt and envy mixed with hatred can be experienced from most of them."[24] The only friends that Hungary had left were the old German soldiers who had become acquainted with the virtues of the Hungarian soldier in World War I, the Germans who had got to know Hungarians during service or through private interactions, or Austrians who still dreamed about the restoration of the Austro-Hungarian Monarchy. The German goal was to make Hungary part of its *Lebensraum* and, for this reason, to solve the Jewish question in the most radical way, to crush the Hungarian intellectuals, to do away with the Hungarian industry, and to create a peasants' state under German control. Therefore, it is not surprising that in both Germany and Slovakia, German soldiers and bureaucrats were gloating over the likely occupation of Hungary.

The German threat led Solymossy to the following conclusion, which was also voiced by Werth:

> By the power of its geographical situation and its political institutions, Germany can exert a decisive influence on Hungary's fate as long as its capacity is unbroken. The content of this "capacity" cannot be

determined ahead of time. Solymossy then defined the road to be taken by the Hungarians as the following: official German intentions towards Hungary should be clarified; Hungarian–German points of friction should be eliminated both in domestic and foreign political issues unless they endanger Hungarian interests; good official and social relations should be established; and among official relations, those between the two military leaderships can be considered the most enduring bridge.[25]

The intensification of the Teleki–Werth controversy accompanied the tense days that preceded the further escalation of the war. Teleki and his circle expected their power base to be solidified by any interruption in Germany's military successes, while the right-wing parties and groups and the army expected that the certain German victory would justify their political efforts and give them a bigger chunk of political power. After the launching of the western campaign both Teleki and Werth watched the developments with optimism. Teleki did not share Werth's joy over German military successes but was reassured to see that the Romanians' hope of avoiding a confrontation with the Germans would make Romania's occupation unnecessary. Therefore, Hungarian participation would not occur. He seemed to be confirmed in these views by Hitler's responding letter, which arrived on May 14. In it the Führer rejected Teleki's earlier proposal for a tripartite conference, and emphasized the importance of peace in the Balkans and the Danube region, which would be of the utmost interest both for Italy and for Hungary. A conference would disturb this. He said that the news about Germany's intention to move militarily into the Balkans was propaganda: "By spreading false news, the propagandists want German troops to be tied down in the Balkans."[26]

Teleki responded to Hitler on May 20, assuring him of his agreement with regard to the probable effect of a tripartite conference. Therefore, taking its allies' interest into consideration, Hungary was willing to postpone the realization of its territorial demands until a more convenient date. Teleki also said that the government wanted to avoid anything that would serve as an opportunity for disturbing the peace of the Danube and the Balkan regions. To this end, it would sacrifice its own interests, because, according to information gained from the military command, it would soon be the appropriate time to assert the Hungarian demands in the east. He was going to stand by this position despite the fact that "every month or, one could say, every day lost will increase the defensive and attack capacity of our possible enemy and it will increase the strength and extent of its fortification system."[27] So far the proof of Hungarian moderation was its modest military arrangements, which were justified because "we cannot leave our country defenseless and hardly prepared for possibilities amidst countries that keep increasing their military strength, constructing fortifications, and further developing existing ones."[28] Teleki also mentioned the fact that preceding the border guard units, only the II. and the VIII. Army Corps—which had needed exercise—and the Mechanized Army Corps had been brought up to full strength. Then, alluding to military preparations made at German request, he continued: "Our General Staff deals only with preventive maintenance such as, for example, the reinforcement of bridges, an activity that neither attracts attention nor causes international havoc. This preventive caretaking, however, serves the interests of the Axis Powers too, not ours only. Only if the situation changed in this half of Europe would we be forced to embrace further regulations, but even then only while we are paying attention to the interests of larger friendly countries."[29]

Teleki, always true to himself in his anti-Soviet sentiments, did not fail to direct Hitler's attention to the Soviet troop concentrations at the Romanian and Hungarian border as a source of danger for Hungary—and to express his resentment.[30] However, his statements were strongly exaggerated and were not actually correct. As he himself could check from the May 15 situation assessment of the 2nd Section of the General Staff, there were no Soviet troops visible along the Hungarian border, as opposed to the substantial concentration of Soviet troops along the Romanian border. The report did speak about five divisions stationed nearby that could be deployed to the Hungarian border within 5–6 days. This was the same situation, as the report emphasized, as the one that applied to the Romanian border as well.[31]

The news about the launch of the western campaign also triggered the mobilization of the Hungarian army. Teleki told Hitler that, preceding the arrangements made for the sake of transporting the Germans across the country, the Hungarian military had kept the II. and the VIII. Army Corps and the units of the Mechanized Army Corps in a near-continuously mobilized status, starting May 13. This partial mobilization was induced by the war atmosphere created by the German attack and ensuing Slovakian, Romanian and Yugoslavian military measures, while obviously the need for careful preparations for a common occupation of Romania—wished for by the Hungarian military command—also could not be ignored.

To no little surprise on the part of the Hungarian military command, the first reports to come in concerned the mobilization of the Slovakian army. The Hungarian side responded with only defensive measures, because the Hungarian General Staff assumed that the whole affair was meant to relieve German occupational forces withdrawn from Poland and to take control of Romania.[32] At any rate, the staff was disturbed by the idea that they might have to share the occupation of Romania with the Slovaks. Since the Hungarian military had supported the proposal and had prepared for the actual transporting of German troops across the country, it could not bring itself to face the assumption that the Slovakian mobilization might be an anti-Hungarian security measure brought about by the uncertainty of Hungary on the transit question. Once again they did not recognize Germany's political method—a tradition by then—whose essence was, in a loaded political situation, that the Germans tried to distance its allies from unwanted political and military measures by threatening them with each other. In this present situation a harried, independent Hungarian military action against Romania was to be avoided, because mistrustful German political and military leaderships alike were concerned that during the preparation for an expected joint occupation the fired-up Hungarian leadership would get carried away. Into this situation the German propaganda machine swung into action. Rumors swept through Budapest that the mobilized Hungarian troops were preparing for occupation of the area in Upper Hungary (Felvidék) that was still in Slovak hands.[33] Over in Slovakia, there were rumors floating around about the re-annexation of lost territories using German help.[34]

After the resignation of Prime Minister Tatarescu the newly formed Romanian government apparently did not want to irritate Germany and the Hungarians, the latter always ready to jump, with large army movements. Consequently, Hungarian intelligence reported only low-scale drafts, while larger activities, such as the withdrawal of the 18th Romanian Division from Transylvania, were detected only towards Bessarabia. Therefore, the Hungarian General Staff came to the conclusion from this and from the troop movements along the Romanian border that the Bessarabian question was soon to be high on the agenda.[35]

A major series of drafting into the military was reported from Yugoslavia, starting in mid-May and continuing afterwards. The Yugoslavian military actions ran along the Italian, German and Hungarian borders all at the same time. After May 20 the strength of mobilized Yugoslavian units reached 600,000 troops.[36]

From May 20 onwards the Romanian troops' movements also picked up. For a new cohort of replacement troops a further 250,000 Romanian reservists were drafted. The strength of the Romanian army now reached 1.5 million.[37]

Although a significant part of the newly drafted forces was directed to Bessarabia and Bukovina, the Transylvanian Hungarian border was reinforced by replacements. Furthermore, the border fortifications were occupied.[38] The Romanian steps along the Hungarian border were in response to the preparations regarding German transit of troops, starting around May 15. A continuous reinforcement of the Arad–Szalonta region, along with the appearance of armored vehicles and the air force in the area, was due to the same reason. The Romanian military command made preparations to fend off parachute troops as well.[39]

Assessing the new situation, the Hungarian generals established that the Romanian forces concentrated in northern Transylvania had, without exception, been brought up to their full strength. Romania accelerated its defensive measures in ways very similar to a general mobilization. According to the staff, and contrary to the news that the Romanian and Yugoslavian mobilizations were targeted at the creation of an "eastern front" against Germany, the preparations of the two countries were really mostly targeted at Russia—completely apart from each other—and for the time being were defensive in character.[40]

The Hungarian military attaché to Belgrade informed Ujszászy that, in the case of a Hungarian–Romanian conflict, Yugoslavia would remain neutral. Furthermore, Yugoslavian officers in the General Staff also said that the Romanians should meet the justified Hungarian demands.[41]

Therefore, under the impact of another wave of Romanian mobilization, on May 27 the Hungarian General Staff passed an order to increase the number of people serving in the hitherto unmobilized III. and IV. Army Corps.[42] However, these troops did not leave their peacetime garrisons, and only the units of the Mechanized Army Corps were placed in northern and eastern Hungary.[43] The 1st Mechanized Brigade was stationed north of Vác, the 2nd Mechanized Brigade was stationed north of the River Tisza, and the troops of the 1st Mounted Brigade remained at their garrisons in the Trans-Tisza area.[44] Deployments both to the north and the east were considered for these units. The deployment itself was inconvenient for the troops, because the majority had just received their tank and motorized vehicle supplies directly from the factories, and taking over these tanks and vehicles and completing the necessary quick, intense training of their operation were extremely complicated tasks to do in the field. They produced wear and tear on the supplies, which substantially decreased their future potential striking power.[45]

As events evolved, the hopes of the General Staff were also slowly destroyed. There were fewer and fewer reasons that they could envision why Germany would occupy Romania in such a manner that would lead to a joint action. Affected by the big German victories of June, the Romanian government struck an increasingly conciliatory tone with Germany. Rumors also began to circulate about the demobilization of the Slovakian troops.

The combined quick completion of the western campaign in June and the spectacular German maneuvers made a great impression on the Hungarian General Staff, although the consequent changes in the Romanian policy stirred some anxiety. Events following the resignation of the Tatarescu government, along with King Carol's desire to create a government of national unity on a new foundation, indicated that Romania was quickly moving towards rapprochement with Germany. Werth had to resign himself to the fact that the recent Romanian moves immobilized the military for the time being and forced the postponement of an armed showdown between the two countries. Executing a revisionist attack independent of Germany was unimaginable for him. Yet he kept a curious eye on the development of the Romanian–Soviet relations.

The suspense caused by the tense Romanian–Soviet relations and the unchanged strength of the Romanian army prevented the Hungarian military command from decreasing the number of mobilized troops. Yet the command still planned to grant 10–14 days of leave to the majority of mobilized units drafted from agricultural areas for the upcoming harvest season. According to the plan of June 17, 10% of the troops in the Trans-Tisza area and 25% of the other units would be allowed to go on leave at the same time during the harvest season.[46] However, four days later another arrangement was made, whereby 33% of the Border Guard units and uniformly 50% of all the other units would go on harvest leave.[47] Nevertheless, the turn of events very soon required the cancellation of these arrangements.

Notes

1. Országos Levéltár (National Archive, OL). K 64-85-23-215/1940. Rp.
2. OL. K 64-88-41-21/1940. Rp.
3. *Ibid.*
4. *Ibid.*
5. Hugh Gibson, ed., *Ciano naplója: 1939–1943: Gróf Galeazzo Ciano olasz külügyminiszter, 1939–1943 teljes, rövidítés nélküli naplói* (Ciano's Diary: 1939–1943: The Full Diary without Shortening of Count Galeazzo Ciano, Italian Foreign Minister, 1939–1943) (Budapest, 1946), p. 232.
6. *Ibid.*, p. 233.
7. Franz Halder, *Kriegstagebuch. Tägliche Aufzeichnungen des Chefs des Generalstabes des Heeres 1939–1942/Generaloberst Halder* (Stuttgart, 1962–1964), vol. I: p. 249.
8. *Ibid.*, p. 256; György Ránki, Ervin Pamlényi, Loránt Tilkovszky and Gyula Juhász, eds., *A Wilhelmstrasse és Magyarország: Német diplomáciai iratok Magyarországról, 1933–1944* (The Wilhelmstrasse and Hungary: German Diplomatic Documents about Hungary, 1933–1944) (Budapest, 1968), p. 840.
9. Halder, *Kriegstagebuch...*, vol. I: p. 256.
10. *Ibid.*, vol. I: p. 251.
11. Ferenc Ábrahám and Endre Kussinszky, eds., *Az Imrédy-per. A vád, a vallomások és az ítélet* (The Imrédy Trial. Charge, Statements and the Judgement) (Budapest, 1945), p. 27.
12. *Ibid.*
13. OL. K 64-88-41-21/1940. Rp.
14. Ránki–Pamlényi–Tilkovszky–Juhász, *A Wilhelmstrasse és Magyarország...*, p. 481. (313)
15. *Ibid.*, pp. 483–484. (315)
16. *Ibid.*, p. 477. (308)
17. Hadtörténelmi Levéltár (Military History Archive, HL). Eln. Vkf.1. 1940/3661.
18. László Zsigmond, ed., *Magyarország és a második világháború* (Hungary and World War II) (Budapest, 1966), p. 236.
19. Halder, *Kriegstagebuch...*, vol. I: pp. 269–270.
20. *Ibid.*, p. 271.

21. *Ibid.*, p. 280.
22. *Ibid.*, p. 308.
23. Kálmán Kéri's personal account to the author.
24. Gyula Juhász, ed., *Diplomáciai iratok Magyarország külpolitikájához 1936–1945* (Diplomatic Writings on Hungary's Foreign Policy, 1936–1945) (Budapest, 1962–1982), vol. IV: p. 783.
25. *Ibid.*
26. Ránki–Pamlényi–Tilkovszky–Juhász, *A Wilhelmstrasse és Magyarország...*, pp. 486–487. (317)
27. *Ibid.*, p. 487. (318)
28. *Ibid.*, p. 489. (318)
29. *Ibid.*
30. *Ibid.*
31. OL. K 64-86-24-391/1940. Rp.
32. HL. Eln. Vkf.1. 1940/3849. 5.sz. tájékoztató (bulletin). The 2nd General Staff Headquarters published its daily situation reports 1–126 under the number above between May 11 and September 16, 1940.
33. Dezső Saly, *Szigorúan bizalmas* (Strictly Confidential) (Budapest, 1945), p. 188.
34. OL. K 149-1940-2-5007/A XXII-513/940/19.
35. HL. Eln. Vkf.1. 1940/3849. 6–8. sz. tájékoztató.
36. *Ibid.*, 12. sz. tájékoztató.
37. *Ibid.*
38. *Ibid.*, 10–11. sz. tájékoztató.
39. *Ibid.*, 22, 24, 29. sz. tájékoztató.
40. *Ibid.*, 20. sz. tájékoztató.
41. Domokos Szent-Iványi, *Emlékirat* (Memoirs), Ráday Levéltár (Ráday Archive), Szent-Iványi hagyaték C/80, p. 98.
42. HL. IV.hdt.1.b. 1940/15534; János Csima, *Adalékok a Horthy-hadsereg szervezetének és háborús tevékenységének tanulmányozásához (1938–1945)* (Additions to Studying the Organizational Structure and the Military Activities of the Horthy Army: 1938–1945) (Budapest, 1961), p. 35.
43. HL. Eln. Vkf.1. 1940/3823.
44. HL. Eln. Vkf.1. 1940/3988.
45. *Hadtörténelmi Közlemények* (1970) 4: pp. 598–601.
46. HL. Eln.Vkf.1. 1940/3823.
47. HL. Eln.Vkf.1. 1940/4015.

MOBILIZATION AND DEPLOYMENT AGAINST ROMANIA: THE SECOND VIENNA AWARD

Both the Hungarian government and the Hungarian military command followed the development of the Romanian–Soviet relationship with increasing concern. The June 21 report of the Hungarian ambassador to Moscow received much attention. In it he called attention to the fact that the Soviet Union planned to enforce its demands for the annexation of Bessarabia, either peacefully or by force, by way of reference to the discussion between Italian Ambassador Rosso and Soviet Commissar of Foreign Affairs Molotov on the previous day. The Soviet government indicated a desire to establish a good relationship with Hungary, and proved to be understanding about Hungarian territorial demands.[1] Therefore, the Hungarians were not surprised that on the evening of June 26 the Soviet Union sent a memorandum to Romania demanding the re-annexation of Bessarabia and Bukovina. The Hungarian reaction was not delayed for long. On June 27 Sztójay handed over a memorandum to Under-secretary Woermann, to be furthered to the German Minister of Foreign Affairs. In this document the Hungarian government pointed out to the Germans that Romania, once under diplomatic pressure, was willing to give territorial concessions to the Soviet Union, although not to Hungary, and the Hungarian government considered this to be discrimination. At the request of the Axis, so far the Hungarian government had tried to maintain peace, and had not exerted any pressure on Romania, nor had it concluded any agreements against Romania. Hungary "wishes and intends to realize its lawful demands through the help of possible agreements with the Axis Powers and in agreement with the two Great Powers."² If Romania initiated discussions with other countries on its own, it ought to include Hungary in these discussions. Woermann accepted the memorandum and relayed German Minister of Foreign Affairs von Ribbentrop's request that Hungary should keep calm. The Hungarian ambassador to Rome also submitted a similar memorandum.

Erdmannsdorff, who had been requested to visit Csáky, also advised calm. In Teleki's presence Csáky called Erdmannsdorff's attention to unforeseeable consequences should Romania decide to give territorial concessions to its northern neighbor while refusing even to discuss Hungary's demands. Csáky referred to his promises to von Ribbentrop and Ciano that Hungary would exercise moderation on the issue and would not attack Romania from the rear even in the case of war. Now, however, a new situation had arisen, because Romania had given territorial concessions towards a neighboring political power while also preparing for war in Transylvania and intensifying its persecution of the Hungarian population. For these reasons Csáky asked whether the Reich still wanted Hungary to wait, whether Hungary could expect the Axis to fulfill its promise on the issue (namely, to support Hungary's demands against Romania), and finally what position it would assume if Hungary were forced into an armed intervention.³ He reassured the German ambassador that thus far no Hungarian military arrangements had been concluded, and that the forces mobilized earlier were now at their peacetime garrisons, except for the VIII. Army Corps. Furthermore, the latter was not deployed directly to the border either. However, it might happen that, considering the possible occupation of Bukovina, the Chief of the General Staff would request these troops to be moved forward.⁴

On June 28 the Hungarian Minister of Foreign Affairs requested that Clodius, who was in Budapest having discussions on economic affairs, visit him. Csáky asked Clodius to relay the message to the relevant German authorities that if Germany supported

Hungarian demands towards Romania, then "after the border revision is completed, the Hungarians will make sure that Germany's economic interests are not harmed, and what is more, that they are furthered. Hungary will make an effort to substantially increase, above the present standard, deliveries of the utmost importance for Germany, even at the expense of instituting limits in our own country."[5] Furthermore, Csáky also held out the prospect of permitting transit across the country towards any southeastern target, under no control on the part of Hungary and carried out by German carriages and personnel.

Csáky also explained to Clodius his concerns about the Soviet advance. He claimed to be trying to seek an agreement through negotiations with the Romanians, which was justified by a need for a common defense of the Carpathians, and stated that he disagreed with the military command's demand for the re-annexation of all of Transylvania.[6] Most certainly, however, he must have exaggerated the intentions of the Hungarian military command.

According to the military's assessment, Romania would fulfill the Soviet demand, since it could not count on help from anyone. In addition, the Soviet measure must have happened only with Germany's knowledge and agreement. If the latter statement was true, it could have been safely assumed that Germany was going to support Hungary's request for discussions relating to its territorial demands, and was also going to support it with demonstrative military measures. The military also believed that preventive military actions might be justified by citing widespread turmoil, the threat of left-wing movements and the protection of the Hungarian population in Romania.[7] However, due to the relative military strengths of the two countries, it was uncertain whether in this case the military command might insist on re-annexing the whole of Transylvania.

These were the considerations that led Werth on June 27 to ask that the Supreme Military Council be convened. During the late evening meeting it was decided to deploy only the border guard units and certain troops of the V. and the VI. Army Corps to the border, contrary to Werth's proposal to deploy all the mobilized units, since no response to the Hungarian position had come from Berlin.[8] The other formerly mobilized units—the II., the III., the IV. and the VIII. Army Corps—were stationed at their peacetime garrisons and received the command to prepare for rail transportation beginning on July 2.[9]

According to the agreement, Soviet troops began Bessarabia's re-annexation on June 28. By the evening all the target posts had been reached without any obstacles. After that, the Hungarian leadership considered a threat towards Hungary the fact that, although the Romanian troops did not show any resistance anywhere and withdrew quietly, on the evening of June 28 King Carol ordered a general mobilization. According to the assessment, it was obvious that "the King has given up on resisting the stronger enemy and, from this point onwards, wants to face any kind of aggressive step from any direction with arms in hand." Furthermore, he must have considered the internal situation as well, which showed the signs of disintegration. New Romanian units now appeared in Transylvania.[10]

The Hungarian Chief of the General Staff found it curious that there was still no official Axis position regarding the Soviet–Romanian events on June 29. But they reasoned that the Axis Powers, and first of all Germany, were preoccupied by the preparations for the offensive against Great Britain. Furthermore, assuming that the Soviet Union might acquire more territorial gains following a possible Romanian collapse might induce the mistrustful Germans to take further steps towards occupying Romania in order to assure for themselves the Romanian oil. Due to the fact that German forces were tied down on the western front, the latter option would coincide with the Hungarian military's desired outcome of a cooperative venture, which this time would be offered with the agreement of the Hungarian government.[11]

Csáky sent for Erdmannsdorff and told him that the Romanian mobilization most certainly targeted Hungary. It might also be assumed that King Carol, with a surprise attack, would attempt to push the Romanian border forward to the line at the River Tisza. Csáky had already instructed the Hungarian ambassador to Bucharest to inquire of the Romanian government what justified the general mobilization, since they had already complied with the Soviet demand in a peaceful manner. Csáky once again repeated his request that the German government should bring home to the Romanian government the fact that they, the Germans, would appreciate it if negotiations were to begin about the Hungarians' demands. Csáky also described the pressure placed on the Hungarian government by leading Hungarian politicians, with Imrédy among them, and by the military on the issue of Transylvania. These circles had already placed an armed solution of the issue in the foreground of events.[12]

A day later, on June 30, Csáky informed the German ambassador about the Romanian response to the Hungarian inquiry, stating that the Romanian mobilization did not target Romania's neighbors. Romania wanted to live in peace with Hungary. Without any further delay the Hungarian government informed Bucharest that the received response was not satisfactory, especially considering that Romania had deployed four more divisions to the Hungarian border within the past few days.[13] Once again he raised with Erdmannsdorff the internal political difficulties in Hungary related to the Transylvanian issue. Csáky also indicated that pro-German circles, the same ones that had criticized the government for its reserved attitude towards solving the Transylvanian question, had now urged the Hungarian government to take steps to acquire Transylvania and to seek German help.

Erdmannsdorff reported back on the discussions that the Minister of Foreign Affairs had told him that Archduke Albrecht, who served as a battalion commander at Pécs, had informed the

Minister about his feelings about the foreign policy of the Hungarian government. The desire to fight for Transylvania was alive in the army. This was the view of many influential personalities and also of the Minister of Defense, who was from Transylvania. It was a generally established view that the Transylvanian issue was a decisive psychological factor both for the Romanian and the Hungarian public. Under such circumstances the government was in a difficult situation in Parliament when it was forced to abstain from taking a direct position on the Transylvanian question.[14]

Speaking about military solutions, the Minister of Foreign Affairs was aware of the difficulties. The number of Hungarian and Romanian forces that could be deployed was relatively equal, although the Hungarian fighting morale was better. Yet in the case of conflict he foresaw strong Romanian resistance. The government, in the meantime, had decided on mobilizing the army corps at Debrecen as well. For the army corps at Szeged, only its units on the Romanian border section were mobilized, while those along the Yugoslavian border were not.

Finally, Csáky also informed Erdmannsdorff that one of the co-workers of the Foreign Affairs Commissariat in Moscow had casually, and expressing a personal opinion, informed the Hungarian ambassador that the Soviet government had no interest in territories in Transylvania and over the Carpathian Mountains.[15]

Csáky's effort to put up a smokescreen for the Germans about Hungarian military steps was unnecessary, since it was obvious from von Ribbentrop's reaction of July 1 that the German Embassy had known about them and reported them to Berlin immediately.[16]

It was not so much the diplomatic but the ongoing Hungarian military steps that urged von Ribbentrop to tell the Hungarian government his opinion concerning developments in the Hungarian–Romanian relationship and to caution them to show patience. He invited Teleki and Csáky for a visit, and asked them to make sure that during the Soviet-Romanian conflict Hungary would keep its calm and not risk a conflict with Romania by aggressively raising its revisionist demands. The Transylvanian question would be discussed during the Munich conferences that were to occur shortly.[17]

One day later—or, rather, in the late hours of July 1—due to its urgent nature Erdmannsdorff delivered a harsher message from von Ribbentrop to Csáky. The major cause of its urgency was the news reaching Berlin that day that, in response to the Romanian mobilization, the Hungarian government had mobilized the I. and the VII. Army Corps, that meant general mobilization in Hungary. The troops had been deployed. Von Ribbentrop's concern was increased by the fact that, in parallel with the news about Hungarian mobilizations, the Romanian government had informed him about incidents along the border and about the fact that the Hungarian government had not found very satisfactory their response to the Hungarian protests against the Romanian mobilization. Von Ribbentrop was afraid that the Hungarian government would launch a military action to take advantage of the Romanians' difficult situation. Even if that did not happen, Hungary's conduct would endanger King Carol's efforts to stabilize the internal and foreign political situations of Romania, which was threatened with a total collapse. King Carol was to solve these problems by giving notice of withdrawal from Western guarantees and by an aggressive rapprochement towards Germany. A Hungarian attack against which the Romanians could barely defend themselves would necessarily lead to more territorial losses, which would in turn lead to an incalculable development in the Romanian situation and would endanger basic German interests in Romania. This should be avoided by all means.

The German Minister of Foreign Affairs was dissatisfied with the conduct of the Hungarian government and resented the

Hungarians' statement to Erdmannsdorff about the mobilization of a few units, while they had mobilized substantial forces. This was happening at a time when the government of the German Reich was not interested in the Balkan question, and so strove to make sure that the Balkans would not become a battle-zone. That was the reason why it welcomed the peaceful agreement between the Soviet Union and Romania. Germany noted that the Hungarian government should know that it was not the intention of Romania to attack Hungary, and therefore the Hungarian mobilization was unacceptable. The German government was sympathetic towards the justified Hungarian revisionist demands, but the Hungarian government should not expect the German army to wage war for them. If the Hungarian government did make an attempt to enforce its demands in an aggressive manner, it would be doing so on its own responsibility, with all the unpredictable developments and consequences that might follow. Furthermore, Germany claimed that Hungary's revisionist hopes could be realized at a more convenient time and without aggression, the type of solution of which "the German government will be in support."[18]

Before the Hungarian government reacted officially, Csáky concentrated all his efforts on reassuring the German ambassador about the "peaceful" nature of the Hungarian military arrangements. Csáky said that the Hungarian government was not planning an attack in order to re-annex Transylvania; the goal of the mobilizations was to force Romania to the negotiating table. However, pressured by public opinion, the government had also taken a military option into consideration. And if events did indeed take a turn towards war, no German military support had been counted on. They were clear about expected losses, but still a people had to make decisions if it wanted to survive. Csáky alluded to a national neurosis relating to the Transylvanian question, denied the news about incidents along the border, and tried to conceal the true proportions of the Hungarian military measures. He claimed that it was all about bringing the troops up to their actual strengths and that it would take as long as twelve days for them to be ready for action.[19] As opposed to what he claimed, the truth was that the actions were meant to bring the troops up to war strengths. Furthermore, transporting them to the Trans-Tisza area, to military operational territory, was to be completed so that they would be ready to launch a campaign against Romania. All this could hardly be kept a secret from Berlin.

On July 2 Erdmannsdorff not only informed the German Ministry of Foreign Affairs about Csáky's statements, but also gave an account of his own experiences and opinion. He said that the general atmosphere was such that if the Germans did not interfere, the weapons might go off by themselves at any time and the occupation of Transylvania might take place. The driving force was "rather in the politicians' hands and not in the hands of the General Staff." Therefore, a decisive stand had to be taken towards the Romanians as well. The Germans should volunteer to make concessions, "considering that the Hungarian government, with the keyed-up expectations of the public in the background, is hardly in a position to disarm without any successes or, at least, without positive and publicly usable promises."[20]

In the wake of the reports of the German ambassador to Budapest, von Ribbentrop commissioned Weizsäcker immediately to send for Sztójay, and then expressed shock at Csáky's intervention, which showed that he had probably not understood the seriousness of the message relayed by Erdmannsdorff and so continued to maintain the possibility of a Hungarian armed action. Therefore, Weizsäcker reiterated to Sztójay that if Hungary initiated any kind of armed conflict in the Balkans, it would remain by itself.[21]

On July 2 the Supreme Military Council was convened to discuss Erdmannsdorff's admonitory diplomatic maneuver and the response to be sent to it.[22] Csáky, who had become very cautious after von Ribbentrop's warning, thought that disturbances to the Hungarian–German relationship should be avoided. A war against Romania could be won, but it was more important not to interfere with Germany's plans and not to destroy their goodwill. Therefore, von Ribbentrop should be reassured about the intentions of the Hungarian government. It was necessary to stress to the Germans that at the forefront of the Hungarian plans was the goal of re-establishing connections with the Romanian government and launching discussions with it. However, it was the uniform view of everyone present that stopping the military arrangements was neither necessary nor possible. Moreover, it would be very reassuring if, after announcing its readiness to negotiate, Romania would immediately evacuate a few cities along the border, to be given over to Hungary as proof of their good intentions.[23]

In the late hours of the evening, following the session of the Supreme Military Council, Csáky handed over his government's official response to von Ribbentrop's message. As it had voiced it several times, the government said that it would like to be in agreement with the Axis in settling its relationship with Romania. This is the reason why Csáky was pleased that the German Minister of Foreign Affairs had said that the territorial revision could be done at a more convenient time and without applying the armed forces. If the German Minister of Foreign Affairs had said it, then of course the German government would endorse it. The Hungarian government, however, wanted to clarify whether the Hungarian demands, including the Székely land [Székelyföld] and the triangle bordered by Marosvásárhely, Bánffyhunyad, the Carpathian Mountains and Nagybánya, would fit within the framework of support of which the Reich held out the prospect. Finally, Csáky spelled out the conditions, as specified in December 1939, that could set off the immediate reaction of the Hungarian government: 1) minority persecution,

2) the outbreak of a revolution in Transylvania, 3) a Russian advance to the Carpathian Mountains, and 4) the forced Romanianization of Transylvania by Romanian refugees moving from Bessarabia and Bukovina.[24] The government's response did not deal with the military actions mentioned by von Ribbentrop, indicating that it did not wish to end them, in view of the threatening Romanian troop movements and in view of what might happen as described above.

Von Ribbentrop's response was relayed by Weizsäcker to Sztójay in Berlin on the afternoon of July 4 and by Erdmannsdorff to Csáky in Budapest during the evening hours. He pointed out that the Hungarian government's position was still vague. Therefore, he indicated that he could no longer help, but emphatically called the Hungarian government's attention to the foreseeable difficulties and complications (perhaps catastrophic consequences under certain circumstances) that the Hungarians might face if they used arms against Romania. Germany would leave them by themselves. Both the German and the Italian government wanted peace in the Balkans. They—the Germans—would examine the issue of territorial revision and would inform the Hungarian government about the result. Von Ribbentrop expected the Hungarian government to follow his advice and to seek a peaceful solution.[25]

Once again the Germans had managed to use the intimidation of the Soviet threat as a successful political tool against the Hungarian government. Sztójay emphasized the portion of von Ribbentrop's message that held out tragic prospects if Hungary, in spite of his advice, got into an armed conflict with Romania, which might provoke the Soviet Union's intervention. In this case Germany could not help. Sztójay also noted that the loss of stability of the western border of Hungary was among the threatened "consequences."[26]

When Csáky requested the source of the last idea, which had never come up thus far during Hungarian–German interactions, Sztójay said that it was his own conclusion. The way that he figured it, if an aggressive revisionist attack were to be initiated without the Führer's preceding endorsement, he would not only abandon the Hungarians but "ruthlessly demand that the 'ethnic border' of Hungary be established."[27]

The coordinated diplomatic offensive against the Hungarian government included military as well as diplomatic channels. Sztójay also called Csáky's attention to Colonel Homlok's assessment of the military situation, which was sent to Werth on July 4. Sztójay said that he agreed with it in general terms, and offered its proposals for consideration.

Homlok reinforced von Ribbentrop's message in his confidential report. Peace in Eastern Europe and in the Balkans was in Germany's interest, and whoever disturbed it could not count on Germany's help. Considering this and his discussion with the Chief of the German General Staff, at the request of Werth, on June 30, Homlok laid down Hungary's military and political situation. First of all he argued that "presently Hungary cannot pursue an independent foreign policy." Considering the countries, one by one, that might influence the development of Hungarian policy, he argued that Germany was the one country to whose goals Hungary had to exclusively adjust and accommodate itself in order "to realize its own foreign political goals, which have become dependent upon Germany." This was true even if nothing could be expected from Germany until it had finished with Great Britain. Hungary's revisionist policy could get no actual help from Italy; at most, it could get promises for help at some future point in time. Homlok considered cooperation with the Soviet Union out of the question. Among the neighboring countries, Romania and Yugoslavia had ceased to pursue an independent policy and were trying to adjust to the new situation, and Slovakia did not count.[28]

A showdown with Great Britain was Germany's main goal; therefore, Germany was trying to avoid anything that might be a hindrance in this process. Homlok argued that war between the Soviet Union and Germany might draw out for years even after Germany took possession of Great Britain. In that case, one had to count on the United States entering the war, and thus the probability that "the German war successes so far and the outcome of the war for the Germans would be in serious danger."[29]

Following that, Colonel Homlok advised that von Ribbentrop's requests be taken to heart, because "they do not leave any doubt that if Hungary harms the peace in Eastern Europe or the Balkans—so important for the German Reich—in order to reach its revisionist goals, Hungary will have sinned from the German perspective, because it will in this way have acted against the eminent interests of the German Reich."[30] He also cautioned against taking any military steps if the Soviet Union appeared in the Carpathian region, and against being confrontational with the Soviets in general, because Hungary could not count on the help of Germany or Italy, which now had a good relationship with the Soviet Union.

Immediately, in the evening of July 5, Csáky responded to Sztójay's telegram of the same afternoon. He wrote to say that the Hungarian government appreciated the message of the German government and wanted to reiterate the fact that it had already communicated three times that, except for certain events, Hungary wanted to deal with Romania in agreement with the German government. Csáky noted that the warnings about Soviet dangers coming from German Foreign Affairs' sources were in sharp contrast with what the Soviet government had stated with regard to the Hungarian–Romanian relationship, and what was once again reinforced by Molotov in Kristóffy's presence: "No one is thinking about a Hungarian–Russian war. Molotov made this statement yesterday to Kristóffy that the Soviets had no demands for Hungary and that they were striving to build a good relationship. The Soviet Union considers that the Hungarian territorial demands are well founded and will support them at a possible peace conference. The Soviet Union will not interfere in a Hungarian–Romanian conflict."[31]

Immediately after delivering von Ribbentrop's message, on July 4 Erdmannsdorff reported to the German Ministry of Foreign Affairs that in his view the Hungarian government finally seemed to understand the seriousness of the warnings. Although the situation continued to be tense due to the mobilizations, they had managed to avoid a crisis.[32]

Werth was not caught by surprise by the reaction of the German government, since it again justified his oft-stated views about the necessity of cooperation of Hungary with Germany's foreign policy. He used every possible opportunity to make his opinion, and that of the army and the officer corps, known to various German political and military circles, in the hope of gaining the goodwill of the German government for the Hungarian army. Once again he wanted to inform the Germans that he and other leaders of the army would do whatever they could to influence the Hungarian government to pursue the right foreign policy. Werth thought that it was high time that he, instead of the helpless government that misread the situation, tell the Germans in a memorandum what he foresaw as the place and role of Hungary in the war alongside the Axis Powers, as well as in the new European order after the successfully fought war. He had decided that if the government would not do it, he would have to assure the Germans that there were many in Hungary who had recognized that it was only together with the Germans that the nation could ensure its future and decisive role in the Danube Basin, also a high priority for the Germans.

On July 6 the Chief of the General Staff handed over to the Minister of Foreign Affairs a lengthy memorandum about

Hungary's revisionist demands and their military justification.[33] It is apparent that the text must have been prepared for the German General Staff with the ulterior motive that it would bring the contents to the attention of the German foreign political leadership.

The Chief of the General Staff's message was based on the presumption of an exclusive German victory and Germany's ensuing decisive role in southeastern Europe, including the Danube Basin, which, of course, would also structure Hungary's future place and role. A strong central power possessing the whole Carpathian Basin, which would include a rebirth of historical Hungary, would be in the foreign political and strategic interest of the Axis.

Werth based his statements most of all on information leaked by sources within the German General Staff. According to this information, after a German victory against Great Britain an intensification of the German–Soviet disagreement could be expected, with the Balkans as a point of impact. When this took place, it was expected that unreliable and shaky Romania would not resist the Soviet designs on the Balkans. Only Hungary, located at the line of the Carpathian Mountains, would be able to influence these efforts and to ensure the balance of power in the region. The area protected by the Carpathian Range would always be a suitable concentration area for the German army in the case of military action against the Soviet Union, and in that it could count on the support of the Hungarian army. But, as Werth emphasized, it should be considered that Germany would have to place the security of the region and the representation of its southeastern European interests in either Hungary's or Romania's hands. The military virtues of the Hungarian soldier, his loyalty and self-sacrificial bond with the allies—qualities with which the German army had had the chance to become acquainted in World War I—could be an asset to Germany's confidence placed in the Hungarians.

According to Werth, separating and restraining the southern and northern Slavic peoples were tasks to be undertaken only by Hungarians. In order to possess the Carpathian Basin, the re-annexation of Transylvania and Slovakia was essential.

In order to justify the importance of the Hungarian role, Werth ventured to analyze the post-war situation of the Western democracies. His description diverged from the Reich's view and could hardly have met with a favorable reception. Werth envisioned a renewed role for the conquered Western states, which could enhance the importance of Hungary's role. After the peace agreement, the Western states would regain their strength and would be ready for revenge. Just as after World War I, they would renew the policy of encirclement with the cooperation of Romania, Yugoslavia, Greece and Turkey in southeastern Europe, countries which would have left the Western alliance due to German pressure. The Balkans once again would become the site of a fire. Hungary's role would be significant here as well. Germany's route to the Balkans led across Hungary, and the circumstances did matter. Werth brought up the situation of the springtime, concerning the issue of the transit of German troops across Hungary, and noting how the Hungarian military leaders supported Germany. Securing the Romanian oil remained a vital issue for Germany. If Hungary possessed the Southern Carpathian Range, the distance to the oilfields would be decreased to 50–100 kilometers, the oil region could be reached within a few hours, and the oil route would be safer.

At the end of the lengthy memorandum, which also laid out the details of future German–Hungarian cooperation, Werth designated himself as the spokesman of the nation. And he, once again, placed Hungary, always and under any circumstances reliable and loyal, in the Axis Powers' goodwill, while describing Hungary as a country that would like to assume the exclusive position of the advance guard of the Axis and to assume a position as a military ally and defender of its eastern interests. Hungary was ready to make sacrifices in the interest of a new European order even at the expense of making certain changes in its internal political and economic life, because Hungary was aware that this was the medium where it would be able to fulfill its role and where it could realize its goal of a total territorial revision.

Teleki informed Mussolini about the strained relationship with the Reich on the issue of Romania, and asked for his support. Colonel László Szabó, the military attaché to Rome, asked for an audience with Mussolini on July 4 to deliver Teleki's letter. Mussolini and Ciano received Szabó while the Hungarian ambassador to Rome was not present. The explanation for Szabó's assignment for this task and for leaving the Hungarian ambassador out was the urgency of the issue, along with the fact that Szabó had been in Hungary and was about to go back to Rome, which meant that Teleki could give him personal instructions. Besides, Szabó's good connections within the highest Italian circles and those of the Duce were well known. It is also important to mention that the content of Teleki's letter, and what Szabó was supposed to add, did not contain details that needed to be kept hidden from the Hungarian military leadership.

Mussolini immediately read the letter and seemed to show understanding towards the Hungarians, "who cannot be condemned to idleness when they can regain Transylvania from Romania in its present state." He also expressed his readiness to inform Yugoslavia that if they interfered in the conflict, they would have to face Italy. Mussolini was also willing to support his Hungarian ally with war material.[34]

Then, following Teleki's instructions, Szabó proceeded to add further details. He pointed out that the Hungarian public had been looking forward to the events with great expectations and had to be reassured. To reassure them, Hungary needed to obtain permission for re-annexing Transylvania either by force of arms or at least a part of it through negotiations to be launched shortly. If the interests of the Axis did not make it possible for Hungary to do so at the moment, then guarantees should be issued later when the situation was more suitable, negotiations would commence and, if they should fail, Hungary would be supported with war materials. The Hungarian government was well aware that peace would be needed in southeastern Europe. However, it was increasingly difficult to make the Hungarian public understand that it was their friends who forbade them from interference and from re-annexing Transylvania. If a conflict was to be avoided, Romania also had to be restrained; Hungary could not be prohibited to act.[35]

Then Mussolini became more cautious and refrained from taking a position. As he said, the question had to be discussed together with the Germans, which was going to be possible in Berlin, where Ciano and the Hungarian statesmen were also present. In any case, Hungary had the right to Transylvania. Sooner or later it would have to receive its share.

Already on July 5 Szabó reported on his mission through the service route: through the Chief of the General Staff. He also added his own impressions to the report. In his view the Duce fully supported the Hungarian position. However, Szabó believed that Ciano "had been heavily worked on by the Romanians" and would do whatever he could so that "we may comply with the command."[36]

Although trying to scare off the Hungarian government from taking military steps against Romania, the German Minister of Foreign Affairs did not bring up the issue of demobilizing the recently mobilized troops. The reason for this obvious lacuna was that von Ribbentrop wanted to exclude the possibility of a Hungarian attack, but still wanted to continue to blackmail Romania with the threatening Hungarian presence along the border in order to hasten the Romanian government's German orientation. It was also clear to him that demands to disarm these troops would embarrass precisely the Hungarian officer corps and politicians who were pro-German.

In the meantime the Hungarian military preparations went on according to the government's plans. The deployment and concentration of troops in the Trans-Tisza area was completed by July 10, and the army commands had been settled on the military operational areas by July 1. The H.Q. of the 1st Hungarian Army under General of the Infantry Vilmos Nagybaczoni Nagy settled at Sóstó near Nyíregyháza; the H.Q. of the 2nd Hungarian Army under General of the Infantry Gusztáv Jány settled at Törökszentmiklós; the H.Q. of the 3rd Hungarian Army under General of the Cavalry Elemér Gorondy-Novák settled in Beregszász. At the new headquarters they immediately began to prepare their troops so that they would be ready for military operations at any time.

Ideological preparation of the troops played an important part in the activities. The paper *Magyar Katonaújság* [Hungarian Military Newspaper] pushed for fighting with articles for Transylvania. These articles described the increasing Romanian oppression that the Hungarian population had to endure on a daily basis, and stated that the time had come to end it all. On July 6 a special issue on Transylvania was published. The main editorial was directed at the troops deployed on the border. It was time to begin Transylvania's liberation, it said: "The integrity of Greater Romania has ceased to exist. Confusion has set in among the Romanian forces, due to the loss of Bessarabia and Bukovina, which creates an ideal situation for intervention... From here it seems that the forest might be burning [and we have to hasten to help] the hard-pressed Hungarian millions... We are alert. We are watching and are ready to do anything to free our Székely brothers from the Romanian hell..." However, the writer of the article had to restrain himself and admit the obvious fact that "the international situation will decide about the time of departure... We cannot engage in half-solutions, and therefore we have to adjust to our allies."[37]

The editorial continued by saying that the military command was saddened that the current favorable situation had to be abandoned. According to the command's assessment, the confusion in Romanian political life and in the army greatly decreased the fighting morale of the Romanian troops, which would make success possible in the case of quick military action. The Soviet troops continued their movements according to plan and finished the occupation of Bessarabia and Bukovina on July 1. The Romanian troops were retreating completely demoralized with their equipment scattered. According to the agreement, the troops from Bessarabia and Bukovina would be disarmed, and therefore several units would have to be reorganized. The consolidation of the difficult situation and the eventual surmounting of the crises in the Romanian army were expected to aggravate the ability of the Hungarians to pull off a successful operation.[38]

From July 4 onwards the daily situation analyses of the General Staff gave an account of the gradual stabilization of the Romanian "front." For Romania, it was of the utmost importance that the ongoing transformation of the country's government meant seeking a closer connection with, and the protection of, the Third Reich in the foreign political arena. This was how Romania planned to secure its borders.[39] In the meantime troop transportation to Transylvania continued at a rapid pace and in an increasingly organized manner. Civilian transportation ceased to exist along the Kolozsvár–Nagyvárad–Szatmárnémeti railway. The main thrust of troop transportation took place in the Maros Valley in the southwestern part of Transylvania. Altogether three or four divisions arrived in the region of Arad and Temesvár between June 30 and July 6. The military grouping that developed in the Maros Valley could not be called defensive, for it showed a counterattacking setup, which, in the case of a Hungarian attack launched into the Szamos Valley, would make a flanking attack on the Hungarian front possible and thus be able to make a sudden advance towards the Szeged and Békéscsaba direction.[40] The dangerousness of this grouping was not diminished by the fact that some of the troops must have arrived from Moldova demoralized, while their equipment was not up to par either.[41]

In Budapest soldiers and politicians alike were forced to acknowledge that it was Germany's first priority to stabilize the Romanian situation and, therefore, would not be able to satisfy Hungarian requests at this point. Hitler's message of July 9, indicating that on the following day he expected to meet the Hungarian delegation in Munich, was of some encouragement for Teleki. This might offer an opportunity to clarify the Hungarian position or perhaps to persuade Ciano, who was also going to be present, with regard to the Hungarian requests.

Germany's victories and stability, France's disintegration, and Great Britain's seemingly hopeless situation following the defeats forced Teleki to engage in a cautious rapprochement with Germany, whose policy had now assumed a decisive role in the Central European region. He could not ignore the jubilation and triumphant activities of the internal opposition following the German victories. Teleki was concerned about the Soviet advance into the region, and was also troubled by the Soviet territorial request and its fulfillment by Romania. His resentment was not changed by the fact that Soviet diplomacy assured the Hungarian government on several occasions about the Soviets' friendly intentions. With Romania giving up the Bessarabian territories and with the quick German–Romanian rapprochement following the cancellation of the British guarantees, Teleki now believed that the earlier rigid Western position towards the Hungarian–German relationship in connection with Romania had changed. Therefore, he could confidently turn to Germany and ask them to put pressure on the Romanian government to engage in negotiations, with the final result that the Germans would be open to independent Hungarian initiatives. In view of these results, further economic concessions to Germany and, if needed, allowing German troops to be afforded transit across Hungarian territory, in order to be deployed to occupy Romania, could be forgiven. However, he did not change his opposition to Hungarian deployment alongside the Germans, an issue about which the Hungarian military command had been very hopeful but Teleki considered inadmissible.

Teleki planned on approaching Germany's leadership with a discussion about the Hungarian extreme right wing and the country's army, both impassioned by the thought of territorial revisionism and both convinced that it would be done with German and Italian support. He wanted to let the Germans know that, unless they wanted these two groups to be disappointed in their German allies, the Hungarian territorial revisionist demands had to be seriously considered.

The tension between Teleki and the Werth–Bartha duo further deepened during the tumultuous weeks preceding the Munich meeting. To Werth's greatest satisfaction, Teleki now was forced to accept some of Werth's proposals, which he had previously flatly rejected. The Hungarian government was willing to offer new economic allowances and to ensure the transit of German troops across Hungary, which not so long ago the General Staff had had to prepare secretly behind the government's back. All this seemed to justify Werth's longstanding assertion that without close cooperation with Germany no territorial revisionism was possible. In his view, the change in the Romanian government's policy left only one alternative for the Hungarian government: to watch closely the development of the Romanian–German relationship, so that any cracks that might develop in the fragile structure could be taken advantage of both politically and militarily. To do this, connections between Germany and Hungary should be solidified through far-reaching economic and other concessions by Hungary and through keeping the *Honvédség* constantly prepared. In spite of repeated failures and von Ribbentrop's protests, Werth did not discount the possibility that German–Hungarian military cooperation could be formulated in order to secure the Romanian oil resources. A probable Soviet southern advance would offer a good opportunity for that.[42]

At this time, several essays were published in the Hungarian military press that analyzed the western campaign and discussed the excellent and exemplary cooperation that had existed and still existed between Germany's political and military leaders. For example, Ferenc Feketehalmy-Czeydner wrote the following: "Understanding the utmost importance of military factors and necessities—the Germans were led to accept—that the military had to participate in all decision regarding important state affairs. When making decisions about state affairs, they do not speak about 'General Staff professionals'—which would be nonsensical—but the military aspect is given priority, and the legal, public administrative, and so on 'professionals' are listened to only with regard to modifications. Their starting point is that war preparation is war itself, and, moreover, it might be the important part of war, which decides the game. Therefore, it is immoral and blind to expose a military leader to the public opinion of a country when the devices of a weak, selfish, discordant and shortsighted peace policy are exhausted, the policy itself has failed, and everyone expects a miracle from the military. This should not happen, because the military will fail and it will be dumped and vilified once again."[43]

On July 10, the Hungarian statesmen who came to Munich at his request were received by Hitler. Teleki presented the Hungarian demands, which the country was willing to negotiate and even compromise as long as the Romanians were ready to engage in serious discussions. He also pointed out that Hungary could solve the Transylvanian question militarily by itself, and this would be the second opportunity after the first one that arose with the occupation of Trans-Carpathia. However, Hungary could also wait as long as it remained in the interest of the Axis and as long as it received assurances that would allow the Prime Minister to advise the nation to "curb its impatience and to wait."[44]

After listening to Teleki's presentation, Hitler, in a long monologue, described his own well-known position, which was only infrequently interrupted by cautious Hungarian objections and by Ciano's interjections of approval. Hitler immediately came to the point—to scare his partners away from an armed action against Romania. He set out to analyze the Hungarian military preparedness and its overall power. He authoritatively raised and immediately answered questions relating to the condition of the *Honvédség*, something that should have included the Hungarian Minister of Defense and the Chief of the General Staff. Hitler, however, was not interested in the Hungarian military's views, and neither was he interested in his discussion partners' objections. Following that, the Führer claimed that he was convinced about the justified Hungarian territorial demands, but that he doubted that the right moment had arrived to push for them. Still, if the Hungarian government thought that it could launch a conflict whose future consequences were not known, it should act according to its liking. However, it should not count on Germany's help, however unfavorably the situation might develop. He also wondered whether the Hungarian politicians present at the discussion were certain about Hungary's defeating the Romanian army by relying only on its own military forces. Teleki's response was a definite "yes," saying that the government "has to rely on the opinion of the country's military authorization, and this opinion—especially that of the Chief of the General Staff—is unambiguously positive."[45]

Following that, Hitler produced a little military pocketbook and proceeded to describe the Romanian army. He called attention to the good equipment that they possessed, which was contributed not only by the Western states but also by Germany itself. Then he brought up the numerical superiority of the Romanian army. He ignored the strategic fact that they were divided along the different borders. Hitler defined the conditions for a successful war as 1) first-rate leadership; 2) excellent organization; either 3) an overwhelming numerical superiority, or 4) a high quality of material equipment, which can crush everything. The first and second conditions would only be manifest during the war, but with regard to the third and fourth conditions he added that the weapons delivered to Romania by the German Reich and Italy and, previously, by the Skoda factory made him convinced that Romania was a definitely well-equipped state. Its army's level of preparedness surpassed that of Hungary's.[46]

At this point Csáky interjected that the morale factor might counterbalance material shortages. He alluded to the collapse of Czechoslovakia, without a shot being fired, and to the German army, where the excellent fighting spirit played an important role in its great victories.

At this point Hitler did not wish to discuss the excellent fighting spirit of the German soldier, and silenced Csáky by saying that although heroism as a military factor was not negligible, it was not a determining one. A machine-gun nest could not be occupied by a bayonet assault, and nor could a brave pilot perform much with a bad airplane. At the end of his thoughts on power relations, Hitler emphasized the point that he trusted the Hungarian government's judgment but "a well-meaning advisor ["Warner"] has called our attention to several questions, and the keen insights gained by his war experience are well founded."[47]

Following that, Hitler turned to Ciano and asked him to elaborate on his own views related to what was said. Ciano indicated that it was not in the interest of Italy—also at war with Great Britain—to have a conflict in the Balkans. There should be a more favorable moment in the future than the present one, when the Hungarian demands towards Romania could be enforced. Finally, he also noted that although Bucharest would find the way to Rome only via Budapest, Italian economic interests—oil—were also connected to Bucharest.

After this spectacular manifestation of cooperation among the Axis Powers, as a conclusion to what had been said Hitler once again cautioned the Hungarian government to assume a position of "all or nothing" in connection with the Transylvanian question.

Teleki noted that the Hungarian government had already requested the support of the German, Italian, and even the Yugoslavian governments to put pressure on Bucharest to stop its discrimination and to carry on negotiations. Yet the Romanian government had not given any straightforward response.

At that point von Ribbentrop jumped into the discussion to contradict Teleki, saying that the Romanians were aware of the need to make territorial concessions to Hungary and showed every sign of being inclined to talk.

Then Hitler once again seized the momentum and carried on along the lines of what von Ribbentrop had said. He tried to reassure Teleki that if the Hungarian government listened to his well-meaning advice, they could count on him to direct Romanian policy, where his influence had increased, into the proper direction complying with the needs of his dear comrades-in-arms from World War I. He had already pointed out to King Carol that he would have to make territorial concessions to Hungary. Carol had written a letter and offered "an alliance of defense and defiance" and, as Hitler continued, had behaved so that it was difficult "to fend off his embracing arms." Hitler had not yet responded to Carol because he wanted to wait for this discussion (with the Hungarians). "You, as our brothers-in-arms in World War I, are closer to us than the Romanians. I am willing to take a step further, and now I will respond to them that in 1918/19 Romania, due to a fortunate coincidence of events and not due to its courage or military power, acquired a larger territorial gain than it was entitled to. Therefore, they should try to get rid of the excess territory, if they want to have something left of Romania. I will tell them that politically I will only be in a situation to establish a closer relationship with Romania if it first fulfills Hungary's territorial demands." He went on to say that he would warn Carol, and that if there were no response, Romania would see "what it means to be left alone."[48] Hitler immediately asked for the Duce's agreement as to what he was going to include in the response to Carol, which Ciano immediately provided.

Teleki thanked Hitler for his goodwill, and added that the Munich invitation and the prospective step towards Romania held out by Hitler would, at the present, satisfy the Hungarian government. However, the situation was far from reassuring for Teleki, and it did not end the uncertainty about the Transylvanian question.

Although in the wake of Hitler's promises Teleki believed that the chances of a solution through negotiations had increased slightly, in agreement with the government's decision he still opposed demobilizing the troops deployed to the Romanian border. Instead, he wanted to use military pressure, because "already at the beginning of the talks one has to assume that, if it does not lead to results, one has to reach for the tools of *ultima ratio*."[49] He tried to preempt Hitler's observations and demands, and wanted to justify the government's decision on the necessity of mobilization and the deployment of troops. Teleki argued that the Hungarian public view had to be reassured, because it had been nervous about the idleness of the government, and, at the same time, the Romanians needed to be warned to refrain from any attack on the Hungarian population. The Transylvanian Hungarian population needed to feel that the Hungarian government was guarding their safety. The possible outbreak of revolution in Romania was mentioned as a final reason by Teleki. Hitler, along with Ciano, reassured the Hungarian Prime

Minister that they did not advise, and moreover that they would disagree with, the demobilization of the Hungarian army.

Arriving home from Munich the disappointed Hungarian statesmen tried to be optimistic in their public pronouncements about the current situation. It was in Germany's interest to keep peace in the southeastern region of Europe. Therefore, it could be expected that Hitler, according to his promise, would put pressure on the Romanian government to participate in negotiations with the Hungarian government where the Romanians would be unable to avoid making territorial concessions. The military leaders agreed with this assessment of the events.[50]

Colonel Homlok's report to Ujszászy on July 18 tried to give a realistic assessment of the situation developing in Berlin after the Munich talks. First of all, he mentioned the fact that while the German press evaluated what was said in a friendly and factual manner, the Hungarian press wrote in a tabloid style that did not fit the seriousness of the situation. He claimed that the military in Germany showed a certain amount of understanding towards Hungary's territorial revisionist aspirations. However, statements made to Homlok by such top German military leaders as General Halder, General Tippelskirch and others did not leave a shred of doubt that the present moment was not suitable for Hungary to act on its dreams. They were concerned about the prospect of Hungary "exclusively considering its own interests" by attacking Romania and thus toppling the cherished peace in the Balkans, with unpredictable consequences for such a move. Homlok was reinforced in his earlier opinion: "Hungarian territorial revisionist aspirations cannot be realized by the force of arms at a date deliberately chosen by Hungary. Instead, the understanding and goodwill of the Axis Powers have to be established, since the date and the extent of our revisionist aspirations are dependent on the Axis Powers. For the time being—and considering the larger picture—a peaceful agreement seems to be preferable."[51]

Analyzing Germany's military situation, Homlok focussed on the imminent operation against Great Britain. However, he also noted that he was starting to doubt it, since the news had been released so many times already. Analyzing the condition and locations of units of the German army, he pointed to troop deliveries from the Reich and even from France going to Poland, which he thought could be explained by the German government's distrust of the Soviet Union. Although it was in Germany's interest to avoid a confrontation with the Soviets—for the sake of a final victory—as could be deciphered from German officers talking to each other, it was certain that after a victory over Great Britain Germany would turn against the Soviet Union.[52]

At the end of July, a period of "great expectations" when the German–Hungarian relationship seemed so "cloudless" to the outside world, the Hungarian government tried to please Germany and gain advantages against the Romanians, who themselves had tried to appease the Germans unsuccessfully. Teleki personally joined the Hungarian–German economic negotiations, ending on June 19, when Hungary offered significant new allowances in order to secure their German ally's goodwill. At Germany's request, the contract valid until June 31, 1941, significantly increased Hungarian agricultural and raw material exports to Germany. At German demands as well, a long-demanded crude oil contractual agreement was also signed.[53]

On June 27 Teleki wrote to Werth and Bartha and reassured them that the discussions had been successful and that the Germans had been given the desired concessions. Werth had worried about the future fuel supply of the army and asked Bartha in April to urge the Prime Minister to permit and undertake exploratory oil drilling in the south of the Alföld and in Transdanubia. At that point the German air force attaché Fütterer, at Göring's request, urged Werth to launch an oil-drilling project, favorable to both armies, by applying German experts and technology that the German government had proposed earlier, a project that had broken down in negotiations. The Germans wanted to dislodge the issue from its impasse by working through the leaders of the *Honvédség*. Werth was immediately ready to take steps, turned to Teleki in a memorandum, and asked for instructions. Werth strongly supported the German proposal, because he also hoped for political advantages beyond tightening the cooperation between the two militaries. He believed that "if Germany gets a share of the production of the discovered areas, it will not need to support Romania against Hungary's aspirations. Because it can gain access to agricultural goods relatively easily, it is not the food supply that is the problem, but the fuel supply. It has to ensure its oil needs via a land route; consequently, it [currently] has to treat Hungarian demands towards its only transporter, Romania, with reservations."[54]

Using economic discussions as smokescreens, the military leadership took an independent route in other areas and made further offers without the knowledge of the government. The Ministry of Defense sent Colonel Jenő Bor to Berlin to gain information about the possible importation of heavy weapons without the knowledge of the Hungarian government. Bor's assignment went so far as to impress the German officials with the prospect of importing raw materials—oil being one—that were part of the existing contract.[55] Letting the Germans use Hungarian military industrial capacities, such as gun and anti-aircraft machine-gun manufacturing, were added bonuses in Bor's offer.[56]

While the Hungarian government made economic concessions and was forced to close its eyes to the most recent manifestations of the army's independence, it also tried to assume a position of patient waiting, in accord with German wishes, on the Transylvanian issue. The government found it most insulting that German war supply transport continued to take place and, moreover, that the older contingence was being complemented by new orders. On July 22 the Hungarian ambassador to Bucharest reported that the Germans had allowed the Romanian government to place an urgent order to the Skoda factory for 350 million infantry bullets, as well as rifles and machine-guns.[57]

On July 23 Csáky instructed Sztójay to raise the issue of more Romanian arms deliveries with the German Ministry of Foreign Affairs. In the current situation, laden with great expectations, this would only strengthen the Romanian resistance both politically and militarily, and hastened the Hungarian government "to bring the issue to a decision, because, once the news hits the public, it will be outraged and demand a quick response from the government."[58]

On July 24 Weizsäcker received the Hungarian ambassador in the company of Clodius, who had just arrived from his Budapest discussions. He said that he was slightly taken aback by the Hungarian government's worries about the consequences of the Romanian weapons delivery, since the Führer himself had elaborated on the German position towards Hungary in the presence of Hungarian statesmen not so long ago. Furthermore, Germany had been supplying arms to Hungary for years, and just within the past few days had endorsed the Hungarian request for the delivery of tanks, howitzers and airplanes. It must also be a well-known fact to the Hungarian government that permitting the fulfillment of Romanian orders was an economic necessity for the German government. It had been going on for years, from the Brno weapons factory, and they were previous orders. Weizsäcker also emphasized the point that there was no connection between the political events of the past two months and the deliveries. On the other hand, the German Under-secretary of Foreign Affairs seemed not to want to understand the actual bone of contention, that is, the urgent new Romanian orders.[59]

Once again the Hungarian military command tried to get over the issue of detrimental Romanian weapons deliveries and to obtain adequate explanations for its own reassurance. The deep friendship between the German and Hungarian armies and their shared past history in World War I—as Hitler himself had mentioned—made the Hungarian *Honvédség* more reliable and valuable than the Romanians for Germany, even if economic issues or the prevention of a possible Soviet advance made strengthening the Romanian relationship and hence the Romanian army a political necessity. It was in Germany's interest to solve the Transylvanian issue through negotiations; if the Romanians did not pay attention to it, it would provoke the Germans' anger and force them into a military intervention. Neither the political nor the military leaders faced the fact, but rather ignored the possibility, that the former Little Entente state Romania could possibly be a more valuable asset for Germany than Hungary at the current time. Obviously, the possibility of using the Romanian army against the Soviet Union had not yet emerged in the prognostic evaluation of the Hungarian military command. Instead, the Hungarian military command assumed that maintaining a Hungarian–Romanian mobilization for a long time could hardly be in the interest of the Germans, since its economic consequences would, by all means, influence the quantity of agricultural products and raw materials available for Germany.

The propaganda was effective in instilling in the population of Hungary, and even more so in the military, the idea that Germany, in agreement with the Italians, would soon solve the Transylvanian question. The basic tone of the propaganda within the army was set by the Chief of the General Staff, who, during his reviews of the troops, held informational meetings about the state of foreign relations and forthcoming developments for officers gathered at army corps headquarters.[60]

In his talk to the 3rd Army on July 23 Werth spoke enthusiastically about the Hungarian–German relationship, saying that it had been good for a long time and essentially friction-free. The fact that in the recent past Hungary was the only country that was willing to participate in a common military operation with Germany in order to deal with the southeastern European issue was instrumental in the good relationship. Exaggerated rumors about conflicts, spread by the liberals in order to taint the atmosphere, were unsubstantiated. The Germans were aware that the anti-German manifestations of these liberal circles—Jews, royalists and the clergy—were not the voices of the Hungarian public, and Germany's friendship towards Hungary was undivided.

Speaking about the Prime Minister's and the Minister of Foreign Affairs' discussions in Munich, he stated that they were of crucial importance for the Transylvanian question. During these discussions, the Führer and Ciano, "without any doubt," recognized Hungary's justified demands on the whole area of Transylvania. Considering, however, that a war conflict in the Balkans would not be convenient for the Axis Powers right then, they had asked Hungary to postpone an armed operation to satisfy its justified demands. Yet, in agreement with Italy, Germany promised to put political and moral pressure on Romania to give up its rigid position and to initiate negotiations with Hungary. This, however, did not mean that the *Honvédség* would not be able to intervene if the security of the country or the safety of the Transylvanian compatriots were in jeopardy. Werth listed the reasons, determined by the Hungarian government and recognized by the German and Italian allies, that might justify when the Hungarian troops "could start immediately" to re-annex Transylvania by force of arms. Amidst the general euphoria he did not even mention the development of the German–Romanian relationship, or developments, such as the weapons deliveries, that would have negative connotations for the army.

Werth also found it necessary to deal with the development of the Hungarian–Soviet relationship; he denied, and considered to be unfounded, news about troop movements against Hungary. The Hungarian–Soviet relationship was exceptional, he said. Although it had not been publicized yet, in the recent past Molotov had declared several times that the Soviet Union recognized Hungary's right to Transylvania. Furthermore, there was no disputed or pending issue between the two countries. The German ambassador to Moscow also told Molotov that Hungary was "a German interest and, therefore, part of the German *Lebensraum*."

In summary, Werth described Hungary's foreign political situation as a brilliant one, from which "there is no road backwards, just forwards." And, he told them, what he had said was no secret and could be spread in public.

The monthly journal of the officer corps, *Magyar Katonai Szemle*, reviewed the Munich meeting in a similar, although slightly subdued, tone. It reported that during the discussions "the just settlement of the open questions about southeastern Europe had to happen at any time, when the peace of southeastern Europe was not disturbed by any external circumstances. During the Munich meeting, Hungary's lasting and reliable loyalty to the Axis Powers was emphasized, and so, as a result of their recognition, the Axis Powers held out the prospect of satisfying Hungary's territorial demands as the first action after the conclusion of the present war."[61]

The columnists of the *Magyar Katonaújság*, the newspaper for the troops, strove to glorify German–Italian–Hungarian friendship and cooperation, and publicized the claim that the Transylvanian question was to be solved by the Axis Powers.

Trusting in the promises that Hitler made during the Munich talks, the military leadership looked forward to the Salzburg talks at the end of July with great anticipation. It was expected that Hitler would convince the Romanians, during the Romanian, Slovakian and Bulgarian statesmen's visit to him, that they could not keep all of Transylvania, and that the Romanians, adjusting to the wishes of the Axis, would be forced to engage in urgent negotiations.[62] In fact, the Hungarian General Staff's analysis of the situation stated on July 28 that the decision would be made within a week.[63]

The military leadership believed that it was not in Germany's interest to destroy Romania, and therefore the solution "is a compromise towards all the Hungarian demands." However, as Colonel Homlok warned from Berlin on July 25, the Axis Powers' mediation had to be accepted at any price, because Hungary could not realize its demands towards Romania by force of arms. The mediation would have its price, and "it would entail a supervisory role or, if needed, a dictating role" in order to maintain the established situation.[64]

However, the situation did not quite evolve according to the Hungarian leadership's expectations. The Romanian ministers, led by Prime Minister Gigurtu, arrived in Salzburg on July 26 and were received by von Ribbentrop, who, first of all, reviewed the development of the German–Romanian relationship.[65] He noted that the British–French guarantee to the Romanians was offensive to Germany. The guarantee was directed at Germany, even though it had never had any territorial demands in the Balkans. On the contrary, Germany wanted to have peace in this part of Europe, which had seen so many storms in the past, precisely because it wanted to strengthen economic connections there. However, the Romanians should not think that their natural resources, such as the oil, would be of crucial importance for Germany. Month by month Germany was becoming increasingly independent with regard to oil supply. This would make it possible to win the war without oil imports.[66] Von Ribbentrop advised the Romanians to come to an agreement with the Hungarians and the Bulgarians through negotiations. This would be desirable, because its postponement would have undesirable consequences for Romania and would make the German–Romanian relationship difficult.

Prime Minister Gigurtu told von Ribbentrop that they had been striving to improve their relationship with Germany and were willing to start negotiations with the Hungarians and the Bulgarians. However, it would not be easy to come to an agreement, due to domestic and foreign political difficulties. Still, he believed that a mutual population exchange and some border adjustments were realistic.

Following the meeting with von Ribbentrop, the Romanians met Hitler. As was customary, Hitler gave an extensive lecture about the European situation, the approaching German victory, and the German–Romanian relationship—all before coming to the Hungarian issue. He stated that he had no doubt about the justified Hungarian demands, and that it had been his intervention in early July that had restrained the Hungarians from attacking Romania. Although he did not go into detail, it could be assumed that the attack would have put Romania in a very difficult military situation, with consequences endangering the peace of the region and Romania's security. Hitler refrained from alluding to either the balance of power between the Hungarian and the Romanian armies or to the prospects of any armed encounter. He said that he wanted to see an agreement on the disputed territorial issues between the two countries, and would be glad to see that an agreement was reached with the Bulgarians as well. Following such agreements, he and Mussolini would guarantee Romania's territorial integrity. Bilateral negotiations should be the path to the agreements, since Germany did not wish to mediate.[67]

Gigurtu proved to be very understanding. Both politically and economically, he said, Romania wanted to fit into the new European order and, therefore, would thus consider its neighbors' demands while it trusted in their reasonable nature. Then the Romanian Prime Minister described to Hitler the Romanian plans to give up 14,000 km² and to propose a population exchange. Romanian Minister of Foreign Affairs Manoilescu interjected that further territorial concessions could also be made. Hitler noted that the Hungarians were speaking about the thousand-year old borders, a restitution of which obviously was impossible. Von Ribbentrop intervened, saying that the Hungarians would even agree to half of the territories that had been annexed at Trianon. Assuming that an agreement would not likely be achieved during negotiations, Gigurtu asked whether he could count on Germany as an arbitrator, an idea that Hitler flatly refused.[68]

The Romanian ministers used the opportunity to raise the question of the equipment needs of their army. After their earlier purchases they had already asked von Ribbentrop to let them continue buying anti-aircraft and anti-tank guns and airplanes. A possible ten-year 600 million Deutschmark loan was also mentioned, which would make further major purchases possible.[69] They now reiterated these wishes to Hitler, who, citing the needs of the 200 division-strong German army, which was engaged in a life-and-death struggle, as well as the needs of the *Luftwaffe*, refused the request but did not exclude the possibility of giving them weapons from the war booty in the future. Responding to the argument that Romania needed anti-aircraft batteries to defend its oilfields and refineries, Hitler said that having a larger force behind Romania to stave off attacks was a more significant form of defense.[70]

Neither von Ribbentrop nor Hitler touched upon the question of the requested armaments loan. A positive response would have overtly encouraged the Romanians and would have had a negative effect on the Hungarians, who had just protested against arms deliveries to Romania a few days earlier. This would have been contrary to Hitler's goal of seeming to understand both parties. Neither did the minutes taken by the discussion mention whether Hitler had responded to an earlier Romanian request that a German military mission provide training for the Romanian army in the use of German weapons.[71]

Back in Romania the delegation made the results of the meeting feel like a triumph, something that was also reinforced by Mussolini in Rome. Hitler had only encouraged the Romanians to negotiate and come to an agreement, and never actually requested anything at all. This fact, and their interpretation that his general attitude was one of understanding and an interest in deepening the relationship with Romania, made them indulge in the hope that Germany would defend them against the Hungarians' exaggerated demands.[72]

The Hungarian government was irritated with the meager results. It was obvious that the German behavior towards the Romanians was not as harsh as the Hungarians had hoped. Moreover, the discussions seemed to build a foundation for further German–Romanian rapprochement. Ciano wrote in his diary: "The Hungarians are nervous about the Romanians' trips to Rome and Berlin. They are afraid that Romania—after being on the Little Entente's side for so many years ...—will request to be admitted to the Axis Powers."[73]

After sharing his plan with his General Staff on July 31, Hitler decided to launch a campaign against the Soviet Union in the spring of 1941, and thus wanted quiet in southeastern Europe. He counted on the Romanian resources and army, as well as Hungary's resources. Therefore, a Hungarian–Romanian armed conflict was not desirable, although it would be desirable if tensions increased to a near-conflict level—when, obliging both antagonistic parties, he would intervene.[74]

Few of the Hungarian political players, let alone the military, recognized Hitler's intentions. Only Teleki and a few of his circle came close to the truth, although without even voicing any ominous words at any forum, which obviously would not have been possible under the circumstances. The completely biased military, on the other hand, continued to believe that Germany could not go into cahoots with Romania, a common enemy until the most recent times, behind the backs of their Hungarian allies.

A special interpretation of what happened in Salzburg made it to the Hungarian public waiting for a decision. Some press organs even spread the news that Hungary's patience as it stood by the Axis Powers had finally earned results: Romania had recognized

Hungary's conditions in Salzburg, and the Romanian government was getting ready to hand over its list, aiming at a settlement with the Hungarian government. The General Staff, however, was forced to consider that Romania was going to stall for time in order to reinforce its Transylvanian forces and to improve its position for negotiations: "Although, for the sake of peace in southeastern Europe, they [the Romanian statesmen] made promises about appropriate territorial concessions and were ready to shoulder any internal or external political obligations," they would do everything to postpone actions. Therefore, they would likely negotiate the Bulgarian territorial settlement before the Transylvanian one. Their capacity for changing directions quickly and their Axis-friendly policy should be kept in mind, because Romania "will do its best to decrease Hungarian territorial demands to the minimum and to ensure the largest possible material advantage to Romania."[75] However, as it was viewed in the General Staff circles, there was no reason to worry, because "the leading politicians of the Axis Powers would decrease their changed policy to a level still acceptable."[76]

On July 30 certain members of the General Staff seemed to know that the upcoming Hungarian–Romanian negotiations would be initiated by Romania. The Romanian press was already preparing the public for the discussions and for the possible unpleasant consequences for Romania. Tension inside Romania was increasing, as was confusion among the country's leadership.[77]

Amidst all its hopes about Transylvania, the Hungarian military leadership still had to tackle political, military and economic issues arising from the extended troop deployment of more than half a million soldiers, a quarter of a million horses, and equipment. Most of the troops were stationed in the poorest regions of Hungary: Békés, Hajdú, Szabolcs-Szatmár, Bereg, Ugocsa and Máramaros Counties. The lengthy deployment—by then, more than two months long—of soldiers, horses and equipment disturbed the everyday life of the villages and local agricultural activities. Field exercises and the construction of dug-outs and fortified positions caused damage to crops as well. Purchases by the troops of local agricultural products aggravated the situation and caused problems with the supply of foodstuffs for the local population. Preventing possible epidemics among so many soldiers placed within a relatively small area and under unfavorable conditions was also of concern. These problems were increasingly present with poorer and more backward ethnic villages, where enthusiasm towards Transylvania nevertheless did not help the population to endure the harsh circumstances. Animosity between the soldiers and the ethnic populations grew, and gave rise to excessive and arbitrary behavior by the soldiers and to mutual recriminations.[78]

The long waiting period, uncertainty, too much free time and inactivity, despite all the efforts of the leadership, damaged the troops' discipline. People had not been prepared to be away from home so long, and the majority of the peasant-soldiers were anxious about the state of agricultural activities, especially the harvest, back home. They began to question the reason for their being there, since they had not been told about being idle for long weeks, nor about all the accompanying problems, but rather had been promised that they would be marching into Transylvania shortly. Under such circumstances it was difficult to keep up military discipline. The atmosphere also deteriorated among the reserve officers. They did not understand either why the departure date had not yet arrived, amidst all the enthusiastic promises, or why the strong goodwill of the Axis Powers had not materialized in concrete form.

The General Staff pointedly called the attention of commanders at different levels to the need to keep order, and did not exclude the application of unpleasant measures. The Chief of the General Staff wrote as follows:

I have experienced certain phenomena that make me conclude that there is a certain laxity in the behaviour of the *Honvédség*. ... I make it the serious obligation of every commanding officer to handle internal order and discipline in the most serious way. Patient moral education is of great significance under the present circumstances. However, a commander also has to consider that often forceful, and sometimes even harsh, disciplinary actions bring faster and more effective results.[79]

In order to comply with their tasks as defined in the operational plans, the commanders engaged their sub-units in military exercises. Army corps and brigade cooperative exercises, which required more mobility, did not take place, because the operational areas were densely occupied by troops. Such exercises would also have provoked suspicions of a military operation in progress among Romanian troops on the other side of the border. After the April–May crash courses, the assault patrols of the infantry battalions assigned to attack in the first echalon, who had major roles in overtaking the fortifications, practiced the occupation of fortifications in the planned breakthrough region.[80] Due to the sparse supply of ammunition, the troops could hardly perform any target-shooting and, in the case of the artillery, the lack of suitable shooting ranges also posed a problem.

It was at this time that the tank battalions received a part of their "Toldi" tank contingence and the mechanized battalions received a part of their "Botond" delivery truck contingence.

The longstanding mobilization burdened the Treasury with significant expenses. In May 1940 the Council of Ministers gave 59.5 million pengős to the army for troop maintenance and other operational expenses, and then in July again it gave 310.7 million pengős to the army for "Transylvanian expenses."[81] About 60 million pengős were already spent by September. By the end of the year the expenses, including the ones related to establishing the IX. Army Corps in Transylvania, had increased to 254 million pengős.

The loss felt in villages due to uncompleted or delayed agricultural work cannot be monetarily expressed, but the dissatisfaction increased there tremendously. The letters of complaint and reports made their way to the Prime Minister's table. An example came from Völcsej: "It breeds great dissatisfaction in the area that strong and able-bodied men, whose families have been living in privation, have been kept within the military for months, seemingly without any serious reason. Measures should be taken to aid those drafted and to make sure that those in need immediately receive help." Another report from Zalamernye suggested that those men drafted into military service, or at least those who would be missed in the harvest, should be sent on leave during the agricultural season. Otherwise, the people might revolt in distress.[82] The circumstances forced the leadership to reinstate for the end of July the earlier-planned but then revoked harvest leave for the end of July.[83]

By the beginning of August the delay in negotiations had increased tensions to the point of explosion. The status quo could not be reconciled with the intensified expectations that the press kept at a high pitch. The deteriorating atmosphere could also be felt in the army. The military leadership tried to deal with the situation by increasingly emphasizing the connections between the allies, by the loyalty and the past and present friendship between the Hungarian army and the German army. Although the real impact on events of the connections between the two armies and their leaders was little more than nothing, allusions to them were not without results. One should be aware that the prestige of the German army among the officer corps and the majority of reserve officers was further enhanced by the early summer victories. Furthermore, German officers showed some interest, which manifested itself in personal relationships and frequent official meetings. All these things fed the hope of the General Staff with regard to the helpfulness of their German counterparts. It did this in spite of Hitler's rapprochement towards the Romanians and the expansion of German–Romanian relationships. The Hungarians felt that the commanders of the German army—with closer links to their Hungarian fellow soldiers—would speak for Hungarian aspirations to Hitler. They also took it as a good sign that earlier, when the plans had been made for Romania's occupation, the German General Staff had considered the possibility of cooperation offered by the Hungarian army, although Hitler himself did not favor it. Moreover, the fact that certain members of the German General Staff relayed confidential information to their Hungarian fellow soldiers, about which the German foreign policy leaders did not want to inform the Hungarian government, was also considered a friendly gesture. They did not realize that in most of the cases it was not a question of benevolent gossiping by German General Staff officers, but a deliberate leakage of the news. All in all, and even if this were based on false ideas, the upper echelons of the officer corps of the Hungarian army were convinced that the German–Hungarian alliance would pass muster amidst the skirmishes about the solution of the Transylvanian question, and it was on this faith that the official position of the army was founded.

Amidst diplomatic and propaganda fights on both sides and in a quandary that they tried to hide from the outside world, the Hungarian government had to face a number of difficult issues: successful negotiations with the Romanians, which would result in an acceptable compromise, the armed annexation of at least a part of Transylvania if the negotiations fell through, or postponement of the Transylvanian question, and the demobilization of the army without any results. The latter solution did not seem to be feasible. The government knew that if it retreated with no results and took no measures, including a military solution, its situation would be gravely shaken in the public eye. Teleki, a champion of territorial revisionism, could not and did not want to accept an unsuccessful retreat. However, he was also uncertain about what was the best solution. He trusted in bilateral conferences and Hitler's promised support, but was not keen on experiencing the Axis Powers' probable interference as a conciliator. It was not in Germany's interest to betray the Hungarian public. Therefore, Germany could not avoid urging Romania towards an acceptable compromise, Teleki believed.

We are not far from the truth when we suppose that Teleki, knowing the relative strengths of the two armies, was afraid of an armed solution. He trusted that if the negotiations failed and a Hungarian attack became unavoidable, it could be stopped before grave losses or failures, since Germany, facing a unwanted situation, would force Romania into a cease-fire and into making concessions. Teleki thought that, in a situation such as that, Romania would ask for a cease-fire and would make concessions to Hungary, since it would have launched the war for justified reasons and on its own volition, and Germany would oblige only Romania with its intervention.

Hitler, however, had counted on this possibility. He could not stand the idea that Hungary would circumvent Germany and so not owe Germany a large debt for the annexed territories. An armed conflict could be avoided. Werth and the military leaders also came close to recognizing this. They were ready to accept any form of German intervention and support. Ending the long-standing mobilization and withdrawing troops without any result threatened to have a demoralizing impact upon the officer corps and among the troops. It would also have endangered the myth of the excellence of the *Honvédség*, its liberating mission and its triumphant execution. It would also have put into question Werth's pro-German activities as Chief of the General Staff and the connections between the two armies.

Werth himself trusted that successful negotiations would take place. The military re-annexation of Transylvania seemed less and less feasible. Werth continued to believe that the crisis situation could only be solved together with the Germans and not against them. Of course, he understood that in early July it was the German pressure that had prevented a Hungarian military action against Romania when the situation looked promising for the Hungarians, and that since then the Romanian army had become stronger and had deployed excess forces across from the Hungarian troops. Their weaponry had improved, in spite of losing their Western allies, as a consequence of the German support. Werth knew that it was in Germany's interest to deliver weapons and it was not its priority to prepare Romania—an ally by then—for defense against Hungary. Germany's interaction in strengthening the Romanian army's weaponry seemed to indicate that Germany had certain goals with the Romanian army that were unknown to the Hungarian General Staff.[84]

The views of the upper echelons of the Hungarian army did not trickle down to the bulk of the army, which had been preparing with increasing impatience to wage a "sweeping" advance into Transylvania. The fact that time was on the Romanian army's side was kept a top secret. So was the fact that the relative strengths of the two armies had changed and that there was less hope for success. The advantageous situation of July had changed dramatically by August.

The troops looked forward to the militarily more advantageous solution—negotiations—with great expectations and with full confidence in their allies. The Romanians procrastinated because they wanted to negotiate from a stronger military position. Sooner or later, however, they would have to give up this treacherous attitude and would have "to consent to the revisionist negotiations according to the will of the Axis," even "if there is no inclination in them towards essential territorial sacrifices."[85] The General Staff also heard rumors that "the Gigurtu government refuses any territorial annexation to Hungary, because they are certain that Germany would prevent a Hungarian attack against Romania."[86] The Iron Guard (*Vasgárda*) was lobbying against any concessions. It was also upsetting that the Bulgarian–Romanian discussions had also begun, even if not without any complications for the other talks. However, some events did indicate the approach of Hungarian–Romanian negotiations, such as Clodius' visit to Bucharest,[87] and the former Romanian ambassador to Budapest Bossy's one-day visit to Budapest to conduct discussions with Teleki. This latter event was immediately considered as an introductory phase to the negotiations.[88]

The Hungarian ambassador to Rome Villani reported on August 9—citing the Duce—the possibility of an upcoming Italian attack on Yugoslavia. The report was substantiated by certain northeastern Italian troop movements.[89] Mussolini did indeed think about an end-of-September operation against Yugoslavia, and instructed his Chief of the General Staff, General Roatta, to draw up the military plans. Following the instructions, Roatta contacted both the German and Hungarian military attachés to discuss military cooperation. Following that, Szabó arrived in Budapest to report and ask for instructions for future reference. Szabó received instructions to offer Hungarian military assistance on behalf of the Prime Minister and the military command in case Italy attacked Yugoslavia, in return for the Italian government's supporting Hungarian territorial demands during the Hungarian–Romanian negotiations.

General Roatta immediately received Szabó upon arriving in Rome on August 12. Roatta was pleased to hear the Hungarian position, and requested that the Hungarian military command appoint the person with whom to start discussions in order to draw up the necessary plans. He also asked Szabó to report the content of their discussions, and requested his consent for the steps to be taken.

To his surprise, the Hungarian military attaché was not favorably received by the Italian leaders. Mussolini did not receive him at all, and Szabó finally managed to meet Ciano only on August 16. As Szabó emphasized in his report to Werth, Ciano "listened to his discourse [about the Romanians' delaying tactics and about the need to make them comply by the threat of war] apathetically." However, "they [the Romanians] well know that the Axis will not let the war happen and, therefore, they will defend their negative positions with all their might during the negotiations." Rumor had it that the case would be taken to conciliation, which was a hopeful development. Ciano commented only on the latter possibility, and said that "the Germans will not want arbitration." Szabó's statements that the Hungarian army could hardly be restrained from taking action, that the impatience of the troops could be curbed only by the Chief of the General Staff's speeches, and that an unfavorable decision "will be followed by an explosion with unimaginable consequences indicating a mood of 'what will be, will be'," did not perturb Ciano either.[90]

Ciano demonstrated slightly greater interest in listening to Szabó's discussion of a common military action. And what Ciano was told would have an impact on cherished future Italian goals. In Szabó's words, the Hungarian General Staff was concerned about a "Balkan catastrophe," including a Yugoslavian–Italian clash. Thus, "starting from a solely theoretical point of view, it is advisable to study the proposed Hungarian armed cooperation within the Yugoslavian context." Then Szabó said that "the Hungarian government would gladly participate in an armed action against Yugoslavia, because the road to Yugoslavia is not across the Carst but across the River Dráva." He stressed that this declaration was made on behalf of the Prime Minister and the Minister of Foreign Affairs, but not on behalf of the General Staff. Obviously, the Hungarian army could not fight on two fronts. Therefore, "the Romanian question must be soon brought to completion, either permanently or temporarily, but in our favor, so that we can withdraw our forces to use against the Yugoslavs." Under such conditions, the majority of the Hungarian military forces could intervene at the proper place and with efficacy that "could initiate the Yugoslavian collapse."

Ciano promised Szabó that he would relay what he had heard to the Duce, but refrained from voicing a definite opinion on the matter, because it was not something that would occur in the immediate future. However, from some of Ciano's unguarded expressions Szabó assumed that, after a successful end of the German operation against Great Britain, the war against Yugoslavia would take place. Although he did not disagree with the idea of a consultative meeting between the two General Staffs, it was Szabó's impression that Ciano "is not sure about the military impact of the offered Hungarian intervention and, therefore, cannot appreciate it properly." He was, however, certain that "when the question is proposed to the Duce, he will fully recognize the value of the support."[91]

Szabó could not have known that, in the meantime, von Ribbentrop had unambiguously informed the Italian ambassador to Berlin, Alfieri, that any planned attack against Yugoslavia or Greece should be dropped. It was Germany's desire that Italy not disturb the Balkan peace while all the German forces were concentrated on crushing Great Britain. Even before that, Ciano had reacted skeptically to Mussolini's plan. He wrote the following in his diary on August 6: "Mussolini speaks a lot about an Italian attack against Yugoslavia to be executed in the second half of September... As for the attack on Yugoslavia, I do not think that Hitler will let the status quo of the Balkans be disturbed unless a new motive emerges."[92]

That the Italians backed down was not unexpected in Hungary. It was the Italian plan that was rather surprising. Hungarian political and military leaders did not know that Germany had earlier taken a position on the Yugoslavian–Italian question in favor of the status quo in the Balkans, with which Mussolini's plan repeatedly collided. There was no sign indicating that the German position had changed. The Hungarian government shaped its relationship with neighboring Yugoslavia in the shadow of a growing German influence there. Similarly, the Yugoslavs strove to develop a good relationship with Hungary. They refrained from any threatening military steps and supported the negotiated solution of the Hungarian–Romanian territorial dispute. This was the situation that made it possible for Hungary, being secured to the south, to deploy its full army at the Romanian border and to prepare for a battle there. The General Staff took this into consideration when drawing up the operational plan against Romania.

Nonetheless, the Hungarian government offered its assistance to Italy and probably considered that during the Hungarian–Romanian discussions, or even should they fail, it was worth luring Mussolini by holding out the prospect of joining a possible Italian attack on Yugoslavia. Similar considerations must have led Werth as well when, despite the German leadership's intentions and risking their reproach, he agreed to a Szabó-type mission aiming at military cooperation and a direct relationship between the General Staffs of Italy and Hungary. Werth was convinced that an Italian–Yugoslavian conflict was quite unlikely, since it went strongly

Mobilization and Deployment against Romania 181

against current German interests. We have good reasons to assume that, even if Teleki had been willing to agree to a separate Italian–Hungarian relationship, Werth and his followers were not likely to have begun serious military preparations without the Germans' knowledge and consent. The question was quickly taken off the agenda without any relevant steps being taken.

After the lengthy waiting period, on August 14 a delegation led by the former Hungarian ambassador to Warsaw, András Hóry, traveled to the site of the negotiations, Turnu-Severin, a place recommended by the Romanian party. The fact that the negotiations had begun at all was solely attributed by the Hungarian military command to the intervention of the Axis Powers.[93]

Two days before the delegation left Budapest, Werth handed over to Csáky the 67-point list of military demands to be achieved during the discussions. The list included compensation for damage caused during the 1919 Romanian occupation. Various institutions and industrial plants, and their equipment, industrial and agricultural products, stocks, and so on, were to be handed over. The Romanian side should make sure that the shipping of these things be not prevented and that they be not destroyed. If they were indeed damaged or destroyed, a specific compensation amount should be set. The Chief of the General Staff also demanded that all the Romanian military constructions, equipment, stores and supplies should be left behind in their entirety, and that "the equipment of military forces should also be given back in proportion to the size of the re-annexed area." This demand was made with reference to the units of the mobilized Romanian army, the border guards and the gendarmerie. A proportional amount of guns, artillery optical equipment, tanks and armored vehicles of mechanized units, along with ammunition, should be handed over, in addition to infantry weapons and ammunition. Moreover, Werth also laid claim to technical, communications and health care equipment, materials, mechanized and horse-drawn vehicles and horses, all in their proper proportions. The list included a part of the pool of the Romanian air force too.⁹⁴ A military committee sent by both parties was to establish the quantity of war materials to be given over, and the mode and time of the transaction. Aside from the insurmountable technical difficulties of executing these transactions, it is unfathomable what political and military considerations Werth assumed would drive or induce the Romanian army, at Hungary's request and in proportion to the re-annexed territories, to voluntarily disarm itself and hand over its equipment. How would he be able to persuade the Romanians at the conference table, and what kind of influence would he have applied to them? Werth also left the probable German reaction out of consideration, since the transaction would have affected a part of the weapons that the Germans had delivered to the Romanians. Under the given circumstances, even raising his demands would have caused the Romanians to balk, and thus led to the breakdown of the talks. The cautious Csáky put Werth's memorandum aside, because he considered that there was hope for a successful negotiation.⁹⁵

Due to the incompatibility of the positions of the two sides, the talks in Turnu-Severin made it increasingly clear that there was no hope for an agreement. The Hungarian government agreed with the Hungarian military that the Romanians were only stalling for time. They did everything that they could politically and, most of all, militarily to reinforce their own rigid position. The General Staff of the Romanian army rejected any agreement and wanted to keep the Transylvanian areas, even at the risk of war. They were so determined that they were ready to sabotage the Romanian government's possible concessions, which, according to rumors, led to a deep rift between the Romanian government and the General Staff. The latter was backed by the Iron Guard, continuously increased its forces in Transylvania, and became increasingly confident.⁹⁶

The Hungarian General Staff watched with concern the growing confidence of the Romanian military command, the appearance of new Romanian troops, and the strengthening of Romanian defenses, all of which decreased the chances of success of a Hungarian attack. They continuously evaluated the strength and quality of the Romanian troops, finding that they were becoming stronger due to foreign arms deliveries as compared to the early July situation, a development unfavorable for Hungary.

The early August analysis about the Romanian army by the Hungarian 2nd General Staff Section[97] concluded favorably for Hungary, establishing that, due to its weaknesses, the Romanian army would not for an extended period of time be able to win a war. After just one or two months of war, Romania would face an unsolvable financial and industrial crisis. This otherwise true statement could not be decisive for the Hungarians to act on, since a Hungarian–Romanian conflict would be a short operation according to the Hungarian General Staff's plans. On the one hand, they considered a longer conflict impossible, due to foreign political reasons. On the other hand, the Hungarian army's industrial base did not make a long war possible.

The Romanian army represented a significant force. Its organization was up-to-date and its degree of training was good, although training with modern war materials had not yet been completed. However, the value of the arms was a significant step forward from the previous situation. "Since early 1939 Romania has received a great quantity of German (Czech), Italian, French and British war materials, which has helped the army to reach unexpected striking power in terms of arms and organization," the report said. Seventy–seventy-five percent of the Romanian army's arms were of modern design. Especially "the arrival of armaments delivered from the Czech protectorate—with Germany's support—had brought the infantry's arms towards uniformity."[98]

The General Staff especially emphasized the point that the Romanians had considerably developed their anti-aircraft capabilities. Almost all of Romania's needs for anti-tank weapons had been met. Furthermore, the Romanian army's artillery showed a "good profile" because, due to German deliveries, significant qualitative and quantitative advances had taken place.

In terms of tanks and airplanes there was a big difference between the two armies. The Romanian modern tank contingence was about 340–350 pieces, while their 500–600 airplanes covered about two thirds of their air force needs.

Mechanization was a serious problem for the Romanian army, although "the mechanized supply of the army corps units, as well as other special units was partly satisfactory, partly basic."[99]

There was, however, one major disadvantage among the many advantages that the Romanian army enjoyed: the military equipment was mostly imported and was composed of several types, especially true for the airplanes. This meant that the spare-part supply was very difficult to keep going, due to blocked British and French imports and due to the underdeveloped Romanian industry. In many instances, this posed unsolvable problems.

Analyzing the Romanian troops' morale, the report of the General Staff stated that "the Romanian soldier is undemanding, obedient and of good military material. However, due to the extended state of 'war without a war' and due to exposure to several disruptive influences, the army's discipline has suffered. Political currents, the differentiation between Transylvania and the Regat, the Bessarabia and Bukovina retreat, a shaken trust in the leaders, the officers' crudeness, and the fact that families at home have not been provided for all have led to the crumbling of the morale of the Romanian troops and have destroyed their resistance." The summary went as far as qualifying ethnic troops as unreliable and not good for fighting, but it cautioned against overestimating factors that looked favorable from the Hungarian point of view, which would be a serious mistake. It could not be ignored that "propaganda boosting the fighting spirit has had its effect on troops originating from the Old Kingdom, and their fighting spirit is high." Therefore, if "Romania fights against only Hungary, one should not completely underestimate the troops' morale." Still, in the case of Hungarian military successes, one could expect a collapse.[100]

Based on what was said, the writers of the summary drew the final conclusion that regarding the soldiers and war materials, the fighting value of the Romanian army reached or surpassed the fighting value of surrounding countries (except for that of the Soviet Union). But in terms of morale, they lagged behind the armies of the surrounding states. This latter statement reflected the dream of the Hungarian military leadership—also spread by their propaganda machine—which dwelled on the lower morale of the Romanian army as opposed to the Hungarian one, which would be of crucial importance in the upcoming military operations. In evaluating the Romanian soldiers they enlarged the negative factors, which they simply ignored in the Hungarians. This was because only the shaky myth of the Hungarian soldier could be compared with the unfavorable change in the relative strengths of the two armies.

The intelligence information of the 2nd General Staff Section could not find anything encouraging to say about the development of the relative power of the two sides. Out of the available 33 infantry divisions and 11 other higher units, the Romanian army would be able to deploy 18–20 divisions and 8 other higher units against Hungary, if the forces left at the Soviet and Bulgarian borders were not counted. Moreover, forces could be withdrawn from there if an agreement were concluded with Bulgaria, which was likely, and due to improved Soviet–Romanian relations.[101]

The situation that had developed in Transylvania by August 25 justified the early August evaluation and forecast. Two days before the planned Hungarian attack on Romania, the following forces were deployed in Transylvania against the Hungarian troops: 16 divisions (out of a total 33), 3 mountain brigades (out of a total 40), 1 fortification brigade (out of a total 1), 1 mechanized brigade (out of a total 2) and 2.5 cavalry divisions (out of a total 4). These forces surpassed the number of Romanian units in Transylvania in the first days of July by 10 divisions, 1.5 cavalry divisions, 2 mountain brigades and a mechanized brigade. Their total strength was 450,000 troops, with new units still arriving.[102]

The Transylvanian Romanian forces were concentrated in the 1st Romanian Army, commanded by General Tzerescu, the former Chief of the General Staff. According to the defense operational plan the army was divided into northern and southern groups as well as army reserves.[103] The northern group, the IV. and the VI. Romanian Army Corps, was under the command of General Ilcusu, a former Minister of Defense, and comprised eight infantry divisions, three mountain brigades and one cavalry brigade (about 32 regiments). By relying with its left wing on the well-developed Carol Line between Érmihályfalva and Nagyvárad, its main task was to confront and eventually to stop—with the help of fortifications in the Szilágyság—the 1st Hungarian Army (28 regiments), advancing in the Szamos Valley, and the 3rd Hungarian Army (12 regiments). Then it was to launch a counterattack against the Hungarian troops that had been stopped and had sustained serious losses. According to Hungarian intelligence, the northern group disposed over 126 light and small tanks.[104] The southern group was concentrated in the Arad region, consisted of five infantry and two cavalry divisions (about 21 regiments) and probably disposed over 150 tanks. Their task was to launch a counterattack against two army corps of the 2nd Hungarian Army (12 regiments), to break into the Trans-Tisza area, to endanger Gyula and Békéscsaba, and to relieve the burdens of the northern group with these actions. The plan was to force the Hungarian forces, halted in the Szamos Valley, to retreat and regroup.[105]

The Romanian troops' superiority was further increased by the strength of their artillery. As opposed to the seven batteries included in a Hungarian brigade, a Romanian division had thirteen batteries, which was a significant difference even if not every Romanian battery was fully manned. Army and army corps artillery units also increased the superiority.

Hungarian reconnaissance learned that about 330 different types of airplanes were landing in Transylvanian airports. About 260 were fighter planes, the rest being bombers and reconnaissance planes. This was a significant force compared with the small Hungarian air force, even if several of the planes were out of order due to problems or missing spare parts.[106]

The Hungarian forces did not possess the military superiority needed for a successful attack. The defenders, relying on the fortifications, had superiority in strength. One should also keep it in mind that while further Romanian forces could be deployed to Transylvania if needed, the Hungarian army did not possess any human or armaments reserves, since the whole Hungarian army had been deployed against Romania.

The Hungarian–Romanian negotiations finally ended without achieving any results. The Hungarian government could not accept the offered 50-kilometer wide border area and population exchange as a basis for further negotiations. Since they had reached a blind alley, the negotiations broke down on August 24. Although the Romanian Committee suggested that the talks go on until August 28, the Hungarian government did not want to engage in futile discussions any longer.

through the defense position of the enemy between Nagykároly and the Szamos River, with a well-concentrated thrust, to defeat the Romanian forces deployed in the Szilágyság, and to reach the Kolozsvár and Dés region in cooperation with the 3rd Army."[109]

The operations of the 1st Army were to be supported by the 3rd Army—the VII. and the VIII. Army Corps and a cavalry brigade—advancing in the direction of Máramarossziget, Nagybánya and Dés. After overcoming the hardship posed by the difficult terrain and reaching the Dés–Beszterce line as soon as possible, the 3rd Army was to attack the right wing of the Romanian forces fighting against the 1st Army and to cooperate with the 1st Army.[110]

Although the Hungarian military operational ideas were correct, they would not work with the forces at hand. Even if the 1st Army—comprising 24 regiments, complemented by two cavalry regiments and two mechanized battalions of the mechanized brigade, and a weak armored force—had managed to break through the fortification line and advance deep into the Romanian defense along the 50-kilometer wide frontline, it would have hardly been able to overcome the far superior Romanian forces deployed there. The situation would not have been much helped by the possible arrival of the 3rd Army, since it might have suffered serious losses in the meantime. Finally, the halted attack would have induced a counterattack of the Romanian forces.

The task of the 2nd Army—the III. and the V. Army Corps—in the south was to fight with delaying tactics with the numerically superior enemy and to prevent it from gaining ground. Later, in parallel with the assumed headway of the 1st Army, it was to attack and occupy Nagyvárad and then to circumvent the Romanian fortification line from the south.[111]

Knowing the size of the Romanian forces facing it, the 2nd Army would have hardly been able to develop a counterattack. Instead, it would have been a success if, within the Békéscsaba–Gyula region, it could have stopped the Romanian attack coming from the Arad region.

Mobilization and Deployment against Romania 191

The troops had to be deployed to the attack on the night of August 26 to 27 and to occupy the designated launching districts so that the attack could be launched along the whole length of the border at dawn on August 28.[112] The attack was to be preceded by Regent Horthy's order to launch the *Honvédség* to liberate Transylvania, due to the imminent danger that the Romanian authority posed to the Transylvanian Hungarians.

After the breakdown of the Turnu-Severin discussions, events accelerated. Csáky informed Erdmannsdorff on August 24 that the discussions had come to a deadlock and had broken down, and that the Hungarian delegation was ready to return to Budapest. Erdmannsdorff conveyed Csáky's announcement to the German Ministry of Foreign Affairs with the remark that, based on his and his Italian colleague's impressions, Hungary would launch a military action around the middle of the following week unless the Axis Powers intervened.[113]

Csáky, who had similar concerns and considerations to Werth's, tried to feel out the German government's reaction following the decision to take military action, and also conveyed the message that he too would favor a solution in Germany's interest. On August 26 he once again sent for the German ambassador and confidentially informed him about the difficult situation that had developed. He was reproached by the Regent and the army for being taken in by the Romanians' delaying tactic, which made it possible for the latter to direct new troops to Transylvania, thereby increasing Hungarian losses in the case of a Hungarian attack. News about the brutal treatment of Hungarian minorities in Transylvania, and unsatisfactory Romanian explanations, strained the situation to breaking point.[114] Csáky also told Erdmannsdorff that the Führer's statement in Munich was thought to have cautioned the Hungarian government about the well-equipped Romanian army, and to have cautioned it due to German interests. The Hungarian government had concluded that it would have a securing the oil resources would be necessary. Hitler was concerned that if the Hungarians crossed the border, the Soviet Union would also launch its own military operation. The German ambassador to Bucharest reported Soviet troop movements along the Romanian border, and the intelligence units of the Germany army gave similar reports.[122] This was a good pretext for Hitler, preoccupied by the plan for Operation Barbarossa, to prepare for the occupation of Romania—a country rich in oil and a good concentration area at the same time.

The news about a possible German military intervention could prove to be a good device to support German diplomatic measures, especially against the Hungarian government, if it did not realize that any conflict in the area would be contrary to Germany's interests. Neither could Germany afford for the Romanian army, a major player in Operation Barbarossa, to waste its forces, equipped with German help, on a fight against the Hungarians, not to mention the expected losses in raw materials and food.

Therefore, on August 28, Hitler ordered the immediate concentration of rapid forces of suitable strength near the Hungarian border, forces that would be transported to Romanian territories by rail and by road, with the agreement of Hungary and Romania and without the use of force. The action was to be executed by using the air force and parachute units as covering forces.[123] He also ordered that forces stationed in Poland should be reinforced: ten divisions were to be transported to the eastern part of the Reich, and two armored divisions, after their armaments were complemented in Germany, were to be transported to the southeasternmost tip of the occupied area. These units were also to stand by for the occupation of the Romanian oil region if the region's defense was necessary.[124] These measures should be considered as preparatory steps for Operation Barbarossa. Consequently, under the pretext of assumed Soviet troop movements and of defending the oil, Hitler did not recoil from executing threatening troop concentrations on the

Mobilization and Deployment against Romania 195

Soviet border. As he said to his immediate circle, he also demonstrated that Germany would not shrink back from anything related to German interests, since Romania was of the utmost importance to Germany. However, preparations should be implemented in such a way that they did not upset the Soviet Union too much.[125]

Complying with Hitler's directives, the High Commands of the *Wehrmacht* and the *Luftwaffe* immediately began preparations, reconciling occupation plans, and concentrating the necessary troops. The XL. Mechanized Army Corps, with two armored divisions and one mechanized division (2nd and 9th Armored Divisions and 13th Mechanized Infantry Division), concentrated near Vienna. The *Luftwaffe* held in readiness a parachute regiment and 270 freight planes to carry them. They were to be deployed to the Ploieşti region.[126]

The units of the XL. Mechanized Army Corps were supposed to reach the Hungarian–Romanian border within three days—as long as they did not come up against any resistance—and to reach the Ploieşti oil region in five days, this having been occupied by the parachutists in the meantime. Ignoring the overcrowded and damaged roads and railways, which would have been exposed to the consequences of a Hungarian–Romanian war, it was planned that wheeled vehicles would reach their targets along two or three routes, while the caterpillars would travel by train.[127]

According to Hitler's August 28 command, preparations had to be completed by August 31 so that the troops could be launched by September 1 if needed. Hitler expedited his military preparations, to emphasize the seriousness of his intentions to the Hungarian and Romanian delegations arriving in Vienna on August 29, and to make them more interested in the discussions. Although the immediate threat of a Hungarian attack had disappeared, the preparations still continued. Jodl, head of the OKW's Operational Section, told the commanders involved in directing the preparations at an August 30 meeting that although an agreement between the tone, he plainly brought it home to the Hungarian ministers that it was in the interest of the Axis Powers to keep peace in the Balkans and to ensure the flow of oil, which would become uncertain in the case of a Hungarian–Romanian conflict. Therefore, there and then everything had to be done to solve the issue. Amidst all the turmoil, neither Hitler nor Ciano were in any position to dedicate too much time to settling the issue. Thus "today the Hungarian government has to express its agreement to unconditionally accepting a conciliator's verdict, so that the verdict can be brought tomorrow."[134] Its rejection would be considered "a dangerous and inexplicable" gesture, which took place when the Axis Powers were involved in heavy fighting. Von Ribbentrop discarded the notion that there might be disagreements with the conciliator, saying that if the conciliator did not propose a viable solution and things continued as before, then Germany would not tolerate that "the oil shipments would sustain even the slightest damage.[135]

Ciano reinforced von Ribbentrop's words and requested that, considering their common interests, the Hungarians unconditionally accept the conciliator's judgment.

Csáky, who appeared to understand and to be ready to unconditionally accept the verdict. Teleki said that Hungary would accept a conciliator's verdict only if it were forced to do so. Then he asked for time to consult with Budapest, and requested that during the consultation he receive both the Regent's and the Council of Ministers' agreements to consent to the intervention of a conciliator.

Although in a more moderate tone, von Ribbentrop also threatened and worked on the unreliable Western-oriented Romanians. In return for their unconditional acceptance of the conciliator's decision, von Ribbentrop held out the prospect of guaranteeing Romania's borders and of sending a German military mission to Romania, as previously requested by King Carol. As Ciano, who also assisted von Ribbentrop in working on the Romanians, wrote in his diary, Manoilescu did not know what to say and was visibly terrified for his country and for himself.[136] He did not know what effect the decision, strongly contrary to Romanian plans, would have in Romania, or how the army, which had been preparing to protect the integrity of the country, would react. By early morning the following day the Romanian Crown Council had given its consent to the unconditional acceptance of the conciliator's decision.

On August 30 in the Belvedere Palace of Vienna, the Second Vienna Award was announced: 43,541 km² were awarded to Hungary, and Romania had to evacuate this area within 14 days. The Hungarian delegation happily acknowledged the decision, which, although not meeting the unrealistic Hungarian idea of re-annexing all of Transylvania as had been suggested by the propaganda machines, nevertheless met Teleki's hoped-for solution of a compromise. However, the mood of the delegation was spoiled by the German ethnic group agreement: all parties had pressure put upon them by Germany to sign this at the same time.

While the Hungarian delegation was happily traveling home, Teleki was considering resignation. The Second Vienna Award marks the failure of his policy toward Transylvania, since it arrived through the Germans and by a conciliatory agreement. What happened was precisely what he had tried to avoid: bargaining had replaced independent Hungarian action. The consequences of this cast a shadow over his joy over re-annexing the Transylvanian territories. He was also informed that General Werth had already announced before the relevant authorities that the Hungarian party would not object to a conciliatory agreement on the Transylvanian question. Teleki felt helpless. He seemed to have been unable to curb various political forces that were contrary to his policies. He was unable to control the military command, which had gradually become a state within the state, had become increasingly influential, and had interfered in major decisions impacting the country in ways contrary to the policy of the country. And Werth was at the head of all those who arrogated rights to themselves far surpassing the sphere of their official role, and this time he had heavily compromised the Hungarian government. Teleki complained to Horthy that "this happened at a time when the government's whole policy was built on the notion that we would not request conciliation, because we hoped that the Romanians would ask for it or that the Axis Powers would express their wish for it. Csáky had told Erdmannsdorff that this statement was contrary to the government's policy. So, once again, we were forced to accept the Chief of the General Staff's political statement."[137]

Notes

1. Raymond James Sontag, et.als., ed., *Documents on German Foreign Policy, 1918–1945* (Washington, 1949–1954), vol. X: p. 22. (21); Országos Levéltár (National Archive, OL). K 64-87-27/a-2653/27/7/1940. Rp.
2. György Ránki, Ervin Pamlényi, Loránt Tilkovszky and Gyula Juhász, eds., *A Wilhelmstrasse és Magyarország: Német diplomáciai iratok Magyarországról, 1933–1944* (The Wilhelmstrasse and Hungary: German Diplomatic Documents about Hungary, 1933–1944) (Budapest, 1968), pp. 327–328. (496)
3. *Ibid.*, pp. 497–498. (329)
4. *Ibid.*
5. *Ibid.*, p. 499. (330)
6. *Ibid.*, p. 500. (330)
7. Hadtörténelmi Levéltár (Military History Archive, HL). Eln. Vkf.1. 1940/3849. 49. sz. tájékoztató (bulletin).
8. Ránki–Pamlényi–Tilkovszky–Juhász, *A Wilhelmstrasse és Magyarország...*, p. 500. (330)
9. HL. IV.hdt. 1940/519/M.
10. HL. Eln. Vkf.1. 1940/3849. 49. sz. tájékoztató.
11. *Ibid.*
12. Sontag, et.als., ed., *Documents on German Foreign Policy...*, vol. X: p. 64. (61)
13. *Ibid.*, p. 76. (69)
14. *Ibid.*, p. 75. (69)
15. *Ibid.*, p. 76. (69)
16. *Ibid.*
17. *Ibid.*, p. 67. (63)
18. Ránki–Pamlényi–Tilkovszky–Juhász, *A Wilhelmstrasse és Magyarország...*, p. 500. (331)
19. *Ibid.*
20. *Ibid.*, p. 502. (332)
21. *Ibid.*, p. 504. (334)
22. *Ibid.*, p. 540. (335)
23. *Ibid.*
24. Sontag, et.als., ed., *Documents on German Foreign Policy...*, vol. X: p. 104. (94)

25. *Ibid.*, p. 117. (105)
26. Gyula Juhász, ed., *Diplomáciai iratok Magyarország külpolitikájához 1936-1945* (Diplomatic Writings on Hungary's Foreign Policy, 1936-1945) (Budapest, 1962-1982), vol. V: p. 292. (171)
27. *Ibid.*, p. 297. (174)
28. *Ibid.*, p. 281. (167)
29. *Ibid.*, p. 282. (167)
30. *Ibid.*, p. 283. (167)
31. *Ibid.*, p. 294. (171)
32. Sontag, et.als., ed., *Documents on German Foreign Policy...*, vol. X: p. 118. (107)
33. Juhász, *Diplomáciai iratok...*, vol. V: pp. 298-306. (175)
34. OL. K 64-85-23-465/1940. Rp.
35. *Ibid.*
36. *Ibid.*
37. *Magyar Katonaújság* (1940) 28.
38. HL. Eln. Vkf.1. 1940/3849. 50, 51. sz. tájékoztató.
39. *Ibid.*, 55. sz. tájékoztató.
40. *Ibid.*, 56. sz. tájékoztató; Vk. Napi jelentések (Daily reports of the General Staff), vol. VII/7 and 8.
41. HL. Eln. Vkf.1. 1940/3849. 57. sz. tájékoztató.
42. *Ibid.*, 50, 51. sz. tájékoztató.
43. *Magyar Katonai Szemle* (1940) 8: p. 315.
44. OL. K 64-88-41-517/1940. Rp.
45. *Ibid.*
46. *Ibid.*
47. *Ibid.*
48. *Ibid.*
49. *Ibid.*
50. Ránki–Pamlényi–Tilkovszky–Juhász, *A Wilhelmstrasse és Magyarország...*, p. 511. (339)
51. Juhász, *Diplomáciai iratok...*, vol. V: p. 344.
52. *Ibid.*, p. 328. (192)
53. Ránki–Pamlényi–Tilkovszky–Juhász, *A Wilhelmstrasse és Magyarország...*, p. 510. (338)
54. *Ibid.*
55. *Ibid.*
56. HL. Eln. Vkf.1. 1940/3502.

57. Domokos Szent-Iványi, *Emlékirat* (Memoirs), Ráday Levéltár (Ráday Archive), Szent-Iványi hagyaték C/80, p. 57.
58. *Ibid.*, p. 58.
59. Sontag, et.als., ed., *Documents on German Foreign Policy...*, vol. X: p. 285. (218)
60. Dezső Saly, *Szigorúan bizalmas* (Strictly Confidential) (Budapest, 1945), pp. 225–226.
61. *Magyar Katonai Szemle* (1940) 8: p. 549.
62. Juhász, *Diplomáciai iratok...*, vol. V: p. 358. (221)
63. HL. Eln. Vkf.1. 1940/3849. 77. sz. tájékoztató.
64. *Ibid.*, 78. sz. tájékoztató.
65. Sontag, et.als., ed., *Documents on German Foreign Policy...*, vol. V: pp. 301–306. (233)
66. *Ibid.*, p. 303.
67. *Ibid.*, pp. 307–316. (234)
68. *Ibid.*, p. 315.
69. *Ibid.*, p. 306. (233)
70. *Ibid.*, p. 314. (234)
71. *Ibid.*, p. 91. (80)
72. *Ibid.*, p. 304. (233)
73. Hugh Gibson, ed., *Ciano naplója: 1939–1943: Gróf Galeazzo Ciano olasz külügyminiszter, 1939–1943 teljes, rövidítés nélküli naplói* (Ciano's Diary: 1939–1943: The Full Diary without Shortening of Count Galeazzo Ciano, Italian Foreign Minister, 1939–1943) (Budapest, 1946), p. 271.
74. Franz Halder, *Kriegstagebuch. Tägliche Aufzeichnungen des Chefs des Generalstabes des Heeres 1939–1942/Generaloberst Halder* (Stuttgart, 1962–1964), vol. II: p. 32.
75. HL. Eln. Vkf.1. 1940/3849. 79, 82. sz. tájékoztató.
76. *Ibid.*, 79, 80. sz. tájékoztató.
77. *Ibid.*, 81. sz. tájékoztató.
78. HL. Eln. Vkf.1. 1940/4536.
79. HL. Eln. Vkf.1. 1940/10413/M. and HL.IV.hadt.79.sz. hdt.parancs
80. HL. Eln. Vkf.1. 1940/3881.
81. HL. HM. Eln. 6.k. 1941/46486.
82. OL. K 37. Teleki-iratok J dosszié. (Teleki documents: Folder J).
83. HL. Eln. Vkf.1. 1940/10660-10662; a 2. gyalogezred iratai. 6. csomó (Documents of the 2nd Infantry Regiment, 6th bundle).

84. HL. Eln. Vkf.1. 1940/3849. 102. sz. tájékoztató.
85. *Ibid.*, 82, 84, 87. sz. tájékoztató.
86. *Ibid.*, 91. sz. tájékoztató.
87. *Ibid.*, 87. sz. tájékoztató.
88. *Ibid.*, 89. sz. tájékoztató.
89. OL. K. 64-1940. Sznlk.
90. Hugh Gibson, ed., *Ciano naplója...*, pp. 273 and 276.
91. OL. K 64-23-1940. Sznlk.
92. *Ibid.*
93. HL. Eln. Vkf.1. 1940/3849. 91. sz. tájékoztató.
94. Juhász, *Diplomáciai iratok...*, vol. V: p. 445. (282)
95. *Ibid.*, p. 438.
96. HL. Eln. Vkf.1. 1940/3849. 105, 107. sz. tájékoztató.
97. HL. Eln. Vkf.2. 1940. Sznlk.
98. *Ibid.*
99. *Ibid.*
100. *Ibid.*
101. *Ibid.*
102. HL. Eln. Vkf.1. 1940/3849. 109. sz. tájékoztató.
103. *Ibid.*, 110. sz. tájékoztató.
104. HL. Vk. Napi jelentések összesített adatai (Summary data of the General Staff's daily reports).
105. *Ibid.*
106. *Ibid.*
107. Carlile Aylmer Macartney, *October Fifteenth. A History of Modern Hungary , 1929-1945* (Edinburgh: Edinburgh University Press, 1961), vol. I: p. 417.
108. HL. Főv.hdm. 40/600.
109. *Ibid.*
110. *Ibid.*
111. *Ibid.*
112. HL. 390/2.hds.I.a.40 and 320/2.dd.I.a.40.
113. Sontag, et.als., ed., *Documents on German Foreign Policy...*, vol. X: p. 534. (384)
114. *Ibid.*, p. 543.
115. *Ibid.*, p. 544.
116. Ránki–Pamlényi–Tilkovszky–Juhász, *A Wilhelmstrasse és Magyarország...*, p. 515. (343)

117. Sontag, et.als., ed., *Documents on German Foreign Policy...*, vol. X: p. 508. (314)
118. *Ibid.*, p. 527. (318)
119. *Ibid.*, pp. 553–555. (400); Ránki–Pamlényi–Tilkovszky–Juhász, *A Wilhelmstrasse és Magyarország...*, pp. 514–515. (343)
120. *Ibid.*, p. 515.
121. Halder, *Kriegstagebuch...*, vol. II: p. 78.
122. Percy Schramm, ed., *Kriegstagebuch des Oberkommandos der Wehrmacht (Wehrmachtführungsstab), 1940–1945* (Frankfurt am Main, 1961–1979), vol. I: p. 48.
123. Sontag, et.als., ed., *Documents on German Foreign Policy...*, vol. X: p. 566. (407); Halder, *Kriegstagebuch...*, vol. II: p. 80.
124. Sontag, et.als., ed., *Documents on German Foreign Policy...*, vol. X: p. 549. (396)
125. Halder, *Kriegstagebuch...*, vol. II: pp. 79 and 83.
126. *Ibid.*, vol. II: p. 80.
127. Schramm, ed., *Kriegstagebuch des Oberkommandos...*, vol. I: pp. 51–52.
128. *Ibid.*, p. 51.
129. *Ibid.*, p. 56.
130. Hugh Gibson, ed., *Ciano naplója...*, p. 278.
131. Ránki–Pamlényi–Tilkovszky–Juhász, *A Wilhelmstrasse és Magyarország...*, pp. 516–519; Sontag, et.als., ed., *Documents on German Foreign Policy...*, vol. X: pp. 566–570. (407)
132. Hugh Gibson, ed., *Ciano naplója...*, p. 279.
133. *Ibid.*
134. Ránki–Pamlényi–Tilkovszky–Juhász, *A Wilhelmstrasse és Magyarország...*, p. 522. (347); Sontag, et.als., ed., *Documents on German Foreign Policy...*, vol. X: pp. 576–580. (410)
135. *Ibid.*, p. 524. (374)
136. Hugh Gibson, ed., *Ciano naplója...*, p. 279.
137. OL. K. 589.I.B.

Part II

HUNGARY ENTERS WORLD WAR II

ANTAGONISM BETWEEN THE MILITARY LEADERSHIP AND THE GOVERNMENT REGARDING THE FURTHER DEVELOPMENT OF MILITARY POLICY

On September 1 Prime Minister Pál Teleki wrote a letter to Horthy offering to resign. The Regent did not accept the resignation, hoping that Teleki's conflict with Werth could be ironed out. Horthy intended to continue to rely on Teleki against the growing pressure from the extreme right, and to pursue a cautious foreign political course that would not alienate the Anglo-Saxon powers in case Germany was indeed not able to create a new European order. Meanwhile, as supreme warlord—that is, supreme commander of the country, but not of the army, since with the abolition of the Army Supreme Command (*Honvédség Főparancsnoksága*) that function now belonged to the Chief of the General Staff—he intended to support the ambitions of the military leaders—in line with his traditional bias towards the army—and protect them against even Teleki.

Horthy continued to consider Werth a well-trained soldier and a good man, one whom he respected and whom he allowed to convince him about things even contrary to Teleki's advice. The German army's successes and Hungary's territorial reannexations, with Transylvania as the most recent example, which had finally materialized due to German help, all seemed to reinforce the increasingly appealing pro-German foreign policy and corresponding military policy that Werth personally represented. All these factors help to explain Horthy's responsiveness towards Werth's demands on behalf of the army and his weakening resistance towards him. Also, by Werth's intervention, by pursuing a pro-German policy, and by acknowledging and supporting the officer corps' desire to play a role in national politics, Horthy was able to keep the increasingly extreme right-wing officer corps on his side. Thus he hoped to curb the advance of elements within the army that posed the danger of an extreme right-wing takeover in the government.

Werth found it reasonable that the supreme warlord, supported and protected the ambitions of the army, which he also represented, even if not at the measure and speed demanded by the situation, since Horthy was also greatly influenced by Teleki-type politicians. Their face-to-face encounters reinforced Werth's belief that his ideas were not too far from those of Horthy. Since events increasingly justified his views, Werth hoped that he could count on Horthy's growing support against Teleki in the future. Werth understood the intimacy of the friendship between Horthy and Teleki, and the role that Teleki played in the political arena of the regime. He also was well aware of the limitations of his own scope of action. Consequently, it seems probable that he never took a strong line against Teleki in front of Horthy. With or without Teleki, he wanted to serve Horthy, and it seemed that the most reasonable way to do so was to go along with the Germans.

Teleki knew well the cause of Horthy's permissiveness, his political concerns, and his need to keep a hand on the military command's aspirations, so that he could turn them to his own use and reinforce his rule. Yet Teleki also saw the dangers of such a policy and wanted to protect the Regent. Werth, whom he despised, and the military leaders lining up behind him were becoming the tools and servants of external and internal forces whose coming to power might be fatal to the country and might sweep Hungarian political life in a direction contrary to the established lawful system, a course that the Regent would not be able to change.

Teleki justified his resignation by saying that in the current tense situation political power should be in the hands of someone who enjoyed the Regent's trust and who "will possess the actual rights of a prime minister and conducts himself in that way." He concluded that "I am probably not suitable for this role, because I have let the military grow on me and, therefore, have less prestige than a new person would have... The new person, whether a military man or civilian, should have your full confidence. That is why—and for this reason only—I have Werth or Lajos Fischer in mind. Otherwise I am far from considering them capable of leading a country, and especially not ours in the present situation. My feelings are the same about Sztójay, who otherwise would be appealing for the Germans and is a military man."[1] He also cautioned Horthy about the dangers of a military dictatorship, which would become a threatening reality under Werth's or Sztójay's leadership, since it was contrary to Hungary's future interests. Finally, Teleki recommended Minister of the Interior Ferenc Keresztes-Fischer, who agreed with all his views.

When Teleki, with wounded pride, emphasized "full confidence" to the Regent, he alluded to the role that Horthy had played in ironing out controversies between Werth and himself, in which he experienced the often exaggerated manifestations of the Regent's confidence in Werth. He also cautioned the Regent about this for future reference: "I would not recommend reconciliation by the head of state when it is done all the time and in every manner of issue... I would not recommend that the head of state be exposed to every issue, whether domestic and administrative or foreign political, because this might lead to dangerous situations."[2]

Teleki also emphasized the fact that he had not spoken up before about the situation between Werth and himself, so that it would not seem as though he harbored any personal antipathy towards Werth. He was sorry to leave, because of his worry about the future of the country: "This is why I have persisted so far and disregarded all these difficulties. This is why I have allowed things to go this far or allowed them to stay this way. But whenever I wanted to say something I was never given the last word against the soldiers, that is, against the Chief of the General Staff. Yet it is my obligation in this position to serve my homeland and my Regent, with whom I am on friendly terms, and to stand ready. However, tasks have multiplied by now and I no longer feel strong enough to face these tasks under such unclear and uncertain circumstances."[3]

On the following day Teleki wrote Horthy another letter, stating the reasons for his resignation in detail and calling attention to the increasing influence that the army exercised over the civilian government.

He stated that after eighteen months of patience he felt fully responsible to declare that "at the present time in Hungary there are two governmental administrations and two governments: one of them is the legal one, and the other one is the military government, this latter expanding into every branch of the administration, while the legal government can neither see nor control its operations." With patience and tact "I have been able to get by among all these difficulties, although I could not stave off numerous harmful effects on the administration and especially on our economic life."[4] One could not responsibly lead under such circumstances. Under such complicated circumstances a new prime minister would be able to act responsibly if he held all the problems in his hands and if, "except for exercising the rights of the Supreme Warlord, he will be the principal actor in every other way."[5]

Teleki felt obliged to speak about the issue of exercising the supreme warlord's rights, in order to reassure the Regent, because just by mentioning it "I seem to have created doubts and fears in Your Grace."[6] Horthy had always rigidly rejected any real or imagined threat to his rights as supreme warlord. He mostly watched out for extra-military political ambitions and political groups, since that was where he had expected threats of a violation of his rights to materialize. He exercised his right as supreme warlord through the military leadership and, more specifically, through the Chief of the

General Staff, who was subordinated directly and exclusively to Horthy and who had to report to him. Anything overstepping the army's boundaries had to originate with the Chief of the General Staff, which would have hardly been possible without at least the silent consent of the Regent. Therefore, Teleki's attack on the Chief of the General Staff's and other military leaders' transgressions directly affected the Regent.

By respecting the supreme warlord's rights and by clarifying the legal boundaries of those rights Teleki tried to point out that Werth and his cronies had abused the Regent's good faith when they intervened in politics on his behalf and in a way that far surpassed the realm of their rights. Teleki asserted that legally "in both peace and war, commanding the army and issues related to the army's internal organization and command are among the supreme warlord's rights and, consequently, these issues are dealt with by the head of state personally, by leaving out the higher-level government." Still, the government was responsible to Parliament "for issues connected with it." However, "it is only the legal government that should deal with all the army activities connected or relating to governing and administrating the state."[7]

Mobilizing personnel and material resources during preparations for war made it unavoidable that the army would acquire a direct role in several areas of state administration, such as control of wartime production, military intelligence and sabotage, registration of popular movements, and so on. This role, however, did not mean the development of an independent military administration. Instead, it would mean the representation and promotion of military interests in different ministries. Army officers undertaking these tasks should be subordinated to their military superiors with regard to disciplinary and personnel issues, yet with regard to their functions in administration they should be under the direction of the relevant minister. If disputes did occur, they should be dealt with by the Minister of Defense, and the relevant government administrator.

In Teleki's view, economic and political actions initiated by the military leadership without the government's knowledge and by circumventing its goals were especially dangerous and produced very unpleasant situations. The military department of the Ministry of Industry was a glaring example of how the military had gained territory and independence in directing industry. This department had expanded from a simple military desk into one employing 100 people, mostly military, under the supervision of both the Minister of Industry and the Minister of Defense, producing a humiliating situation for the government, "a situation which cannot be reconciled with ministerial responsibility, is untenable, and is flagrantly illegal." The two ministers' spheres of responsibility in supervising the department had been blurred.[8] This department sometimes showed up under the Ministry of Defense and again at other times under the Ministry of Industry, which caused confusion. (It was officially the 17th Section of Military Industry at the Ministry of Industry and the 17th Section at the Ministry of Defense.) It often overstepped its boundaries. For example, in Berlin, while conducting negotiations about military orders on behalf of the Minister of Defense, the discussions trespassed into the area of foreign trade, "established export and import agreements which belong to the spheres of authority of the Ministers of Foreign Trade, of Trade and of Industry, while the agreement had not even been acknowledged by the respective ministries." Finally, the agreement could not be revoked during the Hungarian–German economic discussions.[9] With Werth looming safely in the background, Minister of Defense Károly Bartha had not bothered to discuss his initiatives and arrangements necessary for military developments with other government organs, considering post-facto information to them to be sufficient.

Teleki also spoke about factories that had their internal operation disturbed by the Ministry of Defense's unnecessary administrative requests, supervision and increasing interference in their basic functions. The Ministry of Defense declared more factories than necessary as military facilities in order to expand its influence.[10] He also raised complaints about the actions of inadequately trained and overbearing military commanders whose sphere of authority had not been well defined. They would venture out into areas of factory management that they did not understand, thereby disturbing the workflow. They organized workers on a military basis, and held interrogations, which kept people away from production work. Finally, since the commanders belonged to the management of upper military commands, they withdrew themselves from civilian control.[11]

Teleki also raised the complaint that the military authorities often dealt with social-political problems in the factories, thereby interfering in production in a way that did not increase product but rather was instrumental in causing restlessness among the workers, including helping to drive up wage demands. Factory military commanders were at the forefront of this type of activity and increasing numbers of notifications had come in against them. He wrote that "they interfere in workers' issues, support wage demands, and, due to their operations, cause wage hikes to be implemented contrary to the intention of management."[12]

In order to stop difficulties within the Military Industrial Department of the Ministry of Industry, Teleki proposed that the Department be placed under the supervision of the Minister of Industry and that its inflated sphere of influence be downsized.[13] Accepting this proposal amidst the ongoing armament project could have been done by forcing back the military's increasing influence and role within the country and by transforming the established military-industrial structure. This would have led to confrontations between the Prime Minister and the military, something that Horthy believed was unacceptable and unnecessary.

Accusations about the army's superficial and wasteful economic activities occupied a central place in Teleki's letter. The government was responsible for providing material tools at the military's disposal, but it should also be aware of how the army used them. Even in this area the military demanded different treatment. Quoting defense sources, he wrote that the military applied for loans excessively and overspent its resources, while letting necessities go uncovered and withholding information about it all. The Minister of Defense behaved as if he had been insulted when the Prime Minister approached him to request the needed information. A careful budget would preclude the possibilities of events occurring such as what happened the day after the recent military budget had been passed: the army had asked for 28 million pengős for car purchases, which, unfortunately, had been left out of the budget: "The general who came to see me spoke about the 28 million in the manner in which I speak about a matchbox. When we are utilizing the country's economic capacity to its utmost, such events should not occur, in my view."[14] The Prime Minister had noticed similar carelessness when he discovered that the military command had calculated on enough ammunition to last only a month. He had noticed this the previous fall, when he had looked through the ammunition orders at the request of the Minister of Defense.

Teleki considered unnecessary and forced industrial investments aggressively pursued by military institutions to be improper. Scandals like the one at the Diósgyőr gun factory of the *MÁVAG* should not happen again. The director of the factory was obliged to establish increases in production capacity not underpinned by proper orders, leading to deficits at the factory. When the Ministry of Finance initiated an investigation and wanted to hold the leaders responsible, Werth personally intervened for them and stated that they had only fulfilled their patriotic duty towards the army, but then demanded that the process be terminated and that the deficit be paid by state monies.[15]

Teleki was also unhappily affected by the army's illegal foreign political activities. He had been irritated by the military attachés' activities ever since he first occupied office as Prime Minister, but he was even more irritated by the connections that Werth and Bartha kept with the German army and other governmental organs. The officers provided information to their German colleagues when they visited Germany and were eager to be at their service when the Germans visited Budapest. He admitted in his letter that it was unavoidable that the military command receive information and give instructions via its own military attachés. This, however, could not be "a foreign political operation that is divergent, different, or follows a different path from the foreign policy of the government, one every aspect of which is not even known by the Minister of Foreign Affairs." Thus, it followed that the political information of these reports should be known to the government. Furthermore, the instructions given to the military attachés "should be issued only in agreement with the government and with the foreknowledge of the Prime Minister and the Minister of Foreign Affairs."[16] Yet until the spring of that year neither Teleki nor the Minister of Foreign Affairs had received any reports about the activities of the military attachés. Since then the 2nd Section of the General Staff had sent only summary reports, which did not contain insights into the full reports or contain the Chief of the General Staff's instructions of a political nature sent to the attachés.[17]

On several occasions there were General Staff-level discussions with the Germans without either asking the permission of the Prime Minister or the Minister of Foreign Affairs or informing them about the details of the discussions. Otherwise, the results were brought to their attention only much later. On several instances the General Staff's information was different from the well-known position of the government. This created suspicion in the Germans' minds about the Hungarian government. An example was Werth's most recent statement on the issue of mediation, which "did not serve well our later diplomatic efforts... which was again a fact which could only be repaired with much work and, perhaps, through damaging our own interests."[18]

Teleki finally spoke about the necessity of improving cooperation between the Ministry of Defense, the General Staff and civilian organizations. A change was necessary in the atmosphere created in the officer corps and, more closely, in the General Staff. The Prime Minister asked the Regent, in his own way and measure, to call it to the attention of the army's commanders that military issues outside the realm of the Regent's authority "should be managed by the government, and everyone who is connected to the government or other areas of the administration is obliged to follow the government's instructions and is subordinated to them. And the same should be emphasized about political activities as well, whether it is internal or foreign policy—and the latter is to be stressed. In this respect, both the military and the General Staff should be subordinate to the Prime Minister."[19]

The Regent attributed Teleki's resignation to his desperation in the current situation as well as to his poor nervous disposition. He managed to dissuade Teleki from his resignation by promising that he would take his complaints into consideration and by describing the almost unsolvable situation to his good friend. Amidst the festivities following the Second Vienna Award, it would have been difficult to explain a government crisis or the departure of a prime minister who was now considered the father of the successful revision policy and who was celebrated for the results. Furthermore, it would be hard to explain his absence from the celebratory events to the public, and to the Axis Powers, who were counting on Hungary's gratitude for the Award. The most difficult part for Horthy was to make Werth's and Bartha's remaining in office acceptable to the Prime Minister, who saw the source of his problems in them. He must have tried to reassure Teleki that he would change his lenient attitude towards the military, promised to settle the military's relationship with the government, and agreed to clarify different views in the governing elite. The Regent must have reasoned that changes at the head of the army would cause trouble and restlessness there, and that it would be difficult to justify any changes to the officer corps, so satisfied with its leaders.

Horthy must have considered Teleki's complaints about the military to be attributable to forgivable sins on their part, consequences of their ambition in preparing the army and their own inexperience in those issues that needed to be remedied but did not call for radical personnel changes. There was certainly no need for those leaders with whom Horthy was actually satisfied to leave. And he could not discount the lack of comprehension that such changes—as well as Teleki's own departure—would create in German political and military circles.

There were more overarching issues to consider. The development of the army and the mobilization of the country's resources in such a tense situation were things that Teleki simply had to accept. Both the army's development and mobilization continued at an accelerated pace from the fall of 1939 onwards, when the government, authorized precisely by the national defense law (II of 1939), announced extraordinary measures. In fact, it would have been difficult to clearly separate a number of important issues, dealing with army organization, the military organizations' preparation for war, and the associated work that was done under the direction of the Chief of the General Staff but fell within the rights of the Regent, from issues and work areas under the authority of the Minister of Defense and controlled by the government. The goal of clearly separating such issues would have hindered and delayed war preparations even if a will to accomplish this had existed among the military leaders. However, the military leaders did not want to deal with it; their ambition was to complete the country's total mobilization along a German pattern and with Horthy's full consent. They believed that this was how the army's shortcomings in armaments could be made up. Teleki considered such aspirations for totality to be dangerous, and spoke up about it, but then found it difficult to disagree with the military leaders' argument of trying to create the conditions for independent action, since it was a principle that he also advocated. He had come up against an unsolvable task: to curb and to stop a process moving in an undesirable direction and slipping out of control.

Werth had counted on Teleki's actions, but also knew that he still had the Regent's confidence, and so did not change his position. Yet he was troubled by the prospect that Teleki was attempting to have him demoted. Teleki might succeed, but only if he offered a suitable person for the position of Chief of the General Staff, and there was no one else but Vilmos Nagybaczoni Nagy. Although Nagy's nomination to the position of Chief of the General Staff had been ignored by the Regent earlier, because Jenő Rátz, an Imrédy protege, had recommended him, Werth still considered him a rival. Although he entrusted Nagy with the command of the 1st Hungarian Army, which was to undertake the most important part of the planned operation, this did still not prevent Werth from denigrating Nagy in front of the Regent. It also came in handy that General Nagy once again could be compromised for sympathizing with Imrédy, the same "sin" that had harmed his reputation with Horthy previously. Werth hoped that by putting his only potential rival out of the way he had averted that danger for good. Teleki would not be able to come up with a suitable person for Werth's position. Therefore, he would have to continue to cooperate with him during the coming time period, which would lead to the justification of his policy over Teleki's.

Rátz's private letter in July, saying that Imrédy was attached as a reserve officer and train commander to the 1st Hungarian Army, reached Nagy at the Army Headquarters in Sóstó, near Nyíregyháza. Rátz asked Nagy to assign Imrédy to the Army Headquarters and to assign him to a suitable position, appropriate to his previous government role.[20] Nagy satisfied the request, because he did not think that a former prime minister could be left in an insignificant position. He also began to take Imrédy along on parades. However, when the Regent was informed about the development, he ordered Nagy to Gödöllő. Horthy reproached Nagy, claiming that Imrédy was using his position for political activism among the officers. He ordered the surprised Nagy to prevent it from happening and to report to him about his further observations.[21] Returning back to Sóstó, Nagy testified that he had to admit what those around him had long known, that Imrédy, along with extreme right-wing politician Antal Kunder, had campaigned both among the officers and civilians in order to recruit members to his party organization. And this was the direct cause for Vilmos Nagybaczoni Nagy's retirement, which happened very soon after that in January 1941 and which Werth urged.[22] Werth also acted to make Nagy's life unpleasant with petty difficulties during the occupation of Transylvania and during his service following that.[23]

According to plan, Hungary took possession of the re-annexed Transylvanian territories between September 5 and 13. The *honvéd*s were happily celebrated by the local Hungarian population. The infantry units were forced to work extra hard along the bad and dusty roads in order to keep to the prescribed marching goals. The mechanized and cavalry units were the first to arrive at the furthest point—the Székely land—by the given date. The Regent himself and other members of the government also participated in the festive takeover of the largest cities.

The Transylvanian re-annexation festivities and celebrations were still going on when Hitler handed the "bill" to the Hungarian government. When Sztójay gave Hitler Horthy's grateful note on September 10, Hitler immediately grasped the opportunity to warn him about the obligatory gratitude and suitable behavior expected from Hungary. The solution arrived at by the conciliators, which had proved too difficult to convince the Romanians to accept, should satisfy the Hungarian government. Hitler said that he was for the Hungarians with all his heart, but that the need to avoid a Romanian collapse, and to keep the oil resources safe, argued for the division of Transylvania. The victory of the Axis Powers was now of primary significance for Hungary, since the opposite might endanger whatever it had so far won.

Then Hitler set out to describe Germany's situation. He blamed the weather for delays in operations against Great Britain. The proper time should be awaited to destroy the enemy. He had all the necessary tools available, but the economic issues involved should not be neglected either. So, even if it was not a question of life and death, the Romanian oilfields still created an important reserve for the Axis, and setting them on fire would lead to a significant strengthening of the British resistance. In spite of increasing German domestic oil production, the Romanian oil was still a significant factor, which Hitler wanted to secure via "a reconciliation policy in the Balkans." Although it caused problems, he still had to give guarantees for Romania's territorial integrity. Without them the Romanians would not have submitted themselves to the negotiators' decision. Except for the oil nothing else forced him to support Romania, which had "pursued a treacherous policy in the recent past."[24] He fulminated against King Carol as being an unreliable man with whom he—Hitler—had never established any kind of personal relationship. Now the new Romanian dictator General Ion Antonescu would most possibly side with the Axis. In any case, he and the Duce had decided to protect the Romanian oil region. He wanted Hungary's understanding and the recognition of what would have happened if Romania had collapsed and "the East had marched into this area with no foreseeable end." During the course of the conversation Hitler was gradually taken up in describing the issue of the Romanian oilfields, and upgraded it from a complementary factor to a decisive one. Sztójay perceived that Germany would take certain steps in order to secure the oil, and that this would once again bring up the question of German military transit across Hungary, while the obliged and grateful Hungarian ally could not disagree.

During the conversation Hitler also brought up the question of ethnic Germans in Hungary, and advised the Hungarians that it was in their own self-interest to treat them well. Sztójay felt authorized to assure Hitler that, as was evident from the Regent's letter, Hungary was 100% on the Axis side and would act in the spirit of their common fate: "[Hungary] is ready to share your fate even if it has to submit itself to limitations. This cooperation has both a political and an ideological base, reinforced by camaraderie, which is especially true for the soldiers. It cannot be denied that German soldiers and officers who stay in Hungary feel completely at home there."[25] Hungary understood both the German–Romanian relationship and the importance of the oil, and would strive to establish a good relationship with Romania.

In his report to his Minister of Foreign Affairs, Sztójay did not limit himself to describing his conversation with Hitler; he also offered his own opinion on the meeting. Sztójay said that he believed that Hitler would have given the larger part of Transylvania to Hungary had he been able, but now he asked for understanding because "external causes, outside his control, limit his decision." Anyway, he seemed to take a hint from what Hitler said with regard to the Hungarian–Romanian border, which could not be considered final, in spite of the guarantees.[26] Sztójay advised Horthy and the government to be satisfied with the Award, to take a pro-German stand void of critical comments, to avoid endangering the peace of southeastern Europe, and to show the maximum amount of leniency to Germany possible for the sake of further territorial gains. He would find it useful—and he had already mentioned this in his report of September 6[27]—if Hungary declared that it wanted to join the Axis more tightly both militarily and politically. This could always be cited to encourage the Germans.[28]

Sztójay also elaborated on the connection between the *Honvédség* and the German army. He suggested "that, by all means, the relationship between the two armies be further deepened on the basis of total honesty and further military cooperation. In my view, the potential for that exists. The prestige of the *Honvédség*, which was once again damaged after the Czech crisis, has been restored due to its present behavior and fighting spirit."[29]

Finally, in order to sustain his encouragement to support the German connections, he several times elaborated on the speedy strengthening and invincibility of the German army during the weeks following the Second Vienna Award. Sooner or later Great Britain would be broken by the bombings, and Churchill's policy would be shaken. It seemed as if the planned German invasion was playing a secondary role, although everything had been prepared for it, and the Germans might not even wait for the full effect of the bombs. In Sztójay's view the reserves of the German army made it capable of successfully solving other problems in addition to the war against Great Britain.[30]

While trying to smoothly execute the complex task of moving into Transylvania, the General Staff also watched for signals coming from Berlin that might match their own ideas. They did not question Germany's plan to guarantee the crucial Romanian oil through peace in the Balkans, even at the expense of confrontation with the Soviet Union. This would entail settling and solidifying the German–Romanian relationship, including the German occupation of Romania, which would be a decisive factor in the pursued Hungarian policy.

Based on the above considerations, with much curiosity the military analyzed news about the military coup in Romania and how the situation there developed. In its view the Romanian leadership had been taken over by a strong military man in the person of General Antonescu, former Minister of National Defense and Chief of the General Staff, who was now the actual head of state after thoroughly shrinking the sphere of authority of King Michael, who had succeeded the deposed King Carol. In the Hungarian military's view, Antonescu, who was closely connected with the Iron Guard, would surely come to an agreement with Horia Sima, the Iron Guard's leading figure, and, while assuming a completely pro-German line, would solidify his regime through it.[31]

Events proved their prognosis correct. Antonescu immediately set out to reorganize the Romanian army. He demoted twelve generals and appointed reliable replacements from his own clique to the most important positions. He did not hesitate to make connections with Germany and, by holding out the prospect of far-reaching concessions, tried to gain its political support and help in reorganizing the Romanian army.

Antonescu's policy led to the appearance of German training teams in Romania within a few weeks, and the Hungarian leadership drew the conclusion from this that the Romanian dictator's main ambition was to become appreciated by the Germans in order to support his counter-revisionist goals. Thus, the Hungarians should counterbalance this with an adequate pro-Axis policy and with the maintenance of a combat-ready armed force. It did not exclude the possibility of a Romanian armed action in order to re-annex Transylvania, based on merits gained with the Germans in the meantime, or even against German opposition. With German help the Romanian army would be strengthened in every field: organization, training and material.

Besides the Romanian question, the Hungarian military leadership also counted on the unraveling of the German–Soviet agreement about the Balkans, which might escalate into an armed confrontation in which Germany would surely count on Hungary in addition to Romania. Germany would bring Bulgaria and Yugoslavia under its influence, and if they did not give in to

German pressure, they would be occupied. At this point Hungary could immediately offer its help in the hope of another gain in territory, as Werth had already elaborated.

The above military calculation led to demands for further aggressive development of the *Honvédség,* which was in opposition to Teleki's continued policy of advocating armed neutrality. Teleki hoped that he would have the chance at least partially to remedy the country's difficult economic situation, the result of the accelerated armaments policy. He was also wrapped up with concerns about the problems relating to the social and economic re-integration of Transylvania. He did not see any possibilities for new territorial gains. Neither did he plan to extend a significant investment loan to the army, which provoked protests from the military, who viewed the rejection as endangering its ideas relating to the further necessary development of the *Honvédség*. This further deepened the antagonism between the Prime Minister and the military leaders.

Horthy postponed trying to iron out the discord, citing his preoccupation with the Transylvanian takeover. But Teleki could not wait any longer and asked for an audience with Horthy on September 27. He warned Horthy about the troubled relationship between him and the military, which was aggravated by the request for a new so-called Transylvanian army development loan.

Minister of Defense Bartha was surprised to hear that the Prime Minister wanted to have information about how the loan would be used. Teleki informed Bartha about his visit to Horthy. In his letter of response to Teleki on September 28 Bartha indicated that he thought that Teleki's request indicated a lack of trust in him. He felt that Teleki was asking "to terminate the Minister of Defense's special right of a certain freedom of disposal within the framework of the budget and within the overall parameters of the defense portfolio, which he can switch at his discretion according to need." Bartha read the Prime Minister's request as implying that "the Minister of Defense might utilize this possibility to develop the *Honvédség* in a direction that does not correspond to the government's intentions."[32] Bartha seemed to be inclined to give more detailed information about the *Honvédség*'s financial affairs, but also noted to Teleki that "a full and detailed overview and control of such a complicated budget based on reports required by Your Excellency is hardly possible, and Your Excellency will gain reassurances only if you are fully convinced that the reports of your Minister of Defense honestly reflect the real situation."[33] Bartha raised the issue of confidence and noted that a personal change in the job of the Minister of Defense "now, when the *Honvédség* is to prepare for new tasks, will not be a shock from any aspect, and I do not have to be concerned that anyone would come to an unfavorable conclusion about me due to such a change."[34]

Teleki immediately responded that he was sorry that Bartha had "immediately raised the issue of confidence," although Teleki said that he had not given any reason for it based on his cooperation with him and other ministers given with full confidence. What he asked for, he believed, "is not only the most elementary right of a prime minister, but is also his most elementary obligation, because a prime minister has to have an overview of the whole government of the country, and for that he has to see clearly the main features of operations and administrations of all the ministries... If he does not do that, there is not much sense in his being prime minister."[35] At present, neither Teleki nor the Minister of Finance had enough information about the use of the defense budget, and if he was not informed about everything, he would not be able to hold together the affairs of the country responsibly. Finally, he also spoke out against the army's aspirations for independence: "Today, in this social crisis, when state administration also means social administration, it is every citizen's obligation to get closer to each other. This obviously includes the officer corps, because if it does not, and the officer corps follows a separate path, then the view here—as well as in economic issues—is justified that without concentration the military is a state within the state and that there are two governments, a civilian one and a military one."36

Horthy did not postpone acting to clarify the situation. He asked for Bartha on September 29. Bartha reassured him that, contrary to practice so far, in which he had given only the Minister of Finance a rough outline of the use of the defense budgets and loans, he would also now inform the Prime Minister continuously and in detail about the defense budget and different expenses, while respecting his own constitutional rights and obligations.37

Teleki was deeply distressed by the unchanged hopeless situation between him and the military. In October he complained to Ministerial Counselor Szent-Iványi, who had called his attention to the dangers of the military's following a separate path, that "he could not change the situation yet. Others had also called his attention to these dangers, but he could not do anything but follow his own path, whereby he does not want to achieve anything for himself."38

Werth felt that he himself and his aspirations were safe against Teleki and safe with Horthy, who had stuck by him. Yet, similarly to Horthy, he also did not wish for Teleki's or his government's downfall. He did not find Imrédy, whose name came up as a potential prime minister during the fall of 1940, appealing either. Recent events had convinced Werth that Teleki would not be able to oppose the increasing pro-German obligation felt by Hungary and, therefore, he would hardly be able to hinder Werth's pursuing his own military goals. The Germans would have to be assured, possibly with action, about the unconditional loyalty of the Hungarian military leaders, and convinced that a more reliable leadership from the corps of generals and officers than the present ones could not be conjured up even if there were a potential change in government. Werth was highly troubled by a confidential report indicating that in the case of a regime change Imrédy—a trusted friend of the Germans—and his party "would give the state administration into the hands of a military committee of high-ranking officers."[39] He had reasons to suspect that Imrédy would not appoint him as Chief of the General Staff, but instead ask Horthy for his immediate retirement. This report, which most probably came from police organs, listed quite a few officers who were followers and sympathizers of Imrédy, a fact confirmed by Ujszászy. Several of them were retired but could be reactivated at any time. The majority, though, were in active service, and Imrédy got acquainted with most of them during his military service in the summer of 1940.[40]

Notes

1. *Horthy Miklós titkos iratai* (Miklós Horthy's Secret Writings), ed. Miklós Szinai and László Szűcs, (Budapest, 1962), p. 233.
2. *Ibid.*
3. *Ibid.*
4. *Ibid.*, p. 238.
5. *Ibid.*, p. 239.
6. *Ibid.*
7. *Ibid.*
8. *Ibid.*, p. 240.
9. *Ibid.*, p. 241.
10. *Ibid.*
11. *Ibid.*, p. 214.
12. *Ibid.*
13. *Ibid.*
14. *Ibid.*, p. 242.
15. *Ibid.*, p. 215.
16. *Ibid.*, p. 247.
17. *Ibid.*
18. *Ibid.*
19. *Ibid.*, p. 250.
20. Vilmos Nagybaczoni Nagy, *Végzetes esztendők 1938–1945* (Fatal Years, 1938–1945) (Budapest, 1986), p. 38.
21. *Ibid.*, p. 41.
22. *Ibid.*
23. *Ibid.*
24. György Ránki, Ervin Pamlényi, Loránt Tilkovszky and Gyula Juhász, eds., *A Wilhelmstrasse és Magyarország: Német diplomáciai iratok Magyarországról, 1933–1944* (The Wilhelmstrasse and Hungary: German Diplomatic Documents about Hungary, 1933–1944) (Budapest, 1968), p. 528. (351)
25. *Ibid.*, p. 530. (351)
26. Gyula Juhász, ed., *Diplomáciai iratok Magyarország külpolitikájához 1936–1945* (Diplomatic Writings on Hungary's Foreign Policy, 1936–1945) (Budapest, 1962–1982), vol. V: p. 573. (352)
27. *Ibid.*, p. 561. (345)

28. *Ibid.*, p. 577. (352)
29. *Ibid.*, p. 578.
30. *Ibid.*, p. 596. (366)
31. Hadtörténelmi Levéltár (Military History Archive, HL). Eln. Vkf.1. 1940/3849. 49. sz. tájékoztató (bulletin), pp. 116–118, 120, and 122.
32. Domokos Szent-Iványi, *Emlékirat* (Memoirs), Ráday Levéltár (Ráday Archive), Szent-Iványi hagyaték C/80, p. 521.
33. *Ibid.*, p. 522.
34. *Ibid.*, p. 523.
35. *Ibid.*, p. 524.
36. *Ibid.*
37. Carlile Aylmer Macartney, *October Fifteenth. A History of Modern Hungary, 1929-1945* (Edinburgh, 1961), vol. I: p. 433.
38. Szent-Iványi, *Emlékirat*, p. 525.
39. Országos Levéltár (National Archive, OL). K 589 I.D. 15.
40. *Ibid.*

GERMAN TRAINING UNITS IN TRANSIT ACROSS HUNGARY TO ROMANIA

Teleki's policy of neutrality was deeply shaken by letting the German training units cross Hungary. By the end of September it was a done deal that, at the request of General Antonescu, German troops would cross Hungary on their way to Romania to support the government, to protect the oil region, and to reorganize the Romanian army.

In the first days of September the German ambassador to Bucharest proposed to the German Ministry of Foreign Affairs that a German military mission be sent to Romania, at the request of General Antonescu. The details of the request are in the German military attaché's report. The attaché had discussions with General Antonescu on September 7, at which Antonescu conveyed the Romanian army's desire that German officers, as experts, be sent to the Romanian General Staff, military schools and military academies. In addition, he also asked for a mechanized army corps, air units, and anti-air and anti-armor armaments for the Romanian army.[1]

The OKW evaluated the Romanian situation and also considered the view of Canaris, the head of German Military Intelligence, and then stated that Antonescu was in control of the situation and was fully committed to cooperation with the Germans. He claimed that he wanted to mechanize his army with German help and wanted to establish a strong defense on the eastern border of Romania.[2]

On September 15 General Tippelskirch was already having discussions with Antonescu, who complained to him that Romania felt threatened by its neighbors and expected to have its security and territorial integrity protected by the practical manifestations of the German guarantees to it. Therefore, he requested immediate help by the German military, ordering German armored, mechanized, air force and anti-aircraft units to Romania, disguised as German training units. In addition, he requested armaments for his army, along with soldiers who would train the Romanian troops to handle them. Antonescu believed it possible that after fulfilling their tasks with regard to the training of the Romanian forces, the personnel of the troops would return to Germany, leaving their equipment behind. Tippelskirch was taken aback by Antonescu's latter suggestion, and asked for instructions on how to respond to this unusual request in his report to the OKW.[3]

Hitler did not delay much and on September 19 instructed the OKW and the Ministry of Foreign Affairs that a mechanized division jointly with supporting troops be urgently sent to Romania. He was inclined to fulfill Antonescu's request that the troops should be stationed near Romania's eastern borders, with the oilfields to be secured by anti-aircraft guns.[4] However, he rejected Antonescu's request for them to leave war materials behind. The Ministry of Foreign Affairs, in cooperation with the OKW, would take measures to ensure that the troops safely crossed Hungary, and would inform the Soviet government about the German troops' presence, at Antonescu's request.[5]

In compliance with Hitler's instruction, on September 20 Keitel informed the military command in a secret order about Hitler's decision and the tasks of the troops to be sent to Romania. The army and the air force would send a military mission to Romania, and their ostensible task would be to extend help to reorganize and train the Romanian army. Their real task, however, which could not be brought to the attention of either the Romanian or their own troops, was a) to defend the Romanian oilfields against the attack or sabotage of a third power, b) to make the Romanian army capable of solving specific problems in a structured fashion, which would be in Germany's interest for them to do, and c) to prepare for the deployment of German and Romanian forces in case war broke out with Russia.[6]

The Hungarian government was first informed about the plan on September 23. The information arrived from Bárdossy in Bucharest, who referred back to the information of the military attaché, Colonel Oszkár Baitz, and added that his Italian colleague, Chiggi, also found it possible.[7]

Prior to that, Sztójay had reported on Tippelskirch's trip to Bucharest, indicating that the goal of the trip was to discuss the German guarantees given to Romania. On September 26 Sztójay once again sent word and reinforced the news coming from Bucharest.[8] Referring to Colonel Homlok—who had received his highly confidential information from General Marras, Italian attaché to Berlin, and German Lieutenant Colonel Mellethin, chief of the attaché group—Sztójay reported that within one to two weeks a German military mission would depart for Bucharest in order to cooperate in the reorganization of the Romanian army. Following that, a "military group from probably every service branch will occupy the region around the oil resources, in order to defend it against sabotage or other threats."[9] A request for transit via Hungary would be made, and the operation would happen with Antonescu's agreement. Mellethin asked Homlok for the utmost secrecy. Marras, who received his information from Rome and Bucharest, attributed the secrecy of official German circles to the fact that Hitler might not have made a final decision yet.

In the meantime, preparation for the "mission" went ahead at full speed. On September 25 the organizational order for the mission in Romania had been completed, and a day later Lieutenant General Hansen was appointed its leader. The staff of the mission was created in Dresden, with the first segment needing to be ready to travel by September 30, while the second segment had to be ready by October 10. The 13th Mechanized Division and its supporting units also had to concentrate north of Vienna and be prepared to be transported by October 10. This division was to be supported by the 4th Armored Regiment and technical units. The presence of an engineer battalion, two 2B type bridging parties, which were capable of bridging large rivers, an intelligence section, and an intercepting quadrant in the battle order of the division indicated an extended stay in Romania and the prospect of having to overcome large technical and aquatic hindrances.[10]

According to the common plan of the OKW and the Ministry of Foreign Affairs, on September 28 Weizsäcker instructed Erdmannsdorff to request the Hungarian government to permit the transit of these German troops. The ambassador reported on September 30 that agreement had been received. He also let it to be known that the German military attaché, Major General Wrede, was going to start preliminary discussions with Chief of the General Staff Werth.[11]

The Hungarians had no plans to reject the German request.[12] Under the given circumstances Teleki could hardly think about rejecting it. Already in April the question of a German troop transit through Hungary to Romania—at that point still part of the British alliance and enjoying British guarantees—had come up. Although it was his intention, Teleki was very unlikely to have won over the extreme right-wing elements and the army to prevent the German troop transit, and a governmental breakup would have occurred. It is hard to imagine how Teleki could have stood in the way of the German troops, which, after all, Antonescu's Romania had requested after breaking up the alliance and guarantees with the British, even if the troop transit provoked the criticism of the British government.[13]

The British protest was not long in coming. First Csáky tried to fudge the situation to the British ambassador, O'Malley, but when he was finally cornered he said the following: "As far as I know, Romania is neutral and has normal diplomatic relations with Great Britain as well. It is no one's business under what circumstances Hungary lets the armed units of a friendly state cross its territory to a neutral country. Moreover, it is not in Hungary's interest to have turmoil in Romania. The presence of German troops in this mutinous country brings peace and quiet to us too."[14]

The British government's official statement on the issue included threats, which the Hungarian government could count on, should the German troops cross its territory. The road taken had now become risky, but it was difficult to stop. Although the British government did not want to take any further steps at this point, if in the future the Hungarian government allowed foreign forces to deploy across its territory against a country that was in alliance with Great Britain, the British government would terminate diplomatic relations with Hungary following such an unfriendly measure. Furthermore, if Hungary permitted such forces to stay in Hungarian territory or allowed them to use Hungarian military equipment or participated in a joint operation against a country that was in alliance with Great Britain, this would be a *casus belli*. Such an allied nation in Hungary's neighborhood was Yugoslavia, as was Greece, a bit further off. Obviously, it was first of all Yugoslavia that interested the Hungarian military leaders when they analyzed the planned movements of the German troops.[15]

Csáky informed Lieutenant General Littay, Deputy Chief of the General Staff, about the communication with the British ambassador, asked him to inform the German military command, and also sent a message to the German ambassador, Erdmannsdorff. In the period when Hungary was preparing to join the Tripartite Pact, Csáky wanted to assure the Germans that on the question of German troop transit the Hungarian government's position was solid and that the government stood by the decision and would not let anyone influence it.

Contrary to Teleki, Werth had no misgivings, no matter what the British position was. He was happy that the Hungarian General

Staff finally could help the Germans, even if it was only with troop transit. He wanted to fulfill the task to the complete satisfaction of the German army. In his view, the troop transit issue could have been expected to come up, and it coincided with the General Staff's view about German goals in southeastern Europe and Romania. At the same time, Werth had been jealously waiting to see what help the German army would extend to Romania to restructure and modernize its army, and to what extent this would make Romania more powerful. The results might indicate in advance German expectations with regard to the Romanian army in case a conflict broke out in the Balkans or between Germany and the Soviet Union. And this factor could not be left unnoticed in the Hungarian–Romanian competition for the Germans' favor, and he believed that steps would have to be taken to counterbalance Romanian advantages. Further political and economic measures should be taken that would convince the Germans that it was in their interest to promote the development of the *Honvédség*.

The transportation of German training troops began in mid-October. The Central Billeting Office of the General Staff registered the arrival of the first train transporting German troops at Hegyeshalom on October 16.[16] Following that, daily four to six trains were registered, most of which reached the Romanian border within 24 hours. In early November the transportation accelerated, and nine to ten trains crossed the country daily. It was reported on November 10 that the 134th German train left Hungarian territory at Lökösháza.[17] This essentially marked the end of the transportation of the training troops. Until November 20 there was an interval in German troop transportation. However, after November 20 and until mid-December, every day one or two trains (with a total of 53) were reported with Romania as their destination for transporting troops or materials. According to the analysis of the General Staff, thus far a rapid army corps had arrived in the Ploieşti oil region, including one armored or light division, one mechanized infantry division, one fighter division (mostly by air) and part of a bomber division: altogether 45,000–50,000 people.[18]

The transport of German troops and material became more difficult in October due to the transportation of Hungarian units back to their garrisons after participating in the re-annexation of Transylvania.

On November 15 Werth took steps to ensure that mutual respect be shown between the two armies. He asked the German military attaché, Colonel Krappe, to act so that German units in Hungary or in transit could be educated about appropriate military protocol: "It is to the dismay of our officers that the German troops do not acknowledge them at all and do not give any salute to them." The same source indicates that officers from several garrisons invited German officers, who stayed at the train station, for a short sightseeing tour.[19]

Notes

1. Franz Halder, *Kriegstagebuch*. *Tägliche Aufzeichnungen des Chefs des Generalstabes des Heeres 1939–1942/Generaloberst Halder* (Stuttgart, 1962–1964), vol. I: p. 97.
2. *Ibid.*, p. 98.
3. *Ibid.*, pp. 80–81.
4. Halder, *Kriegstagebuch...*, vol. II: p. 98.
5. *Ibid.*, vol. I: p. 83.
6. Raymond James Sontag, et.als., ed., *Documents on German Foreign Policy, 1918–1945* (Washington, 1949–1954), vol. XI: pp. 144–146. (84)
7. Gyula Juhász, ed., *Diplomáciai iratok Magyarország külpolitikájához 1936–1945* (Diplomatic Writings on Hungary's Foreign Policy, 1936–1945) (Budapest, 1962–1982), vol. V: p. 608. (377)
8. *Ibid.*, p. 614. (382)
9. *Ibid.*, p. 621. (386)
10. Halder, *Kriegstagebuch...*, vol. II: pp. 99–100.
11. Sontag, et.als., ed., *Documents on German Foreign Policy...*, vol. XI: p. 226. (131)
12. Gyula Juhász, *Magyarország külpolitikája* (Hungary's Foreign Policy) (Budapest, 1969), p. 230.
13. Carlile Aylmer Macartney, *October Fifteenth. A History of Modern Hungary, 1929-1945* (Edinburgh, 1961), vol. I: p. 441.
14. Juhász, ed., *Diplomáciai iratok...*, vol. V: p. 645. (410)
15. Domokos Szent-Iványi, *Emlékirat* (Memoirs), Ráday Levéltár (Ráday Archive), Szent-Iványi hagyaték C/80, pp. 460–461.
16. Hadtörténelmi Levéltár (Military History Archive, HL). Eln. Vkf.1. 1940/5052, 1940/5080.
17. HL. Eln. Vkf.1. 1940/5550.
18. HL. Eln. Vkf.1. 1941/4181.
19. HL. Eln. Vkf.1. 1940/65444.

THE GROWING GERMAN MILITARY AND POLITICAL INFLUENCE

While German military trains were rolling towards the Romanian border, Hungarian diplomats were working on tying the country even closer to the Axis. In Vienna on November 20 Teleki and Csáky signed Hungary's accession to the Tripartite Pact. The Italians' war against Greece, which had broken out in October, upset Hitler's policy in the Balkans, which had been developed in the name of preparations against the Soviet Union, and also accelerated events in the region. Hitler decided on taking further political and military steps. In addition to energetic secret German diplomatic activity with Yugoslavia, Bulgaria and Turkey, it seemed to Hitler that tying his allies more closely to Germany was a good idea. For this reason he agreed that the Hungarians would be the first to join the Tripartite Pact. The Hungarians had been working on the opportunity since September, because they hoped that it would bring advantages to them.

Following the re-annexation of part of Transylvania, the political leadership decided that solidifying Hungary's commitment to the Axis in a formal agreement seemed to be the most efficient way to demonstrate Hungary's gratitude to Germany, to alleviate German distrust, and to ensure further German goodwill. The Tripartite Pact came in handy, since it did not require additional difficult economic action besides those already existing. It also offered hope for decreasing the German attacks on the Hungarian government's policy and for underpinning further Hungarian territorial revisionist demands.

Following the conclusion of the Tripartite Pact between Germany, Italy and Japan on September 27, 1940, von Ribbentrop made the following statement: "Every country that honestly and gratefully wants to join this bloc and comes with the intention of contributing to the restoration of peaceful relationships is welcome. These countries will participate in the political and economic reorganization [of Europe]."[1]

Sztójay supported the government's intention to join the Axis, and did everything that he could to deal with any obstacles in the way. Already on September 27 he called to Csáky's attention his conviction that Hungary should immediately join the bloc, because "this is the last opportunity to prove our equality with a document—so to speak. This is the only way for us to ensure that we can actively participate in the reorganization of the region when political, economic and, almost certainly, territorial questions are decided." The intention to join should be announced soon, because it would thereby be of double value. It would also be unfortunate if Romania joined before Hungary.[2]

Csáky himself was all for joining the Pact. Although he never received a call from the leaders of the Pact, he submitted Sztójay's message to the Council of Ministers, which decided on joining.

Boosted by von Ribbentrop's call, Csáky immediately instructed Sztójay to inquire whether countries that had not joined thus far could interpret von Ribbentrop's speech as a call to action and, if the answer were "yes," what formalities should be satisfied and what obligations should those wishing to join undertake. Sztójay informed Under-secretary of Foreign Affairs Weizsäcker, who had received him, that indeed the Hungarian government was ready to participate, but first wanted to be informed about protocol.[3]

The Hungarian government was surprised to find that the reception was rather lukewarm and that Germany obviously had no urgent desire for Hungary to join. Although on October 9 von Ribbentrop informed Sztójay that Hitler wanted to make it possible for friendly countries, Hungary among them, to join the Pact, and on October 12 von Ribbentrop once again informed him that Italy and Japan had agreed, the actual signing of the agreement was delayed. This irritated the government, because it was concerned that the Romanians might precede Hungary. In early October an agreement was signed between Hitler and the increasingly important Antonescu about Romania joining the Pact.[4]

Aware that Hungary was going to join a bloc at war with Great Britain, and that Hungary was to give up the so often mentioned armed neutrality, Teleki and Csáky made an attempt to lay down certain conditions in return for joining. In his message to Sztójay on October 13 Csáky asked him to try to make sure that the following conditions were in the document: based on equal rights, Hungary was to join a peace bloc; the European reorganization plan was to include the fulfillment of Hungary's territorial demands against Yugoslavia; the full settlement of the Slovakian and Romanian questions was to be included.[5] Von Ribbentrop returned a message saying that Hungary was obviously joining on an equal basis with existing members, but that no conditions were to be included.[6]

Once again German diplomacy made sure to express Germany's dissatisfaction and reservations towards Hungary. In his reports in early November citing the opinions of the highest political and military circles, including Hitler's, Sztójay once again listed the excuses and demands that increasingly contaminated the Germans' attitude towards Hungary. He argued that Hungary had to dispel German views that Hungary lacked trust in the Axis and was still sympathetic towards the British.[7]

The government tried to justify to Great Britain Hungary's joining the Axis Powers by saying that it was unavoidable, while the Hungarian military command simply avoided trying to make excuses. To the military it was a long overdue move, and joining the Axis was the fortunate realization of a long-awaited gesture, which upcoming expected events would turn into a secure opportunity for Hungary to march alongside Germany. The military wanted to join the Pact as soon as possible, and unconditionally, before it became too late, and so did everything in its power to influence the government. Both Sztójay and Homlok often informed their superiors about Germany's plans, and about possible variations for Hungary's role within these plans, all of which made Hungary's joining the Axis necessary. In his report of October 17 sent to the Chief of the General Staff, Homlok spoke about joining the Tripartite Pact as Hungary's only realistic alternative, emphasized all the advantages that it would bring, and claimed that it would obliterate all the downsides of the German–Hungarian relationship. An Axis victory would become Hungary's victory, although its defeat would become Hungary's defeat, he continued. Hungary would acquire the right to come forward with its own demands during the reorganization of the European order. The Pact meant not only political and economic cooperation, but also military cooperation: "If in the present war of the Great Powers, any other countries should attack the Tripartite Pact, then Hungary should also consider itself to be at war with that country or countries."[8] On the other hand, the Tripartite Pact powers would be obligated to help Hungary militarily if it were attacked. Considering the urgency of the matter, Homlok also stressed that rumor had it that Slovakia, Romania, Bulgaria, Finland and Yugoslavia also wanted to join.[9]

The Hungarian military leadership remained distrustful towards Yugoslavia, was ready to raise territorial demands there, and expected help for this from the Germans. And so it was not willing to review its plans even if Yugoslavia joined the Pact. The military leaders hoped that the oft-mentioned Hungarian "gendarme role" in the Danube Basin—this having been suggested and indeed volunteered to Germany—would give Hungary advantages even towards a Yugoslavia that had taken steps towards rapprochement with Germany. These were Homlok's considerations when he examined Yugoslavia's situation. As far as Yugoslavia was concerned, he wrote, German official circles knew Hungarian territorial claims on it. Even if it joined the Pact, there was still the question of whether settling its territorial problems might not be a prerequisite for Yugoslavia. If an isolated Yugoslavia did not join the Pact, did not bend to pressure during the reorganization of the Balkans, and put up a military defense, its time would come. In the latter case the *Honvédség* could be applied "not for a compromise, but for a total solution." However, to take advantage of such a possibility, "it is necessary to have certain Hungarian military units ready to march at any time. Otherwise, the chance exists of missing the opportunity, because we are well aware of the rapid processes of the Axis Powers and, especially, of the German Reich."[10]

Homlok believed that the German–Soviet relationship was shaky. The German military measures along the Soviet border, which he did not characterize as provocative, had convinced him that, whatever decision the Soviet Union would make, "the German Reich would not long commit itself to idleness towards Soviet Russia's questionable and unclear behavior, even at the expense of war as the ultimate scenario."[11] He found the key to the German–Soviet discord to be the situation in the Balkans. The front composed of those allies meant to prevent the Soviet Union's advance into the Balkans would be complete with the addition of the Romanian army, after it was armed and organized with German help, and after the addition of Hungary. Therefore, as Werth had stated before, Hungary could contribute to the Pact's military operations by defending the Carpathians, with assistance from the Axis. However, Homlok also pointed out that this front was still unstable, due to the Romanian armed forces' weakness, and that it was too early to speak about the Soviet Union's military measures against Germany. There had not been any signs about aggressive intentions from the Soviet Union. Therefore, it was possible that by joining the "preventive" bloc, Hungary would not have to contribute to the "defensive" operations, since they would not take place.[12]

There are obvious similarities between Homlok's views and the military political ideas stated in Werth's memorandum from July. Both men favored the maximum effort to prepare for common action with the German army, in case one of the small neighboring countries resisted Germany's growing influence and military intervention of some sort occurred. Similarly, both held the view that preparations should be made for immediate action in the case of a German–Soviet confrontation. For Werth and his circle, joining the Axis indicated a deepening alliance, a marching forward together with Germany in its eventual expansive actions, and the possibility of alleviating the danger of being left behind others in the competition for Germany's goodwill. They were ready to ignore the explicit terms of the Pact, which obliged Hungary to enter war on behalf of the Axis only if one of the Axis members were attacked by a third country. They were also quite aware of the Germans' methods, including presenting aggression as preventive self-defense, a lie that would be obliterated by the expected future victory. Werth did not miss any chance to elaborate on his views at different high-level staff or commanders' meetings or during his visits to the troops. Therefore, his views acquired official standing and became the guidelines for the army, all the more so because they seemed to be well founded and optimal for the officer corps and they also agreed with the officer corps' own ideas.

Following his fruitless attempts to derail the terms of Hungary's joining the Tripartite Pact, Prime Minister Teleki stood by and watched helplessly as Werth and his circle became increasingly confident and vocal in expressing their views, which were opposed to the views of the government. Their statements that Hungarian policy was now taking a desirable and redeeming course had an impact well beyond the army.

Their views differed not only regarding the utility of the Tripartite Pact, but also regarding the Hungarian–Yugoslavian relationship. While the military had counted on a confrontation between the two countries, the government agreed to postpone dealing with controversial issues that had become more difficult since the Second Vienna Award, hoping to decrease the threat of getting entangled in a conflict in the Balkans.

The Yugoslavian government was relieved by the Second Vienna Award, because it had ended the immediate danger of war in the neighborhood.[13] Belgrade hoped to keep the country out of war and to keep Hungary away from an armed conflict with Romania that might escalate to include Yugoslavia. During the summer of 1940 Yugoslavia adopted a lenient tone towards Hungary, and assumed a neutral position in connection with the Hungarian–Romanian conflict while still acknowledging Hungary's territorial demands on Romania. However, after the Vienna Award there was a palpable change of mood in Belgrade, which was manifest in a growing distrust of Hungary. The image of Hungary as a middle-ranking power that, following territorial revisionist successes in the north and the east, might turn south loomed large in the country. The constantly nurtured Hungarian–Italian plans for a common military action against Yugoslavia might come to fruition now.[14] In his report sent on September 11 about the deteriorating attitude towards Hungary and its causes, Hungary's ambassador to Belgrade, Bessenyei, noted—citing his German colleague—that for the sake of a good relationship Yugoslavia would be willing to make territorial concessions to both Hungary and Bulgaria, but that they were afraid that the Italians would also make claims. Yugoslavia was trying to pursue friendly policies towards Hungary, but it had a permanent fear that the Hungarian government would raise the issue of territorial revision at any time.[15]

The Yugoslavian government was completely encircled by the German troops appearing in Romania in October, by the Italian troops pushing their way into Albania, and by Germany's growing pressure, and so watched its Hungarian neighbor with increasing concern. Since it did not want to strain the situation, Hungarian foreign policy did not exclude settling the two countries' relationship through negotiations. Yet the Hungarians rejected the Yugoslavs' cautious offer of a population exchange.

Hitler, toying with the idea of attacking Greece, wanted to secure his forces from the Yugoslavian direction, and therefore placed diplomatic pressure on the Yugoslavian government while also considering a military solution. At the same time, Hitler's plans forced the Italians to engage in a policy of rapprochement with Yugoslavia, because the Italians had become tied down with the Greek campaign and they also wanted to counterbalance the Germans' presence in the Balkans.

On November 18 in Salzburg Hitler received Italian Minister of Foreign Affairs Ciano, who was on his way to Vienna, where Hungary was to sign the Tripartite Pact. Hitler expressed his deep concern about how the Balkan situation had developed in the wake of Italian military failures. Yet, without the stabilization of the situation and a solution to the Yugoslavian problem, no successful intervention against the British could be imagined. This made winning Yugoslavia over to the Axis necessary. Hitler asked Ciano to persuade the Duce to agree to it, while Hitler also promised to write a letter to him.[16] Hitler also asked Ciano to persuade the Hungarians in Vienna not to raise difficulties and to allow the largest possible number of German trains to cross Hungarian territory, because it would make a quick concentration of German troops in Romania possible. This was essential for a common attack with the Italians on Greece and for keeping Russia and Turkey at bay. Romania would have to recognize that increasing the number of German armed forces on its territory served its own defense.[17]

Germany's military preparations began immediately. On November 4 Hitler announced to German army leaders his decision to launch a relief attack against Greece via Romania and Bulgaria, since the Italian offensive had become bogged down due to the Greek counterattack.[18] He also informed them that, independent of the ongoing Soviet–German discussions, he would launch a campaign against the Soviet Union following the operation against the Greeks.[19] On November 12 he issued his 18th Order, in which he instructed Field Marshal Brauchitsch to take preparatory steps so that, if the need arose, the army could take possession of that part of Greece north of the Aegean Sea by attacking from Bulgaria. Brauchitsch was also to make preparations for the deployment of German air squadrons against targets in the eastern basin of the Mediterranean Sea, most notably those British air bases that might threaten the Romanian oilfields.[20] Finally, the order made it clear that preparations against the Soviet Union had to be continued. To this end, it was stipulated that the forces stationed in Romania be immediately reinforced with ten more divisions. According to Halder, the difficulty in doing this lay in quickly transporting the non-mechanized divisions from Greece to the eastern front after completing the operations in Greece.[21]

Fulfilling Hitler's diplomatic plans, Romania on November 23 and Slovakia on November 24 followed Hungary in joining the Axis. On November 28 Yugoslavian Minister of Foreign Affairs Cincar-Marković visited Hitler, who offered him a non-aggression treaty, albeit without guarantees regarding Yugoslavia's territorial integrity. Hitler tried to gain the trust of the Yugoslavian government through economic incentives and by offering Thessaloniki to it. The Yugoslavian Minister of Foreign Affairs had reservations about Hitler's offer, and the issues remained undecided.

The Hungarian General Staff noted with satisfaction that Hitler had not held out the prospect of guaranteeing Yugoslavia's borders. They thought it likely to be a sign of Germany's mistrust towards Yugoslavia and a tool that Germany wanted to keep in order to blackmail the country.

On the other hand, Teleki was pleased to hear that his desire to form a good relationship with Yugoslavia met with Hitler's approval. After the ceremony on joining the Tripartite Pact, Hitler met with Teleki and Csáky. After a lengthy discussion about the general foreign political situation, which had developed according to Germany's wishes, and the strengths of the German army and the individual armies of the countries that had just joined the Axis, Hitler came to the Balkan issue. The Italians' failure in Greece, which had originated in a poor assessment of the situation, would have to be settled. Germany could not allow the British to set foot in Thessaloniki.[22] In order to clarify the Balkan situation, he urged certain steps to be taken, including reinforcing German units in Romania as well as communicating with Yugoslavia. He requested that Hungary try to settle the Romanian–Hungarian relationship, which had been strained by Antonescu's behavior, for the sake of their common interest in keeping the peace in southeastern Europe. Then he blurted out a request: would Hungary relieve Hitler's southern wing and, for that reason, would it develop a good relationship with Yugoslavia? If so, this should also be sealed by an agreement.[23]

And so, as a result of mutual rapprochement, on December 12 the Hungarians and Yugoslavs signed a treaty of everlasting amity in Belgrade. The parties agreed that "they will discuss any issue that, in their view, affects their mutual relationship." They also established their conviction that "perpetual peace and eternal friendship are established" between the two countries.[24]

The treaty made Teleki happy, since it offered hope for the future. For him, this was an opportunity to establish badly needed peace and quiet in Hungary, and, with tensions decreasing, to end the threat of war in the immediate neighborhood. As for the military command, however, the treaty and ensuing consolidation of the situation between the two countries entailed giving up its hope of territorial revision. For this reason, it tried to give voice to still persistent Hungarian territorial demands.

In his report of December 19 to Csáky, Sztójay expressed shock at the guarded tone of the German press coverage of the treaty. Although it did express satisfaction with the treaty of amity, yet it alluded to it as if it were a specifically Hungarian– Yugoslavian issue, albeit one that obviously had beneficial side effects on the southeastern European situation. Sztójay emphasized to Weizsäcker the point that the treaty was concluded in response to Hitler's request that Hungary establish a state of equilibrium and friendship with Yugoslavia. Sztójay also mentioned this to Undersecretary of Foreign Affairs Woermann, and stressed that Hungary "has not indeed given up on its territorial revisionist claims on Yugoslavia."25

Teleki opposed those who either ignored the treaty or who actively spoke in favor of territorial demands on Yugoslavia. On January 31 he replaced Csáky, who in the meantime had passed away, in giving a very positive evaluation of the treaty to the Foreign Affairs Committee of the Hungarian Parliament. Teleki emphasized the point that the recognition of mutual sympathy and a certain interdependence between the two countries made it possible "to formally express our sympathies and neighborly relations and, thus, to lay the foundation for a future peaceful and friendly cooperation."26 It would not be right to pursue territorial claims on Yugoslavia, which were much less than those on Romania or Slovakia. It should be dealt with differently, "this should happen in a really peaceful and friendly way." He also pointed out that concluding the treaty, which had also been requested by the Germans in Vienna, was important both for the peace in Europe and for the Axis Powers' aspirations to reorganize Europe. He quoted Csáky's speech after signing the treaty, saying that "at least this part of Europe would be saved from a catastrophe." Teleki cautioned the hot-headed and bellicose Hungarians that "we should move ahead without losing breath and without increasing tension to breaking point. We are thinking about the future rather than the present. We will reconstruct the country in a gradual process, step by step, cautiously, wisely and permanently."27

Notes

1. György Ránki, Ervin Pamlényi, Loránt Tilkovszky and Gyula Juhász, eds., *A Wilhelmstrasse és Magyarország: Német diplomáciai iratok Magyarországról, 1933–1944* (The Wilhelmstrasse and Hungary: German Diplomatic Documents about Hungary, 1933–1944) (Budapest, 1968), p. 534. (356)
2. Domokos Szent-Iványi, *Emlékirat* (Memoirs), Ráday Levéltár (Ráday Archive), Szent-Iványi hagyaték C/80, pp. 60–61.
3. Ránki–Pamlényi–Tilkovszky–Juhász, *A Wilhelmstrasse és Magyarország...*, p. 534. (356)
4. Carlile Aylmer Macartney, *October Fifteenth. A History of Modern Hungary, 1929-1945* (Edinburgh, 1961), vol. I: p. 411.
5. *Ibid.*, p. 442.
6. *Ibid.*
7. Szent-Iványi, *Emlékirat...*, pp. 504–505.
8. Gyula Juhász, ed., *Diplomáciai iratok Magyarország külpolitikájához 1936–1945* (Diplomatic Writings on Hungary's Foreign Policy, 1936–1945) (Budapest, 1962–1982), vol. V: p. 671. (425)
9. *Ibid.*
10. *Ibid.*, p. 672.
11. *Ibid.*
12. *Ibid.*, p. 673.
13. Juhász, ed., *Diplomáciai iratok...*, vol. V: p. 582. (354)
14. Szent-Iványi, *Emlékirat...*, pp. 409–410.
15. Juhász, ed., *Diplomáciai iratok...*, vol. V: p. 583. (355)
16. Carlile Aylmer Macartney, *October Fifteenth. A History of Modern Hungary, 1929-1945* (Edinburgh, 1961), p. 299.
17. Raymond James Sontag, et.als., ed., *Documents on German Foreign Policy, 1918–1945* (Washington, 1949–1954), vol. XI: p. 641. (364)
18. Franz Halder, *Kriegstagebuch. Tägliche Aufzeichnungen des Chefs des Generalstabes des Heeres 1939–1942/Generaloberst Halder* (Stuttgart, 1962–1964), vol. I: p. 1181.
19. Andreas Hillgruber, *Hitlers Strategie. Politik und Kriegführung 1940–1941* (Frankfurt am Main, 1965), p. 354.
20. Halder, *Kriegstagebuch...*, vol. I: p. 1181.
21. *Ibid.*, vol. II: p.76.

22. Ránki–Pamlényi–Tilkovszky–Juhász, *A Wilhelmstrasse és Magyarország...*, p. 550. (366); Macartney, *October Fifteenth...*, p. 448.
23. *Ibid.*, p. 552. (367)
24. Juhász, ed., *Diplomáciai iratok...*, vol. V. p. 776. (517)
25. *Ibid.*, p. 788. (530)
26. *Ibid.*, p. 848. (563)
27. *Ibid.*, p. 849.

THE GERMAN ARMY PREPARES FOR WAR
AGAINST THE SOVIET UNION
AND IGNORES THE HUNGARIAN GENERAL STAFF

In compliance with Hitler's decision, the German military began drawing up plans for Operation Marita against Greece. Units designated to participate in this operation had to be concentrated and prepared by mid-December. According to the plan, by January 23, 1941, the mechanized units and by February 4 two infantry divisions and two mountain divisions had to be deployed to the Bulgarian border via Hungary and Romania. In view of possible future military operations against the Soviet Union, the start of the attack was first set for February 11.[1] This, however, was postponed to mid-March in the 20th Order, issued on December 13, 1940. Military operations were planned to last for about three to four weeks, until mid-April. It would then take four more weeks to transport the troops back to Romania and to reinforce them. In this way the troops would be ready for the launch of Operation Barbarossa on May 15.[2]

On December 5, 1940, Hitler made known his final decision about launching an attack against the Soviet Union. His goal was the total annihilation of the Soviet Union and the acquisition of its economic resources. He spoke about his ideas in detail to his military leaders.[3] On December 18 he issued his 21st Order, outlining Operation Barbarossa. Among the troops to attack along the entire length of the Soviet border, he attributed special significance to the forces deployed in the south. He planned to attack with a large force and with the support of Romanian troops on the southern wing. He counted on the cooperation of Finnish forces in the north, but did not consider Hungary's participation necessary. As he explained, the Romanians and the Finns would join the attack, since their future was dependent on Germany.[4]

The transport of German troops designated to execute Operation Marita began on December 14. The transit of two armored and two infantry divisions from the 12th German Army posed a difficult task for the Hungarian railways.[5] Without knowing the parameters or the time period involved, the government nevertheless gave its unconditional agreement to this large-scale transportation project, which could only be executed by significantly decreasing civilian railway traffic. The Hungarian military leadership went out of its way to help the German army. In order to complete the increasingly voluminous traffic, on January 3 the Chief of the General Staff issued an instruction that the lines used be expanded to include more railways running towards the Romanian border that had not been used thus far.[6] He also made arrangements for counterespionage and sabotage activity, and introduced measures for guarding railway-related instruments along the lines used.[7]

On January 3 the German air force attaché Fütterer requested from the Hungarian General Staff the use of the Debrecen airfield in addition to the base used so far in order to resettle 300 different types of airplanes.[8]

The fact that the Hungarian government was so accommodating towards the large-scale transportation was a pleasant surprise for Hitler. He wrote to Mussolini on December 31 that the Hungarian government's position and behavior demonstrated in the Balkan conflict was no less decisive than that of the Romanian one. He noted that since December 13 the ongoing transport of German troops to Romania had not been disturbed. Hungary and Romania both made their railway networks available to the greatest degree possible, and therefore the German forces could occupy their points of deployment in quick succession.[9]

The German military transports indeed followed each other with increasing frequency. While 10 to 15 trains per day crossed the Hungarian border in December, this number grew to between 40 and 50 by January. At the December peak, according to the reports of the central transport headquarters, a total of 1,483 trains crossed Hungarian territory to Romania. The numbers barely decreased in February (984 trains) and March (953 trains). Even with the maximal use of available trains and with the substantially decreased civilian traffic, gridlock and trains stranded at stations could still not be avoided, which did not please the Germans. (On a randomly selected day—January 19—we find that 54 German trains traversed or were stranded in Hungarian territory.[10]) The MÁV (Hungarian State Railway) could barely cope with the huge traffic during the snowy winter time, and the railway infrastructure, along with the weak rail network, could barely carry the heavy transports. Minor and major accidents, collisions and derailments, due to traffic control problems or other technical issues, occurred on a daily basis. The collision near Berettyóújfalu on January 5 stands out from among the many accidents: one train delivering ammunition and fuel collided with another one carrying the belongings of Germans who were resettling from Romania to Germany. According to the report, the ammunition exploded like fireworks, in a process lasting for hours, the fuel caught on fire, two members of the escort died, and several people were injured.[11] In another incident, the train carrying parts of the 30th German Armored Regiment collided with a freight train between Ákos and Érszakácsi on January 23, killing six German soldiers, injuring fourteen more, and inflicting significant material damage.[12] Similarly, the collision at Herceghalom on January 28 entailed injuries and serious physical damage.[13]

Officers of the Hungarian General Staff followed the composition of the transports and their direction with great interest, trying to find out their destination. Already in early January they established that while the previously transported training troops occupied the oilfields, the presently deployed ten divisions would occupy all of Romania's militarily important points. Furthermore, some of the troops were headed for Moldova.[14] Italian assistance and the launching of the German campaign against Greece were expected by spring. The deployment of troops to Moldova could hardly be justified by the tense and uncertain Soviet–Romanian relationship or by the need to secure the upcoming Balkan operations, as German diplomacy liked to claim. The German forces in eastern Romania were deployed in an obvious position pointing to a possible attack against the Soviet Union. This was reinforced by the 50 to 60 German divisions concentrated on the Soviet border. The German deployment towards the east and the weakening of German forces in the west meant that it was possible that Hitler had given up on invading Great Britain and had turned his attention towards the Soviet Union. Therefore, an approaching German military operation against the Soviet Union occupied the General Staff's attention, instead of probable clashes caused by conflicting interests in the Balkans.

However, the General Staff was of the opinion that the recent evolution of the German–Soviet relationship argued against the likelihood of an impending war with the Soviet Union. Both Molotov's visit to Berlin in November and the Soviets' systematic foreign policy were part of the assessment that was included in the General Staff's military political summary: "The Soviet government continues to stand by its neutrality and is keeping away from all sorts of military complications. Economic and political cooperation with Germany continues to remain the basis of its foreign policy."[15] Yet the Soviet Union's mistrust of Germany was not unfounded either, because, besides his friendly exchanges with the Soviet Union, Hitler's ranting remarks and outbursts about obliterating Bolshevism, along with the recent deployment, made a German attack quite probable.

It was unsettling that neither the Hungarian government nor the General Staff received any signals from the German military leaders about their intentions, which increasingly convinced the soldiers that they were observers and helpers in a deployment for an operation in which the participation of the Hungarian army had not been counted on. However, there were obvious signs of German–Romanian military cooperation, and the Hungarian General Staff believed that the Romanian army, as supported by German war supplies, was now an integral part of Germany's anti-Soviet plans. This theory was supported by the fact that Antonescu held discussions with Hitler on January 14, which led to widespread speculation within the General Staff, since it had no information about what had happened at the meeting.

In fact, at the meeting Antonescu offered Romania's full military cooperation with the Germans against the Soviet Union.[16] Allegedly Hitler informed Antonescu, as Commander-in-Chief of the Romanian army, about his intentions towards the Soviets only on June 11, at the beginning of the official meetings between the two governments about Romania's participation.[17]

The General Staff also concluded that the permissiveness with which Germany treated Romania's anti-Hungarian propaganda, as well as the embittered Romanian–Hungarian relationship, gave indications of a Romanian–German rapprochement. Armed clashes on the Romanian–Hungarian border resulting in fatalities became a permanent feature. The General Staff's briefing stated that "Romania's foreign policy has been completely influenced by the Axis, so that the Romanian government is only nominally independent. The country could be considered under German occupation, and its role as an independent European political factor has ceased to exist, at least for now."[18]

Werth wanted to know something certain about Germany's eastern plans, and attempted to obtain confidential information from the members of the German General Staff who had earlier slipped remarks about Hitler's anti-Soviet plans. Yet, due to Hitler's specific order, the members of the German military command refrained from sharing any details with their Hungarian comrades. This, however, did not exclude making unmistakable hints about the approaching military operation during the frequent encounters between the officers of the two General Staffs.

Werth looked forward to Minister of Defense Bartha's visit to Berlin in January with great expectations. The goal of the visit was to gain the Germans' consent to a more efficient armament program for the Hungarian army. Werth hoped that Bartha would become more informed about Germany's future military goals. He was to be deeply disappointed. Bartha was received by Hitler, who, as usual, hardly let his guest open his mouth. When the Hungarian armament program was brought up, Hitler changed the subject to Great Britain, which he said he would mercilessly break. He would begin the invasion during the spring of the same year, as soon as he could count on 10 to 14 days of favorable weather. He considered the Italians' military failures to be temporary, and would send only some air force to help them out. He did not say a word about Operation Marita or its preliminaries, perhaps because it would not have harmonized with what he had said about the Balkans. In the Balkans the situation was not settled, but the current calm situation should be preserved in the interest of the Axis. He did not attach too much significance to the appearance of the British in Thessaloniki, yet he could not watch it idly. Bartha did not dare to disturb Hitler in his monologue by asking why German troops had flocked towards the Bulgarian border. He simply accepted that their probable goal was to assure "quiet" in the Balkans.[19]

Coming to the Soviet Union, Hitler said that he was hopeful of things at the beginning of his lecture: his relationship with Stalin was good and the agreements functioned well enough. "If something happened to Stalin," however, this situation could change. Yet apart from that, he was aware of the dangers of communism and pan-Slavism, both of which threatened the Balkans. Therefore he wanted to secure his position, and so moved the proper military forces to the eastern border of the Reich and into Romania. This was how he planned to deal with any ideas that the Soviets might have, of which he was not afraid in any case. Defending the Romanian oilfields continued to be of the utmost importance for the Axis.[20]

The task of Hungary and its army was the defense of the Carpathians. Therefore, Hungary should reinforce its army and the defense line of the Carpathians. A strong Hungarian army in the direction of Yugoslavia would also be reassuring. In order to say something encouraging, Hitler noted that during the general reorganization of Europe after the war, certain advantages for Hungary could be conceivable.[21]

As for the immediate goal of Bartha's trip—to increase support for the army's equipment and for military industrial production—Hitler had the following to say: "Germany is invincible. Its food supply will not falter, because it is fully secured. It has enough raw materials, and the German army is the largest in the world." He would increase the German army further, and fortify it with new equipment. Therefore, at that time he could not fulfill the Hungarian wish with regard to equipment and armaments for the *Honvédség*, because all the materials were needed for the development of the German armed forces. He would be in such a situation in a few months, when he would be much more able to satisfy the Hungarians' request.[22]

Bartha was thoroughly disappointed when he departed. Not only had Hitler not wanted to use the Hungarian army in the near future, but he would not increase assistance with regard to strengthening it either. Bartha seemed to perceive a planned offensive against the Soviet Union underlying the so-called German defensive measures and in Hitler's suggestion concerning the Hungarian defense of the Carpathians. Neither was Bartha more successful later on with von Ribbentrop, who simply reiterated what Hitler had said.

Hitler demanded that Hungary and all the affected countries were to be informed about the details of the campaign against the Soviet Union at the last possible moment. Romania was the only exception, since its participation in the operations was of vital importance.[23]

As preparations for Operation Barbarossa were going ahead, more and more *Wehrmacht* officers became involved in the work, and more and more bits of news leaked out. Consequently, Hitler's plans became increasingly clear. At the end of February the Hungarian consul to Munich, citing a conversation with a General Staff officer, reported that the outbreak of a Soviet–German war was near: "150 German divisions have been idle and held up for months, which of course carries the danger of demoralizing the troops. They could efficiently be employed for the easy task of occupying the Soviet Union's rich oil, metal and agricultural reservoirs. Then, in the possession of all the necessary raw materials, Germany can set out to starve Great Britain into submission without any invasion."[24] The informer told the consul that his conclusions were based on minor details in his possession and that he had no inside view of the military plans.

Official German foreign policy did its best to conceal Hitler's real intentions and to turn attention towards the invasion of Great Britain. It was repeated again and again that unless Great Britain gave in, the disembarkation would take place in 1941. The German army, as the propaganda parroted, had everything needed to force the British to their knees on their own island. Germany wanted peace in the east and in the Balkans, and its military moves there were defensive. This was the position reflected in Sztójay's January–February report to the Hungarian Minister of Foreign Affairs. He never failed to inform his superior about the increasing strength of the invincible German army. According to his report of February 27, in the spring of 1941 Germany would have at its disposal 250 divisions, about 1,500 airplanes, and 180 to 200 submarines—the latter two ones were of crucial importance in an operation against Great Britain. "In addition, attention is also to be paid to the fact that the firepower of the German divisions surpasses the firepower of any other army's similar units. For example, a German division's firepower is equal to that of a Hungarian army corps, which means that the power of the German land army is roughly equal to that of 750 Hungarian mixed brigades."[25] Sztójay cited Homlok's reports to substantiate his opinion. Homlok, based on his conversation with Halder about the expected German military operational plans, also came to the conclusion that the invasion of Great Britain would happen as soon as weather permitted.

Sztójay's statement, identical to Homlok's, is also worth noting. He said that if the invasion of Great Britain did not happen, "the liquidation of Soviet Russia will occupy a front seat, in order to reorganize the east to acquire further provisions for Germany."[26]

As was his duty, Homlok kept collecting and reporting information regarding Operation Barbarossa. These pieces of information, along with news via other channels, built up enough certainty so that by the end of February Werth became fully convinced that Hitler's offensive against the Soviet Union would occur in the near future. Further details, including the date, were still to be found out, as was the reason why Hitler did not want any Hungarian participation. During a tactical meeting in Budapest, Werth confidentially informed the generals and General Staff officers about the expected outbreak of the German–Soviet war: "Consider what you hear here very seriously. I can confidentially inform you that a German–Russian war will happen within a short period of time, and it is our duty to participate in this war."[27] For Werth it would have been intolerable to be left out of a war against Bolshevism, since that might have grave consequences during the post-victory partitioning of territory. Therefore, everything had to be done to avoid this consequence. For the time being, however, there was nothing much more to do than to complete the military development program called "Huba II" and to have Parliament pass the "Huba III" program with its unheard-of 1,549,600 pengő budget. "Huba III" would accelerate the modernization of the *Honvédség*'s equipment and would further strengthen fortifications along the Soviet border, in keeping with the German wishes. In October Werth himself went to see the fortification work in the Carpathian Mountains. The work had been done so effectively that it could be suspended for the winter by November 1.[28]

The question arises as to why Hitler was so adamant about not including the Hungarian army. It can hardly be explained by Hitler's alleged statement made in Halder's presence during the February 5 conference—publicized by Macartney—that if he involved the pro-British Hungarians in his plans, the British would know about it within 24 hours.[29] We also disagree with Paulus, who claimed that the decision was based on Hitler's desire not to promise the Drohobycz oil region to the Hungarians.[30] Such a Hungarian desire had never emerged at any level of the government. In our view, the reason is buried in the Hungarian–Romanian relationship. Unlike the Hungarian government and public opinion, Hitler considered the question of Transylvanian territorial claims to have been settled by the Second Vienna Award. He also knew that if he asked for the participation of the Hungarian army, the Hungarians would immediately come forward with their demands. And he did not consider the participation of the ill-equipped Hungarian troops in Operation Barbarossa to be necessary at that point. As opposed to that, he was in dire need of the Romanian oil, a suitable area to concentrate German troops, and the participation of both Romanian armies along the right wing of the German

Southern Army Group, which would be attacking from Romanian soil. And it was easy to promise the re-annexation of Bessarabian, Galician and Bukovinian territories to the Romanians. Under such circumstances it was unnecessary to disturb plans involving the Romanians by including the Hungarians. In any case, Hitler was certain that after the Romanians entered the war, the Hungarians would do anything they could to join the campaign, without any previous discussion. As Hitler told Halder at the February 5 General Staff meeting, in return for the appropriate political guarantees, if necessary, Hungary would agree to any German demands anyway.[31]

Notes

1. Franz Halder, *Kriegstagebuch. Tägliche Aufzeichnungen des Chefs des Generalstabes des Heeres 1939–1942/Generaloberst Halder* (Stuttgart, 1962–1964), vol. II: p. 193.
2. *Ibid.*, vol. I: p. 203.
3. *Ibid.*, vol. II: pp. 210–213.
4. *Ibid.*, p. 213.
5. Hadtörténelmi Levéltár (Military History Archive, HL). Eln. Vkf.1. 1941/4181.
6. HL. Eln. Vkf.1. 1941/4031.
7. HL. Eln. Vkf.1. 1941/4005.
8. HL. Eln. Vkf.1. 1941/4018.
9. Raymond James Sontag, et.als., ed., *Documents on German Foreign Policy, 1918–1945* (Washington, 1949–1954), vol. XI: p. 990. (586)
10. HL. Eln. Vkf.1. 1941/4120.
11. HL. Eln. Vkf.1. 1941/4026.
12. HL. Eln. Vkf.1. 1941/4147.
13. HL. Eln. Vkf.1. 1941/4196.
14. HL. Eln. Vkf.1. 1941/4181.
15. *Ibid.*
16. Halder, *Kriegstagebuch...*, vol. I: p. 1189.
17. Andreas Hillgruber, *Hitler, König Carol und Marschal Antonescu* (Wiesbaden, 1954), p. 145.
18. HL. Eln. Vkf.1. 1941/4181.
19. Gyula Juhász, ed., *Diplomáciai iratok Magyarország külpolitikájához 1936–1945* (Diplomatic Writings on Hungary's Foreign Policy, 1936–1945) (Budapest, 1962–1982), vol. V: p. 850. (564)
20. *Ibid.*, p. 851.
21. Vilmos Nagybaczoni Nagy, *Végzetes esztendők 1938–1945* (Fatal Years, 1938–1945) (Budapest, 1986), p. 58.
22. *Ibid.*, p. 59.
23. Halder, *Kriegstagebuch...*, vol. I: p. 299.
24. Juhász, ed., *Diplomáciai iratok...*, vol. V: p. 882. (587)
25. *Ibid.*, p. 889. (589)
26. *Ibid.*, p. 890.

27. Gyula Kádár, *A Ludovikától Sopronkőhidáig* (From the Ludovika [Military Academy] to Sopronkőhida) (Budapest, 1978), p. 343.
28. HL. Eln. Vkf.1. 1941/4784.
29. Carlile Aylmer Macartney, *October Fifteenth. A History of Modern Hungary, 1929-1945* (Edinburgh, 1961), vol. I: p. 461.
30. *Vollmacht des Gewissens* (Frankfurt am Main–Berlin, 1965), pp. 213–214.
31. Halder, *Kriegstagebuch...*, vol. I: p. 299.

JOINING GERMANY'S ATTACK ON YUGOSLAVIA

While Werth and his clique were worried about being left out of the war, Teleki hoped for exactly the opposite, even at the expense of postponing the re-annexation of further territory. He watched the situation in the Balkans with concern, and hoped that both Yugoslavia and Hungary could stay away from a conflict there. He was also concerned about discord between Russia and Germany, but hoped that both parties would become exhausted by it, so that Great Britain would benefit from the aftermath. And he hoped that the unhindered transit of the German troops across Hungary, along with the country's economic concessions, would satisfy his obligations as an ally, and that Hungary could stay away from a military encounter. That is what made him think that letting the Germans cross the country was a forgivable sin, even though he received repeated rebukes from the British government. Minister of Foreign Affairs László Bárdossy, who in the meantime had succeeded the deceased Csáky, could not say anything to the British other than the point that the Hungarian government had issued the permission at the specific request of the Romanian government and that "the British government had not earlier taken issue with the Germans' staying there for a long period of time."[1]

The British response distressed Teleki. Cadogan considered the Hungarian statement as merely a formal explanation, one that did not change the damaging facts. As Bárdossy wrote,

> The fact is that we helped Great Britain's foes to settle its forces in Romania, which consequently became a military basis for further operations. This time Cadogan makes an exception about Romania's request, but our courtesy has really served the

Germans' interests, because by now Romania has lost its independence and became a vassal state of Germany. Cadogan emphasized that he still hoped that the diplomatic relationship with Hungary could be maintained further, but that it will totally dependent on our behavior. If we let the Germans push their way into and settle on our territory and also hand over our military plants to their disposal—as Romania and, to all intents and purposes, Bulgaria also plan to do—we will be judged and treated in the same way as these countries."[2] At Barcza's interjection that for Hungary to reject the German request would have been fatal, Cadogan responded that although it did not want to force small states to choose between fatal alternatives, Great Britain could only allow certain behavior. Great Britain was obliged to consider every state in which enemy forces were creating military bases as enemy territory. Therefore, Great Britain "would attack enemy military objects from the air wherever they are, and would apply all the economic sanctions that it could against occupied countries."[3]

Teleki spelled out the Hungarian government's aspirations in a letter to the Hungarian ambassadors to London and Washington on March 3: "In this European war the Hungarian government's main task is to conserve Hungary's military, financial and manpower force until the end of the war. We have to keep ourselves away from participating in the conflict by all means. The outcome of the war is doubtful. However, whatever the outcome is, it is of the utmost importance for Hungary to stand unruffled when the European conflict is finished. It may easily be the case—especially if Germany loses the war, or even if Germany is not a complete loser—that a chaotic situation sets in in the eastern part of Europe, or all over

Europe for that matter. This would be of the greatest danger for countries that are not protected and had sacrificed their material resources and armies before the conflict finished."[4] He went on to say that Hungary was also threatened by different dangers from its neighbors, and that it could only rely on its own resources against them. Therefore, "it is the Hungarian political leaders' first and almost sole task to keep Hungary stable and strong until the end of the war. We are allowed to risk our country, youth and military power only for ourselves and for no one else."[5] Rejecting the transit of German troops—objected to by the British government—would have been just such a risky undertaking. Hungary had already rejected the German request for transit when the Germans attacked Poland, because Hungarian–Polish friendship and Hungarian honor demanded it. However, to do the same thing in Romania's case "would have meant a misjudgment of Hungary's situation and the Hungarian nation that would have been both offensive and humiliating at the same time, because there is not a single Hungarian who would protect Romania with his own body."[6] Besides, as long as Romania itself had not requested the German troops—and Romania had also informed Great Britain about this step—Hungary had not let through German troops. Furthermore, the German troops were to cross Hungary only by train and were not to take breaks along the way.

The central point that in Teleki's feelings about the Balkan situation was the hope that Yugoslavia would stay away from the Balkan conflict. It could do this by joining the Tripartite Pact. If it rejected joining the Pact then it could not avoid being attacked by the Germans. In that case, the Hungarian government would be unable to deny the transit of some of the attacking German troops across its territory without grave consequences. Moreover, the government would find it difficult to constrain the overly eager military command from joining the attack.

On February 26 on the ceremonial exchange of documents on the Hungarian–Yugoslavian Mutual Friendship Pact Teleki spoke warmly about the Hungarian–Yugoslavian friendship, saying that it would help to further the creation of a new European order, and also to further the goals of their mutual friends, Germany and Italy.[7]

On February 2 a German–Bulgarian agreement was signed, dealing with the German troops crossing Bulgaria towards Greece. Then, on March 1 Bulgaria joined the Tripartite Pact. On the same day German troops built three bridges across the Danube.[8] On March 2 Field Marshal Lišt's 12th Army began its deployment into Bulgaria, and its units advanced quickly towards the Greek border in order to stand by for the execution of Operation Marita.[9] The German troop movements forced Great Britain to take certain steps. On March 7 an expeditionary force of three infantry divisions and an armored brigade set sail towards Greek ports.

On March 8 the Hungarian ambassador to Belgrade reported that there was anxiety in the air due to the German deployments to Bulgaria.[10] Rumors were spreading about a generals' coup. The opposition parties were planning to move against the pro-German government. Mobilization had increased the number of troops in the army to 700,000 and then up to 800,000 during the past two days, when new draft notices had been sent out. The immediate cause of mobilization was the Bulgarians' threatening behavior and the need to reassure the public. However, the main purpose was to prepare for the situation should the discussions with the Germans became critical.[11]

As Hitler became increasingly nervous about the Yugoslavian situation, he needed to secure the deployment of his troops against Greece. Therefore, he could not delay the settling of the German–Yugoslavian relationship. He launched a concentrated diplomatic offensive against the Yugoslavs. He requested that Prime Minister Cvetkovič and Minister of Foreign Affairs Cincar-Markovič meet him on February 14 and, without any further ado, told them that Yugoslavia would have to join the Tripartite Pact. He did hold out the prospect of Yugoslavian territorial gains at Greece's expense.

In parallel with the Bulgarian deployment of the German troops, the Yugoslavian–German negotiations continued on March 2. The Yugoslavs actually joining the Pact, asked for guarantees for their borders and assurances that the German troops would not cross Yugoslavia.

The Hungarian government was insulted by the possible guarantees for Yugoslavia's borders, and immediately protested to the German government. On March 16 Bárdossy sent for the German ambassador, and let him know in forceful terms that just by concluding the Friendship Pact Hungary had not given up its territorial demands. Rather, the second point of the Friendship Pact called for the peaceful settlement of territorial issues. The German Reich's guarantees to Yugoslavia on borders would cause dissatisfaction in the Hungarian public, which would eventually place the Hungarian government in a very difficult situation.[12]

In Berlin, Sztójay immediately went into action and expressed to Weizsäcker and Woermann his surprise that the Yugoslavs would insist on the integrity of their country's borders.[13]

Hitler decided to intervene to soothe the Hungarians, especially because he planned to give them a role in case Yugoslavia decided not to join the line of German satellite states. And so he asked Bárdossy to go to Munich on March 21.

Even before the March 21 meeting took place, Sztójay once again appeared on the scene. In a March 19 telegram he cited Weizsäcker as saying that von Ribbentrop acknowledged the Hungarian position on the question of revising borders. The Germans were not going to double-cross Hungarian interests; furthermore, they planned to act on behalf of them. When Sztójay suggested that this be brought to the Yugoslavs' attention, Weizsäcker requested that the Hungarian government refrain, since this would make a German–Yugoslavian agreement very difficult. Instead, the Germans planned not to stand in the way of any future change in territory and were to establish their respect for Yugoslavia's territorial integrity only within the German–Yugoslavian context.[14]

Hitler received Bárdossy in Munich on March 21, and immediately came to the issue of the Hungarian–German relationship, through which Hungary had accomplished territorial revisionism beyond its dreams. With German intervention a solution had been reached to the Hungarian–Romanian question that, although not completely satisfying, was much better than an armed conflict of uncertain outcome. Peace in the Balkans was in Germany's interest, and therefore a solution had to be found that prevented Romania from total collapse, creating a vacuum into which Russia would step and losing for Germany the oil that it so badly needed.[15]

Hitler said that Germany's Balkan policy was led by the wish to avoid another Thessaloniki. He was sorry about the Greek–Italian conflict, which had made German intervention necessary. If he had been in the Italians' position, he would not have attacked in October without adequate preparation but would have rather turned against Crete. Yet Hitler would not have intervened had the conflict remained only within the realm of the Italians and Greeks. However, the British had "first tried to establish air bases, then tried to deliver war materials to Greece, and finally made an attempt to land troops in order to create a Thessaloniki-type front once again. Therefore, the German army will throw the British out of Greece, so that Greece will become Great Britain's second Dunkirk."[16]

Next, Hitler switched to a harsh tone in connection with Yugoslavia. He was not going to guarantee its borders. He was not an Englishman. He would only say to the Yugoslavs that he was not going to harm them, unless they demonstrated anti-German behavior. Yugoslavia would probably join the Tripartite Pact, and the government of the Reich wanted to make the Yugoslavs' decision easy for them.[17]

Speaking about the general military situation, Hitler established that Germany had already won the war and that the German army was strong. Presently it had 181 divisions that were "without work." He also spoke about invading England, although not with any kind of conviction.

Indirectly, Hitler also alluded to his plans in connection with the Soviet Union. He spoke about the alleged dangers still threatening from the Soviet Union despite the agreement between the two countries. He, however, "trusted above all agreements the 225 divisions at Germany's disposal." If the danger became real, "the divisions stationed at the Russian border would respond... In this case in a few weeks Soviet Russia would no longer exist."[18]

Finally Hitler made friendly remarks about the loyal Hungary. He said that Hungary had allowed and, furthermore, helped the transit of German troops towards Romania. It had done a great service to the Reich, which the Reich was not about to forget. Hungary could always count on Germany's help.[19]

Hitler did not fail to bring up economic requests with the friendly and loyal Hungary. He paid special attention to oil exploration in Hungary: the result of this would make it possible that "Hungary, as an oil and wheat exporter, would become of the utmost significance for Germany."[20]

Bárdossy was satisfied and thanked Hitler for the understanding and friendly tone. He assured Hitler of Hungary's unchanged loyalty and gratitude for the Second Vienna Award, which had necessarily been a compromise, as Bárdossy said he very well understood. However, what he heard gave him hope that ' later, at a more opportune time, we can still count on the modification of the borders as defined in the Vienna Award. Perhaps it will not happen based on historical entitlement, but rather for economic reasons. We do not want to stir up this question, but we expect that its time will come."[21]

Von Ribbentrop had worked on the Hungarian Minister of Foreign Affairs before. This time, first and foremost, he assured him of the invincibility of the German army. Practically, it had already won the war, since Germany now faced only Great Britain and Germany's military force on the continent was unyielding. It had enough ammunition for ten years, so the Führer did not plan to manufacture any more for the time being. And this also ensured that the war would finish the same year.[22]

As far as Yugoslavia was concerned, it would join the Tripartite Pact in a few days. And even if it did not, this was not of any major significance either. Irrespective of the Yugoslavian position, the Greek conflict would be terminated. In order to reassure Bárdossy, who was very sensitive towards enforcing Hungary's revisionist demands, von Ribbentrop came up with a *modus vivendi*. As was well known, the Hungarian revisionist claims were in good hands with the German government, von Ribbentrop said. Therefore, Hungary should not be afraid that Germany would make statements to Yugoslavia that would later prevent the realization of Hungarian territorial demands. However, considering the hard-line, pro-British view of the Yugoslavian public, the government in Belgrade found it difficult to decide to join the Pact. It was in Germany's interest, though, to block British troublemaking in the Balkans as soon as possible by the Yugoslavs' joining, and that was the reason why Germany wanted to make the Yugoslavian decision-making easy. As the discussions stood at that point, it could be reached by giving concessions to the Yugoslavs, which partly entailed agreeing that German troops were not to be transported across Yugoslavia and partly entailed Germany's establishing that it respected Yugoslavia's territorial integrity."[23] But this would not entail anything that would conflict with Hungary's interests. Indeed, the Reich did not have any claims towards Yugoslavia that "cut in or might block the future realization of Hungarian demands.[24]

Finally, the new, reformed Yugoslavian government gave in to the German request and, in Vienna, Prime Minister Cvetkovič, accompanied by Minister of Foreign Affairs Cincar-Markovič, signed Yugoslavia's accession to the Tripartite Pact on March 24. This triggered the explosion of long-simmering dissatisfaction. In the early hours of March 27 Commander of the Air Force General Simovič and the officer corps, dissatisfied with the pro-German policy of the government, toppled it. Peter II then replaced Regent Paul. The mob in Belgrade was thrilled by the change, and showed its agreement by anti-German and anti-Italian demonstrations. The new government formed under Simovič's leadership planned to pursue a policy of neutrality.

The Yugoslavian action outraged Hitler, who thought that it endangered the so-far undisturbed execution of Operation Marita, which had been delayed in any case. The planned date for launching Operation Barbarossa did not allow any delays for Operation Marita. Therefore, Hitler decided to expand Operation Marita to include Yugoslavia. He now counted on Hungary and Bulgaria to help in executing the operation.

On March 27 at 12:30 p.m., Hitler received Sztójay in von Ribbentrop's presence. Without any further preamble he directed the conversation to the Hungarian territorial revisionist demands that the Hungarian government had temporarily given up for the sake of peace in the Balkans but had now become topical again. The machinations of the Serbian military clique had changed the southeastern European situation. Hitler said that he did not want to take up arms against Yugoslavia, but if the Yugoslavs took up a position against Germany then he would "strike them like a streak of lightning and annihilate Yugoslavia."[25] In this case a clear outcome would occur and the operation against Greece would be easier. The military preparations were already underway, and 180–190 first-class divisions were at his disposal to execute his will.

Hitler then asked Sztójay to personally deliver his confidential message to the Regent. In Hitler's view the hour for territorial revision towards Yugoslavia had come for Hungary if he were forced to mobilize against Yugoslavia. Sztójay wrote that Hitler "fully recognizes Hungary's revisionist demands to the extent that His Excellency determines himself." Hitler mentioned Bácska and the Bánát among the territories "to be gained" but also pledged support in the issue of the free port of Fiume, a soft spot for the Regent, which was also claimed by the Italians. Hitler had only one wish—that the Croats receive autonomy.[26]

Hitler left it up to the Regent whether he would take military measures, but also added that "the German military command will probably be in touch with the Hungarian military command within 24 hours."[27]

Sztójay flew to Budapest immediately with Hitler's message, and reported to the Regent in Teleki's and Bárdossy's presence. Horthy received Hitler's message enthusiastically. The discussions about the response to be given to Hitler continued into the morning of March 28, with Teleki, Bárdossy, Bartha and Werth present. Teleki, who dreaded the consequences, tried to restrain the enthusiastic Regent. Teleki was concerned about the responsibility of violating the Hungarian–Yugoslavian pact that had been concluded and ratified not so long ago, about the danger of drifting into the larger European war, and about the necessity of reserving the *Honvéd* forces, since the current situation was laden with Soviet and Romanian threats. He tried to restrain Horthy from expressing immediate, full and unconditional cooperation with the Germans. His efforts bore fruit only with regard to the subdued tone of the response; otherwise he was helpless against the Regent, who was supported by the two soldiers ready for action. Finally, they decided to cite the Tripartite Pact to justify Hungary's allowing the transit of German troops towards Yugoslavia, and to ask the Germans for protection against the expected Yugoslavian and British air raids, because the Hungarian air force was not able to respond properly. Furthermore, they expressed Hungary's inclination to participate in military action against Yugoslavia. The conditions would be drawn up shortly and submitted to the Hungarian Supreme Military Council for a decision. They were to inform the Reich's government about it.[28]

Before even convening and informing the Council of Ministers in the afternoon, the Regent gave his response to Sztójay, who immediately flew to Berlin and delivered it to Hitler that same evening. Horthy assured the Führer that it was the Hungarian nation's decision "to follow the same political path and to stand by the German Reich with unchanged loyalty within its power." The Hungarian territorial demands raised by the message were sustained, and the Hungarian government maintained them in the second paragraph of the Yugoslavian–Hungarian agreement. Horthy also wrote that he agreed that the *Wehrmacht*'s High Command should take up connections with the Hungarian military command. He also noted that Soviet Russian influence might help explain recent Yugoslavian events, and called attention to the hostile sentiments of the Romanian government.[29]

Hitler's calculations had paid off. Without any hesitation, the Regent was willing to ignore the consequences of violating the Yugoslavian–Hungarian agreement recently signed, while expressing joy and satisfaction about the expected military cooperation with Germany. In this way Horthy decided on his own for an armed intervention against Yugoslavia, independent of the upcoming decision of the Council of Ministers and independent of the position of the Supreme Military Council. He must have been aware of the fact that by giving a green light to the common preparations of the Hungarian and German military commands he had started an irreversible process, because Hitler had counted on this cooperation.

During the March 28 session of the Council of Ministers, Minister of Foreign Affairs Bárdossy summarized the recent developments on the Yugoslavian question. According to Werth's interpretation of the meeting, "Hungarian military action against Yugoslavia was decided on, and it was a firm decision, one that no alleged later hesitation made doubtful." Yet the Council of Ministers never agreed on a resolution at that point. After the promises made by Horthy, the Council was not in a situation to bring a resolution, but could only acknowledge the facts of the situation.[30] The Council of Ministers did decide to grant the German request for transit for their army across Hungary. Furthermore, it decided that Hungary would join the war only when Yugoslavia as a political state disintegrated, the Croats proclaimed their independence, and either the Hungarian population of the Southern Region was endangered or a vacuum occurred in the region due to German military action. The Council also decided that military action only in the area between the River Danube and the River Tisza (*Duna–Tisza Köze*) sounded plausible. At the end of the session Teleki announced his resignation, but at Keresztes-Fischer's and Bárdossy's request he rescinded it.

The March 28 decisions opened the road for German–Hungarian military cooperation. Werth was now in his element. What he had long expected had finally materialized, and he would be able to participate in conquering Yugoslavia and, following that, be able to put a curb on the Serbs. Now the opportunity had opened up to acquire military honor and to express the loyalty of an ally. He knew that the Regent was on his side. Furthermore, the Council of Ministers' resolution about restraining the *Honvédség* would hold in reality until it clashed with the Germans' interests in any case. Hitler's promise and the speed at which the military connections were taken up indicated that the Führer had counted on Hungarian participation in the campaign. Neither Teleki nor the Council of Ministers could hinder that for long. In spite of his reservations, Werth would be ready to adjust the operations of the *Honvédség* to the wishes of the German army, since victory would justify it all. It might also have occurred to Werth that steadfastness in pleasing him might change Hitler's mind about the Hungarian military's participating in the likely eastern campaign. Bárdossy alluded to increased pressure on the Hungarian military command in the course of a discussion with Károly Rassay—the leader of the liberal oriented Citizens' Freedom Party—about the possibility of Hungary's entering the war against Yugoslavia. In their view it might be demoralizing for the army if a third mobilization were to be ended without the army's actually fighting.[31]

After Sztójay's departure on March 27 at 1:00 p.m., Hitler discussed the Yugoslavian situation with his army leaders. Both Operation Marita and Operation Barbarossa seemed to be in danger. Considering the consequences to these military plans, and without wondering whether the new Yugoslavian government would be loyal or not to the Axis, he issued the order for military preparations that would lead to the destruction of the Yugoslavian state and the army. The military offensive was planned to begin as soon as the troop preparations were finished. It was of crucial importance that the action be as quick as possible. He would request military support from Italy, Hungary and Bulgaria. His thinking was that the operation was going to be popular in those countries, due to their territorial claims on Yugoslavia. Italy wanted to acquire the Adriatic coast, Hungary claimed Bácska and the Bánát, and Bulgaria wanted Macedonia. Romania was going to have the task of covering the operation on the border with the Soviet Union. Hitler had already informed the Hungarian and Bulgarian ambassadors.

Hitler requested that they convene enough forces to ensure that Yugoslavia collapsed within the shortest possible timeframe, since it was bad enough that launching Operation Barbarossa had to be pushed back by four weeks. The military operations had to be launched from two directions. One wing of the 12th German Army, concentrating west of Sofia, would advance towards Skopje and take up connections with the Italians fighting in Albania. The other wing would advance towards Niš and Belgrade, while cooperating with the very powerful 2nd German Army concentrating in and attacking from the region of Graz and Klagenfurt. German troops attacking from the south would move towards Greece via Yugoslavia and accomplish the goals of Operation Marita at the same time.

The task of the German air force was first to obliterate the Yugoslavian air force—possibly still on the ground—with a surprise attack, and then to attack again in several waves to destroy Belgrade. Hungarian airports and equipment were to be at the Germans' disposal.[32]

Accordingly, on the same day Hitler issued his 25th Order for the military operation against Yugoslavia and Greece, and ordered that the preparations begin immediately.[33] The OKW were immediately to send a liaison staff to the Italian and Hungarian armies. In order to define the air operational space, the *Luftwaffe* would take up connections with the Italian and Hungarian air forces and negotiate with the respective commands. The *Luftwaffe* was immediately to gain access to Hungarian airports and airport personnel. In addition to supporting the *Luftwaffe*, Hungary was also: a) to assist with the deployment of the XLVI. Mechanized Army Corps of the 2nd German Army—concentrating in Graz—to southern Transdanubia so that it could launch its attack from there, b) to secure the swift transit of the XLI. Mechanized Army Corps to the region of Temesvár, and c) to mobilize the necessary Hungarian forces in order to occupy the Danube–Tisza region together with the attacking and advancing German troops from Croatia and the Bánát.[34]

On March 28 General Paulus, as the chief quartermaster of the OKW, was ordered to travel to Budapest. His assignment was to inform the Hungarian General Staff about the tasks of the Hungarian troops and to negotiate the immediate start of the necessary preparations.[35]

On March 29 in Vienna Paulus had discussions with General Lišt and General Weichs, the commanders of the 12th and the 2nd German Armies, respectively, who were assigned to attack Yugoslavia. Paulus informed them about the goals of his trip to Budapest as well. He arrived in Budapest on March 30, where Werth and General Dezső László, Chief of the General Staff's Operational Section, were glad to see him. Their discussions were very successful. They agreed that the *Honvédség* would participate in operations against Yugoslavia and, for that purpose, the Hungarian military command would be under the authority of the OKW. They also established the number of Hungarian army corps to be mobilized, the operational area of these troops, and the methods of cooperation with the different *Wehrmacht* commands. They also discussed the movements of German troops concentrating in southern Transdanubia and crossing Hungary towards the Bánát. Paulus asked Werth to prepare the Hungarian troops to be ready for action when the German troops launched the operations in about a week. While they were meeting, news was delivered about Hitler's decision that the 12th Army in the south under General Lišt would begin the operation on April 5, while the troops of Weichs' 2nd Army were to enter the operations on April 12.[36] Consequently, the start of the Hungarian participation in the action would be April 12. Finally, Paulus informed Werth that, for the sake of better cooperation, a German liaison staff headed by Major General Kurt Himer would arrive in Budapest within a few days.

Following the discussion, Paulus also paid a visit to Horthy and informed him about the results of the discussion. Then Paulus quickly left Budapest.[37]

After the visit Werth immediately got down to work, since time was precious. He wrote the following: "... based on the received authorization on March 30 I conducted discussions with Lieutenant General Paulus, representative of the German High Command, and we came to an agreement regarding military cooperation. The same day I informed the government about the results of our discussions."[38] Having the discretionary authorization of the Regent—and without the knowledge of the Prime Minister or the Minister of Foreign Affairs—he requested the mobilization of the I., the IV., the V. and the VII. Army Corps and the Rapid Army Corps on April 1:[39] "It was important to order the mobilization, because Lieutenant General Paulus informed me that the date of launching the German operation was April 12. Our calculations showed that it was impossible to mobilize and deploy the units of the Hungarian armed forces to participate in the operations at such short notice. Therefore, we had to plan on starting the Hungarian operations on April 15. From this it is obvious that once we had decided on participating in the campaign, ordering the mobilization was of crucial importance."[40] The process of the deployment turned out to be very slow in any case, because the parallel German troop movements both by rail and by road held it up.

The government refused to give its permission for the mobilization of the requested units. At that Werth asked for the Supreme Military Council to be convened. However, he felt that he might be in trouble, because he suspected that the Council might raise objections about the size and employment of the forces to be mobilized. He hoped that Horthy's authority would change the minds of the Council's interfering members.

Meanwhile, on March 31 in Berlin Paulus reported on his discussions with List, Weichs and Werth.[41]

Hungary's compliance with the German requests and its readiness to cooperate made a good impression in Berlin. Hitler spoke to Sztójay at great length about the German–Hungarian relationship and the two countries' "brotherhood-in-arms" relationship, based on a centuries-long common fate, which, in spite of past disagreements, would be firmer than ever before. Reporting on Hitler's reaction, the Hungarian ambassador happily reported that several ministers and generals had also spoken warmly about the recent development of the Hungarian–German relationship.[42]

In the meantime, ominous news arrived for the Hungarian government. On March 29 Barcza reported from London that Yugoslavia planned to enter an open alliance with Great Britain if it were attacked by Germany. The British were keen on being informed as to what consequences Hungary would draw from the Friendship Pact concluded with Yugoslavia.[43]

On Monday April 1 the Supreme Military Council was convened, and it was supposed to have the final word on the questions about cooperation, which Berlin thought had already been resolved, based on Horthy's letter and Paulus' report. During the Council's meeting, presided over by the Regent, Bárdossy introduced the situation, which had already been discussed during the March 28 meeting of the Council of Ministers, and asked for the Supreme Military Council's position regarding intervention in the German–Yugoslavian controversy and, in the case of a positive response, regarding the conditions. Bárdossy also proposed that Hungary should intervene only if there were a provocation on the Serbian side or if, due to a German military advance, the Croats were to secede and establish a counter-government. In the latter situation, the state with which Hungary had concluded a friendship pact would have dissolved, and so that pact would have become null and void. Therefore, Bárdossy continued, it was important to tell the Germans that the Hungarians could start military operations only several days after the Germans did. He urged the Hungarian military leaders to clarify the latter point, because it required military information. He justified his suggestion by the moral inhibition raised by the Friendship Pact with Yugoslavia and by "the unavoidable responsibility raised during the peace talks," even though he had absolutely no doubt that "it was always the loser who bore the responsibility."[44] In the ensuing debate, Minister of the Interior Keresztes-Fischer cautioned against abandoning the Friendship Pact and warned of the possibility of difficulties with the public. The Hungarian troops ought to march into Hungarian regions, but only after the German army. The Hungarian army should take over military administration. "Bárdossy himself saw an armed intervention as unavoidable, obviously at the latest possible date but possibly after the conditions mentioned by himself had been fulfilled. He especially wanted to argue that the Hungarian *Honvédség* was not to cross the line of the River Danube and was not to be employed for the military goals of a foreign power, so that Hungary in the future might enjoy peaceful coexistence with the Serb population living in the neighborhood."[45] Minister of Industry József Varga and Minister of Agriculture Dániel Bánffy also spoke in a similar vein.

Referring to his discussion and agreement with Paulus, Werth sought an immediate order for mobilization. He argued that Hitler would most certainly urge the same thing. From a military point of view he said that it would be very difficult to limit the Hungarian troops' operation to the Danube line. It might happen that the Hungarian troops would have to take over administration in the wake of the Germans advancing south.[46] Werth had every reason to protest, since, during his discussion with Paulus, the two had defined only the major directions of the army's employment and had not spoken about its being contained by any borders. Bartha, Lajos Reményi-Schneller and Bálint Hóman supported Werth's position.

Teleki was the last to speak in the meeting. He agreed with the Minister of Foreign Affairs' proposal, which defined the troops' operational region as being limited by the Danube line, and proposed that "... the intervention is dependent on the German advance into Croatia and, consequently, on the disintegration of the Yugoslavian state, without setting any definite time and while still maintaining our full and immediate freedom of action in the case of a Serb attack or provocation, which also includes the possibility of responding to the persecution of the Hungarian population in the annexed areas."[47]

In compliance with the decision of the Supreme Military Council, Horthy commissioned the Chief of the General Staff to carry out the necessary German–Hungarian military discussions and to make preparations for the mobilization of the five army corps.[48] Horthy kept the final right of ordering the mobilization for himself. He also included the right to command the troops within his own sphere of authority, and this was not to be transferred to the OKW's High Command.

The resolution of the Supreme Military Council as endorsed by Horthy tried to apply restrictions to Hungary s military action. In fact, it tried to detach Hungary from an openly aggressive act against Yugoslavia. Yet the shaky, misleading and self-deluding nature of the decision must have been obvious to Horthy and to Werth. Both of them were aware that the promises given to Paulus, following Horthy's enthusiastic and obliging letter to Hitler, would be mercilessly called upon. The prospective troop mobilization and concentration could be delayed, but not for long How much the Hungarians would participate depended mostly on how the cooperation with the German operations developed. The Hungarians could only hope for quick German victories, which would make a limited Hungarian participation possible. Hitler's definite request for Hungarian military cooperation also included the possibility of a proportionately larger participation by the Hungarian troops in order to complete the operation quickly. Under such circumstances, simply "preparing" for mobilization would not satisfy the Germans, and it was expected that this delaying technique would make the Germans protest.

Horthy was intimidated by his friend Teleki. He did not dare to tell him about the military obligations undertaken at the meeting with Paulus, which he had confirmed, and which called for an immediate mobilization. Horthy consented to a delaying tactic, waiting until the German demand for full mobilization arrived, knowing that it could not be rejected and could be used as a pretext to take the measures so eagerly promised to Paulus behind the

Prime Minister's back. Teleki, however, could not be misled in such a way. He no longer believed that the Supreme Military Council's decision could be upheld against the Germans' pressure. He knew that if it came to a head, neither the soldiers nor the government nor Horthy himself would support him. He felt that he was left alone against an approaching and unavoidable fate.

Werth was irritated by the rejection of his proposal, since he was now unable to satisfy the obligations undertaken in the agreement. He also developed a grudge against Horthy for not standing by him, and so offered his resignation. The Regent, however, did not even want to hear about Werth's resignation, and asked him to stay on.

The discord between Werth and Teleki and the rumor about Werth's resignation quickly leaked out and spread inside and outside the army.[49] Chief of Staff of the mobilized 3rd Army General Frigyes Gyimessy found the uncertainty in the wake of spreading rumors disconcerting. In his view, such rumors should be avoided in the future: "During the days preceding the partial mobilization, unverifiable rumors spread concerning controversies between the government and the military leadership and concerning their foreign policy positions. Since such rumors cannot be prevented in the future, I would find it useful if the relevant central military organs informed the army and army corps commands briefly and confidentially about events."[50]

Barcza's report of April 2 about the expected British reaction to events must have contributed to Teleki's utter despair, which drove him to commit suicide on April 3. For Teleki's letter to Horthy and Churchill's statement on Teleki, see the end of this chapter. Barcza confirmed the earlier British position: if Germany attacked Yugoslavia and Yugoslavia resisted, it would immediately become Great Britain's ally. If Hungary acquiesced or, even more so, facilitated the use of its territory as a base for the German army's use against Yugoslavia, Hungary should count on Great Britain's breaking off diplomatic relations with Hungary and all the consequences that this step might entail. Should Hungary join the offensive (against Yugoslavia), it should expect a declaration of war from Great Britain and its allies. In the latter scenario Hungary would be judged as an enemy of Great Britain and the United States at their final victory.

By the time Teleki received Barcza's message from Bárdossy, presumably in the evening of April 2, the first units of the XLVI. German Mechanized Army Corps had arrived in southern Transdanubia and the head of the XLI. German Mechanized Army Corps was approaching Budapest.

In the evening hours of April 3 Horthy appointed László Bárdossy as Teleki's successor, at István Bethlen's and Keresztes-Fischer's suggestion. Bárdossy also retained the foreign affairs portfolio. The new Prime Minister immediately convened the Council of Ministers regarding the mobilization, and it adopted a resolution ordering the mobilization of the IV. and the V. Army Corps and the Rapid Army Corps, the anti-aircraft units and the river forces. The border guard units had already been mobilized. The Chief of the General Staff set midnight April 4 as the start of the mobilization. Time was short, and the military had to count on the Germans' protesting if the Hungarians did anything less than the exact details that had been agreed to on March 30. The size of the mobilized forces was lagging behind that which had been agreed to, since, in the government's view, the smaller mobilization would be defended as a defensive regulation.[51]

Paulus, who had closely followed the events in Hungary and the execution of the details based on his discussions there, reported on Teleki's death to the OKW in the morning of April 3. At the same time he expressed dissatisfaction about news concerning the Hungarian mobilization, since it seemed that Horthy did not want to mobilize the whole Hungarian army. Instead, he had mobilized only the border guard units and the mechanized army corps. Finally, Paulus also noted that the Hungarian government was acting in an extremely reserved manner.[52] During the day he delivered new information, including the news that participation in an action against Yugoslavia had created serious differences of opinion within the government, which had worn out the sick Prime Minister. Paulus also reported that the mobilization included the IV. and the V. Hungarian Army Corps that day. Horthy was sending a letter to the Führer, with which Minister of Defense Bartha had already set out for Berlin.[53]

In German military circles the news quickly spread during the day that the Hungarian Prime Minister had protested, with his life, the German pressure that had been placed on Hungary to participate in the Yugoslavian campaign. The question came up how much this incident might disturb the planned course of preparations of the German army.[54] Hitler adopted a "wait-and-see" attitude, since he continued to trust Horthy. During his discussions with his military leaders on the same day, Hitler declared that, contrary to earlier decisions, the Hungarian troops were not to be subordinated to the OKW, and Horthy was to be in charge of them. The skeptical Halder wrote in his diary: "What a shame!"[55]

Prompted by a bad conscience, due to Teleki's suicide and his farewell note, and also due to the British threat, Horthy thought that he might attempt once again to clarify with Hitler the conditions of Hungarian participation in the Yugoslavian campaign by citing Teleki's death. Thus, Horthy reasoned, he could at least partially stave off the grave consequences held out by the British. It also seemed to offer a good opportunity to blame the slowness and delays in the Hungarian military preparations on Teleki's misgivings.

Minister of Defense Bartha, who was entrusted with implementing the necessary discussions, delivered Horthy's letter to Hitler on April 4. Horthy blamed Teleki's death on Teleki's guilty conscience, stemming from the fact that "he did not show adequate resistance in connection with the Yugoslavian question"[56] during the meeting of the Council of Ministers two days previously, when the Chief of the General Staff was also present. The whole country was shaken by Teleki's death, and Horthy himself was of the view that for appearance's sake Hungary should intervene only when, in the wake of German attacks, Yugoslavia had ceased to exist. The Council of Ministers also adopted a resolution to this effect.

In compliance with the details included in the March 28 letter, the necessary military preparations were finally completed. However, "his guilty conscience... and the gravity of the situation well proven by the suicide of the Prime Minister" forced Horthy to ask the German High Command "to decide on our troops' tasks in a way that will possibly be reconciled with our conscience."[57]

Horthy now wanted to subject the cooperation promised to Paulus at the discussion on March 30 to certain conditions. Bartha also delivered verbal additions to Horthy's letter to Hitler. A Hungarian military intervention against Yugoslavia would be possible if a *casus belli* situation occurred: if the Yugoslavs attacked the German or Hungarian troops or, more precisely, if such an attack could be provoked; or if Zagreb proclaimed the secession of Croatia, which would terminate the validity of the Friendship Pact.[58] Bartha also tried to reassure Hitler that three army corps had been mobilized, and hence Hungary still intended to cooperate with Germany.[59]

Hitler expressed his sympathy about Teleki's death, and promised Bartha that he would shortly respond to the Regent in writing. Hitler seemed to be understanding about the Hungarian problems; as for the *casus belli*, Hitler believed that it was established when the Yugoslavs de facto breached the agreement on joining the Tripartite Pact. However, he was going to consider the Hungarian views.[60]

Hitler said that he had no doubt that a common military action by the two countries was still important. He did not miss the chance to impress Horthy's vanity, saying that, obviously, the Regent himself would command the Hungarian troops that would cooperate with the Germans. Furthermore, Hitler "would only make suggestions for the sake of, and to ensure, unified action, and would like to make sure that His Excellency the Regent would be in charge for the sake of the prestige of the conquering independent Hungarian kingdom." Hitler also stressed that by re-annexing the Bácska and Bánát territories Hungary would become better off economically.[61]

Then the Führer informed Bartha about the favorable military situation for Germany. He told him not be afraid of a Turkish or a Soviet intervention during the Yugoslavian action, since he would leave strong forces at those borders for security. He was pleased that he would finally have the chance to beat the British in the Balkans and not only in Africa.

Bartha also had talks with the German military leaders. Keitel agreed with Hitler on the question of the *casus belli* against Yugoslavia and held out the prospect of many countries joining them against Yugoslavia. He stressed that quick success was in the common interest of all of them, and so they needed as many troops as possible to participate.[62]

Then the Hungarian Minister of Defense's path led to a meeting with Brauchitsch and Halder. After that meeting, Halder asked Paulus to take care of the Hungarian guest. Bartha told Paulus that Teleki had opposed intervening in Yugoslavia because of the Hungarian–Yugoslavian Friendship Pact and because he was also afraid of the political consequences. Teleki had left a letter behind to Horthy in which he cautioned him about the dangers of not being loyal to Yugoslavia. This was the letter that had shaken Horthy about the consequences of fulfilling what he had promised during the March 30 discussions with Paulus. Now it was Bartha's turn to talk to Paulus in order to reach another agreement. Paulus, who in the meantime had received instructions from Hitler, did not prove to be forgiving on the matter. With no further ado, he called the Hungarians to account regarding the March 30 agreement on which the German army had counted during its military operations.[63] The cornered Bartha promised something new—to mobilize the I. and the VII. Army Corps. He also promised that those army corps would be ready by April 15, while the Rapid Army Corps would be prepared to move by April 12. Although he did not seem to be very satisfied, Paulus disregarded the mobilization of the other army corps for the time being. The German General Staff, however, was surprised to see how tolerant Hitler was towards Horthy with regard to the Yugoslavian military operations.[64]

On April 5 Bartha was already back in Budapest, where he hastened to deliver Hitler's letter to Horthy. Although the letter's content is not known, Hitler must have shown some understanding towards Horthy's concerns, although he did not mention anything on the issue of a *casus belli* against Yugoslavia. Bartha must have spoken in the same vein when he said that he was reproached by the military for not implementing, and in fact delaying, the mobilization, yet did not receive any promises to facilitate the Hungarian government's situation.

In compliance with the German General Staff's wish and with the agreement of the Regent, on April 5 the mobilization was extended to include the 3rd Hungarian Army Command jointly with supporting units. On April 6 it was extended to include the I. and the VII. Army Corps. These units had a shorter time period available to get ready to march than originally planned since the new deadline was set first at April 11, then at April 12.[65] Bartha immediately notified Ambassador Erdmannsdorff about the decision with regard to the extension of the mobilization.[66]

In accord with Paulus' orders, Major General Kurt Himer was commissioned by the OKW on April 3 to set up a liaison staff that would be under the direct command of the OKH (*Oberkommando des Heeres*, the High Command of German Land Forces.) The liaison staff's tasks were to represent the German Command's interests at the Hungarian military command, and to maintain a tight relationship between the Führer and the Regent, on the one hand, and the units of the *Wehrmacht* and the Hungarian military command, on the other. It had to establish and maintain connections with the Commands of the 2nd and the 12th German Armies, and to maintain their cooperation with the Hungarian forces. All the German military supply, intelligence and communications units functioning in Hungary were subordinated to Himer. At the same time, a decision was made to establish an air force communications staff under Himer and led by Fütterer.[67]

Himer arrived in Budapest on April 5 and set to work immediately. It was Himer who relayed the OKW's request that the 19th Brigade concentrating east of the River Tisza be withdrawn to the western bank and that the Tisza be the border between the 19th Brigade and the XLI. German Mechanized Army Corps deployed towards the Bánát. This arrangement was supposed to help to alleviate the tension between Hungary and Romania.[68] Antonescu had protested against the deployment of Hungarian troops in the Bánát region and had threatened military action. Romania held a claim on the Bánát as well, and argued that this area should be occupied by Romanian troops.[69] Hitler accepted the Romanian protest, since he did not consider the presence of Hungarian troops in the Bánát region desirable, in spite of the fact that he had promised the area to Horthy. Yet Hitler also did not find the presence of the Romanian troops there desirable either.

In the evening of April 5 Himer informed the Hungarian military leaders that military action would begin the following day.[70] On April 6 the 12th German Army launched the offensive against central and southern Yugoslavia. At the same time the German air offensive began, with 1,000 airplanes. The attacking troops successfully advanced already during the first day. The 2nd German Army did not move, waiting to swing into action on April 8.[71]

On April 7 the Hungarian General Staff received the following telegram from the OKW: "The behavior of the Yugoslavian government has made it necessary that we occupy Yugoslavia by armed force. Both Hungary and Italy will participate in the actual occupation."[72]

At the news of the offensive, the Hungarian General Staff tried to accelerate the mobilization and deployment of its troops, so that they would be ready to act as soon as possible. In its "deployment and transportation instructions" of April 7 the General Staff announced that, "in the wake of Horthy's decision, Hungary will participate in the military operations against Yugoslavia." Werth told Lieutenant General Elemér Gorondy-Novák, Commander of the 3rd Hungarian Army, "We are late. We have to hurry up not to miss the Germans' offensive starting from Transdanubia and the Bánát on April 12, or maybe even on April 11."[73] Disregarding the resolutions of the Supreme Military Council, Werth wanted to be ready to attack together with the German army. In his view, if Hungary were late, an opportunity would be lost, which might have grave consequences for the future. Horthy, who had been boosted by the German successes, was not far from this way of thinking either. Himer reported to his superiors that Horthy now felt no concern about the application of the Hungarian army in Yugoslavia and was only led by the goal that the Hungarian army not be too far from Hungary and that there not be too much bloodshed.[74]

In the meantime, the telegram coming from Cadogan to the Hungarian government was totally ignored. The telegram called the government's attention to the consequences of allowing German troops to deploy in Hungary.[75]

The German troop movements in Hungary and the use of Hungarian airports caused the Yugoslavian air force to act immediately. In the morning of April 7 it attacked the airports at Szeged, Pécs and Siklós. During the course of the attack, German fighter planes and the Hungarian air defense shot down eight Yugoslavian bomber planes.[76] The Hungarian leadership described these attacks as a provocation and an act of aggression against Hungarian territory. This offered a good opportunity for the press and the radio to join in the psychological preparation of the offensive by creating an anti-Yugoslavian atmosphere in the public.

On April 8 the attack of the 2nd German Army was launched, and therefore the XLVI. German Mechanized Army Corps, concentrating in southern Transdanubia, swung into action as well. Its armored divisions occupied the bridges at Barcs, Koprivnica and Eszék, and created a bridgehead on the other side of the River Dráva. The following day the 14th and the 8th Armored Divisions swung into action and, against weak resistance, quickly advanced in a southern and southeastern direction. The infantry divisions of the 2nd Army, advancing from the west, were hindered mostly by bad road conditions. The Italian army also launched an attack from the Istrian Peninsula. The XLI. German Mechanized Army Corps was ready to proceed towards Belgrade, while the 12th Army turned north with its 11th Armored Division quickly advancing towards Belgrade. The German advance was quicker than expected. On April 10 German troops occupied Zagreb.[77]

The quick success of the 2nd German Army had not been expected either during the planning phase or after the initial launch of the offensive. The operations of the XLVI. and XLI. German Mechanized Army Corps had to be supported by Hungarian forces advancing between the River Danube and the River Tisza. It was the task of Himer and the Hungarian liaison officers who were assigned to the army corps to coordinate these movements. When Paulus and Werth had made arrangements on March 30, they had calculated that the concentration of Hungarian forces would be complete by April 7 or 8 so that those troops could become part of the German attack at any necessary point after that. Since the Hungarian mobilization was delayed, the 2nd German Army launched its operations without the Hungarians.

On April 9 Himer personally delivered Hitler's letter to Horthy, in which the Hungarian *Honvédség* was assigned the task of attacking the Grădiştea–Novi Sad general line in order to break through the enemy's fortifications and take possession of the ridge of hills there. The attacking party was to join the offensive of the XLVI. German Mechanized Army Corps as soon as it could.[78]

This time Horthy did not express any reservations, and accepted Werth's plan that "the majority of the 3rd Hungarian Army—with four to six brigades, two mechanized brigades, and a mounted brigade—should swing into attack on April 12 without waiting for the completion of the planned deployment."[79] They also considered that the 11th Brigade might forge ahead to Eszék.[80]

In the morning of April 9 Erdmannsdorff showed up at Bárdossy's office and asked him to arrange for Hungary to sever relations with Yugoslavia and Greece. At that point Bárdossy could not have known about Horthy's and the Chief of the General Staff's unconditional acceptance of the German plans, and so stated that Hungary's military move—still in the preparatory phase—was conditional upon the disintegration of the Yugoslavian state. He also grasped the opportunity to raise the issue of the threatening Romanian behavior over the Bánát region, which had been promised to Hungary by Hitler. Erdmannsdorff tried to reassure him, saying that Germany would not allow Antonescu to move against Hungary. As for a possible Soviet attack, it was quite improbable, because the Soviets would expose themselves to side attacks from the Germans via the Polish territories.[81]

On the same day in Berlin, von Ribbentrop sent for Sztójay and asked for the immediate severance of diplomatic relations with Yugoslavia. He emphasized "the necessity of a quick, forceful and resolute action that would result in the collapse of Yugoslavia."[82] Weizsäcker also tried to reassure Sztójay, who visited him, about the Romanian behavior. Sztójay voiced Bárdossy's point that it would be beneficial if the Germans preventively told Antonescu that arrangements had been made about the Bánát for Hungary's benefit. Weizsäcker did not think that any "preventive" measures would be necessary, since the situation mentioned by Antonescu could never occur, because the Hungarian troops would not cross the line of the River Tisza to the east and, therefore, would not bump into any Romanian soldiers. Weizsäcker also cautioned Sztójay, alluding to the rumor that "some low-ranking military leaders will not take the River Tisza line so literally." He also objected to the chance that any Hungarian troops might appear in the Bánát even if promised to Hungary by Hitler.[83]

The great moment so eagerly awaited by the Hungarian government had arrived. On April 10, after occupying Zagreb, Yugoslav Colonel Slavko Kvaternik declared Croatia to be an independent state. This came in very handy for the Hungarian leaders, because, for appearance's sake, it could now comply with its earlier resolutions in its decision to launch its troops on April 11. Knowing the precursor events, it seems obvious that if the German troops had not advanced so fast, then Kvaternik's step and Zagreb's occupation would not have happened on April 10. However, Hungary's military action would have started on April 12 at the latest in any case. Urgent messages from the Germans on April 9 to take diplomatic and military action against the Yugoslavs were clear.

We cannot quite agree with any analysis that claims that the April 11 Hungarian military participation in the wake of the German successes was unnecessary, and that Hitler was led only by political considerations, such as preventing Hungary from staying out of the war, which was Teleki's policy. Instead, in addition to the obvious political reasons, there were military ones as well. When launching the 2nd Army's attack on April 8, neither the German High Command nor Hitler foresaw the kind of success of the operations that they enjoyed. They had counted on greater resistance and a slower advance. They had not hoped to occupy Zagreb as early as April 10. However, quite apart from everything else, the deployment of Hungarian troops in the area between the Rivers Danube and Tisza was an organic part of the operational plan.

Starting on April 11, the Hungarian troops were supposed to secure the advance of the XLI. German Mechanized Army Corps from the Bánát towards Belgrade from the right by engaging and defeating the Yugoslavian forces (three infantry divisions and one cavalry division) stationed in Bácska. Hitler had called on Horthy two days before the actual starting date of the Hungarian movement, to remind him that the Hungarian army should live up to its obligation.

Prime Minister Bárdossy convened the Council of Ministers in the late hours of April 10 and announced that, due to Croatia's secession, a new situation had developed in the Hungarian–Yugoslavian relationship. With Croatia's secession, Yugoslavia had ceased to exist. Due to the threatening Yugoslavian behavior—air raids and incursions—it was Hungary's obligation to defend the Hungarians from anarchy in southern Hungary. In the wake of events, Bárdossy asked for an audience with the Regent and suggested that "he give his consent to issuing the submitted governmental proclamation. The development of the general situation has made it possible that we participate in the military action when we want and in the manner in which we want, since Yugoslavia, as a political state, has ceased to exist, and we have regained our freedom of action." The ministers supported the Prime Minister's announcement, since it was in accord with earlier decisions of the military command and the Council of Ministers. The following day the Regent issued a proclamation to the country and gave military orders to the army, emphasizing the point that he had launched the troops in the interest of the defenseless Hungarian population and not against the Serb people.[84]

Without completing the mobilization, the Hungarian troops began their military operations. The troops of the 3rd Hungarian Army—the I., the IV. and the V. Army Corps, and the Rapid Army Corps—reached the set targets after a few small skirmishes on April 14 and completed the occupation of the area between the

Joining Germany's Attack on Yugoslavia

River Danube and the River Tisza and the area of the Muraköz. Their advance was also facilitated by the fact that the Yugoslavian forces feared encirclement and so retreated.

So the troops reached the Danube, which they could not cross, according to the decision of the Supreme Military Council. Bethlen also reinforced this decision on April 11 at the unexpectedly convened, and therefore select, meeting of the Foreign Affairs Committee of the Upper House, where Bárdossy had announced the launching of the military action against Yugoslavia as justified by the formation of the Croat state and the disintegration of Yugoslavia. Bethlen, agreed with the military intervention, emphasized the point that "beyond the set target and on foreign territory, Hungary must not participate in the war against either Serbia or any other country."[85]

Yet, in spite of its intentions and promises, the Hungarian government became more and more entangled in the conflict. Without any protest, it immediately satisfied the German request to deploy part of its troops over the Danube line. This step further aggravated the government's actions and further tarnished its international image. This step could not be justified by the situation arising out of the disintegration of the Yugoslavian state or by the defense of the Hungarian population there. It also lends credence to the idea that the German military command tried to complete the Balkan operation as quickly as possible. And it is in accord with the fact that, three days before the invasion, the Germans insisted on Hungarian participation due to military needs.

On April 12 General Jodl informed Himer that he was not going to deploy the Hungarian infantry brigades over the line of the Danube but that he wanted to ask whether, for a short time, the Hungarians were willing to deploy their Rapid Army Corps in the direction of Sarajevo under the 1st German Armored Group.[86]

The Hungarian General Staff was glad to agree to the deployment, although Colonel Dezső Lászó, Head of the Operational

Section, made reference to politicians who controlled the decision. In his view this issue should be approached on a political level as well, perhaps in the form of a letter from the Führer. Himer immediately reported it to Keitel, who reassured him that a letter would shortly be sent to Horthy spelling out the Führer's request that the mechanized brigades of the Rapid Army Corps continue to be at the German army's disposal.[87]

German Embassy Counselor Werkmeister reported to Horthy in the morning of April 13 and relayed Hitler's telegram request that the Hungarian 1st and 2nd Mechanized Brigades continue their advance in Serbia and participate in defeating the Serb resistance.[88]

Following that, the Prime Minister went to see the Regent and told him that he had misgivings about the German request, in the light of the Regent's April 11 manifesto saying that "my soldiers' action is not against the Serb people, with whom we want to live in peace." If the Hungarian troops crossed the River Danube, it could mean nothing except a military action against the Serbs.

Horthy did not think that he could refuse Hitler's request, yet, he pointed out the difficulties that would hinder the practical realization of the request. The two brigades would not be able to cross the blown-up bridges for a while, and therefore it was questionable whether they could assist the Germans in time.[89]

The German request was not unexpected for either Horthy or the government. Werth had already informed the Regent and, most probably with Horthy's knowledge, prepared a memorandum for the government on April 12 in which he spoke about the necessity and the importance of deploying Hungarian troops beyond the Danube line. He also warned the members of the government that if the Hungarians did not march on with the Germans, they would risk losing everything gained so far. It was clear from Werth's memorandum that the agreement concluded between the two armies had not had factored into it the type of limitations that had been passed by the Supreme Military Council under the influence of Teleki: "We have to count on a call from Germany requiring that, in the spirit of the original agreement, we continue the military operations over the Danube line, towards the direction of Sarajevo, and together with the German and Italian forces." Anticipating disagreements, he also warned that the war would end only after the enemy was fully broken, no matter how modest Hungarian territorial demands would be: "... Keeping them [the re-annexed territories] will be assured only when the enemy is fully broken... The Hungarian army should continue the war until the Yugoslavian armed forces are totally annihilated. Therefore, from where we stand the war against Yugoslavia does not finish upon reaching the Danube line."[90] Werth offered further surprises regarding the German–Hungarian alliance and cooperation. According to him, "within the framework of the military alliance, Hungary has accepted the German High Command. Therefore, directions from this Command will have to be fully accepted, so that we will not commit the mistake of most coalition wars of risking overall success for individual goals."[91]

We do not know of anyone in the Hungarian Council of Ministers who would have flatly rejected Werth's memorandum, which advocated a complete military and political submission to Germany, and which alluded to a non-existent military alliance between the two countries. Reacting to the recent German military successes, Werth disclosed his full-blown pro-German policy, which was created and practiced with the agreement of most of the military leaders. Teleki, who would have responded to this unrestrained suggestion and would have tried once again to hold the Regent back from such irreparable measures, was no longer alive. Bethlen was the only one in the Upper House who, along with Bárdossy, raised the issue of controlling the General Staff and curbing their aspirations, which went way beyond the intentions of the political leadership.

In the early evening hours the Council of Ministers was convened to discuss the German request. Bárdossy immediately pointed out that the decision was in the hands of the Regent, and that it was the government's obligation to cope with his decision. He also thought that "the edge of the German request might be dulled by the developments of the coming days should a situation develop where the Serbs cease to resist and the Serb army capitulates, so that the Hungarian mechanized brigades will not have to be deployed. Yet in the given situation, it would be immensely difficult if we were not willing to fulfill Hitler's request."[92]

Keresztes-Fischer spoke first in the ensuing debate, saying that, although the two mechanized brigades crossing the Danube would not have a major impact on the war, Hungary would irretrievably intervene in the war by their action. Minister of Agriculture Dániel Bánffy seconded Keresztes-Fischer. Bartha tried to buttress the case for fulfilling the German request by saying that the brigades' task was to fill the void left in the Serb part of the Danube region.

Bárdossy reiterated that it would undoubtedly have an adverse effect on the Germans if the request were rejected. He did not want the situation between the Germans and the Hungarians to become strained. And the fact was that "we can only secure and defend our far-reaching plans if we do not raise suspicions about our helpfulness to the Axis."[93] He also spoke about the Russian threat and about Romania's plan to re-occupy northern Transylvania. Therefore, Hungary might be in need of German help in the near future, and the country should not risk losing the Germans' possible assistance. He said that he was convinced that there was no major disagreement among the members of the government on this important issue, and then asked the Council members to strive for a uniform position.

Keresztes-Fischer argued once again that to annihilate the Yugoslavian armed forces was the strategic goal of the German army, while Hungary's goal was to regain the annexed territory up to the Danube line. In his view, this was to be stressed, for it was the cardinal question. After the government agreed, the Hungarian military command should be entrusted with the date and mode of action of the two brigades.

After receiving Horthy's and the government's agreement, the Hungarian military command immediately set out to concentrate the two brigades. The brigades were completely under the authority of the German military command, except for one condition—they were to be deployed for a limited distance only, at a maximum of 150 kilometers from the nearest usable railway station and possibly in the River Száva Valley.

Lieutenant General Béla Miklós, Commander of the Rapid Army Corps, delivered the condition to General Kleist, Commander of the 1st German Armored Group in Belgrade on April 16. The government justified the constraint by noting that the railways and roads could not be used, due to their destruction, and by noting that there were difficulties with providing provisions for the brigades.

The brigades began to cross the River Dráva at Eszék on April 16. Their task was to replace the German 8th Armored Division, so that certain segments could be withdrawn and be able to be transported by April 20. By April 18 certain parts of the brigades had reached Karlovac and Ruma, with others reaching Valjevo. Then the Command of the Rapid Army Corps received a telegram from the Germans ending all further advance because of the ceasefire negotiations. The Hungarian units were withdrawn from Yugoslavia on April 23 and their participation in the operation ended.[94]

The letters sent by Count Teleki Prime Minister of Hungary to Regent Miklós Horthy:[95]
Your Grace!

We committed perfidy—due to covardice—in opposition to the eternal friendship treaty based on Your speech at Mohács. The nation feels it and we throw away it honor.

We joined the rascals—since not a word is true of the fabricated slanders about atrocities committed against Hungarians not

even against Germans. We became body-snatchers, the most despicable nation.
    I did not hold you back.
    I am culpable.
April 3, 1941.   Pál Teleki

Your Grace,
    Even if my action does not succeed fully and would I still be alive, I hereby resign.
    With sincere respect
April 3, 1941.   Pál Teleki

    Prime Minister Winston Churchill's statement on Teleki: "His suicide was a sacrifice to absolve himself and his people from guilt in the German attack upon Yugoslavia. It clears his name before history. It could not stop the march of the German armies nor the consequences."[96]

Notes

1. Gyula Juhász, ed., *Diplomáciai iratok Magyarország külpolitikájához 1936–1945* (Diplomatic Writings on Hungary's Foreign Policy, 1936–1945) (Budapest, 1962–1982), vol. V: p. 685. (9573)
2. Domokos Szent-Iványi, *Emlékirat* (Memoirs), Ráday Levéltár (Ráday Archive), Szent-Iványi hagyaték C/80, p. 489.
3. *Ibid.*, p. 490.
4. Juhász, ed., *Diplomáciai iratok...*, vol. V: p. 893. (594)
5. *Ibid.*, p. 894.
6. *Ibid.*, p. 895.
7. *Ibid.*, p. 883. (588); Országos Levéltár (National Archive, OL). K 64-89-16-85/1940. Rp.
8. Franz Halder, *Kriegstagebuch. Tägliche Aufzeichnungen des Chefs des Generalstabes des Heeres 1939–1942/Generaloberst Halder* (Stuttgart, 1962–1964), vol. II: p. 297.
9. *Ibid.*, vol. II: p. 298.
10. Juhász, ed., *Diplomáciai iratok...*, vol. V: p. 924. (613)
11. *Ibid.*, p. 627. (616)
12. *Ibid.*, p. 643. (628)
13. OL. K 64-89-16-111/1941. Rp.
14. OL. K 64-89-16-118/1941. Rp.
15. Raymond James Sontag, et.als., ed., *Documents on German Foreign Policy, 1918–1945* (Washington, 1949–1954), vol. XII: p. 331. (191); Szent-Iványi, *Emlékirat...*, p. 538.
16. György Ránki, Ervin Pamlényi, Loránt Tilkovszky and Gyula Juhász, eds., *A Wilhelmstrasse és Magyarország: Német diplomáciai iratok Magyarországról, 1933–1944* (The Wilhelmstrasse and Hungary: German Diplomatic Documents about Hungary, 1933–1944) (Budapest, 1968), p. 558. (731)
17. Szent-Iványi, *Emlékirat...*, p. 539.
18. Ránki–Pamlényi–Tilkovszky–Juhász, *A Wilhelmstrasse és Magyarország...*, p. 557. (371); Szent-Iványi, *Emlékirat...*, p. 557.
19. *Ibid.*, p. 359.
20. *Ibid.*
21. Szent-Iványi, *Emlékirat...*, p. 539.
22. *Ibid.*, p. 540.

23. *Ibid.*, p. 541.
24. Juhász, ed., *Diplomáciai iratok*..., vol. V: p. 977. (662)
25. Szent-Iványi, *Emlékirat*..., p. 542.
26. *Ibid.*, p. 543.
27. *Ibid.*
28. Carlile Aylmer Macartney, *October Fifteenth. A History of Modern Hungary, 1929-1945* (Edinburgh, 1961), vol. I: p. 475.
29. *Horthy Miklós titkos iratai* (Miklós Horthy's Secret Writings), ed. Miklós Szinai and László Szűcs, (Budapest, 1962),p. 290; Vilmos Nagybaczoni Nagy, *Végzetes esztendők 1938-1945* (Fatal Years, 1938-1945) (Budapest, 1986), p. 61.
30. Szent-Iványi, *Emlékirat*..., p. 546.
31. *Ibid.*, p. 648.
32. Raymond James Sontag, et.als., ed., *Documents on German Foreign Policy, 1918-1945* (Washington, 1949-1954), vol. XII: p. 373. (217)
33. *Ibid.*, p. 395. (223)
34. *Ibid.*, p. 396.
35. Halder, *Kriegstagebuch*..., vol. II: p. 331.
36. *Ibid.*, p. 337.
37. Kálmán Kéri's personal account to the author.
38. Szent-Iványi, *Emlékirat*..., p. 104.
39. Ránki-Pamlényi-Tilkovszky-Juhász, *A Wilhelmstrasse és Magyarország*..., p. 570. (383)
40. Szent-Iványi, *Emlékirat*..., p. 104.
41. Halder, *Kriegstagebuch*..., vol. II: p. 338.
42. Szent-Iványi, *Emlékirat*..., p. 547.
43. *Ibid.*
44. OL. Filmtár (Film Archive), 7887. Szálasi-per (Szálasi Trial). Hóman napló (Hóman Diary).
45. *Ibid.*
46. Szent-Iványi, *Emlékirat*..., p. 106.
47. *Ibid.*
48. *Ibid.*
49. Dezső Saly, *Szigorúan bizalmas* (Strictly Confidential) (Budapest, 1945), p. 330.
50. Hadtörténelmi Levéltár (Military History Archive, HL). Eln. Vkf.1. 1941/5161.
51. Ránki-Pamlényi-Tilkovszky-Juhász, *A Wilhelmstrasse és Magyarország*..., p. 570. (383)

52. Halder, *Kriegstagebuch...*, vol. II: p. 343.
53. *Ibid.*, p. 344.
54. Percy Schramm, ed., *Kriegstagebuch des Oberkommandos der Wehrmacht (Wehrmachtführungsstab), 1940–1945* (Frankfurt am Main, 1961–1979), vol. I: p. 1200.
55. Halder, *Kriegstagebuch...*, vol. II: p. 342.
56. László Zsigmond, ed., *Magyarország és a második világháború* (Hungary and World War II) (Budapest, 1966), p. 297.
57. *Ibid.*, p. 298.
58. *Ibid.*, p. 301.
59. Nagybaczoni Nagy, *Végzetes esztendők...*, p. 65.
60. Zsigmond, ed., *Magyarország...*, p. 302.
61. *Ibid.*, p. 303.
62. *Ibid.*, p. 305.
63. Halder, *Kriegstagebuch...*, vol. II: p. 348.
64. *Ibid.*
65. János Csima, *Adalékok a Horthy-hadsereg szervezetének és háborús tevékenységének tanulmányozásához (1938–1945)* (Additions to Studying the Organizational Structure and the Military Activities of the Horthy Army: 1938–1945) (Budapest, 1961), p. 51.
66. Sontag, et.als., ed., *Documents on German Foreign Policy...*, vol. XII: p. 479. (282)
67. *Kriegstagebuch des Deutschen Generals beim Oberkommando der Kgl. Ungar Wehrmacht,* published by P. E. Schramm. The Hungarian translation of the diary was published in the journal, *Századok* in József Kun's translation: "A német hadsereg magyarországi politikájához, 1941. március–június" ([Additions] To the German Army's Policy in Hungary, March–June, 1941), *Századok* (1965) 6: pp. 1231–1246.
68. *Ibid.*, p. 1232.
69. Andreas Hillgruber, *Hitler, König Carol und Marschal Antonescu* (Wiesbaden, 1954), p. 151.
70. *Századok* (1965) 6: p. 1232.
71. Halder, *Kriegstagebuch...*, vol. II: p. 351.
72. HL. Eln. Vkf.1. 1941/4856.
73. Csima, *Adalékok a Horthy-hadsereg szervezetének...*, p. 53.
74. *Századok* (1965) 6: p. 1233.
75. Szent-Iványi, *Emlékirat...*, p. 114.
76. HL. Eln. Vkf.1. 1941/4940.

77. Halder, *Kriegstagebuch...*, vol. II: p. 360.
78. *Századok* (1965) 6: p. 1233.
79. Ránki–Pamlényi–Tilkovszky–Juhász, *A Wilhelmstrasse és Magyarország...*, p. 574. (389)
80. Sontag, et.als., ed., *Documents on German Foreign Policy...*, vol. XII: p. 509. (306)
81. Ránki–Pamlényi–Tilkovszky–Juhász, *A Wilhelmstrasse és Magyarország...*, p. 573. (388)
82. Juhász, ed., *Diplomáciai iratok...*, vol. V: p. 1033. (720)
83. Ránki–Pamlényi–Tilkovszky–Juhász, *A Wilhelmstrasse és Magyarország...*, p. 575. (390)
84. Juhász, ed., *Diplomáciai iratok...*, vol. V: p. 1029. (717)
85. *Ibid.*, p. 1037.
86. *Századok* (1965) 6: p. 1234.
87. *Ibid.*, p. 1235.
88. *Ibid.*, p. 1234.
89. OL. Minisztertanácsi jegyzőkönyv (Minutes of the Council of Ministers), April 13, 1941.
90. Szent-Iványi, *Emlékirat...*, p. 585.
91. *Ibid.*
92. OL. Minisztertanácsi jegyzőkönyv (Minutes of the Council of Ministers), April 13, 1941.
93. *Ibid.*
94. Csima, *Adalékok a Horthy-hadsereg szervezetének..*, p. 60.
95. Gyula Juhász, *A Teleki-kormány külpolitikája, 1939–1941* (The Foreign Policy of the Teleki Government, 1939–1941) (Budapest, 1964).
96 Mario D. Fenyo, Hitler, Horthy and Hungary. German–Hungarian Relations, 1941–1944 (New Haven, 1972), p. 10.

THE HUNGARIAN MILITARY COMMAND OFFERS ITS SERVICES TO THE GERMANS

By joining the attack on Yugoslavia the Hungarian government tied itself to Germany and discontinued the policy of armed neutrality as forged by Teleki. Even though there was no declaration, after April 7 there was a breakdown in diplomatic relations between Britain and Hungary, while the United States also strongly expressed its concern about the Hungarian action. On April 12 Deputy Commissioner of Foreign Affairs Vishinski also expressed to Kristóffy the Soviet government's dissatisfaction that Hungary had attacked and occupied a country with which it had signed a friendship agreement just four months ago.[1]

The Soviet government ignored the Hungarian military deployments taken in anticipation of Soviet troop concentrations along the border. In the Carpathians Werth mobilized the 1st Mountain Brigade, the border guard units, and those units of the VIII. Army Corps still at their peacetime station in order to cover the operation against Yugoslavia.[2] Even in the middle of the military operation against Yugoslavia, Werth did not for a moment take his eyes off the movements of German troops on the Soviet border. He was very well aware of Hitler's and his soldiers' remarks about the state of the German–Soviet relationship and remarks alluding to what was obviously a possible anti-Soviet German attack.

The Bánát question was now central to the Hungarian government's foreign policy. Very soon it realized that the Romanians were not the only reason why the German military command did not let the Hungarian troops enter the Bánát territory. Hitler simply did not want to give this territory to Hungary, in spite of his earlier promise. Bárdossy's attempts through the German ambassador to

Budapest and through Sztójay to persuade the Germans otherwise remained unsuccessful.

Erdmannsdorff informed Bárdossy at a meeting on April 14 that the Reich had agreed to a Romanian request that the Bánát be occupied only by German troops, and that this was the reason why Germany could not fulfill the Hungarian request to take it over. And Hitler confirmed this to Sztójay at the German Military Headquarters on April 19. Hitler said that it was in the common Hungarian–German interest that the takeover of the territory promised by Hitler be postponed for a few months. Antonescu's situation was difficult and it was not in Hungary's interest to have turmoil in Romania. Hitler further speculated that he would give some compensation to the Romanians for the Bánát. However, he did not know yet "when or how it would become a possibility." In the meantime, he expected that "in its approach, the Hungarian government would count on this state of affairs."[3]

Hitler also made his position clear to Horthy when he received him in Mönichkirchen on April 24.

While Hungarian diplomats made renewed efforts to prevail on the issue concerning the Bánát, the Hungarian military leaders' attention was occupied by the preparations for Operation Barbarossa. With regard to the Bánát fiasco, Werth came to his usual conclusion that only by joining up with the German army's actions in a timely fashion, without reservations and with the appropriate forces, would Hungary have a chance at a complete territorial revision. The tug of war around joining the attack against Yugoslavia once again decreased the value of the army in the Germans' eyes. Dazzled by another blitzkrieg success of the German army, and trusting in the support of an also enthusiastic Horthy, Werth set out to act decisively. He decided to grasp any opportunity to make an offer of the Hungarian army's joining the upcoming German attack on the Soviet Union.

The Himer Committee seemed to be a good device to use to deepen the connection with the German military command. In Werth's view, the Himer Committee had not stayed in Hungary only to direct the quick transit and regrouping of German troops in their attack on Yugoslavia. In addition, he believed that it was the intention of the German military command to use the Himer Committee to keep up a stable and direct relationship between the two High Commands and to make the preparations for a German attack against the Soviets, possibly to be launched from Hungarian territory, with the participation of Hungarian troops. It was no secret to Werth that several German military leaders—for example, Brauchitsch and Halder—had an opinion different from Hitler's rigid rejection of Hungary's participation.

On March 14 the German General Staff held a meeting about the tasks of the *Heeresgruppe Süd* in participating in Operation Barbarossa and about the military operations of the 17th German Army in an offensive directly north of the Carpathians. The idea came up to mobilize Hungarians and the Slovaks two days before Operation Barbarossa was to begin and then to launch them in parallel with the 17th Army. Their task would be to "make noise" in front of the mountains as a covering diversion on the right wing of the German army. Hitler did not accept these propositions and was not willing to change his position about the Hungarians' role. Two days later he once again threw a fit about the Hungarians, whom he did not consider reliable. In his view the Hungarians had no reason to attack Russia, while the Slovaks should only be counted as an occupying force. Although he did not hold the Romanian army in high esteem either, Hitler still wanted to give them a significant role. In contrast to his earlier ideas, Hitler now decided to leave only the 11th German Army in the region forming the southern wing of Operation Barbarossa. Together with the two Romanian armies, it would be enough to defend Romania until the main forces advanced and then turned south.[4]

Following Hitler's decision, Halder changed the deployment plan for the *Heeresgruppe Süd*. All the mechanized units of the army group were now to be concentrated at Lublin, the Dniester line was to be opened from the east, while the enemy was to be tied down by distracting attacks on the Romanian Siret and Prut fronts.[5] Accordingly, he ordered that eight armored and mechanized divisions be transported from Yugoslavia to Poland and not to Romania. Hitler inquired from Halder only whether he considered the Romanian border defense strong enough for the Soviet troops not to be able to break through and endanger the German wings. The leaders of the OKH were afraid that this outcome was going to happen, especially because Hitler had instructed the southern army group to attack from Romania in a weakened condition.

On April 30 at another General Staff meeting at the Chancery, Hitler finally decided on June 22 as the starting date of Operation Barbarossa. Halder suggested that Hungary should at least be asked to let German troops concentrate on its territory and then cross the defensive line of the Carpathians from Hungary as well.[6] General Rundstedt, Commander of the *Heeresgruppe Süd*, had requested that he be allowed to attack from Hungarian territory with at least parts of his forces.[7] Halder's and Rundstedt's proposal was also supported by General Heusinger, Chief of the Operational Department of the OKH. Hitler rejected the idea.

Werth would not be discouraged by this state of affairs. Through the non-official channels of the German General Staff, he was continuously informed about the differences of points of view between Hitler and his military command voiced at the April 30 meeting with regard to the Hungarian participation in the attack. Werth also perceived that the German General Staff would appreciate it if the Hungarian military command took preparatory steps in order to offer their assistance in case the military situation required it. Most certainly the Hungarian military force would be counted on as a security reserve in the initial phase of the military operation, even if it did not see serious military action.

Werth did not delay in continuing his "military diplomatic" activities, even without the Hungarian government's knowledge or consent. He grasped every opportunity to get information about the details of the oncoming German operation and to inform the German General Staff about his own intentions. The close, daily connection between the high-ranking officers of the Hungarian army and Himer and his staff, as well as the number of discussions with the commanders of German troops regrouping from Yugoslavia via Hungary, provided good opportunities for interactions. Official and private receptions and discussions took place on a daily basis. Among several, on April 19 Werth threw a dinner party for Himer, his staff, and the leaders of other German military units in Hungary at the time to celebrate their common victory. On April 21 the Commander of the XLI. German Mechanized Army Corps and his staff in transit across Budapest and on May 1 the Commander of the 8th German Armored Division were Werth's guests.[8] Cooperation must have been the main topic of conversation between Colonel General Weichs, Commander of the 2nd German Army, and Werth when the German general arrived in Budapest on May 18.

Now in possession of a good deal of information, by May 6 Werth thought that it was time to take the initiative by writing a memorandum to the Prime Minister, summarizing his ideas about the upcoming developments of the German–Soviet relationship, as well as his views on what Hungarian policy ought to be.[9]

In Werth's view, the Soviets were making their relationship with Germany extremely shaky and dangerous for Germany. This "would force Germany to clarify its relationship with the Soviets now that it was the end of the war in the Balkans" and they could not afford to run into any unpleasant surprises from Soviet Russia while at war with Great Britain. He had the impression that Germany had been trying to achieve this through a peaceful agreement, but if it were not successful then Germany would achieve it "through an armed intervention." In his view, it was quite probable that before finishing its current deployment of military forces, Germany was going to make another political offer to Soviet Russia. Although the concentration of German forces on the Soviet border did not indicate that "the Reich would initiate a war right now, its preparations are serious enough to clarify the Soviets' final position..."[10] If there were to be a war, German victory was evident and the participation of Finland, Hungary and Romania seemed to be unavoidable.

Afterwards, in citing the Soviet danger to Hungary, Werth demanded a review of Hungarian foreign and military policies. In his view the country's security policy should be placed in the foreground and "should be built on the Axis Powers and, first of all, on Germany, with no misunderstandings or hesitation." Hungary's geographical situation demanded no less.

Werth made concrete proposals to the Hungarian government about the current situation; the country should do the following: 1) conclude a political and military agreement of mutual guarantees and aid with Germany; 2) "decide Hungary's position right now" because, in a real-life situation, there would not be enough time to consider things; 3) establish the basic principles of Hungary's foreign policy now, so that in any given situation "hesitancy, shakiness, and idleness should neither delay our decisions nor paralyze our efforts."[11]

It was obvious to Werth that Germany "will want to give a share" of the fighting to the Hungarian army in a war against the Soviet Union. He came to this conclusion by considering Hungary's geographical situation as well as the German military command's requests to him about road building and road repair. He finished his memorandum by stressing that if Hungary were to be reluctant to cooperate but instead showed only "its hunger for territory," then it would have lost its hard-won successes perhaps for ever. Thus, he asked the government "as soon as possible, to clarify unmistakably and for good our political position about the German–Soviet relationship." In order to avoid Hungary's isolation when confronted by the Soviets, "we have to stand unambiguously by Germany's side without any reservations during the present development of the German–Soviet relationship."[12]

Prime Minister and Minister of Foreign Affairs Bárdossy did not look kindly on the Chief of the General Staff's venturing into his field of authority with decisive and assertive suggestions. He did not consider it necessary to submit Werth's memorandum to the Council of Ministers. Instead, he dismissed Werth's comment on May 12 without the Council's authorization. To begin with, Bárdossy disagreed with the proposal for a "political and military agreement of guarantees and aid." He wrote that such an agreement did not depend on Hungary's aspirations, but rather on whether Germany was willing to conclude such an agreement based on mutuality. Due to differences in the relative military strengths of the two countries, this could hardly be imagined. As for the suggestion that Hungary and Germany should state the details of their cooperation about the probable war against the Soviet Union "in binding agreements, which would offer a solid foundation during the course of making the Hungarian operational plans," Bárdossy called Werth's attention to the fact that the German government had already proved during the course of the current war that it was not going to give away its political and military plans to anyone, and nor would it enter into conversations about the details of future possibilities. Although he himself agreed that Germany did count on the possibility of war while trying to settle its relationship with the Soviet Union, he did not think that this was yet settled. The confidential reports of the German government had signaled that it still considered the German–Soviet relationship to be satisfactory. If, in this situation, the Hungarian government initiated discussions in connection with future military cooperation, it would obviously expose itself to being rejected.[13]

However, theoretically Bárdossy did not discard the idea of Hungarian–German military cooperation against the Soviets and agreed with Werth that "it would be advantageous for the military leadership if, well ahead of time, they could design the particulars of a military operation to be executed together with the German armed forces." It was unfortunate that "the so-far strictly observed principles of the supreme German military and political leadership and the amazing secrecy that they have kept make it impossible for the Hungarian government to ensure this possibility for our military leadership."[14] In his view, the German military leadership heavily relied on taking advantage of unexpected military situations, and the Hungarian military leadership should accommodate itself to that.

The Prime Minister's response did not divert Werth from his goals, although he had hoped for a better understanding of them. He could not argue against Bárdossy by using the German leadership's non-official and confidential comments to him about a probable military cooperation with Hungary. For the time being all that he could do was to deepen the relationship with the German army, to perform what preparations he could within his authority, and to wait for a favorable moment.

The German High Command paid attention to events in Hungary. It was not only the need "to regulate certain questions" in connection with his staff in Hungary that induced Himer to travel to Berlin on May 15 to see his superiors. Instead he also gave an account of Werth's memorandum and its reception.[15] The Prime Minister's rejection of Werth's suggestions did not fit in with the German military leaders' plans in connection with the Hungarian army. Werth's freedom of action was narrower than they would have liked. Himer returned to Budapest with new instructions that, in compliance with the OKW's early May instructions, he should conduct confidential discussions with the members of the Hungarian General Staff to convince them about the need for border defense fortification.[16] Therefore, he conducted discussions with a number of important Hungarian officers. On May 27 he talked with General Dezső László, Head of the Military Operational Section and on May 28 he spoke with General Staff Lieutenant Colonel Elemér Sáska, Head of the 1st Section of the General Staff, about arrangements to be implemented in case Germany went to war in the east.[17]

On May 29 Himer was received by Werth. The German general initiated the discussion by establishing that his comments were his own opinions and not that of his political superiors. Then they proceeded to overview the region's political and military situation and the "defensive" arrangements that Himer had already discussed in detail with László and Sáska. Considering that a Hungarian mobilization would take about twenty days due to transportation difficulties, Himer suggested that preparations should begin immediately in order to shorten that period of time. Werth received Himer's non-official advice with understanding and promised to take the necessary steps. The following day Himer once again traveled to Berlin to give an account of the results of his discussions.[18]

Himer stressed the necessity of careful preparation, knowing how overcrowded the Hungarian railway would be. Hungarian mobilization could not disturb the ongoing transportation of the German army—running in both directions—which used the Hungarian Railway nearly to its maximum capacity. The regrouping of German armored forces from the Balkans to Poland was continuing at an accelerated pace: 629 units from Romania and 768 units from Yugoslavia entered and crossed Hungarian territory between the end of April and June 15. Trains carrying prisoners-of-war from Yugoslavia to Germany increased the congestion. Simultaneously, 15–20 trains per day crossed Hungary going to Romania.[19]

Werth highly appreciated Himer's activity, and stressed the importance of successful cooperation with Himer and his staff in a speech given on May 24 when he in the name of the Regent presented Himer and his deputy, Major Radtke, with high military medals.[20]

Following his discussion with Himer Werth forced himself to respond to Bárdossy's earlier rejection of his recent proposal. Since he could not reveal the German military command's request transferred to him via Himer, Werth had to enter the debate by only going to the defense of his previous suggestions. He tried to convince Bárdossy about the necessity of preparations for Hungarian cooperation with Germany against the Soviets. In his view, justification for discussions about such military preparations could be found by virtue of belonging to the Tripartite Pact. If talks on this topic were not taken up at the governmental level, then Werth asked for authorization so that he could begin talks at the military level. He continued to consider a German–Hungarian agreement and joint military preparations important, in spite of the fact that a German–Soviet agreement might be reached. He justified his position by saying that a final and reassuring German–Soviet agreement was not yet assured, that a sudden change of the situation ought to be planned for, that German preparations for a war against the Soviet Union were continuing and were to finish soon, that the mobilization of the Romanian army and its concentration at the border under obvious German directions was in process, and finally that German steps taken in the area of air defense and air force cooperation suggested that the Germans intended to involve Hungary in the operations against the Soviets. All these created a need to "raise, clarify and establish the foundation with regard to the war to be fought together."[21]

The Hungarian General Staff did not wait for the authorization of the government to act on the promises that it made to Himer. The Operational Section urgently set out to make preparations for a "defensive plan in the spirit of attack" that would be implemented on the Russian frontline, and then mobilized the units needed by the plan. On June 14 Lieutenant Colonel Sáska showed the plan to

Himer, who did not hesitate to inform Lieutenant Colonel Grolman of the OKH Operational Section about it. On June 15 Himer, accompanied by General Staff Captain Lorx, visited the Carpathians for an on-site inspection of the preparations.[22]

On June 6 Under-secretary of State Vörnle reported to Bárdossy that the *Honvéd* General Staff was venturing out to take undesirable activities. He knew this because Ujszászy had informed him that "in view of the political situation, scouting of the Russian territories will begin, in order to find out what targets should be destroyed in the case of a conflict with Russia. In order to do that, people will be recruited and sent to the Russian areas to do the work." Vörnle immediately informed Ujszászy that he considered such an activity unnecessary and dangerous. Ujszászy, however, cited Bartha, from whom he had the authorization to do the necessary measures. Bárdossy indicated that he also opposed Ujszászy's action.[23] On June 9 Werth himself felt it necessary to correct his Chief of Intelligence: "The military agencies in question solely perform local preparatory work on paper. They study the local situation in their own area and register suitable people." Werth also added that these agencies had been commanded not to work over the border.[24]

In Berlin, Sztójay, who completely agreed with Werth on these issues, was the major supporter of the Chief of the General Staff, along with Homlok. Sztójay's reports sent in May called Werth's attention to the intensifying German–Soviet relationship, which he felt would explode sooner or later. Germany was preparing for a "showdown," prompted by its political, military and, last but not least, economic interests, that is, its desire to get its hands on Soviet food and raw material resources.

Both Sztójay and Homlok tried to direct Hungary's attention to signs that made a military attack possible. In the territory of the Reich, civilian rail traffic was now subordinated to military transportation. The German armed forces in the east received huge reinforcements on a daily basis. The deployed forces included about 130–140 divisions. Every military preparation was seemingly targeted towards the event that the army would be launched in mid-June.[25]

Those who sent the Berlin reports, however, were not satisfied with reporting only the facts and conditions of the situation. Instead, they continuously made suggestions about desirable Hungarian political reactions. The Hungarian ambassador to Berlin reported on June 7 that the "avalanche" could not be held back any longer. The question would inevitably arise of how greatly Hungary would be affected, and what position it should take, during the oncoming German military operation. Based on his discussions with the Führer, Sztójay's impression was that Hitler wanted to give southern Transylvania to Hungary, but that Hungary needed to acquire "new merits" in his eyes, for which the only possibility was cooperation in the war against Russia. If Romania gained distinction in the attack and Hungary did not, not only would the Romanians be able to incorporate Bessarabia, but Romania would demand all of Transylvania as well. Even if Romania did not succeed, the chances of Hungary getting southern Transylvania would hit rock bottom. If Hitler did not call upon Hungary to join the attack, it meant that for some reason he did not want Hungary to gain any more territory. And this, Sztójay believed, should be prevented by all means. Measures should be taken immediately, since it could be expected that the operation would be launched by mid-June. Werth, as well as Sztójay, suggested that "we immediately offer the Chancellor of the Reich our military participation in a probable operation against the Soviets, and in the appropriate form, such as in the form of an alliance."[26]

The idea of lagging behind the Romanians, who would probably gain credit with the Germans and thus forestall any more territorial gains by the Hungarians, as well as the possibility of losing the already re-annexed territories, developed to the point of hysteria in Sztójay's mid-June reports. Antonescu's visit to Hitler especially created major anxiety, because territorial demands on Hungary also came up, in addition to the issue of the Romanian army's participation in the war. Therefore, Sztójay felt that action was needed as soon as possible.

The Hungarian ambassador to Bucharest provided unsettling news. He reported that Romania would join the offensive against the Soviet Union in the near future, and that Romanian nationalist circles hoped to gain new territory in addition to Bessarabia. There were obvious signs of Romanian military preparation, since the Romanian government had introduced a number of measures usually taken only in the case of the danger of war: the number of enlisted men grew on a daily basis, horses and cars were requisitioned, air raid trenches were being dug in Bucharest, and eastbound railways were freed up for troop transportation.[27]

In the strained political atmosphere in the wake of these developments, Werth submitted his second memorandum on June 14, outlining the state of affairs. The time constraint imposed by accelerating events made him submit this second memorandum, because he had never received a response from the government to his earlier proposals.

Since his May memorandum the German–Soviet relationship had become even more strained. Werth argued, Hungary should not stay idle in the war but needed to participate in it.

Once again Werth wanted to make an impact on the government by evoking the Soviet threat, in order to pressure it into making the necessary military arrangements. He stated that it was in Hungary's interest to remove the Soviet danger from its border by cooperating with the German army, since a German victory was inevitable in any case: "We would violate our ideology, based on Christian-nationalistic ideas, if we did not join the fight against Bolshevism."[28]

In his view, joining Germany was Hungary's responsibility, because "we can hope for further territorial gains if we stand by our loyalty to the Axis and, as a reward, we might get back the whole area of historic Hungary. It is imperative for us to join, because Romania has already obligated itself to participate in the war... If, however, our participation is cancelled, not only do we have to give up our revisionist demands towards Romania, maybe for ever, but even our territorial gains so far might be endangered."[29]

Werth requested the government that "Hungary should decide what position it wants to assume and what behavior it will adopt in the case of a German–Russian war. To establish this position soon is necessary, because of time constraints and because adequate military preparations can be done only when the government's position is known."[30] According to his sources the war might break out within ten days, because it was Germany's interest to launch their military operations before harvest time.

Obviously, the Chief of the General Staff did not mention the fact that, in accord with the wishes of the German military command and without the Hungarian government's knowledge, the military regulations had already been prepared. Nor did he inform the government that in his opinion, as formed by the information gained from the German military command, "the German government will not take any initiatives towards us. It will inform us, and perhaps may call us to join, but only at the last moment, some days or hours before launching the war."[31] This was how it happened the last time, before the Yugoslavian campaign, and this was how it would happen again. And if the country waited for that, Werth wrote, Hungary would once again be late with the mobilization, except now it would cause more damage to the country. Once again he suggested that "the government should, without delay, get in touch with the German government and make a formal offer to voluntarily join the German–Russian war." Until then the government should adopt the needed military security regulations, by mobilizing the border guard units, the air force and the domestic air defense, by ordering a domestic air defense alert, and by mobilizing the rapid army corps and, for the time being, the I., the VI., the VII. and the VIII. Army Corps and other supporting units.[32]

Therefore, the secret preparations of the Hungarian General Staff, made in synchronization with the German military command, would have comprised the mobilization of half of the *Honvédség*. When taking into account the employment of Hungarian troops, the German military command took into consideration the development of its own military operations, and counted on those forces that were able to take the initiative against the Soviet forces in the lower Carpathian Mountains. But independently of their operational utility, Werth considered this troop contingent reassuring for the Hungarians, acceptable for the Germans, and comparable with the Romanian contingent with regard to fighting against Bolshevism with an honorable *Honvéd* representation.

By way of finishing up he once again called on the government not to hesitate and not to be influenced by economic interests. The war would come to a quick end, since the German army, as always, would conquer in a short time. In order to achieve his goal, and expecting to be justified by victory, Werth was not stopped by anything, even something that might lead him to compromise himself. Otherwise, he would have never made the irresponsible and irrational statement about the time-frame of the war for Hungary, which surprised even staunch pro-German believers: "... within a few weeks we can count on the gradual demobilization of the mobilized Hungarian armed forces, so that after the demobilization even the conscripted reservists may get home by harvest time."[33]

Werth did not mention the fact that that amidst the indisputable signs of the increasing tension, as well as signs of the impending German offensive, reports suggested that the Soviet government wanted to avoid any clashes with the Germans, even at the expense of sacrifices. After the German deployment the units of the Soviet army also began concentrating in the border region, but their groupings did not indicate any intention to attack. According to the June 16 report of the Hungarian intelligence, the position of the 12 divisions and 5–6 motorized brigades was unchanged. The Soviet army corps' concentration on the border was not visible, they carefully avoided any possible incidents, and they demonstrated a friendly disposition. Yet the conclusion of the intelligence report, concerning troop transportation, signaled caution to the reader. The report said that in the case of war Soviet Russia counted on the appearance of German troops via Hungarian territory and, therefore, "its expected behavior towards Hungary could be hostile. Therefore, it cannot be excluded that the Russian army might even attempt to invade Sub-Carpathia, if it found a soft spot along the Hungarian–Russian border, in order to widen the frontline of the Russian army, to disturb German military movements, and to cut off German groupings deployed to Moldova and around Kraków.[34]

Even if he considered this just to be an extreme statement made by the Chief of the General Staff, in the strained situation the Prime Minister could not ignore it, and so convened an emergency session of the Council of Ministers. This time around the memorandum did not yield the expected result for Werth. Bárdossy reviewed the whole thing and immediately voiced his own disagreement. First of all he emphasized the point that Hungary did not have to prove that it would side with the Axis, because it had already done so. Hitler had emphasized to the Hungarian ambassador to Berlin "how highly he appreciated the service that we had done in the German Reich's interest by transporting the German troops, and by our armed intervention in the Yugoslavian operation, preceding Bulgaria, which had also been interested in the action."[35] Therefore, it was unnecessary to participate in the German–Soviet war as a demonstration of Hungary's pro-Axis friendship.

Bárdossy also said that the German government had not informed him about the development of the German–Russian relationship or about a possible conflict, in spite of his repeated efforts. Weizsäcker, who visited Budapest between June 10 and 14, considered such rumors unfounded, and Woermann expressed a similar opinion to Sztójay in Berlin. Hence, the Germans refused even to share information, let alone to count on Hungary's active collaboration. Bárdossy said he did not have to consider Hungarian military measures reasonable without a clear German request, because they would reveal the Reich's intentions to the Soviet Union or might even induce the Soviet Union's attack on Hungary. Neither of these possibilities would be in Germany's interest. Furthermore, he said that Hungary's participation in the war could not produce the expected result of the re-annexation of southern Transylvania, since in the course of the Vienna Award Germany had guaranteed Romania's borders, and this Romania was now at war on Germany's side.

Finally, the Prime Minister called attention to a glaring contradiction within the memorandum. The Chief of the General Staff counted on the German army's gaining victory within a short period of time, and assumed that the participation of Hungarian troops would develop accordingly, and that the drafted reservists "could return home by the harvest." Yet the Prime Minister noted that it was unimaginable that within two weeks, around June 29, when the harvest would begin in Hungary, the Hungarian soldiers would be allowed to return home.[36]

In agreement with Bárdossy the Council of Ministers rejected Werth's proposals. The thought of participating in a war against the Soviet Union was not alien to the Hungarians, but the Council did not consider it to be as unproblematic as Werth did. Fearing an intensification of economic hardships, they were mostly concerned that the army, developed through tremendous sacrifice and still in the process of modernizing, would be weakened. This would be a major handicap in opposing the Romanians, who, as a result of fighting alongside the Germans, could demand the return of northern Transylvania as well. The situation would be different if there had been a summons for cooperation from the German government. They authorized Bárdossy to inquire about the intentions of the German government.

Bárdossy's rejection of the proposals was motivated both by his antipathy towards Werth and by the criticism of what was proposed. The Prime Minister's vanity was increasingly irritated by the Chief of the General Staff's unmistakable desire to assert his own ideas and suggestions, and by his putting pressure on the Prime Minister and the government by unduly interfering with Hungarian foreign and military policy. In Bárdossy's view, Werth's "diplomatic activities" through independent channels were just too much. He did not wish to share with Werth in directing the government's policy. Bárdossy pointed to the most vulnerable part of the memorandum, which seemed suitable to lessen Werth's exaggerated reputation and military expertise, and thus also to lessen the credibility of the whole memorandum.

In compliance with the Council of Ministers' decision, Bárdossy sent a telegram to Sztójay on the same day, in which he asked Sztójay to go to see Weizsäcker and to bring up the question of the German–Soviet relationship, since, in spite of Weizsäcker's earlier reassurance, the threat of a German–Soviet conflict seemed to be increasing. Sztójay was directed to inquire whether, if the situation became critical, the government of the Reich was going to inform the Hungarian government in time, so that the Hungarians could make the necessary defensive measures desired by the German government.[37]

On June 15 Bárdossy complemented his message from the previous day. He wrote to Sztójay to say that it seemed to be highly improbable that the Soviet army would attack the Hungarian border, but the Hungarian military command did not consider it impossible.

Yet, beyond current work along that section of the border, new preparatory steps could be taken only after preliminary discussions with the German government, so that Hungary would not damage German interests by provoking the Soviets. He noted that Hungary's military preparation would also increase Hungary's economic hardships, since it would endanger agricultural work and agricultural products, and this would also harm German interests. It should also be kept in mind that Hungary's railways were tied up by German troop transits, and therefore deployment of Hungarian troops could only be done at a very slow pace. All these aspects made it necessary that the Reich's government "confidentially inform us at a convenient time about how it judged the situation and about what consequences it wanted to draw, so that any decisions of the Hungarian government would harmonize with German intentions." He asked Sztójay to stay "at the line of inquiry" and to refrain from any kind of offer.[38]

Ambassador Erdmannsdorff reported to the Prime Minister on von Ribbentrop's response on June 16. Considering the Soviet troop concentrations along the border, in early July the German government was forced to raise certain demands to the Soviet government and to take certain steps in order to clarify the German–Soviet relationship. Since the outcome of the discussions could not be known ahead of time, "the German government finds it necessary that Hungary should take the necessary steps to reinforce its borders."[39]

After Erdmannsdorff's visit, Bárdossy immediately contacted Werth and informed him about von Ribbentrop's highly confidential message. Since Werth was going to have talks with one of the most relevant authorities of the German army, Halder, Bárdossy asked Werth to keep in mind the basic principles passed by the government on June 14. The German government only suggested that Hungary take appropriate defensive measures about the border defense and no more. "The German government did not express any wish or desire" for Hungary to participate in military operations. This reinforced the Hungarian government's decision that it would not offer Hungary's participation in a probable German action. This decision would be changed only if Germany requested it from the Hungarian government. Therefore, in terms of implementing the necessary defensive measures, Hungary would want to act in complete harmony with the German government and military command.[40]

Sztójay then spoke up on June 17 after von Ribbentrop's message had been delivered. He called attention to the upcoming settlement in the southeastern part of Europe, which meant that it was important that the government not rest content with the gratitude already earned thus far from Germany. Rather, it should take care "to document our marching along together and our joint interest" with Germany, and thus to secure Germany's gratitude.[41]

On June 19 the Werth–Halder meeting did take place, and during the short discussion Halder informed Werth about the important things to come. Halder said that Germany would take care of the Russian question by force of arms, and this would happen within a short week. It would have been beneficial if the Hungarians had secured the Carpathians more, yet at that point Hungary should not do anything that would alarm the Russians or would hinder German troop transportation. If the German army needed the railways leading across the Carpathians, they should be placed at their disposal. Furthermore, Hungary should permit German radio stations to be set up in Hungary. Finally, Halder noted that if it became necessary for Hungary to implement any more military regulations, the Germans would ask for them through Werth and via General Himer.[42] Halder did not bring up the Hungarian military preparations that had failed due to the Hungarian government's opposition, but also did not exclude the possibility of the Hungarian army's participation in the war.

Werth informed the Prime Minister about his discussions with Halder. Bárdossy sent a relieved telegram to Sztójay, saying that the Germans had not asked for any measures, in order not to alarm the Russians or to hinder the German troop transportation, which justified the government's cautious behavior.[43]

Obviously, the military did not agree with the government's position, and by using the slogan "before it is too late…," it tried to put pressure on the government to change its decision by offering Hungary's help in joining the upcoming offensive. Ujszászy sent Bárdossy a part of the report of the Chief of the General Staff's order, in which anonymous people expressed their surprise that Hungary stood by in the crisis without expressing any special interest when the German offensive was to happen within 48 hours. They said that it was baffling that Hungary had not even activated its air defense and had not taken care to secure its borders in case war broke out, when a Soviet attack threatened.[44]

On June 20 both Sztójay and Homlok spoke up, saying that the tension was palpable and that both the Romanian and the Finnish armies had finished their preparations. The Romanians had deployed 26 divisions. Homlok emphasized the point that he considered Hungary's military participation necessary. Territories should be occupied north of the Carpathians, and then discussions should be held, because otherwise "we will be idle spectators watching when the common German–Romanian border is created." In estimating the length of the campaign Homlok was more cautious than Werth, and cited German sources when he said that although the German General Staff had been preparing for a blitzkrieg, cautious estimates counted on three months until the end of the war. The German military command deployed 124 to 136 divisions and counted on their great firepower and also on the expertise of the German military command.[45]

Notes

1. Domokos Szent-Iványi, *Emlékirat* (Memoirs), Ráday Levéltár (Ráday Archive), Szent-Iványi hagyaték C/80, p. 585.
2. *Századok* (1965) 6: p. 1230.
3. György Ránki, Ervin Pamlényi, Loránt Tilkovszky and Gyula Juhász, eds., *A Wilhelmstrasse és Magyarország: Német diplomáciai iratok Magyarországról, 1933–1944* (The Wilhelmstrasse and Hungary: German Diplomatic Documents about Hungary, 1933–1944) (Budapest, 1968), p. 580. (394)
4. Franz Halder, *Kriegstagebuch. Tägliche Aufzeichnungen des Chefs des Generalstabes des Heeres 1939–1942/Generaloberst Halder* (Stuttgart, 1962–1964), vol. II: p. 319.
5. *Vollmacht des Gewissens* (Frankfurt–Berlin, 1965), p. 213.
6. Carlile Aylmer Macartney, *October Fifteenth. A History of Modern Hungary, 1929-1945* (Edinburgh, 1961), vol. II: p. 17.
7. *Vollmacht des Gewissens*, p. 214.
8. *Századok* (1965) 6: p. 1235.
9. *Ibid.*, p. 1236.
10. Szent-Iványi, *Emlékirat...*, p. 129.
11. *Ibid.*, p. 132.
12. *Ibid.*
13. Gyula Juhász, ed., *Diplomáciai iratok Magyarország külpolitikájához 1936–1945* (Diplomatic Writings on Hungary's Foreign Policy, 1936–1945) (Budapest, 1962–1982), vol. V: p. 1115. (783)
14. *Ibid.*
15. *Századok* (1965) 6: p. 1237.
16. Raymond James Sontag, et.als., ed., *Documents on German Foreign Policy, 1918–1945* (Washington, 1949–1954), vol. XII: pp. 655–656. (431)
17. *Századok* (1965) 6: p. 1238.
18. *Ibid.*, p. 1239.
19. Hadtörténelmi Levéltár (Military History Archive, HL). Eln. Vkf.1. 1941/5466.
20. *Századok* (1965) 6: p. 1238.
21. Szent-Iványi, *Emlékirat...*, p. 604.
22. *Századok* (1965) 6: p. 1239.

23. Szent-Iványi, *Emlékirat...,* p. 607.
24. *Ibid.,* p. 609.
25. Juhász, ed., *Diplomáciai iratok...,* vol. V: pp. 1112–1113. (781–800)
26. Szent-Iványi, *Emlékirat...,* p. 609.
27. Juhász, ed., *Diplomáciai iratok...,* vol. V: p. 1147. (811)
28. Országos Levéltár (National Archive, OL). K 64-90-24-416/1941. Rp.
29. *Ibid.*
30. *Ibid.*
31. *Ibid.*
32. *Ibid.*
33. *Ibid.*
34. HL. Eln. Vkf.1. 1941/5563.
35. Szent-Iványi, *Emlékirat...,* p. 619.
36. *Ibid.,* pp. 620–622.
37. Juhász, ed., *Diplomáciai iratok...,* vol. V: p. 1175. (837)
38. Szent-Iványi, *Emlékirat...,* p. 823.
39. *Ibid.,* p. 824.
40. *Ibid.,* pp. 146–147.
41. Juhász, ed., *Diplomáciai iratok...,* vol. V: p. 1189. (847)
42. Halder, *Kriegstagebuch...,* vol. II: p. 457; Szent-Iványi, *Emlékirat...,* p. 147.
43. Szent-Iványi, *Emlékirat...,* p. 148.
44. Juhász, ed., *Diplomáciai iratok...,* vol. V: p. 1202. (858)
45. *Ibid.,* p. 1199. (855)

OFFENSIVE AGAINST THE SOVIET UNION

On June 22 at 3:15 a.m. the German troops along a frontline several thousand kilometers long attacked the Soviet Union. Early that morning Erdmannsdorff went to see Bárdossy at his home to deliver the news. The Prime Minister expressed his understanding and great satisfaction. Horthy was also pleased with the news when the German ambassador handed Hitler's letter to him during the morning hours. The Regent expressed his gratitude for the "news, which he found excellent," since "he has been pining for this day for 22 years, and now he feels happy."[1]

Hitler justified the decision by the threat that the Soviets posed; he considered himself the savior of European civilization. He did not ask for the Hungarian army to participate this time either, but instead expressed his satisfaction and gratitude to Hungary. As Hitler worded it in his note to Horthy, "As far as Hungary's attitude is concerned, My Dear Excellency, I am convinced that national opinion will appreciate my conduct. I would like to express my thanks for the understanding shown and the arrangements made by the Hungarian armed forces when they reinforced the defense of the border, thus thwarting Russian attacks on our wings and tying down a major part of their forces." Hitler finally promised Horthy that he would document his actions.[2]

At the news the Hungarian General Staff and the German liaison staff immediately went into action. Major Radtke, Himer's deputy, contacted the OKW by phone at the time of the launching of the attack. He was told that discussions with the Hungarian General Staff were now permitted. This measure was necessitated by what the Germans perceived might occur if the 17th German Army did not make the headway envisioned. Therefore, the deployment of Hungarian troops might be necessary to relieve them against the Soviet troops.[3]

In the midday hours General Himer and General László met to take an overview of the new situation. László complained to Himer that the Hungarians had not been told why they had not been invited to participate in the operations. Neither the German government nor Halder had said anything regarding the Hungarian participation, yet this could be changed by the OKW's decision.[4] While László was having discussions with Himer, Major Kuthy, Ujszászy's deputy, reported on measures implemented by the 2nd Section of the General Staff to seal off the frontier and to stop rail and telephone communications.

At 5 p.m. Himer informed Paulus about the capabilities of those Hungarian forces that Germany might request to be mobilized and used if necessary. The Chief of the Hungarian General Staff appointed the Commander of the VIII. Army Corps to direct any possible operations. The following units, presently on a peacetime footing, could be quickly mobilized and deployed: units of the VIII. Army Corps itself, parts of the 2nd Mechanized Brigade stationed in the area of the VIII. Army Corps, the 1st Cavalry Brigade deployed in the northern part of the Trans-Tisza area, the infantry and artillery of the IX. Transylvanian Army Corps, and the mountain and border guard brigades in the Sub-Carpathian area.[5]

At 6:20 p.m. Himer called General Jodl, the Chief of the General Staff of the OKW, to inform him about the Hungarian army's situation. In the meantime, Jodl had been informed about things from Paulus. At Himer's remark that the Hungarian army was waiting for instructions, Jodl said, "We will accept any Hungarian assistance at any time. We do not want to demand anything. However, we gratefully accept everything that is offered voluntarily. We certainly do not rule out Hungary's possible participation."[6]

Himer immediately tried to find Werth with the message. However, he was not available, nor was Bartha. Himer finally managed to reach Dezső László, who always seemed to be available, and gave him Jodl's message in written form. It was only after lengthy searching that László managed to reach Werth and give him the message. At 9 o'clock László reported to Himer with Werth's response: for the time being he could not do anything, because the Regent had offered his support three times to Hitler, who had said that he would inform the Regent when and on what scale he would use the Hungarian assistance. Furthermore, the need for Hungarian participation had not come up during a personal conversation with General Halder not such a long time ago.[7]

On June 23 Bárdossy convened the Council of Ministers, which agreed with his submitted proposal, and decided to break off diplomatic relations with the Soviet Union. Only Keresztes-Fischer, among those present, suggested thinking over the issue. Bárdossy called on Bartha to offer his expert opinion about the German–Soviet war. In Bartha's view the German army would gain a full victory within six weeks.

The decision of the Council of Ministers was immediately delivered to Ambassador Erdmannsdorff by Bárdossy, who asked him to immediately inform his government. He also asked him "whether the German government had any remarks or wishes in connection with it." Erdmannsdorff did not have anything to say, because he considered the breaking off of diplomatic relations to be a self-evident act.[8]

The same day Deputy Minister of Foreign Affairs János Vörnle summoned the Soviet ambassador, Saronov, and informed him that Hungary was immediately breaking off diplomatic relations with the Soviet Union.

An exchange of messages and discussions continued between the two General Staffs on June 23. At 12 p.m. Colonel General

Halder himself called Himer by phone. Referring to Werth's statement from the previous day, he said that it was clear that the Hungarian political leadership was not adamant about joining the attack on the Soviet Union, and that only Horthy's opinion would force them. Therefore, "everything is dependent on whether the leading Hungarian military organizations are able to mobilize the country's political organs so that they themselves would offer their assistance." Halder reiterated the German military command's position as delivered by Jodl: the German military would not demand help from Hungary but would accept any voluntary support—especially that of the Rapid Corps—with gratitude. He asked Himer to clarify with the Hungarian General Staff exactly what forces might be available. If it indeed happened, then the Command of the Southern Army Group would regulate the details of the Hungarian troops' tasks because the Hungarian troops would be under the command of the *Heeresgruppe Süd*.[9]

On the second day of the campaign Halder, the Chief of the General Staff of the OKH, set aside some time to give weight to the OKW's and OKH's ideas in connection with using the Hungarian troops. He personally considered it important to clarify what Hungarian troops could be mobilized and be at the disposal of the *Heeresgruppe Süd* as early as possible. Since the 17th German Army had advanced only 10–12 kilometers on the first day of the campaign, and since there was uncertainty about the operational development of the 11th German Army and two Romanian armies constituting the southern wing, then it might be necessary to deploy Hungarian forces to tie down Soviet forces threatening their wings—as Halder and Brauchitsch had tried to convince Hitler. Clearly the German military command had a free hand to call openly on the Hungarians for a voluntary offer of assistance, even though Hitler at that point considered it due to the military's poor-spiritedness and desire to over-secure the operation. Based on general information and earlier experience, Halder was also aware that mobilizing larger numbers of Hungarian forces would take at least two or three weeks. Therefore, he was mostly interested in the Rapid Army Corps, which could be mobilized and deployed in a shorter period of time.

Himer met Werth at 1 p.m., handed over Halder's message, and reiterated the position of the German military command. Werth admitted that he did not know what Horthy's letter from Hitler contained. If it did not contain an open call for military cooperation, then it might be very difficult to encourage the Hungarian politicians to act. He found it unfortunate that he had not received adequate warning from the politicians four weeks earlier. If it had occurred, then he would have been in a better position with the army and could have crossed the border on the previous day (June 22). Although ten days earlier Werth had initiated political inquiries, the Führer had not wanted Hungary's participation in the war.[10]

Himer's quick response to Werth's complaint about the poor political preparations was "now the ball is in the military's court." Werth sadly remarked that the Hungarian help would be late anyway. Himer, however, consoled him by saying that it was not too late to act and that Hungary could still participate in the war against Bolshevism The task to be fulfilled by the *Honvédség* was in front of the Carpathians.[11]

Werth immediately informed Bárdossy that the leaders of the German army considered Hungary's participation in the war desirable. In the early afternoon hours he and Bartha traveled to Kenderes to report to the Regent about the German military command's wish and to convince him to authorize Werth to take the necessary measures suitable for the situation. The conversation distressed the Regent, who allegedly complained to those around him that his guest had threatened that if Hungary did not participate in the war, a revolution might break out within the officer corps, since the honor of the *Honvédség* demanded that the army act. In spite of everything, Werth did not manage to bring the Regent round to his position.[12]

According to the diary of the German liaison staff, Werth immediately informed Himer about the unsuccessful visit, and Himer relayed it on to the OKW's and OKH's operational sections and added that every sign shows that "General Werth cannot cope with the greatness of the moment."[13]

While in Budapest the military did everything in its power to divert Hungary onto the fatal road of war, which the government also aggravated by breaking off diplomatic relations, a crucial event took place in Moscow. On June 23 People's Commissar of Foreign Affairs Molotov asked for Hungarian Ambassador Kristóffy and inquired about Hungary's position towards the Soviet–German conflict. Just as he had done several times before, he once again informed Kristóffy that "the Soviet government has no demands towards or intention to attack Hungary, has no comment about Hungary's demands to be realized at Romania's expense, and will not have any in the future either." However, he said that the Soviet government would like to know as soon as possible whether Hungary planned to participate in the war or planned to remain neutral.[14]

Kristóffy expressed his own private views and said that it was unlikely that Hungary would enter into a war with the Soviet Union. He asked Molotov to make it possible that he—Kristóffy—re-establish connections with his own government.

The connection was re-established by the evening of June 23, so Kristóffy's telegram with Molotov's message was on Bárdossy's desk by the morning of the following day. Yet the Prime Minister left the telegram unanswered. He informed neither the government nor the Regent about its content, although he testified differently later before a People's Court.[15] In his memoir Horthy reproached Bárdossy for concealing Kristóffy's telegram from him, saying that he learned about it three years later, in 1944, when Bárdossy acknowledged it to him.¹⁶ Before the People's Court Bárdossy claimed that the decision-making did not take place in this way in any case. He argued that in the meantime events had overrun the content of the telegram, and a non-response was also a kind of response. By breaking off diplomatic relations, Hungary had formally given up its neutrality anyway. Hungary did not want to launch a war against the Soviet Union, but to reveal that would have been impossible because of the negative reaction by the Germans, the Hungarian military command and the extreme right wing. Besides, if Hungary had attacked the Soviet Union under German pressure, it would have been considered a breach of trust. Still, however Bárdossy tried to justify himself post facto, he cannot be acquitted of the fatally heavy sin of hiding Molotov's message.¹⁷

On June 24 Kristóffy received Bárdossy's telegram about breaking off diplomatic relations dated on the previous night. In the morning of June 25 Kristóffy tried to speak with the Soviet Commissar of Foreign Affairs, but Molotov was busy and so his deputy, Vishinski, saw Kristóffy and received the Hungarian government's statement breaking off diplomatic relations with the Soviet Union.¹⁸

In the meantime, the Soviet Union did everything that it could not to cause an incident at the Hungarian–Soviet border. The General Staff's daily report of the situation described complete quiet on June 23 and 24. The Hungarians experienced only friendly behavior from the Soviet troops.¹⁹

After hearing about the messages of high-ranking German military leaders, Bárdossy still wanted to be reassured from foreign affairs sources as well with regard to German intentions. On June 24 he asked for the German ambassador and reminded him that he had made several attempts to gain information about the German government's position towards Hungary in the case of a German–Russian conflict. He had asked the ambassador himself. However,

German official circles—probably due to the need for secrecy—had avoided all responses. Moreover, Woermann had even declared that "there was no Russian question at all." On June 14 von Ribbentropp had requested only the reinforcement of the borders. During Halder's visit Werth had openly asked him whether the German military command "wanted anything from us on the military field" and Halder had responded with a "no." Therefore, he was surprised to hear Werth's communication that General Himer had visited him with a message from the German military leaders saying that "our participation in the military action would be desirable."[20]

Bárdossy also found it unusual that the German military leadership stated this wish via the General Staff, even though "this is a primarily political question and as such is a governmental or constitutional issue and not that of the General Staff." The government felt that it was necessary to clarify politically "whether the government of the Reich really wanted us to participate in a military action against Russia and, if the answer is 'yes,' what exactly they want."[21]

Bárdossy would not refuse to consider an accidental German "wish" if it came from the German political leadership, but he wanted to call the Reich's attention to a few urgent issues that would increasingly be present if the Hungarian army were deployed.

First of all the German government should be cautioned about the catastrophic state of Romanian–Hungarian relations, the constant border incidents, and the counter-revisionist ambitions voiced by authoritative Romanian statesmen. Under such circumstances a Romanian incursion should be counted on at any time along the southern border, which "is difficult to defend militarily." The Slovaks also should be considered, because they also intended to come up with revisionist demands in the course of a final southeastern European territorial settlement.

Bárdossy believed that the country's economic situation was grave, due to the bad weather of the previous year, and due to military measures that negatively affected the agricultural sector. "Our economic situation is grave, and its hardly bearable consequences are visible everywhere. And I do not know whether there will not be greater problems before we harvest the crop." The economic situation was further aggravated by that fact that "we have given almost all of our rail network over to the disposal of the German army, although we are pleased to bear its consequences as a sacrifice to Germany."

In such a situation it was the Hungarian government's obligation to preserve the nation's forces and its military preparedness. This was the only way to secure the situation in the Danube Basin, in agreement with Germany's interests. He could honestly declare that the Hungarian government "is on the side of the Axis Powers with unchanged loyalty and solidarity," as evidenced by the breaking off diplomatic relations with the Soviets, but would still have difficulty in deciding on participation in a military action. However, Bárdossy was going to consider the Reich's wishes.[22]

Without any further delay Erdmannsdorff reported on his discussions with Bárdossy to the German Ministry of Foreign Affairs. Bárdossy had been urged by an alleged remark of Himer, the liaison officer of the Hungarian General Staff, that "the participation of the Hungarian troops in the advance against the Soviet Union is desirable. The Hungarian Prime Minister wants to clarify whether a request for the Hungarian troops' participation was true and, if so, on what scale."[23]

The German government did not hurry with its response. On June 26 Bárdossy asked the ambassador to report to his government that he—Bárdossy—would appreciate an immediate response, because it was imperative for the Hungarian government to adjust to German plans.[24]

Following Erdmannsdorff's rebuke,[25] Himer immediately contacted the operational sections of the OKW and the OKH to excuse himself for being misunderstood. At the same time he also informed his superiors about the Bárdossy–Erdmannsdorff conversation to reinforce his argument that the Hungarians wanted to be directly called upon to participate in the war. He noted that Hungarian officers had several times expressed their disapproval about the German government's hesitancy.[26]

The Hungarian General Staff was growing more impatient. The view that "once again we will be late" prevailed among the General Staff and was strengthened by the news that Slovakia had entered the war against the Soviet Union on June 25, although no one had requested them to do so. Sztójay reported from Berlin that talk about German–Romanian "brotherhood-in-arms" was ubiquitous in the German press. Following Slovakia's entering the war, the Hitler–Tiso correspondence was widely discussed in the press. Some circles in Berlin were showing gradually growing interest on whether "Hungary, one of the champions of anti-Bolshevism, would participate in the fight." Colonel Szabó from Rome also reported that "The Italian public and the Italian officer corps are perplexed, and consider the fact that we, a bordering country, do not actively fight the Russians with a certain irony."[27] Marosi, the Hungarian ambassador to Zagreb, furthered General Horstenau's confidential remark to Bárdossy: "It is unfortunate that Hungary does not participate in the offensive against the Soviet Union with one or two divisions."[28]

The idea of setting up a volunteer corps was raised by some soldiers dissatisfied with the government and by some in the *Volksdeutsche* circles. Archduke Albrecht, who wanted to establish a volunteer corps within the Waffen SS, toyed with similar ideas.[29] On June 25 Himer held a brunch where the German ambassador, several leaders of the *Volksbund*, Werth, Miklós and László were present. Werth elaborated on the plan for establishing a Hungarian volunteer force with the organization and direction given to Himer and his staff. Lacking any other opportunity, the Hungarian military leaders wanted to participate in the war at least through a volunteer corps. Since neither the Chief of the General Staff nor other high-ranking officials were to be volunteer corps leaders, they wanted Himer to be one. They also hoped that the organizational work would sober up the responsible Hungarian politicians. The following day, on June 26, Himer contacted his superiors and asked for instructions on the volunteer corps issue.[30] In just a day the issue was no longer relevant, because the long desired *casus belli* had been created for the "hesitant" political leadership.

The air attack against Kassa on June 26 at 13:16 offered Hungary the opportunity to enter the war. Three unknown bombers without markings flew over Kassa, a town 17–20 km from the Slovakian border, and dropped 29 100 kg bombs on the town.[31] The train station and railway bridge—primary targets and of high importance for the German army—were not bombed, as would have been expected.

In addition, it was reported to the General Staff prior to the Kassa attack that at 12:10 three Soviet fighter planes strafed the Kőrösmező–Budapest train between Tiszaborkút and Rahó.

The news of the Kassa attack, which in terms of the nationality of the people involved is still a mystery, was received at 13:40 by the duty officer of the General Staff. At the same time the command of the I. Anti-Aircraft Army Corps in Budapest reported to the General Staff that Kassa had been attacked by unknown planes, which had dropped bombs on the artillery barracks and the post office. This command was in charge of the country's anti-aircraft center, with air reconnaissance and air warning duties, as well as anti-aircraft and fighter units that were assigned the air defense of the country. Directly after the I. Anti-Aircraft Army Corps' report a short piece of news can be found in the news register: "According to subsequently arriving reports the attack planes were Russian, dyed yellow." This is the only information among the reports, without any indication of its source or date; nor is it mentioned in what way the news came to the General Staff's attention after the fact. Although the report speaks about unknown planes, the General Staff immediately qualified them as Soviet ones, and that was how the information was sent to the Chief of the General Staff. In their earlier analyses the Hungarians had counted on the possibility of a Soviet attack on Hungary, and therefore had no doubts about this. Consequently, the command of the I. Anti-Aircraft Army Corps did not reveal the source of its information when at 14:40 it laconically reported on Russian planes dyed yellow approaching Miskolc.

Following the attack on Kassa the northern Hungarian airspace suddenly became very tumultuous. The reports on June 26 between 14:00 and 18:00 show that the anti-aircraft observation stations reported unknown airplanes in the regions of Kassa, Ungvár, Sátoraljaújhely, Miskolc and Ózd to the anti-aircraft center in Budapest, which ordered air-raid warnings eight times in these towns. Another mysterious plane approached Vác, but it turned back at 16:30. Previously, an air-raid warning had been ordered in Budapest at 16:15.

At 17:05 the regional anti-aircraft center in Miskolc reported to Budapest that Hungarian fighters had opened fire on four unknown planes in the region of Erdőbénye. The planes, however, "turned westward so quickly that they could not catch up with them, nor could they recognize their insignias." Obviously, the question arises whether this was possible, when, as had been established, they had come so close to the planes that it was worthwhile to open fire at them.[32]

Without any reservations Werth considered these events to be acts of Soviet aggression, and immediately set out to act. Without waiting for any detailed information, he, probably accompanied by Bartha, rushed to Horthy and asked for an audience. He was certain that the news of the attack would appall Horthy. As usual, he did not consider that any preliminary information of the Prime Minister was necessary. Werth was wary lest the Prime Minister's reservations would make the Regent hesitate. Werth and Bartha arrived at the Palace at 14:00, and a few minutes later Werth informed the Regent about the air raid on Kassa. Horthy had never doubted his Chief of the General Staff's assessment of the situation, nor did he feel the need to inquire about the identity of the attackers. Therefore, he did not consider any further investigation into the affair necessary. He adopted Werth's suggestion that it was time to act, since Hungary could not stay idle in the war against the Soviets, especially since there had to be some sort of retaliation against the unprovoked attack. Werth's calculations worked: he managed to convince the Regent to order the deployment of the army beyond the border and to declare war on the Soviet Union. The Regent possessed this right under the second paragraph of Article 1920: XVII/2, which also prescribed that he could ask for Parliament's subsequent approval. The law stated that in the case of immediate danger the Regent could order the employment of the army beyond the borders of Hungary, which should, without delay, be subsequently endorsed by the Hungarian Council of Ministers and the national assembly. Once in possession of the Regent's decision, Werth immediately gave the order to retaliate. He assumed that the Regent's decision would not cause too much surprise or disagreement in the government or Parliament.

In this situation the Prime Minister had to be immediately notified. The Regent asked for Bárdossy, who arrived at about 2:30 p.m., after Werth and company had left. Horthy declared to Bárdossy that he would not have the effrontery not to respond to the attack and to stay idle. He also informed him that Werth had already ordered the air force to launch a retaliatory attack.[33] Bárdossy warned him that the government's support was needed. But Horthy's response was that "There is no time left. The government will acknowledge it." Bárdossy realized that his reservations were useless and he would not be able to make the Regent change his decision or make him modify it. He did not have a chance against Werth, who had already convinced Horthy. Yet Bárdossy was also relieved, because the Regent's decision presented him with a *fait accompli* and relieved the pressure that had been on him.

Werth rushed to the General Headquarters and, in response to his immediate order, the appointed units of the air force moved into action. Orders were issued for the mobilization of the mountain and border guard brigades of the VIII. Army Corps and the Rapid Army Corps. Werth did not consider it necessary to wait for the government's endorsement, even though it was still in session when the General Staff's order was issued.[34]

The Prime Minister convened the ministers to an emergency Council meeting at 3:00 p.m. Before the session Bartha pointedly warned Bárdossy that if the Council of Ministers did not endorse the declaration of war, he and Werth would resign. Bárdossy distantly responded that the ministers would decide about the issue.[35]

During the Council meeting Bárdossy informed the ministers about the Soviet air raid against Kassa and about the Regent's decision. He asked the ministers to acknowledge the Regent's decision and to declare that in the wake of the attack Hungary was at war with the Soviet Union.

Following that, Bartha informed them about what was known so far about the circumstances of the attack. He said that the attack was a hostile act, which required a response. Hungarian planes would have to respond to the attack, and it would have to be declared that the Soviet Union had launched an unprovoked attack against Hungary, which "created a state of war against us, and therefore we also consider ourselves at war." Romania and Slovakia were already at war, and the Italians were also getting ready to become involved. Therefore, this unprovoked attack served as an opportunity for Hungary to join the war against the Soviet Union, which was also substantiated by the fact that the

Regent had been the first to declare war on Bolshevism. Bartha asked for the mobilization of only parts of the armed forces, including the entire Rapid Army Corps.

Lacking the original documents on the evolving debate, we have to rely on the tendentious minutes of Under-secretary of State István Bárczy, the permanent recorder of the minutes, written at the request of the People's Court after 1945. According to Bárczy's reconstructed minutes, Minister of the Interior Ferenc Keresztes-Fischer considered the declaration of war to be too early. He did not doubt the fact that there was a Soviet attack on Kassa, but he did not consider it so serious that it justified a declaration of war. And, in his view, it was not in Hungary's interest to declare war on a great power like Russia. To respond with a few airplanes as a retort was an acceptable idea. However, Hungary did not have serious offensive forces to participate in the war, and serious consequences could ensue in the case of a war with a great power. Keresztes-Fischer disagreed with both the mobilization of forces and the declaration of war without asking Germany about it. It would have been totally different if the German political authorities were in perfect accord with the military ones and a unified German leadership requested that Hungary enter the war.

Minister of Agriculture Dániel Bánffy agreed with Keresztes-Fischer, while both Minister of Industry József Varga and Minister of Justice László Rodocsay expressed doubts as well.

The pro-German ministers argued in favor of the declaration of war. Minister of Religion and Public Education Bálint Hóman emphasized the point that "from a higher point of view, and considering precisely the Hungarian–Romanian issue, he agreed with the Minister of Defense's position. He was convinced that if Bessarabia were joined to Romania, the question of southern Transylvania would come up as well." Minister of Finance Lajos Reményi-Schneller also enthusiastically argued for the declaration of war and for the mobilization of limited forces, adding that it would be unimaginable for only Hungary to be left out of the war.

Bárdossy argued that after what had happened "we must consider ourselves at war with the Soviet Union." In Hungary's present foreign political situation he also found it unimaginable to be left out of the war against the Soviet Union. He also pointed out that such precursor events as Sztójay's reports, the circumstances of Werth's and Halder's discussions, and the demonstrative manifestations of the German *Heeresleitung* all argued for Hungary's joining the war. He said that Hungary should participate in the war against the Soviet Union but with limited forces.

As mentioned above, our knowledge of the debate comes from Bárczy's recreation from memory years later. The ministers who were present seem to have accepted the Prime Minister's and the Minister of Defense's announcements about the events that had happened just two hours earlier without much reservation or without demanding confirmation. They did not require anyone to explain that mistakes had not been made, and nor did they require proof about the nationality of the planes. Instead, they took the Prime Minister's words for granted and accepted the fact of Soviet aggression. Most significantly, the fact that Horthy had already decided what the ministers then only had to reinforce with their agreement was of crucial importance. It was not possible for any of them to turn on Horthy, except at the price of resignation.

Following the discussion, the Council of Ministers—in agreement with Horthy's decision—proclaimed that a state of war existed with the Soviet Union and gave a free hand to the military to act within the given contingency.[36]

Since the German ambassador was out of town, after the session of the Council of Ministers Bárdossy informed Counselor of the German Embassy Werkmeister about recent Hungarian events. Bárdossy explained that the government had decided that the Hungarian air force would execute a retaliatory attack against Soviet territory and had also decided that Hungary was at war with the Soviet Union. He asked the counselor to urgently inform his government about it, even though the Hungarian government's decision would be issued only later, due to military reasons. He also required that the German government should consider his comments to Erdmannsdorff on June 24 as null and void.[37]

Sztójay sought contact with Budapest in the evening, since he had not been informed about events. He did not know that he was preaching to the converted when he reported on his meeting with Weizsäcker, who had finally reacted to the discussion of June 24 between Erdmannsdorff and the Prime Minister. Weizsäcker had tried to fend off any possible rebuke that either he or any other German had deliberately tried to mislead the Hungarian government. Although Germany could not give the Hungarians concrete facts about the situation, due to military confidentiality, it also did not assume anything that would have excluded the possibility of a Hungarian military action.[38]

Interpreting Weizsäcker's words as an official warning, Sztójay once again checked in, at 2 a.m., saying that "it would be good to march along with the Germans against Bolshevism with at least certain parts of the *Honvédség*."[39]

The Hungarian government's response was dispatched to Berlin on June 27. Sztójay was informed about the state of war, which, at the request of the military command, was not to be revealed to the public before the Hungarian air force's retaliatory attack the next morning. In the rest of the message Bárdossy responded to Weizsäcker's comments, saying that although he did not assume that the Germans wanted to mislead the government on the Russian issue, it was quite obvious that they did not want to involve the Hungarian governing leaders in deciding an issue that had finally been decided. Still, the Hungarian government intended to act in complete harmony with the Reich's government. It would follow the guidelines set on June 18 by General Halder, as requested in the course of his discussion with the Hungarian Chief of the General Staff when he requested that the Soviets not be alarmed. The Hungarians had interpreted this to mean that their task was of a defensive character. But now the Hungarians did not hesitate to draw the appropriate conclusions from the recent Soviet attack, thus revealing their solidarity with Germany: "Our military action obviously will involve sacrifices, which we will gladly bear, being convinced that we can count on the Reich's government's understanding and active help in solving our difficulties originating from our special political and economic situation."[40]

On June 27 in the morning, 19 bombers of the 8th and 9th Tactical Reconnaissance Companies bombed Lavocsne, Tatarov, Nadvorne and Stanislav. The airplanes could only partially execute their missions. Several of them did not even reach their target areas, due to mechanical breakdown; one accompanying fighter plane was also shot down by Soviet air defense.[41]

At 10 o'clock that same morning, Hungarian Radio announced that the Hungarian air force had executed a successful retaliatory air raid against Soviet targets, and that the Hungarian government considered Hungary to be at war with the Soviet Union.

During the morning in the House of Representatives, Prime Minister Bárdossy demanded to have the floor before discussion on the agenda began, and announced Horthy's and the Council of Ministers' decision amidst great enthusiasm from the legislators.

The same day the Hungarian military command began to deploy troops to participate in the offensive. The Carpathian Group (*Kárpát-csoport*) was formed under the command of Lieutenant General Ferenc Szombathelyi, Commander of the VIII. Army Corps. The 1st Mountain and 8th Border Guard Brigades—in the Carpathians and placed on alert earlier as well—and the 1st and 2nd Mechanized and 1st Cavalry Brigades of the Rapid Corps were also under Szombathelyi's command. The units of the Rapid Army Corps had to be deployed in the region of Rahó, Huszt and Máramarossziget by July 1.

At midday on June 27 Himer informed Halder about the Hungarian preparations. Halder set the target of the Hungarian troops' advance—soon to be started—as reaching the Stanislav–Kolomea line. He also emphasized the point that the Hungarian deployment should not, under any circumstance, disturb the German army's troop transit to Romania, an important issue because the Italian contingent also had to reach the front by crossing Hungary. Himer immediately informed Lieutenant Colonel Sáska, Chief of the Operational Section.[42]

The 17th German Army, thrusting its way from the Carpathians, failed to advance at a speed desired by the German military leadership. After crossing the River Prut the German and Romanian troops attacking from Romania advanced very slowly and with severe losses. One thing that Halder had anticipated did occur: the flank of the 17th German Army needed to be secured. In the evening of June 27, the OKW telegrammed a request to the Hungarian General Staff that, before completing its deployment, the Carpathian Group move into action in order to tie down the Soviet forces to be deployed against the *Heeresgruppe Süd*.[43]

Himer engaged in discussions with the General Staff about sending out liaison officers and about the modes of their employment. One of Himer's staff, Major Siegler, contacted the 2nd Section of the Hungarian General Staff and got Captain Kollány to agree that the daily military reports of the General Staff would be shown to him on a daily basis so that he could inquire with Berlin whether any changes might be necessary. Kollány was glad to make this promise; in view of past German objections, he also pledged that "from now on the Hungarian newspapers will release German, Italian and Hungarian military reports and not third- or fourth-hand ones."[44]

On June 28 the Hungarian General Staff informed Himer about the ongoing mobilization and deployment indicating that the units of the Rapid Army Corps would finish deployment by July 3 and would be concentrated in designated districts ready to take the offensive. Conforming to the German request, the mountain and border guard units had already crossed the border and were advancing northeast following the Soviet troops towards Strij.

General Jodl and Colonel Heusinger, Head of the Operational Group of the OKW, were satisfied with Himer's report about the Hungarian preparations. They stressed how important it was that the Hungarian rapid troops complete their deployment by July 3 and move into action. They asked Himer to urge them on so that they would not arrive late, or otherwise they would no longer be needed. The Command of the OKH expressed similar views.[45]

Himer conscientiously relayed the German High Command's messages to the Hungarian General Staff, which did not want to be "late" for the war under any circumstances.[46] Berlin's position about Hungarian participation had changed. Now the Hungarians had entered the war voluntarily, without the Germans holding out the prospect of anything in return. Suddenly dissatisfied voices, complaining that Hungary was inadequately participating in the war, were amplified.[47] On June 29 Sztójay complained that the German press had commented more warmly on the participation by Romania, Slovakia and Italy than on that by Hungary.[48] Homlok was also warned by one of his German fellow officers that certain people were keen on exploiting Hungary's passive behavior. The source, therefore, recommended that Hungary take further "spontaneous" steps, including offering a more substantial participation in the attack.

Hitler himself changed his earlier position. Since Himer was holding an inspection on the front, Major Radtke delivered a letter from Hitler to Horthy in Kenderes on July 2. Hitler thanked the Regent for the Hungarian troops joining the war effort which Horthy, like the other allies, ordered on his own volition. Hitler continued that the common fight would make it possible to stabilize the situation and diminish the tension between Hungary and Romania. No longer considering Hungary's participation as merely demonstrative or superfluous with respect to the German army,

Hitler now emphasized its importance and required that after reaching the Stanislav–Kolomea line the Hungarian *Honvédség* would continue advancing together with the German troops. The Hungarian units were to be subordinated to the *Heeresgruppe Süd*, as they were during the Serb campaign, so that the command structure would be solved similarly. Hitler also said that he had given his consent for Commander of the *Heeresgruppe Süd* Rundstedt's posing his requests regarding the military cooperation directly to the Hungarian military command in order to save time.[49]

Horthy was pleased with Hitler's letter. In his reply of July 5 he assured Hitler about their complete identity of views, expressed understanding towards his requests, and wished him luck with further military operations. Horthy also stated that the Hungarian troops would receive the appropriate information about their ongoing tasks, agreeing with the necessity of a common command structure.[50]

The units of the Rapid Army Corps had reached the River Dnester by July 6 and began crossing the river. At the request of the *Heeresgruppe Süd* the Rapid Army Corps separated from the Carpathian Group and came under the command of the German army group. The staff and certain units of the Carpathian Group temporarily took over the role of regional and administrative command in the area between the Carpathians and the border of the Rapid Army Corps' region. The Rapid Army Corps was not under Rundstedt's direct command for long, because from July 16 onwards it became part of the 17th German Army as its rapid force unit.[51]

Notes

1. György Ránki, Ervin Pamlényi, Loránt Tilkovszky and Gyula Juhász, eds., *A Wilhelmstrasse és Magyarország: Német diplomáciai iratok Magyarországról, 1933–1944* (The Wilhelmstrasse and Hungary: German Diplomatic Documents about Hungary, 1933–1944) (Budapest, 1968), p. 594. (412)
2. *Ibid.*
3. *Századok* (1965) 6: p. 1239.
4. *Ibid.*
5. *Ibid.*, p. 1240.
6. *Ibid.*
7. *Ibid*; Raymond James Sontag, et.als., ed., *Documents on German Foreign Policy, 1918–1945* (Washington, 1949–1954), vol. XIII: p. 63. (54)
8. Gyula Juhász, ed., *Diplomáciai iratok Magyarország külpolitikájához 1936–1945* (Diplomatic Writings on Hungary's Foreign Policy, 1936–1945) (Budapest, 1962–1982), vol. V: p. 1231. (866)
9. *Századok* (1965) 6: p. 1240.
10. *Ibid.*, p. 1241; Sontag, et.als., ed., *Documents on German Foreign Policy...*, vol. XIII: p. 64. (54)
11. *Századok* (1965) 6: p. 1241.
12. Miklós Horthy, *Emlékirataim* (My Memoirs) (Buenos Aires, 1953), p. 128.
13. *Századok* (1965) 6: p. 1241.
14. Juhász, ed., *Diplomáciai iratok...*, vol. V: p. 1241. (867); *Új Látóhatár* (1975) 1: p. 34.
15. *Bárdossy László népbírósági pere* (László Bárdossy's Trial in the People's Court) (Budapest, 1946), p. 9.
16. Horthy, *Emlékirataim*, p. 226.
17. László Bárdossy, *A nemzet védelmében* (In Defense of the Nation), (Fahrwangen, 1976), p. 52.
18. *Új Látóhatár* (1975) 1: p. 34.
19. Hadtörténelmi Levéltár (Military History Archive, HL). Eln. Vkf. 1941/5567.
20. Domokos Szent-Iványi, *Emlékirat* (Memoirs), Ráday Levéltár (Ráday Archive), Szent-Iványi hagyaték C/80, p. 155.

21. *Ibid.*, p. 156.
22. *Ibid.*, pp. 157–158.
23. Sontag, et.als., ed., *Documents on German Foreign Policy...*, vol. XIII: p. 13. (10)
24. *Ibid.*, p. 24. (21)
25. *Ibid.*, p. 15. (11)
26. *Századok* (1965) 6: p. 1241.
27. Juhász, ed., *Diplomáciai iratok...*, vol. V: pp. 1222–1223. (874–875)
28. Szent-Iványi, *Emlékirat...*, p. 154.
29. *Bundesarchiv* (BA) NS 19 neu 2069.
30. *Századok* (1965) 6: p. 1241.
31. HL. Eln. Vkf.1. 1941/5567.
32. *Ibid.*
33. Carlile Aylmer Macartney, *October Fifteenth. A History of Modern Hungary, 1929-1945* (Edinburgh, 1961), vol. II: p. 25.
34. *Ibid.*, p. 30.
35. *Ibid.*, p. 25.
36. Szent-Iványi, *Emlékirat...*, pp. 643–644.
37. *Ibid.*, p. 646; *DGFP*, vol. XIII: p. 25. (22).
38. Országos Levéltár (National Archive, OL). K 64-91-24-431/1941. Rp.
39. *Ibid.*
40. OL. K 64-91-24-431/1941. Rp.
41. HL. Eln. Vkf.1. 1941/5615 and 1941/5813.
42. *Századok* (1965) 6: p. 1242.
43. *Ibid.*
44. *Ibid.*
45. *Ibid.*, p. 1243.
46. *Ibid.*
47. Szent-Iványi, *Emlékirat...*, p. 649.
48. OL. K 64-90-24-437/1941. Rp.
49. *Századok* (1965) 6: p. 1244.
50. Macartney, *October Fifteenth...*, vol. II: p. 31.
51. János Csima, *Adalékok a Horthy-hadsereg szervezetének és háborús tevékenységének tanulmányozásához (1938–1945)* (Additions to Studying the Organizational Structure and the Military Activities of the Horthy Army: 1938–1945) (Budapest, 1961), p. 87; *Századok* (1965) 6: p. 1244.

Part III
THE FAILURE OF THE NEW HUNGARIAN MILITARY POLITICAL EXPERIMENT

COLONEL GENERAL FERENC SZOMBATHELYI AT THE HEAD OF THE GENERAL STAFF: AN ATTEMPT TO CREATE A NEW HUNGARIAN MILITARY POLICY

By July and August 1941 it had become clear that a blitzkrieg on the eastern front was out of the question. In spite of their substantial territorial gains, the German troops were unable to attain a decisive victory. Their losses were increasing, as was the resistance of the Soviet troops, while the German advance had slowed down. The fighting spirit had been dampened as a result of the first losses and the extended military operations. In July Sztójay was compelled to make the following observation: "The Russian forces' resistance and, especially, their technical expertise had not been expected by the Germans. But now relevant people have pointed out the danger that would have struck, had the Reich's Chancellor not recognized the situation and thus not preceded the Russians."[1] Homlok also called attention to the difficulties involved.

In the meantime, the Rapid Army Corps fought its increasingly hopeless fight alongside the Germans. It received a series of tasks that far surpassed its capabilities, due to its relatively small size (40,000 men) and the level of its equipment, which included a total lack of medium and heavy tanks. While advancing several hundred kilometers, the Rapid Army Corps suffered increasingly serious losses, lost a major part of its equipment, and suffered a dramatic decrease in its fighting capability. The German High Command completely ignored all these factors, and continued to assign it tasks. By the end of August it had become obvious that the Rapid Army Corps could only escape a total collapse by withdrawing from the operational zone and being transported home. The

Rapid Army Corps Command raised these issues at the end of August, saying that the Corps should be replaced by different units of the *Honvédség*.[2]

In the increasingly difficult battlefield situation, Werth came to the conclusion that the Germans could be helped by increasing Hungary's participation in the attack. The hope of a blitzkrieg had been shattered, and the necessity had arrived for the Hungarians to be at the German army's disposal with at least half of the *Honvédség*. In this way the mistake committed by the Hungarians' delay in entering the war with only moderately sized forces would be remedied.[3] This could also be a good opportunity to ask for the restoration of Hungary's thousand-year old borders, and also to share in Soviet raw materials resources, in return. Werth's eagerness had increased, due to the requests arriving directly to him from the German military command. As Horthy agreed in his letter to Hitler in early July, German officers at many levels of the German army sent their requests to the Hungarian General Staff, and the requests were not limited to the military operations of the Carpathian Group, but included the Rapid Army Corps, due to the unfavorable development of the battlefield situation and to the Corps' increasingly grave losses. This "direct link" made Himer's and his staff's activities in Budapest unnecessary, and they departed at the end of July. Their departure elevated the role of the German military attaché to Budapest, who thus far had been pushed rather into the background. Werth felt free to engage in discussions that circumvented the Hungarian government. For example, he promised Canaris on his visit to Budapest that the Hungarian forces would be reinforced at the front and that an army corps of appropriate size would be deployed. He also raised the issue of deploying them as occupying forces behind the front and as replacements for German troops in Serbia, and not just as fighting units.[4]

While Werth was urging that the army participate in the war with more forces, a part of the government, along with Horthy himself gradually, had become wary of the war, cautioned by the postponement of the blitzkrieg, the danger of further entanglement in a long war of doubtful outcome, and the unfolding coalitional character of the war. The pro-British circles in Hungary called Horthy's attention especially to the latter situation. Bárdossy, now that he had become increasingly irritated by the Chief of the General Staff's role and now that the war had not developed as expected, tried to attribute his and his government's position on the war to Werth's professional opinion, which had deceived both the Regent and himself. Bárdossy claimed that, as opposed to Werth, the government was of the view that the deployment of further forces was not advisable, because it would weaken the defensive power of Hungary.

The government paid more attention to news coming from southern Transylvania, indicating an increasing military concentration by the Romanians in parallel with increasing anti-Hungarian propaganda. Before the beginning of the war against the Soviet Union almost all Romanian military forces had been withdrawn from southern Transylvania, but by July these forces were to be transported back. By mid-July the force of almost four divisions was now stationed along the Transylvanian border. In August, when the Romanian army's front narrowed to just the Odessa region, Hungary received news and rumors about these forces.[5] Important Romanian politicians spoke more openly about the approaching armed re-annexation of Transylvania. This obviously did not lack the silent consent of German politicians.[6]

Werth argued that increasing Hungarian assistance to the Germans would be the most effective countermove. By August he wanted to have a decision on the question of which troop contingent to deploy. He had counted on the objections of the government, but also relied on the Regent's support. Pretty soon he realized that he had misjudged the situation. In the wake of his memorandum submitted to the government on August 19, a clash with the Prime Minister became unavoidable.

In his memorandum Werth held the government to blame, because, "in spite of its traditional anti-Bolshevist attitude, Hungary entered the war reluctantly and only after it was in fact attacked [in the Kassa bombing]. Even then, the fact that the country applied only a small military force might be a political disadvantage for Hungary that is hard to repair... This mistake [of the government] cost the Germans a lot of blood. For example, the lack of Hungarian assistance had a disadvantageous effect in the battle of Lemberg [Lvov, L'viv]... The full extent of its effect and significance will be only known after the war, when the Germans reproach us."[7]

In his letter to Horthy on August 26 Bárdossy wrote that he was appalled at, and rejected, the tone that the Chief of the General Staff once again allowed himself to use towards the government. In Bárdossy's view Werth criticized the government and dealt with its internal and foreign political tasks "as if they belonged to the General Staff's sphere of authority." Bárdossy claimed that he had warned Werth several times that the government's policy and measures should not appear in a false or crooked light due to his behavior, and that "it is unseemly for the Chief of the General Staff to act as if he supervised the government's measures or could hold the government responsible for them, because under our constitutional arrangements the General Staff does not and should not have any right to do so."[8] In spite of this warning, Werth once again wandered from the right path in his memorandum, and hurled heavy accusations at the government, presenting his internal and foreign political suggestions in an "emphatic" form. This was what led Bárdossy, as he stated in his capacity as head of the government and in full knowledge of his responsibility, to bring the issue to the Regent's attention.

Bárdossy wrote in his letter that he considered it appalling, unprecedented and unpardonable that the Hungarian General Staff raised an accusation against the Hungarian government concerning the issue of how much the country should participate in the war, something that had never been objected to by the Germans. He felt gravely personally insulted. It was also clear that he desired the issue should be decided by Horthy so that he—Bárdossy—would come out victorious. This was only possible if he made Werth seem impossible in Horthy's eyes. Bárdossy also knew that Werth had agreed with Horthy on the question of entering the war and on the scale of participation, and that the government had only nodded to say "yes." Therefore, any kind of relevant criticism or pointing out of responsibility would primarily affect the Regent. Werth had not noticed this. Bárdossy called Horthy's attention to the development of events that would help to clarify the issue of responsibility.

Bárdossy continued to explain that the government had decided on the extent of the country's participation in the war against the Soviets by considering both the given situation and the strength of the country. As a result, the most valuable and most modern equipped segments of the Hungarian army, the Rapid Army Corps and a part of the air force were made available for the fight against Bolshevism. From the Hungarian point of view it was a significant sacrifice, which should not be proportionately compared with the size of the German army or with Romanian or Finnish forces participating in the war. Therefore, the Chief of the General Staff's statement that Hungary had participated "with only a small force" should be flatly denied. All these considerations, as well as the strength of Hungary's participation in the war, must be made clear to the authorities in the German government and those in the German army.[9]

As Bárdossy continued to write, the accusation raised by Werth was especially strange because in the afternoon of June 26 Werth himself suggested—with the Minister of Defense present—that Hungary participate in the war against the Soviet Union with the Rapid Army Corps: "As far as I know, he made a similar proposal to the same effect to you, Your Grace, on the same day." What was more, in the presence of the Minister of Defense Werth also declared that he was "fully convinced that the deployment of even this limited segment of our armed forces would be necessary for only a short period of time, and that we will be abundantly compensated for the possible losses of technical equipment of the Hungarian units participating in the war by valuable pillage from the Soviet army." The government did not want to hold the Chief of the General Staff responsible at all, but noted with protest the fact that just two months after the Chief of the General Staff's hearing before the government, he now accused it of "failing to act" and stated that "it caused a political disadvantage to Hungary that will be difficult to remedy."[10]

Now Werth came up with the idea that Hungary's failure to act properly so far should be remedied by offering half of the army (four or five army corps) to participate in the war. According to Werth, this should not depend on whether the Germans asked for it or not, because "Germany will never approach us with such a request" and because "in the Germans' opinion, a sovereign country should come to such a crucial conclusion by itself." Rather, it was in Hungary's interest to do it because after the war individual countries would be rewarded according to how much each participated in the war.[11]

Bárdossy rejected Werth's reasoning. He argued that it did not conform with the fact that the German military command, even if needed, would not turn to Hungary with a request to increase its forces on the eastern front. If the Reich's government counted on Hungary's participation, it would speak up, just as it had done before launching the military campaign against Yugoslavia. Still, on June 24 the German military command also had informed General Himer that "our certain participation was considered desirable." Bárdossy thought it was most curious of the Chief of the General Staff to forget about this detail, although he had informed the government about it in written form. Nothing substantiated the supposition, or made it plausible, that "the German government or the German army expected us to participate with larger forces in the ongoing war or wanted us to volunteer to do so."[12]

As Bárdossy went on, the Germans had taken over administration even in areas occupied by Hungarians, and therefore they did not even need a larger Hungarian presence as an occupying force. Yet if the German army did need a proportionately larger Hungarian participation, it would be brought to Hungary's attention based on the confidential and good relationship between the two countries. In that situation the Hungarian government would certainly strongly consider fulfilling the request if it had the means. Until then, however, Hungary was not in a position to participate in the war with larger forces, because "it would obviously have an adverse effect on the condition of our national forces, internal politics and economic production." Bárdossy considered it curious that the Chief of the General Staff "would want to risk all these things by making a volunteering offer that would force us to join the anti-Soviet war with a larger number of forces."[13]

As Werth had written in his memorandum, sovereign states "decide themselves" on crucial questions. This was precisely why, Bárdossy thought, the government had to take the country's internal situation and security readiness into consideration. "After seriously considering these things, it has to come to a conclusion, and not merely in order to gain 'credits' or to receive 'rewards' later on." The Germans had been made aware, by the situation in southeastern Europe, of the importance of the Hungarians, and there was no reason to ask for special rewards for that.[14]

As a conclusion to his anti-Werth indictment, Bárdossy said that based on his earlier experiences he could not see any possibility of cooperation with the Chief of the General Staff, since the latter had overruled the government's decisions and instructions. This placed Horthy in the difficult position of having to choose between Bárdossy and Werth.

The news that a disagreement had developed into a government crisis leaked out and offered many opportunities for guessing games.[15] The Germans, who had been aware of the reasons for the crisis, also paid close attention to the development of the situation. Werth's attempts floundered at the government's resistance. Urged on by the dire needs of his army, Hitler decided to turn to Horthy to clarify the question of further German–Hungarian military cooperation. On September 1 von Ribbentrop instructed Ambassador Jagow to invite the Regent to the General Headquarters on behalf of the Führer. Mussolini had also visited there a few days previously. It was up to Horthy to decide about the exact time of the visit, and to choose whom to take along.[16]

Horthy thanked him for the invitation, expressed eagerness to go, and said that he would decide about his escort later.[17] Hitler's invitation urged him to solve the tense situation in his government. During the visit mostly military questions were to be discussed, and therefore the presence of the Chief of the General Staff was necessary. The decision could not be delayed, and Horthy, feeling personally hurt, took the step: he dismissed Werth. Horthy came to the conclusion that Werth had been striving to gain an improper leading political role. He had made a series of statements against the government's policy without first informing or seeking agreement from Horthy or the Prime Minister. And, overstepping and misunderstanding his own sphere of authority, he had made binding promises that had questioned and compromised (before the Germans) the Regent's and the government's earlier instructions.

This time around Horthy was concerned about the government's authority and legality, and he himself called Bárdossy's attention to Werth's mobilization ideas and the promises that he had made to the Germans, without informing the government or the Supreme Military Council, which Horthy did not endorse. Bárdossy asked for Werth and informed him that he was obliged to report to the Prime Minister before he submitted any matter of political consequence to the supreme warlord. Werth concluded that he had fallen out of grace from the way the situation had developed, from the rejection that he received to his suggestions about increasing the country's participation in the war, and mostly from the Regent's changed attitude towards him. He handed in his resignation due to health reasons on September 5.[18]

Jagow reported to the German Ministry of Foreign Affairs that Werth had resigned and that his successor, Lieutenant General Ferenc Szombathelyi, the former commander of the VIII. Army Corps and the Carpathian Group, was an eminent pro-German soldier. Jagow concluded that Werth's resignation must have been in connection with disagreements about the size of Hungarian troops to be deployed to the Soviet front.[19]

Jagow sent a second report that day, which went into further detail. When he handed Keitel's invitation to visit the German Headquarters to Werth, he thanked him for the honor and "added that since he was not physically in top shape, he had resigned from his office." Arrangements had been made for his successor to respond to the invitation. Jagow noticed that there was great anxiety in the General Staff. One of the staff officers noted that "this is a juicy bit for the British." Jagow was also informed that the prestige of Lieutenant General Szombathelyi, the successor, could not be compared with that of Werth, and it was questionable whether he was capable of exerting as much energy as Werth did.[20]

Why exactly did Horthy choose Szombathelyi? Szombathelyi had not been much at the forefront of events, although the Germans knew him as the Commander of the Carpathian Group. So why did Horthy risk the resentment of three higher-ranking generals, one of whom was Gusztáv Jány? As Szombathelyi confirmed in his "speech for the defense" in 1945, he had come into the limelight by accident. As an army corps commander in Kassa, he had hosted the visiting István Horthy, the Regent's son. After dinner they had a long conversation, during which Szombathelyi elaborated on his views of the war and its probable development. In his view the Germans had underestimated the Soviet forces, a successful blitzkrieg was out of the question, and the war would last for years. One could not envision the war's outcome, he said, but a complete victory was improbable. It would have been better if Hungary had stayed out of the war, but once it was in it then the preservation of forces would be the most important issue for the future. This would be the only way to ensure that after the end of the uncertainly developing war, Hungary would be able to secure the country's territorial integrity and its internal order. We have to be prepared for the eventuality that following the war—or even during the war—Hungary would have to fight its own war with its neighbors, he said. The young Horthy attentively listened to Szombathelyi's elaboration and asked him to write a memorandum that he could show to his father, who was dissatisfied with Werth for insisting on a total mobilization and deployment of the *Honvédség*. And Szombathelyi indeed gave his own notes to the young Horthy.[21]

Finally the Regent had found a man who found it necessary to preserve the country's military forces as much as possible—as opposed to Werth, who wanted to sacrifice everything.

Szombathelyi's appointment gave reassurance to Bárdossy and his government. In order to emphasize the importance of his new Chief of the General Staff, Horthy personally appeared at his introduction at the Council of Ministers, something which had not previously been customary. Szombathelyi also got a favorable reception from the pro-German members of the government, due to his assumed definite pro-Axis attitude. He "is also aware of the country's national interests, and is a suitable choice to maintain friendly relations with the Germans, which will serve our common affairs without offending Hungary's self-respect." They were looking forward to seeing his reception by the Germans, which took place when Horthy himself introduced his new Chief of the General Staff at the German Military Headquarters. The news about the visit was reassuring. In Hungary Bárdossy declared that Szombathelyi was received with "the greatest congeniality and affection." The Germans proved to be understanding towards Werth's departure, which was thought to be due to Szombathelyi's role as the Commander of the Carpathian Group, which required Szombathelyi to satisfy the German military command.[22]

On the way to visiting the German Military Headquarters, Bárdossy felt reassured that the Hungarians were going along with a new Chief of the General Staff, who identified his views with those of the government. He knew that, in addition to the future role of the Rapid Army Corps, raising the Hungarian war contingent would be the main topic of conversation with Hitler. It was obvious to him that the German leaders were the driving force behind Werth's eagerness to make voluntary offers, something for which he had now been rebuked. Bárdossy believed that the German leaders had unsuccessfully wanted to take a road that was simpler for them, and void of diplomatic negotiations. Bárdossy was prepared to attempt to minimize the Germans' expected requests, even though it could not be, and would not be, practical to flatly reject them. He hoped for Szombathelyi's "professional" support in this undertaking.

The Hungarian delegation, complete with Counselor Szentmiklósy, visited the German Main Headquarters between September 7 and 10 and met members of the German leadership in succession. Besides Hitler, Göring and von Ribbentrop, they had the chance to meet Keitel, Jodl, Brauchitsch and Halder. As expected, their partners tried to dissuade them from withdrawing the Rapid Army Corps from the front.

The essence of the discussions can be condensed based on the short notes of the Bárdossy–von Ribbentrop meetings, on the draft summary prepared by the Ministry of Foreign Affairs, and the agreement reached.

The first Bárdossy–von Ribbentrop discussion took place on September 9. The German Minister of Foreign Affairs immediately came to the point and asked Bárdossy whether it was true that the Hungarian government wanted to withdraw the Rapid Army Corps fighting on the eastern front. After an affirmative response, Bárdossy listed all the arguments that made the withdrawal unavoidable: between 50% and 80% of its equipment had been destroyed; the *Honvédség* had no other rapid unit with which to replace it; due to a shortage of war materials the equipment could not be replaced; the Hungarian government was also not able to deploy regular forces to replace the mechanized units, since it would so weaken Hungary both militarily and economically that it would not be able to fulfill its role in southeastern Europe, something not in Germany's interest.

Von Ribbentrop found it morally reprehensible for Hungary to withdraw from the anti-Bolshevist war. As a solution—assuming the Führer's and the military leadership's consent—he raised the possibility of re-arming the rapid troops at the front, which would make it possible to extend their stay. After finishing the ongoing military operation, the Rapid Army Corps could be withdrawn, and in the future Hungarian units would only have security roles behind the front.[23]

During their second discussion on September 10, Bárdossy returned to the topic of Hungary's southeastern European role as a primary Hungarian strategic goal, and tried to convince von Ribbentrop about its significance. The Hungarian rapid force was the only one able to curb the various anti-German movements that were still to be found in the region and were re-invigorated time and again. Therefore, it was in Germany's interest to save this Hungarian force. Bárdossy also tried to turn von Ribbentrop against Romania, by saying that Romania's role was tied to Antonescu and that without him their siding with Germany was unimaginable. Romanian officials still did not accept the Second Vienna Award, which was a warning sign both for Hungary and Germany. Bárdossy also raised the Bánát issue, which could easily become a factor in the Pan-Slavic movement if its re-annexation were made difficult.[24]

All the German leaders maintained a friendly tone towards Romania, which dampened the spirit among the members of the Hungarian delegation. It was clear that the Germans trusted Antonescu and held him in high esteem. The main emphasis was on the Romanian oil, without which the military operations would come to an end: 50,000 tons of oil per month came from Romania.

After lengthy bargaining, an agreement was concluded on the issue of Hungarian units on the eastern front, which under the given circumstances sounded like an appropriate solution, but turned out not to be the last word in terms of future Hungarian military participation. The agreement signed by Szombathelyi stated the following: 1) The Germans would supplement the equipment of the rapid brigades so that they would remain in action until the end of the present military operations, which would not be beyond October 15; 2) The Germans would place the equipment of a whole armored division at Hungary's disposal; 3) The occupation units of the four peacetime brigades would be replaced by twelve infantry battalions.[25]

The Germans' insistence on employing the now weakened and worn-out rapid brigades alluded to their own weakness. Halder said that it was a selfish action on the part of Hungary to withdraw the army corps before the upcoming grandiose military operation. And as far as their equipment was concerned, in the *Heeresgruppe Süd*'s view it was not any worse than that of the German units.

The Hungarian delegation returned home successfully, or at least that was how they felt, since they had let themselves be convinced by the Germans' optimism and now also had a promise for the immediate re-armament of the Rapid Army Corps.

Szombathelyi could meet the members of the Hungarian General Staff in his new appointment only after returning home from the German Main Headquarters. The officers of the General Staff received him with suspicion. He had to confront Werth's legacy, as he made clear in his 1945 testimony at the People's Court: "Except for a few, both the generals and the General Staff were imbued with my predecessor's spirit, and with the conviction that Hungary's fate and future were to be decided at Germany's side. The officer corps of the army, and especially the General Staff, were completely pro-German even in their political ideology. They kept up a strong relationship with one of my predecessors, a leading personality of the Hungarian right wing, Colonel General Rátz, who consequently could have been considered a second Chief of the General Staff of the Hungarian army. High-ranking officers and generals in my immediate vicinity were completely pro-German, and to a certain extent I was under their control."[26] Under such circumstances, in order to pursue his own ideas he had to change the leading echelon of officers, gradually, step by step. The question was where to acquire reliable people and on what basis to demote those who had acquired "merits" earlier. The danger was that those officers promoted would think much like those demoted. For example, on November 1 Lieutenant General János Vörös replaced Dezső László, who was assigned to a different position. Vörös proved to be as pro-German as his predecessor had been. The new Chief of the General Staff had to realize that things were not going to change quickly. He said later, "Often I felt that I had come too late, and could hardly change the spoilt public spirit."[27]

General Szombathelyi in his orientation to the leaders of the army on September 25, spoke about the danger that an anti-revisionist group of states led by Romania meant for Hungary. He planned to defend the country against such a grouping, which obviously would have to have Germany's consent in order to be created, only from Hungary's own resources. "Therefore," he wrote in the orientation material, "our country has to be prepared to defend itself against the newly forming 'Little Entente' under all circumstances—by itself if needed—to retain its relative position of strength, to secure its territorial integrity, and to realize its military political goals."[28] He spoke more realistically about the Soviet army: "The perfection of the equipment, technical readiness and advanced mechanization of the Soviet armed forces surprised both us and the German leadership." It was quite obvious that Szombathelyi considered the German army's fight of primary interest to Hungary, although one to be given limited support.[29]

Szombathelyi's attention was very soon occupied by the problem of fulfilling new German demands. Reports coming from the front convinced him that the war would be expanded and will give rise to new demands. Therefore, he asked for the German military attaché, Toussaint, in mid-October, and told him that the German military leadership needed to inform him, through the military attaché, about what Hungary could expect in the coming year. In this way it could avoid having to deal with new problems unprepared.[30]

Toussaint then inquired of his superiors and was instructed to ensure that the two General Staffs be in contact on the issue of reinforcing occupation forces and the issue of the manner of deploying technical units. The attaché was also authorized to say that the German military command would offer assistance to equip and train a "smaller size" armored division.[31]

The two General Staffs were in contact pretty soon, something that the German General Staff initiated because they had misunderstood Szombathelyi's request. The Germans obviously thought that Szombathelyi would go on from the point where Werth had stopped. In the morning of October 20, Lieutenant General Paulus, Leader of the Operational Section of the OKH, called Dezső László and relayed Staff Colonel Halder's request to ask for Szombathelyi's theoretical consent to the deployment of further two brigades beyond the four brigades already at the Germans' disposal. Paulus "emphasizes the point that the requested Hungarian troops are very much needed" and expected an urgent response, preferably on the same day.

Colonel Roeder, Head of the German Transportation Command in Hungary, also paid a visit to the 7th Section of the General Staff Headquarters, and presented a request from the commander of the German railway troops for the deployment of railway construction units in large numbers.[32]

On both October 20 and October 21 Paulus urged the Hungarians to respond. Finally, to fulfill Szombathelyi's instructions, László informed Halder on October 22 that he should initiate the request along political lines with the Hungarian government, via an ambassador or otherwise.[33]

Ritter, a representative of the German Ministry of Foreign Affairs at the German Main Military Headquarters turned to Jagow on the issue on October 26. Ritter told Jagow about the antecedents; in his view allusions to a political meeting were surprising and unjustified. Apparently not even considering the possibility that the Chief of the General Staff could have acted in agreement with the Hungarian government when he turned the request to diplomatic channels, Ritter followed earlier expectations in drawing the conclusion that the misunderstanding "was caused by the different attitudes of the Hungarian military and political authorities, as we have stated before. Considering that the deployment of technical units is important for the OKW, we cannot avoid conducting the negotiations on a diplomatic level." Jagow was instructed to clarify with the Hungarians that they had initiated the discussion between the General Staffs, and that the German proposal would become null and void if they wanted to raise political, economic or military conditions. Jagow ought to discuss the issue with the German military attaché, and in the case of agreement he was to tell the Hungarian Minister of Foreign Affairs that the Hungarian General Staff had asked the OKW to inform them as soon as possible about the probable gradual deployment of Hungarian forces the following year. In compliance with the request, the OKW proposed that further units earmarked for occupation areas and more technical units be deployed. Since the Hungarian General Staff now declared that the Hungarian government expected to discuss the matter along diplomatic lines, the OKW commissioned the ambassador to tell the Minister of Foreign Affairs that it was ready to deploy the above-mentioned Hungarian troops to the eastern front.

Should the Hungarian government agree without any further ado, the ambassador was to acknowledge it and to suggest that for future reference the two General Staffs were to agree. However, should the Hungarian government set up conditions, Jagow was to explain that there must have been some misunderstanding, since he was under the impression that the *Wehrmacht* had agreed to the deployment of Hungarian troops at the Hungarian General Staff's initiative and that Germany was unlikely to conduct discussions about the deployment of Hungarian troops with the Hungarian government. The ambassador was not authorized to do that in any case, and he was to relay the Hungarian communication to Berlin.[34]

Following his commission, Jagow paid a visit to Bárdossy on October 27. Bárdossy responded to Jagow's message by saying that a clear agreement between the two military commands had been achieved at the German Headquarters with regard to the number of units to be deployed to the eastern front. If the German military command wished or felt it necessary to deploy further units, the Hungarian government would consider it. Following Ritter's instructions, Jagow then responded that, as far as he knew, "the Hungarian military command had expressed its wish to be able to increase the number of Hungarian military units available in the east."[35]

Bárdossy thought that there had been a misunderstanding. He said that he was convinced that with regard to the General Staff "it was an expression of readiness and willingness to satisfy the German request as much as we can, and it was not a case of offering new troops to be deployed voluntarily." He could safely say this, he continued, because he had had the chance to discuss the issue with the Chief of the General Staff and was familiar with his understanding. It was possible that "irresponsible people from the General Staff had made some statements, but these statements could only be interpreted as mentioned before."[36]

Jagow proceeded to tersely inform the German Ministry of Foreign Affairs that Bárdossy had unambiguously declared that the Hungarian government "did not and does not" intend to offer further troops and that the OKW was in error.[37]

On October 30 Sztójay reported from Berlin that he had had the chance to speak with Clodius, who confidentially described the negative attitude towards the Hungarians that he had experienced in the German Ministry of Foreign Affairs, provoked by the fact that the German military command had not received an appropriate response to its request. The Hungarian Prime Minister had tried to shift the issue to the diplomatic sphere. However, presently, Clodius said, the issue was not to be discussed on the level of foreign affairs, since "there is not such a great need for this help." Clodius was not familiar with the German Military Headquarters' reaction but, as far as he knew, the issue might have come to a deadlock there as well.[38]

On October 31 Bárdossy sent for Szombathelyi, who told him about the message exchanges between the two General Staffs and established that the OKW had misunderstood things. Neither responsible or other officials of the General Staff had made any offers.[39] Szombathelyi stood by his subordinates.

Following the discussion with the Chief of the General Staff, Bárdossy responded to Sztójay on November 2, informing him about his discussion with Jagow and lashed out at the General Staff: "I can find an explanation for the German action in the probability that one of the officers of the Hungarian General Staff might have made the statement—obviously in order to gain merit—that we wanted to increase our participation in the Russian operation. The Hungarian government, in agreement with the Chief of the General Staff, wants to terminate such irresponsible individual offers... Should the German military command truly need Hungarian technical troops and should it bring it to our attention, the Hungarian government will not rule out fulfilling the request. We are not trying to initiate diplomatic discussions, but we want to make sure that the Hungarian government, aware of actual requests, will take a position without the intervention of unauthorized mediators."[40] He asked Sztójay to inform Clodius and to indicate that the message was highly confidential and private information from Budapest, and also to ask him for absolute secrecy.

Hardly had Sztójay received the telegram when a new instruction came. The Prime Minister modified the section of the telegram dealing with the role of the General Staff. Since "he could clearly state, based on the examination conducted with the Chief of the General Staff, that officers of the General Staff or the Hungarian military command had not made statements—not even as private views—that could have been interpreted as meaning that we would like to increase the level of our military participation," Sztójay should consider Bárdossy's speculation with regard to the German action as superceded, and should concentrate on the rest of the telegram in his further discussion with Clodius.[41]

The situation of the Rapid Army Corps on the front was becoming critical. Its withdrawal was cancelled according to the September agreement. On September 13 Szombathelyi sent Major General János Vörös to the Army Corps Headquarters to review the condition of the army corps and to give confidential information to Lieutenant General Béla Miklós, the Commander of the Rapid Army Corps. Miklós and his senior commanders could not have been overjoyed at the Chief of the General Staff's message: 1) Until a new decision was made concerning the southern wing of the frontline, the Rapid Corps would participate in further mobile operations; 2) After that the Rapid Corps would be sent home; 3) According to the OKW's promises, the Germans would supplement their missing war materials, since the lack of it was hindering their fighting efficiency. Therefore, they should urgently claim these materials from the Germans.[42]

Following that, the units of the Rapid Army Corps provided defense on the bank of the River Dnieper until the end of September. They hoped that this would be the end of their frontline service. Their hopes were fed by the fact that their fighting efficiency deteriorated even further, due to a delay in receiving the promised German materials.

On October 5 the Rapid Army Corps received a new task, which was to advance to the River Donec. By then it had lost even its name, because the Rapid Corps had been subordinated to the IV. Army Corps of the 17th German Army, under the name of the "Schwedler" Group. The mechanized brigades had lost their whole armored materials and some of their cars, and yet still struggled forward over a difficult terrain in deep mud. Their losses made the cavalry brigade unfit for further employment, and on October 16 Lieutenant General Miklós made arrangements for its immediate withdrawal and its transportation home. At the expense of huge sacrifices, the mechanized brigades reached the River Donec at Izjum on October 30, but the prospect of their continued presence on the frontline threatened them with total annihilation. In this critical situation Miklós traveled to Budapest on October 27 to ask for permission for the urgent and immediate withdrawal of the brigades.

Szombathelyi began negotiations with the OKW; as a result, on November 6 the order came that the Rapid Army Corps would be replaced by German units. The process was completed by November 15, so that on that day they began their transportation home. The OKW had realized that the units of the Rapid Army Corps were not usable in their present state.[43] The loss was substantial: 180 officers and 3,825 men had been killed; 100% of small tanks, 80% of light tanks, and 90% of armored vehicles had been destroyed; 1,200 vehicles and 28 guns had been made unusable.[44]

The withdrawal of the Rapid Army Corps forced the Germans, who had sustained serious losses in the October offensive, to take further steps. On November 9 Ritter got in touch with Jagow and reminded him of Bárdossy's statement that the Hungarian government would not rule out deploying new troops if the Germans expressed a need for a new contingent. He asked Jagow to immediately contact the Hungarian Minister of Foreign Affairs and relay to him the *Wehrmacht*'s request that in addition to the four brigades promised, the Hungarian army would deploy two more brigades at the disposal of the German army. Furthermore, the *Wehrmacht* wanted technical military units to be deployed, the numbers and the location to be decided by the two General Staffs. If the Hungarian government inquired about the transportation of the promised German equipment, Jagow should allude to ongoing discussions about the equipment and about the training of a Hungarian armored division.[45]

It was impossible to sidestep this issue, since it was submitted through diplomatic channels. Bárdossy assured Jagow, who came to see him on November 11, that "we will evaluate your request with our best intentions while considering the situation and our capabilities."[46]

On November 12 the Hungarian government agreed to the deployment of two more occupational brigades. The Chief of the General Staff also consented, with his only request being that the Germans hold the brigades together both organizationally and in the same area.[47]

On the day of the decision Bárdossy contacted Sztójay to inform him that the Hungarian government was willing to fulfill the

German request. He said that he also hoped that his decision would end the Germans' negative views about the Hungarians, about which Sztójay had spoken in his latest report.[48]

In early November three (the 121st, the 124th and the 105th) of the formerly mobilized occupational brigades were already in the military operational zone, and the transportation of the fourth (the 108th) had already begun. The transportation of the two brigades mobilized in the wake of the most recent agreement (the 102nd and the 111th) was to begin in early December. By December 17 the 102nd Brigade had arrived at the operational zone, while only part of the 111th Brigade had arrived, due to transport difficulties. The defeat of the German army and the December retreat had necessitated the urgent deployment of reserves, which completely tied down the capacity of the railways. In parallel with the Soviet attack, vigorous partisan activity also began in areas behind the front. Hungarian units became heavily entangled with these partisans. In their difficult situation, the Germans did not adhere to the Hungarian Chief of the General Staff's conditions, and applied the Hungarian units to proportionately oversized military areas, under German command.

Equipping the armored division with German materials remained only a promise. The Hungarians were promised that the Germans would look into the matter.[49] In October General Becker, Commander of the Armaments Department of the German Land Forces, could only say to Homlok that he had not received any relevant instructions from the OKW.

The German army's situation began to turn critical on the eastern front. Operation Typhoon, led by General Guderian and launched in October in order to occupy Moscow, collapsed. The German army incurred colossal losses both in human lives and in destroyed equipment, and ran through a major part of its reserves. By the end of November the losses included 735,000 men, or 22.96% of the forces fighting on the eastern front. At the same time the German offensive wound down on the southern front as well.

The counterattacking Soviet troops re-occupied Rostov. Rundstedt asked Hitler for permission to retreat. In response, he was replaced by the Commander of the *Heeresgruppe Süd* Reichenau, who, however, also failed to avoid further retreats.[50] The Soviet counteroffensive launched at Moscow on December 5 increased the German losses to catastrophic proportions; for the first time during the war, the *Wehrmacht* was forced to flee.

The failure below Moscow, the fact that the advance had come to a deadlock on the southern front, the major German losses, the retreat and the shortage of deployable reserves were known facts to the Hungarian military command and the Prime Minister. Therefore, Bárdossy must have expected to be asked for a greater Hungarian participation in the war during his trip to Berlin to sign the five-year extension of the Anti-Comintern Pact. This was the background when he met von Ribbentrop on November 26.

After Bárdossy had expressed his gratitude and thanks for the honor of participating in such historic times in Berlin, von Ribbentrop immediately began to analyze the political situation and the situation at the front. He did not speak about the lack of success or its causes, yet claimed that the Führer had planned to deal the final blow to the enemy in the following year. Then he proceeded to discuss financial matters, and emphasized the point that the war was also being fought to obtain the Soviet oil, without which Germany could not continue fighting. This presented a good opportunity to speak about Hungarian oil shipments. He asked Bárdossy to make sure that Hungary make the largest possible amount of oil available for Germany. An increase of deliveries by the relatively small amount of 40,000 tons would be very important. Following that, he looked into a precise review of ongoing Hungarian wheat and food transports, and called his guest's attention to numerous unexploited possibilities.[51] Von Ribbentrop claimed that in the common fight the Germans had borne the brunt of the burden and had suffered the most sacrifices. Consequently, Germany "expected its friends to extend all the possible help and support to it."[52]

Bárdossy promised that the Hungarian government would do everything in its power to increase oil and wheat shipments. However, he pointed out that weather conditions, as well as organizational and other unforeseeable factors, might affect the Hungarians' ability to satisfy the German requests.

In spite of Bárdossy's expectations, the German Minister of Foreign Affairs did not bring up the question of increasing Hungary's military contribution. He did, however, speak about the painful Hungarian–Romanian relations, which might get in the way of the efforts that everyone had to exert in the interest of their common goal. The Minister of Foreign Affairs might have found the issue important because the Hungarian government had justified avoiding a greater participation in the armed sacrifice by citing the tense relationship between the two countries.

At this point Bárdossy complained about Antonescu and the other Romanian leaders at great length, because they did not seem to have accepted the Second Vienna Award, but rather had pursued an openly counter-revisionist policy.

Von Ribbentrop asked for Bárdossy's understanding towards the Romanians, who had landed in a very difficult situation following the Second Vienna Award. Although it had not satisfied either party, arbitration was necessary, because in this way both countries had avoided a critical situation. The Hungarian army would have been unable to solve the issue by itself, and an armed clash would have provoked the danger of the Soviets' intervening. The family rivalry should be put aside, since winning the war was the only important issue at that moment. After the war, the Romanians would be occupied with rebuilding Bessarabia and other eastern areas, and not with Transylvania. Antonescu would understand the situation. Von Ribbentrop also noted that the Romanian troops had done a good job in the war against Soviet Russia.[53] Bárdossy was not reassured by von Ribbentrop's words. Even if he had not said it in words, he had hoped for a definite promise from Germany that would assure him about the protection of Hungarian interests against the Romanians.

On November 28 the Hungarian Prime Minister was received by Hitler at the German Main Military Headquarters. Hitler's flood of words to Bárdossy told him that he had actually won the war, and that only the reorganization of the new Europe after the victory was left to be done. Hitler spoke appreciatively about the Hungarian troops, who had been fighting brilliantly on the front and would now deserve "to be the first to have some rest and to recuperate." After this remark, which did not lack sarcasm, Hitler did not speak about future Hungarian sacrifices.[54]

Bárdossy was satisfied when he returned home. Having the units of the Rapid Army Corps finally at home was considered to be a success, as was the fact that Hungary, despite German losses, had got away with deploying only six occupying brigades—for the time being. After the December defeats for Germany, rumor spread that the spring continuation of the eastern campaign would not be possible without the deployment of substantial Hungarian forces.

Soon Hungary had to undertake further political obligations attached to the Axis policy following the extension of the Anti-Comintern Pact. On December 7 the British government declared war on Hungary. On December 11, four days after Pearl Harbor, Germany and Italy—in solidarity with Japan—declared war on the United States. On the same day Bárdossy proposed to the government that Hungary express its solidarity with the Axis and that, without waiting for the German request, Hungary should sever diplomatic relations with the United States. Instead, the government decided to express its solidarity with the Axis by recalling its ambassador, in order to avoid a final breakdown in diplomatic relations. The decision was immediately delivered to the ambassador of the United States. Bárdossy's speed was only surpassed by Sztójay, who telegrammed from Berlin already in the evening of December 11 to state that the German Reich emphasized its insistence that

Hungary should declare war just as Romania and Slovakia were about to do. On December 12 German Embassy Counselor Werkmeister and the Italian ambassador went to see Bárdossy and, on behalf of their governments, almost demanded that Hungary declare war. They argued that failure to do so would cause Hungary to exclude itself from a group of countries in solidarity with Germany. Bárdossy was scared by their determined attitude, and on the same day—without asking the Regent or the government—he informed the ambassador of the United States that the government's declaration of the previous day should be considered a declaration of war. Bárdossy announced this step only at the regular session of the Council of Ministers, where the ministers acknowledged it without protesting against its unconstitutional nature. Horthy behaved similarly, although he resented the fact that he had been circumvented. In fact, since it was not a case of an attack on Hungary, Parliament should have decided the issue of the declaration of war. Since Bárdossy did not consider it necessary, he violated the law.

Notes

1. Országos Levéltár (National Archive, OL). K 64-60-24-527/1941. Rp.
2. Franz Halder, *Kriegstagebuch. Tägliche Aufzeichnungen des Chefs des Generalstabes des Heeres 1939–1942/Generaloberst Halder* (Stuttgart, 1962–1964), vol. III: p. 217.
3. Carlile Aylmer Macartney, *October Fifteenth. A History of Modern Hungary, 1929-1945* (Edinburgh, 1961), vol. II: p. 54.
4. György Ránki, Ervin Pamlényi, Loránt Tilkovszky and Gyula Juhász, eds., *A Wilhelmstrasse és Magyarország: Német diplomáciai iratok Magyarországról, 1933–1944* (The Wilhelmstrasse and Hungary: German Diplomatic Documents about Hungary, 1933–1944) (Budapest, 1968), p. 611. (431)
5. Hadtörténelmi Levéltár (Military History Archive, HL). Eln. Vkf.1. 1941/5827.
6. OL. K 64-90-27-762/1941. Rp.
7. *Horthy Miklós titkos iratai* (Miklós Horthy's Secret Writings), ed. Miklós Szinai and László Szűcs, (Budapest, 1962), p. 302.
8. *Ibid.*, p. 301.
9. *Ibid.*, p. 303.
10. *Ibid.*
11. *Ibid.*, p. 304.
12. *Ibid.*, p. 305.
13. *Ibid.*
14. *Ibid.*
15. Dezső Saly, *Szigorúan bizalmas* (Strictly Confidential) (Budapest, 1945), p. 388.
16. Ránki–Pamlényi–Tilkovszky–Juhász, *A Wilhelmstrasse és Magyarország...*, p. 615. (437)
17. *Ibid.*, p. 615. (438)
18. HL. Filmtár (Film Archive) 1729. *Hóman naplója* (Hóman's Diary).
19. Ránki–Pamlényi–Tilkovszky–Juhász, *A Wilhelmstrasse és Magyarország...*, p. 617. (440)
20. *Ibid.*, p. 617. (441)
21. Gyula Kádár, *A Ludovikától Sopronkőhidáig* (From the Ludovika [Military Academy] to Sopronkőhida) (Budapest, 1978), p. 424.

22. HL. Filmtár (Film Archive) 1729. *Hóman naplója* (Hóman's Diary).
23. Domokos Szent-Iványi, *Emlékirat* (Memoirs), Ráday Levéltár (Ráday Archive), Szent-Iványi hagyaték C/80, pp. 687–688.
24. *Ibid.*, p. 689.
25. *Ibid.*, p. 688.
26. *Szombathelyi Ferenc visszaemlékezése* (Ferenc Szombathelyi's Memoirs) (Washington, 1988), p. 15.
27. *Ibid.*; Kádár, *A Ludovikától...*, p. 407.
28. HL. Eln. Vkf.1. 1941/6317.
29. *Ibid.*
30. Ránki–Pamlényi–Tilkovszky–Juhász, *A Wilhelmstrasse és Magyarország...*, p. 622. (449)
31. *Ibid.*
32. Szent-Iványi, *Emlékirat...*, p. 694.
33. *Ibid.*
34. Ránki–Pamlényi–Tilkovszky–Juhász, *A Wilhelmstrasse és Magyarország...*, p. 622. (449)
35. Szent-Iványi, *Emlékirat...*, p. 692.
36. *Ibid.*, p. 693.
37. Ránki–Pamlényi–Tilkovszky–Juhász, *A Wilhelmstrasse és Magyarország...*, p. 623. (450)
38. Szent-Iványi, *Emlékirat...*, p. 695.
39. *Ibid.*
40. *Ibid.*, p. 696.
41. *Ibid.*
42. HL. Eln. Vkf.1. 1941/6218.
43. János Csima, *Adalékok a Horthy-hadsereg szervezetének és háborús tevékenységének tanulmányozásához (1938–1945)* (Additions to Studying the Organizational Structure and the Military Activities of the Horthy Army: 1938–1945) (Budapest, 1961), p. 98.
44. *Ibid.*, p. 99.
45. Szent-Iványi, *Emlékirat...*, p. 624. (452)
46. Szent-Iványi, *Emlékirat...*, p. 697.
47. Ránki–Pamlényi–Tilkovszky–Juhász, *A Wilhelmstrasse és Magyarország...*, p. 625. (453)
48. Szent-Iványi, *Emlékirat...*, p. 698.
49. HL. Eln. Vkf.1. 1941/6466.
50. Halder, *Kriegstagebuch...*, vol. III: p. 286.

51. Ránki–Pamlényi–Tilkovszky–Juhász, *A Wilhelmstrasse és Magyarország...*, p. 626. (454)
52. *Ibid.*, p. 627.
53. *Ibid.*, p. 628.
54. *Ibid.*, p. 629.

GERMAN–HUNGARIAN DISCUSSIONS: PUTTING THE 2ND HUNGARIAN ARMY AT GERMANY'S DISPOSAL

Following the German army's retreat and the solidification of the front in late 1941, the German military command immediately began to replace its losses and to deploy its reserves so that the war could continue in the spring. According to the German plans, however, these reserves included the forces of satellite countries such as Hungary.

On January 1, in a letter to Horthy, Hitler asked for the Hungarian army's participation in the spring military operations. On January 6 the letter was followed by von Ribbentrop's arrival for a visit, at Horthy's earlier invitation. Officially the visit was due to an invitation announced with a big fanfare in December. Its delay had been very unpleasant for Bárdossy. In December he remarked to Ambassador Jagow that the internal "opposition" and the Romanians would be overjoyed with the delay and would use it against the Hungarians.[1] As soon as the door of the conference room closed behind him, the long-awaited dear guest, von Ribbentrop, set about submitting heavy military and economic demands on his hosts. In the spring, he said, Germany was preparing for crucial military operations that would lead to the annihilation of Bolshevism, for which it needed the help of its allies such as Hungary. Since the fight was still being fought primarily by the *Wehrmacht*, which had sacrificed a lot, Germany's allies were now obliged to have their armies participate in the war as much as they could.[2] Hungary was now requested to mobilize its whole army and send it to the front. He warned the Hungarians that 'if we did not submit our whole armed forces to their disposal... since we did not know Hitler's fair but passionate nature... we do not know what effect our decision might have on him. It might well happen that under such circumstances the Führer would no longer count on the Hungarians for help and take the position that the German army itself would undertake and execute the task in the east. He proceeded to say that he could not hide the effect that such a decision would produce in the whole German public, the Party and the German government."[3] Obviously, the size of the sacrifice would be closely related to the future fulfillment of Hungarian territorial claims.

Von Ribbentrop also had abundant economic demands. Just as in November, he urged an increase in the oil and wheat shipments. The quantity of the oil shipped was to be increased by 60,000 to 80,000 tons per year.

The German Minister of Foreign Affairs brought up the issue of the *Volksdeutsche*. He asked the Hungarian government to make it possible that 20,000 *Volksdeutsche* be drafted into the Waffen SS.[4]

It was clear to Bárdossy that he could not reject the German demands, and could only attempt to bargain down the size of the Hungarian contingent. The deployment of the complete Hungarian armed forces would entail giving up Hungary's expected increasing superiority over the Romanian army, due to its losses so far and due to Hungary's proportionately larger absence from the military operations. The Romanians also recognized this fact; based on their proportionately larger sacrifice, they demanded an increase in the participation of the Hungarians from the Germans. The Romanians had pledged to mobilize their whole army if Hungary did the same. If the Hungarian government did not fulfill the German request, then the Romanians would think that Hungary was getting ready to attack southern Transylvania, and would revoke their pledge. And for that outcome the Hungarian government would be responsible.

Bárdossy lined up a whole slew of arguments to tone down the German Minister of Foreign Affairs' requests. He referred to the strategic role of the Hungarian armed forces in the Danube Basin, which also served Germany's interests, to the danger threatening from the Balkans and from Romania, to the substandard armament of the Hungarian troops, and to the country's economic hardship. He hoped that his arguments would convince von Ribbentrop to give up on the deployment of the whole Hungarian armed forces to the front.

After lengthy bargaining on the last day of the discussions, Bárdossy relayed the Hungarian government's response to von Ribbentrop: "Even though Hungary cannot sacrifice one hundred percent of the Hungarian army to the goals of the eastern campaign, it is willing to go as far as possible and to participate in the campaign with forces much larger than before."[5]

Von Ribbentrop was satisfied when he departed from the Hungarian capital. He had managed to gain the Hungarian government's agreement on the most important military question, and had received promises to increase the oil and wheat shipments. The Hungarian government seemed to be willing to agree to the SS recruitment of the *Volksdeutsche*. He hoped for calmer Hungarian–Romanian relations now that he had managed to obtain a promise from Horthy that he would not take a strong line against Romania.[6]

Following von Ribbentrop's departure, Horthy responded to Hitler's letter of January 1 and assured him that he was showing his loyalty with arms, and that they shared a common fate, as exemplified by Hungary's participating in the common war. First, Horthy spoke about the Rapid Army Corps, which Hungary had equipped at great sacrifice, but which had arrived home from the front totally destroyed. He continued, saying that in spite of the substantial sacrifice thus far, it was Hungary's determination to participate further in the war according to its ability.

The Regent continued with a detailed analysis of the situation in the Balkans, which carried danger for Hungary, and called Hitler's attention to the tense Hungarian–Romanian relations. He emphasized the point that Germany should not underestimate these dangers, which increased the significance of the Hungarian strategic situation in the Danube Basin, for which the Hungarian armed forces had to be prepared and kept in readiness. This was what limited the size of Hungary's forces to be sent to the eastern front. The Hungarian public would not understand and would not accept it if the country did not have enough military forces to protect the country from these dangers.[7]

In connection with the military forces at the country's disposal for the common fight, Horthy pointed out that Hungary had substandard equipment, so the country was at a disadvantage against the modern equipped enemy, and even a generous martial spirit could not alter that fact. It was, therefore, essential that the German military command immediately provide suitable armaments for the troops.

Finally, the Regent once again assured Hitler that "we will enthusiastically participate in the spring offensive as long as the armaments and the enemy surrounding us make that possible." Military experts were scheduled to discuss the details.[8]

Von Ribbentrop had briefly informed Keitel before he departed for Budapest that Hungary was ready to participate in the spring operations "up to the extreme limit of its possibilities," even though not with its complete armed forces: "The way I interpreted this promise is that at least two thirds of the Hungarian defensive forces will participate in the eastern campaign," he said, and instructed Keitel that this should be the starting point for his talks. Von Ribbentrop had also informed Ambassador Jagow, asking to inform him when Keitel ran into difficulties and a ministerial intervention was needed.[9]

Keitel arrived in Budapest in the morning of January 20. He began by paying a visit to the Prime Minister. First of all, he informed him about the general military situation, which he considered advantageous for Germany, and then proceeded to inform him about the eastern front in a fashion that seemed extremely honest to Bárdossy. He acknowledged that the German leadership had miscalculated things several times, "calculating that the Soviet armed forces would be overcome by early December. Moreover, it had drawn incorrect conclusions even with regard to Soviet industrial capacity." The decision was left for the coming year, and that was when the Hungarian army would be needed. He said that von Ribbentrop had already informed him that Hungary was ready to participate in the war.

Since Keitel did not speak about the Balkans, Bárdossy asked him whether von Ribbentrop had mentioned to him the Hungarian reservations relating to the threatening danger from the Balkans. Keitel gave a negative response and said that he had not had the chance to speak with the German Minister of Foreign Affairs at great length. Then Bárdossy repeated his concerns about the Balkans to Keitel, and added that not only was he wary of a landing by British troops, but he would not be surprised if Soviet troops suddenly turned up on the Bulgarian or Romanian coast. Keitel tried to reassure him that Hungary was completely protected from the Balkans and that he should have no concerns about any disembarkation attempts.

In spite of Keitel's efforts Bárdossy did not perceive the situation as being so clear-cut. He continued to emphasize the danger coming from the south, pointing out that this concern lived in the general consciousness of the Hungarian people, and that it "should be taken into consideration in determining the size of forces to be deployed." Although Keitel showed sympathy towards popular fears, he noted that "one should do something to wipe out these unreasonable fears from the people."[10]

After his visit to the Prime Minister, Keitel visited the military. The dinner party at the Hotel Ritz went exceedingly well. Both hosts, Szombathelyi and Bartha, came to the conclusion that their guest had counted on about six brigades and perhaps an armored division, which would be equipped by the Germans. This size of force coincided with what had been agreed on with the Prime Minister when they had decided to hand over as many as nine brigades during their discussions.

It then came as a surprise during the official meeting at the Hungarian Ministry of Defense when Keitel asked for the use of eight army corps (each with three brigades), the Rapid Army Corps, and a mountain brigade—the entire Hungarian army. Recovering from their surprise, Szombathelyi and Bartha told him that it was impossible and that they had already explained this to von Ribbentrop. Keitel seemed to have misjudged the nature of the Hungarian army, since, at present, the Hungarian army was organized only horizontally and not in depth. The necessary organization work would be finished by the end of 1944. The available forces were only half armed and their training was scattered. Therefore, it could not compete with the Soviet army, which, after all, had presented the Germans with a difficult task as well. Beyond all that, the Hungarian army simply did not have 28 brigades, as said in the battle order familiar to Keitel. It had only 21 brigades, because the Transylvanian Army Corps had not yet been set up and two brigades of the I. Army Corps had been divided in order to set up the armored troops. The mountain brigade was also under development, and the Rapid Army Corps had been divided to create two armored divisions. Furthermore, five brigades had already been sent as occupying forces to the front.

All in all, as Szombathelyi stated, the Hungarian army was not prepared for an application of force at such a remote place, either psychologically or organizationally. Nor could Hungary remove all the forces from the country, because that would mean that the

Danube Basin would remain undefended, and so if Anglo-Saxon forces landed, a very dangerous situation would develop for all. The Romanians constantly threatened Hungary with an attack, which was another reason why Hungary could not dedicate all its forces to the cause of the eastern front.

Keitel tried to reassure the two military men as well. He kept saying that they should not be concerned about an attack from the Balkans. Romania also did not pose a danger, since it would participate in the war with a large force. And as far as the Soviet army was concerned, during the winter months it had become extremely weak, suffering losses both in artillery and armored vehicles. Thus, even the Hungarian army could confront it.

Szombathelyi contested Keitel's statements, disagreeing with his evaluation of the Soviet army, since it was precisely the war during the last winter that had proved that its strength was undiminished. For Hungarian troops to face them would definitely necessitate that the German army extend help to equip the troops.

Finally, Keitel changed his extreme demands and an agreement was reached that a force of three army corps, including nine light divisions, one armored division and five occupying brigades, would be sent to the East. An agreement was also signed on replacing the missing armaments of the Hungarian army, with the details to be discussed between the two General Staffs. The light divisions consisted of two regiments each.

Following the agreement, Keitel also met Bárdossy, who emphasized the point that the agreed troop contingent surpassed what he had counted on and that it "imposes too grave a political and economic hardship on the government." Szombathelyi, however, was pleased with the outcome of the bargain. He later said that "our impression was that we could not have given a smaller force without making the Germans angry at us." This was the minimum that they were willing to accept.[11]

The army that the Hungarian government gave to the disposal of the Germans did not reach two thirds of the available Hungarian forces, as predicted by von Ribbentrop's original measure. When informing Jagow about the process and about the results of the negotiations, Keitel told him that after having considered the equipment shortage and difficulties of the Hungarian troops he found the number of Hungarian units adequate and did not wish to increase them numerically. In addition to that, Hungarian political factors also contributed to the agreement, so the help would be devalued if "demands or limitations are raised conditional to making the units available to our disposal."[12]

The OKW could not help the Hungarian government with arms, to secure its acceptable level.

Keitel made it very clear to the Hungarian leaders that the OKW would dispose over the Hungarian troops, and that no conditions or intervention with regard to their application would be tolerated. Yet the Hungarian leadership was relieved to acknowledge the result of the bargaining. It managed to preserve the bulk of their forces, and it was the immediate prerogative of the Hungarian industry to complement and modernize their equipment.

Before mobilizing the army to be deployed to the front, the Minister of Defense and the Chief of the General Staff went to see the Regent to relay the Council of Ministers' request that the troops of the three mobilized army corps and their "M" (for mobilization) reserves not be recruited just from their designated geographical areas but evenly from the entire country. The only condition that the Regent imposed was that the mobilization should not affect the VI. and IX. Army Corps on the Romanian border.[13]

With the Regent's consent in hand, the mobilization of the 2nd Hungarian Army to be deployed to the front began in February. This army was not the same as the one in the battle order of the *Honvédség*. The goal was that the 2nd Hungarian Army would minimally affect the most valuable regular and reserve troops of the

Honvédség, and its deployment would upset the least the forces that stayed behind, in terms of their ability to mobilize and move into action.

The mobilization of the *Honvédség* took place according to the so-called "twinning" system in which all units of the peace organization were doubled at mobilization. For example, the 6th Infantry Regiment mobilized not only its own subunits but the entire 36th Infantry Regiment which did not exist in peace time. The serial numbers of the army corps and the light divisions did not change. In spite of the railway transportation difficulties a mobilization would be executable within a week.

With the help of monthly registers from 1942 one can follow the implementation of the plan. The August and October data are especially of representative value. It was in August that the entire 2nd Hungarian Army arrived and took up its position on the frontline, and during the fall months the number of people was more or less unchanged.

Effective Force	August 1-	October 15
The number of regular soldiers in the *Honvédség*	218,400	254,500
Of that, the number of soldiers in the 2nd Hungarian Army	44,150	41,800
Percentage of the total number	20.4%	16.4%
Total number of soldiers in the 2nd Hungarian Army	193,850	195,000
Percentage of the effectives	23.3%	21.7%

Three army corps had been designated for mobilization. Two of the three—the III. and the IV. Army Corps—had originally been part of the 3rd Hungarian Army, while only the VII. Army Corps had originally belonged to the 2nd Hungarian Army. The three army corps included three light divisions each.[16]

It took almost three months to organize, mobilize and equip the new 2nd Hungarian Army, with so many factors at play. Therefore, it began transporting to the front as late as April 11 and only finished it on July 27. Horthy appointed Colonel General Gusztáv Jány as its commander.

Jány undertook a confusing task, since both operationally and in terms of provisions it was subordinated to the Germans. Its deployment was totally dependent upon Colonel General Weichs, Commander of the *Heeresgruppe Süd*. The 2nd Hungarian Army's location of deployment, its regional role and how long it would be deployed had not been clarified in advance. The Hungarian leadership could only hope that due to its weak equipment it would not be deployed in the main direction of the front and, furthermore, that until decisions were made about the military operations it would survive without any personnel or material losses. The hope was that no major replacements from Hungary would be necessary and that the 2nd Hungarian Army could be withdrawn after a few months. There were a few observers who viewed the expected situation and expected losses of the 2nd Hungarian Army in a darker light, but still refrained from dwelling on them. However, no one considered its total devastation likely.

Since there had been no written agreement between the two governments or the supreme commands of the two armies, in the beginning the authorized officials of the two countries' General Staffs and ministries discussed the details of the 2nd Hungarian Army's deployment. But very soon the commanders of the *Heeresgruppe Süd*, as the competent authorities, became the discussion partners of the Hungarians. In March Colonel Weinknecht, Representative of the Army Group, arrived in Budapest to discuss armament, equipment, and provision issues. He was informed about the army's readiness regarding armaments and war materials. It was also clarified that the Germans would take care of provisions. Only special ammunition and materials replacements would be sent from Hungary, while everything else, including food, would be provided by the German army. Hungarian food deliveries to compensate for the food service would be sent to Germany.[17]

During the discussions Weinknecht's attention was emphatically called to the armament and equipment shortages of the army and, by citing Keitel, the Hungarians tried to get Weinknecht to promise to take care of them. It could hardly escape the Hungarian party's attention that the German colonel was reluctant to make concrete promises, even though he also did not reject their request. Weinknecht claimed that such arrangements could only be made when the 2nd Hungarian Army arrived at the frontline and came under the command of the Army Group. He also claimed that he was not authorized to provide the requested equipment to the Hungarian units before they departed for the front

The equipment of the light divisions of the 2nd Hungarian Army conformed in every way to the "M" equipment of the *Honvédség* standardized in those days. This equipment lagged behind the equipment of German infantry regiments in several regards. There seemed to be an especially great shortage of anti-tank guns, which the Germans had promised to provide to the units. German help had also been expected in modernizing the units' battle and food trains. Since the Hungarians lacked enough motorized vehicles, it was impossible for them to fully provide for the troops with the help of horse-drawn vehicles.

According to the agreement the 1st Hungarian Armored Division was also deployed to the front. A significant part of the army's existing and repaired motor vehicles were concentrated here. However, the tank unit of the division, the 30th Armored Regiment, was not equipped, due to the inadequate development of the country's heavy industry. Therefore, the regiment received its tanks from the Germans. The 22 "Pz-IV" tanks and the 89 "T-38" tanks, which were light tanks given to Hungary as medium ones, added up to quite a feeble and outdated armored regiment.

Under such circumstances the gradual transportation of the 2nd Hungarian Army to the front began on April 11. In his speech to the commanders of the 2nd Army on April 11, Szombathelyi enthusiastically urged the soldiers ready to depart for the front with high spirits. He spoke about the soldiers' careful and professional preparation and training, during which, "compared with the available time and available equipment, we did everything in our power to prepare the 2nd Army for its expected tasks." In the field of armaments and organization, he said that "considering our resources, we have given the army everything that it might need in a modern war and against the expected enemy."[18] He also pointed out the *Honvédség*'s shortcomings in terms of leadership and training, which would need to be remedied. However, although his orders to them also served to reassure the Hungarian military leaders as much as to reassure himself, they still did not quite conceal his worry about the fate of the army, which was totally defenseless both operationally and materially. As Szombathelyi wrote, "In every respect the leadership did its best so that our 2nd Army would not be dispatched like an unfavored child, but as a favored one, on its long trip, which no Hungarian armed forces had taken before." Then he continued: "And when it is at the front, we do not want the soldiers to feel like motherless children, and we will try to do our best in terms of keeping up communications."[19]

Notes

1. György Ránki, Ervin Pamlényi, Loránt Tilkovszky and Gyula Juhász, eds., *A Wilhelmstrasse és Magyarország: Német diplomáciai iratok Magyarországról, 1933–1944* (The Wilhelmstrasse and Hungary: German Diplomatic Documents about Hungary, 1933–1944) (Budapest, 1968), p. 634. (461)
2. *Ibid.*, p. 464. (475)
3. Domokos Szent-Iványi, *Emlékirat* (Memoirs) Ráday Levéltár (Ráday Archive), Szent-Iványi hagyaték C/80, p. 702.
4. Ránki–Pamlényi–Tilkovszky–Juhász, *A Wilhelmstrasse és Magyarország...*, p. 647. (475)
5. *Ibid.*
6. *Ibid.*
7. *Horthy Miklós titkos iratai* (Miklós Horthy's Secret Writings), ed. Miklós Szinai and László Szűcs, (Budapest, 1962), p. 317.
8. *Ibid.*, p. 318.
9. Ránki–Pamlényi–Tilkovszky–Juhász, *A Wilhelmstrasse és Magyarország...*, p. 648. (476)
10. OL. Filmtár (Film Archive) 7887. *Szálasi-per anyaga* (The Szálasi Trial).
11. *Ibid.*
12. Ránki–Pamlényi–Tilkovszky–Juhász, *A Wilhelmstrasse és Magyarország...*, p. 649. (477)
13. OL. Minisztertanácsi jegyzőkönyv (Minutes of the Council of Ministers), January 27, 1942.
14. HL. HM. Eln.6.k. 1942/48819.
15. HL. HM. Eln.6.k. 1942/66573.
16. HL. HM. Eln.1.a. 1941/41000.
17. HL. HM. Eln.6.k. 1942/145 and 1945/177.
18. HL. Eln. Vkf.5. 1942/63579.
19. HL. HM. Eln.20. 1942/113341.

THE HUNGARIAN–ROMANIAN DISCORD INTENSIFIES: ASPIRATIONS TO RETAIN POWER IN THE CASE OF AN ANTI-ROMANIAN ACTION

At a central festive ceremony, Miklós Kállay—Prime Minister since March 9, 1942—said goodbye to the Hungarian troops on their way to the front. Kállay spoke about the "sacred mission" of the troops and about the eternal and sheltering care of their home, which would accompany them on their way. Kállay believed that sending the 2nd Hungarian Army to the front was a sacrifice that his predecessor had been forced to offer at the altar of common war, but he also considered it to be a necessary sacrifice from the point of view of his own policy.

On March 7 Prime Minister Bárdossy had submitted his resignation, due to health reasons, after Horthy had finally convinced himself to ask for the former's resignation, due to a disagreement between them regarding the selection of the Vice Regent. Horthy believed that Bárdossy was no longer suitable to pursue these policies of the politicians who had congregated mostly around Bethlen. These circles needed a prime minister and government capable of carefully adjusting and pursuing a foreign policy that included contacts with the West and was capable of defending the status quo against rightist or leftist attacks and against internal or external attacks. It also needed to be able to salvage the existing system under the changed foreign political circumstances, impacted by military events. And to do all that, this ideal prime minister and government would have to be able to prepare and implement a radical change while retaining and organizing the existing political forces. The assumption was that Kállay would be able to make Germany accept this new policy, and that Szombathelyi, who had promised changes in the military leadership, and the new Minister of Defense (to replace the pro-German Bartha) would support the governments' new plans.

The German leaders were sorry to hear that Bárdossy, who was favored by them and who "had pursued Count Csáky's longstanding policy," was compelled to resign due to health reasons. The Germans had hoped that he would at least retain the minister of finance's portfolio in the new Kállay government. Von Ribbentrop expressed this hope in his private letter to Bárdossy on March 17. On behalf of Hitler and himself, he assured Bárdossy of their true affection and friendship, and conveyed their best wishes for his recovery.[1]

Berlin was disturbed by the new appointee to head the Ministry of Foreign Affairs as well. The Germans found unacceptable Antal Ullein-Reviczky, who, according to rumor, was going to be the new Minister of Foreign Affairs. In order to avoid complications, Kállay kept this portfolio, of crucial importance to his policy, for himself.[2]

In this way the Prime Minister traveled in both roles to attend an introductory meeting with Hitler. Kállay's intention was to raise and discuss the most important issues affecting both countries, hopefully in such a way as to avoid any further obligations and to avoid undertaking new burdens.

Hitler received Kállay at his eastern Prussian Headquarters in Rastenburg. Kállay arrived accompanied by Permanent Deputy Minister of Foreign Affairs Andor Szentmiklósy and Lieutenant General János Vörös, Head of the Military Operational Section of the General Staff. During his private conversation with Kállay, Hitler proved to be patient and understanding, which made it easier for Kállay to quickly come to the most important issues.

Speaking about the 2nd Hungarian Army, which was already being deployed, Kállay pointed out that its armaments and equipment would hardly make it possible for it to be deployed to the frontline. In its present state it could only be used for occupying tasks and security tasks behind the front, and Kállay asked Hitler to take these facts into consideration. Kállay also expressed the hope that after the summer offensive the 2nd Hungarian Army would be able to return to Hungary, just as the Rapid Army Corps had done the previous year. He did not consider the deployment of new occupation divisions possible, due to equipment shortages of catastrophic proportions. Yet he assured Hitler that Hungary would continue to stand by its allies in the future too. He said that the food deliveries would continue to be sent, and that their quantity would not lag behind what had been delivered before the war. However, he claimed that loyalty could not entail fully giving up the country's foreign political independence.

Speaking about the unsolved Romanian–Hungarian relations, Kállay asked Hitler to intervene so that the anti-Hungarian actions and propaganda supported by the Romanian government would not lead to a further deterioration of the tense Romanian–Hungarian relationship. The Hungarian government's concern was also heightened by the fact that Romanian units arriving back from the front were being transported to southern Transylvania, where they were newly re-armed before being deployed, probably to the eastern front. Kállay was also disturbed by news about the weakening German occupation forces in the Balkans.

Hitler tried to reassure Kállay, saying that he found it implausible that Romania would not recognize the Second Vienna Award, which Romania had asked for in the first place. Yet he would warn Antonescu, because it was in their common interest that the relationship between the two countries improve. The outbreak of a possible armed conflict would not disturb the common effort of the two countries' armies on the eastern front. He believed that the Romanian troops could certainly be counted on, and he was satisfied with the performance of the Romanian troops as trained and led with German help. He added that the Hungarian army, which had not utilized the offered German help, had shown quite a bit of inexperience. Hitler then proceeded to say that conflict between the two countries should definitely be avoided until the end of the war. From this remark Kállay inferred that the German guarantee to the Romanians would stay valid only until the end of the war, and from then onwards Hitler would give a free hand to the Hungarians against Romania. Finally, Hitler also promised that German foreign policy would be geared towards doing everything possible to settle the Hungarian–Romanian issues, as indeed he himself would do everything in his power to save them. As for the Romanian troops in southern Transylvania, there was no reason to worry, since they were there only to rest and to be re-armed. He also admitted that he had withdrawn troops from southeastern Europe, but not in a measure that would make the region's situation uncertain.

Then Hitler proceeded to inform his guests about the situation on the fronts. He went into great detail about the offensive on the eastern front, where he said that he had gained the initiative once again, and for good. Keitel and Jodl, who were also present, enthusiastically nodded during the monologue and limited themselves to saying "yes" and "no" whenever Hitler asked them about something.[3]

During Kállay's discussion with von Ribbentrop, the German Minister of Foreign Affairs set a harsher tone and mostly spoke about the issue of the German minority in Hungary. Finally, Kállay made a promise to increase the number of troops drafted into the Waffen SS by 10,000 men, in addition to the already permitted 20,000 men.

The fact that Hitler did not even raise the issue of a new troop contingent, and thus that no obligations had to be undertaken in this area, was considered the most important event by Kállay.[4] He also considered Hitler's approach to the Romanian issue to have been positive as well, and he considered that the discussions had been harmonious with regard to political and military issues

Either he was not informed by Vörös or, what was even more probable, Kállay did not want to acknowledge the fact that the issue of deploying new Hungarian troops had indeed arisen at the German Headquarters. During their discussions with Vörös, Hitler's military leaders raised the issue of increasing the number of Hungarian occupation forces at the front, in addition to the matter of Hungarian–German military industrial cooperation and war materials transportation. The German General Staff requested the mobilization of the two occupation brigades—now light divisions—on which Keitel had given up in January, due to the equipment difficulties of the 2nd Hungarian Army, and which, due to the increase in the numbers of supply lines, had become essential.[5]

After the Hungarians had returned to Budapest, the German military attaché, Pappenheim, immediately contacted Vörös on the issue of the two occupying divisions. Vörös told him what he had already alluded to at the German Headquarters, that is, the fact that deploying the two divisions was hindered by equipment shortages. Pappenheim did not easily accept the rejection. On July 15 he turned to Colonel General Bajnóczy, Deputy Chief of the General Staff, and reiterated the German General Staff's request, again without any results. Bajnóczy told him that even if he were able to secure the troops, there were simply no weapons and equipment for this purpose. The troops of the 2nd Hungarian Army had been equipped to a level surpassing the usual level of armaments, at the expense of troops staying home, and so reinforcing the troops at home was very difficult. All the existing weapons were needed for the training and equipping of the 60,000 reserves and 80,000 new recruits.[6]

After achieving no results with the General Staff, Pappenheim turned to Bartha, who, not adhering to the government's position, which emphasized the preservation of forces, proved to be sympathetic. In Bartha's view, equipping the divisions was in fact a problem, but one that could be easily solved with recourse to the

Russian military spoils. He suggested to Pappenheim that the issue be submitted through diplomatic channels.

Ambassador Jagow, who was informed about Bartha's suggestion by the attaché, expressed the conviction that, due to the continuing tense Romanian–Hungarian relations, all the country's military equipment, material and food stocks should be preserved in preparation for any possibility. It was highly doubtful that the Hungarian government would send any kind of new force to the eastern front before tensions were reduced.[7]

The tensions in the Hungarian–Romanian relationship did not ease. During the Hungarian–German discussions, Kállay had explained to Clodius that sooner or later Hungary would have to go to war with Romania, and that he—Kállay—would not take the responsibility of Hungary's being defenseless. He also requested that Germany satisfy its obligation and provide the necessary armaments for the troops at the front and make it possible that equipment shortages for units in Hungary be eased. Clodius promised that he would intervene at the OKW, and said that demands on the frontline would most certainly be filled. Other needs, he said, could be satisfied only to a limited degree, due to Germany's own needs.[8]

Jagow reported on the increasing anti-Romanian concern within Hungarian government circles. Kállay considered a Hungarian–Romanian war to be possible, independent of finishing the anti-Soviet war. In his view, some events might occur that would force Hungary to act. Discussion of preparations against Romania would be the main topic of the July 24 Hungarian Crown Council.[9]

Led by Horthy, the Crown Council indeed passed a resolution about preparations for a possible war against Romania and about the implementation of the relevant military and economic measures. The resolution was justified by the intensification of anti-Hungarian propaganda, by increasing provocation, and by the increasing number of measures brought against Hungarians in southern Transylvania.[10]

The German government resented the intensification of the Hungarian–Romanian discord, and so protested against Kállay's statement, saying that, in the case of a Hungarian–Romanian conflict, Hitler would certainly not intervene before the completion of the war against the Soviet Union. However, beyond that he also did not see any solution but an armed showdown, which he would not hinder. He would guarantee the Romanian border until only the end of the war.[11]

Jagow, who had been informed directly by Bartha about Kállay's statement, immediately reported it to von Ribbentrop. He, in turn, rushed to Hitler, who agreed with him that it was intolerable that such news be spread without refutation in Budapest "because it also will reach Bucharest—probably in a different variation—where it might cause significant political harm. Furthermore, a variation might get to Bucharest, suggesting that the German guarantee given to Romania would not be valid after the war."[12]

Von Ribbentrop instructed Jagow to tell the Prime Minister that both he and the Führer were surprised that news had been circulating about the confidential discussions in Budapest, and a false version at that. The Führer had not indicated to Kállay that after the war he would not do anything to prevent an armed showdown. At Kállay's complaint that the ongoing Romanian provocations would lead to an armed conflict sooner or later, Hitler had responded that the Second Vienna Award was uniformly obligatory for everyone. And Hitler had added that everyone should strive to destroy the common enemy, and "if, after the war, anyone still felt like starting a new war in Europe, one could not help it."[13] Von Ribbentrop claimed that he himself had unambiguously indicated to Kállay that Germany would effectively intervene in the case of a Hungarian–Romanian conflict. Jagow was instructed to approach Kállay and tell him "to correct things" and to make sure that in the future even those people who received information about important discussions should adhere to the confidential nature of those discussions.[14]

On July 23 Kállay stated to Jagow, who went to see him, that "the Führer spoke very clearly, and he thought that he had understood him." Moreover, according to his sources, the same opinions prevailed among the political élites of Berlin. For example, Weizsäcker conducted a discussion in a similar vein with Ambassador Sztójay. All in all, Kállay promised Jagow that he would consider whatever he heard at the Main Headquarters as confidential, as would just be obvious. He said that thus far he had only informed Bartha, from whom Jagow had acquired his information.[15]

In spite of Hitler's statement that Kállay—according to German official circles—had so sadly misunderstood him, Kállay must have observed that the Germans continued not to support Hungary's anti-Romanian plans. Furthermore, he had to witness a deepening of the German–Romanian relationship. He indignantly stated at the meeting of the Council of Ministers that the Romanians continued to pursue their anti-Hungarian actions and "strengthened their foreign political positions both with the Germans and with the Italians. If the Hungarian government did not receive a satisfactory answer and support with regard to the Hungarian–Romanian conflict, he would soon approach Hungary's Romanian policy in a different way."[16]

German diplomacy did try to curb the Hungarian–Romanian conflict, so that it would not go beyond what they wanted. The Germans were of the view that by consciously exaggerating the Romanian threat and by repeatedly bringing up the concentration of Romanian forces in connection with the Romanian threat, Hungary was scrambling for excuses to avoid any future contribution to the common fight. The same opinion could be heard from Rome as well. After the Hungarian ambassador, Máriássy, had visited Ciano and informed him about the tense Hungarian–Romanian relations, Ciano wrote in his diary that "the Hungarians only pretend to be concerned, so that they might avoid undertaking any major responsibility in the offensive against Russia."[17]

As a matter of fact, in this situation it was indeed the Hungarian government's main objective to fend off German requests for the deployment of new troops to the front and to make up for the equipment sent to the front with the 2nd Hungarian Army, so that a major portion of its armed force at home would be able to fight. Major effort was applied to the manufacture of armaments for the 2nd Armored Division, so that it would be able to fight as soon as possible. It was planned that the 2nd Armored Division would have an important role in the event that an armed conflict broke out with Romania. As a report analyzing the Transylvanian situation stated, this would have unpleasant consequences for the Hungarian population in southern Transylvania, unless "a Hungarian armed intervention occurred in the form of a blitzkrieg—in its real sense—and suppressed any possible attack on civilians."[18] This operation would be possible with armed forces and with an air force capable of air defense. Using considerable loans, the government financially stimulated factories involved in armored and mechanized vehicle and airplane production, in order to increase their capacities and to accelerate production.

In July, after a long march and following several clashes involving major losses, the 2nd Hungarian Army reached the River Don and occupied a 200-kilometer long frontline. The troops received tasks far surpassing their capabilities, which they would not be able to undertake even at the price of bloody sacrifices. The Hungarian military leaders watched the evolving events with helpless resignation, not speaking out against the impossible situation. They tried to reassure themselves that from a strategic and tactical point of view the 2nd Hungarian Army was subordinated to the Germans, and therefore the German military leadership was responsible for them.

During the summer of 1942 an ever-growing network of German agents, in addition to the German ambassador and military attaché, churned out report after report about the conditions in Hungary. These reports called attention to the turncoat policy of the

Prime Minister, influenced by pro-Western and anti-German social and political forces. Caution was justified. The report claimed that beyond his statements misleading the Hungarian public about the common fight against the Soviets and about the loyalty to the country's allies, Kállay had sought contact with the Anglo-Saxon countries. Kállay's government secretly worked on breaching the country's obligations under their alliance, and secretly tried to concentrate its armed forces towards its true goals. All sorts of government officials, politicians, high-ranking soldiers, including generals, were cited as sources of what was occurring. According to the German spies, some of the Hungarian generals and high-ranking officers followed Kállay's policy, while younger and lower-ranking officers stood by the German allies without reservation and believed in the coming victory.

In spite of the repeated rejection, the issue of the two occupational divisions were kept on the two countries' agenda, and Commissioner of the German Ministry of Foreign Affairs at the German Headquarters Ritter sent a letter on September 21 to Jagow asking for the divisions from the Hungarian government via diplomatic channels. The two General Staffs had already agreed to set up the divisions using German and looted materials, but the Hungarians expected the request to be submitted through diplomatic channels. Ritter said that the issue of the two divisions was not mentioned during Hitler's and Kállay's discussion, which must have given the impression that the Germans were not interested in the deployment of any more Hungarian troops. This must have happened because, at the time of the visit, the issue was in its preparatory phase between the various military organs, and so the Führer avoided mentioning it.[19]

But Kállay continued to dodge the question. When Jagow went to see him on September 22, he claimed that he had been under the impression that in the future he would not even have to take care of reinforcing the Hungarian troops at the front. But in the meantime it turned out that he was mistaken, as the Chief of the General Staff learned during his recent visit to the front. Instead, he would have to secure 20,000 men as replacements. Kállay claimed that it was not clear at this point whether, after sending this contingent, the *Honvédség* would be in a situation to provide two more divisions for occupation purposes. However, he promised to discuss the possibilities with the Chief of the General Staff and, following that, on September 29 he would submit the case to the Supreme Military Council. Kállay was going to inform the ambassador about the decision within a short period of time.[20]

On the day of the planned Supreme Military Council session, Embassy Counselor Werkmeister sent a telegram to the German Ministry of Foreign Affairs. In a memorandum the previous day, Kállay had reassured Ambassador Jagow that he had already contacted the Chief of the General Staff, who had just returned from the front with the new Minister of Defense Vilmos Nagybaczoni Nagy. The decision was going to be discussed by the Supreme Military Council to be convened in the following few days. According to Werkmeister, Kállay's memorandum was sent ostensibly to correct the date of the Supreme Military Council session, but it might also have been written because "he wanted to secure an alibi for himself in case the Supreme Military Council refused to fulfill our request, because he [Kállay] emphasized the point that he would do everything in his power to support our common cause."[21]

The session of the Council took place on October 5; at the request of the Chief of the General Staff, a decision was reached there about the mobilization of the 1st and 201st Occupational Light Divisions. The German request could not be postponed any longer. Therefore, the mobilization work had to be initiated, since it would take a while, due to the well-known problems with the equipment. And this was exactly what happened. The divisions did not begin their deployment to the operational region until January 5, 1943, finishing by the end of the month.

Chief of the General Staff Szombathelyi's report of his review trip to the 2nd Hungarian Army was also on the October 5 agenda. Szombathelyi returned with rather bad impressions from his trip, which had included a visit with Hitler at his Main Headquarters. Szombathelyi was surprised to see how nervous Hitler was, and to note that he did not speak much, and that he let Keitel do most of the talking. Szombathelyi tried to raise the topic of the 2nd Hungarian Army and warn Hitler of its difficult situation. Szombathelyi claimed that without significant re-armament—which had been promised by the German General Staff—the Hungarian troops would not be able to fulfill their tasks along the rather objectionably long front. The typical promises from the Germans, which always seemed to avoid the facts, did not satisfy the Hungarian Chief of the General Staff. Still, he could not escape giving two occupational divisions to the war effort.

On the prospects of the war, Szombathelyi said that his experiences on the eastern front confirmed his conviction that the era of blitzkriegs had undeniably come to an end: "Consequently, the military goals have changed, and so have ideas about the possible date of the end of the war… We have to be prepared for the fact that the war might last for years."[22] In Szombathelyi's view, the Germans would not be able to force out a decision on the eastern front, the frontline would remain in place, and the 2nd Hungarian Army would remain at the front, fighting, even into 1943. In his view, Hungarians should draw a sharp conclusion from these facts, because "the country's present intellectual and material preparedness for war compared with tasks to be executed by us are far from being in balance."[23] But learning from the experiences of World War I, Hungary "definitely needs an unused and capable army, one that in the case of an unexpected turn of events, can defend the nation's interests and achieve exclusively Hungarian goals."[24] In Szombathelyi's view, Hungary's military political situation was not reassuring, in spite of the fact that Hungary was surrounded by allies. Also, some of Hungary's neighbors were only waiting for the occasion to realize their own goals against the country.

The fighting morale of the 2nd Hungarian Army made a positive impression on the Chief of the General Staff, although it had suffered significant losses. The army's missing weapons had not been replaced, and more losses were to be expected. (Szombathelyi visited the front in early September, before the second unsuccessful attack was launched against the Uryv bridgehead.) Colonel General Jány, Commander of the 2nd Hungarian Army, had requested the immediate deployment of 30,000 men to make up for the losses and to accumulate reserves behind the long (almost 200-kilometer long) frontline. However, as Szombathelyi had told Jány, no more than 20,000 men would be deployed, even after taking the German demands for occupying divisions and the new military political situation into consideration.

The Council listened to Szombathelyi's review and accepted it. At his recommendation the Council decided to mobilize 20,000 men in order to replace the army's losses. However, it decided not to replace all the troops, even though it seemed certain that the troops would remain at the front during the following year as well. In practice, this meant that the situation of the 2nd Hungarian Army, at the mercy of the German military command, would become intolerable sooner or later, its combat value would rapidly decrease, and it would perish should the Soviets mount an attack.

The new Minister of Defense, Colonel General Vilmos Nagybaczoni Nagy, participated in the council meeting, having succeeded Bartha on September 24. Bartha's dismissal was inevitable, due to his dubious role as a member of the government, including his eager support of deploying the occupation divisions, his informing the German ambassador about the Prime Minister's confidential information, and, on top of all this, his compromising the government in the debate over the German supervision of the Hungarian military industry. The reason for the procrastination in dismissing Bartha was only partly due to tactfulness towards the suspicious Germans. It was also due to the difficulty of choosing the right person to replace him, as well as convincing the Regent to accept Nagy as the only suitable person for the job when he resented him somewhat.

The commission of the retired Nagy was reactivated by the Regent, taking him away from his well-paid position as Chairman of the Board of Directors of the Danube Airplane Factory. His earlier discord with Werth and his antipathy towards the Germans and the Hungarian extreme right were well known, and he also had good relationships with pro-British circles. All of the above and his rich military experience made him suitable to try to promote the government's policy as the head of the Ministry of Defense.

The Regent, who received Nagy at Gödöllő on September 20, told him that he was expected to restore the spirit and discipline of the *Honvédség*, which had deteriorated, developments for which Bartha had been blamed. According to Nagy's recollections, at the end of the short visit Horthy asked him the following: "How are you getting along with Imrédy?" That was the point when Nagy realized that his assumed relationship with Imrédy, who had become the chief of one of the parties of the extreme right wing, was the pretext that Werth had used to convince Horthy to send Nagy into retirement, since Horthy was angry at Imrédy.[25]

As happened to Szombathelyi with the General Staff, Nagy was also received with suspicion and antipathy in the Ministry of Defense by Bartha's numerous followers. Among his measures, those relating to the improvement of the conditions of Jewish labor battalions caused especial resentment. It was his goal to improve the 2nd Hungarian Army's situation, and in order to do that he needed to gather information on site. And so he announced that he would inspect the army at the front and then pay the traditional visit to Hitler.

Prior to Nagy's departure from Budapest on October 15, he had a lengthy conversation with Kállay, who tried to inform and prepare his new minister for the visit. First on the agenda was the German–Hungarian relationship and questions likely to be raised by Hitler. As Kállay said, the relationship had deteriorated because Hungary had not submitted itself totally to the German ideology and did not completely fulfill all of Germany's demands. The zealous Romanians had an advantage in this area. Antonescu continued to speak about revising the Second Vienna Award as a reward for Romania's participation in the war and also tried to revive the Little Entente. He had already entered into an alliance with Slovakia, and tried to include Croatia as well. The Romanians' behavior gave rise to a constant disquiet among the Hungarian public. The Prime Minister also raised the idea of creating a second front in the Balkans. If that indeed happened, the scattered South-Slav peoples would join the enemies of the Axis, and the situation in the whole Balkan region might become questionable, creating danger for Hungary. Hitler should be convinced that settling the Hungarian–Romanian controversy and directing Romania's expansionism to the east were in Germany's interest as well. This was the only way to get a southward concentration of Hungarian forces. The Romanian–Hungarian tension hindered Hungary from participating more intensively in the sacrifices on the eastern front. With regard to sending reinforcements to the 2nd Hungarian Army, Kállay asked the Minister of Defense to limit it to 30,000 men and the two occupational divisions to be deployed soon.[26]

Hitler received Nagy at his Headquarters near Vinnica. Once again he seemed to be very talkative about the situations of the different fronts and about his ideas on the further development of the war. Success for the Axis would be completed at Stalingrad within a few days, he claimed. Following that, the Soviet oil region would be occupied. Hitler also tried to dazzle his guest with the outstanding achievements of the German war industry. He spoke about new weapons, including powerful airplanes that would be especially suitable for forcing Great Britain to surrender. Hitler also spoke about the Hungarian troops, and said that after overcoming initial difficulties and their dread of tanks, they had successfully fulfilled their duties. Anticipating Nagy's expected questions, Hitler reassured him that the Hungarian troops would receive the necessary effective anti-tank weapons and, beyond that, attention would be given to increasing the fighting capacity of the 2nd Hungarian Army. After the arrival of Italian and German reserve divisions, the long frontline of the Hungarian troops would be shortened, while the troops' defensive depth would be increased as well. Nagy could hardly open his mouth during the visit, and left without discussing the most important issues. He had to make do with Hitler's declarations.[27]

Nagy found the 2nd Hungarian Army in their 200-kilometer long defensive positions after the unsuccessful Uryv bridgehead battles. Jány informed him about the army's situation and about his tasks, which he would be unable to accomplish without proper reinforcements. The Hungarians were unable to withstand the attack of the Soviet troops, and therefore, under the given circumstances, he was unable to assume responsibility for the fate of the army. Jány asked Nagy, who was also his friend, to use his influence with the Regent to accept his request to be replaced. Nagy tried to reassure Jány; however, he could not promise much beyond the 20,000 reserves.[28]

Nagy could have hardly remedied all the complaints flooding to him from the officers and the troops with regard to weapons and supply shortages and the increasingly unbearable circumstances. "I have listened to the many wishes," he wrote in his memoir. "There was no variety in the food... It would be nice if certain courses were prepared in the Hungarian style. Obviously, I considered complaints about tobacco and bread to be serious, and promised to do my best to remedy them... The officers were justified in complaining that their defense against Russian armored vehicles was helpless. They also said that our artillery was minimal and that we did not have heavy mortars. But there were complaints about provisions for the animals as well. Oats were missing. Automobiles also caused a lot of problems, and an important issue was the accelerating of engine repairs. It was a basic problem that the Germans had not kept their promise, and that they had hardly delivered any of the promised materials and weapons. Without proper defensive weapons, the extensive frontline cannot be defended."[29]

Nagy also voiced his opinions to the officer corps about the treatment of the troops and members of Jewish labor battalions, and held out the prospect of punishment for those who abused their situation or committed acts of cruelty. This created resentment in some of the officers, which was increased by the fact that Nagy also spoke with members of the labor battalions and inquired about their circumstances.

Before leaving for Hungary, Nagy went to see Colonel General Weichs, Commander of the German Army Group B. He asked him to end the shortages of the 2nd Hungarian Army subordinated to him. Weichs seemed to be a sympathetic listener, but refrained from making promises, since the Germans themselves had also been struggling with shortages.[30]

The Minister of Defense gave an account of his experiences to Horthy and the government. Nagy considered it necessary to improve the 2nd Hungarian Army's general situation, to gradually replace its staff, and to urgently take care of its armaments shortages. He stated that without doubt, in the present state of the army it would not be able to defend its frontline and that the Russians would break through it.[31]

By empathizing with the troops' miserable condition on the front and by asserting their need for reinforcements and for improvements in their situation, Nagy came into conflict with the government's policy of conserving forces, a policy that he himself had condoned. The dilemma could not be solved. The 20,000-strong reinforcement proved to be too little even to replace the losses. The materials and equipment sent as replacements were even more scanty. The government and the military command rigidly held themselves to the agreement with the Germans, and deferred the performance of this task to them, even though it would have been in their own interest as well to do it. Instead, they held firmly to the position that weakening the forces under development in Hungary was out of the question. The country's industrial production was tied down with equipping the latter forces in their entirety, which was no secret to the Command of the 2nd Hungarian Army either. It repeatedly asked in vain for weapons replenishment from what had already been manufactured. For example, it asked to be re-supplied with the new "Turán" tanks and for the reinforcement of a new tank battalion to fill the grave gaps of the battle-weary armored division, the only mobile reserve of the 2nd Hungarian Army. The General Staff flatly rejected the request saying "We do not suggest sending out new units, and especially not tanks."[32] The tanks being manufactured were meant for the two armored divisions under development in Hungary. As Chief of Military Operational Section of the General Staff János Vörös said on behalf of Szombathelyi, "I do not intend to deploy them before they reach their full material and staff readiness." Manufacturing directly for the 2nd Hungarian Army from the limited supplies was out of the question.[33]

During the process of being introduced to the chief officials of his new Ministry, Nagy very soon realized that it would be hard to work with his predecessor's confidantes, who, in the majority, held both pro-German and extreme right-wing views. He also came to realize that he would be unable to make the necessary changes according to his own ideas. The officers both in the Ministry and on the General Staff continued to be convinced that Germany would be victorious. As Nagy described it, the only exception was

Lieutenant General István Náday, who, even early on, had openly stated his conviction that the Anglo-Saxon countries would win. But Nagy also saw that a major part of the politicians—and not only the extreme right-wing ones—believed in the German victory. Therefore, only a very few of them would sympathize with the government's most important military-political goal, which was the development and retention of enough armed forces so that in the case of a possible German defeat, or even in the case of a German victory, there would be military resources to defend Hungary's interests.

Nagy first officially met the cabinet representatives when the 900 million pengő budget of the defense portfolio was submitted. Zsolt Beöthy, who presented the budget, emphasized the point that the defense budget, which had surpassed the previous year's budget by 30%, did not include all the expenses incurred by the mobilization and deployment of the army, but served only to maintain and modernize the forces in the hinterland. As was well known to the representatives, the government also spent billions on equipping the army, using various other loans. Beöthy also spoke about Hungary's *realpolitik*, which during the "settlement" after the war necessitated the existence of "a well-equipped army, which was ready for anything and which demanded respect."

The right-wing opposition claimed that the submitted budget did not go far enough even in a minimalist way to make up for the several-year backwardness of spending on the military, which the representatives, surprisingly, had only now realized.[34] Long-time extreme right-wing politicians such as Andor Jaross, Gábor Vajna, László Baky, Zoltán Meskó, and others who expressed their views in the ensuing debate said that the major—and only—issue of importance for them was that the government sacrifice more on the army in order to fully stand by the Germans and to do it more successfully this time than before. They urgently wanted to modernize the armored and mechanized units as well as the air force.[35]

Endre Bajcsy-Zsilinszky from the democratic wing rose to speak in the debate. He also considered that the sum submitted in the budget was too little, and attacked the Minister of Finance, who had not budgeted enough to equip the army, meaning that the country was becoming vulnerable to external attacks. He demanded a well-equipped army of one and a half million men, which would be the only security against a now organizing—although this time not under "French leadership"—anti-Hungarian Little Entente. This army was needed "to fend off the increasingly provocative and bold Romanian threats and dangers" mostly supported by the Germans.[36] In harmony with the government's military political goals but totally ignoring Hungary's economic situation, Bajcsy-Zsilinszky condemned the policy, now several years long, of negligence in the area of arming the army, as well as the policy of not striving for complete self-sufficiency. The result was that the country was at the Germans' mercy. He demanded that the government terminate the food exports, in order to force Germany, which had plentifully provided arms to the Romanian army, to fulfill its obligations towards Hungary as well.[37]

Notes

1. György Ránki, Ervin Pamlényi, Loránt Tilkovszky and Gyula Juhász, eds., *A Wilhelmstrasse és Magyarország: Német diplomáciai iratok Magyarországról, 1933–1944* (The Wilhelmstrasse and Hungary: German Diplomatic Documents about Hungary, 1933–1944) (Budapest, 1968), 651 (480) and 653 (482).
2. *Ibid.*, p. 652. (481)
3. Miklós Kállay, *Hungarian Premier. A Personal Account of a Nation's Struggle in the Second World War* (New York, 1954), p. 141.
4. Ránki–Pamlényi–Tilkovszky–Juhász, *A Wilhelmstrasse és Magyarország...*, p. 661. (489)
5. *Ibid.*, p. 670. (496)
6. *Ibid.*
7. *Ibid.*
8. BA DZA A.A. Büro des Staatsekretars Rolle 16171/105379.
9. Ránki–Pamlényi–Tilkovszky–Juhász, *A Wilhelmstrasse és Magyarország...*, p. 671. (497)
10. BA DZA A.A. Büro des Staatsekretars Rolle 14080/452362.
11. *Ibid.*
12. Ránki–Pamlényi–Tilkovszky–Juhász, *A Wilhelmstrasse és Magyarország...*, p. 671. (498)
13. *Ibid.*, p. 673. (498-1)
14. *Ibid.*
15. *Ibid.*, p. 676. (501)
16. Országos Levéltár (National Archive, OL). Minisztertanácsi jegyzőkönyv (Minutes of the Council of Ministers), October 13, 1942.
17. Hugh Gibson, ed., *Ciano naplója: 1939–1943: Gróf Galeazzo Ciano olasz külügyminiszter, 1939–1943 teljes, rövidítés nélküli naplói* (Ciano's Diary: 1939–1943: The Full Diary without Shortening of Count Galeazzo Ciano, Italian Foreign Minister, 1939–1943) (Budapest, 1946), p. 454.
18. Hadtörténelmi Levéltár (Military History Archive, HL). Az olasz–német bizottság iratai (Documents of the Italian–German Committee), 1942/5041 (4. doboz)

19. Ránki–Pamlényi–Tilkovszky–Juhász, *A Wilhelmstrasse és Magyarország...*, p. 693. (513)
20. *Ibid.*, p. 693. (514)
21. *Ibid.*, p. 695. (516)
22. Ferenc Adonyi, *A magyar katona a második világháborúban. 1941–1945* (The Hungarian Soldier in World War II: 1941–1945) (Klagenfurt, 1954), p. 94.
23. Vilmos Nagybaczoni Nagy, *Végzetes esztendők 1938–1945* (Fatal Years, 1938–1945) (Budapest, 1986), p. 77.
24. *Ibid.*
25. *Ibid.*, p. 86.
26. *Ibid.*, p. 86.
27. *Ibid.*, pp. 96–97.
28. Interview with Kálmán Kéri by the author.
29. Nagybaczoni Nagy, *Végzetes esztendők...*, pp. 104–105.
30. *Ibid.*, p. 108.
31. *Ibid.*, p. 109.
32. HL. Eln. Vkf 1. 1942/5848.
33. HL. Eln. Vkf 1. 1942/5909.
34. *Az 1939. évi országgyűlés naplója, XV. 1942. november 18-i ülés* (Minutes of the 1939 Parliamentary Meeting: XV. Session of November 18, 1942).
35. *Ibid.*, Session of November 19, 1942.
36. *Ibid.*
37. *Ibid.*

A RADICAL TURNING POINT IN THE COURSE OF THE WAR: THE DESTRUCTION OF THE 2ND HUNGARIAN ARMY

On November 19, 1942, the offensive of the Soviet troops at the River Don and along the southeastern fronts was launched. The German and Romanian fronts were both broken through, north and south of Stalingrad. On November 21 the Soviet troops occupied Kalach and completely encircled the 300,000-strong 6th German Army. The Battle of Stalingrad, which had a great impact on the outcome of World War II and proved to be a radical turning point in the war, was underway. Paulus and the generals of the German General Staff recognized the grave situation and suggested to Hitler either an attempt to break out or an attempt to withdraw, but he did not even want to hear about it. On November 24 his final decision was that the 6th German Army would remain at its position and fight. The numerous failures of the German relief efforts, and the strength of the Soviet army's ring, which squeezed the Germans into smaller and smaller areas, eventually made it evident by the end of December that the total annihilation of the 6th German Army was only a question of a few weeks' time.

In the meantime, the 8th British Army also swung into action in northern Africa, broke through the German frontlines, and after heavy fighting in the first days of November completely defeated Rommel.

The news coming from the front once and for all shattered the pro-Western and pro-Kállay circles' belief in a possible German victory. Even stronger efforts were made to avoid any further unnecessary sacrifice, to retain Hungarian forces at home, to carefully prepare for a separation from the German alliance, and, in order to do this, to take special initiatives towards the Anglo-Saxon powers.

The Nagy–Szombathelyi military leadership also agreed that new opportunities should increasingly be sought, due to emerging events, on which new Hungarian military political ideas could be built.

Szombathelyi gave a talk on the new theory and practice of upper and middle level military leadership in December 1942. During this confidential talk with general staff-level officers, he surprised quite a few who were present by strongly stating that the blitzkrieg war of the Germans was over. It had failed in the enormous Russian space, in the cauldron battles there, and due to the tough resistance of the Russian soldier, he said. Furthermore, it had failed due to the "enfeebling" slow warfare of the Anglo-Saxon countries, based on their immeasurable material reserves. In this new situation the Hungarian soldier had to think with his own head and not with the head of a people of 90 million. Hungarian soldiers needed to know that in order to finish the war "not only the winning of great and dazzling battles is needed, but also the fortunate recognition and utilization of emerging political situations, as well as a clever way of weaving the texture of diplomacy.." He also added that whatever he had said was his honest personal opinion, and that he expected the participants not to tell anyone else.[1]

Szombathelyi may have been reinforced in his earlier view that Germany would not win the war, but he did not have a catastrophic defeat in mind either. The prestige of the German army was too great for him to think that.

At the end of January, after analyzing the grave military situation and its consequences, Szombathelyi explained to Rudolf Andorka that, in his view, it was time to oppose the Germans on certain questions, but it was not yet time for a complete breakup of the alliance. Should the Hungarians break the alliance, the Germans would definitely place the Hungarian extreme right in power, even by applying military force if needed. In his view, Germany had not lost the war yet, and still had the opportunity to reach a compromise. And he hoped that the Soviet army would be held up somewhere, because "otherwise we are finished."[2]

The Hungarian military and political leadership assumed a "wait-and-see" position, standing by helplessly at the increasingly worrisome situation of the 2nd Hungarian Army. They were resigned to the fact that they could not do anything about the 2nd Army, because the Germans controlled it, because of the pending Soviet offensive, and because they had learned that it was futile to approach the leaders of the OKW or the Command of Army Group B. The Hungarian military and political leadership failed to press the Germans for the promised but still missing effective defensive weapons or for enough reserves to be placed in the appropriate depth, without which the defense would collapse.

On December 24 Hitler sent a letter to Horthy telling him that it was of crucial importance that the Hungarian troops hold out and relieve the German troops, even at the expense of sacrificing themselves. He tried to reassure Horthy, calling the Soviet successes transient ones, which would be corrected by the new German divisions to be deployed soon. In the meantime, every sign indicated that the Soviet attack would spread out in front of the Hungarian army's line. As Hitler wrote, "The battles of recent weeks repeatedly proved that the prerequisite for a successful resistance in the case of an overwhelming attack is for the defenders to hold out in their positions, even if the enemy breaks through their defense lines and only isolated wedges survive. If every base holds out to the last man—even if he is disconnected from his unit—significant portions of the enemy's forces remain tied down and cannot build on their initial successes. In the meantime, they [the soldiers holding out] make it possible for their own leadership to rectify the situation by a counterattack with newly deployed troops." If the troops do not fight in this manner, Hitler continued his strategic line of thought, then "the area of incursion will grow, and it will make it difficult to clarify the situation later, while increasing the danger for the soldier holding out who withdraws, because he might perish in the infinite depth of the Russian space." Therefore, he asked Horthy to try to prevent "even the idea of withdrawal from occurring" among the troops.[3]

Hitler once again did not fail to promise to send the weapons that would increase the resistance of the Hungarian troops. Then, not trusting that the Hungarian troops would hold out in their positions, in spite of Horthy's expected encouraging command, he asked for the Regent's consent for the exchange of some divisions of the 2nd Hungarian Army with divisions of the neighboring 2nd German Army, a measure that he believed would increase the troops' fighting spirit.

Szombathelyi did not procrastinate, and immediately sent Jány a command to the troops to unconditionally persevere. He repeated Hitler's platitudes about the utility of troops holding out, saying the following: "Our supreme warlord orders that in the case of an attack all the positions and bases should be held under all circumstances. No one is allowed to turn back. There is no backwards, only forwards. Every *honvéd* should be imbued with the idea that defeating the danger of Bolshevism, keeping it away from our dear homeland and fighting for a happier future all depend on his perseverance at the place where he has been placed. Accordingly, the troops are ordered to stand their ground. The German military command has held out the prospect of reinforcing our defense line."[4]

Not much was said about the Hungarian army in Berlin, when Minister of Defense Vilmos Nagybaczoni Nagy participated in the festivities for Göring's fiftieth birthday in early January. Following the instructions of Kállay, Nagy talked to Göring about the issue of the continuing strained Hungarian–Romanian relationship and about the issue of the airplanes. He also asked for anti-aircraft guns to reinforce the Hungarian air defense. The German Air Marshal refused to supply any weapons, saying that he would give them only to troops on the front, because otherwise the Hungarian government would use them for an attack against Romania. Nagy refuted rumors that he said were spread by the Romanians, and reproached Göring for his distrust, based on these false Romanian rumors, which he demonstrated towards the Hungarian government.[5]

But then Keitel brought up the issue of the 2nd Hungarian Army. By then the news about the Soviet offensive had arrived in Berlin, and the German Field Marshal ventured out to reassure Nagy by promising German reinforcements, which would soon arrive at the front in order to help with the 2nd Hungarian Army's situation.[6]

On January 12, 1943, the offensive of the Soviet army began against the 2nd Hungarian Army. The Soviet troops broke through the 2nd Army's positions at several places, and within a few days wiped out the desperately resisting Hungarian units or forced them to retreat. The troops of the defeated 2nd Army retreated in disarray. In compliance with Szombathelyi's order Jány had given his own orders to defend the positions until the very end, prohibiting any withdrawals. At the command of Hitler, who personally intervened in directing the battle, several times Jány prevented the Hungarian units from retreating in time, increasing the losses. Jány had offered his resignation, due to the non-executable tasks facing the army, and due to grave armaments shortages, which prevailed in spite of all the German promises. On January 24 he issued an unfortunate order: "The 2nd Hungarian Army lost its honor because, except for a few men loyal to their oaths and obligations, it did not deliver what could have rightly been expected from it." He said all these even though he knew that the German army had broken all the brotherly loyalty, had behaved inhumanly, and had also fled in terror. Jány instructed the commanders and field security police to restore order and iron discipline at all costs, even at the expense of putting people to the sword. He told everyone 'to stay wherever your concentration was ordered, where the reorganization is to be made; where everyone should stay until he recovers or perishes."[7]

Jány's command caused a great uproar. Certain commanders, such as Major General László Kuthy, Commander of the 13th Light Division, immediately protested against the accusations made against the army. He asked for an investigation to determine whether his division, which had fought until the last possible moment, had created a backdrop for the German troops, and had finally been completely destroyed, had not fulfilled its obligation but rather had lost its honor.[8]

Jány gradually calmed down and tried to "rehabilitate" his own soldiers with a speech on March 12 in which he spoke of soldiers "who fought with honor and stood the test."[9]

On January 22 Hitler ordered the withdrawal of the remnants of the defeated 2nd Hungarian Army from the frontline, and the army's immediate reorganization. The OKW designated the Belgorod region as the army's concentration area. Szombathelyi agreed with the arrangement and promised to arrive at Hitler's Headquarters on February 1 in order to discuss activities in connection with the reorganization.

However, the Chief of the General Staff's main task when he set out to meet Hitler was to try to get the remnants of the 2nd Hungarian Army sent home immediately and to avoid any agreement on deploying new troops.

During the discussion the Führer called the recent past events "unpleasant incidents," and tried to disarm Szombathelyi. Then he proceeded to speak about the ally's loyalty and obligations, and did not miss the chance to covertly threaten any unfaithful allies.

While listening to Hitler, Szombathelyi became convinced that it was impossible to fully dodge the German "requests" without certain negative consequences, and all that he could do was to make reference to the army's losses and to the ensuing necessary reorganization and re-armament, which might moderate or delay the extent to which Hungary could fulfill the Germans' wishes. Then Hitler broached the subject and suggested the following: the remnants of the 2nd Hungarian Army would be convened into an army corps including two divisions, while twelve construction battalions would also be set up. Units that would not be needed could be sent home. He also suggested that the Command of the 2nd Hungarian Army establish a Hungarian occupying armed force of six divisions by using the two divisions and the Hungarian occupying forces already on the front.[10] Szombathelyi knew that these divisions would not be used just for occupational tasks against the partisans, since the German military command was in such a grave situation. He also knew that these divisions, battle-weary and disorganized, lacking the most basic weapons, were unsuitable even for occupation tasks. Yet he did not dare to disagree; although he was not authorized to do so, he promised to fulfill the request.

During the discussion Hitler also asked for occupying divisions in the Balkans, and Szombathelyi once again agreed to that. He allowed himself to be convinced by Hitler that sooner or later the Allies would land in the Balkans and, as a result, Hungary's strategic situation would change. He hoped to satisfy Hitler with the Hungarian divisions to be deployed to the Balkans, and hoped that the Hungarian troops stationed there could be used for special Hungarian strategic goals. He was also enticed to comply by Hitler's offer to immediately equip the Hungarian divisions to be deployed in the Balkans.

Szombathelyi did not think that the Hungarian *Honvédség* could withdraw from the war at that point. These appear to have been his internal motives when, by himself and not accompanied or supported by anyone else, he faced Hitler with the unpleasant government commission.[11]

The result of Szombathelyi's mission caused dissatisfaction in Hungary. The Prime Minister resented the fact that Szombathelyi could not get the 2nd Hungarian Army fully withdrawn and removed back home, and that he was also willing to participate in the occupation of Serbia. The OKW turned to the General Staff on February 11 and requested that three divisions be deployed to Serbia, while indicating that two of them should replace the German troops as early as March. On February 13 the German military attaché, Pappenheim, went to the OKW and reported that he had held discussions with Chief of the General Staff Szombathelyi on this matter, and that Szombathelyi did not think that the request could be satisfied. Szombathelyi's justification was that forces should be held in reserve in the case of a possible Allied landing in the Balkans or in case Romania expectedly changed sides. Pappenheim also added that equipping four divisions would certainly exhaust all of Hungary's armaments, material and human resources. However, if material and training support were offered, Szombathelyi considered it possible to have five divisions at Germany's disposal by May.

With some difficulty, the OKW agreed that the Hungarian General Staff would provide two divisions for the occupation of Serbia and three divisions as military operational reserves ready for action beginning on May 1.[12]

Finally, on February 24, Szombathelyi's letter arrived at the OKW; in this he stated that at the moment he did not have a single division suitable for frontline service, and that new divisions could be set up later only with German support. He also said that badly trained and poorly equipped divisions could not take over the German troops' role in Serbia. How much the insufficiently equipped troops were worth on the battlefield had been proved by recent events. Szombathelyi also added that whatever weapons the *Honvédség* possessed would be sent to the reorganized troops of the 2nd Hungarian Army, since it was considered vital to concentrate the scattered Hungarian troops on the eastern front under Jány's command.[13]

In his memorandum of February 12 to Horthy, Szombathelyi tried to justify his actions. He gave an overview of Hungary's participation in the war thus far, and pointed out that because of the quality of its equipment the 2nd Hungarian Army was unsuitable to fight in the war into which it had been forced. The Germans had never fulfilled their promises to raise the quality of the Hungarian army's armaments to the level of the German ones. Szombathelyi claimed that the Germans themselves had misjudged the Soviet army's combat efficiency. Keitel had always reassured the Hungarian military command that the Russian forces had weakened. And it was only the Soviet offensive launched during the fall that had had a sobering effect on the Germans, leading to a clear recognition of the situation. Szombathelyi thought that his earlier position that "the demands of the war in Russia are overstraining the Hungarian nation and the Hungarian armed forces" had been proved correct. Therefore, as early as the Christmas of the previous year, he had compiled an information bulletin for the Chief of the General Staff of the OKW, General Jodl, pointing out that "the equipment and training of the Hungarian army and our manufacturing capacity are in such a condition that we are unable to send new forces to the Russian front. Moreover, if future battles of the 2nd Hungarian Army inflict major losses, replacing them will entail the greatest difficulties."[14]

Following that, he tried to convince Horthy about the strategic advantages of sending troops to the Balkans in return for the troops withdrawn from the Soviet front: "By the power of its geographical situation the southern front is suitable for Hungary to intervene in. Within the framework of the allied command and the war, Hungary will find those tasks there that fit its military situation, goals and capabilities. Within this strategic framework Hungary is a strategic reserve in the Danube Basin facing south and southeast."[15] In Szombathelyi's view, in this new situation Germany would recognize Hungary's importance and would "give more effective support and help both for the rearmament of the 2nd Hungarian Army and for our forces in the hinterland. And, in a given situation, our troops fighting on the eastern front could also be deployed to the southern front."[16] He considered this a primary Hungarian interest for several reasons, including the view that, if the Anglo-Saxon forces came ashore in the Balkans, one should count on the Romanians' changing sides and immediately attacking Hungary in order to gain respect from the Anglo-Saxon nations. Hungary should be prepared for the eventuality that "these attacks will probably be waged against larger towns along the border and in the Székely land, and we will counterattack them. Moreover, we will harshly respond to any attack. Therefore, within the frame of a Balkan war, an intervention against Romania would be the first step for which we have to prepare and through which, along with the common war, we can realize our own special Hungarian goals: the occupation and securing of Transylvania. This anti-Romanian stand falls in line with the German ideas, as manifested in the expression of 'strategic reserve'."[17]

Therefore, in Szombathelyi's view, troops could be withdrawn from the eastern front only "if we are confronted with a task of so-far unknown characteristics, and if this task is of crucial importance with regard to the common war, Hungary's particular goals, and Hungary's national interest, one for which we should make a major sacrifice. This is the circumstance that imparts to us an especially heavy obligation. It is heavier than we have ever had before. This is the recognition with which I came away from the German Main Headquarters, and this is the recognition that guides me in my suggestions."[18]

The request that Hungarian soldiers replace the German divisions in the Balkans was submitted to the Council of Ministers on March 10 and 30, and was flatly rejected both times. Even in his submission, Minister of Defense Nagy rejected participating in the Balkan occupation. He did not agree with the Chief of the General

Staff's proposal, even though Szombathelyi thought that "the Germans would equip three divisions, the Serbs would like us to occupy their area as opposed to a German occupation, and this fact would gain sympathy for us from the Serbs."[19]

Prime Minister Kállay did not accept Szombathelyi's argument either, resented the fact that he had conducted discussions on this topic without the knowledge of the Prime Minister or the Minister of Defense, resented the fact that he had made promises to the Germans, and especially resented the fact that he had made propositions to the Regent.

After that, the government refused to fulfill the German requests, since they could not be reconciled with Hungarian interests. Acceding to them would irreversibly damage the government's relations with the Anglo-Saxon governments and the Yugoslavian government in exile. It would also be impossible to morally justify an intervention to the Hungarian public. As for the German promise of equipping the three divisions, even "if they truly kept their promises, it would have absolutely no consequences for our *Honvédség*, because these troops would be stationed outside the borders of the country."[20] In any case, it was noted that the equipment was assured by standing contracts with the same military industry that also worked for the Germans. If the Germans did not fulfill older contractual obligations, what would guarantee that they would keep a new promise?[21]

Szombathelyi must have been surprised by the Prime Minister's rigid rejection of his proposal, since, at the time of his visit to Hitler, he would have been justified in thinking that participating in a possible Balkan action would not contradict the Prime Minister's foreign policy goals. This is what Kállay's report to the Foreign Policy Committee of Parliament on February 18 confirmed. *Inter alia*, Kállay told the members of the Committee that the government's focus of attention was shifting towards the Balkans, since it was expected that a second front would open up there. He also said that, in connection with the Balkan events, it could also be expected that the Romanians would become active against Transylvania, and so the remaining forces of the *Honvédség* should be reserved for this. At the same time he also stated that some rapprochement had been shown from the direction of the Serb national forces towards Hungary, which "kept [Hungarian political life] busy."[22] Although Kállay did not say much about the nature of the connection or what it was geared towards, still it is certain that after discussing the issue within a confidential circle—and with the Chief of the General Staff knowing about it—the question of cooperation between Hungarian troops and Draža Mihailovič's Serbian "Chetnik" guerrilla forces on the side of the Allies must have come up. While the process of sending out feelers about Hungary's changing sides was happening, discussions about cooperation with Mihailovič were very soon—after the visit to Hitler—taken off the agenda. Szombathelyi heard about this only later, and therefore he primarily viewed it as a manifestation of suspicion towards him. On the other hand, as one can see from his letter to Horthy, he held onto his opinion, even under changed circumstances, and considered a military presence in the Balkans necessary to safeguard Hungarian interests. This whole situation confirmed his aversion towards the pro-British Hungarians supporting Kállay. The distrust was mutual—consequently, Szombathelyi was less and less counted on to help the government change the situation. He was not included in confidential circles, since he was trusted by the Germans, and he was only included marginally in sharing ideas even on a social level, which hurt his pride.

Under such circumstances it was not surprising that he felt obligated to warn Horthy that the war was not finished. He cautioned him about people who lived in a fantasy world, thinking that "the war for us has lost its concrete form and now our task is to watch events and to dedicate ourselves to speculations about whom to join."[23]

Bringing up the military force to an effective level was a crucial question for Szombathelyi, since the military's current equipment did not allow it to fight with much force. He was convinced that everything should be done to put at least the V. and IX. Army Corps and the mounted division onto a state of alert. Equipping the armored divisions, the new three-regiment divisions, and the air force would have to be finished within a short period of time in order for them to reach acceptable level of military preparedness. This would be dependent on Germany's support, in spite of the fact that even on industrial issues the fulfillment of German promises could not be trusted.[24]

The issue of the Hungarian military presence in the Balkans did not divert the country's attention from the 2nd Hungarian Army's fate. Although the official governmental organs and the press tried to keep silent about it, while the military reports of the General Staff only spoke about heavy fighting in the rear and about a flexible withdrawal, what had happened could not be covered up forever. Hungary's population was shocked to face the tragic reality. All over the country thousands expected news about their loved ones and the return of those who had survived.

At the end of February 1943 Minister of Defense Nagy informed the government about the situation of the 2nd Hungarian Army. About 70,000 men had survived, the material loss was 70%, the loss was 100% in heavy weapons, and the financial loss was estimated at 367 million pengős. He dramatically described the miserable demise of the Hungarian troops, and condemned the German military command that had first placed the troops in an impossible situation and then let them down. Now, he went on, the Hungarian military command's approach was that "no more people or equipment will be sent to the front."[25]

Due to the increasing tension and uproar in the country, Kállay and Nagy considered it to be of the utmost importance that the government follow its original intention of bringing the surviving troops of the 2nd Hungarian Army back home, even at the expense of deploying new Hungarian occupational divisions. In early March, after convincing Horthy about it, they instructed Szombathelyi to conduct discussions with the OKW accordingly.

In the meantime, according to the agreement of February, the OKW took the necessary measures to reorganize Hungarian forces on the front. On March 5 Keitel informed Szombathelyi that the 2nd Hungarian Army was being resettled west of the River Dnieper, where the troops would be reorganized. Keitel had already contacted Major General Gyula Kovács, Chief of the General Staff of the 2nd Hungarian Army. All the Hungarian units on the eastern front would be under the Command of the 2nd Hungarian Army, which, in turn, was going to receive instructions directly from the OKW.[26]

At that point Szombathelyi had not counted on the Council of Ministers' deciding that the offer of deploying new divisions would allow the units of the 2nd Hungarian Army to be brought home to Hungary. Instead, he issued guidelines relating to the reorganization to the Command of the 2nd Hungarian Army and ordered the Chief of the General Staff of the 2nd Hungarian Army to go to Budapest to clarify the details.[27]

According to the basic principles issued by the Chief of the General Staff under the order 1622/M. hdm. I. Vkf. 1943, the Command of the 2nd Hungarian Army had to create an army corps, including two full divisions, for occupying duties, made up of the remaining units, together with their staff, of the 2nd Hungarian Army.

The Chief of the General Staff was concerned that the soldiers arriving home would have a destructive effect on their environment, and so a thorough "re-education" was needed. "Units designated to come home will remain at military operational areas for six to eight weeks, and will receive a thorough disciplining re-education. Patriotic education is to be increased. Enhanced propaganda and the sending out of field chaplains and judge-advocates might be

A Radical Turning Point in the Course of the War 433

necessary." This, however, was not enough, because, according to the order, more "re-education" awaited the troops at home, who "after disciplining re-education should be transported home in closed units. At home these units and some troops on non-active service will not be discharged immediately but will receive further disciplinary re-education under their commanders in training camps. From the middle of the second month onwards, they will be deployed to their peacetime station and will be merged with their own substitute units, while soldiers on non-active duty will be demobilized after the second month."[28]

Although the decision had been made behind the scenes that all the units and troops of the 2nd Hungarian Army should be brought home, and only the military command would remain on the front to coordinate all the Hungarian occupying forces, the meeting to discuss questions about the reorganization took place in Budapest on March 14, 1943. Chief of the Operational Section Major General Géza Vörös represented the Chief of the General Staff, and Major General György Rakovszky represented the Minister of Defense. The Chief of the General Staff of the 2nd Hungarian Army, Major General Gyula Kovács, was also present, as were other section leaders of the General Staff and the Ministry of Defense.

Major General Kovács had arrived to Budapest to discuss the details of the execution of the original order. Accordingly, he reported about the future course of the war, about the role of the 2nd Hungarian Army in it, and about discussions on direct tasks ongoing with the Germans. He was quoted as saying "Based on the general evaluation of the situation and based on several discussions with the German leaders, I am of the view that Hungary should continue to have an armed participation in the war; we cannot watch from the theater as history is made. From this statement it follows that the Hungarian army should be set on its feet as soon as possible, its organization and equipment should be modernized, and once it is done we must once again request a place on the frontline. We will bitterly pay for any other solution if our German ally finishes this war with victory or even with an outcome that could be considered victorious." Based on the above reasoning, Kovács reported that the military command had ordered the reorganization of the army into three-tier divisions, so that—as was emphasized in Smolensk during the meeting with the Germans—they would be of equal value with the German divisions in case they were involved in the war. Kovács also said that agreement had been concluded with the Germans so that "the most up-to-date training would accompany the most modern equipment along with German support."[29]

Vörös and Rakovszky warned Major General Kovács that for the time being no action should be taken about equipping and training the 2nd Hungarian Army as a frontline army, since, according to the order, only occupying forces should be formed from the remnants of the army.

After acknowledging this, Kovács requested that "the Command of the 2nd Hungarian Army become the Command of all the Hungarian military forces in the east with regard to service, administration and provision, and deployment as well. This is the only way to avoid having different small German commands tear the battle order of the occupying forces into pieces and waste Hungarian blood in disjointed military operations. The Hungarian military command should represent and support with its prestige all the Hungarian forces alike." Kovács said that the occupying task also necessitated a change to three regiments for a division, because, "whether we want it or not, Hungarian troops once again will be at the frontline within a certain amount of time."[30] The meeting ended essentially with agreement on Kovács's points.

Following that, the participants held a discussion on the reorganization of the 2nd Hungarian Army, based on the Chief of the General Staff's principles. Kovács said that in order to fulfill the conditions of the Chief of the General Staff's basic principles, the best solution would be to transport home the whole army and to deploy new troops to take care of the necessary tasks, because not even two of the current divisions were in a fit shape to be deployed. He did not think that there was any danger in deploying any new troops, since the Hungarian leadership would only deploy them for occupying tasks, and military experience was not crucial for such tasks. The participants of the meeting agreed with Kovács. They also agreed that bringing home the 2nd Hungarian Army not only made the long-awaited restructuring of the army's battle order possible, but "it also ends the injustice of a part of the country's population's having been fighting for almost a year while the larger proportion had stayed at home."[31] Then the conference submitted a proposal to the Chief of the General Staff and the Minister of Defense to bring the 2nd Hungarian Army home. Both of them agreed to the proposal on March 16, while Horthy agreed to it on March 18.

Kovács elaborated at great length on how appalled he was to see the homeland's warped view of the army: "Neither under siege nor after an attack was this army an undisciplined revolutionary gang by which the homeland should feel threatened." Therefore, he protested against plans to discipline the remnants of the army on the eastern front for about two months followed by another one and a half to two months at home." This was not only unnecessary but downright harmful. He requested that this plan be dropped, and the participants agreed.[32]

On March 23 the Minister of Defense informed the ministers that the remnants of the 2nd Hungarian Army would return home in the near future, but in return two occupying divisions would stay on the front, complemented by two more occupying divisions in April. Nagy thought that this would satisfy the Germans' requests, because he categorically established the following: "We cannot and will not submit more than these forces at the disposal of the eastern front. The new deployment is to be launched when the majority of the remnants of the 2nd Hungarian Army has arrived home."[33]

With no further ado, the OKW agreed to Szombathelyi's new proposal that the units of the 2nd Hungarian Army would be replaced by rested divisions. On March 28 Keitel informed the Chief of the General Staff that the Führer had agreed to transport the remnants of the 2nd Hungarian Army—with the exception of its staff—back to Hungary, replacing them with two new divisions and twelve construction battalions. He instructed the OKW that the new troop transports would start in mid-April.[34]

Notes

1. *A m. kir. honvéd vezérkar főnökének előadása a vezetésről az 1942. december 14-15-i tábornoki és vezérkari megbeszélésen* (The Lecture Held by the Chief of the Hungarian Royal General Staff on Leadership at the General and General Staff Level Meeting of December 14 and 15, 1942) (Budapest, 1942).
2. Rudolf Andorka, *A madridi követségtől Mauthausenig* (From the Madrid Embassy to Mauthausen) (Budapest, 1978), pp. 289–290.
3. Elek Karsai, *A budai vártól a gyepüig* (From the Buda Castle to the Border-land) (Budapest, 1965), pp. 229–230.
4. *Ibid.*, p. 231.
5. Vilmos Nagybaczoni Nagy, *Végzetes esztendők 1938–1945* (Fatal Years, 1938–1945) (Budapest, 1986), p. 123.
6. *Ibid.*
7. Hadtörténelmi Levéltár (Military History Archive, HL). A 2. magyar hadsereg anyaga (Material of the 2nd Hungarian Army).
8. *Ibid.*
9. *Ibid.*
10. Carlile Aylmer Macartney, *October Fifteenth. A History of Modern Hungary, 1929-1945* (Edinburgh, 1961), vol. II: p. 138.
11. HL. Békeelőkészítő Bizottság iratai. A/II/1. (Documents of the Peace Preparatory Committee).
12. Percy Schramm, ed., *Kriegstagebuch des Oberkommandos der Wehrmacht (Wehrmachtführungsstab), 1940–1945* (Frankfurt am Main, 1961–1979), vol. III: p. 134.
13. *Ibid.*
14. *Horthy Miklós titkos iratai* (Miklós Horthy's Secret Writings), ed. Miklós Szinai and László Szűcs, (Budapest, 1962), p. 347.
15. *Ibid.*, p. 348.
16. *Ibid.*
17. *Ibid.*, pp. 349–350.
18. *Ibid.*
19. Országos Levéltár (National Archive, OL). Minisztertanácsi jegyzőkönyv (Minutes of the Council of Ministers), March 10 and 30, 1943.
20. *Horthy Miklós titkos iratai*, p. 364.

21. *Ibid.*
22. György Ránki, Ervin Pamlényi, Loránt Tilkovszky and Gyula Juhász, eds., *A Wilhelmstrasse és Magyarország: Német diplomáciai iratok Magyarországról, 1933–1944* (The Wilhelmstrasse and Hungary: German Diplomatic Documents about Hungary, 1933–1944) (Budapest, 1968), p. 707. (526); BA DZA – Potsdam – II.14080/452420-452427.
23. *Horthy Miklós titkos iratai*, p. 349.
24. *Ibid.*, p. 333.
25. OL. Minisztertanácsi jegyzőkönyv 1943 (Minutes of the Council of Ministers), February 23 and March 2, 1943.
26. Schramm, *Kriegstagebuch...*, vol. III: p. 187.
27. *Ibid.*, p. 255.
28. HL. A 2. magyar hadsereg anyaga (Material of the 2nd Hungarian Army).
29. *Ibid.*
30. *Ibid.*
31. *Ibid.*
32. *Ibid.*
33. OL. Minisztertanácsi jegyzőkönyv (Minutes of the Council of Ministers), March 23, 1943.
34. Schramm, *Kriegstagebuch...*, vol. III: p. 243.

FAILED ATTEMPTS TO BREAK AWAY
AND THE MILITARY COMMAND

Hitler considered the Hungarian refusal to deploy an occupational division to the Balkans to be an unfriendly step, and he rebuked both Kállay and, most of all, Nagy. He also expressed his dissatisfaction during Horthy's visit in April, 1943. As the Prime Minister explained to the Council of Ministers, the goal of the visit "obviously was to make an impact on the Regent, so that we deploy all our forces and also allow nothing to indicate that Hungary's foreign political stance had become shaky."[1]

During the visit Hitler emphatically asserted that Germany's military power remained unbroken, and presented the Regent with a whole list of sins indicating the turncoat policy of the Kállay government. The Hungarian peace feelers sent out to the Allied governments constituted the set of biggest crimes, and the surprised Horthy had to confront every instance of breach of trust from the "well-informed" Hitler. Hitler also attacked the Hungarian government for speaking only about the common fight against the Soviets and not mentioning the common fight against the Anglo-Saxon countries, with which, moreover, it had tried to establish connections. He also alluded to the insufficiency of Hungarian sacrifices, which Horthy, mentioning the 80,000 Hungarian dead, denied. During the rest of the meeting Hitler did not touch upon the Hungarian participation in the war, nor did he discuss new requests for more forces. However, he managed to get Horthy's agreement to expand the SS recruitment to include the *Volksdeutsche* serving in the *Honvédség*.[2]

In the meantime Keitel conducted discussions with Szombathelyi, who had accompanied the Regent, but their discussions were later deleted from the official statement. During this discussion Szombathelyi refuted the German charges, also reiterated by Keitel, and reproached him for giving equipment for eight divisions to the Romanians while the Hungarian army received almost nothing, although the Hungarian troops had lost most of their equipment during the Don fights. After a while, he agreed with Keitel that the two "will not reproach each other for anything." Szombathelyi must have been invited due to the need for Hungarian troops to participate in the Balkan occupation and the need to discuss all related issues. Hitler probably wanted to present the request to the Regent after a preliminary discussion between Szombathelyi and Keitel. However, by referring to Horthy's stubborn resistance and probable rejection of the request, and by offering new, although inefficiently equipped, occupational divisions to be deployed against the Soviet partisans, Szombathelyi managed to prevent Hitler from raising the request with the Regent.[3]

While trying to find a way to break away from the war, the Prime Minister and his circle knew that without winning over the Hungarian military command to their idea, they could hardly be successful. They also were aware that a thorough cleansing of the military leadership would also be unavoidable in order to succeed. In this, Kállay and his circle counted on the help of Szombathelyi, who continued to enjoy the Regent's confidence. Indeed, when Horthy appointed him Chief of the General Staff, he expected Szombathelyi to pursue a more heedful and less pro-German policy and leadership of the army. Szombathelyi tried to fulfill these expectations, but came up against increasing numbers of stumbling blocks, various people and factions who balked at executing his plans. His evaluation of the expected outcome of the war usually turned out to be right.

When he became Chief of the General Staff in the fall of 1941, Szombathelyi enjoyed the undivided trust of the Anglophile circles. Under-secretary of State Antal Ullein-Reviczky had tried to feel out his attitude towards the war and the Anglo-Saxon nations. At that point Szombathelyi gave a definite and non-hesitant response, saying that if it were up to him, no Hungarian soldier would shoot at either a British or an American soldier; instead he would have the Hungarians lay down their arms and change sides. At Ullein-Reviczky's request Szombathelyi agreed that his statement could be used to inform the British, with whom Ullein-Reviczky had been in contact through his father-in-law, an official of the British Embassy in Istanbul. During the following months a very tight bond developed between Szombathelyi and Ullein-Reviczky, who continuously informed the Chief of the General Staff about Anglo-Saxon-related events.

During the fall of 1942 Ullein-Reviczky came up with the suggestion that Szombathelyi make contact with the British military command through the American mission in Istanbul, because the British were only willing to speak with soldiers. The attempts by Hungarian politicians to establish contacts had failed. Szombathelyi was pleased with the possibility, but he was also distressed that the Germans might get wind of it through their man posted at the 2nd Section of the Hungarian General Staff. To find the suitable person for establishing the connection was also troublesome. It was months by the time the appropriate person, Lieutenant Colonel Jenő Tömösy, was ready to get going, during the spring of 1943. At that point, however, the Prime Minister, who had become distrustful of the military, intervened and cancelled Tömösy's trip. So, for the time being, Szombathelyi was left outside the circle of contacts that were established with the Anglo-Saxon powers, which he considered militarily unacceptable. He was afraid that the civilians would do something resulting in dire consequences.[4]

In this atmosphere of increasing distrust, it is difficult to comprehend Kállay's and his circle's expectations about changes in the military leadership or about convincing the army to change sides. It is quite surprising how much they misjudged the prevailing atmosphere and conditions. At the beginning they hoped that the pro-German commitment and the extreme right-wing attachment in the army were lower than they actually were. They also hoped to find numerous reliable generals and General Staff officers who would assist in implementing the necessary reorganization. Moreover, they also hoped that the morale of the General Staff and, through them, that of the whole officer corps could be changed, and that was what they informed their British partners about.

However, the necessary reorganization and regrouping was of such a large scale that it was impossible for the Hungarians to successfully implement it. An incident in 1943 reveals how uninformed, in this regard, people were. In February 1943, in Ankara, Albert Szent-Györgyi informed the British emissaries that 25 pro-German General Staff officers or officers of German ethnic origin would have to be removed from the General Staff so that he and his contacts could count on the Hungarian army's support.[5] In April Károly Schrecker did not judge the situation so optimistically, in a memorandum handed over to the British ambassador to Ankara for the British government. He described the officer corps as "the population's most savagely pro-German segment," of whom at least 70–80% were of German ethnic origin or harbored "German sentiments behind their Hungarian masks." In order to mitigate the hopeless picture, he also informed the British about the following: "It would be unjust not to say that a small portion of the officer corps—that of the higher-ranking ones—behaves exceptionally towards the government. For a while the government has been promoting the latter and has achieved immediate results."[6] In a May letter delivered by a Dutch ambassador to Turkey, based on unidentified experiences, Schrecker informed the British about some progress, in order to increase the chances of the British government's benevolence and readiness to negotiate: "The Hungarian government has been working hard for a year to establish a real Hungarian spirit in the army, to exclude the pro-German elements from the officer corps, and to decrease the officer corps' pro-German inclinations. It has already achieved results worth mentioning, especially among high-ranking officers."[7] Schrecker's statement was correct only with regard to the government's intentions. What he said about achieved "results" was unfounded and misleading, since in reality the government did not have proper data about the proportion of generals and General Staff officers within the officer corps who would presumably be loyal to the Regent, about their identity or about the size of the ensuing necessary reorganization.

Military historians have not investigated the issue, and so we are unable to draw a proper contemporary political picture of the officer corps of the *Honvédség*. The question is what proportion of generals and officers, among both the General Staff and the regular officers, had pro-German or extreme right-wing connections or sympathies versus the proportion that were more reliable to the Regent and who might, at the Regent's request in a given situation, even turn against the Germans. Based on our years of research, we have concluded that about two thirds of the generals were loyal to the government, while only one third of General Staff officers can be characterized as such. Professional advancement also helped to motivate the commitment of the latter group to the Germans and the Hungarian extreme right wing. In our view, this proportion was even lower with the General Staff officers: with them it was below one third. The situation is further complicated if we approach this question by looking at the most important commanding posts. The Germans and their Hungarian friends made sure that only trusted officers occupied these positions in large numbers, and if any of them should face the threat of replacement, the Germans immediately launched countermeasures. It is even more difficult to figure out the division of lower ranking officers, who in any case had no significant impact on commanding the army. It can be assumed that, depending on the influence of their immediate commanders and on contacts established at their service sites, they tended between the right wing and the extreme right wing.

Purging the General Staff, the Ministry of Defense and the higher commands of the army of pro-German and extreme right-wing elements did not take place, in spite of promises and timid initiatives. During his interrogation in 1945 Szombathelyi said the following: "I set out to change the General Staff officers who had been in close cooperation and quasi-friendly relationships with the Germans. However, I had to be very slow and certain in the steps taken, because the Germans raised obstacles by immediately asking about the reason for the replacement and about what new position the replaced officer would receive."[8] Although there were indeed changes and transfers, everything happened extremely carefully and slowly, and not at all at the speed that the situation demanded.

The careers of such well-known General Staff colonels as Elemér Sáska, András Zákó, Jenő Tömöry, Ferenc Szász and Ferenc Deák were in their ascent during this period of time and went totally undisturbed. All of them were pro-German and held extreme right-wing views, and they all later became generals under Szálasi.

Apart from Gyula Kádár's appointment, no movements in the leadership can be pinpointed as proof that reliable people replaced unreliable ones. The proof is the fact that, except for Kádár, no one else in a high position was compromised enough for the Germans to demand their replacement after they occupied Hungary.

The ubiquitously present Germans closely watched events within the Hungarian military and tried to prevent the "cleaning up" process from happening at all, since they counted on the officer corps and the army as major factors in the implementation of their goals. In his report of April 30 Veesenmayer analyzed the situation in Hungary and called his superiors' attention to increased anti-Axis political forces there, which had brought increasing danger to the alliance, dreamed about breaking away from the war and hindered the country from properly participating in the common bearing of wartime burdens. According to his report, the Regent was surrounded by aristocrats, Jewish capitalists and religious people, and he would not be the true ruler of the situation until he was freed from them. A change in government seemed to be necessary but, for the time being, plans for this had encountered difficulties. Veesenmayer claimed that Germany could not seriously count on the Hungarian right's "national" parties. Although he did not hold the Hungarian army, which had failed on the front and had produced the most disastrous result from among the "Balkan" peoples, in high esteem, he still placed emphasis on the army as the only mass organization to be able to play a role in Hungary. According to him, the army was the only tool that the regime had not fully contained yet. That was the reason why the government tried to remove every officer of "national" sentiment and why their replacements were closely watched, with every movement choked off. Not long before, at Keresztes-Fischer's suggestion, the Regent had censured four generals and four officers. General Vörös was the one who tried to keep defeatism out of the army. Consequently, Veesenmayer claimed, at that point neither the leadership nor the troops were homogenous enough to count as an independent political force.[9] Taking every factor into consideration, Veesenmayer said that if push came to shove, external force should be applied. In his view an SS division in Budapest would be enough to execute a change of regime.

Veesenmayer's claim that there was an attempt to clean up the army was an exaggeration. Most of the relevant planned changes remained only plans, although it would simplify the issue for us if their causes were narrowed down to just the issue of German influence. The Chief of the General Staff was also hindered by the fact that he could not share his honest views with anyone outside a few generals and General Staff officers—such as Gyula Kádár— because he did not know their views: how committed they were to the Germans and how they might be connected with the different groups of the extreme right. A good General Staff officer was disciplined, provided excellent work, fully complied with his commands, and acted on the basis of allied loyalty, and thus he would be lavishly praised by his superiors and given the appropriate awards. Behind these qualities it was difficult to discern if a man held anti-German sentiments, and under these circumstances it was difficult to choose General Staff officers who would be reliable in serving a new and more complicated political situation that might be antithetical to the one thus far. Every single reorganization provoked the General Staff's suspicion. Without a proper excuse—which was difficult to find—it was impossible to remove heavily decorated General Staff officers from their positions within the sections of the General Staff.

Loyalty to the Axis allies was demanded from the officer corps, which had been educated to hold anti-Soviet, anti-Semitic and pro-German views. Many officers were closely connected with the Arrow-Cross, were pro-Imrédy, or were connected with other extreme right-wing parties, groups or cliques. Through these channels the Hungarian extreme right wing and German intelligence services were immediately informed about events or the mood within the army, and could use their friends there to aptly bring to bear influence.

Under such circumstances Szombathelyi had to be careful if he wanted to avoid a "palace revolution" by the General Staff that could have threatened even his own position. He had to face the fact that even if there were some officers of the General Staff, at the Ministry of Defense or among the troops who thought soberly and were open-minded, they were pretty much isolated among their peers. Although a willingness "to open up to the left" could be discovered among a few generals and General Staff officers, their careful attempts never led to any concrete action. As Kádár wrote in his memoirs, "The saddest characteristic of their behavior was that they hardly knew each other, and concealed their views. And they had to conceal them, because the statements by their officials and high superiors glorified standing one's ground in the war. If the statements and commands of the Commander-in-Chief, of all the military superiors, and of government officials demand that, then an openly contrary position is impossible from a soldier."[10]

He was especially disturbed by the dilettantism of both right- and left-wing politicians in military issues. He often gave free rein to bitter and angry outbursts, which made cooperation between him and civilians working on how to break away from the war impossible.

He often had disagreements with the army's generals. He had an especially reserved relationship with Vilmos Nagybaczoni Nagy, which had been aggravated by the General Staff section chiefs' various machinations.

Yet he had excellent relations with the next Minister of Defense, Lieutenant-General Lajos Csatay, who was a well-trained soldier without any political flair. Csatay felt inferior towards Szombathelyi, completely submitted himself to Szombathelyi's views, and was the voice for Szombathelyi's opinions in the Council of Ministers. More than once he landed himself in an awkward situation when, after interpreting Szombathelyi's views to the Council, he had to face the contrary opinions of most of the ministers.[11]

In his memoirs Gyula Kádár also spoke about one of Szombathelyi's attitudes, one that often repelled even left-wing circles close to him. He would immediately reject any charge or accusation against an army officer by civilians, an attitude that often brought about serious consequences. He tried to retain his belief in an officer's honor, in loyalty towards one's superiors, and in the dictum of full compliance with commands. He was angry at anyone who proved to him his officers' misuse of power or rowdiness, or who forced him to take them to task. He did not want to believe that there might exist a situation in which the officer corps might not follow the instructions of its commander-in-chief or chief of staff.

Nothing ever materialized from the sporadic attempts at rapprochement with the Western Allies or feelers for peace that were sent out. No idea was formulated or plan developed for military cooperation should a British–American disembarkation occur in the Balkans, nor was a plan ever developed for resistance against an expected German occupation or a probable takeover attempt by the extreme right. Under the prevailing circumstances, making the necessary military preparations within the upper echelon of the *Honvédség* and the officer corps without the Germans' or the extreme right's getting wind of it and immediately applying countermeasures was impossible. Szombathelyi or another high-ranking general, at Horthy's instruction, could have involved a few of the reliable generals, such as Nagy, Náday, Lakatos, Dálnoki Veress or Rőder, as well as General Staff officers, in such preparations. However, such a narrow circle would have necessarily been isolated, and taking the necessary steps to realizing their ideas—such as instructions to the troops—carried the danger of an immediate exposure. But the basic requirement, the supreme warlord's command, was the thing that was missing. It never occurred to Horthy to issue such a command directed against his German ally. And he could not force himself to do it even much later.

In the summer of 1943 Szombathelyi commissioned Kádár to prepare a plan for how the military would switch sides, with some probable help from the West. The plan had to include "how much assistance by air would be needed, where and with what direction of advance an Allied force would land, what should be taken in hand, how and with what forces the *Honvédség* could connect to these military operations, and so on." Kádár wrote that "three divisions transported by air would be the necessary minimum, along with parachutist securing troops, freight planes, a landing area on the *Hortobágy*, and defense along the River Tisza. Measures would have to be taken so that the army corps in eastern Hungary would partly join and partly offer security against the Romanians."[12] The Chief of the General Staff quickly returned the plan as not being topical and as being too "romantic." As Kádár put it, Szombathelyi probably needed it for his usual meditation. He wanted to be convinced—or this is what he had said anyway—that the prerequisites for the execution of such a switchover did not exist and was that the whole idea was not timely.

The parties of the extreme right launched a campaign against Minister of Defense Vilmos Nagybaczoni Nagy. They blamed the destruction of the 2nd Hungarian Army on Nagy's parsimoniousness, saying that it also seriously affected the German troops. He was blamed for his earlier roles in the country's economy, his pro-Jewish views, and measures that were taken in the interest of the forced labor battalions. All this was topped off by legal proceedings brought by the Minister of Defense against Imrédy and Rajniss for dishonorable behavior as reserve officers. The two were also parliamentary representatives.

In Parliament the pro-Imrédy representatives signed up for questions against Nagy, who, in return, offered his resignation first to Kállay and then to Horthy himself. He wanted to prevent an attack on the government initiated through an attack on him. He asked for an audience with Horthy, and handed over a memorandum that included a list of the causes of the campaign against him: "According to the right wing, my behavior on the Jewish issue does harm to the universal interests of the Hungarian nation. And since I refuse to fulfill the German military's demands, I hinder a full and complete cooperation with the Germans, which therefore threatens the interests of the Hungarian nation... Based on confidential reports I am aware that the attack by Imrédy's group on me is not an isolated affair of certain representatives but a long-decided party-alliance program to overthrow me. Imrédy's circle considers the Regent, the Minister of the Interior and me alike as their enemies.

In their view the Hungarian government relies for support on these three factors... Our removal is the most important prerequisite of the party-alliance's future role."[13] He went on to say that the Germans were behind Imrédy's circle, which hoped for their support and therefore went out of its way to serve them in order to gain favor: "Here at home the leaders of the right-wing party alliance do not make a secret of the fact that they would ensure a much larger military contribution for the common fight than the present government. They present the campaign against me as their attempt to thwart the government's procrastinating policy and to make a Hungarian mobilization on the Axis side possible. Certain signs have shown that a concrete agreement was concluded for the campaign against me—or at least that there is a silent consent between the two Arrow-Cross camps—although in the case of a successor to my position there is a vital difference."[14]

Finally Nagy warned the Regent that the fight alongside the Axis, which had strained Hungary's capabilities so far, should not be allowed to go on until the country was destroyed. At the threshold of the final outcome of the war, Hungary should not be further weakened. He asked the Regent not to agree to deploy any more military forces to the front. Hungary had to prepare for the possibility of Romania's turning against it should the Allies land in the Balkans or due to some other turn of military or political events. This was the reason why more forces should not be deployed outside the borders of Hungary, and "that is the reason why I consider the offer by Imrédy's circle to the Germans not only to be based on military ignorance, but also to be a downright sinful abrogation of the interests of the Hungarian nation."[15]

Horthy did not accept the Minister of Defense's resignation, and, for the time being, Kállay reacted the same way.

Before the May 4 session of the House of Representatives, when Nagy's questioning was supposed to occur, Kállay convened a session of the Council of Ministers. He announced that the excessive behavior of the parties of the extreme right was disturbing the government's work and would not be allowed to continue. He claimed that it was equally intolerable that the Minister of Defense be questioned. Therefore, he had requested from Horthy that the session be postponed.

Yet the campaign against Nagy did not stop. The text of the postponed questioning time was printed and disseminated by the extreme right. Kállay gave in and, in the interest of political peace and in order to stabilize his government's situation, tried to convince the Regent to accept Nagy's resignation. Horthy, however, did not budge. Keresztes-Fischer then warned Nagy that Kállay had been working against him behind the scenes.

The Germans' growing demand for the dismissal of the Hungarian Minister of Defense was the main factor behind the strengthening of the extreme right's campaign. The 2nd Section of the General Staff secretly tapped Italian Ambassador Anfuso's radiogram to Mussolini and sent it to Kállay and Nagy. Anfuso reported on a discussion with Jagow, conducted in mid-May, in which Jagow said he hoped that Kállay and his government would soon be toppled from the inside. Until this happened he would request from Kállay the "solution" to the Jewish question and request Nagy's dismissal.[16]

Kállay sent for Anfuso and confidentially informed him that the German ambassador, or the German Embassy, had urged the right-wing opposition to stage a parliamentary attack on the Minister of Defense, and that it would not withdraw the interpellation, even at the request of the Regent and the Prime Minister. Anfuso, who immediately reported to Jagow about his private conversation with Kállay, castigated Kállay for not being responsive to the Germans' requests, and warned him about Germany's crucial influence. Kállay supposedly responded that, except for the Jewish question, he was willing to fulfill Germany's requests.[17]

Finally, at Hitler's and Mussolini's prodding Kállay persuaded Horthy to accept Nagy's resignation. Nagy's successor, General Lajos Csatay, occupied his new position on June 12. The reliable and apolitical Csatay was considered to be a good soldier and was never charged with undue sympathy towards the Germans. He was reticent by nature and usually assumed a neutral position; therefore he was acceptable to everyone, including the extreme right. Based on favorable information from the army, the opinion of one of the German Embassy's co-workers was that Csatay was suitable to fill the chair of the portfolio: "He has no political role; he is a troop commander. He is entirely pro-German and definitely an anti-Semite, although a bit lazy, quiet, clever and cautious. He stubbornly insists on the implementation of decisions. Archduke Albrecht, who highly respects him, called my attention to him. He considers him to be accountable."[18]

Following the Anglo-Saxon armies' debarkation in Sicily and Mussolini's downfall, the Germans, distrustful of the Hungarian government, paid close attention to how events were received in Budapest. They were especially interested in the military's opinion and attitude towards a possible debarkation of the Allies in the Balkans.

The German military attaché, Pappenheim, spoke with both Foreign Affairs and General Staff officials about the situation after Mussolini's pull-out. They agreed that Italy was not at all in a situation to continue the war without help. Besides, in their view, any switch on the part of the new Prime Minister of Italy, Field Marshall Pietro Badoglio, over to the Allies was not likely, because he would clearly remember events following World War I and what a country could expect after quitting the war. In addition, the threat of the Italian communist movement also tied him to Germany, since an unconditional surrender would open up the way for the communists. On the other hand, Germany was also motivated to get rid of the burden of the Italian ballast, since it led to a military disadvantage. It should also be taken into consideration that if Italy were occupied, it would be possible for the Allies to bomb both Germany and Hungary from the south.[19]

According to the German intelligence's evaluation of the situation, Mussolini's pull-out originally had a stimulating effect on the Hungarian followers of the Western Allies. Yet this impact was now vanishing, because Italy's immediate collapse had not taken place. The political forces behind the Italian government's readiness to pull out had assumed a "wait-and-see" position. With a typical approach of leaving the military issues behind, the Western-oriented Hungarians hoped to divert the advance of the Allies expected to land in the Balkans towards Hungary by political methods and by using their connections. In this way the Hungarian government could "sail into neutrality." Although the Hungarians expected to lose Sub-Carpathia and the Bácska, they hoped to re-annex Transylvania in return for their better cooperation and behavior than that of the Romanians.

German intelligence claimed that the Hungarian government counted on using the army of 18 infantry regiments (9 of which were providing occupational tasks in Ukraine) to implement its plan. They also had two armored divisions, although one was still under development. The government would probably make an attempt to have its divisions transported home, so that all its army corps would be inside Hungary in case there were an Allied debarkation in the Balkans. If the Reich demanded that Hungary participate in the military defense of the southeast, the Hungarian government would probably refuse the demand by referring to military materials shortages and the necessity of securing the country's internal situation.

German intelligence warned the German leadership not to count on involving the Hungarian forces too much in the fight against the Allies. At present there was no assurance that the Hungarian military leadership wanted to fight them, and nor was the Hungarian army easing up its demands with regard to equipment. In terms of artillery, the divisions in Ukraine were only half as well equipped as the now destroyed 2nd Hungarian Army had been. They were experiencing shortages in mortars, tanks, and so on. According to the report of the Group Chief of the Hungarian Material Supply, the equipping of the divisions in Hungary would only be finished by May 1944. And by then their armaments would be irretrievably obsolete.

Furthermore, in order to conceal its goals, the Hungarian government was trying to avoid any demonstration against the Reich. This explains Clodius' successful economic conferences.[20]

On July 30 Szombathelyi gave a talk to his highest-level commanders in the Officers' Club. The event ended with Csatay's concluding remarks; he grasped the opportunity to reassure everyone about the position of the army. It seemed that the situation was being stabilized in Sicily and, supposedly, Badoglio had no plans to capitulate. Therefore, Germany would win significant time to remain in a favorable position in Europe. The equipping of the *Honvédség* should be accelerated, but the principle of having fewer but better-equipped units should be kept in mind. The Hungarian army ought to be prepared for securing the internal front at all times.

It caused quite a stir at the end of his presentation when, in speaking about the strength of the German–Hungarian friendship-in-arms, Csatay stated that Horthy would never break his promise. Since Csatay had always tried to avoid making political statements, many interpreted this to mean that he had been authorized to make the statement.[21]

According to Pappenheim it must have been said in the spirit of the July 29 Crown Council, where Horthy made a similar statement during an analysis of the post-Mussolini situation. On the other hand, it might also be possible that this statement was given to the well-meaning Csatay to say, in order to alleviate Germany's cautiousness.[22]

During General Csatay's introductory visit in August, Hitler renewed his demand for Hungary's participation in the occupation of Serbia. Hitler elaborated on the military situation, which he considered satisfactory and even reassuring, in spite of the territorial losses and the Italian breakaway. After dispersing Csatay's doubts, Hitler came to the point: "The defense of the Balkans' shores will be taken over by the Germans. We would like the Hungarians to take over the defense and coverage of the German soldiers. In order to discuss this and to have talks about it, Szombathelyi is expected at the General Headquarters."[23]

At home Csatay informed the government of his impressions of the visit and the fact that even though the Germans' situation was difficult, they still persisted. He also made reference to the Germans' goodwill, which the Hungarians could not afford to lose, since all the "important armaments" were from them. Furthermore, it was in Hungary's interest that the Germans would fight the Russians as successfully as possible. All things considered, Csatay wondered whether it would not in fact be more advantageous for Hungary to withdraw 100,000 men from the eastern front so that they would rather be deployed in Yugoslavia: "This would be of serious help to the Germans, and it would not be a greater sacrifice for us than [what we have done] so far, and nor would it be a less favorable situation than the present one."[24]

The Council of Ministers did not agree with Csatay, and once again the German request remained unfulfilled. Keresztes-Fischer made the sharpest remark of all against the renewed German request, as noted in the meeting's minutes: "As far as the German wish that we function behind the German army in the Balkans is concerned, he took the most definite stand against it... This would be the complete and final destruction for us... That is why he personally would not take any responsibility and would come to certain conclusions about his own situation. On the other hand, we can only deal with our own interests. We have to be prepared for the final moment."[25]

Szombathelyi shared the Minister of Defense's opinion. The Germans seemed to have reached their goal in Hungary, and with Nagy's departure the Hungarian military command had become more unified and tolerant towards the Germans. Yet they were disappointed: once again the military was not able to persevere against Kállay and Horthy.

Kállay himself was pondering the possibility of fulfilling the Germans' request, and tried to harmonize it with his hopes of breaking with the Axis. In the case of a possible Anglo-American disembarkation, the possibility of establishing an immediate contact with them seemed to be favorable. The Prime Minister's pondering and his odd remarks indicating interest induced Csatay, in agreement with Szombathelyi, to inform the Germans that this time the Balkan affair was moving along in the best possible way towards succeeding. However, when Kállay raised the issue with the Allies and asked for the Americans to provide a supporting mediating role, he was flatly rejected, and so he quickly discarded the thought of a Balkan maneuver.[26]

The letter written to Szombathelyi by the Permanent Deputy of the Minister of Foreign Affairs, Andor Szentmiklósy, indicated a definite stand against participation in the Balkan occupation. Szentmiklósy emphasized the point that "the state of war between the Anglo-Saxon powers and Hungary can rather be defined as technical in nature, because we have not, so far, in fact participated in the war between Germany and the Anglo-Saxon powers. This situation would not be essentially changed by the fact of whether the Anglo-Saxon air forces attacked Hungary, because their air forces have launched air attacks against countries such as France, Belgium, Holland and so on, considered to be occupied by the enemy. Accepting the Minister of Defense's suggestion would transform this prevailing situation, and it would add an even heavier burden to Hungarian foreign policy at a time when the final outcome of the war is doubtful to say the least. Sooner or later the

Anglo-Saxon forces will appear in the Balkans, and the Hungarian army could encounter them on foreign territory. One of the principles of the Hungarian government is that, with the exception of Russia, it does not use the *Honvédség* beyond the borders of Hungary. We cannot break this principle without the gravest consequences. On the contrary, we have to target our attention towards doing away with the Russian exception."[27]

The Crown Council also passed a negative resolution, urging the Germans to transport the Hungarian occupational forces home. If this were not permitted, the resolution instructed the Chief of the General Staff to order their partial withdrawal home or their full withdrawal to an area nearer to the Hungarian border.[28]

It was unpleasant for Szombathelyi to inform the Germans about all the above; in order to protect himself from reprisals, he tried to disclaim any responsibility. In his analysis of the situation at the September 4, 1943, session of the Supreme Military Council—also recorded as a memoir—he pointed out the possible German reprisals, which it would be beneficial to avoid. In the introduction he said that events made it evident to him that the Germans had lost the war. He claimed that Germany was on the defensive on all fronts and the growing numerical superiority of the Allies did not make it possible that the Germans could initiate or wage a decisive blow anywhere. His goal was "to drag through the war until we reach an acceptable peace agreement."[29] However, he did not want to deal with the possibility of a complete collapse of the Germans, and went on believing that the German army was strong enough to squeeze out an acceptable peace. He did not see any other way out but to persist with the Germans, and to share their defeat or, as he hoped, an "acceptable" peace. Accordingly, he remained inclined "to deploy occupational forces to the Balkans so that Hitler 'would hand over' the occupational Hungarian divisions in Russia, which could then be utilized in defense of Hungarian soil."[30]

The Chief of the General Staff reiterated his earlier warning that no one should be under the illusion that with the withdrawal of the 2nd Hungarian Army the war was over for Hungary. There were newer and more difficult tasks for which to prepare. He also warned the officer corps in an earlier confidential command: "While the Russian war, with its extraordinary circumstances, made several phenomena understandable—even if not forgivable—an armed conflict taking place nearby should be judged from another angle. Here it will not be forgiven or appreciated."[31]

He further elaborated that during the peace following the war Hungarian interests would be endangered by neighboring peoples, and so Hungary should prepare to encounter that challenge: "Whichever party should win, neither will bring matters to a head. We will have to fight for it. Therefore, the nation must be awakened, so that it does not fare as it did in 1918."[32] Then he stated that the country's internal order had to be solidly preserved.

Szombathelyi once again cautioned the pro-Anglo-Saxon politicians that the German army's fighting spirit and strength were still unbroken, although it was in a tight spot. It was a vain hope that the alliance between Hungary and Germany could be dissolved by risking the danger of a German occupation, which, according to some speculators, would last for only a short time. The German army could inflict "cruel blows on anyone who revolts against it... Those who advocate this trend of thought do not think it over, because otherwise they would soon be taken aback. First of all, it would not be the Germans who would occupy us but the Romanians, the Slovaks and—in spite of their miseries—the Croats who would soon take back the areas that, according to the Treaty of Trianon, were theirs, and some more... They would do whatever they can to destroy our armed forces, the only support of our defense and sovereignty. They would disarm the army and would rob us of our weapons... Probably, Germany would only keep Budapest and, where the defense is stronger, would bomb it.

Obviously, in reaction to that, the Anglo-Saxons and the Russians would also bomb us. A few months would be enough to totally destroy us. Hungary would lose its sovereignty and could never reclaim the soil that its neighbors take away."[33]

According to Szombathelyi, this did not mean "senselessly" serving them: "We should not engage in adventures but, if needed, we have to make sacrifices in the interest of our sovereignty and to maintain our armed forces, and we should not even recoil from a task in the Balkans."[34]

Prime Minister Kállay responded to Szombathelyi's stern warning in a letter. Kállay thought that it should be considered whether the government should confront the threat of German occupation, which an open action might produce. However, he agreed with the views in connection with the Balkans, and asked Szombathelyi to do the same: "I fully share your reasoning and opinion with regard to military matters and with regard to national and military spirit and morale in every aspect. However, I do not see any causal relation between these matters and undertaking the Balkan job. With regard to the survival of the Hungarian nation, however, I consider any such enterprise as risking annihilation or irreparable harm. I cannot give my consent to it under any circumstances." Furthermore, he requested Szombathelyi that in compliance with the Crown Council's decision, "you should try to persuade the German military command to place the Hungarian troops in a situation where they can be utilized for the defense of the Hungarian borders, if needed. However, even the appearance of Hungary's intention to withdraw from the war in Russia should be avoided."[35]

Finally, Kállay emphatically asked Szombathelyi to be cautious at the Main Military Headquarters, and to keep the guidelines in mind, because "the Hungarian Royal government will not be able to accept anything that diverges from them." In a situation when a result could not be reached, Szombathelyi should strive to adhere to the established situation and try to negotiate for any humanly possible relief for the troops.[36]

In agreement with Szombathelyi, and hoping to be able to convince the Regent and Kállay before Szombathelyi left for the German Headquarters, Csatay told German Ambassador Jagow and Military Attaché Pappenheim that the Hungarian government's response would be positive. Therefore, already on September 6 both Jagow and Pappenheim reported to the OKW that the Regent had agreed with Csatay's suggestion. Csatay "has expressed his opinions in the Cabinet, and everywhere, as confidently and decisively as he has to our ambassador. This fact once again proves that, in our interpretation, the Minister of Defense is the most positive factor in Hungary." Furthermore, Pappenheim stated that he would mention the deployment of the Hungarian troops in the Balkans in connection with the withdrawal of some of the occupational forces in Ukraine during the Chief of the General Staff's upcoming visit: "The Germans' courtesy, or even some reference to it shown in this issue, would stabilize the situation of the *Honvédség*'s leaders vis-à-vis the politicians."[37]

It was clear from the above that the Germans held a favorable impression of the Hungarian military leadership. And, the Germans' good opinion about Csatay was also an expression of satisfaction with the Chief of the General Staff, since it was well known that Csatay primarily voiced the Chief of the General Staff's opinion. The Germans also recognized the controversy caused by a lack of confidence, which fundamentally characterized the relationship between the military and the political leadership. Furthermore, they also recognized that the supreme military leadership had not initiated, and had been left out of, the process of sending out peace feelers. They were afraid that this controversy would lead to a break between Kállay and the military leadership. Pappenheim wrote the following: "It should be recognized that the military command's situation is not firm. Therefore, in my view, our courtesy in the issue of withdrawing the Ukrainian divisions should not go so far that the Hungarian political leadership comes under the impression that Hungary can completely withdraw itself from the fight in the east. Furthermore, it should also be considered that, in the uncertain situation in Hungary, those Hungarian troops deployed in German districts form a valuable pawn."[38]

According to Kádár, Szombathelyi delivered the negative response to Pappenheim right before his departure on the train setting out for the German Headquarters. As Pappenheim's telegram of September 15 forwarded to the OKW clearly states, Szombathelyi transferred the odium of the affair to Kállay and his government's "civilian" members, since they had convinced Horthy to change his position: "The Chief of the General Staff is not authorized to promise to send troops to the Balkans... The general attitude of the Hungarian military in connection with the common warfare continues to remain positive, and this is especially true with regard to the sending of Hungarian troops to the Balkans. In opposition to the government and especially to Minister of Foreign Affairs Ghyczy, the Minister of Defense and the Chief of the General Staff could not prevail with the Regent, and are appalled by their government's cowardice—as they put it. The Chief of the General Staff declared that under these circumstances he was ashamed to travel to the Headquarters."[39]

This was Pappenheim's exaggerated interpretation of Szombathelyi's opinion, when, in an awkward situation, he tried to place himself and his "informer" Szombathelyi in a favorable light before the OKW. However, knowing Szombathelyi's nature, his prejudice, his anxiety when he had discussions with Hitler and the German military leaders at the German Headquarters, and his wounded vanity and anger at Kállay, the angry outburst cited by Pappenheim must have occurred.

Jagow also proposed to the German Ministry of Foreign Affairs that Germany take a hard stand if Szombathelyi rejected the proposal of deploying Hungarian troops in Serbia or if he asked for the withdrawal of the eastern security forces. He considered an appropriate response to be the threat of taking away from Hungary all the territories re-annexed after 1938, in order to impress the Hungarian government, which dreaded the loss of its freshly retrieved territories and would thus be ready to do anything to keep them. In Jagow's view, Szombathelyi should be told that, according to the German military command's interpretation, "Hungary did not wish to continue the armed fight, in Europe's interest, and wished to play the role of a neutral country to a certain extent. Such a position fundamentally changes Hungary's relationship with Germany. We interpret a withdrawal from the war effort as Hungary's giving up its territorial demands and, practically, re-establishing its Trianon borders. We will draw the appropriate conclusions and will occupy, and involve under our administration, territories allotted to Hungary since 1938 through German decisions or through the action of German troops."[40]

Szombathelyi was given the cold shoulder when he arrived at the German Headquarters on September 18. Hitler, who by then had been informed about the Hungarian position, did not even raise the request in connection with the Balkans, simply acknowledging the Hungarian government's rejection. He said that he would turn the originally grave Italian situation to his advantage. He expected to receive one million workers, and he would, as a result, be able to free half a million Germans for his army. The Anglo-Saxon armies might carry out their operations in Italy, although a landing in the Balkans was not out of the question, in which case he would immediately launch a counterattack in Italy.

Hitler emphasized to Szombathelyi the point that, in order to reinforce the Balkans and the Italian front, Axis forces had to be withdrawn from the eastern front, leaving it without reserves. He continued that he would avoid heavy fighting on the eastern front so as to be able to establish central reserves in the Balkans. As far as the British were concerned, he would launch a devastating submarine offensive against them, while also significantly decreasing the efficiency of their air attacks by the gradual expansion of the German air defense.

When Hitler proceeded to inquire about the Hungarian occupational troops, Szombathelyi mentioned the fact that one division was fighting on the first line while the others were being regrouped behind the lines. He cautioned Hitler that the VIII. Army Corps, which was located further north, should join the VII. Army Corps in withdrawing, so that the whole Hungarian occupational force would get back to its natural communication line, the Kiev–Lemberg line.

The Führer listened to Szombathelyi's analysis about the occupational forces without making any remarks, and became animated only when Szombathelyi spoke about the great concern that Hungarians felt at the news of air raids on German cities. Hitler went into detail in explaining how excellently the Germans behaved in enduring the blows. He claimed that the loss of industrial production was only about 15–20%, which would be made up within a few weeks.

In finishing the audience, Hitler spoke about the period following the expected victory, when he would teach everyone a lesson, just as he had done with the Italian traitors.[41]

Listening to Hitler, Szombathelyi could hardly be reassured. Although Hitler did not offer a contrary view on sensitive issues, Szombathelyi did not consider his mission successful, because he thought that he had heard blame from Hitler during the detailed Balkan analysis. And silence in connection with the occupying Hungarian troops was not exactly a clear agreement with the implementation of the Hungarian plans.

The Hungarian decision not to contribute to the Balkan forces was a bad disappointment for the OKW as well. To replace the grave losses following the Kursk defeat, and to confront the quickly advancing Soviet troops who had liberated Harkov on September 22 and Smolensk on September 24, an urgent deployment of reserves was needed in order to solidify the front. The OKW was deeply concerned about the Italian cease-fire following the Anglo-Saxon forces' landing in Calabria and Salerno, which had required the Germans to occupy northern and central Italy.

After seeing Hitler, Szombathelyi was received by Keitel in the company of General Kurt Zeitzler, the Chief of the General Staff of the OKW. The tasks awaiting the Hungarian troops in the Balkans were given a general outline, and a new German request was introduced: Hungary was requested to assist with the settling of the training units of the *Luftwaffe*; in this way at least, it would increase its contribution to the common war effort. These units could at least be used for the defense of Hungarian airspace. Szombathelyi did not give a straightforward response, but noted that people in Budapest were extremely scared of the Allies' air raids, which would definitely occur if the Hungarian troops were put into action beyond the River Dráva. He did not add that settling the German air bases in Hungary would have the same consequences, eliciting Allied air raids. After all this, Szombathelyi only cautiously dared to mention the issue of transporting the occupational Hungarian divisions home from Ukraine. Keitel rigidly rejected the request, since the replacement of the troops would pose inextricable difficulties for the Germans. Finally, Szombathelyi set out to discuss just how important the German help was to the Hungarians in producing the armaments and equipment for the newly developing Hungarian army. He said that he fully realized why Germany—considering all its hardships—could not fulfill its promises, but asked Keitel that they would nevertheless be fulfilled.[42]

After the departure of the Chief of the Hungarian General Staff, the OKW did not hesitate to take what it considered to be the necessary steps in the situation. The OKW was convinced that an intention of breaking away from the Axis underlay the rigid rejection by the Hungarian government of the German request, and preventing that was in Germany's basic interest. A repeat of the Italian breakaway could not be tolerated. Germany could not give Hungary up, since it was a strategically important area and economic base, and nor could it ignore the possibility of utilizing the remaining Hungarian forces. Therefore, General Warlimont of the OKW, received instructions to prepare for Hungary's occupation. In preparing Operation Margarethe, both Hungary's and Romania's occupation—perhaps both at the same time—had to be considered. Warlimont established that the situation would pose many difficulties and would surpass the capabilities of the German army.[43]

Similarly, Romania, also pondering the idea of breaking away and so trying to establish connections with the Western powers, became the object of suspicion by the German military command. The OKW viewed the region with growing unease, in spite of the fact that, during his discussions at the German Headquarters on September 2 and 3, Antonescu assured Hitler about his and his country's steadfast loyalty and about the undiminished fighting spirit of the Romanian troops.[44]

The OKW had prepared the first version of Operation Margarethe by October 30, during which time it realized that in spite of the most careful preparation it would not be able to avoid having to improvise during the implementation of the plan, which recommended three operational zones:[45]

1) the region spreading as far as the River Tisza, including Budapest and the bulk of the Hungarian army's garrisons, was to be occupied by the *Wehrmacht*;
2) the region east of the River Tisza would be occupied primarily by the Romanian army;
3) the region north and northeast of the River Tisza was to be occupied by German and Slovakian troops.

It was calculated that eight days would be needed for the necessary troop concentration, which was to be performed as a troop maneuver so as to distract the Hungarian military command's attention. The forces thrusting up from the south would concentrate for a large-scale anti-partisan offensive north of Belgrade.

The plan indicated that the German army's attitude towards the Hungarian army would depend on how the situation developed. It spoke about "ruthless quenching" and the disarmament of Hungarian troops in the case of resistance. However, it also held that a favorable political solution was possible, which would make an armed intervention and disarmament of the Hungarian troops unnecessary. In the latter case, the chance to win over the Hungarian troops should be kept in mind.

The plan had to be redrawn several times. While the main goals and directions of the plan remained through each revision, an important principle emerged that every four weeks the plan would be re-evaluated and the troops would be re-designated for Operation Margarethe, according to the most recent troop movements along the fronts.[46]

A new version was completed by November 7, and on November 11 the OKW drafted a memorandum of the units available starting on December 1. In spite of the greatest efforts taken, only units at the level of battalions and divisions of poor combat value could be held in readiness, along with tank units and other battle-weary units under development. The German army could not afford to keep units representing important military value in one place at readiness with the intention of withdrawing them from the battle, since the situation on the fronts kept absorbing all new reserves. Thus, the only approach that the OKW could take was to reckon that, if Operation Margarethe were to be implemented, these weaker forces placed on alert could be reinforced by mostly armored troops of high combat value that were temporarily withdrawn from the front and detailed to the operation.[47]

While the OKW was issuing the command to draw up Operation Margarethe, Pappenheim, who thought that he had been misled by the Hungarian government, along with the military command, wrote an angry memorandum about the Hungarian situation to his superiors, which was also sent to Lieutenant Colonel Oswald, German liaison officer at the headquarters of the Hungarian occupational forces. In this memorandum Pappenheim claimed that the Hungarians and their government were sitting on the fence in the war and expected the country to break away from the Axis at the right moment. Pappenheim also called attention to the unreliability of the Hungarian occupational forces, which made it necessary to pay increased attention to them and to place them at the furthest possible point from the Carpathians. They should possibly be wedged amidst German units. In the case of a Hungarian break-away from the Axis, they could serve as hostages in the hands of the German military command.[48]

The encoded report also made way into the hands of Colonel General Géza Lakatos, the commander of the occupational forces, who considered it to be an insult to his and his troops' honor. He placed a complaint with Szombathelyi, requested that he lodge a protest with the German military command against Pappenheim's despicable aspersions, and initiated demands that Pappenheim be recalled from office.[49] However, it was all unnecessary. The OKW could not understand how the memorandum got into Hungarian hands or how it was deciphered, and Pappenheim was blamed for all that. The attaché was compromised in Budapest, and was therefore unfit for further service; he was recalled on October 8. General Hans Greiffenberg was dispatched to Budapest as his successor.[50]

Returning from the German Headquarters, the Chief of the General Staff experienced a feeling of growing distrust coming from the Prime Minister, who had commissioned Gyula Kádár—also travelling with Szombathelyi—to pay close attention to his boss's behavior at the Headquarters. After returning home, Kádár was to report immediately if Szombathelyi had made any promises beyond the instructions given to him.[51] As opposed to Kállay, Szombathelyi viewed the Italian developments and the military's failure in arranging a cease-fire as the justification of his own views. The fact that Germany had the strength to occupy Italy, to disarm the Italian units, and to open up a new front against the Anglo-American troops disembarking in southern Italy reinforced his conviction that a mistaken step by Hungary or straining the Germans' patience might result in a German occupation. Such a situation, however, would make the free movement and free use of the Hungarian army impossible, and would facilitate the extreme right's coming to power. All this would offer unimaginable advantages to the Romanians, who were supported by the Germans in any case. He was gradually losing faith in the possibility of an Anglo-American landing in the Balkans, and believed that staying with the Germans was the only way to save the regime.[52]

The Italian events did not just affect Szombathelyi; they also unnerved the precious few in the army who had been contemplating the possibility of a military breakaway from the Axis. At the same time, the extreme right was jubilant and more and more noisily demanded full power in order to be able to prevent a "betrayal" like the one that had occurred in Italy.

Kállay was not in any position to propose Szombathelyi's dismissal, even though he had opposed his policy for the second time in front of the Regent. On the one hand, Kállay could not find anyone with whom to safely replace Szombathelyi; on the other, such a step might have induced the immediate intervention of the Germans, who were near the end of the tether in terms of their distrust of Kállay in any case. Werth could be sent away due to his extreme pro-German policy, but this could not be done with Szombathelyi at that point. However, a few months later Szombathelyi did leave, but at the Germans' request, when they withdrew their confidence in him because he had not been aggressive enough towards the Hungarian government in getting their requests fulfilled.

The result of the so-called "Veress-mission," which had come to his attention in the meantime, also convinced Szombathelyi about the necessity of keeping up a pro-German orientation. On August 16 in Istanbul, Hungarian Commissioner László Veress delivered a message to the Allies in which, under the impact of the Italian events and counting on the immediate appearance of Anglo-American troops in the Balkans and in Hungary, a group consisting of the Prime Minister, the Minister of the Interior, the Minister of Foreign Affairs, the head of the Political Department of the Ministry of Foreign Affairs and the Chief of the General Staff informed the Allies about Hungary's terms for surrender: "Hungary accepts the form of unconditional surrender and will try to realize it as soon as possible. The group declares that the Hungarian army is ready to defend [the Hungarian] borders against the Germans, fully submits its airports and other military establishments to the Allies' disposal, and will fully cooperate with the Allies to facilitate their occupation of the country."[53]

The writers of the message, completely detached from reality as they were, counted on an Anglo-American occupation of Hungary executed by forces and airborne operations larger than any experienced during the war thus far. Such an operation, however, was not among the plans of the Anglo-American military leaders even in the event of a possible Balkan landing. This hope was cherished by Prime Minister Kállay and circles around him based only on the hope of a miracle, and it was totally unfounded. In order to encourage the Anglo-American operation in their own way, they tried to exaggerate its expected success and, irresponsibly, they spoke about being prepared to turn on the German troops, although they well knew that the *Honvédség* had not at all been prepared for the promised cooperation with the Allies.

Szombathelyi was aware of the condition of the *Honvédség*, and therefore the idea of his alleged participation in the group's work, or at least in drawing up the military segment of the message, should be taken with a grain of salt. He could not have believed in the militarily unfounded operations for which Kállay and his circle had hoped, and Szombathelyi must have informed Kállay about it. Therefore, it was unlikely that he would have contributed to writing such a false and irresponsible promise. It is quite likely, however, that including the Chief of the General Staff among the writers of the message was done without his knowledge, or at least without his agreement, since without him whatever had been stated about the Hungarian army would have been even less convincing to the Allies.

The Allies' response of August 23, relayed from the British, which contained the preliminary armistice conditions, came like a cold shower to the Hungarians. It said that a Hungarian capitulation—synchronized with the Italian one—would be favorable for the Allies, because it would force the withdrawal of German troops from the front, especially the eastern front. In addition, it would have a favorable demonstration effect on all the other satellite countries pondering the same issue. Yet the Allies also said that they could neither send troops nor extend armed help to Hungary. Consequently, they did not really think that it was possible that Hungary would undertake the capitulation, since it would entail a German occupation. Therefore, they modified their preliminary armistice conditions in the following way: the Hungarian government should deny the transport of German troop and war materials across Hungary, and Hungary itself should not deliver raw materials to Germany. Furthermore, Hungary should prove its good intentions "by ending every cooperation with Germany and by hindering and delaying each one of its actions. Moreover, Hungary should possibly pursue minor sabotage." Finally, they also required that Hungary would facilitate the operation of the Allies' intelligence in Hungary.[54]

As the absence of the allied troops in the Balkans and in Hungary and the lack of armed help became more certain, Szombathelyi, who had not had much trust in them in any case, came to view it as impossible for Hungary to fulfill Great Britain's conditions, because it would induce Germany to occupy Hungary, which would not be able to defend itself against it. The Germans would make it impossible for the Hungarian war industry to function, and would merge it with the German industrial complex, with unfortunate results. This would completely end the equipping of the *Honvédség*, which had been beset with major problems in any case. The Germans would also force the Hungarians to deploy the whole *Honvédség* to the eastern front. Therefore, in order to maintain the existing military forces and their freedom of action, he suggested staying with the Germans and cautiously fulfilling their requests.

The Hungarian response to the Allies' conditions was delayed. Kállay did not dare to agree to their fulfillment. However, on September 7 the Allies urged Hungary to respond and, in the case of a favorable response, they requested that a Hungarian military envoy travel to Istanbul in order to discuss the military issues involved.[55]

The Allied governments became increasingly aware of the fact that the Kállay government was delaying in answer, while trying to avoid any step that would entail a break or a clash with the Germans. The government found itself caught in contradictions caused by previously giving false information about the army. Its reputation was now damaged. The Hungarian government soon recognized that the image of the army's condition that it had given at the encouragement of the Allies could not be maintained, since, in the meantime, the Allies must have informed themselves about the army. In the absence of outside Anglo-Saxon armed help, there were no suitable and available military or political forces on which the government could rely.

Since the fall of 1943 the government had striven to convince the Allied governments that its hands were tied by the possibility of grave consequences following any potential German occupation. It was one of the primary tasks of Antal Ullein-Reviczky, who had just been appointed Hungarian ambassador to Stockholm, to maintain connections with the Allied governments through the British government and to try to convince them about the measures that Hungary had planned to take by deploying all its resources against the Germans as soon as the Allies reached the Hungarian borders. "Every action" executed before the arrival of the Allied troops "would be hasty and would be of harmful consequences for the Allies as well." The fact was that the Germans would also occupy the important military points, which would be followed by the liquidation of pro-Western elements in the country as well as the Jewish population. A total ransacking of the country could not be avoided, and "the million-strong army, which had potentially been prepared to fight against Germany at the side of the Allies, would be paralyzed."[56]

The Allies received the negative Hungarian response to their demands only in October. Their October 27 summary established that the Hungarian Cabinet had been lethargic about dealing with the Italian events and about the postponement of a military action. It was now forced to admit—contrary to its earlier statements and to its own excuse—that it did not trust the army's leadership and could not complete its ongoing campaign to purge or demote pro-German commanders: "The Hungarian government is compelled to honestly point out that the Hungarian army did not keep pace with the political development of the public, and that there is a methodical cleansing going on in the military at key positions, which is the main cause of the Germans' suspicion. These measures have not been completed yet and, consequently, presently there are hindrances with regard to establishing military relations with the Allies." Therefore, the government could not establish connections between the Hungarian General Staff and a British military mission, even though it attributed great importance to this, nor could it secure or guarantee the mission's security in Hungary. As for the future, the government could only promise a gradual decrease of cooperation with the Germans, while "geographical and historical factors will decide the speed at which it can be fully dissolved and the date when Hungary can be handed over to the Allies as a military base."[57]

During the autumn months of 1943 Szombathelyi's views about the developing Hungarian military policy underwent a certain modification, and he also moved towards a rapprochement with the government's guidelines; all this was primarily manifested in changes in his earlier approach towards, and understanding of, the deployment of the Hungarian troops in the Balkans. Analyzing the post-Teheran (November 28, 1943) military situation, as well as expected developments, he came to recognize that by deciding on a landing in the western European theater of war, the Allies had effectively discarded any plans for a Balkan disembarkation. This fact was reinforced by the slowing down of the Italian operations. At the same time Soviet troops were quickly approaching the Carpathians, which made Szombathelyi focus on the fact that the military situation necessitated concentrating all the mobilizable Hungarian military forces within the country's borders.

During the October 14 session of the Council of Ministers, Csatay announced that the Chief of the General Staff found it necessary to mobilize five infantry regiments and seven artillery battalions as well as the Rusinsko Mountain Brigade. But these units would remain at their garrisons for the time being.[58]

On November 8, trusting that Hitler would agree, Szombathelyi gave instructions to Colonel General Lakatos, the commander of the occupational forces, to start regrouping the troops to districts nearer to the border. On November 12, in order to gauge the German reactions, Szombathelyi sent a telegram to

Keitel indicating that he expected that his repeated request would now find understanding in the OKW and, therefore, he had already issued the command to withdraw the 18th and 19th Light Divisions. However, he did not meet with the understanding for which he had hoped. On the very same day Greiffenberg reported that Szombathelyi had modified his command and agreed that Hungarian troop movements would take place only with the agreement of the affected German military commands. The OKW issued an instruction that every Hungarian troop movement that lacked the OKW's permission should be hindered, by force if needs be.[59]

The Germans were not satisfied with the Hungarians' fighting spirit in any case. The Hungarians wanted to avoid fighting, and in some places they even tried to conclude an agreement with the partisans. Colonel General Lakatos' command of October 23 ordered his troop commanders to avoid atrocities: "The spirit of Hungarian chivalry and the military law inherited from our predecessors do not tolerate cruelty or inhuman treatment of the defeated enemy. Therefore, we have to be especially careful that, while fighting and annihilating the enemy, we do not commit unnecessary murders and should especially refrain from eradicating whole villages in vengeance."[60] The Hungarian troops should differentiate the partisans from the civilians.

In November, most probably on November 21, Szombathelyi once again visited the German Headquarters. In concord with the government's most determined instruction, he made an attempt to negotiate the withdrawal and transportation home of all the Hungarian occupational forces. He tried to convince Hitler that the stability of the southeastern front could essentially be guaranteed by relying on the Carpathians, where a decisive role was awaiting the Hungarian troops, who themselves would be able to take care of the task by utilizing the characteristics of the terrain if they had possession of the appropriate weapon replacements. Therefore, it was in Germany's interest to develop the Hungarian troops' armaments. He also requested an increase in German raw and war materials shipments to Hungary and a decrease in the number of Germans using the already contracted Hungarian war materials and raw materials.[61]

Hitler let Szombathelyi know that for want of rolling stock it was not possible to withdraw the Hungarian occupational forces at that moment. He also made him understand that the troops on the eastern front also filled the role of hostages in the case of a "careless" Hungarian step.[62]

In the meanwhile, Soviet troops occupied Kiev on November 6 and advanced westward, which resulted in the withdrawal of the Hungarian occupational forces to the Rovel–Kovno line. It was unlikely that the retreating Germans, who were in a very difficult situation themselves, would have agreed to withdraw the Hungarian troops.

In addition to the development of the military situation, and not independently of it, the deteriorating public atmosphere and restlessness in Hungary also induced Szombathelyi to try to concentrate the Hungarian forces within the country. There were reports coming in to the Ministry of Defense about the increasing dissatisfaction of the working class. The workers were becoming politically active, and the Social Democratic Party had started organizing variously sized movements within military industrial sites. The disciplinary situation within the war factories had also deteriorated, which threatened the *Honvédség*'s reinforcement with armaments. Szombathelyi attempted to reinforce order on the civilian frontline by "demanding discipline, the ruthless fulfillment of obligations, and order."[63]

Minister of Defense Csatay also expected that the "disciplinary" situation of the workers could be stabilized by the introduction of a heavy-handed policy. In November 1943 he requested the Council of Ministers' consent "to collect into labor units and to deploy to military zones the obstinately regressing and subversive workers. This was necessary because "in war industries the propaganda and machinations of the enemy, with the aim of breaking up the workers' discipline, is already increasing, with harmful consequences in the form of labor movements."[64]

Thus, Szombathelyi finally gave up his former role as fulfiller of German wishes when German demands towards the country became more and more impatient and serious. The Germans' distrust towards the government increased; in fact, they were already debating the modes and dates of the unavoidable occupation of Hungary. In spite of the rumors about German intentions, which reached both Szombathelyi and Kállay, they hoped that by voicing the necessity of the common defense against the Soviet troops and the preparations for that, by stabilizing the internal front in Hungary, and by fulfilling some of the German requests, they would be able to convince Hitler about the honesty of Hungarian intentions and persuade him that a German occupation was unnecessary. Even the *Wehrmacht*'s leaders recognized the change in Szombathelyi's behavior.[65]

During the autumn, the reports of German agents and their Hungarian supporters that were sent to Berlin multiplied. They reported on the unreliability of Hungarians, on the government's obvious intent to break away from the Axis, and on the preparatory secret conferences, while also urging Germany's decisive intervention in Hungary. Independently of each other, the German Ministry of Foreign Affairs, the Security Office of the SS, and the German army diligently produced analyses of the situation for the Führer, while also making plans to execute them.

In his October 26 summary analysis of the situation to German Minister of the Interior and SS Chief Heinrich Himmler, Head of the Chief Security Office of the Reich Kaltenbrunner gave an analysis of the Hungarian breakaway plans and measures taken thus far. He indicated that his sources included high-ranking military and civilian circles. The report referred to people and secret discussions that had occurred in a confidential body created around

Horthy, yet minus any important military leader. This body's final analysis resolved that if, due to the military successes of the Anglo-Saxon armies, the situation along the southern border of Hungary turned critical, then it would appoint a new government headed by the Germanophobe Lipót Baranyai. All the existing ministers would be members of the new government except for Csatay, Reményi-Schneller and Szász. The task of the new government would be to dissolve the alliance with the German Reich and to conduct separate peace negotiations with the Allies. With that interest in mind, there were already extensive discussions going on with the British government through Istanbul, Switzerland and Lisbon. According to the report, the circle around Bethlen and Kállay hoped "to use Horthy, who was the Führer's weak spot, as a shield, while in the background the governing body would work to realize its goals essentially unchanged." Consequently, Hungary's reluctance to deploy troops to the Balkans "is only an introductory step to its earlier decision to turn away from the Reich," the report concluded.[66]

The Hungarian attempt to break away could happen at any moment, and it was in Germany's vital interest to prevent it. And so the report argued that the necessary political and military steps to act should be prepared. The situation must be precisely assessed, especially the situation of the Hungarian army, because the Germans did not have a consensus view, despite the established connections and the presence of reliable and capable men in the General Staff and officer corps. It was an open question how divided the Hungarian army and its leadership would be in the case of an open break with Germany, and in what proportion it would turn against the Germans should Horthy command it. This was not a negligible question, especially in view of the awareness about the weak quality of the troops assigned to Operation Margarethe, where success perhaps might partly depend on whether an organized resistance developed.

In his analysis of the situation on December 10, Veesenmayer was of the view that even though politically the army was only conditionally under the control of the government, still "the leadership and the troops are heavily contaminated and, in its present state, it is not the appropriate tool with which to establish a military dictatorship without any further ado." He went on to say that the reorganization of the army and the replenishment of its armaments would be necessary, so that the troops could be applied according to German demands, but that it could all still be sabotaged by unreliable elements within the command of the *Honvédség*. The Hungarians "carefully avoid applying strong personalities to head the army. However, they tolerate more or less good soldiers among the leadership, so that this admittedly important institution will not be discredited, all the more so because they never know when a new deployment will take place."[67] Here Veesenmayer was alluding to the assumed desire of the Hungarian military command not to compromise the army with the Western Allies by increasing commitments towards the Germans. What was more, it was Veesenmayer's assumption that the Hungarian military command was ready to turn the army against the Germans in any given situation. All in all, in the case of a regime change performed with German military help it would be quite possible that, "on the part of the army, we cannot count on any kind of armed support at the beginning." In that case, he continued, they would need to organize independent legions made up of reliable elements and leadership, who would fight wholeheartedly along with the German soldiers and would form the basis of a *Honvédség* newly organized according to the German system. A thorough screening of the officer corps would be indispensable.

Veesenmayer proposed to his superiors that Germany engage in suitable and multifaceted propaganda as a means to destroy the enemy by threats and promises or even military exercise-like troop concentrations at the Hungarian border. Horthy should be invited to meet Hitler and be brought to his senses by the method of specious offers followed by a verbal lashing. The main aim was to make him reform the government by an ultimatum-like demand. According to Veesenmayer, one should allude to the increased Bolshevik threat, both internally and externally, and to the unique role that the Regent might play in fending it off. One should also appeal to his weaknesses, such as his dynastic plans and the hope of a Hungarian free port, and so on. He should be won over for the reorganization of the *Honvédség* and for the establishment of proposed legions, for which the Reich would supply first-rate equipment.[68]

A December summary by the *Abwehr* sent to the OKW Chief of the General Staff based on Greiffenberg's reports also examined the situation of the *Honvédség* from the perspective of a probable occupying maneuver.[69] It stated that the Hungarian occupational units on the front now at their new districts were of poor fighting quality. They were too poorly trained to engage in battle with regular Soviet units. Their leadership was also weak, and many young active officers were missing. The equipping and training of reorganized divisions in Hungary was going on at a furious pace. Presently, eight infantry divisions of three segments, two armored divisions, one cavalry division and two mountain brigades were more or less available. The High Military Command planned to finish manning them, including the appropriate staff and subordinated units, by the spring of 1944. However, the view prevailed in industrial circles that the intense armament program necessary for these divisions could hardly be completed by the planned date.

Veesenmayer acknowledged that most of the members of the officer corps were indeed adherents of Germany; however, this did not mean that in certain situations they would not come to contrary conclusions. The Hungarian officer corps looked at events from a Hungarian viewpoint: therefore, the intense situation on the eastern front, the feared Balkan landing, the fear of air raids, and the country's inadequate anti-aircraft defense might lead to a situation where even officers definitely complying with superior commands would falter. The court-martial trials, initiated once again for foreign political reasons, against *honvéd* and police officers who were blamed for the Hungarian cruelties in Újvidék in 1942, were also a major burden for the spirit of unity of the officer corps. In spite of these unfavorable signs, the officer corps, and therefore the troops, still seemed to be the surest bet with regard to defending German interests in Hungary, and most probably they would remain so. As the report emphasized, the utilization of Hungarian troops beyond their own borders could not be envisioned either in the Russian or the Balkan region within the confines of the present approach of Hungarian policy. On one occasion the Chief of the General Staff stated to the German military attaché that, "in the worst possible scenario, the Hungarian army will honorably perish here, that is, at the border."

Hungary had reinforced its eastern border, and the so-called Árpád Line was being built in the Carpathians, while the mobilized mountain brigades were being trained on site for its defense. The value of these positions was not more than that of a more or less completed system of hindrances. As a mobile reserve, the 2nd Armored Division was to be deployed from the region of Budapest behind the Carpathians, in the area of Munkács.

The analysis finally underlined the fact that Horthy, who enjoyed great prestige, would determine the further development of Hungarian policy and the expected role of the army.

Furthermore, the *Abwehr* had examined Hungary with a view to the preparations needed for a German military occupation, and then set out the tasks that urgently needed to be done. Hungary's transportation and communication equipment fully met the demands of the German army. Although Hungarian demands of a few weeks earlier that Budapest not be stocked up with *Wehrmacht* deliveries, which could be seen by the outside world, and that Budapest should be declared an open city, had been dropped, no necessary preparations had been made for the reception and supply of larger German troop concentrations staying in Hungary for an extended period of time or moving towards the Balkans. The surveying and registering of stocks that could be used, the location of camps, and supplies acquisition had not yet been done. The only step taken was for the establishment of a German hospital base in southern Hungary. General Greiffenberg asked for urgent instructions on what kind of information and assessment tasks he should carry out.

Veesenmayer's trust in the Hungarian Generals was shaken. That was the reason why he did not think that the alternative of using the army to establish a government of pro-German soldiers was possible, as he studied the possibilities of "a way out." There were a number of soldiers on whom Germany could count in the case of a change, but no one among them seemed to be suitable to line up a significant part of the army against Horthy with any hope of success. He did not think that Archduke Albrecht, who had established strong contacts with the SS and provided continuous verbal and written news for the Main Security Office of the Reich, would be capable, even though he was drawing up and presenting plans to prevent the country from changing sides.

In September Albrecht reported that it was certain that the Hungarian government was going to choose the Italian way. He had already discussed the applicable necessary rules of conduct with high-ranking right-wing officers. At the right moment he, along with the officer corps, the majority of whom did not agree with the political course of the government, would switch over to the German side. Their action was proposed on the grounds that the government's intention of breaking away was obvious.[70]

Albrecht's promises of recruiting the officer corps did not convince the SS leaders in contact with him, and even less the officials of the German Ministry of Foreign Affairs and the army. It was not difficult for them to figure out that they were witnessing the careless promises of a political swashbuckler. Albrecht himself might have noticed their attitude during the conversation that he conducted in October with Berger, the Head of the Department of the SS Main Office in Berlin. Brenner reported to Kaltenbrunner that because of his—Albrecht's—merits he could not avoid seeing him. And as Brenner said, Albrecht had informed him about the situation in Hungary, about the increasing leftist orientation of the government, and its intent to break away from the Axis. This time Albrecht did not repeat his offer with regard to mobilizing the officer corps. It seemed to Brenner that Albrecht himself had not trusted the army's officer corps, because he burst out that the soldiers would be ashamed of themselves because of the failures of the army and the government's policy. Similarly, his belief in the Hungarian right wing was shaken because, according to him, it could not be brought together on a common platform. He thought that an irregular group established under the auspices of the SS would be the best way out. He suggested that Jenő Rátz be its commander. Besides, he saw the gendarmes as a reliable force that could be utilized in the case of a change headed by Jenő Ruszkay.[71]

Berlin's distrust was misplaced. Even though they could not find a resolute personality to lead their proposed regime change, the spirit of the officer corps continued to be predominantly pro-German. Prime Minister Kállay and circles around him received no support from the leadership of the army. In the political arena, in the case of a difference of views between the government and Germany, the military command mostly supported the Germans. But the change of view by Germany of the Hungarian army and its leaders was not based only on Veesenmayer's opinion. German intelligence units and people active in Hungary also substantiated the German Headquarters' brewing suspicion. After several times failing to get the Hungarian government to accept the most important German requests, Szombathelyi slowly lost credibility with Hitler and the German military command, he came to be seen as serving the cause of the Kállay clique.

In the meantime the German secret service took steps to find out whether the Hungarian military command continued to be unequivocally negative towards Kállay's policy and his established Western contacts, and whether the Hungarian military command also intended to make its own contacts with the Allies.

Already during the spring of 1943, when Antal Ullein-Reviczky suggested that the military should contact the Americans, the Chief of the General Staff was willing, but the distrustful Kállay refused to deal with the issue, and asked for an immediate cancellation of the preparations for the Tömösy mission, saying that "the soldiers should not interfere with it."[72]

In September Szombathelyi gave instructions to establish the contact with the Americans. The contact and exchange of messages established between Szombathelyi and the Americans during the fall of 1943—via Lieutenant Colonel Ottó Hatz, the military attaché to Sofia—might have come to the Germans' attention even before Hatz informed Szombathelyi about the developments. It was also possible that by using Hatz the Germans themselves wanted to set a trap, so that in the intensifying political situation Szombathelyi, of whom they had become suspicious, would be forced to take a stand, and so the Germans would be able to figure out his real intentions.

The contact with the American envoys via Hatz had been established as a result of rather confusing scheming. Hatz relayed their conditions, which did not include anything new compared with the British preliminary armistice conditions handed over to the Hungarian government in September, and which were also known by Szombathelyi. Prime Minister Kállay suspected a German provocative ploy when the military people, aware of their usefulness, handed over the information gathered by Hatz to him.

The details of Hatz's mission and discussions are known only indirectly from the reports of the German ambassador to Sofia, Beckerle, to his Ministry of Foreign Affairs. Hatz's later excuse was that he had given an account to the Germans, who had revealed his connections, only under pressure, and had not revealed the most important parts of his conferences. However, if one compares the Beckerle reports with Hatz's reports to Hungary described by Gyula Kádár, with Kádár's and Szombathelyi's response to them, and with their consequent instructions, it turns out that Hatz did not hide any essential detail of the Istanbul discussions before the Germans.

Hatz had discussions with the American envoys in Istanbul on December 18 and, returning to Sofia on December 22, he immediately informed Delius, the *Abwehr's* envoy to Sofia, and Ambassador Beckerle. Consequently, Hatz fulfilled both Szombathelyi's and the Sofia *Abwehr* envoy's instructions in Istanbul. He "repeatedly and emphatically" asked Delius and Beckerle to keep his report to them away from Hungarian organs, because otherwise as an officer he would be in a very difficult situation.

Ambassador Beckerle's report about Hatz's account arrived at the German Ministry of Foreign Affairs in the evening of December 22. He shared with Delius the information that his Istanbul discussion partners, referring to their earlier conferences, warned him that it was time for Hungary, along with the other small states, to immediately decide whether they would switch over to the Allies' side; if they decided to do so, they should act now. The benevolent judgment of Hungary's intentions would be dependent exclusively upon its actively hostile behavior towards the Reich. Hatz, in return, told the Americans that he had reported their demands, as elaborated during their previous discussions, to the Budapest authorities and that he was authorized to state that Hungary would never engage in any spying activity against the Reich, and nor would it turn against the Reich in an armed fight. It would always support Germany's fight against communism. Hatz tried to convince the Americans that dealing with this danger was in their primary interest as well.[73]

After the discussions had come to an impasse, Hatz promised to inform his Budapest superiors about the unchanged American position and maintained the possibility of further successful conferences. The Americans warned him that "there was not much time left, because, in their view, the war would be finished within a few months, and therefore Hungary should most urgently make a decision."[74] They asked Hatz to keep the discussions secret from the Germans, because it would be disadvantageous both for Hatz and the Hungarian state if Germany got wind of them.

At the conclusion of the conference, Hatz asked whether the Allies would fulfill his requests and guarantee Hungary's traditional thousand-year old borders against Bolshevism if Hungary accepted the Americans' offer. According to Beckerle, the Americans cynically responded that Hungary should not build castles in the air, because they could not undertake such guarantees even if Hungary stood on the Allies' side: "They are of the view that at the end of the war every nation should have a claim on what it deserves."[75]

At home Hatz gave an account of his Istanbul discussions to Szombathelyi, although he did not mention the fact that he had informed Delius and Beckerle as well. Following the discussion held on December 31, 1943, with the Prime Minister, Hatz received instructions from the unsuspecting Szombathelyi to make the Americans understand that their demands could not be fulfilled, because disclosing information about the Germans would simply be treachery, which the Regent and the government rejected as unworthy of the Hungarian nation. First of all, from the Hungarian point of view, what they were attempting was a political step. With this step Hungary would like to leave its alliance in a dignified manner, and it needed help for this departure. The withdrawal of Hungarian troops beyond the country's border back home was impossible, because the Germans would prevent it. As far as a partisan movement was concerned, the small size and inadequate terrain of the country would make this impossible. Nor could an appropriate person be found to lead such an activity. The government would not be able to make the Germans believe that it could not suppress a partisan movement. Yet, in spite of the repeated negative responses, Hatz was instructed to try to maintain the connection with the Americans and to have them send a commissioner to Hungary, who should be briefed about the situation and with whom the question of Hungary's needed help could be discussed.[76]

Szombathelyi was not suspicious of Hatz, who was promoted to colonel on January 1, when Homlok reported from Berlin that German circles were speaking about the fact that Hungary was pondering the idea of breaking away from the Axis and that Hungary had been conducting talks via its military with the Americans in Turkey. The news scared Szombathelyi, who was afraid of a German reprisal. He did not look for the source of the information that the Germans received. Instead, he decided to send Kádár and Hatz to Canaris to inform the Chief of German Military Intelligence about the American connection as if it had been mere orientation, which could be useful for Canaris himself, since in this way they could receive valuable data, such as the expected location and date of the expected Balkan invasion. Kádár and Hatz should also seek Canaris' agreement to continue the conferences in Turkey.

Probably Hatz smelled a rat, fearing that it was a German ploy and that he had really met fake Americans, who had not told him anything more than what the Allies' earlier message had contained. His suspicions might have been increased by the fact that thus far it had been exclusively the British, and not the Americans, who had been in contact with the Hungarians and had relayed the messages of the Allies. This must have been what led him to inform Beckerle to stave off any major reprisal. After hearing the news from Berlin, Szombathelyi decided on similar steps. But why did he not inform his superiors in Hungary?

Hatz was recalled to Budapest and then, accompanied by Gyula Kádár, he traveled to Munich, where they met Canaris on January 9. Hatz presented the goal of their trip, since Canaris had known him from earlier and showed a favorable disposition towards him. The German spy chief listened to him without showing any emotion, and most decidedly declared to the two dumbfounded colonels that "permitting anything like that is out of the question. The whole idea is naïve; the Americans are cunning enough to give nothing away. The only thing that would come from the connection is that we are driven into the suspicion of spying on each other, with unforeseeable consequences."[77]

According to the German ambassador to Sofia, Szombathelyi then sent Colonel Hatz back to Istanbul with the instruction to tell the Americans about the Hungarian government's unchanged position and to close the discussions. Once again Hatz sent him the information after meeting this time with the Allies' southeastern European informant, called Roberts, a.k.a. Randow, and an American called Colmann, who was the U.S. Secret Service expert on Eastern European resistance movements. Once again the Americans emphasized to Hatz their insistence that they "were willing to discuss the armed resistance unconditionally and exclusively with military personnel, and not with politicians." The Hungarian army should pursue active intelligence against Germany, and should be prepared to fight the Reich at the right possible moment. They also warned Hatz that "their relationship is confined to these two points." At the moment they could not even discuss whether, if Hungary fulfilled their demands, this help would be credited to the country at the upcoming peace conference, because "the Allies can only judge Hungary's achievements after the Allies' victory."[78]

True to his assignment, Colonel Hatz could only repeat what he had earlier elaborated on to the American envoy—that Hungary would never take up arms against the Reich. Although they considered any further discussion pointless under the circumstances, the Americans asked him to relay to his superiors the information that they, the Americans, "insist that Hungary make a final decision by early February 1944. Lengthy discussions should not take place, because the Allies' military plans could not be delayed or changed, either with regard to time or militarily, because they definitely were following their pre-determined paths."[79] To Hatz's note that Hungary was kept at the side of Germany by the fight against Bolshevism, which the Western Allies should take into consideration, the Americans responded that "it was out of the question to pursue a double-dealing policy against the Soviets, because the Soviets are equal members of the Allied Great General Staff and carry a meaningful role in that they democratically participate in every decision affecting the military command."[80]

Finally, the Americans reproached Hatz for the information that they had received from Washington, from an alleged German source, indicating that Hatz was working for both sides. Hatz did not deny his German contacts, but defended himself by saying that certain indiscretions committed in connection with his role forced him to inform the Germans, and in this way to identify himself. The Americans cautioned him against continuing the double-dealing.

After Hatz had given a detailed account in Sofia about the Americans' suspicions towards him, which allegedly originated from German sources, he reassured Beckerle about his services, telling him that "it was his steadfast decision to continue to watch the Allies' attempts to get in touch with Hungarian circles. He will always give an account of them and by drawing all the conclusions, he would prevent Hungary's possible disloyal behavior."[813]

However, the German Ministry of Foreign Affairs distrusted Hatz, who worked for the *Abwehr*. It cautioned against him because his confidential reports "contain contradictions and describe a picture about the process of the negotiations that seems to be improbable in several respects. Besides, the government of the Reich cannot be certain whether the German security officer's information in Sofia was not given with the purpose of trying to provide an alibi, while the most important moves of the negotiations are left unsaid. Such an assumption seems to be reasonable, because it was only two months after engaging in discussions that the first information was released. But it is unheard-of that a Hungarian military attaché commissioned by his own government would enter into connection with the enemy in Turkey behind the back of the allied German Reich."[82]

It seems, however, that the German distrust was groundless, and can be traced back to the Ministry of Foreign Affairs' aversion to the *Abwehr* and its agent, since, when in Hungary, Hatz did not give a report on the Sofia interlude. The American offer remained unacceptable both for the Prime Minister and for Szombathelyi and his circle. However, despite all the warnings and not fully giving up the possibility of the Allies' appearing in the Balkans, they still found maintaining the connection to be necessary. Hatz was unable to persuade Szombathelyi to sever the connections. On the contrary, from February 1 onwards he became the military attaché in Ankara. Szombathelyi, who had been uneasy about the Germans, made arrangements so that at his new post Hatz would be in contact with the Americans only indirectly or through his alleged friend Lothár Köves, a travelling tradesman. The contact with the American envoys was maintained until the German occupation of Hungary in March 1944. Szombathelyi requested an American military envoy to be dispatched to Hungary, but he failed to achieve this. According to both Hatz and Kádár, they and the American envoys in Turkey had nothing to do with the American officers who landed in the Csáktornya region on March 16. According to Kádár, Hatz's last message from Ankara was that they should turn to the Soviet Union.[83]

At the time of the German occupation Hatz happened to be in Budapest. He then went back to Ankara and in June, he became the aide-de-camp to the Minister of Defense.

Hatz's conferences confirmed for Szombathelyi as early as January that the prospect for an Anglo-Saxon landing in the Balkans had no chance of occurring. At the same time, Soviet troops were quickly approaching the Hungarian border. However, this way of breaking away from the war was not feasible for him. Szombathelyi and the part of his military command that could be counted on to attempt to break from Germany allowed themselves to drift helplessly with the tide at the turn of 1943/1944. One thing was certain: the idea of turning arms on the Germans did not even occur to them. Szombathelyi thought that he was justified when he advocated the policy of "wait-and-see" in the shadow of the Germans as long as possible. For the circles of Kállay, and for those from the military command who were thinking more soberly, salvaging the system became their common ambition in a situation where "a double fear squeezed the representatives in power: on the one hand, fear of a German occupation, which would lead the extreme right to move into power, with all its political, economic and military consequences, and on the other, an even greater fear of a possible left-wing takeover if the Soviet army appeared. These fears produced the confusion of self-defensive reflexes."[84] Both the political and military leadership became incapable of action in this hopeless situation.

On December 31 Jagow reported to von Ribbentrop that, affected by the quick German counteractions in Italy and by the news coming from the Teheran and Moscow resolutions, the Hungarian government must have realized that its interests tied the country to Germany. Besides these turns of events, Veesenmayer's negotiations and his restraint must have had "a sobering effect." Therefore, Jagow suggested that steps should be taken to more closely tie the Regent and the government to Germany. He said that it was desirable that "the Reich's Minister of Foreign Affairs, or another relevant and suitable official, visit the Regent to discuss with him—and thus with the Hungarian government as well—the seriousness of the situation and the good chances for victory. And, at the same time, he should inform him about Germany's military, economic and propaganda requests, which all should be defined clearly. Simultaneously, to dispel all the doubts, we should also give something to Hungary, for example, assurances about its sovereignty and our repeated direct promises of later transferring the Bánát to it. Furthermore, the Hungarian government should awake to its responsibility, which it has not done so far. This is how we could acquire an effective influence that can be once again solidified. The Hungarians are volatile and unreliable, and therefore we cannot move ahead without them being tied down closely and permanently."[85] Jagow added that the situation would be different if Hungary became an area for the concentration of troops. In that case Germany could demand the introduction of a state of emergency. Horthy would be forced to endow a military person, probably the Chief of the General Staff, with dictatorial authority, so that he would form a professional cabinet from among the ranks of the pro-German opposition.

Jagow was right in pointing out the uncertainty and confusion of Kállay and those surrounding him, and in pointing out that the extreme right was becoming active. Therefore, he thought that the time was right for diplomatic counteraction.

During the turn of events Kállay had to realize that if he wanted to break away from Germany, then seeking some connection with the Soviet Union was unavoidable. Anglo-Saxon warnings had also kept multiplying, saying that the government should seek connections with Moscow. On January 12 Barcza, the former ambassador to London, relayed the British message from Switzerland: the Hungarian government should listen to reason and should not wait until the Soviet troops reached the Hungarian border. Nor should it commit the worse blunder—or rather sin—of attempting an armed resistance or defense against the Soviet troops. Such reckless behavior would lead to the complete annihilation of the army, and would place the Hungarians in the same category as the Germans.[86]

However, Kállay did not face the facts. He did not even want to hear about turning to Moscow, and hoped that he could make the Allies accept the necessity of the Hungarian defense of the Carpathian line against the approaching Soviet troops and convince the Germans about that as well. The Hungarian occupational forces should be brought home, in his view, and deployed to the eastern border together with the home troops. Szombathelyi also shared his view on this. He did not take any steps to prepare the army for a possible break from Germany. As he frequently declared, he viewed every confrontation with Germany as improper and potentially posing tragic consequences. He urged the withdrawal of troops from the front exclusively for the sake of internal order and for the sake of the defense of the Carpathians. Moreover, pressed by the Germans, he did not take a stand in the military command against the strengthening extreme right wing and against those who insisted on a common fight against the Soviets.

At the end of January Lieutenant General János Vörös, Commander of the II. Army Corps and former Chief of Logistics, turned to Szombathelyi with a memorandum. After stating that Germany would overcome its temporary difficulties and referring to the ever-triumphant German army, which would deploy new armaments, he called the Chief of the General Staff's attention to the dangers that would occur should "the Hungarian government become more and more removed from Germanophilia and not participate in the war with the forces with which it is able to do so. Although he was aware that the Chief of the General Staff is not responsible for political changes of directions, he is nevertheless obliged to warn him that, at the end of the day, he will also be responsible for the shift to the left."[87]

Szombathelyi was hardly mistaken when he thought that Lieutenant General János Vörös' memorandum was in the same bracket as Jenő Rátz's and his German contacts' warning to him, because they all swam in the same stream. Convinced that whatever he said would get to the Germans within hours, he responded briefly and in a reserved fashion: "I would have appreciated it if Your Excellency had given me advice within the authority of your position. However, your statements on political issues go far beyond your sphere of authority."[88]

Vörös was deeply offended, and asked for a three-month medical leave, which he was granted. He interrupted it during the days before the German occupation and reported back to service.

The desertion to Germany of General Ferenc Feketehalmy-Czeydner, General József Grassy and Gendarmes Colonel Deák, who had all been prosecuted for the Újvidék massacre, was also a warning sign for Szombathelyi. Mainly for foreign political reasons, the government could not postpone questioning their responsibility any longer, and urged Szombathelyi to review once again the proceedings against them, which had been terminated earlier, and to start the trial. Szombathelyi wanted to keep the case within his own sphere of authority, and wanted to bring them before the separate court of the General Staff, although the Minister of the Interior had warned him that this case did not belong to the Military Court, because "it is not an issue of defection, but of murder and robbery." The defendants were not arrested, because, as he later wrote in his written defense, "I considered the thought of arrest to be as undeserving of a Hungarian general as the thought that he would flee from taking responsibility. But there was another circumstance that I had to consider. The Germans were behind the whole affair, most probably as instigators..." And they also could have freed them, which "I did not want to provoke." But Szombathelyi also had to consider the popularity of the accused within the non-negligible circles of the officer corps.[89]

The leaders of the Újvidék massacre who were helped to flee to Germany constituted a valuable reserve for the German rule in

Hungary. They were received as the guests of the German Chief of the SS, Himmler. Allegedly Hitler himself dealt with the issue of their escape. In any case, at the request of the SS the OKW instructed the German military attaché in Budapest not to deal with the issue, because it was definitely a police matter. Other leading officials of the German Embassy received similar instructions.[90]

Therefore, it was useless for Szombathelyi to complain to Werkmeister and Greiffenberg, who had shown complete ignorance and lack of interest in the matter, about what an unpleasant situation it was in which Grassy and friends had landed him with their escape from taking responsibility. As he told them, "I find it incomprehensible that these generals 'simply took to their heels.'" Shortly before the event, they had declared that they would take full responsibility for everything. Now they simply fled and would, he had no doubt, reappear as martyrs abroad. He was so depressed by the issue that he toyed with the idea of resignation.[91]

The December 24 offensive of the 1st Ukrainian Front destroyed the 4th German Panzer Army and broke through the front. The 1st Ukrainian Front occupied Zsitomir on December 31 and Berdicsev a few days later. The German troops could only stop the advancing Soviet troops after a 200-kilometer long retreat by cooperating with forces deployed from other sections of the front. The 2nd Ukrainian Front also swung into action and occupied Kirovograd on January 8. The front rapidly approached the Hungarian border. The January 10 situation analysis of the Hungarian General Staff stated the following: "We have to count on the fact that, in the case of dire need, the space in which our defense will have to work will reach across the Danube delta, the ridge of the Carpathians, and the River Vistula line, all according to the German plan. Therefore, possible events on the eastern front may move the Russian front to the Hungarian border. In this case, we cannot escape our historic destiny, and have to deploy all our available forces to defend our thousand-year-old borders."[92] The General Staff analysts shared the view with Kállay that the final goal of the Russian attack would be Berlin and the Balkans: "The shortest and geographically most advantageous thrust of attack does not lead to either target across the Carpathians but beside them. Therefore, most probably the Hungarian border will not be affected by the Russian main thrust but by the diversionary attack of the Russian securing forces."[93] Thus the task determined by the situation should convince the Germans that they should entrust the Hungarian troops with the defense of the Carpathians, the analysts felt. The Germans should allow the withdrawal of the Hungarian occupational forces and their concentration on border defense.

In mid-January Horthy and Kállay commissioned Szombathelyi to travel to the German Headquarters and gain the Germans' agreement to the defense of the Hungarian borders described above. In his memoirs Kállay described his last hope as being that Szombathelyi would be able to convince the Germans to entrust the defense of the Carpathians exclusively to the Hungarian troops, which would make it unnecessary for the German army to stay within the Carpathian line and on Hungarian territory. This way the Germans would be able to deploy all their forces north and south of Hungary. Even at the point of writing his memoirs in the 1950s Kállay still believed that if they had managed to make Hitler accept the proposal, the Soviet troops would not have considered it necessary to break through the reinforced and defendable defensive line of the Carpathians at all costs. In his view, in this case both the occupation of Hungary and the country's becoming a battle-zone could have been avoided. This naturally leads to the obvious conclusion—not written down by Kállay—that in the political and military vacuum that developed the regime could have survived, because it would not have been bothered directly by anyone and it could have obtained an "adequate" armistice. Later on Kállay considered it probable that whatever Szombathelyi presented at the meeting might have contributed to the finalization of the German decision: the occupation of Hungary.[94]

According to his commission, on January 17 Szombathelyi turned to Greiffenberg and asked him to intervene at the OKW so that he could travel to the German Headquarters for informational talks. The attaché conveyed the request to General Zeitzler, who discussed it with Keitel. They decided that since none of them was interested in the Hungarian Chief of the General Staff's visit, they would give him an evasive response and feed him with the promise of a visit on a future date.[95] On January 22 Zeitzler also informed Hitler about his and Keitel's position, but to his surprise Hitler was interested in Szombathelyi's visit. Hitler personally wanted to speak with him and promised "to tell him off."[96]

Szombathelyi wanted to meet in order to clarify and register the tasks that had to be done in connection with the withdrawal of Hungarian occupational forces and the defense of the Carpathians. Similarly to Kállay, he also thought that the Hungarian defense of the Carpathian line was possible, and that it would allow the Germans to concentrate their forces south and north of the line. He made up his mind to convince Hitler and his military commanders about this theory.

Hitler received the Hungarian Chief of the General Staff in the late hours of January 24. He carefully listened to what Szombathelyi presented as the Regent's request, and then flatly refused to fulfill it. Hitler claimed that at that point he did not have at his disposal forces that could replace the occupational Hungarian troops. After hearing what was presented about the defense of the Carpathians, he called Hungarians fainthearted. Hitler claimed that a Russian advance to the Carpathians was unthinkable. If it happened, both the war and Europe were lost. He continued to say that fifty divisions of German reserve troops had been under training and that new weapons were being manufactured. In the spring he would launch a new eastern offensive with these forces. He only wanted the Hungarians to provide their occupational tasks and economic support.[97]

Hitler showed his strong and determined self, which proved to be effective. Szombathelyi once again let himself be convinced that Germany still had reserves. He arrived back at his quarters in a visibly good mood, as if Hitler had not rejected his request, the goal of his mission. His mood was not dampened by Kádár's and Homlok's report on their experiences in the German situation recording office, where the situation was not described as optimistically as Hitler had described it.[98] The forces at Germany's disposal were less and less able to cover the gaps created in the front, let alone able to stop any further Soviet attacks or to swing into a counteraction. They warned Szombathelyi in vain, because he wanted to believe that Hitler would launch the offensive in the spring, and would not want the Hungarian troops to participate in it. Following that, the stabilization of the front would make the withdrawal of the Hungarian troops possible.

Szombathelyi and Keitel also had a discussion in which Keitel also found the suggestion laughable that the frontline would be withdrawn to the line of the Carpathians. He claimed that the Russians had been weakened and had no fresh reserves. As opposed to that, from March onwards Germany would deploy 42 new *Wehrmacht* and 33 new SS divisions. Keitel also doubted that the Anglo-Saxon powers would at all attempt to land in the west. Therefore, it was unnecessary to discuss the Hungarian troops' withdrawal and the defense of the Carpathians.[99]

The offensive of the Soviet troops continued. The synchronized offensive of the 1st and 2nd Ukrainian Fronts waged a shattering blow on the German defense and closed the Germans in a giant cauldron at Cherkassi. The troops suffered irreplaceable human and material losses. In early February the troops of the 4th Ukrainian Front also swung into action in the Dnieper bend. They destroyed six German divisions and occupied Nikopol. The Germans' "Eastern Wall" collapsed, a gap was created between the Southern and Middle Army Groups, and the complete German evacuation of the Dnieper bend began. The troops of the 3rd Ukrainian Front occupied Krivoj Rog. By the end of February all the new Soviet positions were 200 to 300 kilometers "behind the Eastern Wall."[100] There was no sign of Hitler's offensive. Moreover, the deployment of German reserves was barely sufficient to fill the huge gaps in the front and to prevent a complete collapse. The Hungarian military command was watching the unfolding events with growing concern. To organize the defense of the Carpathian line and to withdraw the occupational forces for that purpose seemed to be inevitable. News about the increasingly hopeless situation of the occupational forces induced Horthy to write a letter to Hitler in the interest of the troops.

Colonel General Géza Lakatos, the commander of the occupational forces, had urged both the German and the Hungarian military commands—several times and without any results—to withdraw his troops, which had been involved in heavy fights, had suffered increasingly major losses, and were threatened by complete destruction. On his own authority, already at the end of January he turned to Colonel General Zeitzler, but did not receive any response. Lakatos could not accept its being left at that, and kept the issue on the agenda through the German liaison staff, while the Soviet advance began to wipe out his troops. On February 9 Lakatos went to meet Szombathelyi in Budapest to inform him about the untenable situation and to ask for appropriate action. However, Szombathelyi had just arrived from the German Headquarters and could not say anything encouraging. He could not do anything without the Germans' permission, and hoped that the Regent's letter would break the ice.

Lakatos was also received by Horthy, who showed him the draft of his letter to Hitler. Lakatos also had discussions with Kállay and Csatay. Kállay suggested that Lakatos, as the commander of the occupational forces, should travel to meet Hitler, because he might be more successful than Szombathelyi. Csatay agreed and hoped that if Lakatos' mission succeeded, the Regent would appoint him to replace Szombathelyi, with whom, as Csatay confided to Lakatos, Csatay had growing difficulties in cooperating. Following that, Lakatos also went to see Greiffenberg and asked him to pave the way for him at the German Headquarters.[101]

The Regent sent his letter to Hitler on February 12. He wrote to explain that, with the war quickly approaching the Hungarian border, he was obliged to take the necessary measures in order to defend the borders. Therefore, in the near future he intended to mobilize the border guard units and to deploy them to endangered areas: "Your Excellency will find it obvious that saving my country from the horrors of war and keeping it, with all its devastation and destruction, as far away as possible are my most important problems." He claimed that the Carpathians offered an ideal site, where, he firmly believed, "we are able to keep the front by ourselves without German help, and then our centralized military industry and transport roads, important for both of us, may not be exposed to air raids."[102] However, in order to take this step, which would also be advantageous for the German troops, once again the issue of the withdrawal of the Hungarian troops providing occupational tasks behind the German troops should be brought up, even though it had been raised several times without any results, he said. By now these troops were in direct battle contact with the Soviet troops and were in a situation that was very upsetting. Horthy continued to say that they were not armed properly to tackle the tasks faced and were in danger of being "totally destroyed and scattered." These six poorly equipped divisions' replacement at home would be impossible. "Therefore, I most emphatically ask Your Excellency, to order back the Hungarian divisions from the front in time, and in compliance with our agreement, to the foot of the northeastern Carpathians, where we could secure the Lemberg–Odessa railway and could keep all our troops together. Later these troops would also be available for the defense of the Carpathians, which now seems impossible with the scattered forces."[103] Finally, the Regent assured Hitler that he would support the *Wehrmacht*'s heroic fight with all the forces at his disposal.

At the same time Szombathelyi, whose optimism was not justified, turned to Keitel in a letter written on February 14 to describe the gravity of the situation. He pointed out that holding onto and defending the Danube Basin was a common Hungarian–German interest. Alluding to the promised, but by then obviously cancelled, spring offensive, Szombathelyi assumed that the Germans were paying their full attention to the western frontline as they waited for the Anglo-Saxon landing there, and were pursuing only delaying battles with the eastern enemy, as if "they were striving to drag them behind themselves, and thus put them in a disadvantageous situation, so as to then strike a crucial blow against them." However, the "delaying" retreat, which had been going on since November 1943, created a situation that endangered the Hungarian regions, since the front was only 250 kilometers from the Hungarian border. Consequently, a further withdrawal should be counted on. According to Hungarian intelligence, Soviet troops, still possessing 60 divisions, could easily break through the frontline in the region of Rovno and Vinnica, which could consequently be divided into two parts south and north of the Pripjaty marshland.

The mobilization and deployment of the Hungarian military force would take a long period of time, he said, and that was the reason why Szombathelyi had tried to receive some information from the Headquarters as early as January. In case the eastern frontline retreated further towards the Carpathians, the Chief of the Hungarian General Staff should be aware of the tentative circumstances of a possible deployment of the *Honvédség*. Szombathelyi considered the defense of the Carpathians to be the special task of the Hungarian troops, and he expected them to put up a substantial fight. This would certainly necessitate the withdrawal of the six divisions being engaged in occupational duties.

In order to gain Keitel's confidence, he expressed his conviction that, similarly to World War I, once again only the Germans and Hungarians would be fighting together until the end of the war. This statement corresponded to his earlier—and, with time, increasingly justified—opinion that, due to the growing lack of interest of the Western powers, Germany remained the only trustee of an anti-Bolshevist fight.[104]

On February 14 Jagow also reported to the Reich's Ministry of Foreign Affairs that the Hungarian government had determined to defend its eastern borders. As the German military attaché was informed by the Hungarian General Staff, if the Russian offensive gained more westward territory, the Chief of the General Staff would propose the silent mobilization of a mountain brigade and two Transylvanian divisions—the Nagyvárad and the Kolozsvár—to the government, which would obviously agree. These divisions would be deployed to the security region behind the Carpathians as a first step.

Jagow warned the Germans that in case the German military command had calculated on the deployment of the Hungarian *Honvédség* along the ridge of the Carpathians, he calculated that it would be crucial "to dot the Hungarian frontline with German troops, because the *Honvédség*'s military capabilities do not comply with our needs." Even if the Hungarian response to a further Russian advance could be envisioned, it was difficult to form an educated opinion of the possible situation that might occur, in which political changes would take place, such as in the case of Finland's breakaway. This would primarily be something that stimulated circles that did not trust that Germany would be victorious. However, the landing of the Allies in Bulgaria, Romania, or Trieste would also have a damaging effect on the Hungarian government's military determination and probably on the troops as well.[105]

Once again Jagow's information was not quite correct. The Hungarian General Staff indeed began the mobilization of certain units of the First Hungarian Army. On February 18, 40,000 people were called up to continue the replenishment of mountain brigades partially mobilized and deployed to the border. Also, the partial mobilization of the 16th Szolnok Division and the 24th Ungvár Division began; these had been on an elevated war footing in any case.[106] The mobilization of the divisions to be deployed in the region of Uzsok and Ökörmező was accelerated by the 35,000 people joining on March 13.[107]

Notes

1. Országos Levéltár (National Archive, OL). Minisztertanácsi jegyzőkönyv (Minutes of the Council of Ministers), April 20, 1943.
2. Ibid.
3. Ibid.
4. Domokos Szent-Iványi, *Emlékirat* (Memoirs), Ráday Levéltár (Ráday Archive), Szent-Iványi hagyaték C/80, p. 839.
5. Gyula Juhász, *Magyar–brit titkos tárgyalások 1943-ban* (Hungarian–British Secret Discussions in 1943) (Budapest, 1978), p. 149.
6. Ibid., p. 120.
7. Ibid., p. 144.
8. Hadtörténelmi Levéltár (Military History Archive, HL). Békeelőkészítő Bizottság iratai (Documents of the Peace Preparatory Committee), A/II/1.
9. BA NS 19 neu 1529.
10. Gyula Kádár, *A Ludovikától Sopronkőhidáig* (From the Ludovika [Military Academy] to Sopronkőhida) (Budapest, 1978), p. 500.
11. Ibid., p. 524.
12. Ibid., p. 536.
13. Vilmos Nagybaczoni Nagy, *Végzetes esztendők 1938–1945* (Fatal Years, 1938–1945) (Budapest, 1986), p.138.
14. Ibid., p. 139.
15. Ibid., p. 141.
16. BA NS 19 neu 2114.
17. György Ránki, Ervin Pamlényi, Loránt Tilkovszky and Gyula Juhász, eds., *A Wilhelmstrasse és Magyarország: Német diplomáciai iratok Magyarországról, 1933–1944* (The Wilhelmstrasse and Hungary: German Diplomatic Documents about Hungary, 1933–1944) (Budapest, 1968), p. 719. (540)
18. BA NS 19 neu 2114.
19. Ibid.
20. Ibid.
21. Ibid.
22. Ránki–Pamlényi–Tilkovszky–Juhász, *A Wilhelmstrasse és Magyarország...*, p. 728. (549)

23. OL. Minisztertanácsi jegyzőkönyv (Minutes of the Council of Ministers), August 24, 1943.
24. Ibid.
25. Ibid.
26. Nagybaczoni Nagy, Végzetes esztendők..., p. 179.
27. Ibid.
28. Carlile Aylmer Macartney, October Fifteenth. A History of Modern Hungary, 1929-1945 (Edinburgh, 1961), vol. II: p. 189.
29. Nagybaczoni Nagy, Végzetes esztendők..., p. 172.
30. Ibid.
31. HL. Eln. Vkf 1. 1943/5373.
32. Nagybaczoni Nagy, Végzetes esztendők..., p. 175.
33. Ibid., p. 178.
34. Ibid.
35. Ibid., p. 179.
36. Ibid., p. 180.
37. Ránki–Pamlényi–Tilkovszky–Juhász, A Wilhelmstrasse és Magyarország..., p. 728. (549)
38. Ibid.
39. Ibid., p. 732. (553)
40. Ibid., p. 732. (554)
41. Nagybaczoni Nagy, Végzetes esztendők..., p. 183.
42. Percy Schramm, ed., Kriegstagebuch des Oberkommandos der Wehrmacht (Wehrmachtführungsstab), 1940–1945 (Frankfurt am Main, 1961–1979), vol. III: p. 1119.
43. Ibid.
44. György Ránki, ed., Hitler hatvannyolc tárgyalása, 1939–1944, I–II. (Hitler's Sixty-eight Discussions, 1939–1944) (Budapest, 1983), vol. II: p. 149.
45. Schramm, Kriegstagebuch..., vol. IV: pp. 187–188.
46. Ibid., vol. IV: p. 212.
47. Ibid., vol. III: p. 261.
48. Ibid.
49. Kádár, A Ludovikától..., p. 623.
50. Schramm, Kriegstagebuch..., vol. III: p. 1185.
51. Kádár, A Ludovikától..., p. 619.
52. Miklós Kállay, Hungarian Premier. A Personal Account of a Nation's Struggle in the Second World War (New York, 1954), p. 141.

53. Juhász, *Magyar–brit titkos tárgyalások...* p. 189. (45)
54. *Ibid.*, p. 219. (47)
55. *Ibid.*, p. 236. (3). For the circumstances of writing and delivery of the message, see pp. 60–65.
56. *Ibid.*, p. 249. (72)
57. *Ibid.*, pp. 276–277. (86)
58. OL. Minisztertanácsi jegyzőkönyv (Minutes of the Council of Ministers), October 14, 1943.
59. Mario D. Fenyo, *Hitler, Horthy, and Hungary. German–Hungarian Relations, 1941–1944* (New Haven–London, 1972), p. 156.
60. *Ibid.*, p. 157.
61. Kállay, *Hungarian Premier...*, pp. 315–316.
62. Juhász, *Magyar–brit titkos tárgyalások...*, p. 286. (92)
63. *Horthy Miklós titkos iratai* (Miklós Horthy's Secret Writings), ed. Miklós Szinai and László Szűcs, (Budapest, 1962), p. 352.
64. OL. Minisztertanácsi jegyzőkönyv (Minutes of the Council of Ministers), November 16, 1943.
65. Ránki–Pamlényi–Tilkovszky–Juhász, *A Wilhelmstrasse és Magyarország...*, p. 733. (551–1)
66. *Ibid.*, p. 740. (559)
67. *Ibid.*, p. 750. (561–1)
68. *Ibid.*, p. 754. (561)
69. BA RM 7/98.
70. BA NS 19 neu 2067.
71. *Ibid.*
72. Ránki–Pamlényi–Tilkovszky–Juhász, *A Wilhelmstrasse és Magyarország...*, p. 750. (561–1)
73. *Ibid.*, p. 756. (562)
74. *Ibid.*, p. 758. (562)
75. *Ibid.*
76. Kádár, *A Ludovikától...*, p. 607.
77. *Ibid.*, p. 609.
78. Ránki–Pamlényi–Tilkovszky–Juhász, *A Wilhelmstrasse és Magyarország...*, p. 766. (571)
79. *Ibid.*
80. *Ibid.*, p. 767.
81. *Ibid.*
82. *Ibid.*, p. 777. (578)
83. Kádár, *A Ludovikától...*, pp. 629–630.

84. Juhász, *Magyar-brit titkos tárgyalások...*, p. 71.
85. Ránki-Pamlényi-Tilkovszky-Juhász, *A Wilhelmstrasse és Magyarország...*, p. 759. (564)
86. Macartney, *October Fifteenth...*, vol. II: p. 209.
87. Kádár, *A Ludovikától...*, pp. 629-630.
88. *Ibid.*
89. *Szombathelyi Ferenc visszaemlékezése* (Ferenc Szombathelyi's Memoirs) (Washington, 1988), p. 310.
90. Ránki-Pamlényi-Tilkovszky-Juhász, *A Wilhelmstrasse és Magyarország...*, p. 761. (565)
91. *Ibid.*, p. 763. (566)
92. Ferenc Adonyi, *A magyar katona a második világháborúban, 1941- 1945* (The Hungarian Soldier in World War II, 1941-1945) (Klagenfurt, 1954), p. 97.
93. *Ibid.*
94. Kállay, *Hungarian Premier...*, pp. 315-316.
95. Ránki-Pamlényi-Tilkovszky-Juhász, *A Wilhelmstrasse és Magyarország...*, p. 763. (567)
96. *Ibid.*, p. 765. (570)
97. Nagybaczoni Nagy, *Végzetes esztendők...*, p. 186; and Kádár, *A Ludovikától...*, p. 633.
98. Kádár, *A Ludovikától...*, p. 633; and Nagybaczoni Nagy, *Végzetes esztendők...*, p. 177.
99. Nagybaczoni Nagy, *Végzetes esztendők...*, p. 186.
100. György Ránki, *A második világháború története* (The History of World War II) (Budapest, 1973), pp. 297-298.
101. Géza Lakatos, *Ahogy én láttam* (As I Saw It) (Munich, 1981), p. 67.
102. *Horthy Miklós titkos iratai*, p. 409.
103. *Ibid.*, p. 410.
104. Nagybaczoni Nagy, *Végzetes esztendők...*, p. 187.
105. Ránki-Pamlényi-Tilkovszky-Juhász, *A Wilhelmstrasse és Magyarország...*, pp. 767-768. (572)
106. HL. HM. Eln.6.k. 1944/19124.
107. HL. HM. Eln.6.k. 1944/28040.

HUNGARY'S OCCUPATION

Soviet troops had crossed the River Dniester and approached the Hungarian border, and so Hungary's strategic importance became a crucial factor. If Hungary dropped out of the war at the same time that Soviet troops appeared in the region, then the German connection with the Romanian oil and the German troops to the south of the eastern front would be severed. The collapse of the southeastern front also had to be counted on. György Ránki writes the following:

> Even if the German political and military command had been aware of the anti-Soviet bent of the Hungarian government, this [aforementioned] possibility could not be ignored. They knew about the Hungarian government's intention of breaking away from the Axis, and feared that the Hungarians would come to the only logical solution: the conclusion of an armistice with the Soviet Union. Not only was their suspicion strengthened by the repeated attempts made for the withdrawal of Hungarian troops at the front, but they also considered suggestions for the independent defense of the Carpathians as a first sign of desertion, in spite of Horthy's emphatic statement in his letter: " ... I am determined to defend the Hungarian borders with every available force and device against a possible invasion."[1]

The Germans had other motivations in addition to the Hungarian government's very hesitant steps to break away from the Axis, about which Hitler must have been concerned. Apart from that, Hitler did not agree to the Hungarian government's and military command's plan to concentrate the Hungarian troops in the Carpathians and to deploy them as an independent defense, a move for which the Hungarian occupational forces would be withdrawn. Hitler wanted not only to use the Hungarians as occupational forces, but to deploy them soon, in order to fill the gaps in the frontline and to solidify his defense. The German military command was especially carefully watching how the two Hungarian armored divisions were equipped. The question was, however, in what shape the army would be following the occupation of Hungary. In the case of resistance, a total reorganization of the *Honvédség* and its submission under the German military command would have to be undertaken.

The other possibility for which Hitler hoped was that the Hungarian army and its command would accept the German occupation without resistance and so could be mobilized for German goals. Besides this, Hitler also wanted to secure an unlimited access to Hungarian industry and agriculture for German use. Solving all these questions, in an increasingly grave military situation, could not be delayed. Political bargaining with the Hungarians was no longer feasible, and so a radical military intervention remained the only option. A Hungarian government was needed that would fully satisfy Hitler's demands and join in a common effort with Germany.

On February 19 the OKW issued a memorandum in which it emphasized the inadequacy of forces available for Operation Margarethe. The plan could only be executed with the available forces—even if the Romanians were involved—if the concentrated defense of the Hungarian troops did not have to be feared. But the Hungarian troops should be counted on to resist. The fact that the Hungarian troops' weapons were only partially up-to-date, and at the same time the troops did not have access to anti-armor heavy weapons, also improved the chances of the German troops. On

February 24 the list of forces needed to secure the execution of plans under every conceivable circumstance was presented.[2]

Antonescu's visit to and discussions with Hitler on February 26 and 27 in Klessheim were closely related to the preparations for Hungary's occupation. After discussing the general military situation and specific questions about common German–Romanian warfare, such as the evacuation of the Crimea, Hitler brought up the Hungarian question as well. Hitler had promised Antonescu that the Hungarian troops, just like the other alliance troops, would be deployed.[3] Antonescu cautioned Hitler not to trust the Hungarians, and urged that "the Hungarian question should be taken seriously." Hitler repeatedly reassured Antonescu that he could rest assured that he, the Führer, would deal with the Hungarians intensively and seriously.[4]

Antonescu expressed his views to von Ribbentrop about the Hungarians even more openly, and proposed measures against them: "If Hungary, small as it is, dared to openly request the withdrawal of all the Hungarian troops to Hungary in the Regent's letter to the Führer, then in his [Antonescu's] view, it means that Hungary must have received some promise from the other side. The demand of the enemy that his own Romanian troops should be withdrawn from the front had also been relayed to him. He responded with an open refusal and with a 'never' in written form. The Hungarians seem to have behaved differently. Their demanding the withdrawal of their troops equals the cancellation of the alliance. Therefore, measures have to be taken against Hungary, and the sooner the better, because, in case the situation worsens on the eastern front, an uncertain Hungary behind the front may pose an extraordinary danger. We must not allow events to overtake us." Alluding to the Führer's words, von Ribbentrop reassured the Romanian dictator, who, however, was unable to learn what concrete measures were being considered against Hungary, either from Hitler or von Ribbentrop. Therefore, he could not offer to intervene, but "casually" remarked that "one million Romanian soldiers are available to fight as soon as the Hungarian threat is cleared away."[5]

Even if Hitler did not share his plans with his Romanian guest and, for reasons of secrecy, did not ask him to intervene, Hitler must have established that he did not have to be concerned about a possible Romanian breakaway from the Axis. On February 28, in his instructions to draw up the final and working version of Operation Margarethe, he stated that there was no political incentive to act on Operation Margarethe II and it was therefore to be abandoned. Yet the following points had to be considered:

- the deployment should take place within Hungary, so that it would create the appearance of troop transportation, hence the codename "Trojan Horse";
- the transportation should be concealed as a southeastern-eastern troop movement;
- the units to be deployed should be reinforced by parachutist, armored and mechanized units, as well as police forces;
- the most important military economic and political targets should be determined in advance.[6]

The OKW began to organize the operation and to designate the troops to be used. At the situational analysis discussion, Hitler was informed about the measures being implemented. Thinking that the end of March was late, Hitler issued an order to accelerate the preparations. He also took steps to include further divisions in the operations.

The OKW did time calculations the same day, and acknowledged that if the units received their marching orders on March 5, the troops from the southern, southwestern and western military units would reach their concentration districts by March 12 at the earliest, while the northern units would get there five days later.

On March 7 General Foertsch, the Commander of the Balkan Army Group F, who had been appointed leader of the military operations, was ordered to the Headquarters in order to discuss the details of the execution of Operation "Trojan Horse." Trains carrying troops would cross the Hungarian border from the south and the west, and at a designated point in time, and under a certain pretext, they would unload in the Budapest region and occupy the designated points. The cooperation of the *Wehrmacht* and the Security Service had also been harmonized. The latter would infiltrate 500 people into the country prior to the attack. They decided that, for the time being, only the zone up to the River Tisza would be occupied. For secrecy, the other members of the alliance would not be informed. Finally, they settled on the starting date of the action. Foertsch suggested March 18 as the closest possible date, but then finally March 19 was accepted as an advantageous day. The following day, on March 8, Foertsch set up his headquarters in Vienna.[7]

On March 12 Hitler issued the command for the occupation. He justified the necessity of the attack by noting Kállay's and his government's upcoming treachery, which certain (unnamed) high-ranking officers of the *Honvédség* were also ready to join. They had been planning to change sides, and not only to let down the alliance, but even to stab it in the back. Repeated warnings, he noted, had not brought results. The treachery had not taken place the previous year because the rapid and energetic German handling of the Badoglio groups had scared off "the Hungarian traitors." "I cannot tolerate any possibility that their plan might develop to a point where, similarly to the Italian situation, we are surprised by an attempt to act treacherously. Therefore, I have decided to remove the treacherous clique. German troops will march into Hungary and will temporarily occupy the country." This would make way for the formation of a Hungarian government that, "true to an ally's obligation, and in the spirit of our old friendship and brotherhood-in-arms, will invest all the strength of the country in the interest of the final victory of the common cause."[8]

Then the order explained in details the execution of the military operation and the various tasks of the attacking units. The attack should be quick and surprising, and would have to secure the necessary railways and bridges for the eastern and southeastern front. For this reason, all opposition should be ruthlessly crushed.[9]

Hitler kept the right to dispose over all forces participating in the operation to himself, and demanded the utmost secrecy from everybody. The southern and southwestern attacking groups' preparations had to be concealed, disguised as actions against partisans, while the preparations of the northwestern and northern groups had to be concealed as preparations for the spring eastern offensive.

Concerning behavior towards Hungarian soldiers, the OKW issued an order on March 11 that prescribed that every Hungarian soldier was to be disarmed and locked in the barracks. All opposition was to be ruthlessly crushed, using all available arms. The leaders of resisting units should be shot during the fighting, and the rest of the soldiers should be taken as prisoners-of-war.[10] A supplementary instruction on March 13 issued by Keitel established that in case the troops resisted, they should be interned and transported to Germany to do forced labor, and that Hungarian volunteers could be accepted for German auxiliary service. Contrary to the original order, resisting Hungarian officers were to be disarmed, put under observation, and as soon as possible sent to the Reich, where they would be placed in specialized camps.[11] But the OKW hoped that all these sanctions would not need to be implemented, that the Hungarian army would change sides without any resistance, and that it would then be deployed to the eastern front as soon as possible.

The numbers of people and weapons of the concentrated German forces participating in the occupation are not available. This difficulty is further enhanced by the fact that the units made it to Hungary in a partially replenished state, which makes it impossible to assess the forces from the perspective of the regular soldiers.[12] Nevertheless, we estimate that a force of 40,000 to 50,000 men, whose equipment was comparable with that of the average German units deployed to the front in 1944, took part in the operation. The number of armored vehicles—"Párduc," (Panther) "P-IV" tanks, and a variety of assault guns at the disposal of the troops—can be estimated at 300 to 400. This powerful group, waging a concentrated attack from four different directions, was not to be underestimated, and could have engaged in a successful fight even if the Hungarians had resisted.[13]

Géza Lakatos' visit to Hitler also served as a cover-up of Operation Trojan Horse. After the antecedents described above, Lakatos received Zeitzler's invitation to Berchtesgaden on March 9, he left on March 10, taking an information bulletin with him, including detailed data documenting the necessity of an immediate withdrawal of the Hungarian occupational forces from the front.

Zeitzler received Lakatos on March 11. He struck a seemingly optimistic chord in analyzing the situation on the front. He stated that he continued to hope to hold the Dniester front. He said that it would be a piece of cake to stabilize the eastern military situation by transferring ten to twenty divisions from the west. Therefore, it would be desirable that the invasion of western forces would be launched soon, which surely would be repelled within a short period of time.

On March 12 Hitler received Lakatos, accompanied by Homlok, in Ober-Salzberg. Keitel, Jodl and Zeitzler also accompanied Hitler. Hitler called upon Lakatos to present verbally what he had described in written form. Lakatos briefly described the situation, and then asked Hitler to put an end to the existing disadvantaged situation of the Hungarian troops. He also requested that, should a later military situation occur, the *Honvédség* be allowed to defend the Hungarian borders itself.

Hitler then gave a speech lasting half an hour. He spoke about victory, divisions to be deployed, and armaments, which would also sweep away the Anglo-Saxons. But he did not speak about the fate of the Hungarian units.

Once he held the floor again, Lakatos brought up the issue of the Hungarian troops. He said that he did not feel competent "to take a position with regard to Hungarian political goals or to Hungary's further sacrifice. I have arrived, at the cordial invitation of the Chief of the General Staff, to conclude a healthy agreement about the further deployment of the Hungarian occupational forces."[14]

After returning home Lakatos immediately rushed to Horthy to report on the uncertain outcome of his mission. He concluded with the following statement: "My general impression is that we are dealing with an aggressive madman who is inevitably driving the German Reich to a catastrophe, which will also drag us along."[15]

The Hungarian government listened nervously to news coming from different sources about German troop concentrations around Vienna, and turned for an explanation to the employees of the German Embassy in Budapest. Colonel General József Bajnóczy, Deputy Chief of the General Staff, asked to meet with Fütterer on March 13. Fütterer was substituting for Greiffenberg, who had gone to Berlin for instructions. Bajnóczy informed him that German officers had told railway officials that the goal of German troop concentrations around Vienna was to occupy Hungary. Between forty and fifty trains with German troops had arrived in the region of Wiener-Neustadt–Eisenstadt.[16] Fütterer immediately inquired at the OKW, which, as he told Bajnóczy, was surprised that the Chief of the General Staff was taken aback by the unloading of an armored training division around Vienna.

Bajnóczy apologized for daring to throw suspicion on the German General Staff, and pointed out that it was not the military but the civilian authorities, "that are restless and constantly seek more information." He himself, however, found the response reassuring.

Jagow also reported on disquiet in Hungary. He said that the source of it was to be found in the helplessness created by the German troop concentration, as well as in the fact that neither Horthy nor Szombathelyi had received a reply to their letters to Hitler and Keitel. He also noted that information about the troop concentration was intentionally not requested by the Chief of the General Staff, but by his deputy, so that the Hungarian military would demonstrate that "the military authorities are not unquiet."[17]

Jagow brought up the restlessness that he saw and its cause to Minister of Foreign Affairs Ghyczy, expressing surprise that "such careless rumors should have raised the concern of the relevant civilian authorities ... [and] that such rumors can spread at all."[18]

Without thinking, Ghyczy cast the blame on the military. He said that actually it had not created any disquiet among the civilian authorities, which was proved by the fact that a short time ago the transportation of German war materials had been permitted without delay. The Minister of Foreign Affairs declared that "the cause of the Deputy Chief of the General Staff's interest is not so much disquiet, but rather curiosity. He wanted to know whether the transportation of the troops concentrating on the border would happen across Hungary. The Hungarian government did not think about the possibility that was rumored."[19]

Consequently, the scared Hungarian government and military command did not institute any kind of counteraction at the news of the threatening German troop movements; they tried to hide their anxiety, and accepted the Germans' assurances. Moreover, they were concerned that their distrust would provoke the Germans: "Both I myself and the government considered an occupation almost impossible, because the Germans could not undertake the intensification of new military and political tensions to the point of an open breakup. Unfortunately, we were wrong." Szombathelyi wrote these lines later, in 1945, but Kállay also made similar statements in his memoirs. He, along with Szombathelyi and Keresztes-Fischer, thought that the Germans were only threatening Hungary and wanted to exert pressure on them, even if it were just a first step in their removal. Szombathelyi declared that an occupation would never serve the Germans' military interests, it would be a political and tactical mistake on their part, and it would lead to a further fragmentation of their forces. In his view, the right moment to occupy Hungary would come only when the war reached the Hungarian border. Then the German troops, under the pretext of supporting military operations, would appear in the country without any further ado. If the Germans marched in before that, they would create the impression that they had lost their senses, and would convince the Allies that they simply did not count on Hungary at all.[20]

Yet Kállay did ask Szombathelyi whether there were any chance for Hungary to resist a German occupation. The response was a definite "no." No resistance could be attempted with the troops on a peacetime footing. Most of the troops were not on location and were not provided with heavy weapons or equipment. The Chief of the General Staff did not dispose over a single combat-ready regiment for the defense of Budapest. One of the two army corps replenished to war strength was in Transylvania, and the other one was in the process of deployment to the northeastern Carpathians. Their transportation to the west would take weeks. Yes, these forces would be able to resist an attack of the German troops concentrated near Vienna, but only if the Germans did not muster other troops. However, Szombathelyi was convinced that in the case of a German attack the Romanians would also mobilize in Transylvania against Hungary, and they were stronger than Hungary's two army corps.[21]

At this point the Hungarian leaders did not count on the German groupings' attacking from the north and the south. The German forces deployed for the hunting of partisans beyond the

River Dráva had escaped their attention, and the northern grouping had not even appeared near the Hungarian border.

Following the March 15 gala performance at the Opera in the late evening hours, Jagow asked for an audience with Horthy in the Castle. He gave him Hitler's invitation to visit him in Klessheim on March 18.

The Regent hesitated whether to accept the invitation, and sent for Kállay, Ghyczy, Szombathelyi and Csatay. Kállay was against the trip, and suggested that it be postponed until the goal of the German troop concentration was clarified. Kállay thought that Horthy might simply be held prisoner there, which would completely paralyze the actions of the government and the army. Szombathelyi represented the opposing view, which could not imagine rejecting a German invitation. Moreover, he thought that the visit was a good opportunity for Horthy to persuade Hitler to withdraw the Hungarian troops to the defense of the Carpathians. At first Horthy leaned towards Kállay's view, but finally he decided to accept it.

Horthy arrived in Klessheim on March 18 in the company of Ghyczy, Csatay and Szombathelyi. Sztójay joined them there. Hitler immediately received Horthy and came to the point by telling Horthy that he could not tolerate the repeat of the Italian case, or the idea that treachery would be plotted behind his back. Yet his impression was that Hungary was going to switch over to the enemy's side. Horthy was appalled, and denied the accusation, but could not convince Hitler, who indicted Hungarian policy in an even sharper tone. He enumerated all the contacts that the Hungarian government had established with the Allies, he declared, he had decided on an occupation of Hungary, for which there were Romanian, Slovakian and Croatian troops available in addition to his own. The discussion broke down at that point, because the deeply offended Horthy rushed out of the room.

In the meantime, Keitel had a discussion with Szombathelyi and told him that the Führer was not satisfied with Hungary's behavior and was concerned "especially, that Hungary should be a reliable rear support for the German army, which was fighting under difficult circumstances in the east. They needed guarantees in Hungary and, therefore, will implement certain measures."[22] What kind of measures these would be, Keitel did not specify, but he hinted that they were military.

Szombathelyi tried to point out that if they planned military measures, these would have unfortunate consequences for the Hungarian and for the German people, and might even have fatal consequences. Whatever disagreement had arisen should be dealt with in a friendly manner. Thus far no unpardonable step had been taken within the relationship between the two countries. Both the foreign and domestic news reports about Hungary's behavior were exaggerated: "I, for myself, can say that I have not detected anything that would be a serious indication of Hungary's changing sides or would offer any guarantees." He said that an aggressive measure would open up the arena for political denunciations and destroy Hungary's unity, and the political situation would become unstable, and the present quiet and peaceful relationship between the two countries would be upset. Allied carpet bombings would start against Hungarian industrial and transportation targets, which would gravely damage German interests also.

Keitel refused to analyze the political aspect of the question, and reiterated the point that they had made up their minds to tidy Hungary up, so that things would not go as they had in Italy.

Szombathelyi then shifted the conversation to the eastern front, where larger reinforcements should be sent, because, "if Keitel and the German military command do not watch out, a terrible landslide will happen there within a short period of time, with which Romania, the whole Balkans and perhaps also us will be entangled."[23]

Keitel listened attentively to the elaboration and stated that they fully trusted Romania. During his last visit Antonescu promised that he would hold out beside Germany until the final moment.

In the midday hours Horthy sent for his entourage, and informed them in great agitation about what had happened during his visit with Hitler. He said that he was going to resign if Hitler pursued his plans. Szombathelyi and Csatay tried to convince him to continue his negotiations with Hitler and to "try to convince him that we are fully standing by [the Germans] and doing everything that we can to facilitate their victory" and, therefore, that the occupation was unnecessary.[24]

Convinced by his companions, Horthy decided to continue. He tried to convince Hitler to refrain from occupying Hungary, since there had occurred in Hungary neither strikes nor anti-German actions to indicate the country's intention of changing sides. If Hungary were occupied, the Allies could be counted upon to bomb the country, which would be disadvantageous for Germany as well. The occupiers would also have to be concerned about a potential partisan movement. When Hitler proved to be hard-set, Horthy indicated that he would like to leave for home at 6 p.m. Hitler then repeated his request that Horthy sign a proclamation "according to which the German occupational troops have come to Hungary in agreement with the Germans and with his [Horthy's] consent." Horthy refused and once again left Hitler.[25]

In the meantime, Hitler issued the order for the execution of Operation Trojan Horse. According to the plans, the Germans tried to delay the departure of the Hungarian delegation for home by means of an excuse of air raids and a broken telephone connection with Budapest.

After listening to the Regent, so agitated by the failure of the afternoon discussion, Szombathelyi decided to take the initiative into his own hands. He believed the complete and stubborn rejection of Hitler's demands to be dangerous. If the Hungarians broke the conferences off, it would only aggravate the situation. Isolated from Budapest and the government, it was ridiculous to make arrangements that would lead to increased disturbances in the country or to unnecessary bloodshed. If Hitler could not be persuaded to drop his plans, then the solution was to accept the occupation with the least possible shock. An attempt should be made to ensure that, as the price for acquiescing to the forced transformation of the government and the sacrificing of certain politicians, the Regent could be saved as the only security of the legal continuity of the regime and its possible future dénouement. The army should be spared from an aggressive reorganization and submission under German command following the German occupation. They should attempt to gain some flexibility in how the army would be disposed, so that it might be used in the future for Hungarian purposes, depending on how the situation developed. However, any kind of resistance, even scattered, to the German troops entailed unnecessary victims and did not fit into this picture. These were the considerations that induced Szombathelyi to ask the Regent to let him have a private audience with Hitler. Keitel also agreed to the idea, and immediately arranged for it with Hitler.

Szombathelyi began by saying that the centuries-long Hungarian–German relationship was facing a tragic turn and that it was his obligation to "hinder [its fulfillment as best as he could] so that there would not be any fatal consequences. I have always considered it my task to take good care of the relationship."[26] He asked Hitler to clarify the situation, since the Regent would have to decide on a crucial question in a situation where they were not even sure what it was about. Hitler repeated that "his decision to clarify the situation in Hungary through occupation was irreversible, and he would not postpone it. His troops would be launched tomorrow morning."[27] Hitler claimed that he had warned Horthy about Kállay's policy, but that nothing had happened. He was sorry that the Regent wanted to resign, since he had wanted to proceed in agreement with him. Then he changed to a threatening tone: "The consequences of His Excellency's resignation would be totally uncertain as far as he or his family is concerned. Moreover, in the case of an armed resistance, Hungary might be able to resist for a few days, but I can assure you that within ten to twelve days Hungary's fate would be sealed. Furthermore, its neighbors would also intervene. Under such circumstances Hungary could not secure its future."[28]

Szombathelyi realized that there was no room left for argument, yet he asked for 24 hours of delay so that the Regent could travel home and come to a decision there. Hitler, however, considered this to be impossible, since he had already issued the command to launch the troops the following day and it could not be retracted. Keitel, who had just entered the room, also reinforced the latter statement. The German trains were irreversibly rolling towards the Hungarian border. Finally, Hitler concluded the audience by saying that he was ready to continue negotiations until 8 p.m.

After leaving Hitler, Szombathelyi also went to see von Ribbentrop. He asked him to let the Regent leave. The German Minister of Foreign Affairs said that in his view it was not a problem. However, whether the Regent was expected among the troops he could not tell, since Horthy did not want to cooperate. The Regent should agree to the issuing of a common proclamation in which he would declare that the German troops' entry into Hungary had occurred in agreement, and then the case would be settled. Szombathelyi tried to use a loophole saying that the head of state's declaration would have constitutional power if the government also countersigned it. That was one of the reasons why it was necessary that the Regent travel home to arrange the matter. He had already proposed Sztójay, who had conducted discussions with von Ribbentrop on the political aspects of the situation in the afternoon, as the new prime minister. Von Ribbentrop remarked that he would also like to see such a development. Then Sztójay joined the conversation and the two of them asked von Ribbentrop to make it possible that the Regent would once again meet the Führer so that they could finally clarify what the whole situation was about.[29]

At 8 p.m., the third discussion took place between Horthy and Hitler. They kept silent for a long time. Finally Hitler broke the silence and "asked the Regent to stay in his place and not leave it under any circumstance ... He had always loved Hungary, and even the idea that the Germans wanted to make a province of Hungary was laughable. He had ordered Romanian Conducator Antonescu to himself who, at the request that Romania should dedicate new divisions to the ongoing efforts against the Russians, had turned him down by saying that Romania could not do it because the Hungarians wanted to attack the Romanians in the back. He would send a telegram to Antonescu today so that he would immediately deploy his divisions against the Russians."[30]

Although no common declaration was signed, mostly at Szombathelyi's urging the broken Regent accepted the unchangeable situation. Hitler's ace, the covert threat that Antonescu and his troops would be sent to the front after the situation was clarified, might also have been effective. Since Horthy, at that point, did not repeat his protest, Hitler took his silence as acceptance of the occupation.

Later, during the Nuremberg trials, von Ribbentrop made the following statement about the events: "When in the evening Horthy once again visited Hitler, they arranged the whole situation between themselves. I think that by the end Horthy was quite satisfied that the situation had developed thus. I think in retrospect that we found that things had been going quite smoothly."[31]

On their way home, Jagow showed up in Horthy's train compartment. He announced that he had been relieved from his job as ambassador. He introduced his successor, Veesenmayer, the new ambassador with the plenipotentiary power of the Reich.

From the slow-moving train, in Linz, Szombathelyi issued a command that the troops should not resist the entering German troops. In defense of himself later on he justified it in the following way: "Resistance would have led to unnecessary bloodshed, but only in sporadic cases, because, considering the spirit of the armed forces and especially that of the officer corps, which were completely under right-wing influence, one could hardly speak about a unified and forceful resistance, even if we could have issued a command for it. Spiritually the army was completely on the German side and was waiting for the maturing of right-wing politics. It would not have undertaken a fight against the Germans. We had lost the political battle before we could have entered a bloody military one, and we have to acknowledge that."[32]

At four a.m. on March 19 the German troop transport trains crossed the border, reached their destination undisturbed in the area of Bicske and Cegléd, and began unloading. In the early morning hours the German troops occupied the most important strategic points in Hungary without any sign of resistance. The unsuspecting Hungarian garrisons were taken prisoner in their own barracks and the Tisza line was closed down. The occupation of Hungary was implemented within a few hours, without a shot's being fired and under optimal circumstances for the occupiers.

While the special train was approaching the border, Prime Minister Kállay was alerted that there had been several reports about German units approaching Budapest on the road and by train. After a short discussion with Minister of the Interior Keresztes-Fischer, who had also been alerted, Kállay asked to meet the relevant officials of the Ministries of Defense and Foreign Affairs, since their ministers had been away.

The soldiers arrived one after the other at the call of the Prime Minister, including the following: Colonel General Imre Ruszkiczay-Rüdiger, Deputy Minister of Defense; Colonel General Sándor Magyarosy, Commander of the Air Force; Colonel General

István Náday, Commander of the 1st Hungarian Army; Colonel General Károly Beregfy, Commander of the 3rd Hungarian Army; Lieutenant General Béla Aggteleky, Commander of the I. Army Corps; Colonel General Béla Miklós, Head of the Regent's Military Office. Colonel General József Bajnóczy, Deputy Chief of the General Staff, could not be found for the time being. According to Kállay's memoirs, Lieutenant General János Vörös, Commander of the II. Army Corps, was also present. After a while Colonel of the General Staff Lajos Nádas, Head of the 1st Section of the General Staff, and Colonel of the General Staff Gyula Kádár, Head of the 2nd Section of the General Staff, also joined the discussion. Nádas handed over Szombathelyi's telegram to Kállay.

Minister of the Interior Ferenc Keresztes-Fischer, Deputy Minister of Foreign Affairs Andor Szentmiklósy and István Bethlen were there also.

The Prime Minister's dilemma was whether he should make arrangements by himself or wait for the Regent. The fact that the occupation had actually occurred now became evident. The incoming reports, Szombathelyi's telegram, and the coded telegram handed over by Szentmiklósy, in which Ghyczy wrote that the German occupation was to be expected, all served as proof. Kállay asked the high-ranking soldiers who were present whether they would be ready to issue commands for resistance to the army at his order. Their responses were unambiguous. In Budapest and in its surrounding area no resistance was possible, because the army did not dispose over any notable military force. There had been no preparations in the garrisons, and the soldiers had spent the night in their barracks, probably surrounded by German troops. The generals unanimously declared that in the absence of the Regent and not knowing his intentions, and while in possession of the Chief of the General Staff's orders to the contrary, they were not willing to issue such a command. Moreover, they would prevent those troops subordinated to them from executing anything in this regard. They said that their oath obliged them to do this. Only Colonel General Náday held a more flexible position, although practically speaking he also supported the others. He said that as far as he was concerned he would be willing to accept the Prime Minister's position and would agree to the resistance, provided that the whole armed forces would undertake it. But it would be dangerous to break up the Hungarian *Honvédség* with different measures before the Regent arrived home. A rushed resistance would fail now in any case, and would make a later and potentially successful one in Transylvania and the Carpathians impossible. General Magyarosy emphasized the impossibility of using the air force. Colonel General Bajnóczy, who had arrived at the last moment and who commanded the *Honvédség* in the absence of the Regent and the Chief of the General Staff, also agreed with the position taken by the others.[33]

Confronted with these views, the Prime Minister gave up on the idea of resisting the occupation. He recognized that in the absence of the Regent he did not have the constitutional right to preside over the army. The Chief of the General Staff, who did have the constitutional right, had already issued an order to the contrary, although Kállay did have doubts about the authenticity of the telegram. The army commanders rejected the prospect of resisting, or considered it unlikely to succeed. Finally, the assembled leaders decided that the *Honvédség* would remain in its barracks, but that if the barracks or different military institutions were attacked, then the army would put up an armed resistance. For further action the Regent's instructions would be needed.

The Prime Minister also considered whether the police, gendarmerie or the general population should resist the occupation, but he had to admit that it was completely impossible. The German army would crush any unprepared and improvised resistance within hours, endangering hundreds of lives and preventing a possible positive outcome led by the Regent.

At the last moment General Greiffenberg also arrived and handed over Keitel's letter. According to the letter, Regent Horthy and Hitler had agreed that German troops would occupy Budapest. The Regent was to arrive in the morning with the new German envoy. The German troops were to be assertive but not hostile, yet would mercilessly crush any kind of resistance. Keitel warned the government that along with the German troops, the troops of allied countries on the northern, eastern and southern borders of Hungary were also standing by and could also move towards Budapest if necessary. At Greiffenberg's inquiry about what position the Prime Minister would then assume, Kállay responded that until the Regent's arrival home he was responsible for what happened, although he did not wish to discuss it with the attaché.[34]

In the early morning hours the unloaded German units occupied the most important strategic points in the country and locked the unsuspecting Hungarian soldiers in their barracks. They also occupied the airports and closed the corridors across the River Tisza.

By 9 a.m. on March 20, when the special train arrived at Kelenföld, everything had been decided. German guards received the Regent, who drove up to the Castle in Kállay's company.

The German troops met almost no resistance everywhere, and the few and scattered exchanges of gunfire were mostly due to misunderstandings. Hearing the news, von Ribbentrop sent a telegram to the German Ambassador in Bucharest already in the morning of March 19. Von Ribbentrop asked him to see Antonescu that morning and to tell him that in order to secure common military interests German troops had entered Hungary. The Führer had agreed on this with Regent Horthy. The German ambassador to Pozsony (Bratislava) appeared with a similar task before Slovakian President Tiso.

The Regent gave an account of the preliminaries and event of his Klessheim trip at a Crown Council meeting that began at 12:45

p.m.[35] He complained about the impossible situation in which he had landed with Hitler, whose intention had been to lure him out of Hungary so that he would not be able to organize a resistance. Considering the situation, Horthy had discarded the idea of a resistance. Hungary did not have appropriate military forces, but even if it did, they would not have been aptly prepared for such an unexpected situation, and even if they had been so prepared, the Germans would have taken possession of the country in any case. This might be a better solution, because the resistance would have cost a lot of blood and perhaps even the loss of the country. A resistance would also have entailed the involvement of Romanian troops, but as things now stood the Hungarians would not have to be concerned about their incursions, because hopefully the Romanians would be deployed against the Russians.

Then the Regent accepted the resignation of the government, and requested that the members carry out their affairs until a new one was formed. He also expressed the hope that the nation would successfully deal with the difficult situation. The war would not last forever, he said, and it would be even worse if the Russians inundated the country.

Members of the Klessheim delegation reiterated what the Regent had said. Csatay stated that when they arrived the Germans spoke about the occupation of Hungary as a finished affair, and his counter-arguments were futile. The Germans insisted that the Regent stay as the head of the country and not leave his position. In the case of resistance they held out the prospect of the saddest consequences. They also alluded to the fact that in the case of disturbances the Romanians, Slovaks and Croats were ready to intervene. Ghyczy and Szombathelyi reiterated what Csatay had said.

Sztójay felt that he would have to speak about the events and their precursors in more detail. He listed all the charges that Hitler and his colleagues had presented to the Hungarian delegation, which had motivated them to act. While the Regent was visiting

Hitler, Minister of Foreign Affairs von Ribbentrop had received him. Von Ribbentrop had asked him whether he had reported to the Hungarian government the complaints that the Germans had expressed. In von Ribbentrop's view nothing had happened in connection with them; they had never received a concrete response in any of the cases. *Inter alia*, they had expected, but in vain, that the Jewish question would be answered. Furthermore, foreign broadcasting services had come to see Hungary's behavior as resembling that of the Italians, and kept announcing that Hungary was going to break away and join the Allies. Furthermore, the Hungarian government did not react to this news adequately. Both the government's and the press's attitude induced the government of the Reich to deal directly with the idea that Hungary would change sides and that adequate measures had to be taken to prevent it. Von Ribbentrop deeply regretted the fact that the Hungarian government had not taken the German official circles' warnings to heart.

Sztójay assured those present that he had tried to bring von Ribbentrop around and had tried to convince him about the Regent's pro-German sentiments. He had asked von Ribbentrop to reveal any damning evidence that he possessed. Von Ribbentrop had left that comment without response and had repeated that if the Regent did not agree to the occupation, it would have serious consequences for the country. Therefore, during their afternoon discussion he had asked Sztójay to try to speak with the Regent to get him to reconcile himself to the fact that the occupation was irreversible and that he should not resign, because it would be catastrophic for Hungary. The new Hungarian government should engage in the politics of friendship and agreement with the German government.

Sztójay said that he had told von Ribbentrop that he did not exclude every form of intervention, but wanted written guarantees from the German Minister of Foreign Affairs, which should include a statement that Hitler did not want to affect Hungary's sovereignty with the occupation. He said that it would also be necessary to postpone the German troops' entry until the Regent had thought about the grave situation and come to a decision. Von Ribbentrop considered this latter element to be impossible, because the command had already been sent to the troops and the action had begun. He, however, promised to submit the issue of guarantees to Hitler. Sztójay did not specify why von Ribbentrop had discussed all these issues with him and not with Minister of Foreign Affairs Ghyczy, also present.

Next, Minister of the Interior Keresztes-Fischer informed those present about the police measures already instituted by the *Gestapo*. He said that all the police functions had already been taken out of the hands of the Minister of the Interior, and that under such circumstances he could not carry on the Ministry's affairs any longer.

The Regent closed the Crown Council's session by saying that the main task was to clarify the situation. They needed to find out who exactly among the Germans in Hungary was "in command." Finally, it would be necessary to issue a declaration to the nation, "because something should be said to our unfortunate homeland."[36]

Veesenmayer, however, did not leave any doubt about who exactly held the plenipotentiary authority to execute the German Reich's commands in the country. Already on March 20 he started discussions with the Regent about establishing the new government. Von Ribbentrop's candidate was Béla Imrédy. Veesenmayer had called the Regent's attention to him already on the train. However, the Regent flatly refused to accept Imrédy, but considered a bureaucratic government led by Sztójay or Csatay to be acceptable. Any other solution would force him to breach his oath taken on the constitution and the laws. He would defy Imrédy's nomination even at the expense of a German attack on the Castle.

Veesenmayer protested the unnecessary delay. He did not understand the Regent's delaying behavior or why the installment of an Imrédy government would be a breach of oath for him. So the negotiations broke down. Veesenmayer made menacing statements and sent a telegram to von Ribbentrop: "After conducting three lengthy discussions with the Regent within 24 hours, I am becoming more and more convinced that, on the one hand, Horthy is an excessive liar and, on the other hand, he is already physically unable to take care of his duties. He keeps repeating his words, often contradicts himself within a few sentences, and sometimes comes to a sudden stop in speaking. What he has to say sounds like a well-rehearsed formula. I am afraid that he will be difficult to convince, let alone to win over."[37]

During the same day Veesenmayer sent another telegram to the German Ministry of Foreign Affairs. He was notified by Greiffenberg that one German division was already on its way back to Germany. Veesenmayer considered this to be too early, due to the drawn-out discussions on forming the new Hungarian government. He was afraid that once the news spread the Hungarians would assume that the German occupation had just been a bluff and that the German divisions were now needed somewhere else. "Considering the so-far totally unclarified situation, I think that it would be beneficial to disregard any planned withdrawal of German divisions until our aspiration to form a new government is satisfied. With regard to any further discussions about the restructuring of the government, the German *Wehrmacht*'s presence in Hungary is crucial."[38]

Veesenmayer's report produced results. The military pressure increased, and Hitler detailed another division from the Belgrade area to Hungary.

The stubborn resistance of the Regent finally led to a compromise. Since it was also in Germany's interest to come to an agreement with the Regent and to stabilize the situation, they dropped Imrédy and accepted Sztójay, whose name as a potential prime minister had already come up in Klessheim. In German circles Sztójay was considered to be reliable. Horthy also viewed him as *persona grata* for Hitler. Sztójay's military past also added to his value. At first he hesitated because of his illness, but finally gave in to the Regent's persuasion and accepted the appointment.

Squeezed for time, von Ribbentrop was forced to backtrack, yet he still placed some conditions on the composition of the new government. He insisted on including experienced extreme right-wing people, including Jenő Rátz as Deputy Prime Minister, Colonel General Jenő Ruszkay as Minister of Defense, and László Baky or László Endre to handle the Ministry of the Interior's ministerial portfolio.

Veesenmayer also tried to push the right-wing agenda, but in vain. The Regent refused to accept Imrédy even as a minister without a portfolio, and both Baky and Endre were unacceptable to him. He was willing to appoint only Csatay as Minister of Defense.

In the evening of March 21 the Regent received a space of 36 hours to set up the Sztójay government. In the meantime, the occupational forces had held out the possibility of occupying the Castle unless the government was created. Allegedly, General Foertsch had already made a plan that would have been implemented on March 24. This, however, was only a pretext to keep up the pressure towards a peaceful solution.

Finally, after all the compromises, on March 22 the new government was formed. It was headed by Döme Sztójay, who took the oath of office that same evening.

The average Hungarian citizen only knew about things because of the presence of German soldiers; because of the ban on assembling, and on theater and cinema performances, and from scattered rumors about what was going on behind the scenes. Finally, on March 23, the MTI issued the news about the formation of the new government and informed the public that, "In order for Hungary to gain support in the war fought by nations allied in a tripartite agreement against the common enemy and especially [attempting] to overcome Bolshevism by mobilizing all its forces and after laying out comprehensive guarantees, German troops have arrived in Hungary, based on mutual agreement."[39]

Cooperating with the police organs of the German occupiers, the new government immediately began to arrest left-wing and liberal politicians and intellectuals. Prime Minister Kállay fled to the Turkish Embassy. Under-secretary of the Interior Baky issued an order on March 31 that within 48 hours all communist sympathizers, leading members of extreme left-wing movements, and people considered dangerous due to state security or public security reasons should be arrested and interned. Several thousand people were then put under arrest. Extreme right-wing politicians were placed in important posts in the state leadership. Several government party parliamentary representatives were asked to resign.

The German leadership immediately set out to take possession of the Hungarian military industry and to remodel it according to its own needs. Common German–Hungarian military and economic bodies were established to direct the industry. But Allied air raids, which began in March, caused serious damage to the military industry and the railway equipment. Industrial productivity declined.

The fate of the *Honvédség* was a question yet to be decided. Apart from a few people to be pushed to the sidelines, Veesenmayer trusted the pro-German and anti-Soviet leanings of the Hungarian generals and officers. He still considered the *Honvédség* capable of contributing to the common fight. Therefore, he disagreed with von Ribbentrop's view that the unreliable Hungarian army should be disarmed. Colonel General Weichs, Commander of the German Forces occupying Hungary, also supported Veesenmayer's position. Weichs tried to convince the OKW that the Hungarian units under the difficult quarantine should be freed and deployed to the eastern front as soon as possible, to help the German troops in the increasingly grave situation there. Weichs' point was that the Hungarian officer corps did not comprehend the situation, considered the occupation to be unnecessary, and wanted to fight. His position was reinforced by the fact that on March 25 the Hungarian General Staff made a voluntary offer to mobilize eight divisions and to deploy them to the front. On March 26 Military Attaché Greiffenberg requested that the Hungarian troops that had been mobilized earlier and detailed in the Carpathians be deployed to Galicia. Szombathelyi agreed, but said that he needed to have his freedom of activity restored and to have the barracks quarantine immediately end, so that he could take the necessary measures to make the requested troops available. On March 25 the German military command declared the Trans-Tisza Area a military operational zone and placed the Hungarian units there under German command.

The fate of Hungarian troops was decided at a conference held with Hitler on March 28. Weichs and Veesenmayer suggested to Hitler, Keitel, Jodl, von Ribbentrop, and Himmler that the Hungarian army be utilized, although under a strong German influence and direction. Hitler, ever-distrustful towards Horthy and his army, finally allowed himself to be convinced. Considering the military situation, disarming the troops was not desirable, and the best possible solution was to squeeze out as much as possible from them. For the time being, he ordered the deployment of three Hungarian divisions to the front and arrangements for the maximum utilization of Hungarian economic resources. The latter became the responsibility of Veesenmayer, the plenipotentiary commissioner to Hungary, who was now responsible for organizing, directing and controlling Hungarian politics and the Hungarian economy according to the interests of the German Reich, by applying all the organs of German power available in Hungary. Accordingly, General Greiffenberg requested from Szombathelyi the immediate mobilization of the 20th, 25th and 27th Divisions.

On April 19 General Greiffenberg was appointed the *Wehrmacht*'s emissary to Hungary. He, cooperating with

Veesenmayer, was to enforce the OKW's interests by commanding the German occupational forces still remaining in Hungary. He maintained connections with the Hungarian military leadership, passed down instructions received from the OKW, and ensured that they were implemented. It was also his task to cleanse the Hungarian military command of undesirable people. He persuaded the Regent to relieve the unreliable Szombathelyi of his post on April 19 and to appoint Lieutenant General János Vörös (Colonel General from May 1), acceptable to the Germans, as the new Chief of the General Staff. Szombathelyi's deputy, Colonel General József Bajnóczy, was replaced by Lieutenant General Dezső László, known for his strong pro-German views. In April, due to his participation in establishing connections with the Western powers, the *Gestapo* arrested Major General István Ujszászy, Chief of the State Security Center, as well as Colonel Gyula Kádár, Head of Vk. 2. [2nd Section of the General Staff] and his deputy, Major Károly Kern. Moreover, there were additional replacements within the leadership of ministries and troops, which were supposed to assure a greater degree of German influence.[40]

In the meantime, the situation at the front deteriorated further. The Soviet army was approaching the Hungarian border. The government mobilized and deployed the 1st Hungarian Army to the front. After István Náday's resignation, the Regent appointed Colonel General Géza Lakatos as its commander. The 1st Hungarian Army, reinforced by the 2nd Armored Division, launched an offensive on April 17, which, however, tapered out within two weeks. Very soon the troops were in the middle of serious defensive battles, suffering a great toll. During the summer, through a slow retreat, they joined up to the Hunyadi entrenchment position, and then later to the Árpád Line, thus preventing the Soviet troops from breaking through the passes of the Carpathians.

While the Regent tried to prevent the military from being commanded by people with divided loyalties, the OKW demanded that further Hungarian troops be deployed to the front in order to ease the shortages there and to weaken the Regent's hinterland. Greiffenberg requested that the Regent's favorite cavalry division be deployed to the front on April 24, because the OKH wanted to deploy it under German command in the region of the Pripjaty marshland. The Regent rejected this, and would only consent to the cavalry division's staying within the formation of the 1st Hungarian Army at the forefront of the Carpathians. The German demands, supported by Sztójay and Vörös, could not move him from his decision. Vörös noted in his diary that "the Regent let me know that he would agree to the transportation of the 1st Cavalry Division only on the condition that it is subordinated to the 1st Army. Furthermore, he does not intend to deploy more divisions outside of the country. Finally, he expressed resentment towards the commanding style of the German military command, and said, with regard to the question of using the *Honvédség* in the manner that they have proposed, that they have to learn to use a different tone."[41] Finally, the bargaining was ended by Hitler, who did not agree to the idea that the division would be detailed to its planned site of deployment while being subordinated to the 1st Hungarian Army. At this Vörös then declared that the division's case had moved from being a military to a political issue, and that any further opposition would have damaging consequences. Finally, at Sztójay's persuasion, Horthy succumbed: "During the afternoon the Prime Minister managed to persuade His Excellency to change his position and to agree to the Führer's request in terms of using the cavalry division."[42] Under the command of Lieutenant General Vattay, the 1st Cavalry Division was deployed to the front on June 12; there, under German command, it found itself at the center of heavy fighting, entailing heavy losses.

The Council of Ministers on March 29, 1944, passed a resolution to solve the Jewish question according to the Germans' demands, and then issued the necessary regulations. With this, the destruction of Hungary's Jewish population began. A number of regulations made the life of Hungary's Jewish citizens very hard. On April 26 the Council of Ministers sanctioned the ongoing gathering of Jews into ghettos, depriving them of their property. With the intervention of Hungarian police organs, on May 15 Eichmann and Baky began deporting the Jews from the ghettos of the country according to the five zones into which the country had been divided. With 70 to 75 people crammed into each freight car, under inhuman conditions, more than 10,000 people were transported daily from Hungary towards Auschwitz. By July 8 the deportation of the Jews from the countryside had ended. Thus far 437,402 people had been deported.

Baky and circle also made preparations for the transportation of the 200,000 Jews living in Budapest. In order to implement it, 5,000 gendarmes were concentrate in Budapest by July 2. In the wake of increasing internal and external protests, and after finally finding out about the aim of the deportations and about the manner in which it was done, the Regent decided to take action to stop them. On July 5 he notified Colonel General Vörös, Chief of the General Staff, that he intended to stop any further deportations of the Jews, so that at least the Budapest Jews would remain in the country. At his command, Lieutenant General Szilárd Bakay, Commander of the Budapest Garrison mobilized the *honvéd* units in Budapest on July 5. Furthermore, the units of the 1st Esztergom Armored Division were ordered to Budapest on July 6. The gendarmerie was forced to withdraw without accomplishing anything.[43]

Notes

1. György Ránki, *1944. március 19. Magyarország megszállása* (March 19, 1944: Hungary's Occupation) (Budapest, 1979), p. 95.
2. Percy Schramm, ed., *Kriegstagebuch des Oberkommandos der Wehrmacht (Wehrmachtführungsstab), 1940–1945* (Frankfurt am Main, 1961–1979), vol. IV, p. 214.
3. György Ránki, ed., *Hitler hatvannyolc tárgyalása, 1939–1944*, I–II. (Hitler's Sixty-eight Discussions, 1939–1944) (Budapest, 1983), vol. II, p. 210.
4. *Ibid.*, p. 222.
5. *Ibid.*, p. 223.
6. Schramm, *Kriegstagebuch...*, vol. IV, p. 215.
7. *Ibid.*, p. 216.
8. Hoover Institute (Stanford, USA). Háborús bűnösök anyaga (Materials of War Criminals): Ministerial Case Veesenmayer V/a167. See Ránki, *1944. március 19...*, pp. 103-105.
9. *Ibid.*
10. Mario D. Fenyo, *Hitler, Horthy, and Hungary. German–Hungarian Relations, 1941–1944* (New Haven–London, 1972), p. 160.
11. *Ibid.*, p. 161.
12. Schramm, *Kriegstagebuch...*, vol. IV, p. 222.
13. *Ibid.*, p. 223.
14. Géza Lakatos, *Ahogy én láttam* (As I Saw It) (Munich, 1981), p. 72.
15. *Ibid.*, p. 74.
16. György Ránki, Ervin Pamlényi, Loránt Tilkovszky and Gyula Juhász, eds., *A Wilhelmstrasse és Magyarország: Német diplomáciai iratok Magyarországról, 1933–1944* (The Wilhelmstrasse and Hungary: German Diplomatic Documents about Hungary, 1933–1944) (Budapest, 1968), p. 780. (582)
17. *Ibid.*
18. *Ibid.*, p. 781. (582)
19. *Ibid.*
20. Miklós Kállay, *Hungarian Premier. A Personal Account of a Nation's Struggle in the Second World War* (New York, 1954), vol. II, p. 410.
21. *Ibid.*

22. László Zsigmond, ed., *Magyarország és a második világháború* (Hungary and World War II) (Budapest, 1966), p. 418.
23. *Ibid.*, pp. 418-419.
24. *Ibid.*, p. 421.
25. *Horthy Miklós titkos iratai* (Miklós Horthy's Secret Writings), ed. Miklós Szinai and László Szűcs, (Budapest, 1962), p. 424.
26. Zsigmond, *Magyarország és a második világháború*, p. 422.
27. *Ibid.*
28. *Ibid.*, p. 423.
29. *Ibid.*, pp. 424-425.
30. *Ibid.*, p. 426.
31. *Ibid.*, p. 429.
32. *Szombathelyi Ferenc visszaemlékezése* (Ferenc Szombathelyi's Memoirs) (Washington, 1988), pp. 24-25.
33. The following memoirs serve as resources for the events: Gyula Kádár, "Emlékezés az ország német megszállására, 1944. március 19" (Memoirs of the Country's German Occupation: March 19, 1944) (*Hadtörténelmi Közlemények*, 1974, No. 1), pp. 75-91; and Kálmán Kéri, "Visszaemlékezés 1944. március 19-re" (Memories of March 19, 1944) (*Hadtörténelmi Közlemények*, 1974, No. 1.), pp. 92-103.
34. Kállay, *Hungarian Premier...*, vol. II, p. 178.
35. *Horthy Miklós titkos iratai*, pp. 422-430.
36. *Ibid.*, p. 430.
37. Ránki–Pamlényi–Tilkovszky–Juhász, *A Wilhelmstrasse és Magyarország...*, p. 787. (590)
38. *Ibid.*, p. 788. (591)
39. In *Pesti Hírlap*, March 24, 1944.
40. Ránki–Pamlényi–Tilkovszky–Juhász, *A Wilhelmstrasse és Magyarország...*, p. 824. (633)
41. OL Filmtár 16 732 396 kk. János Vörös' diary: note of July 7, 1944.
42. *Ibid.*, note on April 24, 1944.
43. Ránki–Pamlényi–Tilkovszky–Juhász, *A Wilhelmstrasse és Magyarország...*, p. 872. (690) János Vörös' diary: note of July 5, 1944.

THE REGENT'S UNSUCCESSFUL ATTEMPT TO STABILIZE HIS REGIME AND TO BREAK AWAY FROM THE WAR: THE FAILURE OF THE OCTOBER 15, 1944, PROCLAMATION

Affected by the approaching Soviet troops and by the invasion of the Western powers, the Regent decided that it was time to enforce his will and to confront the Sztójay government. He also wanted to take the command of the *Honvédség* out of Vörös' hands and to entrust it to a loyal follower. His goal was to preserve the forces still available and to have something to rely on in case the situation changed. He was also encouraged to act by the messages of Hungarian diplomats, such as György Bakách-Bessenyei and others, in neutral countries, which stated that Hungary had to break away from the war before it was too late. The Regent still believed in Churchill's proposal for a landing in the Balkans, and did not even want to hear about unconditional surrender. He wanted to seek an armistice with the Anglo-Saxon nations only, which would allow Hungary to avoid a Soviet occupation. At István Bethlen's suggestion he planned to appoint a military government, which would restore the country's sovereignty and prepare it for pulling out of the war.

On July 5 Vörös and Sztójay tried to dissuade him from his intentions, claiming that Hungary was helpless against the might of the SS and the *Wehrmacht*. Their intervention would lead to a second "Mongol invasion" of Hungary, which would also open the way for the Soviet troops. Two days later, according to his diary, Vörös tried to divert Horthy with references to the Anglo-Saxons: "We are doing the best service to the civilized Western states if, even if with blood, we hold up Bolshevism. Even our present political enemies, for example the English, will appreciate that."[1]

On July 6 Horthy also informed Veesenmayer about his dissatisfaction with the German government. He asked him to implement a further reduction of German troops, to downsize the *Gestapo* in Hungary, and to restore the independence of the country. He expressed concern about the deportations, and asked for their immediate termination. Veesenmayer informed his superiors that Horthy wanted to appoint Colonel General Géza Lakatos as head of the new government. Veesenmayer was also getting ready to inform Hitler about Horthy's plans when, on July 17, he learned about Hitler's opinion regarding the issue. Hitler most definitely opposed the removal of the Sztójay government, which had been established based on a mutual agreement.[2]

Yet Horthy did not give up on his plan to reform the government. He was waiting for a favorable moment to implement his plan. The German army's tight situation on the front encouraged him, because that decreased the German presence in Hungary and made German military action difficult. Yet asserting his will would require that combat-ready troops were available and that the newly issued Hungarian replacement units were being deployed to the front. He had also let go the 1st Armored Division, deployed to Transylvania, the last efficient force, which had already been successfully deployed for policing tasks in July. Still, Horthy tried to assert his influence over his troops on the front through his loyal followers. On August 1 he appointed Colonel General Béla Miklós to replace Beregfy as Commander of the 1st Hungarian Army. On August 28 Colonel General Lajos Veress was appointed as Commander of the 2nd Hungarian Army, which was stationed in Transylvania, and also designated as the Regent's successor. In this way the situation became more tense between Horthy and Veesenmayer, who ceaselessly sent warning messages to Berlin.

The news of Romania's switching sides on August 23 also gave a boost to events. The strengthening of the internal anti-war opposition, the latest warning messages coming from Hungarian ambassadors in neutral countries, and the views of Bethlen's circle all pressured Horthy to form a new government. Its most important task, pushing everything else into the background, would be to shape and execute a military policy that would make the preparation and implementation of pulling out of the war possible.

The Regent did not wait any longer, but made the ailing Sztójay sign his resignation. On August 25 he appointed Colonel General Lakatos to form a new government, which took the oath of office on August 29. Lieutenant General Gusztáv Hennyei, Minister of Foreign Affairs, and Csatay, who retained his position, represented the military and enjoyed the Regent's unconditional trust. Although he felt that he was obliged to accept the appointment, Lakatos viewed it as a leap in the dark. His feelings were substantiated by the government's composition, by the fact that the military government was missing the one ingredient that gave a rationale to its existence, a military force, and by the power of the extreme right, supported by the German presence in the country.

Although he could not prevent the appointment of the government in the given critical situation, Veesenmayer was able to see that two of his loyal friends, Minister of Finance Lajos Reményi-Schneller and Minister of Agriculture Béla Jurcsek, were also part of it.

Simultaneously with the formation of the government, the Regent also tried to strengthen the intimate circle, made up mostly of soldiers, that he had formed around himself. Lieutenant General Antal Vattay, who had been ordered back from heading the cavalry division and who was also the decisive figure of the circle, became Chief Aide-de-Camp and Head of the Military Office. There was also Lieutenant General Szilárd Bakay, who took over commanding the I. Budapest Army Corps in early August. He was expected to ensure the execution of the Regent's will, with the help of the troops concentrated in the Budapest garrison. Lieutenant General Károly Lázár, Commander of the Guards, and retired Colonel

General István Náday, who, however, was not in the vicinity of the Regent in the crucial days due to his Italian mission, were also members of the internal circle.

The cautious new government assured the command of the German army that it intended to continue the common fight. The Council of Ministers decided that Hungarian troops would launch a southern offensive together with the Germans in an attempt to seal off the passes of the Southern Carpathians before the Soviet troops arrived. After initial successes against the Romanian troops, the attack of the 2nd Hungarian Army, launched south of Kolozsvár on September 5, halted and then turned into a defensive military operation against the arriving Soviet troops. In order to deal with the situation the Hungarian government asked, in vain, for the urgent deployment of German divisions. Soviet troops had finally forced their way onto Hungarian territory.

The situation was further aggravated by the national uprising that broke out in Slovakia, by Finland's signing a cease-fire with the Soviets, and by Romania's declaring war on Hungary on September 7.

The increasingly critical situation induced the Regent to announce at the September 8 session of the Crown Council that if the requested German help did not come and the military situation proved hopeless, then he would ask for a cease-fire. However, Minister of Defense Lajos Csatay proposed waiting and requesting the deployment of five German armored divisions within 24 hours as an ultimatum. Only if the request was not fulfilled, he said, should they take this grave step. His proposal was accepted. And although the divisions never arrived, on September 11 the Council of Ministers did not accept the idea of a cease-fire, and offered its resignation in protest. On September 12 the Regent sent Chief of the General Staff János Vörös to German Headquarters, hoping that he would get the promised armored divisions, which would stabilize the front, would gain time for the leadership, and would at least postpone the cease-fire.

On September 13 the Hungarian troops deployed in the south of the *Alföld*, headed by the 1st Hungarian Armored Division, were given the command to attack in the direction of Arad–Lippa. The operation began successfully here as well as at Arad. However, just as at Torda, the operation faltered when it bumped into Soviet troops. The Hungarian troops began to retreat towards the Hungarian border.

Since Vörös' mission had also failed to obtain the requested divisions, a decision was made by a narrow circle around Horthy that Colonel General István Náday should fly to Italy to contact the Allies and prepare the cease-fire. Due to the uncertain behavior of the government, the action was not taken until September 22. Náday arrived at the Allies' base without written authorization, and his mission proved to be unsuccessful. He was told to turn to the Soviet Union for a cease-fire.

Seeing the absence of the promised German help, on September 28 the Regent finally consented to sending a delegation led by Lieutenant General Gábor Faragho to Moscow. Even then he took this forced step in an ambiguous way, and by setting unrealistic cease-fire conditions. The Faragho delegation also arrived without the necessary written authorization. Horthy still thought that it was possible to obtain Anglo-Saxon participation in the occupation of Hungary, as well as securing the free withdrawal of German troops, based on the Finnish example. Only following another exchange of telegrams was the delegation granted the authority to sign the preliminary cease-fire conditions, which obliged the Hungarian government to end all connections with Germany and to declare war on it, and to instruct Hungarian troops to stop operations against the Soviet troops and to turn their arms against the Germans.

Led by the Regent's son, Miklós Horthy, and with the assistance of the Regent's confidential circle, the "breakaway" office came in existence in the Castle. The confidential circle consisted of the Regent's daughter-in-law, the Chief of the Cabinet Gyula Ambrózy, Aide-de-Camp Gyula Tost, Chief Aid-de-Camp Antal Vattay, and Lieutenant General Károly Lázár, Commander of the Guards. Later Lieutenant General Szilárd Bakay, Commander of the I. Budapest Army Corps, also joined the circle. Their tasks were the military preparations for the cease-fire and the organization of the resistance against the expected German countermeasures.

But the military preparations were already late. Neither the military measures necessary for the breakaway nor the execution of those steps included in the cease-fire agreement ever happened, and the timid steps taken towards them proved to be too little too late. The delayed concentration of troops in Budapest and its region against the opposition of that part of the General Staff not involved in breaking away, as well as the intervention of the Germans, doomed the effort to failure. The 10th Infantry Division was deployed to Budapest, but did not arrive, and it proved impossible to deploy the cavalry division to defend Budapest. It had unloaded in the region of Nagykőrös and Kecskemét on October 13 and had moved to the frontline. The commander of this division Lieutenant General Mihály Ibrányi considered it to be impossible to concentrate his troops, which were located among the German units, during the night of October 14, or to lead them to Budapest by the morning. And nobody could line up the battle-weary and retreating fragmented units under reconstruction around Budapest for the defense of Budapest.

However, the guards' battalion, as well as the 9th Infantry Regiment, all assumed to be loyal to Horthy and ordered up to defend the government, were in Budapest. The latter, however, turned against the Regent at the crucial hour. The loyalty of the Budapest gendarmerie battalion was uncertain and it was not counted on. The reliable 1st Parachutist Battalion, on the other hand, arrived only on October 15 and so did not become main role-players in the events. In the final analysis, the only armed unit that took up arms to defend the Castle was that of the guards.

Commander of the 1st Army Béla Miklós and Commander of the 2nd Army Lajos Veress were the only commanders of armies on the front who were on the inside on the breakaway issue. Even they could follow the events only circumstantially, and did not receive any instructions on what preparations to make that would have made it possible to turn against the Germans and to take up connections with the Soviet troops following the announcement of the cease-fire. As experienced soldiers, they well knew that such a measure could not be executed from one hour to the next. Short of a command from the Regent, they would not independently set out to take any preliminary measures, which would have produced an uncertain result in any case and would have been expected to induce an immediate German reaction. They also had doubts as to how the officer corps, which dreaded the Soviet army, would react, and whether they would fully implement the command. The October 15 proclamation on the radio was unexpected for them as well. With the help of his own officers Lajos Veress was immediately arrested by the Germans, while Béla Miklós went over to the Soviet troops in order to avoid arrest.

It was a fatal mistake that the Regent and his Prime Minister could not agree on the content of the proclamation. Consequently, it was not clearly included in the proclamation that, according to the conditions of the cease-fire, Hungary had to break away from Germany and had to commence war against the Germans while cooperating with the Soviet army. Instead, Horthy informed Veesenmayer about his intention of signing the cease-fire and its imminent announcement. He would not have considered it to be fair to stab a former ally in the back.

But the Regent was unable to control events or to implement the cease-fire, which he himself feared as well. He could not reasonably hope that the abandoned and confused army would react appropriately to his radio proclamation, which might or might not get through to the troops on the frontline, to whom he had obscurely hinted that they should obey their commanders but had not given decisive instructions. Even on hearing the proclamation, the troops and their commanders could only be informed about the intent to sign a cease-fire and not about changing sides.

On the other side, the Regent and his confidantes could not prevent the police forces of the Germans and the army, well informed about every nuance of the preparations for the cease-fire, from suppressing the attempt to change sides. General Bakay, who was supposed to organize and direct the opposition, was arrested by the Germans. The same happened to the Regent's son. German troops—including the "Tiger" tanks of the 503rd Heavy Tank Division and the 22nd Cavalry Division—were directed towards Budapest. These soldiers agreed with Szálasi, and put on alert the Arrow-Cross. The Regent was helpless towards them, and he and his circle could not hinder anything that they did. Under such unfavorable circumstances, the Regent decided to read his proclamation on the radio at noon on October 15. Since the Regent could not agree with his Prime Minister about the content to be included in the proclamation, he told the nation only about the cease-fire, and did not include the unambiguous command that the troops on the front should turn against the German troops and begin fighting them in cooperation with the Soviet army. The proclamation was this:

> Ever since the will of the nation put me at the helm of the country, the most important aim of Hungarian foreign policy was, through peaceful revision, to repair, at least partly, the injustices of the Peace Treaty of Trianon. Our hopes in the League of Nations in this regard remained unfulfilled.
>
> At the time of the beginning of a new world crisis, Hungary was not led by a desire to acquire new territories. We had no aggressive intention against the Republic of Czecho-Slovakia, and Hungary did not

wish to regain territories taken from her by war. We entered Bácska only after the collapse of Yugoslavia and at that time in order to defend our blood brethren. We accepted a peaceful decision of the Axis powers regarding the eastern territories taken from us in 1918 by Romania.

Hungary was forced into war against the Allies by German pressure, which weighed upon us owing to our geographical situation. But even so we were not guided by any ambition to increase our own power and had no intention to snatch as much as a square meter of territory from anybody.

Today it is obvious to any sober-minded person that the German Reich has lost the war. All governments responsible for the destiny of their countries must draw pertinent conclusions from this fact, for, as a great German statesman, Bismarck, once said: "No nation ought to sacrifice itself on the altar of an alliance." Conscious of my historic responsibility, I have the obligation to undertake every step directed to avoiding further unnecessary bloodshed. A nation that would allow the soil inherited from its forefathers to be turned into a theater of rearguard actions in an already lost war, defending alien interests out of a serf-like spirit, would lose the esteem of public opinion throughout the world.

With grief I am forced to state that the German Reich on its part broke the loyalty of an ally toward our country a long time ago. For a considerable time it has launched ever- new formations of Hungarian armed forces into the fight outside the frontiers of the country against my wish and will.

In March of this year, however, the Führer of the German Reich invited me to negotiation in consequence of my urgent demand for the repatriation of Hungary's armed forces. There he informed me that Hungary would be occupied by German forces and he ordered this to be carried out in spite of my protests, even while I was retained abroad. Simultaneously German political police invaded the country and arrested numerous Hungarian citizens, among them several members of the legislative assembly as well as the minister of the interior of my government then in office.

The Premier himself evaded detention only by taking refuge in a neutral embassy. After having received a firm promise from the Führer of the German Reich that he would cancel acts that violated and restricted Hungary's sovereignty, in case I appointed a government enjoying the confidence of the Germans, I appointed the Sztójay government.

Yet the Germans did not keep their promise. In the shelter of German occupation the Gestapo tackled the Jewish question in a manner incompatible with the demands of humanity, applying methods it had already employed elsewhere. When war drew near the frontiers, and even passed them, the Germans repeatedly promised assistance, yet again they failed to honor their promise.

During their retreat they turned the country's sovereign territory into a theater of looting and destruction. Those actions, contrary to an ally's loyalty, were crowned by an act of open provocation when in the course of measures for the maintenance of order in the interior of Budapest, Corps Commander Field Marshal Lieutenant Szilárd Bakay was treacherously attacked and abducted by Gestapo agents who exploited the bad visibility of a foggy October morning when he was getting out of his car in front of his house.

Subsequently German aircraft dropped leaflets against the government in office. I received reliable information that troops of pro-German tendency intended to raise their own men to power by using force to effect a political upheaval and the overthrowing of the legal Hungarian government which I had appointed in the meantime (Premier Lakatos) and that they intended to turn their country's territory into a theater of rearguard actions for the German Reich.

I decided to safeguard Hungary's honor even in relation to her former ally, although this ally, instead of supplying the military help he had promised, meant to rob the Hungarian nation finally of its greatest treasure—its freedom and independence.

I informed a representative of the German Reich that we were about to conclude a military armistice with our previous enemies and to cease all hostilities against them.

Trusting your love of truth, I hope to secure in accord with you the continuity of our nation's life in the future and the realization of our peaceful aims.

Commanders of the Hungarian army have received corresponding orders from me. Accordingly, the troops, loyal to their oath and following an order of the day issued simultaneously, must obey the commanders appointed by me. I appeal to every honest Hungarian to follow me on the path beset by sacrifices that will lead to Hungary's salvation.[3]

Without the intervention and support of the Hungarian military command, the successful implementation of the cease-fire was not imaginable. And they did their best to destroy the cease-fire by hindering the mobility of troops commanded to move to Budapest, and tried to gain control over the troops already there. The General Staff officers considered cooperation with the Soviet troops to be unacceptable, and believed that a Soviet occupation would be fatal both for themselves and for the system. Even at that point they considered sticking with the Germans to be the best solution. Therefore, some of them considered it to be necessary to inform the German leadership and the Arrow-Cross about events, and to support the activities that would prevent a cease-fire.

János Vörös, who had done everything even during the summer of 1944 to support the common fight and to prevent the Regent from taking careless steps towards the German army, behaved passively towards preparations for a cease-fire when he became aware of it. However, since the Regent considered him to be unreliable, he was not involved in the affair. He did not comply with the instructions of the General Staff, did not prevent his subalterns' arrangements to hinder the cease-fire, and also did not call the Regent's attention to them. Following the Regent's proclamation, Vörös did not keep the soldiers at the front and in the hinterland in uncertainty for very long. He quickly issued the following counter-command:

> The Order of the Chief of the Hungarian General Staff as Regards Laying down Arms
>
> The expression of "laying down arms" included in the radio proclamation [of Regent Horthy] does not mean that everyone throws his arms away. No order was issued to cease the fighting, only proposal for armistice was made.
>
> To be sent to the 1st, 2nd, and 3rd Armies and to all the independent commands and organizations of the *Honvédség*.
>
> Budapest, October 15, 1944.
>
> Colonel-General János Vörös[4]

After the unsuccessful attempt, the German troops—with Arrow-Cross help—immediately occupied the main points of Budapest. General Aggteleky, Commander of the Budapest Army Corps, was arrested by his own subordinates. Horthy was also carried to the German Embassy after the German troops advanced on the Castle and broke down the resistance of the guards. The attempt to pull out of the war was crushed. On October 16 the Regent was blackmailed by threats to his son, and was forced to recant his proclamation of the previous day and to appoint Szálasi to form a new government.

The ill-considered, ambiguous, and militarily unprepared proclamation was doomed to fail. With the intervention of the General Staff, the supreme warlord of the *Honvédség* became isolated from his troops and officer corps, and was unable to establish contact with them. The Regent, who had taught the officer corps and the staff of the army for 25 years to hate Bolshevism and the Soviet Union, acted in an uncertain and hesitant fashion when in Moscow it was pointed out that turning against the German army was a basic and unavoidable condition for obtaining a cease-fire, under the terms of "unconditional surrender." Therefore, the majority of the officer corps did not even have to face the problem of choosing which alternative to accept, since the command whose fulfillment would have proved their unconditional loyalty to the Regent was never issued. The Regent also failed to secure his army for his own defense. The supreme warlord—deprived of his ranks as Regent and Commander-in-Chief, abandoned by his troops, disappointed, and in German custody—had to leave the country, thus ensuring the collapse of the regime that he established and that was connected to his name.

Notes

1. OL Filmtár 16 732 396 kk. János Vörös' diary: note on July 7, 1944.
2. György Ránki, Ervin Pamlényi, Loránt Tilkovszky and Gyula Juhász, eds., *A Wilhelmstrasse és Magyarország: Német diplomáciai iratok Magyarországról, 1933–1944* (The Wilhelmstrasse and Hungary: German Diplomatic Documents about Hungary, 1933–1944) (Budapest, 1968), p. 884. (700)
3. www.hungarian-history.hu/lib/montgo/montgo20.htm.
4. Hadtörténeti Intézet és Múzeum, Hadtörténeti Levéltár (Institute and Museum of Hungarian Military History, Military History Archives), 1591/Főv. hdm. 44. 10. 15. (Supreme Command Section of Operations, October 15, 1944).

BIBLIOGRAPHY

Ábrahám, Ferenc and Endre Kussinszky, eds. *Az Imrédy-per. A vád, a vallomások és az ítélet* (The Imrédy Trial: Charge, Statements and Judgement). Budapest: Híradó Könyvtár, 1945.
Adonyi, Ferenc N. *A magyar katona a második világháborúban. 1941–1945* (The Hungarian Soldier in World War II: 1941–1945). Klagenfurt: Ferdinand Kleinmayr, 1954.
Andorka, Rudolf. *A madridi követségtől Mauthausenig* (From the Madrid Embassy to Mauthausen). Budapest: Kossuth Könyvkiadó, 1978.
Bárdossy László népbírósági pere (László Bárdossy's Trial in the People's Court). Budapest, 1946.
Bárdossy, László. *A nemzet védelmében* (In Defense of the Nation). Fahrwangen: Duna Kiadó, 1976.
Csima, János. *Adalékok a Horthy-hadsereg szervezetének és háborús tevékenységének tanulmányozásához (1938–1945)* (Additions to Studying the Organizational Structure and the Military Activities of the Horthy Army: 1938–1945). Budapest: Honvédelmi Minisztérium Központi Irattár, 1961.
Fenyo, Mario D. *Hitler, Horthy, and Hungary. German–Hungarian Relations, 1941–1944.* New Haven–London: Yale University Press, 1972.
Gibson, Hugh, ed. *Ciano naplója: 1939–1943: Gróf Galeazzo Ciano olasz külügyminiszter, 1939–1943 teljes, rövidítés nélküli naplói* (Ciano's Diary: 1939–1943: The Full Unabridged Diary of Count Galeazzo Ciano, Italian Foreign Minister, 1939–1943). Budapest: Athenaeum, 1946.
Hadtörténelmi Közlemények (1977) 1.

Hadtörténelmi Közlemények (1974) 1.

Halder, Franz, *Kriegstagebuch. Tägliche Aufzeichnungen des Chefs des Generalstabes des Heeres 1939–1942/Generaloberst Halder,* 3 vols. Stuttgart: Kohlhammer, 1962–1964.

Hillgruber, Andreas. *Hitler, König Carol und Marschal Antonescu.* Wiesbaden: Steiner, 1954.

———. *Hitlers Strategie. Politik und Kriegführung 1940–1941.* Frankfurt am Main: Bernard u. Graefe, 1965.

Horthy Miklós titkos iratai (Miklós Horthy's Secret Writings). Ed. Miklós Szinai and László Szűcs. Budapest: Kossuth Könyvkiadó, 1962.

Horthy, Miklós. *Emlékirataim* (My Memoirs). Buenos Aires: own publishing, 1953.

Juhász, Gyula. *Magyar–brit titkos tárgyalások 1943-ban* (Hungarian–British Secret Discussions in 1943). Budapest: Kossuth Könyvkiadó, 1978.

———. *Magyarország külpolitikája* (Hungary's Foreign Policy). Budapest: Kossuth Könyvkiadó, 1969.

———. *A Teleki-kormány külpolitikája, 1939–1941* (The Foreign Policy of the Teleki Government, 1939–1941). Budapest: Akadémiai Kiadó, 1964.

———, ed. *Diplomáciai iratok Magyarország külpolitikájához 1936–1945* (Diplomatic Writings on Hungary's Foreign Policy, 1936–1945). Budapest: Akadémiai Kiadó, 1962–1982.

Kádár, Gyula. *A Ludovikától Sopronkőhidáig* (From the Ludovika [Military Academy] to Sopronkőhida). Budapest: Magvető Könyvkiadó, 1978.

Kállay, Miklós. *Hungarian Premier. A Personal Account of a Nation's Struggle in the Second World War.* New York: Columbia University Press, 1954.

Karsai, Elek. *A budai vártól a gyepüig* (From the Buda Castle to the Borderland). Budapest: Táncsics Könyvkiadó, 1965.

Lakatos, Géza. *Ahogy én láttam* (As I Saw It). Munich: Auróra Könyvkiadó, 1981.

Macartney, Carlile Aylmer. *October Fifteenth. A History of Modern Hungary, 1929-1945.* Edinburgh: Edinburgh University Press, 1961.

Magyar Katonai Szemle (1940) 8.

Magyar Katonaújság (1940) 28.

A m. kir. honvéd vezérkar főnökének előadása a vezetésről az 1942. december 14-15-i tábornoki és vezérkari megbeszélésen (The Lecture Held by the Chief of the Hungarian Royal General Staff on Leadership at the General and General Staff Level Meeting of December 14 and 15, 1942). Budapest: Hadtudományi Könyvtár, 1942.

Nagybaczoni Nagy, Vilmos. *Végzetes esztendők 1938-1945* (Fatal Years, 1938-1945). Budapest: Gondolat, 1986.

Pesti Hírlap, March 24, 1944.

Ránki, György. *1944. március 19. Magyarország megszállása* (March 19, 1944: Hungary's Occupation). Budapest: Kossuth Könyvkiadó, 1979.

———. *A második világháború története* (The History of World War II). Budapest: Gondolat Könyvkiadó, 1973.

———, ed. *Hitler hatvannyolc tárgyalása, 1939-1944* (Hitler's Sixty-eight Discussions, 1939-1944), I-II. Budapest: Magvető Kiadó, 1983.

———, Ervin Pamlényi, Loránt Tilkovszky and Gyula Juhász, eds. *A Wilhelmstrasse és Magyarország: Német diplomáciai iratok Magyarországról, 1933-1944* (The Wilhelmstrasse and Hungary: German Diplomatic Documents about Hungary, 1933-1944). Budapest: Kossuth Könyvkiadó, 1968.

Saly, Dezső. *Szigorúan bizalmas* (Strictly Confidential). Budapest: Anonymus, 1945.

Schramm, Percy, ed. *Kriegstagebuch des Oberkommandos der Wehrmacht (Wehrmachtführungsstab), 1940-1945.* Frankfurt am Main: Bernard und Graefe Verlag für Wehrwesen, 1961-1979.

Sontag, Raymond James, *et. al.*, eds. *Documents on German Foreign Policy, 1918-1945.* Washington, DC: U.S. Government Printing Office, 1949-1954.
Századok (1965) 6.
Szent-Iványi, Domokos. *Emlékirat* (Memoirs). Ráday Levéltár (Ráday Archive), Szent-Iványi hagyaték C/80.
Szombathelyi Ferenc visszaemlékezése (Ferenc Szombathelyi's Memoirs). Washington, DC: Occidental Press, 1988.
Új Látóhatár (1975) 1.
Vollmacht des Gewissens. Frankfurt am Main–Berlin: Europäischen Publikation, 1965.
www.hungarian-history.hu/lib/montgo/montgo20.htm.
Zsigmond, László, ed. *Magyarország és a második világháború* (Hungary and World War II). Budapest: Kossuth Könyvkiadó, 1966.

THE AUTHOR

Lóránd Dombrády was born in Szatmárnémeti (today Satu Mare, Romania) on April 3, 1931. He worked as a teacher after taking his degree in History–Hungarian language. He was a research fellow at the central office of the Society for Popularization of Scientific Knowledge, with the desk of history, military science and the popularization of knowledge of international policies from 1966. He was then a research fellow from 1972, later a senior member, and finally, between 1990 and 1991, that is, until his retirement, the director of the Institute of Military History, Budapest. His fields of science are the military policy and war economy of the period between 1920 and 1944. A candidate (1975) then doctor (1990) of military science, he is also a member of the Committee on Military Science of the Hungarian Academy of Sciences and the editorial board of the periodical *Hadtörténelmi Közlemények* (Publications on Military History).

Major works: *Magyar gazdaság és hadfelszerelés, 1938–1944* (Hungarian Economy and the Equipment of the Army, 1938–1944) (1981), *Hadsereg és politika Magyarországon, 1938–1944* (Army and Politics in Hungary, 1938–1944) (1986), *A magyar királyi honvédség, 1919–1945* (The Hungarian Royal Honvédség, 1919–1945) (1987), *A legfelsőbb hadúr és hadserege* (The Supreme Commander and his Army) (1999), *Katonapolitika és hadsereg, 1920–1944* (Military Policy and the Army, 1920–1944) (2000), *A magyar hadigazdaság a második világháború időszakában* (Hungarian War Economy in the Period of the Second World War) (2003).

BIOGRAPHIES

Aggteleky, Béla (1890–1977)
: Hungarian major general. He was arrested on the morning of October 15, 1944 by his adjutant, who turned him over to the *Gestapo*.

Alfieri, Dino (1886–1966)
: Italian politician. He was a member of the Fascist *Gran Consiglio*, and ambassador to Germany in 1939–1943.

Ambrózy, Gyula (1884–1954)
: Hungarian writer of international law. He worked as chief of the Cabinet Office of the regent from 1942.

Andorka, Rudolf (1931–1997)
: Hungarian university professor and sociologist. He was imprisoned after the 1956 Hungarian Revolution. He became a corresponding member of the Hungarian Academy of Sciences in 1990.

Antonescu, Ion (1882–1946)
: Prime minister and dictator of Romania during World War II from 1940 to 1944.

Apor, Gábor, Baron (1889–1969)
: Hungarian diplomat. Ambassador to the Vatican in 1939–1944. He resigned when Hungary was occupied by Germany, and stayed in Rome.

Badoglio, Pietro (1871–1956)
: Italian soldier and Fascist politician. He was created viceroy of Ethiopia and duke of Addis Ababa in 1936. He resigned in 1940 and succeeded Mussolini as prime minister of Italy from 1943 to June 1944, negotiating the armistice with the Allies.

Bajcsy-Zsilinszky, Endre (1886-1944)
: Hungarian politician. First a racialist right-wing MP, later an anti-Fascist, he was arrested and executed by the Fascist government.

Bajnóczy, József (1888-1977)
: Hungarian colonel general. Deputy chief of the General Staff in 1941-1944, and deputy minister of defense in 1943-1944.

Bakách-Bessenyey, György, Baron (1892-1959)
: Hungarian diplomat. Ambassador to Belgrade (1938), to Vichy (1941) and to Bern (1943). He resigned when Hungary was occupied by the Germans, and stayed in the West.

Bakay, Szilárd (1892-1946)
: Hungarian lieutenant general. He was one of the key figures of the attempt to break away from the war, and so the Germans took him to Mauthausen. In early 1946, the Soviet authorities arrested him and executed him as a war criminal because of his role in the Ukraine.

Baky, László (1898-1946)
: Hungarian gendarme and politician. Secretary of state of the interior in the Sztójay government. An MP of the Arrow-Cross Party in 1939. After March 19, 1944, he led the deportation of the Hungarian Jews. He was executed as a war criminal.

Bánffy, Dániel, Baron (1893-1955)
: Transylvanian landowner and conservative politician. Minister of agriculture in the Teleki, Bárdossy and Kállay governments.

Baranyai, Lipót (1894-1970)
: President of the Hungarian National Bank, and a member of the Hungarian Academy of Sciences. The Germans arrested him. He left Hungary in 1948.

Barcza, György (1888-1961)
: Hungarian lawyer and diplomat. Hungarian ambassador to the Vatican and to the United Kingdom in 1927-1938, and special envoy of the prime minister in Switzerland in 1943. He lived in Austria after 1945.

Bárczy, István (1866–1943)
　Hungarian politician. Minister of justice (1919–1920).
Bárdossy, László (1890–1946)
　Hungarian diplomat and politician. Minister of foreign affairs, and then prime minister in 1941–1942. After World War II he was condemned for war crimes by the People's Court and executed.
Bartha, Károly (1884–1964)
　Hungarian professional army officer. Minister of defense in 1938–1942.
Beck, Ludwig (1880–1944)
　German officer. Chief of the German General Staff from 1935. He opposed attempts by Hitler and the Nazi Party to take over the army. When Hitler discovered that he was plotting against the regime, he was removed from office. Suspected in being involved in the abortive 1944 July Plot (an unsuccessful putsch against Hitler), he was arrested and was ordered to commit suicide.
Beckerle, Adolf Heinz (1902–?)
　German officer. Envoy in Sofia. Commander of the SA from 1928 to 1945.
Beregfy, Károly, Berger (1888–1946)
　Hungarian colonel general. Before the Arrow-Cross takeover he was commander of the 3rd Hungarian Army. He became minister and chief of the General Staff under Szálasi. He was executed as a war criminal.
Bethlen, István, Count (1874–1946)
　Hungarian statesman. A member of the Hungarian peace delegation in 1920. Prime minister of Hungary in 1921–1931. He opposed one-sided pro-German attitudes, being a leading politician of Anglo-American orientation. He was deported to the Soviet Union by the Red Army.

Brauchitsch, Walther von (1881–1948)
: German field marshal and commander-in-chief of the German armed forces during the first part of World War II. He was instrumental in planning and carrying out the campaigns against Poland, the Netherlands, Belgium, France, the Balkans and the Soviet Union.

Canaris, Wilhelm (1887–1945)
: German naval officer. Head of the *Abwehr* (German military intelligence) in 1935. He enlisted some of the anti-Hitler conspirators into the *Abwehr* and shielded their activities. After the 1944 July Plot against Hitler, he was arrested and executed.

Carol II, King (1893–1953)
: King of Romania from 1930 to 1940.

Ciano, Galeazzo, Conte di Cortellazo (1903–1944)
: Italian politician and diplomat. Minister of foreign affairs in 1936–1943. He was executed on Mussolini's orders.

Csáky, István, Count (1894–1941)
: Hungarian diplomat and minister of foreign affairs. He played an important role in signing the Anti-Comintern Pact, the Second Vienna Award and the Hungarian–Yugoslavian Treaty of Eternal Friendship.

Csatay, Lajos (1886–1944)
: Hungarian general. Minister of defense in 1943–1944 in the Kállay, Sztójai and Lakatos governments. Arrested by the *Gestapo*, he committed suicide together with his wife.

Dálnoki Miklós, Béla (1890–1948)
: Hungarian colonel general. Commander of the 1st Hungarian Army in 1944. Prime minister of the provisional national government in 1944–1945.

Dálnoki Veress, Lajos (1889–1976)
: Hungarian colonel general. Commander of the 2nd Hungarian Army in 1944. He was imprisoned in 1947–1956, and later emigrated.

Eichmann, Adolf (1906–1962)
: German SS lieutenant colonel. Chief of the Jewish Office of the *Gestapo*, which aimed at the total extermination of European Jewry. He prepared the *Anschluss*. He was able to escape to Argentina, but was abducted from there and taken to Israel in 1960, where he was sentenced to death for crimes against the Jewish people and crimes against humanity.

Erdmannsdorff, Otto von (1888–1978)
: German diplomat. Ambassador to Budapest in 1937–1941.

Faragho, Gábor (1890–1953)
: Hungarian colonel general. Military attaché to Moscow in 1940–1941, a leader of Horthy's delegation that signed the preliminary armistice agreement in Moscow on October 11, 1944, and minister of public supply in 1944–1945. He was sent into retirement in 1945.

Foertsch, Hermann (1885–1961)
: German general. Chief of the General Staff of the Army Group E in 1942, and then of the Army Group F from 1943. Planner and leader of the occupation of Hungary.

Fütterer, Kuno Heribert (1894–1963)
: German officer. Air attaché to Budapest from 1940 to the end of World War II.

Gafencu, Grigore (1892–1957)
: Romanian politician and journalist. Minister of foreign affairs from 1939. He emigrated after the war.

Ghyczy, Jenő (1893–1982)
: Hungarian politician. Foreign affairs under-secretary from 1941, and minister of foreign affairs in 1943–1944.

Gömbös, Gyula (1886–1936)
: Hungarian professional army officer and politician. Minister of defense in 1929–1932, and prime minister in 1932–1936. As prime minister, he announced a National Work Plan based on contemporary German and Italian models. He brought Hungary into an alliance with Italy, Austria and Germany.

Gorondy-Novák, Elemér (1885–1954)
    Hungarian officer. Inspector of the Rapid Troops and the Cavalry in 1938–1940, and commander of the 1st Hungarian Army, then of the 3rd Hungarian Army, in 1940–1941. He retired in 1942, and emigrated after the war.
Göring, Hermann (1893–1946)
    Prussian prime minister and minister of the interior in 1933–1934. Marshal of the German Empire. He was a leader of the Nazi Party and one of the primary architects of the Nazi police state in Germany. He was sentenced to death, but committed suicide in prison.
Grassy, József (1894–1946)
    Hungarian *Honvéd* officer. Commander of the 15th Infantry Brigade in 1941–1942. He was court-martialed in 1943 because of the Újvidék atrocities, but escaped to Germany in January 1944, and became brigadier general of the Waffen SS and commander of the "Hunyadi" and "Hungária" SS Divisions in 1945. He was executed in Yugoslavia.
Greiffenberg, Hans von (1893–1951)
    German officer. Chief of the General Staff of the 12th German Army and the Central Army Group in 1941, and of the Army Group A in 1942. Military attaché to Budapest from 1943. Plenipotentiary general of the *Wehrmacht* in Hungary in 1944–1945.
Grolman, Helmuth von (1898–1977)
    German officer. Chief of the General Staff of the Southern Ukraine Army Group and Southern Army Group in 1944–1945.
Guderian, Heinz (1888–1954)
    German general. Chief of the General Staff of the OKH (*Oberkommando des Heeres*, the High Command of German Land Forces) in 1944–1945.

Halder, Franz (1884–1972)
: German officer. Chief of the General Staff of the OKH in 1938. He organized the offensive against Poland and helped to plan Operation Barbarossa. Commander-in-chief of the German army until September 1942. He was arrested by the *Gestapo* in 1944 and was sent to Dachau. He was a witness in the Nuremberg War Crimes Trials.

Halifax, Edward Frederick Lindley Wood, Earl of Halifax (1881–1959)
: British viceroy of India in 1925–1931, foreign secretary in 1938–1940, and ambassador to the United States in 1941–1946.

Hennyei, Gusztáv (1888–1977)
: Hungarian general and military diplomat. Commander of the II. Army Corps in 1941–1942, inspector of the Infantry in 1942–1943, and minister of foreign affairs in 1944. He was arrested and deported to Germany after the Arrow-Cross takeover.

Himer, Kurt (1888–1942)
: German officer. Military attaché to Warsaw in 1938–1939, and commander of the 216th Infantry Division in 1940. During the Balkan operations and the attack against the Soviet Union, he was assigned to the headquarters of the *Honvédség*.

Himmler, Heinrich (1900–1945)
: German Nazi leader. The head of the SS. Minister of the interior in 1943. After the 1944 July Plot, he became chief of the army's home organization. In April 1945, Hitler ordered his arrest because he had tried to propose peace to the Allies. He poisoned himself.

Hitler, Adolf (1889–1945)
: German politician. Leader of the Nazi (National Socialist) Party and dictator of Germany in 1933–1945. He was directly responsible for World War II. One of the greatest genocides of human history is connected to his name.

Hóman, Bálint (1885–1951)

Hungarian right-wing politician and historian. A member of the Hungarian Academy of Sciences from 1918 to 1945, he was minister of religion and public education in 1932–1938 and 1939–1942, and minister without portfolio in 1938. He was sentenced to life imprisonment as a war criminal, and died in prison.

Homlok, Sándor (1892–?)

Hungarian lieutenant general. Military attaché to France (1927–1933), to Sweden (1940–1941), to Finland, Estonia, Latvia and Lithuania (1941) and to Germany and Switzerland (1941–1944).

Horstenau, Edmund Glaise von (1882–1946)

German historian.

Horthy, István, vitéz nagybányai (1904–1942)

Hungarian military and political figure. The elder son of Regent Miklós Horthy. An engineer, he became vice-regent of Hungary. He died in an air accident at the Soviet front.

Horthy, Miklós, Jr., vitéz nagybányai (1907–1993)

Hungarian diplomat. The younger son of Regent Miklós Horthy. Leader of the Hungarian Embassy in Rio de Janeiro from 1939 to the beginning of the war. He was one of the leaders of the attempt to break away from the war, and so he was deported to Mauthausen by the Germans, as they could blackmail the regent in this way.

Horthy, Miklós, vitéz nagybányai (1868–1957)

Hungarian navy officer and statesman. Admiral of the Austro-Hungarian Fleet and regent of Hungary from 1920 to 1944. He joined the Berlin–Rome Axis and entered World War II. In 1944 he attempted to leave the war, but failed, as a result of which German troops occupied Hungary. After World War II he lived in Portugal.

Hóry, András (1883–1971)
: Hungarian diplomat and political journalist. Ambassador to Warsaw in 1936–1939. He was a representative of the Hungarian government at the Turnu-Severin Hungarian-Romanian negotiations in 1940.

Ibrányi, Mihály (1895–1962)
: Hungarian lieutenant general. Commander on the eastern front. Inspector of the Infantry in 1945.

Ilcusu, Ioan (1883–?)
: Romanian lieutenant general. Minister of war in 1939–1940, he retired in 1940 and died in prison.

Imrédy, Béla (1891–1946)
: Hungarian financial expert and politician. Minister of finance in 1932–1935, president of the Hungarian National Bank in 1935–1938, and prime minister in 1938–1939. After World War II he was condemned for war crimes by the People's Court and executed.

Jagow, Dietrich von ("*Der Degen*") (1892–1945)
: German officer. SA *Obergruppenführer*. German minister in Budapest in 1941–1944. Nazi courier to Meran in 1945. He committed suicide.

Jány, Gusztáv (1883–1947)
: Hungarian general. Commander of the 2nd Hungarian Army destroyed at the River Don in 1943.

Jaross, Andor (1896–1946)
: Hungarian right-wing politician. Minister without portfolio of Upper Hungarian affairs in 1938–1940, and minister of the interior in 1944. He was executed as a war criminal.

Jodl, Alfred (1890–1946)
: German officer. Chief of the *Wehrmachtführungsamt* in 1939–1945, and colonel general from 1944. He was executed.

Jurcsek, Béla (1893–1945)
: Hungarian Fascist politician and landowner. Secretary of state of public supply in 1942–1944, and minister of food and agriculture in 1944–1945. He committed suicide.

Kádár, Gyula (1898–1982)
: Hungarian officer of the General Staff. Chief of the Second Section of the General Staff (Intelligence) in 1943–1944. He was arrested by the German authorities in 1944, and was arrested again by the Germans after the Arrow-Cross takeover. He was kept in a forced labor camp after the war until 1956. He was made a posthumous colonel general in 1992.

Kállay, Miklós (1887–1967)
: Hungarian politician and landowner. Minister of agriculture in 1932–1935, and prime minister in 1942–1944, as well as minister of foreign affairs in 1942–1943.

Kaltenbrunner, Ernst (1903–1946)

: Austrian Nazi officer. Minister of state security and chief of the police in Vienna after the *Anschluss*. Commander-in-chief of the SS in Vienna in 1938–1941. As head of the SD (from 1942), he controlled the *Gestapo* and the concentration camp system. He was found guilty of crimes against humanity and executed.

Kánya, Kálmán (1869–1945)
: Hungarian diplomat and politician. Minister of foreign affairs in 1933–1938.

Keitel, Wilhelm (1882–1946)
: German field marshal and head of the OKW (*Oberkommando der Wehrmacht*, the German High Command of the army) during World War II. One of Hitler's most loyal and trusted lieutenants, he became chief of the Führer's personal military staff, and helped direct most of the Third Reich's World War II campaigns.

Keresztes-Fischer, Ferenc (1881-1948)
    Hungarian lawyer and politician. Minister of the interior in 1931-1935 and 1938-1944. He was arrested after the German occupation of Hungary. After 1945 he lived in Austria.
Kéri, Kálmán (1901-1994)
    Hungarian General Staff officer. Commander of the Central Transportation Staff in 1938-1941, and military attaché to Bratislava in 1941-1942. Aide-de-camp to the minister of defense from 1942. Chief of the General Staff of the 1st Hungarian Army, he went over to the Soviets. Military chief of the new Ministry of Defense in 1945. He became a colonel general in reserve in 1991. President by seniority of the Hungarian Parliament in 1990-1994.
Kinzel, Eberhard (1897-1945)
    German general of the Infantry. Chief of Department of Foreign Armies East at the Army General Staff in 1938-1939, chief of the OKH in 1939-1942, chief of the General Staff of the Northern Army Group in 1943-1944, and chief of the General Staff of the Vistula Army Group and of OKW Operations Staff A in 1945. He was a member of a German delegation negotiating with General Montgomery in early May 1945. He committed suicide.
Kovács, Gyula (1893-1963)
    Hungarian General Staff officer. Chief of the General Staff of the III. Army Corps in 1940-1941, chief of the 3/a Section of the Ministry of Defense in 1941, brigadier general in 1942, commander of the Military Academy in 1943-1944, and plenipotentiary general of the Supreme Command in 1945. An American prisoner-of-war after World War II, he was later an active emigrant in the United States.
Kristóffy, József (1890-1969)
    Hungarian diplomat. He was envoy in Warsaw in 1937-1939, and ambassador to Moscow in 1939-1941. He informed

Bárdossy, by telegram, that the Soviet Union did not have claims against or any intention of attacking Hungary, but Bárdossy withheld that from the regent.

Kunder, Antal (1900–1968)

Hungarian politician and engineer. An MP from 1938 to 1944, he was minister of trade and traffic in 1938–1939 and 1944, and minister of industry in 1938–1939. He was sentenced to forced labor for life after the war, but managed to emigrate to Rio de Janeiro.

Kvaternik, Slavko (1878–1947)

Croatian field marshal. Austrian-Hungarian colonel in World War I. He declared the independent state of Croatia in 1941. He emigrated to Slovakia. He withdrew from political and military positions in January, 1943. He was executed.

Lahousen, Erwin (1897–?)

Austrian officer. Lieutenant colonel of the German General Staff (Intelligence Division). He served in the *Abwehr* after the *Anschluss*. He belonged to the "Canaris circle," who were opposed to Hitler's policies. He was an important witness in the Nuremberg War Crimes Trials.

Lakatos, Géza (1890–1967)

Hungarian general. Commander of the 1st Hungarian Army in 1944. Prime minister in 1944, he participated in preparing the failed breakaway attempt. He was arrested by the Arrow-Cross in 1944–1945, and then by the Soviets in 1945–1946. He died in Austria.

László, Dezső (1893–1949)

Hungarian general. Chief of the Military Operations Section of the *Honvéd* General Staff in 1941, and commander of the Military Academy in 1941–1943. He took part in overthrowing the breakaway attempt. He became a colonel general and commander of the 1st Hungarian Army in 1944–1945. He was sentenced to death and executed after the war.

Lázár, Károly (1890–1968)
: Hungarian major general. Commander of the Guards of the Regent from 1936. He opposed the Arrow-Cross with arms, and was deported to Mauthausen. He was made a posthumous colonel general in 1992.

Lengyel, Béla (1897–1988)
: Hungarian general. Military attaché to Warsaw in 1933–1939, and chief of the General Staff of the Rapid Army Corps in 1940–1941. Chief of the Tenth Section of the Ministry of Defense. He took part in the battles in Galicia, then became commander of the II. Reserve Army Corps in 1944. He was known for his friendly feelings towards Poland. He emigrated after the war.

Lišt, Wilhelm (1880–1971)
: German general. Commander of the 14th German Army during the battles against Poland, and of the 12th German Army on the western front. He was commander-in-chief in the Balkan operations in 1941, and leader of the Army Group A on the Soviet front in 1942. He was sentenced to death, but pardoned because of his illness, in 1952.

Littay, András (1884–1967)
: Hungarian general of the Infantry. Commander of the VII. Army Corps from 1936, and deputy chief of the General Staff from 1940. Deputy minister of defense in 1941–1943, he retired in 1943 and left for Germany in 1944. He emigrated to Australia.

Magyarosy, Sándor (1891–1972)
: Hungarian infantry officer. Commander of the air force in 1943–1944, and Hungarian royal governmental commissioner acting in Germany until 1945. He emigrated to the United States.

Manoilescu, Mihai (1891–1950)
: Romanian economist and university professor. Minister of foreign affairs at the time of the Vienna Awards.

Máriássy, Zoltán (1891–1970)
: Hungarian ambassador to Iraq, Iran and Turkey in 1936–1940.

Markó, Árpád (1885–1966)
: Hungarian military historian, and a member of the Hungarian Academy of Sciences from 1934 to 1949.

Meskó, Zoltán (1883–1959)
: Hungarian politician. He established the first Hungarian Arrow-Cross party and its journal.

Michael I, King of Romania (1921–)
: The last king of Romania, from 1927 to 1930 and from 1940 to 1947. He was only nominal king, at the side of Antonescu, until 1944. Under his leadership, Romania went over to the Allies. He had to abdicate the throne in 1947, and emigrated to Switzerland.

Mihailovič, Draža (1893–1946)
: Yugoslavian military politician and royalist guerilla leader. He organized Chetnik groups from the dispersed army in 1941, and was minister of defense of the Yugoslavian government in exile in London in 1942–1944. He was executed.

Molotov, Viacheslav Mihailovich (1890–1986)
: Soviet politician. A member of the CPSU CC and PB in 1926–1957, president of the Council of People's Commissars in 1930–1941, and people's commissar and minister of foreign affairs in 1939–1949 and 1953–1956.

Mussolini, Benito (1883–1945)
: Italian politician. Prime minister and Fascist dictator of Italy in 1922–1943. Leader of the "Salo Republic" in 1943. He was executed by partisans.

Nádas, Lajos (1902–1968)
: Hungarian artillery officer. Head of the Military Operational Subsection in 1941–1942, and head of the First Section of the *Honvéd* General Staff in 1943–1945. He helped the Arrow-Cross to take over, and participated in its activities. He emigrated to Canada.

Náday, István (1888–1954)
: Hungarian general. First deputy of the chief of the General Staff in 1939. Commander of the 1st Hungarian Army in 1942–1944. He retired in 1944, but flew to the headquarters of the Allies in the hope of negotiations for a cease-fire in the same year. He returned in 1945.

Nagy, Vilmos, nagybaczoni (1884–1976)
: Hungarian colonel general. Army commander in 1940–1941, and minister of defense in 1942–1943.

Paulus, Friedrich (1890–1957)
: German field marshal on the eastern front, whose capture at Stalingrad in early 1943 with his entire army became one of the turning points of World War II and substantially contributed to Germany's defeat.

Peter II, King of Yugoslavia (1923–1970)
: The last king of Yugoslavia, from 1934 to 1945. After the capitulation of Yugoslavia in 1941, he escaped to London and founded the government in exile. He helped the Chetniks until 1944. In spite of British assistance, he had to abdicate, and emigrated to the United States.

Rajniss, Ferenc (1893–1946)
: Hungarian journalist and right-wing politician. An MP from 1939 to 1945. The articles of his journal, the *Magyar Futár*, were directed against the Jews and the Allies. He opposed the breakaway attempt. A member of the Cabinet Council of the Arrow-Cross, he was minister of religion and public education in 1944–1945. He was executed as a war criminal.

Rakovszky, György (1892–1962)
: Hungarian diplomat and officer. Military attaché to France (1933–1938) and to Switzerland (1935–1938). Commander of the 8th Border Guard Brigade (1941) and the III. Army Corps (1942) on the eastern front. Commander-in-chief of the air force in 1941–1942, and head of the Bureau of the Ground Forces of the Ministry of Defense in 1943–1944.

Rassay, Károly (1886–1958)
: Hungarian liberal politician and journalist. An MP from 1929 to 1944, he spoke against the Germans and right-wing ideas in the Parliament. He was arrested and deported to Mauthausen in 1944.

Rátz, Jenő (1882–1952)
: Hungarian politician. Chief of the General Staff in 1936–1938. He played a role in spreading the Arrow-Cross ideas among the officers. He was minister of defense in 1938, minister without portfolio in the Sztójay government, and president of the Upper House in 1944–1945. He died in prison.

Reményi-Schneller, Lajos (1892–1946)
: Hungarian financial expert and politician. An MP from 1935 to 1945, he was minister of finance in 1938–1945. One of the most important men trusted by the Germans in the Hungarian governments, he was executed as a war criminal.

Ribbentrop, Joachim von (1893–1946)
: German politician. Ambassador to London in 1936–1938, and minister of foreign affairs in 1938–1945. He was executed.

Roatta, Mario (1886–1968)
: Italian lieutenant general. Military attaché to Berlin in 1939. Deputy chief (1939–1941) and then chief (1941–1943) of the Italian General Staff. Commander of the 2nd Italian Army in Yugoslavia (1942), in Slovenia-Dalmatia (1942–1943), and in Sicily (1943).

Rőder, Vilmos (1881–1969)
: Hungarian colonel general. Minister of defense in 1936–1938, he opposed joining the war. He voted for the cease-fire in 1944.

Rommel, Erwin (1891–1944)
: The most talented German military officer who was not a Nazi. His forces fought successfully in the German invasion of France and in north Africa (*Afrika Korps*) against the British.

Hitler did not allow him to evacuate his troops from there. He was sent to France to improve the coastal defenses in Normandy. He cared about both his troops and his prisoners. He agreed that Hitler must be removed from power. Hitler ordered him to commit suicide.

Rundstedt, Karl Rudolf Gerd von (1875–1953)
    German field marshal. Commander-in-chief of the Southern Army Group during the invasion of France and that of the Soviet Union. Commander-in-chief of the Western Army Group and the Army Group D in 1942–1944. He became a prisoner-of-war in the United Kingdom until 1949.

Ruszkay, Jenő (1887–1946)
    Hungarian artillery officer, military diplomat and politician. A member of the Arrow-Cross Party. The main inspector of the Hungarian SS groups and general of the Waffen SS in 1945. He was executed.

Ruszkiczay-Rüdiger, Imre (1889–1957)
    Hungarian general. Deputy minister of defense in 1943–1944. He was arrested by the *Gestapo* and the Arrow-Cross, and then retired in 1945. He was a prisoner-of-war in the Soviet Union from 1945 to 1948, then a prisoner in Hungary until 1953.

Sáska, Elemér (1898–1985)
    Hungarian General Staff officer. Commander on the eastern front in 1942–1943, and commander of the Ludovika Military Academy in 1943–1944. Deputy chief of the General Staff after the Arrow-Cross takeover.

Sima, Horia (1906–1990)
    Romanian Fascist leader. Leader of the Iron Guard in 1938. He fled to Germany, but then returned in 1940. He established the national legionary government with Antonescu. His policy was directed against the Jews. He tried to take over the government, but Antonescu put down his Iron Guard revolt. He was sentenced to death, but was able to escape to Spain.

Sónyi, Hugó (1883–1958)
: Hungarian general. Commander-in-chief of the *Honvédség* in 1936–1940, and a member of the Upper House. He emigrated to Germany.

Stalin, Joseph (Yosif Vissarionovich Dzhugashvili) (1879–1953)
: Bolshevik revolutionary of Georgian origin. Absolute dictator of Soviet politics after Lenin's death. One of the greatest genocides of human history is connected to his name.

Szálasi, Ferenc (1897–1946)
: Hungarian military officer and politician. Hungary's prime minister as National Leader in 1944–1945. He was executed in 1946.

Szent-Györgyi, Albert (1893–1986)
: Hungarian biochemist, whose discoveries concerning the role played by certain organic compounds, especially vitamin C, in the oxidation of nutrients by the cell brought him the 1937 Nobel Prize for Medicine.

Szent-Iványi, Domokos (1898-1980)

: Hungarian diplomat. Foreign policy advisor of Horthy's son. He served in the provisional government set up by the Soviet occupational forces.

Szentmiklósy, Andor (1893–1945?)
: Hungarian diplomat. Head of the Political Section of the Ministry of Foreign Affairs in 1942–1943, deputy minister of foreign affairs in 1943–1944, and leader of the anti-German group in the Ministry. He died in Dachau.

Szombathelyi, Ferenc (1887–1946)
: Hungarian general. Commander of Hungarian troops attacking the Soviet Union in 1941, and chief of the *Honvéd* General Staff with the rank of colonel general in 1941–1944.

Sztójay, Döme (1883–1946)
: Hungarian politician and general. Hungarian ambassador to Berlin in 1935–1944, and prime minister and minister of foreign affairs in 1944. He was executed for war crimes.

Tatarescu, Gheorghe (1886–1957)
    Romanian diplomat and politician. As premier of Romania in 1934–1937 and 1939–1940, he was unable to stem the tide of fascism.
Teleki, Pál, Count (1879–1941)
    Hungarian geographer and politician. A prominent statesman of the Horthy era. Prime minister in 1920–1921 and 1939–1941. He committed suicide on April 3, 1941, in protest against Hungary's drifting into World War II.
Tiso, Jozef (1887–1947)

    Slovakian Roman Catholic priest and head of state. Prime minister of Slovakia from 1938, and president of the Republic in 1939–1945. Chief commander of the Slovakian army and the Hlinka Guard. He called the Germans into Slovakia in 1944; this caused the Slovakian national uprising. He was executed as a war criminal.
Ujszászy, István (1894–?)
    Hungarian General Staff officer. Head of the State Security Center in 1942–1944. One of the defendants in the trial against Szombathelyi. After the unsuccessful breakaway attempt he escaped to the Swedish Embassy. He was deported to the Soviet Union, where he disappeared.
Ullein-Reviczky, Antal (1894–1955)
    Hungarian diplomat. Head of the press department at the Ministry of Foreign Affairs in 1939–1943. Hungarian ambassador in Stockholm in 1943–1944. He resigned his post after the German occupation of Hungary.
Utassy, Lóránd (1897–1974)
    Hungarian *Honvéd* lieutenant general. Military attaché to London until 1945, and then to Washington DC.
Vajna, Gábor (1891–1946)
    Hungarian politician. An MP of the Arrow-Cross Party from 1939 to 1945, he was minister of the interior in 1944–1945. He was executed as a war criminal.

Varga, József (1891–1956)
: Hungarian chemical engineer and university professor. A member of the Hungarian Academy of Sciences from 1932. An MP from 1939 to 1944, he was minister of industry and minister of trade and traffic in 1939–1943.

Vattay, Antal (1891–1966)
: Hungarian general. Deputy chief (1939) then chief (1944) of the military office of the regent of Hungary from 1939. Commander of the 1st Cavalry Division and inspector of the Cavalry in 1942–1944. He was arrested by the Germans, by the Americans (1944–1945) and in Hungary (1951–1956).

Veesenmayer, Edmund (1904–1977)
: German politician. Hitler's plenipotentiary in Hungary from March 1944.

Veress, László (1908–1980)
: Hungarian lawyer and diplomat. Head of the public relations office of the prime minister, then that of the Foreign Ministry, from 1939. He took part in the Hungarian mission for peace in Ankara in 1943. He went to Istanbul, where he received the conditions of cease-fire from the British.

Villani, Frigyes, Baron (1882–1964)
: Hungarian ambassador to Italy in 1935–1940, and to Albania in 1935–1939.

Vörös, János (1891–1968)
: Hungarian military officer. Colonel general. Army Corps commander in 1943–1944, and Chief of the General Staff in 1944 and 1945–1946. Minister of defense in 1944–1945. He was in prison from 1949 to 1956.

Weichs, Maximilian, Baron (1881–1954)
: German field marshal. He led the *Weichsarmeegruppe* (Weichs Army Group) at the eastern front in the summer of 1942 and the Army Group B until July 1943, and was commander of the Army Group F from August 1943 and

commander-in-chief of the southeastern territories. As such he directed the occupation of Hungary on March 19, 1944.

Werth, Henrik (1881–1952)
: General of the Hungarian army, of German descent. Chief of the General Staff of the Hungarian army when the Germans attacked the Soviet Union. He was openly pro-German.

Zákó, András (1898–1968)
: Hungarian infantry officer. Chief of the Secretariat General of the Supreme Council of National Defense from 1939. Teacher at the General Staff Academy from 1940. Chief of the General Staff of the VI. Army Corps from 1942. Head of the State Security Center in 1944. He was a prisoner-of-war of the Americans, and then lived in the United States.

Zeitzler, Kurt (1895–1963)
: German officer. Chief of staff of the 12th Grenadier Army Corps and the Kleist Panzer Group in 1940–1942, and of the Southern Army Group in 1942. Head of the OKH in 1942–1944, he retired in 1945.

Name Index

Aggteleky, Béla 524, 551
Albrecht of Habsburg, Archduke 136, 339, 452, 481-482
Alfieri, Dino 179
Ambrózy, Gyula 544
Andorka, Rudolf 12, 14-16, 29, 42-43, 420
Anfuso, Filippo 451
Antonescu, Ion 222, 224-225, 232-235, 242, 249, 257, 291, 294, 308, 319, 366-367, 378, 399, 411, 465, 509, 519, 522, 526
Apor, Gábor, Baron 188
Badoglio, Pietro 452, 454, 511
Baitz, Oszkár 91, 234
Bajcsy-Zsilinszky, Endre 416
Bajnóczy, József 74, 401, 514, 524-525, 534
Bakách-Bessenyei, György 88, 246, 539
Bakay, Szilárd 536, 541, 544, 546, 548
Baky, László 415, 531-532, 536
Bánffy, Dániel 283, 300, 344
Banfield 50-51
Baranyai, Lipót 111-112, 477
Barcza, György 50-52, 90-92, 267, 282, 285-286, 491
Bárczy, István 344-345
Bárdossy, László 33, 59-61, 66-68, 88, 91, 93-94, 234, 266, 270-273, 275-278, 282-283, 286, 294, 296-297, 299-300, 307-308, 313-314, 316-317, 322-325, 327, 330, 332, 334-339, 342-343, 345-347, 357-362, 364-367, 371-373, 375, 377-380, 384-386, 388, 390, 397-398
Bartha, Károly 401-404, 409-410
Beck, Ludwig 32
Becker, Karl 376
Beckerle, Adolf Heinz 483-486, 488
Beöthy, Zsolt 415
Beregfy, Károly 524, 540
Berger, Gottlob 482
Bessenyei, György, see Bakách-Bessenyei
Bethlen, István 286, 297, 397, 477, 524, 539, 541
Bodenschatz, Heinrich 27
Bor, Jenő 161
Bossy, Raoul 67-68, 177
Brauchitsch, Walter 48, 248, 289, 309, 333, 365
Brenner, Hildegard 482
Cadogan, Alexander, Sir 52, 266-267, 292
Canaris, Wilhelm 232, 356, 486-487
Carol, King 128, 135-136, 138, 157-158, 198, 222, 225
Chiggi, Ludoviko 234

Name Index

Ciano, Galeazzo, Conte di Cortellazo 13, 36, 38, 55, 58, 65, 76-78, 99-100, 105, 111-112, 133, 148-149, 152, 155-156, 158, 164, 169, 178-180, 196-198, 247, 404
Cincar-Markovič, Aleksander 248, 269, 274
Clodius, Carl von 80, 116-117, 133-134, 162, 177, 372-373, 402, 454
Colmann, informant 487
Crutescu, Gheorghe 93-94
Csáky, István, Count 24-27, 32-34, 36-41, 52, 55, 57-64, 66-71, 73, 75-77, 87-89, 93, 100-101, 109, 111, 133-134, 136-144, 156, 162, 181-182, 191-192, 197-198, 200, 235-236, 240-242, 249-250, 266, 398
Csatay, Lajos 447, 452, 454-456, 460, 473, 475, 477, 498-499, 517, 519, 527, 529, 531, 541-542
Cvetkovič, Dragisa 269, 274
Dálnoki Veress see Veress
Darré, Richard Walter Oskar 192
Deák, Ferenc 444, 493
Delius 484-485
Eichmann, Adolf 536
Endre, László 531
Erdmannsdorff, Otto von 11, 13, 63, 68, 70-71, 80, 133, 136-140, 142, 145, 191-192, 200, 235-236, 290, 294, 308, 325, 330, 332, 338-339, 346
Faragho, Gábor 76, 92, 543
Feketehalmy-Czeydner, Ferenc 154, 493

Fischer, Lajos 211
Foertsch, Hermann 510-511, 531
Fütterer, Kuno Heribert 160, 254, 291, 514
Gafencu, Grigore 59-60, 99-100
Ghyczy, Jenő 45, 461, 515, 517, 524, 527, 529
Gigurtu, Ion 166-168, 177
Göring, Hermann 27, 41, 73, 160, 365, 422-423
Gorondy-Novák, Elemér 150, 292
Grassy, József 493-494
Greiffenberg, Hans von 467, 474, 479, 481, 494, 496, 499, 514, 526, 530, 533, 535
Grolman, Helmuth von 317
Guderian, Heinz 376
Gyimessy, Frigyes 285
Halder, Franz 112-113, 118-120, 159, 248, 261-263, 287, 289, 309-310, 325-327, 331-334, 337, 345-348, 365, 367, 369-370
Halifax, Edward 52
Hansen, Erich 234
Hatz, Ottó 483-490
Hennyei, Gusztáv 541
Heusinger, Adolf 310, 349
Himer, Kurt 280, 290-293, 297-298, 309, 311, 314-317, 326, 330-335, 337-340, 347-349, 356, 360
Himmler, Heinrich 476, 494, 533
Hitler, Adolf 5, 8, 25-26, 30-31, 40-41, 48, 55, 58, 90, 92, 112, 118-120, 122-125, 152, 154-159, 163, 165, 167-169, 174-175, 180, 188, 193-196, 198, 221-223, 233-234, 240-242,

Name Index

247-250, 253-254, 256-263, 269-272, 274-281, 283-284, 287-291, 293-296, 298, 300, 307-310, 318-319, 322, 330, 332-334, 339, 349-350, 356, 362, 365, 377, 379, 384-387, 398-401, 403-404, 406, 408, 410-412, 419, 421-425, 429-430, 439-440, 452, 455, 457, 461-465, 473-476, 479, 482, 494-500, 507-514, 515, 517, 519-522, 526-531, 533, 535, 540

Hóman, Bálint 283, 344

Homlok, Sándor 10, 94, 119-120, 143-144, 159-160, 166, 234, 243-245, 261, 317, 327, 349, 355, 376, 486, 497, 513

Horstenau, Edmund Glaise von 339

Horthy, István 16, 363-364

Horthy, Miklós, Jr. 16, 543

Horthy, Miklós, Regent 3, 15, 18, 20, 31, 90, 96, 113-114, 191, 200, 209-213, 215, 218-221, 223, 226, 228-229, 275-277, 280-282, 284-294, 296, 298, 301, 308, 330, 333-335, 341-343, 345, 347, 349-350, 356-359, 361-364, 380, 384, 386-387, 393, 397, 402, 410, 413, 421-422, 427, 430, 432, 435, 439-440, 448-452, 454, 456, 461, 477-478, 480-481, 491, 495, 498-499, 507, 514-515, 517, 519-522, 526-527, 530, 533, 535, 539-541, 543-545, 550-551

Hóry, András 43, 181

Ibrányi, Mihály 544

Ilcusu, Ioan 186

Imrédy, Béla 3-4, 11-12, 14-16, 18, 24-26, 42, 73-74, 136, 220-221, 228-229, 410, 446, 449-450, 529-531

Jagow, Dietrich von 362-363, 370-372, 375, 384, 387, 391, 402-404, 406-407, 451, 460-462, 490-491, 501, 515, 517, 522

Jány, Gusztáv 150, 363, 393, 409, 412, 422-424, 426

Jaross, Andor 415

Jodl, Alfred 195, 297, 331-333, 349, 365, 400, 427, 513, 533

Juhász, Gyula 41

Jurcsek, Béla 541

Kádár, Gyula 444-449, 461, 467, 484, 486-487, 489, 497, 524, 534

Kállay, Miklós 397-404, 406-407, 411, 419, 422, 429-431, 439-441, 449-452, 456, 459-461, 468-471, 476-477, 482-483, 490-492, 494-496, 498, 511, 516-517, 520, 523-526, 532

Kaltenbrunner, Ernst 476, 482

Kánya, Kálmán 12-13, 24

Keitel, Wilhelm 47, 62, 233, 289, 298, 363, 365, 387-391, 394, 400-401, 408, 423, 427, 432, 436, 439-440, 464, 474, 496-497, 500-501, 512-513, 515, 518-521, 526, 533

Keresztes-Fischer, Ferenc 16, 18, 80, 96, 211, 277, 282, 286, 300, 332, 344, 445, 451, 455, 516, 523-524, 529

Kéri, Kálmán 120-121

Kern, Károly 534

Kinzel, Eberhard 113, 115, 117, 119
Kleist, Ewald 301
Kollány, Károly 348
Kovács, Gyula 432-435
Köves, Lothár 489
Krappe, Günther 238
Kristóffy, József 144, 192, 307, 335-336
Kuhl, Lajos 48
Kunder, Antal 221
Kuthy, László 331, 424
Kvaternik, Slavko 295
Lahousen, Erwin 29
Lakatos, Géza 448, 467, 473-474, 498-499, 513-514, 534, 540-541, 549
László, Dezső 42-43, 74, 280, 315, 331-332, 339, 368-370, 534
Lázár, Károly 541, 544
Lengyel, Béla 43
Lišt, Wilhelm 269, 280-281
Littay, András 236
Lorx, Viktor 317
Macartney, Carlile Aylmer 262
Magyarosy, Sándor 523, 525
Manoilescu, Mihai 167, 198
Máriássy, Zoltán 404
Marosi, Ferenc 339
Marras, Efesio 234
Mellethin, Horst 234
Meskó, Zoltán 415
Michael, King 225
Mihailovič, Draža 430
Miklós, Béla 301, 339, 373-374, 524, 540, 545
Molotov, Viacheslav Mihailovich 132, 144, 164-165, 192, 256, 335-336

Mussolini, Benito 13, 36-38, 40, 55, 57-58, 99, 111-112, 118, 148-149, 167-168, 177-178, 180, 197, 254, 362, 451-454
Nádas, Lajos 524
Náday, István 42-43, 415, 448, 524-525, 534, 542-543
Nagy, see Nagybaczoni Nagy
Nagybaczoni Nagy, Vilmos 104, 150, 189, 220-221, 407, 409-415, 420, 422-423, 428, 431, 435, 439, 447-452, 456
O'Malley, Owen St.Clair 235
Oswald 467
Pappenheim, Friedrich Rabe von 401-402, 426, 452, 454, 460-461, 467
Pariani, Alberto 56-57
Paul, Regent 274
Paulus, Friedrich 262, 279-284, 286-290, 293, 331, 369-370, 419
Peter II 274
Radtke 316, 330, 349
Rajniss, Ferenc 449
Rakovszky, György 433-434
Ránki, György 507
Rassay, Károly 278
Rátz, Jenő 15, 18-19, 220, 368, 482, 493, 531
Reichenau, Walter von 377
Reményi-Schneller, Lajos 283, 344, 477, 541
Ribbentrop, Joachim von 13-14, 24-26, 30, 38, 41, 63-64, 66, 68-71, 75, 133, 137-138, 140-145, 149, 154, 157, 166-168, 179, 193, 196-198, 240-242, 260, 270, 273-274, 294, 325,

326, 337, 362, 365-366, 377-378, 384-389, 391, 398, 400, 403, 490, 509, 521-522, 526, 528-533
Ritter, Karl 370-371, 375, 406
Roatta, Mario 177-178
Roberts, a.k.a. Randow, informant 487
Rőder, Vilmos 448
Roeder, Werner 370
Rommel, Erwin 419
Rosso, Augusto 132
Rundstedt, Karl Rudolf Gerd von 310, 350, 377
Ruszkay, Jenő 482, 531
Ruszkiczay-Rüdiger, Imre 523
Saronov, Nikolai 332
Sáska, Elemér 348, 444
Schrecker, Károly 442-443
Seeckt, Hans von 6
Siegler 348
Sima, Horia 225
Simovič, Dusan 274
Solymossy, Ulászló 121-123
Sónyi, Hugó 72-73, 104
Stolz, Otto 29
Szabó, László 12-13, 37, 40, 56, 148-149, 177-180, 339
Szálasi, Ferenc 7, 444, 546, 551
Szász, Ferenc 444, 477
Szent-Györgyi, Albert 442
Szent-Iványi, Domokos 228
Szentmiklósy, Andor 365, 398, 456, 524
Szombathelyi, Ferenc 347, 355, 363-365, 367-370, 372-374, 389-390, 395, 397, 408-410, 414, 420, 422-432, 436, 439-441, 444, 446-449, 456-464, 467-471, 473-476, 482-487, 489-490, 492-500, 515-524, 527, 533-534
Sztójay, Döme 11, 13-14, 27-30, 34, 44-46, 48, 60, 62, 66-68, 72, 79, 86, 92, 104, 108, 132, 140, 142-144, 162, 192-193, 211, 221-224, 234, 241-243, 249-250, 260-261, 270, 274-276, 278, 281, 294-295, 308, 317-319, 323-327, 339, 345-346, 349, 355, 372-373, 375-376, 379, 404, 517, 521-522, 527-531, 535, 539-541, 548
Tatarescu, Gheorghe 126, 128
Teleki, Pál, Count 3-4, 19-21, 24, 26, 29-30, 34, 38, 40-42, 46-51, 55, 58-59, 64-65, 73, 76, 80-81, 85, 88-91, 95-96, 104, 108-111, 113-119, 121, 123-125, 133, 137, 148, 152-155, 157-158, 160-161, 169, 175, 177, 181, 188, 197-200, 209-220, 226-228, 232, 235-236, 240, 242, 245, 248-250, 266-269, 275, 277, 283-289, 295, 298-299, 301-302, 307
Thomas, Georg 120
Tippelskirch, Kurt von 98-99, 102, 108, 159, 232-234
Tiso, Jozef 30, 70, 339, 526
Tömöry, Jenő 444
Tömösy, Jenő 441, 483
Tost, Gyula 544
Toussaint, Rudolf 369
Tzerescu 186
Ujszászy, István 42, 78, 91-93, 98-99, 119, 121, 127, 159, 229, 317, 327, 331, 534

Ullein-Reviczky, Antal 398, 440-441, 472, 483
Utassy, Lóránd 50-51, 91-93
Vajna, Gábor 415
Varga, József 283, 344
Vattay, Antal 535, 541, 544
Veesenmayer, Edmund 444-445, 478-479, 481-482, 490, 522, 529-534, 540-541, 545
Veress, László 468
Veress, Lajos, see also Dálnoki Veress, Lajos 448, 540, 545
Villani, Frigyes, Baron 13, 36, 38, 76-77, 91, 105, 111, 177
Vishinski, Andrei Yanuarievich 307, 336
Volosin, Ágost 32
Vörnle, János 317, 332
Vörös, Géza 433-434, 445
Vörös, János 368, 373, 398, 401, 414, 492-493, 524, 534-536, 539, 542-543, 550
Warlimont, Walter 465
Weichs, Maximilian 280-281, 311, 393, 413, 532-533
Weinknecht, Friedrich-August 393-394
Weizsäcker, Ernst von, Baron 45-46, 71, 105, 140, 142, 162, 235, 241, 250, 270, 294-295, 323-324, 346, 404
Werkmeister, Karl 298, 345, 380, 407, 494
Werth, Henrik 3-9, 12, 14-21, 24-31, 34-35, 37, 42-44, 46-50, 55-58, 60-62, 64-66, 68-69, 73-78, 80, 85-90, 93-97, 104, 109-110, 113-117, 119-123, 128, 134-135, 143, 145-147, 153-154, 160-161, 163-165, 175-176, 178, 180-182, 191, 199, 209-211, 213-214, 216-218, 220-221, 226, 228, 235-238, 244-245, 257-258, 261-262, 266, 275, 277-278, 280-281, 283-285, 292-294, 298-299, 307-327, 332-335, 337, 339, 341-343, 345, 356-365, 368-369, 410, 468
Winter, August 112-113
Woermann, Ernst 11-12, 45, 48, 62, 67, 132-133, 193, 250, 270, 323, 337
Wrede, Theodor, Baron 80, 235
Zákó, András 444
Zeitzler, Kurt 464, 496, 498, 513

Place Index

A - Austria; B - Bulgaria; BH - Bosnia-Herzegovina; C - Croatia; Cz - Czech Republic; D - Germany; F - France; G - Greece; I - Italy; Ir - Iran; L - Lithuania; M - Macedonia; P - Poland; Po - Portugal; R - Romania; Ru - Russia; S - Sweden; Sk - Slovakia; T - Turkey; U -Ukraine; UK - United Kingdom; USA - United States of America; Y - Yugoslavia

Ákos (Aciş; R) 255
Ankara (T) 442, 489
Arad (Arad; R) 127, 151, 186, 190, 543
Auschwitz (Oświęcim; P) 536
Bánffyhunyad (Huedin; R) 141
Barcs 293
Békéscsaba 121, 152, 187, 190
Belgorod (R) 424
Belgrade (Beograd; Y) 88, 127, 246, 249, 269, 273-274, 279, 293, 296, 301, 466, 530
Berchtesgaden (D) 196, 513
Berdicsev (Berdicsiv; U) 494
Beregszász (Berehove; U) 150
Berettyóújfalu 255
Berezna (U) 33
Berlin (D) 11, 13, 24-26, 28-29, 40-41, 46-48, 56, 60-62, 66, 68, 72, 77, 80, 94, 111-112, 119, 135, 137-138, 140, 142, 149, 159, 161, 166, 169, 179, 192, 214, 224, 234, 256, 258, 270, 276, 281-282, 287, 294, 314-315, 317-318, 322-323, 339, 346, 348-349, 371-372, 377, 379, 398, 404, 422-423, 476, 482, 486, 495, 514, 540
Beszterce (Bistriţa; R) 190
Bicske 523
Bisztra (Bistra; R) 33
Bled (C) 14
Brăila (R) 112
Bratislava, see also Pozsony 526
Brno (Cz) 45, 162
Bucharest (Bucureşti; R) 29, 33, 60, 67-68, 78, 136, 157, 161, 177, 192, 194, 232, 234, 319, 403, 526
Budapest 11-13, 25, 29, 32, 57, 67, 79, 93, 98, 105, 111-113, 115-116, 126, 133, 140, 142, 152, 157, 162, 177, 181, 191, 198, 217, 261, 275, 279-280, 286, 290-291, 308, 311, 314, 323, 335, 340-341, 346, 356, 373-374, 387-388, 393, 401, 403, 411, 432-433, 445, 452, 458, 464-465, 467, 480, 484-485, 487, 489, 494, 498, 511, 514,

516, 519-520, 523-524, 526, 536, 541, 544, 546, 548, 550-551
Cegléd 523
Cherkassi (U) 497
Constanţa (R) 112
Csáktornya (Čakovec; C) 489
Danzig (Gdańsk; P) 43
Debrecen 137, 254
Dés (Dej; R) 190
Diósgyőr (Miskolc) 216
Drohobycz (U) 262
Dresden (D) 234
Dunkirk (Dunkerque; F) 271
Eisenstadt (A) 514
Eperjes (Prešov; Sk) 34
Erdőbénye 341
Érmihályfalva (Valea lui Mihai; R) 186
Érszakácsi (Săcăşeni; R) 255
Eszék (Osijek; C) 293-294, 301
Esztergom 536
Fiume (Rijeka; C) 275
Galaţi (R) 112
Gödöllő 221, 410
Grădiştea (R) 293
Graz (A) 279
Győr 9
Gyula 121, 187, 190
Harkov (Harkiv; U) 464
Hegyeshalom 237
Herceghalom 255
Huszt (U) 33, 347
Istanbul (İstanbul; T) 441, 469, 471, 477, 484-485, 487
Izjum (U) 374
Kalach (Ru) 419
Karlovac (C) 301

Kassa (Košice; Sk) 11-12, 34, 69, 340-344, 358, 363
Kecskemét 544
Kelenföld (Budapest) 526
Kenderes 334, 349
Kiev (Kijiv; U) 463, 475
Kirovograd (U) 494
Klagenfurt (A) 279
Klessheim (A) 509, 517, 526-527, 530
Kolomea (U) 348, 350
Kolozsvár (Cluj-Napoca, R) 151, 190, 501, 542
Koprivnica (C) 293
Kőrösmező (Jasina; U) 32-33, 340
Kovno (Kaunas; L) 475
Kraków (Cracow; P) 322
Krivoj Rog (Krivij Rih; U) 498
Kursk (R) 463
Lavocsne (Volócz; Volovec; U) 347
Lemberg (Lvov; L'viv; U) 358, 463, 499
Linz (A) 523
Lippa (Lipova; R) 543
Lisbon (Lisboa; Po) 477
Lökösháza 237
London (UK) 50, 58, 90-92, 116, 267, 282, 491
Lublin (P) 310
Máramarossziget (Sighetu-Marmaţiei; R) 190, 347
Marosvásárhely (Târgu Mureş, R) 141
Miskolc 341
Mönichkirchen (A) 308
Moscow (Ru) 76, 132, 137, 165, 335, 376-377, 490-492, 543, 551

Place Index

Munich (München; D) 9, 138, 152-154, 158-159, 164-165, 188, 191, 260, 270-271, 487
Munkács (Mukachevo; U) 11, 24, 480
Nadvorne (U) 347
Nagybánya (Baia Mare; R) 141, 189
Nagykároly (Carei; R) 189
Nagykőrös 543
Nagyszalánc (Slanec; Sk) 69
Nagyvárad (Oradea; R) 151, 186, 190, 501
Nikopol (B) 497
Niš (Y) 278
Novi Sad see also Újvidék 293
Nuremberg (Nürnberg; D) 522
Nyíregyháza 150, 220
Nyitra (Nitra; Sk) 34
Ober-Salzberg (D) 513
Odessa (U) 357, 499
Ökörmező (Mezsgorje; U) 501
Ózd 341
Pécs 136, 292
Ploieşti (R) 99, 118, 195, 237
Pozsony (Bratislava; Sk) 526
Pripjaty (U) 500, 534
Rahó (Rahiv; U) 340, 347
Rastenburg (Kętrzyn; P) 398
Rome (Roma; I) 12-13, 35-39, 56-57, 66, 77, 99-101, 105, 111-112, 133, 148, 157, 168-169, 177-178, 234, 339, 404
Rostov (Ru) 377
Rovel (U) 475
Rovno (U) 500
Rozsnyó (Rožňava; Sk) 12
Ruma (Y) 301
Salerno (I) 464
Salzburg (A) 165-166, 169-170, 247
Sarajevo (BH) 297, 299
Sátoraljaújhely 341
Siklós 292
Skopje (M) 278
Smolensk (Ru) 434, 464
Sofia (B) 278, 483-484, 487-489
Sóstó 150, 220-221
Stalingrad (Volgograd; Ru) 411, 419
Stanislav (Ivano-Frankovsk; U) 347-348, 350
Stockholm (S) 472
Strij (U) 349
Szalonta (Nagyszalonta, Salonta; R) 127
Szatmárnémeti (Satu Mare; R) 151
Szeged 137, 152, 292
Szolnok 502
Tarpa 10
Tatarov (U) 347
Teheran (Tehrán; Ir) 473, 490
Temesvár (Timişoara; R) 151, 279
Thessaloniki (Saloniki; G) 112, 248-249, 258, 271
Tiszaborkút (Kvasi; U) 340
Torda (Turda; R) 543
Törökszentmiklós 150
Trieste (I) 501
Turin (Torino; I) 56
Turnu-Severin (Drobeta-Turnu Severin; R) 181-182, 191-192
Újvidék (Novi Sad; Y) 480, 493
Ungvár (Uzgorod; U) 11, 32, 341, 502
Uryv (Ru) 409, 412
Vác 128, 341
Valjevo (Y) 301

Vásárosnamény 10
Vienna (Wien; A) 1, 10-11, 13-14, 113, 132, 193, 195-196, 199, 218, 224, 234, 240, 246-247, 250, 262, 272, 274, 280, 323, 366, 378, 399, 403, 411, 511, 514, 516
Vinnica (U) 411, 500
Völcsej 173

Warsaw (Warszawa; P) 29, 43, 181
Washington D.C. (USA) 267, 488
Wiener-Neustadt (A) 514
Zagreb (C) 288, 293, 295, 339
Zalamernye 173
Zsitomir (U) 494
Zsolna (Žilina; Sk) 59

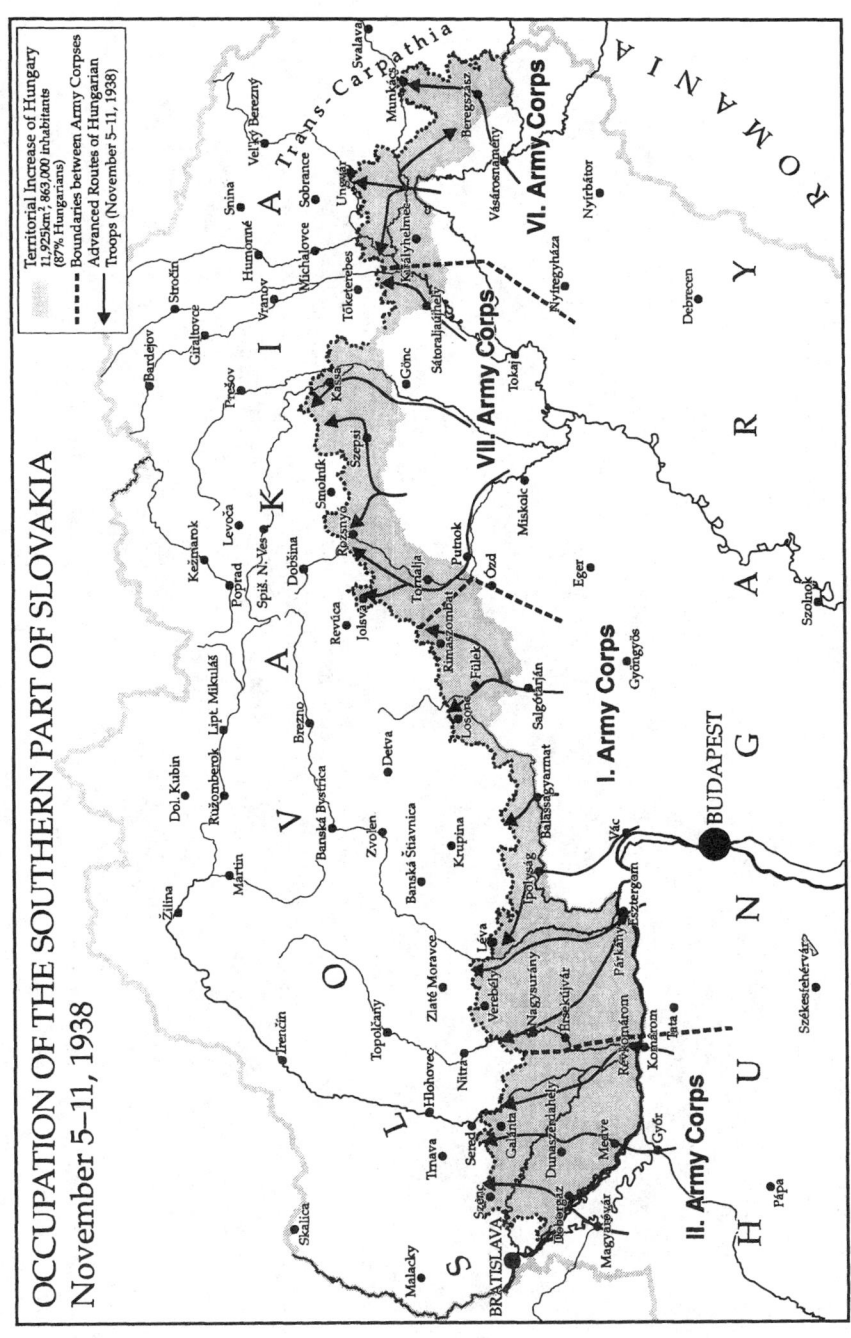

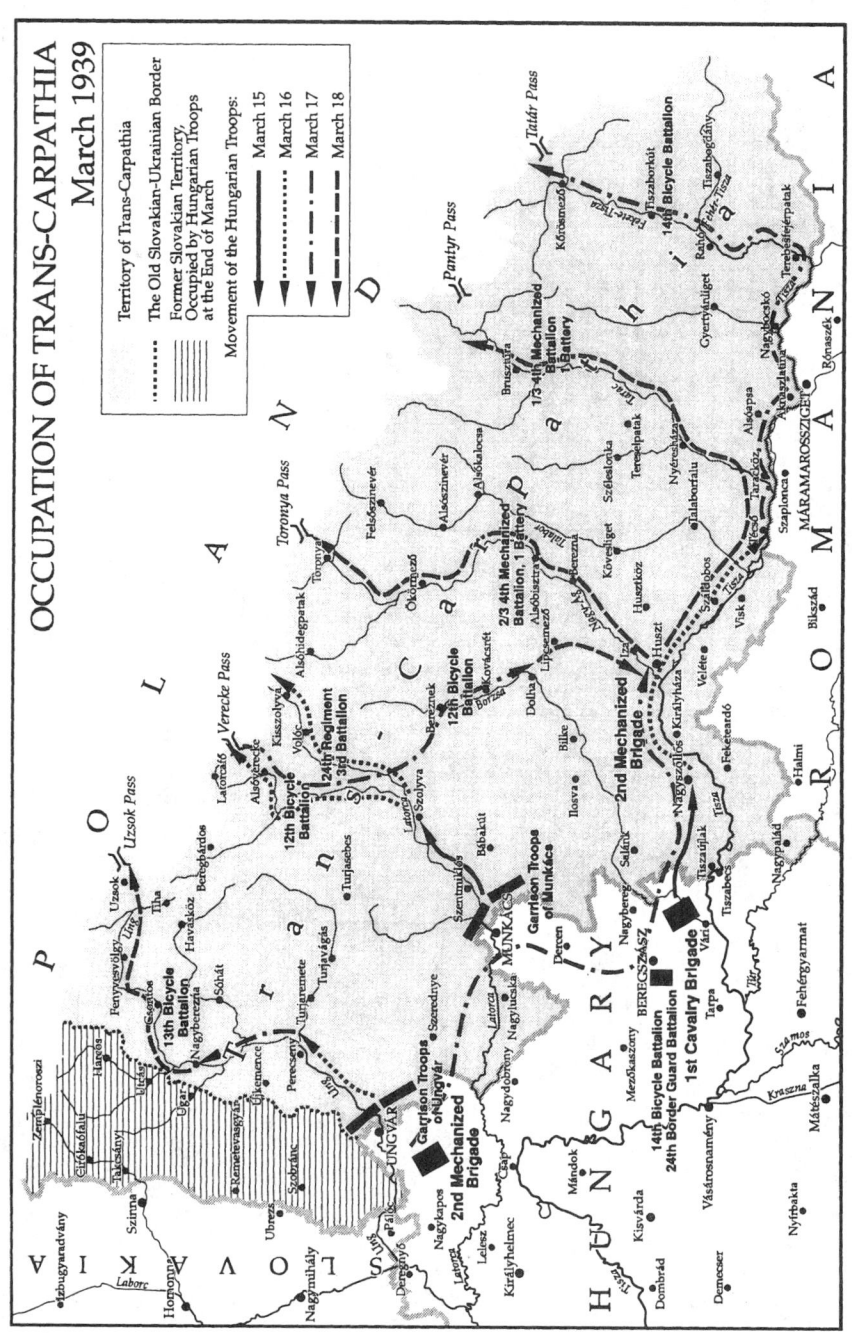

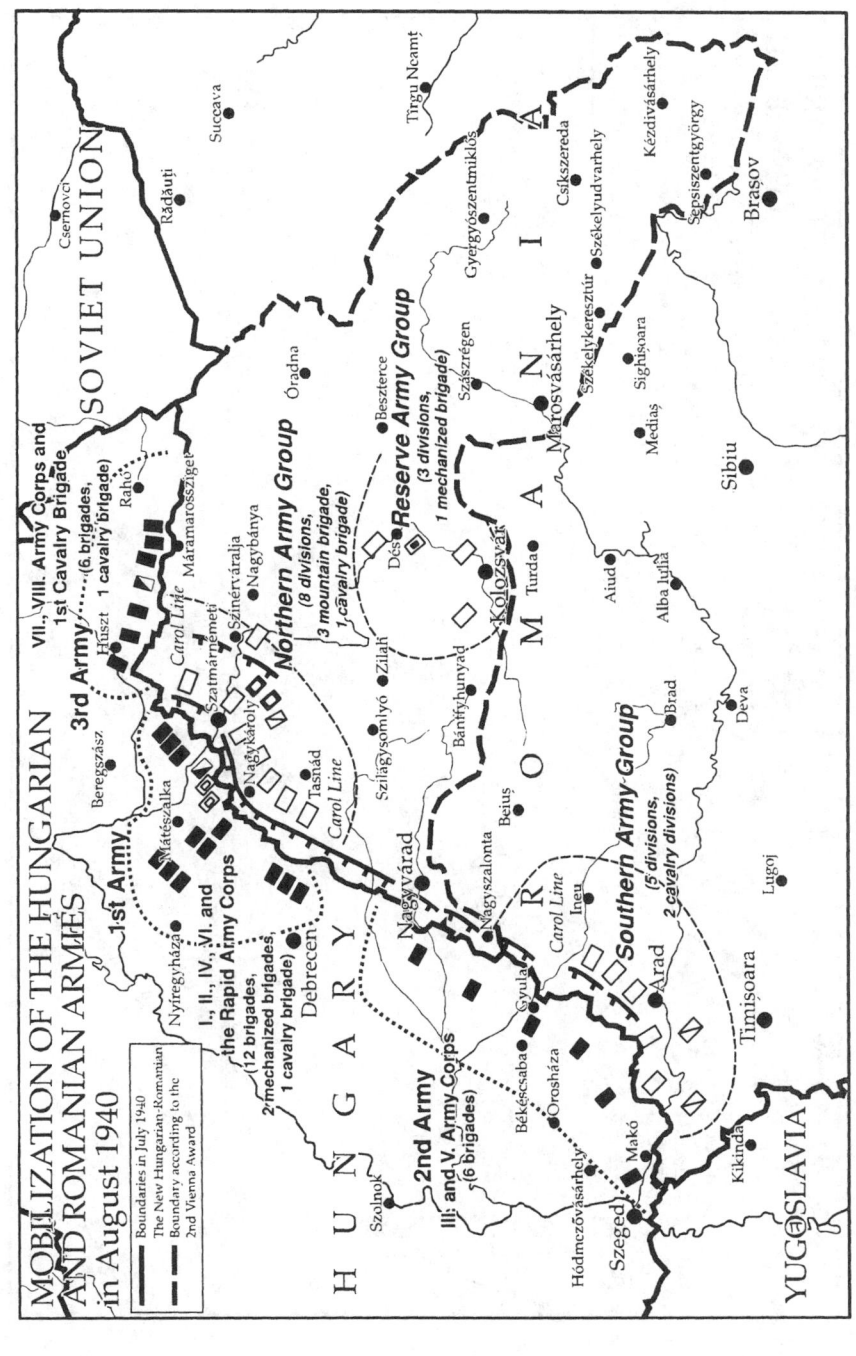

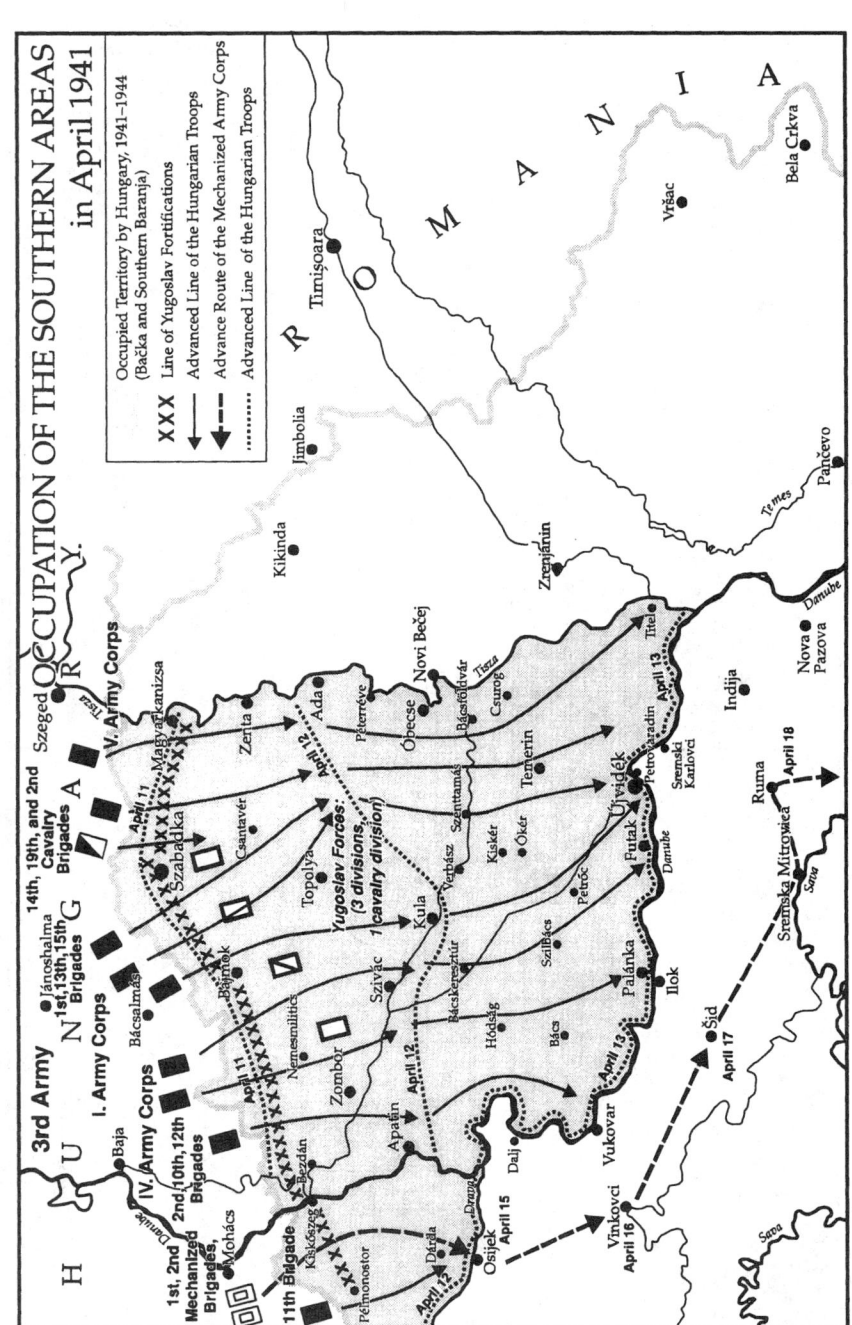

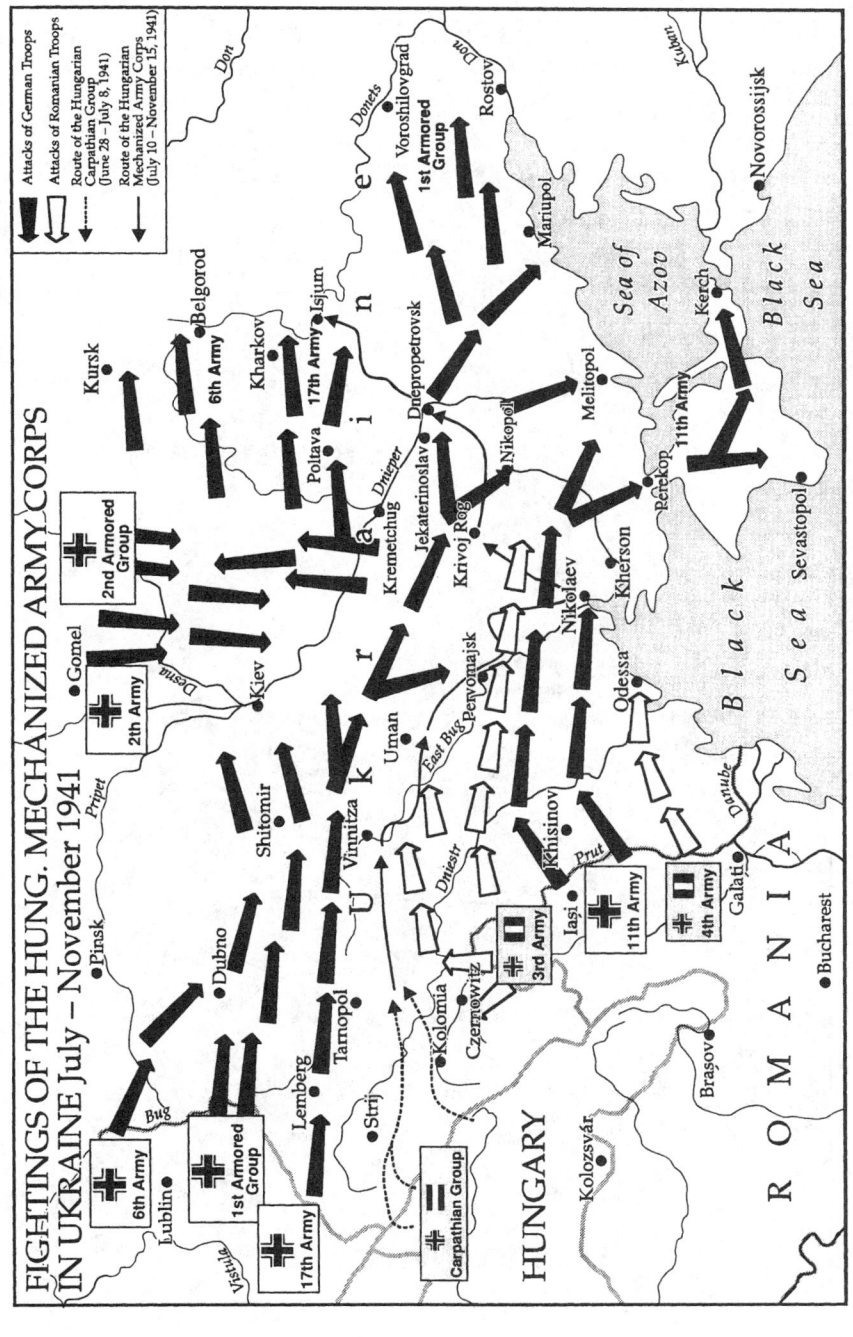

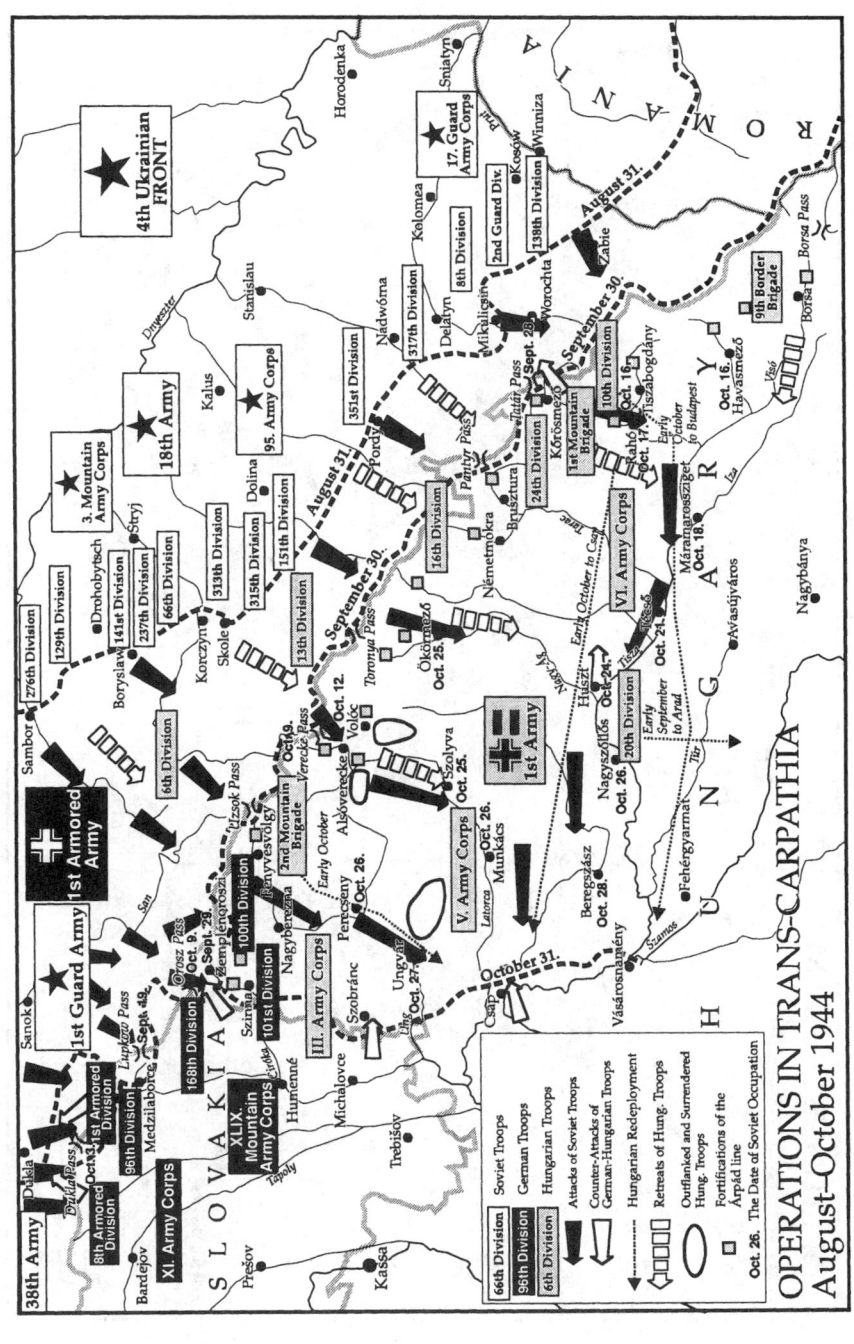

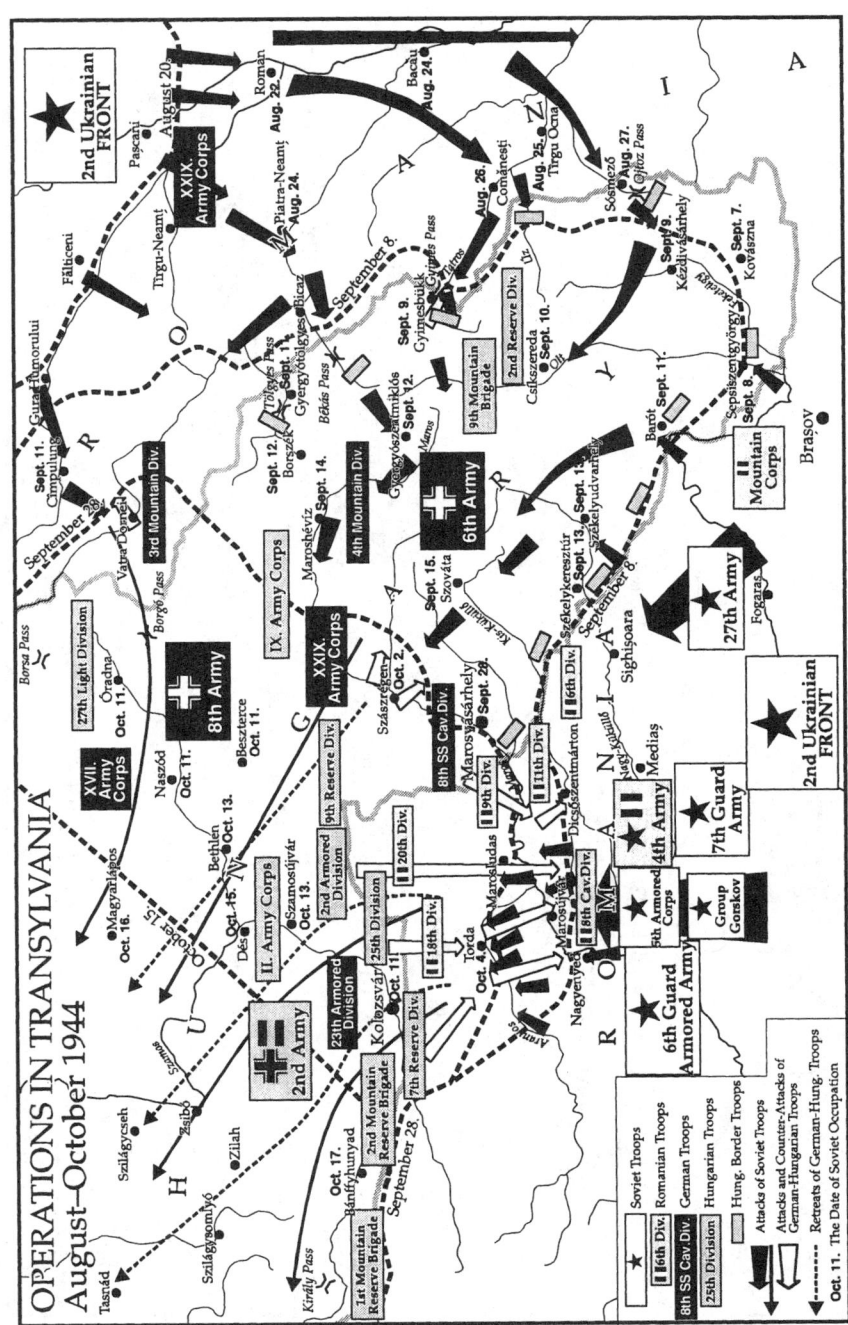

Volumes Published in
"Atlantic Studies on Society in Change"

No. 1   *Tolerance and Movements of Religious Dissent in Eastern Europe.* Edited by Béla K. Király. 1977.

No. 2   *The Habsburg Empire in World War I.* Edited by R. A. Kann. 1978

No. 3   *The Mutual Effects of the Islamic and Judeo-Christian Worlds: The East European Pattern.* Edited by A. Ascher, T. Halasi-Kun, B. K. Király. 1979.

No. 4   *Before Watergate: Problems of Corruption in American Society.* Edited by A. S. Eisenstadt, A. Hoogenboom, H. L. Trefousse. 1979.

No. 5   *East Central European Perceptions of Early America.* Edited by B. K. Király and G. Bárány. 1977.

No. 6   *The Hungarian Revolution of 1956 in Retrospect.* Edited by B. K. Király and Paul Jonas. 1978.

No. 7   *Brooklyn U.S.A.: Fourth Largest City in America.* Edited by Rita S. Miller. 1979.

No. 8   *Prime Minister Gyula Andrássy's Influence on Habsburg Foreign Policy.* János Decsy. 1979.

No. 9   *The Great Impeacher: A Political Biography of James M. Ashley.* Robert F. Horowitz. 1979.

No. 10   *Special Topics and Generalizations on the Eighteenth and*
Vol. I*   *Nineteenth Century.* Edited by Béla K. Király and Gunther E. Rothenberg. 1979.

No. 11   *East Central European Society and War in the Pre-*
Vol. II   *Revolutionary 18th Century.* Edited by Gunther E. Rothenberg, Béla K. Király, and Peter F. Sugar. 1982.

* Vols. no. I through XXXVII refer to the series *War and Society in East Central Europe*

No. 12 Vol. III	*From Hunyadi to Rákóczi: War and Society in Late Medieval and Early Modern Hungary.* Edited by János M. Bak and Béla K. Király. 1982.
No. 13 Vol. IV	*East Central European Society and War in the Era of Revolutions: 1775-1856.* Edited by B. K. Király. 1984.
No. 14 Vol. V	*Essays on World War I: Origins and Prisoners of War.* Edited by Samuel R. Williamson, Jr. and Peter Pastor. 1983.
No. 15 Vol. VI	*Essays on World War I: Total War and Peacemaking, A Case Study on Trianon.* Edited by B. K. Király, Peter Pastor, and Ivan Sanders. 1982.
No. 16 Vol. VII	*Army, Aristocracy, Monarchy: War, Society and Government in Austria, 1618-1780.* Edited by Thomas M. Barker. 1982.
No. 17 Vol. VIII	*The First Serbian Uprising 1804-1813.* Edited by Wayne S. Vucinich. 1982.
No. 18 Vol. IX	*Czechoslovak Policy and the Hungarian Minority 1945-1948.* Kálmán Janics. Edited by Stephen Borsody. 1982.
No. 19 Vol. X	*At the Brink of War and Peace: The Tito-Stalin Split in a Historic Perspective.* Edited by Wayne S. Vucinich. 1982.
No. 20	*Inflation Through the Ages: Economic, Social, Psychological and Historical Aspects.* Edited by Edward Marcus and Nathan Schmuckler. 1981.
No. 21	*Germany and America: Essays on Problems of International Relations and Immigration.* Edited by Hans L. Trefousse. 1980.
No. 22	*Brooklyn College: The First Half Century.* Murray M. Horowitz. 1981.
No. 23	*A New Deal for the World: Eleanor Roosevelt and American Foreign Policy.* Jason Berger. 1981.
No. 24	*The Legacy of Jewish Migration: 1881 and Its Impact.* Edited by David Berger. 1982.
No. 25	*The Road to Bellapais: Cypriot Exodus to Northern Cyprus.* Pierre Oberling. 1982.
No. 26	*New Hungarian Peasants: An East Central European Experience with Collectivization.* Edited by Marida Hollos and Béla C. Maday. 1983.

No. 27	*Germans in America: Aspects of German-American Relations in the Nineteenth Century.* Edited by Allen McCormick. 1983.
No. 28	*A Question of Empire: Leopold I and the War of Spanish Succession, 1701-1705.* Linda and Marsha Frey. 1983.
No. 29	*The Beginning of Cyrillic Printing — Cracow, 1491. From the Orthodox Past in Poland.* Szczepan K. Zimmer. Edited by Ludwik Krzyżanowski and Irene Nagurski. 1983.
No. 29a	*A Grand Ecole for the Grand Corps: The Recruitment and Training of the French Administration.* Thomas R. Osborne. 1983.
No. 30 Vol. XI	*The First War between Socialist States: The Hungarian Revolution of 1956 and Its Impact.* Edited by Béla K. Király, Barbara Lotze, Nandor Dreisziger. 1984.
No. 31 Vol. XII	*The Effects of World War I, The Uprooted: Hungarian Refugees and Their Impact on Hungary's Domestic Politics.* István Mócsy. 1983.
No. 32 Vol. XIII	*The Effects of World War I: The Class War after the Great War: The Rise of Communist Parties in East Central Europe, 1918-1921.* Edited by Ivo Banac. 1983.
No. 33 Vol. XIV	*The Crucial Decade: East Central European Society and National Defense, 1859-1870.* Edited by Béla K. Király. 1984.
No. 35 Vol. XVI	*Effects of World War I: War Communism in Hungary, 1919.* György Péteri. 1984.
No. 36 Vol. XVII	*Insurrections, Wars, and the Eastern Crisis in the 1870s.* Edited by B. K. Király and Gale Stokes. 1985.
No. 37 Vol. XVIII	*East Central European Society and the Balkan Wars, 1912-1913.* Edited by B. K. Király and Dimitrije Djordjevic. 1986.
No. 38 Vol. XIX	*East Central European Society in World War I.* Edited by B. K. Király and N. F. Dreisziger, Assistant Editor Albert A. Nofi. 1985.
No. 39 Vol. XX	*Revolutions and Interventions in Hungary and Its Neighbor States, 1918-1919.* Edited by Peter Pastor. 1988.

No. 41 Vol. XXII	*Essays on East Central European Society and War, 1740-1920.* Edited by Stephen Fischer-Galati and Béla K. Király. 1988.
No. 42 Vol. XXIII	*East Central European Maritime Commerce and Naval Policies, 1789-1913.* Edited by Apostolos E. Vacalopoulos, Constantinos D. Svolopoulos, and Béla K. Király. 1988.
No. 43 Vol. XXIV	*Selections, Social Origins, Education and Training of East Central European Officers Corps.* Edited by Béla K. Király and Walter Scott Dillard. 1988.
No. 44 Vol. XXV	*East Central European War Leaders: Civilian and Military.* Edited by Béla K. Király and Albert Nofi. 1988.
No. 46	*Germany's International Monetary Policy and the European Monetary System.* Hugo Kaufmann. 1985.
No. 47	*Iran Since the Revolution—Internal Dynamics, Regional Conflicts and the Superpowers.* Edited by Barry M. Rosen. 1985.
No. 48 Vol. XXVII	*The Press During the Hungarian Revolution of 1848-1849.* Domokos Kosáry. 1986.
No. 49	*The Spanish Inquisition and the Inquisitional Mind.* Edited by Angel Alcala. 1987.
No. 50	*Catholics, the State and the European Radical Right, 1919-1945.* Edited by Richard Wolff and Jorg K. Hoensch. 1987.
No. 51 Vol.XXVIII	*The Boer War and Military Reforms.* Jay Stone and Erwin A. Schmidl. 1987.
No. 52	*Baron Joseph Eötvös, A Literary Biography.* Steven B. Várdy. 1987.
No. 53	*Towards the Renaissance of Puerto Rican Studies: Ethnic and Area Studies in University Education.* Maria Sanchez and Antonio M. Stevens. 1987.
No. 54	*The Brazilian Diamonds in Contracts, Contraband and Capital.* Harry Bernstein. 1987.
No. 55	*Christians, Jews and Other Worlds: Patterns of Conflict and Accommodation.* Edited by Philip F. Gallagher. 1988.
No. 56 Vol. XXVI	*The Fall of the Medieval Kingdom of Hungary: Mohács 1526, Buda 1541.* Géza Perjés. 1989.

No. 57	*The Lord Mayor of Lisbon: The Portuguese Tribune of the People and His 24 Guilds.* Harry Bernstein. 1989.
No. 58	*Hungarian Statesmen of Destiny: 1860-1960.* Edited by Paul Böval. 1989.
No. 59	*For China: The Memoirs of T. G. Li, Former Major General in the Chinese Nationalist Army.* T. G. Li. Written in collaboration with Roman Rome. 1989.
No. 60	*Politics in Hungary: For A Democratic Alternative.* János Kis, with an Introduction by Timothy Garton Ash. 1989.
No. 61	*Hungarian Worker's Councils in 1956.* Edited by Bill Lomax. 1990.
No. 62	*Essays on the Structure and Reform of Centrally Planned Economic Systems.* Paul Jonas. A joint publication with Corvina Kiadó, Budapest. 1990.
No. 63	*Kossuth as a Journalist in England.* Éva H. Haraszti. A joint publication with Akadémiai Kiadó, Budapest. 1990.
No. 64	*From Padua to the Trianon, 1918-1920.* Mária Ormos. A joint publication with Akadémiai Kiadó, Budapest. 1990.
No. 65	*Towns in Medieval Hungary.* Edited by László Gerevich. A joint publication with Akadémiai Kiadó, Budapest. 1990.
No. 66	*The Nationalities Problem in Transylvania, 1867-1940.* Sándor Bíró. 1992.
No. 67	*Hungarian Exiles and the Romanian National Movement, 1849-1867.* Béla Borsi-Kálmán. 1991.
No. 68	*The Hungarian Minority's Situation in Ceausescu's Romania.* Edited by Rudolf Joó and Andrew Ludanyi. 1994.
No. 69	*Democracy, Revolution, Self-Determination. Selected Writings.* István Bibó. Edited by Károly Nagy. 1991.
No. 70	*Trianon and the Protection of Minorities.* József Galántai. A joint publication with Corvina Kiadó, Budapest. 1991.
No. 71	*King Saint Stephen of Hungary.* György Györffy. 1994.
No. 72	*Dynasty, Politics and Culture. Selected Essays.* Robert A. Kann. Edited by Stanley B. Winters. 1991.

No. 73	*Jadwiga of Anjou and the Rise of East Central Europe.* Oscar Halecki. Edited by Thaddeus V. Gromada. A joint publication with the Polish Institute of Arts and Sciences of America, New York. 1991.
No. 74 Vol. XXIX	*Hungarian Economy and Society during World War Two.* Edited by György Lengyel. 1993.
No. 75	*The Life of a Communist Revolutionary, Béla Kun.* György Borsányi. 1993.
No. 76	*Yugoslavia: The Process of Disintegration.* Laslo Sekelj. 1993.
No. 77 Vol. XXX	*Wartime American Plans for a New Hungary. Documents from the U.S. Department of State, 1942-1944.* Edited by Ignác Romsics. 1992.
No. 78 Vol. XXXI	*Planning for War against Russia and Serbia. Austro-Hungarian and German Military Strategies, 1871-1914.* Graydon A. Tunstall, Jr. 1993.
No. 79	*American Effects on Hungarian Imagination and Political Thought, 1559-1848.* Géza Závodszky. 1995.
No. 80 Vol. XXXII	*Trianon and East Central Europe: Antecedents and Repercussions.* Edited by Béla K. Király and László Veszprémy. 1995.
No. 81	*Hungarians and Their Neighbors in Modern Times, 1867-1950.* Edited by Ferenc Glatz. 1995.
No. 82	*István Bethlen: A Great Conservative Statesman of Hungary, 1874-1946.* Ignác Romsics. 1995.
No. 83 Vol. XXXIII	*20th Century Hungary and the Great Powers.* Edited by Ignác Romsics. 1995.
No. 84	*Lawful Revolution in Hungary, 1989-1994.* Edited by Béla K. Király. András Bozóki Associate Editor. 1995.
No. 85	*The Demography of Contemporary Hungarian Society.* Edited by Pál Péter Tóth and Emil Valkovics. 1996.
No. 86	*Budapest, A History from Its Beginnings to 1996.* Edited By András Gerő and János Poór. 1996.
No. 87	*The Dominant Ideas of the Nineteenth Century and Their Impact on the State. Volume 1. Diagnosis.* József Eötvös.

	Translated, edited, annotated and indexed with an introductory essay by D. Mervyn Jones. 1997.
No. 88	*The Dominant Ideas of the Nineteenth Century and Their Impact on the State.* Volume 2. *Remedy.* József Eötvös. Translated, edited, annotated and indexed with an introductory essay by D. Mervyn Jones. 1997.
No. 89	*The Social History of the Hungarian Intelligentsia in the "Long Nineteenth Century," 1825-1914.* János Mazsu. 1997.
No. 90 Vol.XXXIV	*Pax Britannica: Wartime Foreign Office Documents Regarding Plans for a Post Bellum East Central Europe.* Edited by András D. Bán. 1997.
No. 91	*National Identity in Contemporary Hungary.* György Csepeli. 1997.
No. 92	*The Hungarian Parliament, 1867-1918: A Mirage of Power.* András Gerő. 1997.
No. 93 Vol. XXXV	*The Hungarian Revolution and War of Independence, 1848-1849. A Military History.* Edited by Gábor Bona. 1999.
No. 94	*Academia and State Socialism: Essays on the Political History of Academic Life in Post-1945 Hungary and East Central Europe.* György Péteri. 1998.
No. 95 Vol.XXXVI	*Through the Prism of the Habsburg Monarchy: Hungary in American Diplomacy and Public Opinion during World War I.* Tibor Glant. 1998.
No. 96	*Appeal of Sovereignty in Hungary, Austria and Russia.* Edited by Csaba Gombár, Elemér Hankiss, László Lengyel and Györgyi Várnai. 1997.
No. 97	*Geopolitics in the Danube Region. Hungarian Reconciliation Efforts, 1848-1998.* Edited by Ignác Romsics and Béla K. Király. 1998.
No. 98	*Hungarian Agrarian Society from the Emancipation of Serfs (1848) to Re-privatization of Land (1998).* Edited by Péter Gunst. 1999.
No. 99	*"The Jewish Question" in Europe. The Case of Hungary.* Tamás Ungvári. 2000.
No. 100	*Soviet Military Intervention in Hungary, 1956.* Edited by Jenő Györkei and Miklós Horváth. 1999.

No. 101 *Jewish Budapest*. Edited by Géza Komoróczy. 1999.

No. 102 *Evolution of the Hungarian Economy, 1848-1998.* Vol. I. *One-and-a-Half Centuries of Semi-Successful Modernization, 1848-1989.* Edited by Iván T. Berend and Tamás Csató. 2001.

No. 103 *Evolution of the Hungarian Economy, 1848-1998.* Vol. II. *Paying the Bill for Goulash-Communism.* János Kornai. 2000.

No. 104 *Evolution of the Hungarian Economy, 1848-2000.* Vol. III. *Hungary: from Transition to Integration.* Edited by György Csáki and Gábor Karsai. 2001.

No. 105 *From Habsburg Agent to Victorian Scholar: G. G. Zerffi (1820-1892).* Tibor Frank. 2000.

No. 106 *A History of Transylvania from the Beginning to 1919.* Vol. I. Edited by Zoltán Szász and Béla Köpeczi. 2001.

No. 107 *A History of Transylvania from the Beginning to 1919.* Vol. II. Edited by Zoltán Szász and Béla Köpeczi. 2001.

No. 108 *A History of Transylvania from the Beginning to 1919.* Vol. III. Edited by Zoltán Szász and Béla Köpeczi. 2002.

No. 109 *Hungary: Governments and Politics, 1848–2000.* Edited by Mária Ormos and Béla K. Király. 2001.

No. 110 *Hungarians in the Voivodina, 1918–1947.* Enikő A. Sajti. 2003.

No. 111 *Hungarian Arts and Sciences, 1848–2000.* Edited by László Somlyódy and Nóra Somlyódy. 2003.

No. 112 *Hungary and International Politics in 1848–1849.* Domokos Kosáry. 2003.

No. 113 *Social History of Hungary from the Reform Era to the End of the Twentieth Century.* Edited by Gábor Gyáni, György Kövér and Tibor Valuch. 2003.

No. 114 Vol.XXXVII *A Millennium of Hungarian Military History.* Edited by László Veszprémy and Béla K. Király. 2002.

No. 115 *Hungarian Relics. A History of the Battle Banners of the 1848-49 Hungarian Revolution and War of Independence.* Jenő Györkei and Györgyi Cs. Kottra. 2000.

No. 116 *From Totalitarian to Democratic Hungary. Evolution and Transformation, 1990-2000.* Edited by Mária Schmidt and László Gy. Tóth. 2000.
No. 117 *A History of Eastern Europe since the Middle Ages.* Emil Niederhauser. 2003.
No. 118 *The Ideas of the Hungarian Revolution, Suppressed and Victorious, 1956-1999.* Edited by Lee W. Congdon and Béla K. Király. 2002.
No. 119 *The Emancipation of the Serfs in Eastern Europe.* Emil Niederhauser. 2004.
No. 120 *Art of Survival. Hungarian National Defense and Society in Modern Times.* Béla K. Király. Edited by Piroska Balogh and Tamás Vitek. 2003.
No. 121 *Army and Politics in Hungary, 1938-1945.* Lóránd Dombrády.
Vol.XXXVIII Edited by Gyula Rázsó. 2005.
No. 122 *Hungary and the Hungarian Minorities (Trends in the Past and in Our Time).* Edited by László Szarka. 2004.
No. 126 *The Occupation of Bosnia and Herzegovina in 1878.* László
Vol.XXXIX Bencze. 2005.
No. 127 *Wars, Revolutions and Regime Changes in Hungary, 1912-2004. Reminiscences of an Eyewitness.* Béla K. Király. Edited by Piroska Balogh, Andrea T. Kulcsár and Tamás Vitek. 2005.